An Introduction to Arabic Translation

Combining theory and practice, this book is a model for Arabic translation and prepares students for the translation industry.

Containing 22 approaches, *An Introduction to Arabic Translation* provides the normative principles to guide training in Arabic-English-Arabic translation. It revitalizes Arabic-English-Arabic translation through its empirical textual reality, hinged upon Arabic and English authentic contexts and their linguistic, discoursal, and cultural incongruity. The exercises in each chapter provide practical training supported by translation theory. The translation commentaries included represent a critical translation quality assessment based on an analysis of discourse and textual features to highlight the process of translation, the translation approach adopted, and why. Such commentary invites students to reflect on their understanding of the translation process and the approach required for a given Arabic-English-Arabic translation problem.

Providing a methodologically comprehensive course of Arabic-English-Arabic translation studies, and insightful discussion of high value for both students and teachers, this book will be invaluable to anyone seeking to learn or improve their Arabic and translation skills.

Hussein Abdul-Raof is a Professor of Linguistics and Translation Studies at Taibah University, Saudi Arabia, who has worked in the United Kingdom as a practitioner since 1976, a translation and interpreting instructor in Specialist Language Services (York, 1984–1992), the University of Salford, Manchester (1985–1992), the University of Leeds (1993–2012), and as a PhD supervisor to postgraduate students of translation studies at the University of Leeds (1993–2012).

An Introduction to Arabic Translation

Translator Training and Translation Practice

Hussein Abdul-Raof

LONDON AND NEW YORK

First published 2023
by Routledge
4 Park Square, Milton Park, Abingdon, Oxon OX14 4RN

and by Routledge
605 Third Avenue, New York, NY 10158

Routledge is an imprint of the Taylor & Francis Group, an informa business

© 2023 Hussein Abdul-Raof

The right of Hussein Abdul-Raof to be identified as author of this work has been asserted in accordance with sections 77 and 78 of the Copyright, Designs and Patents Act 1988.

All rights reserved. No part of this book may be reprinted or reproduced or utilised in any form or by any electronic, mechanical, or other means, now known or hereafter invented, including photocopying and recording, or in any information storage or retrieval system, without permission in writing from the publishers.

Trademark notice: Product or corporate names may be trademarks or registered trademarks, and are used only for identification and explanation without intent to infringe.

British Library Cataloguing-in-Publication Data
A catalogue record for this book is available from the British Library

Library of Congress Cataloging-in-Publication Data
A catalog record for this book has been requested

ISBN: 978-1-032-21546-4 (hbk)
ISBN: 978-1-032-21555-6 (pbk)
ISBN: 978-1-003-26895-6 (ebk)

DOI: 10.4324/9781003268956

Typeset in Times New Roman
by Apex CoVantage, LLC

For: Noah & Aiden

Contents

Acknowledgements	x
Preface	xi

Introduction   1
I.1 Translator training and translation practice 1
I.2 Rationale and description of the target market 4
I.3 How this book is different from available ones 6

1 Translation as process and product   9
1.1 Introduction 9
1.2 What is translation? 9
1.3 Monitoring and managing translation 13
1.4 False friends 17
1.5 Overview of translation approaches 19
1.6 Translator training and translation practice 54

2 Stylistics and translator training   73
2.1 Introduction 73
2.2 Stylistic analysis and translation 74
2.3 Tight texture and loose texture 74
2.4 Stylistic idiosyncrasies of conjunctions 74
2.5 Translation and stylistic variation 80
2.6 Translation of hyperbole pattern 93
    2.6.1 Translation of morphologically based hyperbole 94
2.7 Translator training and translation practice 98

3 Stylistic literalness in Qur'an translation   134
3.1 Introduction 134
3.2 What is stylistic literalness? 134
3.3 Natural and easy style 136

viii   *Contents*

3.4   *Sources of stylistic literalness 137*
3.5   *Translator training and translation practice 142*

4   Translation beyond the full-stop 149
4.1   *Introduction 149*
4.2   *Punctuation and translation 149*
4.3   *Translation of punctuation 151*
4.4   *Conjunctions in Arabic and English 151*
4.5   *Punctuation, texture, and translation 157*
4.6   *Learning objectives 158*
4.7   *Translator training and translation practice 160*

5   Translation of cohesion 187
5.1   *Introduction 187*
5.2   *Translation and cohesion 187*
5.3   *Translation of reference 188*
    5.3.1   Types of reference 189
5.4   *Translation and conjunctions 190*
5.5   *Translation of ellipsis 191*
    5.5.1   Translation of anaphoric ellipsis 192
    5.5.2   Translation of cataphoric ellipsis 193
    5.5.3   Translation of nominal ellipsis 195
    5.5.4   Translation of verbal ellipsis 198
5.6   *Translation of substitution 201*
    5.6.1   Types of substitution 201
        5.6.1.1   Translation of verbal substitution 201
        5.6.1.2   Translation of nominal substitution 203
        5.6.1.3   Translation of clausal substitution 205
5.7   *Lexical cohesion 207*
    5.7.1   General noun 207
    5.7.2   Reiteration 209
    5.7.3   Synonymy 210
    5.7.4   Antonymy 211
    5.7.5   Collocation 211
    5.7.6   Hyponymy 211
    5.7.7   Meronymy 212
5.8   *Translator training and translation practice 212*

6   Jargon translation 220
6.1   *Introduction 220*
6.2   *The birth of a jargon 220*
6.3   *Word formation processes 221*
6.4   *Important observations 223*
6.5   *Types of jargon 224*

Contents ix

6.6 Jargon production approaches 224
6.7 Proliferation of jargon 234
6.8 Translator training and translation practice 234

Appendix 1	245
Appendix 2	300
Bibliography	322
Index	326

Acknowledgements

I wish to thank Mr Joe Whiting, the Acquisitions Editor for Middle Eastern, Islamic & Jewish Studies, Routledge Taylor & Francis Group, and Professor Ian Richard Netton of the Institute of Arab and Islamic Studies, University of Exeter for their much-appreciated support and insightful feedback on the book proposal. Particular thanks go to the President of Taibah University, Dr Abdul-Aziz Bin Qablan Al-Sarrani, for his interest in my research and for his continuous support. I would also like to thank Grace Rollison, the editorial assistant, for her valuable administrative work on the publication of the manuscript, and Euan Rice-Coates, editorial assistant, Middle East, Islamic and Jewish Studies. A special word of appreciation goes to Marie Louise Roberts, the project manager from Apex CoVantage, for her challenging work and much needed assistance during the production stage of this book. Thanks are also due to Andrew and Avann for their much appreciated assistance in checking the language of the English translations of the Arabic texts.

Preface

An Introduction to Arabic Translation is a model for Arabic translation. It aims to provide intensive translation training to students and equip them with insight into translation theory through the thorough discussion and examples of the major translation approaches which can be adopted in any translation process as well as the main characteristics of major translation approaches. The student is introduced to 22 translation approaches, two of which (stylistic literalness approach and jargon translation approach) are put forward by the author and are specific to Arabic translation.

The present book puts theory into practice and prepares students for the translation industry through the detailed analysis of numerous Arabic and English examples on full-stop, particle, word, phrase, sentence, paragraph, and text levels. Each of the six chapters is allocated a section at the end of the chapter (Translator Training and Translation Practice) where many different exercises are given for the purpose of providing practical training supported by translation theory. Each exercise is given a translation commentary that represents a critical translation quality assessment based on an analysis of discourse and textual features of the source text (ST) to make the student aware of what has taken place during the translation process, what translation approach is adopted by the translator, and why. The translation commentary on examples invites students to reflect on their understanding of the translation process and the translation approach required for a given Arabic-English-Arabic translation problem.

Textual geography and text typology have been taken into account in the selection of STs where different genres are translated and analyzed, such as journalistic, literary, legal, descriptive, instructional, advertisement, scientific, medical, and Qur'anic text types. The examples selected to equip the student with an insight into the ST culture.

In addition to the insightful discussion of the different, and at times overlapping, translation approaches, *An Introduction to Arabic Translation* equips the translation student with valuable details on translation studies notions such as the distinction between stylistic literalness and literal translation, the notion of tight and loose texture, the notion of jargon translation, the translation of punctuation, the translation beyond the full-stop, the translation of cohesion, inter-sentential cohesion, which is concerned with the employment of conjunctions between consecutive sentences, and intra-sentential cohesion, which is concerned with the employment of conjunctions within the same sentence. The student is also made aware of the fact that some translation approaches represent different labels but in fact refer to the same translation approach and notion (i.e., old wine in new bottles).

An Introduction to Arabic Translation plugs the research gap and answers the market need for a model for Arabic translation supported by a textbook with practice-based exercises that can be used by translation teachers. This book fills the research gap and offers a valuable

xii *Preface*

pool of exercises where STs are translated and analyzed thoroughly. These exercises primarily aim for nurturing a culture of critical analysis among translation students, and can be used either for in-class discussion or as homework assignments. Some exercises require a contrastive analysis of some Qur'anic Arabic STs, writing a critical translation quality commentary, or a correction of a TT. This book provides the translation student with the tools of ST analysis, an insight into translation quality assessment, and the remedies that stem from translation theory.

Introduction

I.1 Translator training and translation practice

This manuscript aims to provide a model for Arabic translation. It offers normative translation strategies to guide Arabic-English-Arabic translator training. Strengthened by translation theory, the book offers an in-depth account of Arabic-English-Arabic translation strategies at word, phrase, sentence, paragraph, and text levels, as well as explicated analyses of English, Arabic and Qur'anic Arabic translation problems and their solutions. The book provides insightful discussion of high value for both students and teachers of translation, culminating in a methodologically comprehensive course of Arabic-English-Arabic translation studies. Analysis of examples invites students and teachers of Arabic translation to reflect on their understanding and knowledge of the translation process.

The greatest emphasis is on the solutions of Arabic-English-Arabic translation problems, which are explained in the light of major theoretical notions of translation theory supported by critical comments on goal and strategy. This book is a prescription for training translators, equipping them with a solid theoretical foundation during the translation process to achieve the required goal of translation output. The book introduces the reader to the textual analysis of varied Arabic and English text types followed by their translations and critical discussion of the approaches adopted. The textual analysis demonstrates the distinctive textual features (linguistic, discoursal, and cultural), which are the norms employed by both the source language (SL) and the target language (TL). The strategies for training involve the maneuverability of the translator who aims to address and accommodate the linguistic, discoursal, and cultural incongruity between Arabic and English through a stylistically innovative translation. Thus, the students and teachers of Arabic translation need to be aware of the concordant relationships between Arabic and English where the same SL word should not always be translated by one and only one TL word. The translator may resort to paraphrastic (exegetical) translation of culture-bound, ideologically oriented expressions, and Qur'an-specific style, rather than literal translation. The discussion of Arabic-English-Arabic translation problems demonstrates how faith in the translation of cultural and ideologically centered individual words can almost never fully reproduce the meaning they denote in the ST. With regards to Qur'an translation, however, fidelity, on the textual level, will lead to stylistic literalness; in other words, the adherence by some Qur'an translators to the style of Qur'anic genre. Some Qur'an translations have become examples of interlinear (ultraliteral) translations, where the same Qur'anic style is rendered in English, violating the TL linguistic and stylistic norms. Such translations are unique examples of foreignizing SL style and syntactic patterns.

The section "Translator Training and Translation Practice" at the end of each chapter is a valuable practical exercise combining theory and practice and equips students with

DOI: 10.4324/9781003268956-1

2   *Introduction*

translation training to prepare them for the translation industry. The STs and their proposed translations aim to provide a translation commentary based on a contrastive stylistic and linguistic analysis of the ST and the TT, and provide insight into what has taken place during the translation process and what translation approaches have been adopted. Critical analysis of examples provide a translation quality assessment guiding the translator towards the achievement of a context-based, pragmatically adequate, and semantically accurate translation that satisfies the TL audience and the ideological implications (performative intent) of the SL text producer, especially with regards to Qur'anic Arabic translation and how "to come to terms with the foreignness of languages and the solution of this foreignness that remains out of the reach of mankind" (Benjamin 1968:19). The translation strategies that aim to address the incongruity problems between Arabic and English "consist in finding the intended effect *[intention]* upon the language into which the translator is translating which produces in it the echo of the original" (ibid:20).

An Introduction to Arabic Translation aims to equip translation students with fundamental translation notions and procedures, summarized as:

1   Minor adjustments in content comprise a translation strategy through which the translator makes the SL message both intelligible and meaningful to the TL audience through slight modifications in ST content. However, the student is made aware that minor adjustment is different from exegetical translation where the latter is concerned with adding additional details that are not explicitly conveyed in the ST – an explication and expansion of the SL expression.
2   The domestication of the SL message is a translation strategy through which we aim to make the SL message intelligible to the TL audience. It is a form of cultural transposition where the student is advised to leave literal translation and replace ST features and replace them with TL features to reduce the foreignness of the TT.
3   The foreignization of the ST message is concerned with opening up the target text (TT) to us in its utter foreignness. It involves the verbatim transfer of SL content and form into the TT.
4   The notion of equivalence (TL-reader-oriented, communicative translation) emerged in the 1960s and 70s, and is a functional variety of correspondence, considering translation as a process of communicating the ST by a semantically analogous (equivalent) TT. However, students are made aware of the fact that there can be no absolute correspondence between languages. Hence there can be no fully exact translations. Students are also advised to undertake a change in SL word order to meet the TT grammatical and stylistic norms. This is similar to faithful translation, which aims to provide complete naturalness of the SL expression.
5   Context-based and naturalness of the TT aims to relate the TL audience to modes of behavior relevant within the context of his/her own culture; it does not insist that he/she understands the cultural patterns of the SL context in order to comprehend the message. This is similar to faithful translation, which aims to provide complete naturalness of the SL expression.
6   Functional equivalence provides the student with insight into the fact that the translation process needs to be based on a thorough syntactic, semantic, pragmatic, and stylistic analysis of the ST.
7   Formal equivalence (structural equivalence, gloss translation) focuses attention on the ST form and content. The student is warned about the disadvantages of this translation approach because it requires a relatively close approximation to the structure of the ST

Introduction 3

in form (syntax and idioms) and content (themes and concepts), and numerous footnotes in order to make the TT fully comprehensible. The student is told that formal equivalence translation contains much that is not readily intelligible to the average TL reader.

8 Anachronism produces unsmooth translation, such as using old-fashioned language in the receptor language and hence giving an unrealistic impression.

9 Natural translation (transposition, shift) involves adaptation in grammar and lexicon. In general, the grammatical modifications can be made the more readily, since many grammatical changes are dictated by the obligatory structures of the TL. The translator is thus obliged to make adjustments such as shifting word order, using verbs in place of nouns, and substituting nouns for pronouns.

10 Naturalization translation is distinct from the natural translation method. Naturalization is concerned with transliteration and is similar to the transference approach in that they are both forms of cultural borrowing, where the ST expression is taken to the TT verbatim in a transliterated form. For instance, the SL word is transferred phonetically (transliterated) and adapted to the TL morphology.

11 Stylistic literalness is an unnatural TL style which aims to imitate the ST with disregard to TT linguistic norms. It typifies the structural equivalence with the ST.

12 Verbal and nominal substitution is concerned with the clause cohesion system. Verbal substitution in English is concerned with the verbal substitutes (do, be, have). However, Arabic does not have verbal substitution. Nominal substitution is concerned with how a noun or noun phrase is replaced by another noun. Both Arabic and English have nominal substitution;

13 Jargon translation approaches are applied when the student of translation is made aware of the seven linguistic approaches we have proposed for the creation of a jargon in the TL.

14 Translation of punctuation and the textual geography of the ST and the TT are concerned with ST sentence demarcation; how to create the sentence boundaries in the ST, especially the Arabic sentence. It provides an insight into the translation of punctuation as a stylistic idiosyncrasy of English, as well as how English is an asyndetic language while Arabic is polysyndetic. Thus, the textual geography of Arabic is totally different from that of English.

15 Inter-sentential cohesion is concerned with the employment of conjunctions between consecutive sentences. Intra-sentential cohesion is concerned with the employment of conjunctions within the same sentence.

We recommend for any translation course syllabus and translation commentary the following teaching materials based on authentic STs:

(1) the translation approaches adopted by the student during his/her translation process, (2) managing and monitoring mechanisms, (3) false friends, (4) sentence demarcation (textual geography), (5) Arabic and English stylistic idiosyncrasies, (6) texture features in the ST and the TT (tight/loose texture, asyndeton/polysyndeton), (7) morphologically based translation problems, (8) sources of stylistic literalness, (9) Arabic-specific linguistic features (active/passive participle, hyperbaton, foregrounding, absolute object), (10) punctuation translation problems, (11) cohesion translation problems (ellipsis translation problems (cataphoric/anaphoric, nominal/verbal), substitution translation problems (verbal/nominal/clausal), synonymy translation problems (Arabic semantic redundancy; verb, noun, adjective, adverb), (12) jargon translation problems and approaches (solutions),

4   *Introduction*

(13) major rhetorical features (metaphor, metonymy, proverb), (14) anachronism and natural/unnatural style, (15) exegesis/paraphrase-based translation, and (16) domestication/foreignization-based translation.

An Introduction to Arabic Translation has provided all the above in addition to extensive details for the translation instructor and the translation student, in addition to exercises with their solutions as well as exercises for homework assignments and in-class discussion.

I.2   Rationale and description of the target market

An Introduction to Arabic Translation is a training manual and a roadmap for translation students and translation instructors. The book aims to provide normative translation strategies to guide in Arabic-English-Arabic translation practice and to provide enlightening discussion valuable for translator training. It is an in-depth account of Arabic-English-Arabic translation approaches supported by translation theory. The current work is an explicated analysis of English, Arabic and Qur'anic Arabic translation problems and their solutions backed up by translation theory. It provides insightful discussion of high value for both students and teachers of translation. The book provides a methodologically comprehensive course of Arabic-English-Arabic translation studies. Analysis of examples invites students and teachers of Arabic translation to reflect again on their understanding and knowledge of the translation process and the translation approach required for a given translation problem at word, phrase, sentence, and text levels.

The greatest emphasis of the book is on the solutions of Arabic-English-Arabic translation problems which are explained in light of major theoretical notions of translation theory backed up by critical comments (translation commentary) on goal and approach. Thus, the book is a prescription for training translation students and translators, and equipping them with a solid theoretical and practical foundation during the translation process in order to achieve the required goal of translation output.

An Introduction to Arabic Translation introduces the translation student and translation instructor to the textual and discourse analysis of varied Arabic and English text types followed by their translations and critical analysis of the strategies adopted in each translation problem. The textual and discourse analysis demonstrates the distinctive textual features (linguistic, discoursal, and cultural) which are the norms employed by both the source language (SL) and the target language (TL). The strategies for training involve the maneuverability of the translator who aims to address and accommodate the linguistic, discoursal, and cultural incongruity between Arabic and English through a stylistically innovative, faithful, and context-based translation. The proposed book makes the students and teachers of Arabic translation aware of the concordant relationships between Arabic and English where the same SL word should not always be translated by one and only one TL word. The translator may resort to paraphrastic (exegetical) translation of culture-bound, ideologically based expressions, and Qur'an-specific style rather than literal translation. The discussion of Arabic-English-Arabic translation problems demonstrates how faithfulness in the translation of cultural and ideologically oriented individual words can almost never fully reproduce the meaning they have in the ST. With regards to Qur'an translation, however, fidelity, on the textual level, will lead to stylistic literalness; the adherence by some Qur'an translators to the style of Qur'anic genre. Some Qur'an translations have become examples of interlinear (ultra-literal) translations where the same Qur'anic style is rendered in English violating the TL linguistic and stylistic norms. Such translations are

Introduction 5

unique examples of foreignizing TL style and syntactic patterns. Students of translation and translation teachers will be provided with extensive examples from Qur'anic Arabic where different Qur'an translations are compared, analyzed, and critically assessed, and problems are provided with proposed solutions; thus, a comprehensive translation commentary is provided for each example.

The critical analysis of examples from different types of text aims to guide the translation student and translation instructor towards the achievement of a pragmatically adequate and accurate translation that satisfies the TL audience and the ideological implications of the SL and how "to come to terms with the foreignness of languages and the solution of this foreignness that remains out of the reach of mankind" (Benjamin 1968:19). The translation approaches that aim to address the incongruity problems between Arabic and English "consist in finding the intended effect *[intention]* upon the language into which the translator is translating which produces in it the echo of the original" (ibid:20).

An Introduction to Arabic Translation is hinged upon two key factors: (1) my translation expertise as a freelance translator (from 1976 until the present time), and (2) my teaching expertise (from 1985 through the present time). To verify the value of the proposed book, I will outline my expertise in translation and translation training, since this has been the foundation of the present book and, in terms of transferable skills, I would like to pass on my expertise to translation students and translation teachers.

An Introduction to Arabic Translation provides a wealth of practical examples and has benefited from both my teaching experience and teaching materials. The major aim of the proposed book is to help translation students and translation teachers through the extensive examples and commentaries on the translations of various text types. The discussion includes textual and discourse analysis of the source text (ST) and how the translation process has been made, and what translation approach is adopted by the translator.

The present book is pitched at the intermediate level and is suitable for ungraduated translation modules, translation programs, and short translation training courses. In the view of Jeremy Munday (2001:6), there are two very visible ways in which translation studies has become more prominent. First, there has been a proliferation of specialized translating and interpreting courses at both undergraduate and postgraduate levels. In the UK, the first specialized university postgraduate courses in interpreting and translating were set up in the 1960s. In the academic year 1999/2000, there were at least 20 postgraduate translation courses in the UK and several designated "Centres of Translation". Caminade and Pym (1998) list at least 250 university-level bodies in over 60 countries offering four-year undergraduate degrees and/or postgraduate courses in translation. These courses, which attract thousands of students, are mainly oriented towards training future professional commercial translators and interpreters, and serve as highly valued entry-level qualifications for the translating and interpreting professions. Other courses, in smaller numbers, focus on the practice of literary translation. In the UK, these include major courses at University of Leeds, University of Salford, Manchester University, Herriott Watt university, Sheffield University, Middlesex University, and the University of East Anglia (Norwich), the latter of which also houses the British Centre for Literary Translation. In Europe, there is now a network of centres where literary translation is studied, practiced, and promoted. Apart from Norwich, these include Amsterdam (the Netherlands), Arles (France), Bratislava (Slovakia), Dublin (Ireland), Rhodes (Greece), Sineffe (Belgium), Stralen (Germany), Tarazona (Spain), and Visby (Sweden). There is also a proliferation of conferences, books, and journals on translation in many languages.

6   *Introduction*

I.3   How this book is different from available ones

An Introduction to Arabic Translation is the first Arabic translation textbook that puts translation theory into practice and provides extensive practical training exercises, insight into all translation approaches, a detailed textual and discourse analysis of the ST and the TT, and thorough translation quality assessments and commentaries. The book is of high value to undergraduate and postgraduate students, translation instructors, practitioners, and scholars. There is no such textbook of Arabic translation available on the market for Arabic translation students and Arabic translation instructors.

Throughout the long past years of my work, I have encountered numerous books and textbooks on translation studies. However, they all have either mixed up translation approaches, allocated more space to theoretical discussion with minimal examples, discussed a limited number of examples and translation approaches, or they have provided no or limited exercises for training translation students and assisting translation teachers. When the exercises are given in some of the books on translation studies, there are no answers, no analysis of the translation, no translation commentary based on textual and discourse analysis, no discussion of why a given translation approach is adopted, and what translation approach is recommended. The available books cannot be adopted as a roadmap for translation students and translation teachers.

The numerous books on translation studies thus far have not dealt with in-class, practice-based training, and have overlooked valuable discussion and analysis of core translation problems facing translation students and translation instructors, such as joining the sentences within a paragraph (i.e., translation beyond the full-stop), the relationship between stylistics and translation, the translation of the cohesion system, a thorough list of all translation approaches (past and modern) with extensive Arabic and English examples, and most importantly, guiding the student through the different approaches and making him/her aware of the fact that it is, at times, old wine in new bottles; in other words, explaining to the translation student and the translation teacher that most of the translation approaches overlap with each other, and although the labels are different, the approach is the same.

Based on my long experience in translation teaching and freelance translation, I have included 32 exercises in Chapter One in addition to the numerous examples for each translation approach. Sixty-nine exercises related to Chapter One are provided in Appendix 1. All the exercises include the proposed translations of all the STs followed by a thorough textual and discourse analysis of the ST and of the TT, alternative translations, and at times, back-translations. A large number of exercises will also be provided for each chapter with solutions (proposed translations), textual and discourse analysis of the STs, and an informative translation commentary. This research methodology and extensive pool of training resources are not available in any available Arabic translation book.

The in-depth translation commentary in each exercise is of huge value to translation projects at undergraduate and postgraduate levels. They are of high value for translation training, and also of interest to researchers in translation studies. The examples cover variegated texts like sentences taken from TV shows and news, journalistic, instructional, and literary texts, TV adverts, other types of adverts, and Qur'anic texts. This research methodology, practical training exercises, and in-depth translation commentaries are a model to be followed by other researchers in other languages. Thus, *An Introduction to Arabic Translation* is a training manual and a roadmap for Arabic translation students and translation instructors.

Introduction 7

Structure of the book. The present book includes the following chapters and two appendices:

Introduction: This constitutes the rationale of the proposed book and also sets the scene for the translation student and translation teacher. It provides a bird's eye view of the book as well as the research methodology adopted in this work.

Chapter One: Translation as Process and Product. This sets the scene for what takes place during the translation process and how the translation product is received by the consumer, based on the translation approach adopted and the translated type of text. It provides a thorough definition of translation and many major translation notions related to translation as process and product, such as monitoring and managing – and, most importantly, the major translation approaches the translator adopts during any translation process. We have put forward two new translation approaches: stylistic literalness approach and jargon translation approach.

Chapter Two: Stylistics and Translator Training. The present chapter provides practical training for the translation student and the translation teacher in critical translation quality assessment through contrastive stylistic analysis between the ST and the TT. The stylistically based translation quality assessment is a vital measurement tool that aims: (1) to enhance the translation student's skills in critical translation analysis, and (2) to train him/her in how to employ stylistic analysis in the assessment of the translation process and product and the assessment of the ST and the TT. This translation assessment approach is of high value to other languages. Thus, there is universality in our approach where translation students and teachers can apply this approach to their own languages. Our assessment approach is also of value to the translation projects required from undergraduate and postgraduate translation students.

Chapter Three: Translation beyond the Full-Stop. This chapter is concerned with the TT sequence of sentences, their word order re-shuffle, and rearranging them according to a coherent and cohesive TL sentence/paragraph structure with the main idea reproduced in a fresh form with equivalent effect. It aims to rid the TT of the ST clumsiness and structural complexity in order to enhance clarity and meaning. This chapter also accounts for the translation of punctuation and how punctuation plays a major role in the TL textual continuity and coherence. Arabic and English depict two distinct linguistic and textual systems. Thus, different SL and TL punctuation and cohesive systems designate distinct stylistic preferences in the two languages and may reflect different illocutionary force and the text producer's performative intent.

Chapter Four: Stylistic Literalness. The landscape of Qur'an translation reflects the contrast in translation strategies between the literalist and spiritualist translations. The chapter accounts for the foreignization of Qur'anic style by some Qur'an translations. In some Qur'an translations, we encounter a greater focus of attention upon SL stylistic features (form). Such translations are unique examples of foreignizing the SL style and syntactic patterns. Different Qur'an translations give distinct considerations to content and form. As a Qur'an translation strategy, the foreignization of Qur'anic style (stylistic literalness) has favored form over content, giving style (stylistic features) a higher priority in the TT. For such Qur'an translations, the importance of TL form far exceeds the consideration of the content of the SL message. There is abundance of evidence of such a translation strategy with regards to

8 *Introduction*

the Qur'anic stylistic features of foregrounding and hyperbaton, which have alienated the TL audience.

Chapter Five: Translation of Cohesion. This chapter examines the different types of cohesive devices like substitution, ellipsis, reference, lexical cohesion (lexical repetition), and conjunction. It questions whether overrepresented SL additive conjunctions like و are necessary in the TL or whether textual continuity and TL lexical cohesive system are undermined. The ST (the Qur'an) is marked by dense texture where some of its elements – such as nominalization, the active participle, the no-main-verb nominal sentence, and the subject noun-initial sentences with a main verb – have inherent performative intent that may not be possible to reproduce in the TL. Shift is a case in point. The chapter accounts for the unnatural TT style and how the TL audience is alienated by the TT that does not observe the TL linguistic norms and cohesion system.

Chapter Six: Jargon Translation. This chapter provides a detailed analysis with numerous examples of the different linguistic approaches through which the SL jargon (terminology) is produced in a given TL; how a jargon is born in the TL. It accounts for the creation of a jargon, as a notion, in Arabic. The proposed TL jargon-generation approaches are universal mechanisms which can be of high value to other languages. The semantic relationship between the SL and the TL jargon is also explained. The discussion deals with whether the literal (foreignization) translation approach, through phonetic borrowing (transliteration), can always be adopted in the birth (production) of a new jargon, or whether the naturalization (domestication) translation approach, through semantic borrowing, is an option for the translator to deliver the new jargon. The chapter also provides many recommendations for the creation of new Arabic jargon and how the newly adopted lexical items can be disseminated in the Arab countries.

Appendix 1: This is for practice-based exercises aimed at training translation students and translators. Appendix 1 is related to Chapter One.

Appendix 2: This is for practice-based exercises aimed at training translation students and translators. Appendix 2 is related to Chapter Two.

Bibliography: This provides a wealth of useful major and minor resources on translation theory and will be of high value to students in terms of their assignments and translation commentary projects.

1 Translation as process and product

1.1 Introduction

The present chapter sets the scene for what takes place during the translation act and the end product consumed by the receptor audience. It provides a thorough definition of translation and many major translation notions related to translation as process and product, such as monitoring and managing and false friends. However, the pivotal part of this chapter is concerned with the major theory-based translation approaches that can be adopted during a translation process and can justify the end product. Twenty-two translation approaches are provided with different examples. Thirty-four training-based exercises in this chapter and 70 exercises in Appendix 1 of Chapter 1 are provided as a valuable pool of learning and teaching resources which can be effectively employed for in-class discussion, homework assignments, or for translation commentary projects.

1.2 What is translation?

Translation is concerned with linguistic architecture where the linguistic architect (the translator) is concerned with the design of a new linguistic construction at the particle, word, phrase (TL jargon production), sentence, and text levels (re-modelling). The linguistic architect attempts to piece together the ST linguistic jigsaw (translation beyond the full-stop, the translation of punctuation), and is busy with the beautification of his/her construction (the text) in the hunt for the most glamorous dress to clothe the new building and provide an attractive façade through various TL aesthetic devices. The architectural joy produced by the ST should be shared by the TL reader, too. This bliss cannot be attained without the translator's competent linguistic architectural skills.

Translation is an act of communication bridging different nations and cultures. Translation is a process in which a text in one language is replaced by a functionally equivalent text in another. In other words, translation is the transfer of the intended meaning of a text from one language – called the source language (SL) – to another – called the target language (TL). It is also the transfer from one culture to another. Therefore, the translator is a communicator and a mediator between two languages and two cultures. We are reminded by Nida (1964:160) of the dangers emanating from the translation between two linguistically and culturally incongruous languages, as is the case with Arabic and English.

However, a translation does not have to be longer than the ST; it should not be an over-translation. A translation is either the rendering of a ST in another TL, or the communicating of a SL message to a new TL audience. In the view of Dickins et al. (2002:29), translation involves not just two languages, but a transfer from one culture to another, and general

DOI: 10.4324/9781003268956-2

10 *Translation as process and product*

cultural differences are sometimes bigger obstacles to successful translation than linguistic differences. This supports Beaugrande's claim (2003:13) that translation is a utopian activity. However, Wilss (1982:49) argues that the limited ability of the translator with regards to text analysis is the major cause of mistranslation.

Translation gives priority to meaning over the SL stylistic idiosyncrasies and SL syntactic category word form. However, any translation is only an approximation of the ST meaning. Moir (2009:43) concludes that whatever level of equivalence may be achieved, the translation will necessarily be an imperfect or approximate rendering of the ST. Translations commonly misrepresent their source texts by either failing to do justice to all the aspects of the original, or by augmenting the original's effect (Shuttleworth and Cowie 1997:69).

Thus, a translation should pass itself as an original piece of writing. An effective translation is the one which can produce the closest natural equivalent of the ST in terms of meaning and style. Therefore, a translation should affect the TT readers in the same way the ST has affected its readers. Translation should also read with the same ease and pleasure of the ST; the TT should have TL fluency, and should not smell of foreignness.

In the view of Reiss (1971; cited in Venuti 2000:160), translation is a bilingual mediated process of communication which aims at the production of a TL text that is functionally equivalent to an SL text.

Translation is the study of applied semantics. In other words, it examines meaning, the strategies, and problems of conveying meaning from one language to another. Although the unit of translation is the sentence (i.e., we translate sentence by sentence), we must ensure that it is the TT as a whole that is taken into account at the end of the translation process. We need to read the TT aloud, if possible, to guarantee three important criteria:

1   Upon the completion of the translation, we have achieved a natural TT genre that matches the ST genre;
2   Upon the completion of the translation, we have achieved a natural and fluent TT that meets the TL grammatical and stylistic norms; and
3   Upon the completion of the translation, we have achieved a natural TT that meets the TL cohesion system.

Translation is not a mechanical process. It is not a ST and a dictionary. It is a creative process and is both science and art. In other words, we follow translation approaches according to translation theory (science), and we use our artistic linguistic and stylistic skills in the TT (art).

Based on the notion of equivalence which emerged in 1960s and 70s, translating is generally seen as a process of communicating a foreign text by a semantically analogous (equivalent) text. For Nida (1964), there can be no absolute correspondence between languages. Hence there can be no fully exact translations. The total impact of a translation may be reasonably close to the original, but there can be no identity in detail. A good translation should aim for pragmatic success and the pragmatic success of the TT should correspond with that of the ST. The TT should employ pragmatic effects which are perlocutionary effects; they are the effects of the text on the reader's behavior, feelings, beliefs, attitudes, or actions. Thus, the perlocutionary effects of a given text are defined by Hickey (1998a:8) as the thoughts, feelings, and actions that result from reading a text. A pragmatically successful TT should be eloquently forceful. However, pragmatic failure is the inability of the TT to decode the context in which the ST has evolved; the inability to package in the TT the linguistic, semantic, textual, cultural, and emotional elements of the ST.

Translation as process and product 11

Concerning lexical equivalence across languages when things or events are unknown in the TL, Beekman and Callow (1974:191–211; cited in Venuti 2000:387), list three main options:

1 Equivalence by modifying a generic word;
2 Equivalence using a loan word; and
3 Equivalence by cultural substitution.

Looking at the first option, this involves the addition of a "descriptive modification" to a "generic term" to supply a specific meaning absent from the generic term itself. For example, the word جُنُبًا (Q4:43) is given a number of descriptive equivalent translations such as: a state of ceremonial impurity (Ali 1934:no page), polluted (Pickthall 1930:no page), a state requiring total ablution (Asad 1980:169), a state of *janabah* (Saheeh International 1997:107), and a state of major ritual impurity (Abdel Haleem 2005:55).

Let us also consider يُظاهِر (Q58:2), which has different semantic components, such as divorcing wives by *zihar* (calling them mothers) (Yusuf Ali), saying to one's wife "You are to me like my mother's back" (Abdel Haleem), to pronounce zihar (Saheeh International 1997), to put away one's wife (by saying she is like his mother) (Pickthall). Gutt (ibid:390), however, puts forward his "translation principle": do what is consistent with the search for optimal relevance.

Throughout history, Brisset (1996; cited in Venuti 2000:343–344) argues that translators have had to contend with the fact that the TL is deficient when it comes to translating the ST into that language. Such deficiencies can be clearly identified as lexical, morpho-syntactic deficiencies, or as problems of polysemy. The difficulty of translation does not arise from the lack of a specific translation language. Rather, it arises from the absence in the TL of a sub-code equivalent to the one used by the ST in its reproduction of the SL.

Based on Arabic translation, we can identify lexical, syntactic, and morphological deficiencies in English, as in words whose meanings are

1 morpho-syntactically oriented, as in مُطَهَّرَةٌ, (Q2:25, Q3:15, Q4:57); مُطَهِّر, Q:2:25; يطهُر Q2:222; طَهَّرَ, Q3:42; يتطهَّر Q7:82; مُتطهِّر, Q2:222; مُطَهِّر Q9:108; طهور, Q14:22, مُصرِّخ Q36:43; يصرُخ, صريخ, Q28:18; يستصرخ Q35:37; يصطرخ Q25:48, عجيب, Q11:72 and عُجاب, Q38:5;
2 related to polysemy, partial synonymy and shades of meaning, as in إنفَجَرَ, Q2:60 and إنبَجَسَ, Q7:160; الحُسنى, Q16:62, Q10:26; الكريم, (Q44:49, Q82:6 and 11); and
3 case marking (حركات الإعراب), which can influence a major semantic distinction, as in الضُّرُّ in Q21:83 where the letter ضَ has the short vowel الضمة /u/, and its counterpart الضَّرُّ where the letter ضَ has the short vowel الفتحة /a/. The word الضُّرُّ in Q21:83 semantically entails [+ Disease] – it is specific; while الضَّرُّ entails [+ Suffering] – it is generic. This is because أيوب (Job) was afflicted with a disease for 18 years. Thus, the accurate meaning of الضُّرُّ in Q21:83 is "disease". These examples demonstrate that English lacks a sub-code equivalent to that in Arabic.

With the emergence of the notion of equivalence in the 1960s and 70s, translation has been generally seen as a process of communicating foreign text by a semantically analogous (equivalent) text. Based on the notion of equivalence, Eugene Nida distinguishes between "dynamic (functional)" and "formal" varieties of "correspondence" (Nida and Taber 1969).

12 *Translation as process and product*

The ST, according to Vermeer (1978; cited in Venuti 2000:222), is usually composed originally for a situation in the source culture; hence its status as ST, and hence the role of the translator in the process of inter-cultural communication. This remains true of a ST which has been composed specifically with transcultural communication in mind. The ST is source culture oriented. However, the TT is target culture oriented. Thus, the ST and TT diverge from each other quite considerably, not only in content formulation and distribution but also in terms of the content arrangement.

Newmark (1991:43–44) talks about the "purposes of translation" and claims there are five purposes:

1   Political: to promote peace and understanding among nations,
2   Technological: to transmit knowledge (transfer of knowledge),
3   Cultural: to mediate between cultures,
4   Artistic: to translate world's classics, and
5   Pedagogical: to use it as a teaching aid in teaching/learning a foreign/second language.

In the view of Gutt (1991; cited in Venuti 2000:376), a translation is a receptor language text which interpretively resembles the original without unnecessary processing effort on the part of the TL reader.

In the view of Tancock (1958:29), translation is to meet the four basic requirements of: (1) making sense, (2) conveying the spirit and manner of the original, (3) having a natural and easy form of expression, and (4) producing a similar response.

Based on Arabic translation, the following discussion will demonstrate that the semantic relations between Arabic and English are always "many-to-many, with plenty of scope for ambiguities, obscurities, and 'fuzzy' boundaries" (Nida 1994:147), that there is seldom a complete match between languages (Larson 1984:57), and that whatever level of equivalence may be achieved, the TT will necessarily be an imperfect or approximate rendering of the ST (Moir 2009:43).

Among the major criteria of translation are faithfulness to the performative intent of the ST and effectively natural style. A good translation achieves a balance between content (meaning based on ST context and culture) and form (linguistic and stylistic TL norms). A translator should always aim for a target-oriented translation, fidelity to the ST meaning, making the translation intelligible to TT reader, and conformity to the ST genre.

During the translation process, the translator should be aware of three useful translation procedures:

1   *Addition*: The translator is allowed to add a word or two in any TT sentence in the interest of clarity, naturalness, and equivalent effect in the TT.
2   *Deletion (omission)*: The translator is allowed to take out an intra-sentential full-stop, a conjunctive particle (cohesive device), some words, or punctuation marks (such as commas, full-stops, semi-colons) from the ST in order to naturalize and domesticate the TT whose linguistic, cohesion system, and stylistic norms do not need them.
3   *Adaptation*: The translator needs to naturalize and domesticate the TT in order to:

   (i)   suit the TL audience,
   (ii) meet the TL linguistic, stylistic, semantic, and cultural norms, and
   (iii) provide a natural TL style (i.e., make the translation enjoy the sound fluent in the TL).

1.3 Monitoring and managing translation

Monitoring and managing are concerned with linguistic prejudice and the abuse of semantics. They are situational factors that can influence the TT. This is due to the fact that "discourse is the vehicle of attitudinal expression" (Hatim 1997:206). Translation borders, at times, with politics, and the translator is influenced by his/her political views with regards to a given notion (concept) embodied in an expression. Thus, in such a situation, the translator is either an impartial or a biased mediator between the ST and the TT. For examples and more details, see the Concluding remarks at the end of this section. It is worthwhile to note that the notions of managing and monitoring are also encountered in journalism. For instance, the *Khaleej Times*, a UAE newspaper, reports of "Bomber kills two settlers, 18 May 2003" as a monitoring (neutral) journalistic mechanism. However, Western newspapers report of "Terrorists (Suicide bombers) kill two Jews in Hebron" as a managing journalistic technique.

Any given translation involves either monitoring or managing a situation; either objectivity/impartiality or mediation/persuasion prevails. Thus, in terms of translation studies, we encounter two types of contextual factors:

1   **Situation monitoring**: In monitoring a ST situation, the translator provides objective, impartial, and neutral transfer of a situation in which the overtone designates an ideological stance towards a contentious political, religious, or social issue. The output of such a translation process based on situation monitoring is a faithful translation to the ST producer's performative intent, since the translator has provided an unmediated account of the ST situation. Thus, we can claim that the situation monitoring is similar to the faithful translation approach proposed by Gutt (1991; cited in Venuti 2000:378) where the TT preserves the ST implicature to the TL reader. Situation monitoring pertains to situations like reporting, narrating, describing, informing, greeting, or instructing. Thus, the translation is dominated by an atmosphere of impartiality and objectivity, as in the following examples:

Example 1:
The <u>bombing</u> of a Pan AM jetliner over Lockerbie in 1988 killed 270 people.

If the translation is based on situation monitoring, the TT is

أدى <u>انفجار</u> الطائرة بان آم فوق لوكربي الى مقتل 270 شخصا.

where the translator has adopted the dogmatic or political standpoint in a given country where he/she lives or which he/she supports. Thus, the translator has employed انفجار as a nominalized noun مصدر derived from the intransitive verb اِنفَجَرَ: The airliner exploded on its own due to a mechanical fault and there is no third party involved. The intransitive verb semantically signifies the absence of a doer (Agent) to an action denoted by the verb: There is no one behind the action of blowing up the jetliner. The above translation can be clarified through *Case Grammar* and the semantic roles undertaken by the noun (phrase). Agent is a semantic role assigned to a noun (noun phrase). It means the actual doer of an action embodied in an action verb like "break, write, build". Agent refers to the typically animate instigator of the action identified by the verb. In other words, there is volition (i.e., will,

14 *Translation as process and product*

desire) on the part of the doer of an action. However, الطائرة بان آم (Pan AM jetliner) has the semantic role of "Patient" because a "Patient" undergoes an action and changes its state due to an action by an "Agent". Since there is no Agent mentioned, then no country can be held responsible for the إنفجار (explosion).

Such a translation appeared in Libyan newspapers and media and in many Arabic newspapers across the Middle East in support of Libya. Such a translation does not implicate Libya in the death of 270 people.

The same applies to تفجير مرفأ بيروت where we can have a translation process based on situation monitoring "the explosion at Beirut port" where no third party is involved. The ST makes an implicit reference to an Agent behind the action of تفجير. However, the translation has made no reference to the implicit Agent who caused the تفجير (explosion). Thus, this translation failed the ST, which implicitly implicates a third party.

> Example 2:
> "The <u>withdrawal</u> of the Turkish forces", whose translation based on situation monitoring, is انسحاب القوات التركية الإنسحاب التكتيكي للقوات التركية إعادة تموضع القوات التركية.

> Example 3:
> "Sa'dah is the Huthi <u>stronghold</u>", whose translation based on situation monitoring, is بُعتبر صعدة <u>معقل</u> الحوثيين.

> Example 4:
> "The <u>liberation</u> of Iraq in 2003", whose translation based on situation monitoring, is تحرير العراق في عام 2003.

> Example 5:
> "Wuhan was the <u>center</u> of the novel coronavirus", whose translation based on situation monitoring, is كانت ووهان مصدر فيروس كورونا الجديد.

> Example 6:
> Smoking <u>kills</u>, whose translation based on situation monitoring, is التدخينُ مُضرٌ.

> Example 7: The use of the nominalized noun تسمُّم "unintentional 'food' poisoning" – a reflexive act on the part of the person who has suffered food poisoning where there is no third party involved. This word has occurred recently when the Russian opposition leader Alexei Navalny suffered from "poisoning" on 20 August 2020. To monitor the expression, Arab media employs تسمُّم to relay the message that the Russian government is not a suspect and is innocent of "poisoning" Alexei Navalny.

2 **Situation managing**: This is to steer (guide) the ST situation in a manner which is favorable to the translator's dogmatic goals. In other words, the translator attempts to steer the ST message to his/her interest and favor. By twisting the ST producer's performative intent, impartiality and bias prevail in the TT. This is due to the fact that the translator, via managing the ST situation, attempts to persuade the TT reader towards a certain ideological stance regarding a contentious political, religious, or social issue.

The translator engages the TT reader in a situation management and guides him/her in a manner favorable to the translator's political, religious, or social goals. In situation managing, the translator's intention is to steer his/her TT reader into accepting (through persuasion) the "twisted" performative intent of the TT. The output of such a translation process based on situation managing is an unfaithful translation – an intentionally subjective, mediated, and biased transfer of the ST situation that does not represent the ST producer's performative intent, as in the following examples:

Example 1:
The <u>bombing</u> of a Pan AM jetliner over Lockerbie in 1988 killed 270 people.

If the translation is based on situation managing, the TT is

أدى تفجير الطائرة بان آم فوق لوكربي الى مقتل 270 شخصا.

where the translator has adopted the ST producer's performative intent. Thus, the translator has employed تفجير as a nominalized noun مصدر derived from the transitive verb فجَّرَ: Someone deliberately planted a bomb on the airliner. Such a translation implicates Libya in the death of 270 people. The transitive verb semantically signifies that there is a human doer (Agent) to an action denoted by the verb: There is someone behind the action of blowing up the jetliner.

The same applies to انفجار مرفأ بيروت, where a translation process based on situation management (Beirut port has been blown up) suggests that a third party (the semantic role Agent) is implicitly involved. This translation "Beirut port has been blown up" has failed the ST انفجار مرفأ بيروت, which does not politically implicate a third party.

Example 2:
"The <u>withdrawal</u> of the Turkish forces", whose translation based on situation managing, is تقهقُر اندحار القوات التركية.

Example 3:
"Sa'dah is the Huthi <u>stronghold</u>", whose translation based on situation managing, is تُعتبر صعدة بؤرة الحوثيين.

Example 4:
"The <u>liberation</u> of Iraq in 2003", whose translation based on situation managing, is احتلال العراق في عام 2003.

Example 5:
"Wuhan was the <u>center</u> of the novel coronavirus", whose translation based on situation managing, is كانت وهان بؤرة فيروس كورونا الجديد.

Example 6: Smoking <u>kills</u>.

On the cigarette packet, however, we find the translation التدخين مُضرٌ بالصحة, the back-translation of which is "Smoking is harmful to health". Thus, the ST situation of a stern warning against smoking has been managed in Arabic, since it minimizes the deadly health

16 *Translation as process and product*

hazards of smoking. For instance, "junk food" can be "harmful to health" but "smoking kills". Thus, the illocutionary force of the two adverts are widely distinct.

> Example 7: The use of the nominalized noun تسميم "intentional poisoning": There is a third party involved in deliberately putting poison in someone's food/drink. This word has occurred recently when the Russian opposition leader Alexei Navalny suffered from "poisoning" on 20 August 2020. To manage the expression, the media employs تسميم to relay the message that the Russian government is a suspect and is involved in the "poisoning" of Alexei Navalny – "toxins were poured into his tea". Kira Yarmysh, Navalny's press secretary, says she suspects poison was added to a cup of tea that he drank at the airport. The managing of the expression تسميم is based on the fact that Alexei Navalny has been the Russian president Putin's arch-rival.

Concluding remarks: The translator shows his/her true colours when the ST is politically sensitive. When translation borders with politics, the two types of contextual (situational) factors of managing or monitoring translation play a significant role in translation decision making: The translation process is either managed or monitored. However, the victim of such a situation is always the translation output (TT). The expression "the six-day war in June 1967" is a case in point. For an impartial translator who wants to monitor the ST, we find an unmediated account of the ST situation and the TT is "حرب الأيام الستة في عام 1967". However, for an Israeli translator we get "Milhemet Sheshet Ha Yamim" ملحمة شيشة هياميم, meaning "the Six-Day War", which is based on situation monitoring and has a Biblical overtone; and for an Arab translator we get "نكسة 'حزيران عام 1967", which is based on situation managing. This is because of the word نكسة نكبة, meaning "setback", because in the six-day Arab-Israeli war (5–10 June 1967), the Arab armies suffered defeat and losses in territory.

Similarly, for an Arab translator, the ST expression "terrorist" may have a situation managing where we get فدائي/مُجاهد, the back-translation of which means "a freedom fighter/a fighter in the cause of God". However, if we apply the monitoring situation translation, we get ارهابي/متطرف. The same applies to the SL expression "suicide bomber". The same applies to the ST expression "Covid-19 in Europe", which has been given a situation managing translation by some Arab TV channels as فيروس كورونا في القارة العجوز where the expression القارة العجوز is connotatively derogatory. However, a translation based on situation monitoring is فيروس كورونا في أوربا.

During the early days of August 2021, the sentence: "The withdrawal of American troops from Afghanistan" became an interesting example in Arabic translation with regards to monitoring and managing the ST. We have observed two different translations:

(i) A translation based on monitoring the above ST situation. Thus, we have

انسحاب القوات الأمريكية من أفغانستان.

(ii) A translation based on managing the above ST situation. Thus, we have

هزيمة (اندحار) القوات الأمريكية في أفغانستان.

Thus, the difference is ideologically and politically based: We have إنسحاب versus هزيمة.

Similarly, ". . . to evacuate US citizens and Afghan allies fleeing the Taliban", where "allies" can be monitored as الخُلَفاء "allies" or managed as الجواسيس، العُملاء، الخونة "traitors, collaborators, spies".

1.4 False friends

False friends are false cognate words in two or more languages. False friends

1 look alike – they are orthographically similar;
2 sound similar – the phonetic form of the SL word is apparent in the TL; but
3 differ in meaning significantly.

For instance: the English word "embarrassed" and the Spanish word "embarazada", which means "pregnant"; the English word "parents" and the Portuguese word "parentes", which means "relatives"; and the English word "sensible", which means "reasonable" in English, but it means "sensitive" in French, German, and Spanish. Additional examples include: English "demand" and French "demander", English "ignore" and Spanish "ignorer", English "virtue" and Latin "virtus", and English "deacon" and Greek "diakonos". Thus, in bilingual situations, a false friend refers to a borrowed or cognate word – a word which appears borrowed from another language at face value, but has a semantic shift. It has become a loan word but has acquired an additional meaning.

> Example 1: "casino" in English and كازينو in Arabic.

In English, "casino" means "night club; gambling-house; a public building for gambling and entertainment". However, in Arabic, it means "a café where tea and coffee are served", and sometimes hookah شيشة is served, too. Thus, the two words are semantically distinct in terms of their respective connotative meaning. The English word "casino" is a loanword in Arabic which has developed a new meaning not found in the SL. While "casino" designates a negative social connotation in English, كازينو in Arabic has a positive social connotation.

> Example 2: "gymnasium" is a Latin word which can mean both (i) a place of education, and (ii) a place for exercise.

However, in Arabic and English, the Latin word is used to designate the second meaning, but in German, "gymnasium" is used to mean the first meaning.

> Example 3: "club" in English and نادي in Arabic.

The most recurrent meaning of "club" in English is "a nightclub with dance and music". However, in Arabic, it denotes "an association of people who meet regularly to take part in a particular social activity such as نادي الطلاب (student club) or sports (gym, swimming)".

There is linguistic and cultural distance between Arabic and English. However, consider languages and cultures which are comparatively closely related, such as Arabic and Hebrew. We must beware superficial similarities; translations done under these circumstances are often quite poor. Nida (1964) argues that "differences between cultures cause many more severe complications for the translator than do differences in language structure".

18 *Translation as process and product*

> Example 4: After the First World War, when the British and the French colonized some Arab countries, they framed the situation such that they were not occupiers but rather empowering the people to re-build their countries. Their claims drew on Qur'anic intertextuality in order to win the hearts and minds of Arabs:
>
> هو أنشأكم من الأرضِ واستعمركُم فيها.(هود 16) – He has produced you from the earth and made you settle down in it, Q11:61.

where the verb استعمر "to enable someone to settle down somewhere" is employed in the Qur'an with a positive connotative meaning. Having realized that the occupation of the British and the French was for different political and economic ends, the Arabs have developed a negative connotative meaning for the Qur'anic word إستعمر. Thus, it has become a false friend (Newmark 1988:72). The Qur'anic expression إستعمر has now been clothed with the negative politically oriented meaning "to colonize". To achieve cultural or functional equivalence, Newmark (ibid:83) calls for a cultural componential analysis as the most accurate way of translating or de-culturalizing a cultural word.

> Example 5: The expression كازينو in the Arab world is used for places where tea or coffee is served; the intended meaning of كازينو is "café". However, the expression has been borrowed into Arabic without realizing that the culture-based meaning of casino in English is a facility where alcohol is served, women are working there, and the place is mainly used for gambling, card games, or other games like Roulette, Craps, Blackjack, Poker.
>
> Example 6: The expressions مُبشّر/تبشير/الحركات التبشيرية are false friends in Arabic. This is because these expressions have a different intended meaning from their original meaning. These expressions have an intertextual relationship with the Qur'anic expression بشير/مُبشّر of Q2:119 and Q17:105, whose meaning is "a bringer of glad tidings, i.e., the Islamic faith and the winning of paradise", which refers to the Prophet Muhammad. When the missionaries started their work in the Arab world in the 17th century, they introduced the false-friend expression بشير/مُبشّر. The Arabs have been using this expression without realizing that it signifies Jesus Christ and the spread of the glad tidings of Christianity. However, the context-based, culture-specific intended meaning of the false friend مُبشّر/تبشير is مُنصّر/تنصير, whose translation is "missionary". The back-translation of مُنصّر/تنصير is "the one who spreads Christianity/the movement of spreading Christianity". The meaning based on back-translation would have been rejected by Muslims in the Arab World. Thus, the false-friend expressions مُنصّر/تنصير are readily acceptable by the Muslims, although semantically deceptive and misleading.

The verb يستقطب has the common (expected) meaning of (i) "to attract" and (ii) "to recruit the talented ones". However, recently, the nominalized noun إستقطاب has taken a distinct semantic signification in political discourse. The noun إستقطاب has adopted a false friend meaning: "the divergence of political attitudes to ideological extremes", as in ظهرَ استقطاب بين التيار الأسلامي والتيار الليبرالي في الوطن العربي "Polarization has emerged between the Islamists and the liberals in the Arab world".

Translation as process and product 19

1.5 Overview of translation approaches

We are now, as Bassnett (1998:26) rightly claims, at a watershed in translation studies, where there are all kinds of shifting and conflicting concepts of translation being continually reassessed and revised. Up until the second half of the 20th century, translation theory seemed locked in what George Steiner (1998:319) calls a "sterile" debate focused on the distinction between "word-for-word" (i.e., "literal") and "sense-for-sense" (i.e., "free") translation, which goes back to Cicero (first century BCE) and St Jerome (late fourth century CE), and forms the basis of key writings on translation in centuries nearer to our own (Munday 2001:19). Among the different translation approaches are

1   **Anachronism translation approach** produces unsmooth translation, using old-fashioned language in the TL, and hence giving an impression of unreality. Anachronism is a feature of some Qur'an translations, as in

وقلنا ياآدمُ اسكُن أنتَ وزوجُكَ الجنَّةَ وكُلا منها رَغَدًا حيثُ شئتُما (البقرة 35)

And We said: O Adam! Dwell thou and thy wife in the Garden, and eat ye freely (of the fruits) thereof where ye will (Pickthall 1930:no page).

We said: "O Adam! dwell thou and thy wife in the Garden; and eat of the bountiful things therein as (where and when) ye will" (Ali 1934:no page).

And We said, "Adam, dwell thou, and thy wife, in the Garden, and eat thereof easefully where you desire" (Arberry 1955:35).

O Adam, dwell thou and thy wife in this garden, and eat freely thereof, both of you, whatever you may wish. (Asad 1980:33).

خَلَقتني من نارٍ وخَلَقتَهُ من طينٍ (ص 76)

I am better than him. Thou createdst me of fire, whilst him Thou didst create of clay (Pickthall 1930:no page).

Thou createdst me from fire, and him thou createdst from clay (Ali 1934:no page).

Thou createdst me of fire, and him Thou createdst of clay (Arberry 1955:206).

I am better than he: Thou hast created me out of fire, whereas him Thou hast created out of clay (Asad 1980:954).

The above TTs demonstrate unsmooth translations because of the employment of old-fashioned language and violation of modern stylistic norms in the TTs. This is illustrated through the lexical level where we encounter archaic words like "thou, ye, thy, createdst, didst, hast" as well as at the grammatical and word order levels, as in "whilst him Thou didst create of clay", "him thou createdst from clay", and "I am better than he".

Let us also consider Q51:58 إنَّ اللَّهَ هوَ الرزاقُ ذو القوَّةِ المتين (الذاريات 58), whose translation is based on anachronism translation approach: "Lo! Allah! He it is that giveth livelihood, the Lord of unbreakable might" (Pickthall 1930:no page).

2   **Literal translation approach**: The major characteristics of literal translation are as follows.

   (i)   The literal meaning of the SL expression is given out of context in the TT: This approach provides the literal meanings of the SL words out of context. Thus, literal translation is the opposite to localization, which is SL context and culture-based

20 *Translation as process and product*

translation in which a ST is stripped of its culture-specific features – as in "the tip of the iceberg", wrongly translated literally as قمة الجبل الجليدي, while its correct and context-based meaning is غيضٌ من فيضٌ. Another example is قالَ نُسوةٌ, where the subject noun is a plural of paucity جمع قلة because in the context of the women mentioned in Q12:30 of the story of Joseph, there were only five. However, English lacks this grammatical mechanism; English, unlike Arabic, does not differentiate between two types of plural. Arabic does: جمع قلة/جمع كثرة or plural of "paucity"/ plural of "multitude", respectively. Thus, a literal translation approach is adopted "Women said" without reference to their very limited number. On 12 April 2013, the satellite TV channel العربية used a literal translation أدلة صلبة of the expression "hard evidence" when reporting on the Syrian regime's use of chemical weapons. The correct non-literal translation is (أدلة قاطعة (دامغة. In Q21:90, we encounter the verb أصلحَ which is given the literal translation of "to amend" while its accurate context-based meaning is "to cure".

An example of context and meaning is تخصيب/يُخصِّب which should be translated as "to fertilize, fertilization" when the context is about soil or an egg (sperm) where we say "to fertilize the soil; to fertilize an egg". However, when the context is about uranium, we should use "to enrich uranium, the enrichment of uranium".

Another example of a literal translation approach is أبو الخيمة الزرقة whose literal meaning out of context is "The father of the blue tent". The translation of metonymy suffers from literal translation when transferred to the TL out of the SL context. The above example is a metonymy expression used in Iraq whose context-based (intended) meaning is "Allah – God" because the sky is blue, God is the owner (father) of the blue sky, and the sky is likened to a tent under which all people shelter.

We encounter in some Arab countries the expression نأسف على الإزعاج on signs where road work is taking place. However, its translation "Sorry for the annoyance" provides a literal meaning of the ST expression out of context. The context-based TT is "Sorry for the inconvenience".

An interesting example of an out-of-context, literal meaning of a SL expression is "a hand-to-mouth existence", whose out-of-context literal translation is "حياة "عيشٌ" من اليد الى الفم". However, a context-based non-literal translation is الكفاف, as in

يعيشُ الكثيرُ من الناس على الكفاف "Many people live a hand-to-mouth existence"

Similarly, in the Arab Gulf, when X does a favour to Y, Y says ما قصرت, whose out of context literal translation is "You have not shortened". Similarly, we have تختلط سلمى كثيرا, whose out of context literal translation is "Salma mixes with a lot of people".

Literal translation in Arabic has been a source for jokes. Jokes they may be, but they are examples of literal translation, which provides the literal meanings of the SL words out of context, as in ظروف قاهرة, whose literal translation is "Cairo envelops". The context-based translation is "mitigating circumstances, hard times". Also, an airplane hostess asks a passenger: "Would you like beef or chicken, sir?", the passenger replies: "Monday". The airhostess is baffled and the other passenger next to him tries to help and explains to him what she meant. The passenger becomes defensive and says: "I want Monday". However, the passenger's context-based response should be: "Both". To provide a translation commentary on both examples, we say:

(a) Both "Cairo envelops" and "Monday" are literal translations; and

(b) The plural noun ظروف is a polyseme which means either (a) envelops, or (b) circumstances, situations;

(c) The noun الإثنين is a polyseme which means either (a) Monday, or (b) both.

Thus, the literal meaning of an expression out of context leads to the wrong meaning.

Another example of literal translation found in an herbal medicine shop is حَب ينسون with its literal translation "They forgot love". The error has resulted from the out-of-context translation of the herb noun ينسون which means "aniseed". However, the translator has thought the initial letter ي of ينسون represents a verb and has treated the noun ينسون as a verb with a plural subject pronoun "they forgot". The translator has also misunderstood the noun حَب, which means "seeds", because he/she has read the initial letter ح with a short vowel /u/ – حُب ضمّة – while it should have been read with a short vowel /a/ – حَب فتحة – so that the meaning is "seeds".

In Qur'an translation, we also encounter the literal meaning of the SL word out of context, as in يتماسَّا من قبل أن (Q58:3, 4):

> Before they touch one another (Saheeh International 1997:782).
> Before they touch each other (Ali 1934:no page).
> Before the two of them touch one another (Arberry 1955:248).

Here the Qur'anic expression يتماسَّا is given a literal, out-of-context meaning "to touch one another". However, stylistically, يتماسَّا is a rhetorical device of metonymy كِناية whose context-based meaning is "to have a sexual intercourse".

Another example of an out-of-context, literal meaning of a SL expression given in the TT is "The Prime Minister said he agreed to make it easier to do business with our friends across the pond". The translation problem lies in the noun "the pond" whose literal (denotative) meaning out of context is بُركة, where we have the literal translation:

صرَّحَ رئيسُ الوزراء بأنه وافق على تيسير عقد صفقات تجارية مع أصدقائنا في الجانب الآخر من البركة.

However, a context-based translation would provide a context-based meaning, which makes the TT easily understood where the expression بركة means "the Atlantic, i.e., the USA":

صرَّحَ رئيسُ الوزراء بأنه وافق على تيسير عقد صفقات تجارية مع أصدقائنا في الجانب الآخر من المحيط الأطلسي.

or even better:

صرَّحَ رئيسُ الوزراء بأنه وافق على تيسير عقد صفقات تجارية مع أصدقائنا في الولايات المتحدة الأمريكية.

Another example of meaning out of context is the expression "Guinea pigs", whose literal translation is خنازير غينيا.

22 *Translation as process and product*

Examples of context-based, intended meaning, and non-literal translation are

"to tread the water", whose non-literal translation is يجس النبض rather than يخوض في الماء.

"in custody", whose non-literal translation is قيد التحقيق rather than في السجن.

"Turkish official TV has fallen off air", whose non-literal translation is انقطعَ التلفاز التركي الرسمي عن البث rather than سقط من الهواء.

"Rumors had swirled around the capital", whose non-literal translation is تخيُّم الإشاعات على العاصمة rather than تدور الإشاعات حول العاصمة.

"Another "bimbo eruption" will be revealed", whose non-literal translation is سيتمُّ الأعلان عن ثوران بركان (الكشف) عن فضيحة جنسية أخرى rather than سيتم الأعلان عن امرأة غبية ذات جمال.

أُحِبُّكَ في الله, whose non-literal translation is "I love you for the sake of God" rather than "I love you in God".

Another example of an out-of-context literal meaning of a SL expression is أمسكَ أحمد لسانهُ, whose literal translation is "Ahmad held his tongue".

In Qur'an translation, literal translation is encountered frequently, as in حرثَ الآخرة الشورى 20, where the noun حرث is literally translated as "tilth, harvest" – "the tilth 'harvest' of the hereafter" – while its context-based meaning is "reward, deeds which lead to reward".

The classical Arabic expressions بيت المال and بيت الله can be given an out of context literal meaning as "the house of money" and "the house of God" respectively. Similarly, the expression "cornerstone" is given an out-of-context literal translation as حجر الزاوية.

During the recent American presidential election campaigns and the polarization between Democrats and Republicans, we have encountered the slogans: "Black Lives Matter", "Blue Lives Matter", and "Back the Blue". To provide an out-of-context literal meaning of such SL expressions, we have: حياة السود مهمة/حياة الزرق مهمة/ساندوا الزرق respectively. However, a context-based translation is different for the last two SL expressions: "Blue Lives Matter" → حياة الشرطة مهمة, and "Back the Blue" → ساندوا الشرطة, which are the slogans of the US Republicans. The context of "Black Lives Matter" is based around the murder of George Floyd, a 46-year-old Black man on 25 May 2020 in Minneapolis, USA, by a white police officer.

(ii) The word order and stylistic structure of the ST are kept to their nearest TL word order and stylistic structure. Upon the completion of the literal translation, the TL style is not natural, the TL cohesion system is not met, and the meaning may not be accurate, as in:

الله يعلمُ وأنتم لا تعلمون – "Allah knows, while you know not" (Q2:216), where the ST stylistic structure is preserved in the TT. The ST involves the reiteration of the same verb يعلم "to know" and the TT violates its cohesion and structural norms of verbal substitution where the second verb تعلمون should be substituted by the auxiliary verb "do". Thus, we should have "God knows and you <u>do</u> not", which is a non-literal translation approach.

وإذ يرفعُ إبراهيمُ القواعدَ من البيتِ وإسماعيلُ

Translation as process and product 23

Let us consider the following literal translation with an unnatural style due to the ST word order being preserved:

> And when Abraham was raising the foundations of the house and Ishmael (Q2:127) (Saheeh International 1997:24).

Next we encounter a natural, non-literal translation which has taken into consideration the word order norms of the TL:

> And when Abraham and Ishmael were raising the foundations of the House (Pickthall 1930:no page).

A unique example which illustrates how a TT style is not natural due to literal translation is Q28:24 as follows:

ربِّ إنِّي لِما أنزلتَ إليَّ من خيرٍ فقيرٍ (القصص 24)

> My Lord, indeed I am, for whatever good You would send down to me, in need (Saheeh International 1997:535).

It is worthwhile to note that we have two lexical items خير and فقير ending with the same consonant /r/(الراء حرف) . This is evidence that this particular word order, which is called in stylistics a "hyperbaton", has been employed for the purpose of rhyme. Q28:24 could have ended with the lexical item خيرٍ, and the other lexical item فقير placed after the subject pronoun إنِّي, (I). Thus, we get ربِّ إنِّي (فقيرٌ) لِما أنزلتَ إليَّ من خيرٍ. However, the lexical item فقير has behaved for the achievement of the rhetorical device of hyperbaton (placed at the end of the sentence) to establish the illocutionary force of attracting the reader's attention. In other words, this lexical behavior resulting in word order change in the sentence structure is employed for the perlocutionary effects of focus, saliency, affirmation, and vivid depiction of the idea depicted by the word فقير that has been moved from its original position and placed at the end of the sentence, rather than to its original initial position of the sentence. This lexical behavior is for focusing the notion of لِما أنزلت إليَّ من خيرٍ "for whatever good You would send down to me" and give it prominence.

Having provided textual and discourse analysis of the ST (Q28:24), we suggest the following more natural TL style:

> TT: My Lord, I am in need of whatever good thing You may send down to me.

Let us consider this next example of a literal translation whose word order and stylistic structure of the ST are kept to their nearest TL word order and stylistic structure in Q66:11:

رَبِّ ابن لي عِندَكَ بَيتًا في الجنّة – My Lord, build for me near You a house in paradise.

It is worthwhile to note that upon the completion of the translation, the TL style is natural.

In literal translation, according to Newmark (1988:46), the SL grammatical structures are converted to their nearest TL equivalents, but the words are translated singly out of context. In literal translation, according to Dickins et al. (2002:16), the denotative meaning

24 *Translation as process and product*

of words is taken as if straight from the dictionary, out of context, but TL grammar is preserved, as in:

الدُنيا شمسٌ – It is sunny.

Here the TT employs the dummy subject "It" while the ST has the noun الدُنيا literally meaning "the world", and the TT employs the adjective "sunny" while the ST has a noun شمسٌ.

It is worthwhile to note that the term "literal" is used to denote a TT which is overtly close or influenced by the ST or SL, and the result is what sometimes known as "translationese" (Hatim and Munday 2004:12). Thus, a literal translation is not so common when the SL and the TL are linguistically unrelated, like Arabic and English. Literal translation, however, can take place between linguistically related languages like Catalan and Spanish.

> **(iii)** Literal translation is word-for-word translation and sticks very closely to the ST lexis and syntax (Newmark 1981:63), as in جُزُر القَمُر which is literally translated as "the Moon Islands" while it should be "The Comoro Islands or Comoros".

For Newmark (ibid:39), literal word-for-word translation is not only the best – it is the *only* valid method of translation, provided that equivalent effect is secured. However, Newmark (ibid) distinguishes between semantic translation and literal translation. Semantic translation, in his view, "respects context" as it interprets the ST.

An example of a word-for-word translation that sticks very closely to the ST lexis and syntax is the translation of the Arabic expression لا ناقة لي فيها ولا جَمل, whose literal and word-for-word translation is "Neither a female camel do I have in this matter nor a male one". However, contrary to what Newmark claimed that in such a translation equivalent effect is secured, we can argue that this is *not* the case: equivalent effect is *not* secured by the TT due to the culture-specific ST words ناقة/جَمل (female camel/male camel).

A SL noun phrase "Adam's apple" is translated word-for-word literally as تفاحة آدم.

3 Stylistic literalness translation approach: We have diagnosed this approach in Qur'an translation. This approach aims to imitate the Qur'anic stylistic structure with disregard to TT linguistic norms. Stylistic literalness approach completely typifies the structural equivalence with the ST; it is structural equivalence through which the translator attempts to reproduce as literally and meaningfully as possible the form and content of the Qur'anic text. We have provided five sources which lead to stylistic literalness in Qur'anic Arabic translation. These are (i) hyperbaton, (ii) foregrounding, (iii) the absolute object, (iv) verbal substitution, and (v) the detached pronoun. For more details, see Chapter 3.

4 Communicative translation approach: The major characteristics of communicative translation are as follows.

> **(i)** Communicative translation is a target-oriented translation: It renders the exact contextual meaning of the ST in such a way that both source content and language are acceptable and comprehensible to TL readership (Newmark 1988:47), as in (piggy bank) which is rendered to Arabic as حَصَّالة. Other examples are
>
> تختلط سلمى كثيراً, whose context-based communicative translation is "Salma mingles with a lot of people". However, its out-of-context literal translation is "Salma mixes with a lot of people".

Russia has flexed its muscles in Libya – تَستعرضُ روسيا عضلاتها في ليبيا

crewed space shuttle – مركبة فضاء مأهولة

أمسَكَ أحمدُ لسانَهُ, whose communicative translation is "Ahmad kept quiet".

In the Arab Gulf, when X does a favour to Y, Y says ما قصَّرت in appreciation to what X has done to him. The target-oriented translation is "Much appreciated". However, its out-of-context literal translation is "You have not shortened".

Examples of translations based on contextual meaning:

"Herd immunity" in the medical context is translated as مناعة القطيع, while "diplomatic immunity" in the diplomatic context is rendered as حَصَانة دبلوماسية.

Similarly, the word "center" has two different context-meanings: (i) negative connotative meaning "Wuhan was the center of the novel coronavirus", whose context-based meaning is كانت وهان بؤرة فيروس كورونا الجديد, (ii) positive connotative meaning "Baghdad was the center of translation studies", whose context-based meaning is كانت بغداد مركزًا لدراسات علم الترجمة.

Also, the polyseme word حُجَّة occurs in two different contexts, but in English, the translator needs to use

(a) (pretext) when the context designates a negative connotative meaning "The US attacked China under the pretext of the coronavirus" هاجمت الولايات المتحدة الصين بِحُجَّة فيروس كورونا;

(b) (conclusive evidence) when the context designates defense and the need for a proof "China demanded conclusive evidence" طالبت الصين بحجة دامغة.

The Prime Minister outlined a £24 billion austerity package وضع رئيس الوزراء خطة تقشف قيمتها 24 مليار جنيه استرليني.

The British economy will grow by one percent in 2020 despite the debt storm tearing through the Euro-zone سوف ينمو الأقتصاد البريطاني بنسبة 1% على الرغم من زوبعة الديون التي تعصفُ بمنطقة اليورو,

where the contextual meaning of the ST expressions "package" خطة and "the debt storm tearing through the euro-zone" زوبعة الديون التي تعصفُ بمنطقة اليورو is provided and the TTs are acceptable and comprehensible to the TT audience.

Communicative translation is the opposite of the literal translation approach as illustrated by the translation of Q58:3–4 من قبل أن يتماسا, whose communicative translation is: "Before they have a sexual intercourse", where the translator has considered the context of the ST and translated the intended meaning of the metonymy rather than the literal and out-of-context meaning of يتماسًا. However, the literal meaning of Q58:3–4 is "Before they touch one another".

The expressions بيت المال and بيت الله can be given communicative translations as "the Treasury" or "the Ministry of Finance".

(ii) The communicative translation approach provides the contextual meanings of the SL words, the intended meaning of the ST author, and a natural TL style. The

26 *Translation as process and product*

two criteria of SL natural style and cohesion are achieved through communicative translation.

Communicative translation reads like an original in terms of meaning and style, as in:

لم يكُن لهُ كُفواً أحَدٌ (الإخلاص 4)

whose communicative translation is: "No one is comparable to Him". (Abdel Haleem 2005:444), where complete naturalness of the TT is achieved.

However, Arberry (1955:281) has provided a translation "And equal to Him is not any one", which is not a natural style; it is literal and very close to the ST structure and word order.

Similar, in terms of natural TL style, is the translation "I am most forgiving towards those who repent", (Q20:82) (Abdel Haleem 2005:199) for the ST إني لغفّارٌ لمن تابَ. However, we encounter translations which provide a style which is alien to the TL reader, as in "I forgive him who repents" (Ahmad 2010:417).

Another example of a communicative translation approach which provides the contextual meaning of the SL words, the intended meaning of the ST author, and a natural TL style is the expression "a hand-to-mouth existence", whose communicative translation is الكفاف, as in

"Many people live a hand-to-mouth existence" يعيشُ الكثيرُ من الناس على الكفاف

(iii) Communicative translation is TL-culture-based: It provides an equivalent target culture situation, as in رَجَعَ بخُفّي حُنَين, whose communicative translation is "He came back (returned) empty handed". For Dickins et al. (2002:234), a communicative translation is a mode of free translation. It is produced when, in a given situation, the ST uses an SL expression standard for that situation, and the TT uses a TL expression standard for an equivalent target culture situation. In their view (ibid:17, 35), communicative translation is a normal approach in the case of culturally conventional cliché, such as إن شاء الله, where the literal translation "if God wills" may seem unnatural. The same applies to نراكم على خير, whose literal translation is "We will see you on prosperity" which seems unnatural, while its TL culture-based rendering "see you soon" sounds normal. For this reason, rephrasing should be avoided, and a communicative translation is adopted which is "I hope" although it lacks the religious concept of the SL. The communicative translation approach is adopted because the TL does not have a cultural equivalent – a corresponding cliché – to the one employed in the SL. Thus, communicative translation may be said to be an example of "dynamic equivalence" (Nida 1964:166), as in:

No smoking – ممنوع التدخين
To kill two birds with one stone – ضربَ عصفورين بحجر
Don't mention it – لا شُكر على واجب
I have nothing to do with this matter – لا ناقة لي فيها ولا جَمَل

Therefore, the communicative translation approach is a localization translation process in which a ST is stripped of its culture-specific features.

Translation as process and product 27

5 **Metaphrase, paraphrase, and imitation translation approaches**: Dryden (1680/1992:17; cited in Munday 2001:25) proposes a triadic model which offers three categories of translation approaches:

(i) **Metaphrase translation approach**: This is word by word and line by line translation which corresponds to literal translation.

(ii) **Paraphrase (minor adjustments) translation approach**: This is a translation with latitude (freedom) where the author is kept in view by the translator, so as never to be lost, but his/her words are not so strictly followed as his/her sense. This involves changing whole phrases and more or less corresponds to faithful or sense-for-sense translation, as in "super bug" whose translation is جُرثومة مَقاومَة للمُضادات الحيويّة, which is based on a paraphrase translation approach. We have arrived at this translation after we have done a lexical analysis of the medical expression. Consider the expression's semantic componential features, which are: (1) The bug is not affected by antibiotics, and (2) The bug is resistant to any antibiotics.

Another example of a paraphrase translation where the ST intended meaning is followed but the ST words are not strictly observed:

تمَّ بيع (نفدت) جميع مُنتجاتنا ولن تتوفر حتى شهر – .We're completely sold out until August أغسطس (آب) القادم.

Another example of paraphrase translation is خروج بريطانيا من الإتحاد الأوربي, a paraphrase translation of "Brexit". This translation is based on the semantic components of "Brexit", which are "Britain exiting (leaving) the European Union" where we have not strictly followed the words of the expression "Brexit" but have provided a faithful (sense-for-sense) translation of the expression. Another example is "parliament", whose paraphrase translation is مجلس الأمة/مجلس النواب/مجلس الشورى/مجلس الشعب. In Q35:13, we encounter the noun قطمير, which is a lexical void for English. Thus, it has been paraphrased as the skin of a date stone/the thin cover around the seed of a date.

This approach, also called the minor adjustments translation approach, is a translation strategy that allows slight modifications in content and aims at making the SL message both intelligible and meaningful to the TL audience.

(iii) **Imitation translation approach**: In this approach, the translator abandons both words and sense and corresponds to free translation and adaptation. However, Dryden favors the paraphrase translation approach over the other two translation approaches, metaphrase and imitation.

6 **Exoticizing translation approach**: Nord (1988:73; cited in Munday 2001:81) proposes "exoticizing translation" where certain culture-specific lexical items in the ST are retained in the TT in order to maintain the local colour of the ST, such as food items like quark, roggenbrot and wurst from a German ST. For Dickins et al. (2002:29, 236), exoticism signals cultural foreignness in the TT. This translation approach involves the importing of linguistic and cultural features from the ST into the TT with minimal adaptation. Thus, the exotic source culture is vividly signaled in the TT. Therefore, exoticism in translation is more or less literal translation (ibid:30).

28 *Translation as process and product*

It is worthwhile to note that the exoticizing translation approach is similar to the adequate translation approach proposed by Toury (1995; cited in Venuti 2000:201), where the translator adopts the linguistic and cultural norms of the ST.

Examples include كيف حالك؟, whose exotic (literal) translation is "How is your state?"; the Iraqi Arabic شلونك؟, whose exotic (literal) translation is "What is your colour?"; ما قصرت, whose exotic (literal) translation is "You have not shortened"; السلام عليكم, whose exotic (literal) translation is "Peace be upon you"; and أمسكَ أحمدُ لسانهُ, whose exotic translation is "Ahmad held his tongue". However, if we adopt alternative translation approaches such as a communicative translation, a dynamic equivalence translation, an acceptable translation, or a cultural transposition translation approach, then the translator needs to transfer the ST cultural content (meaning) to the TT culture where TL features indigenous to the TL culture are adopted. Thus, we get "How are you?", "How are you?", "Much appreciated", and "Hello" respectively. In other words, we may say that the ST has been domesticated in the TT in terms of intelligibility and familiarity by the TL audience. Through the alternative translation approaches, we have managed to include the TL cultural norms in the TT. For more on these translation approaches, see the following details.

7   **Gloss translation approach**: In this approach, the translator attempts to reproduce the ST form and content as literally and meaningfully as possible. This approach is designed to permit the TL reader to identify himself/herself as fully as possible with a person in the SL context, and to understand as much as he/she can of the customs, manner of thought, and means of expression. For example, a phrase such as "holy kiss" (Romans 16:16) in a gloss translation would be rendered literally, and would probably be supplemented with a footnote explaining that this was a customary method of greeting in New Testament times. An interesting example of gloss translation is provided by Saheeh International (1997:304) for Q11:100. The source of the translation problem is the ST expression حصيد.

A gloss translation approach is encountered in Q33:4 and Q58:2 (Abdel Haleem 2005:266, 362):

ما جعلَ أزواجَكم اللائي تظاهرونَ مِنهُنَّ أمهاتِكم.

He (God) does not turn the wives you reject and liken to your mothers' backs into your real mothers.

الذين يظاهرونَ منكم من نسائهم ما هُنَّ أمهاتهم إن أمهاتهم إلا اللاتي ولدنهم.

Even if any of you say to their wives: "You are to me like my mother's back", they are not their mothers; their only mothers are those who gave birth to them.

The above translations are supplemented with footnotes explaining that الظِهار was a customary method of divorce in pre-Islamic Arabia. In pre-Islamic Arabia, the husband sometimes said to his wife: "From now on, you are to me like my mother's back", by which he meant that he refused to have further conjugal relations with his wife, yet did not divorce her and so gave her the freedom to remarry. The pagan Arabs used to separate themselves from their wives by saying: "You are to me like my mother's back" – a form of divorce which deprived the wife of her marital rights, preventing her from marrying again (Abdel Haleem 2005:266, 362).

Another example of gloss translation is the term "street artist", which is translated literally as فنانُ الشارع. However, this is a SL culture-specific expression and needs to be explained in a footnote to the TT audience: الشخصُ الذي يقدم الفن في الأماكن العامة ويشمل فناني الرسوم ورسامي الكاريكاتير وفناني الجرافيتي والموسيقيين والبهلوانيين والمشعوذين.

8   **Formal equivalence translation approach**: The major characteristics of formal equivalence are as follows.

(i)   Formal equivalence produces a source-oriented translation. It aims for structural equivalence with the ST. Formal equivalence (structural equivalence, gloss translation) focuses attention on the SL message itself, in both form (grammatical structure and stylistic pattern) and content. In such a translation, one is concerned with such correspondences as poetry to poetry, sentence to sentence, and concept to concept. The translator is concerned that the TL message should match as closely as possible the different elements in the SL. This means that the message in the TL culture is constantly compared with the message in the SL culture to determine standards of accuracy and correctness. The type of translation which most completely typifies this structural equivalence might be called a "gloss translation", in which the translator attempts to reproduce as literally and meaningfully as possible the form and content of the original. Such a translation requires

(a)   a relatively close approximation to the structure of the ST in form (syntax and idioms) and content (themes and concepts); and

(b)   numerous footnotes in order to make the TT fully comprehensible.

Let us consider the following example which demonstrate the structural equivalence with the ST:

الله يعلمُ وأنتم لا تعلمون – Allah knows, while you know not, (Q2:216), where the ST stylistic structure is preserved in the TT.

الى الله مرجعُكم – To Allah is your return, (Q11:4),

where the TT is a close approximation to the stylistic structure of the ST. The ST begins with a foregrounded prepositional phrase الى الله "to Allah" for the illocutionary effect of saliency given to the notion of the theological concept of monotheism التوحيد. Thus, the above TT represents structural equivalence – formal equivalence translation has produced a source-oriented translation. The Qur'an translation above has focused attention on the form and content of the ST message. Thus, the TT of Q11:4 can be called a "gloss translation". In Arabic, this is a marked (unusual, unexpected) word order whose unmarked (usual, expected) word order is مرجعُكم الى الله, which does not convey the same illocutionary force nor the ST producer's performative intent.

Another example of a formal equivalence translation that is source-oriented is نأسف على الأزعاج, which is displayed as a sign where road work is taking place. However, its translation "Sorry for the annoyance" provides a literal meaning of the ST expression out of context

30 *Translation as process and product*

where the translator has reproduced as literally and meaningfully as possible the form and content of the ST. The context-based TT is "Sorry for the inconvenience".

An interesting example of formal equivalence through which a source-oriented translation is provided and which aims for structural equivalence with the ST is

تباعُدنا اليوم يقرّبُنا غداً whose formal equivalence translation is (Our distancing today brings us together tomorrow).

Stylistically, the ST involves the rhetorical device of oxymoron where two contrasting expressions, phrases or sentences are placed next to each other. This is represented by تباعُدنا اليوم, which is semantically in contrast with يقربنا غداً. This ST stylistic structure has been well-preserved in the TT.

> (ii) Formal equivalence translation attempts to reproduce several formal elements, including: (1) grammatical units, (2) consistency in word usage, and (3) meanings in terms of the source context. The reproduction of grammatical units may consist in:
>
> > (a) translating nouns by nouns, verbs by verbs, etc.;
> > (b) keeping all phrases and sentences intact (i.e., not splitting up and readjusting the units); and
> > (c) preserving all formal indicators, e.g., marks of punctuation, paragraph breaks, and poetic indentation.

For instance, "herd immunity" and "diplomatic immunity" are both noun phrase grammatical units which are also translated as noun phrase grammatical units in Arabic: مناعة القطيع and حَصانة دبلوماسية respectively.

> (iii) Formal equivalence translation reproduces the ST more or less literally, as in some Qur'an translations. The following examples demonstrate how formal equivalence is primarily concerned with equivalence of style (form) between the ST and the TT:

"في" السماء رزقُكم – In the heaven is your provision (Q51:22) (Saheeh Internatioal 1997:741).
السماءَ بنيناها . . . الأرضَ فرشناها – The heaven We constructed . . . The earth We have spread out (Q51:47–48) (ibid).

where the grammatical units like the ST foregrounded prepositional phrase في السماء"in the heaven" and the direct objects السماءَ . . . الأرضَ "the heaven . . . the earth" are reproduced in terms of word order in the TT.

In many instances, however, as in Qur'an translation, one simply cannot reproduce certain formal elements of the source message, such as the dislocated adjective (left dislocation) in the ST, as in

وإنَّنا لفي شكٍّ مما تدعونا اليه مُريب (هود 62)

> TT: And indeed we are, about that to which you invite us, in disquieting doubt (Saheeh International 1997:298).

In this example the ST involves three innate Arabic-specific features:

(a) A noun phrase شكٌّ مُريبٌ whose structure is noun + adjective;
(b) The rhetorical device of hyperbaton represented by the dislocated adjective (مُريب) "disquieting", which is taken off its natural position and placed at the end of the sentence;
(c) The relative clause مما تدعونا اليه (that to which you invite us) enjoys the textual feature of saliency (focus), has the semantic relation of cause, and is placed next to the semantic relation of effect شَكّ (doubt).

Thus, the above ST formal features cannot be reproduced in the TT.

(iv) Reliance on footnotes: Formal equivalence translation contains much that is not readily intelligible to the average TL reader. The translator, therefore, usually supplements such translations with marginal notes not only to explain some of the formal (grammatical) features which could not be adequately represented in the TT, but also to make intelligible some of the formal equivalents employed. An example of formal equivalence is interlinear renderings. Thus, formal equivalence is similar to gloss translation.

Let us consider Q30:30, whose translation has been supplemented with marginal notes (footnotes) to make intelligible some of the formal equivalents employed:

فأقم وجهك للدين حنيفاً فِطرَتَ اللهِ التي فطرَ الناسَ عليها لا تبدلَ لخلق الله ذلكَ الدينُ القيِّمُ

(الروم 30)

And so, set thy face[1] steadfastly towards the [one ever-true] faith, turning away from all that is false,[2] in accordance with the natural disposition which God has instilled into man:[3] [for,] not to allow any change to corrupt what God has thus created[4] – this is the [purpose of the one] ever true faith (Asad 1980:486–487).

The following TT represents a formal equivalence translation which is supplemented by a marginal note to explain why the abstract noun (darkness) is employed in the plural (darknesses), which violates English grammatical norms. In attempting to reproduce consistency in word usage, a formal equivalence translation usually aims at so-called concordance of terminology; it always renders a particular term in the ST, such as ظُلمات, by the corresponding term in the TT. This SL term which always occurs in the plural form is dogmatically and theologically oriented. In other words, it conveys the ST producer's performative intent, and whose perlocutionary force is polytheism (disbelief). It has occurred 23 times in the Qur'an, as in Q2:257 and Q21:87, with mostly the same Qur'an-based theological notion (theme, concept). Thus, a formal equivalence translation approach needs a helping hand through a footnote, as in Saheeh International (1997:53, 447) formal equivalence translation: "The light of truth is one, while the darknesses of disbelief, doubt and error are many" and "The darknesses are that of the night, of the sea, and of the fish's interior". Thus, using the plural noun in the TT aims to achieve the correspondence of concept to concept, and the TL message should match as closely as possible the different elements in the SL at the expense of violating the TL linguistic norms. Formal equivalence is a source-oriented translation approach.

32 *Translation as process and product*

Therefore, the formal equivalence translation approach is the opposite to the localization translation process in which a ST is stripped of its culture-specific features. In other words, while formal equivalence produces a source-oriented translation, localization aims to produce a target-oriented translation.

An example of formal equivalence translation needing a footnote is "street artist", which is translated literally as فنان الشارع. This is a SL culture-specific expression and, therefore, needs to be explained through a footnote to the TT audience: الشخص الذي يقدم الفن في الأماكن العامة ويشمل فناني الرسوم ورسامي الكاريكاتير وفناني الجرافيتي والموسيقيين والبهلوانيين والمشعوذين.

9 **Dynamic equivalence translation approach**: The major characteristics of dynamic equivalence translation are:

(i) Dynamic equivalence translation is a TL-reader-oriented approach which aims for the complete naturalness of the SL expression. This has been put forward by Nida (1964). In his view, a translation of dynamic equivalence aims at complete naturalness of expression, and tries to relate the receptor to modes of behavior relevant within the context of his/her own culture – as in "life vest", which denotes a survival tool in aviation incidents. Thus, this mode of behavior should be relevant to the context of survival and therefore requires the TT to be natural: سترة النجاة, whose back-translation is "survival vest". Similarly, we have رَجَعَ بخُفّي حُنَين, whose dynamic equivalence translation is "He came back 'returned' empty handed". Another example is "to sell coal in Newcastle", whose dynamic equivalence translation is يبيع الماء في حارة السقّائين.

Another example is the expression "a hand-to-mouth existence", whose dynamic equivalence translation aims for the complete naturalness of the SL expression (الكفاف), as in "Many people live a hand-to-mouth existence". The dynamic equivalence translation is يعيشُ الكثيرُ من الناس على الكفاف

Additionally, the ST expression (pond) is naturalized and given a target-language-oriented meaning (the Atlantic, or the United States). For example,

> The Prime Minister said he agreed to make it easier to do business with our friends across the pond.

The translation problem lies in the noun (the pond), whose literal (denotative) meaning out of context is بُركة where we have the literal translation:

صرّحَ رئيسُ الوزراء بأنه وافق على تيسير عقد صفقات تجارية مع أصدقائنا في الجانب الآخر من البُركة.

However, a dynamic equivalence translation would provide complete naturalness of the SL expression:

صرّحَ رئيسُ الوزراء بأنه وافق على تيسير عقد صفقات تجارية مع أصدقائنا في الجانب الآخر من المحيط الأطلسي.

Translation as process and product 33

or:

صرَّحَ رئيسُ الوزراء بأنه وافق على تيسير عقد صفقات تجارية مع أصدقائنا في الولايات المتحدة الأمريكية.

The expression "Guinea pigs" has been given complete naturalness in the TT. Thus, we have got فئران تجارب, rather than its unnatural, literal, and out-of-context translation: خنازير غينيا. Also, "Ahmad kept quiet impatiently" is a dynamic equivalence TL-reader-oriented approach which aims for the complete naturalness of the ST أمسكَ أحمدُ لسانه, whose out-of-context literal translation is "Ahmad held his tongue".

The expressions بيت المال and بيت الله can be given dynamic equivalence translations as "the Treasury" or "the Ministry of Finance".

Based on the dynamic equivalence translation approach – a TL-reader-oriented approach which aims for the complete naturalness of the SL expression – we provide the following examples:

بدل غلاء المعيشة – "cost of living benefits 'allowances'"
بدل البطالة – "unemployment benefits"
بدل السكن – "accommodation benefits"
بدل الأطفال – "child benefits"
بدل النقل – "transport benefits"
وزارة النقل – "transport secretary"
التباعُد الإجتماعي – "social distance 'distancing'"
كمامات الوجه – "face masks"
أمر البقاء في المنزل – "stay-at-home order"
فيروس كورونا الجديد ليس من صنع الإنسان – "the novel coronavirus is not man-made"
(الحجر الذاتي (الحجر المنزلي – "to self-isolate"
احجر نفسك في المنزل إذا شعرت بالأعراض – "If you have symptoms, self-isolate."
تخفيف قيود الإغلاق – "to ease lockdown measures"
جائحة كورونا – "coronavirus pandemic"
ارتفعت حصيلة الوفيات الى 70 – "fatality count jumps to 70 'official death toll rises to 70'"
الإغلاق بسبب فيروس كورونا – "the coronavirus lockdown"
تدابير احترازية – "containment measures"
ينجو من الموت بإعجوبة – "'to have' a brush with death"
يُلقي بظلاله على – "to overshadow"
(خضروات طازجة (في متجر مواد غذائية – "fresh produce"
شِجار كلامي بين اثنين – "a stand-off"
على قدم وساق – "to be in full swing"
الذي يوسوسُ في صدور الناس – "who plays with people's minds"
(بارقة (بصيص) أمل – "a glimpse of hope"
رئيس الوزراء المكلف – "the prime minister-designate"
(التصويت بالبريد (الغيابي – "mail-in ballot"

34 *Translation as process and product*

فرز الأصوات – "vote counting"

إعادة فرز الأصوات – "vote recounting"

الولايات المُتأرجحة – "swing states"

حقَّقَ تقدماً طفيفاً في الإنتخابات – "He held slim 'narrow' leads in the election."

المُجمَّع الإنتخابي – "the Electoral College"

الرئيسُ المُنتهية ولايتهُ (المُنصّرف) – "the outgoing President"

الرئيسُ المُنتخَب – "the President-elect"

(ii) Dynamic equivalence does not insist that the TL reader understands the cultural patterns of the source-language context in order to comprehend the message (Nida 1964; cited in Venuti 2000:129). For instance, wearing leather socks is an Arab cultural pattern. Thus, we encounter the proverb رَجَعَ بخُفّي حُنَين, which, if translated literally, will lead to alienating the TL reader "He came back 'returned' with the Hunain's leather socks". Therefore, dynamic equivalence is the solution to the SL proverb: "He came back 'returned' empty handed". Another example is "This is a non-smoking area", whose translation also relates the TL reader to a mode of behavior relevant within the context of his/her culture; he/she is not required to understand the SL context since the TL message is clear to understand: هذا المكان مُخصَّص لغير المُدخنين.

(iii) Dynamic equivalence aims to reduce the foreignness of the TT in order to achieve complete naturalness of TL expression, as in رَجَعَ بخُفّي حُنَين, whose dynamic equivalence translation is "He came back 'returned' empty handed".

Another example of a dynamic equivalence translation that aims at minimizing the foreignness of the TT is the expression نأسف على الأزعاج, which is displayed as a sign where road work is taking place. However, its translation "Sorry for the annoyance" is source-oriented, which provides a literal meaning of the ST expression out of context. The context-based target-oriented translation that does not smell of foreignness is "Sorry for the inconvenience".

The above example هذا المكان مُخصَّص لغير المُدخنين, for instance, demonstrates that dynamic equivalence is similar to cultural transposition and cultural transplantation introduced by Dickins et al. (2002:29, 32, 235), which involves departure from literal translation and the replacement of SL-specific features with TL-specific features to reduce the foreignness of the TT. In other words, the translator deletes source-culture details that have occurred in the ST and replaces them with target-culture details in the TT. We can observe the following in terms of complete naturalness of expression:

(a) The ST has employed مكان for the TL word "area" instead of مكان;

(b) The ST is in the indefinite form through the indefinite article (a) while the TT is in the definite form through the definite particle ال;

(c) The addition in the TT of the expression مُخصَّص;

(d) The back-translation of the ST is "This is a place allocated for non-smokers" – an adaptation of the ST – where (non-smoking) has been transferred to the TT as "non-smokers" in the interest of complete naturalness of expression; and

(e) Regardless of the adaption procedure in the TT, the translation has provided the closest natural equivalent to the SL message.

Translation as process and product 35

An example of dynamic equivalence translation that aims to reduce the foreignness of the TT in order to achieve complete naturalness of TL expression is "piggy bank", which translates to Arabic as حَصَّالة, where the other word "piggy" is dropped in the TT.

An interesting example of dynamic equivalence translation "cultural transposition/cultural transplantation" is "to sell coal in Newcastle", whose dynamic equivalence translation is يبيعُ الماءَ في حارة السقَّائين.

Thus, a dynamic equivalence translation aims at complete naturalness of expression, and tries to relate the TL audience to modes of behavior relevant within the context of his/her own culture; it does not insist that he/she understands the cultural patterns of the SL context in order to comprehend the message. One of the modern English translations which seeks for equivalent effect is John Bertram Phillips' rendering of the New Testament. In Romans 16:16, he translates "greet one another with a holy kiss" quite naturally as "give one another a hearty handshake all around" (Nida, Principles of Equivalence).

Cultural material expressions can also be given a dynamic equivalence translation for the purpose of complete naturalness of expressions like (toothbrush) and (air freshener), to which we recommend the dynamic translations of مِسواك and بُخور respectively.

To minimize the foreignness in the TT and attain complete naturalness, the expression "blue-collar voters" should be translated as الناخبون من الطبقات العُمالية instead of the literal "out of context, formal equivalence" translation الناخبون من ذوي الياقات الزرقاء. Similarly, the expression "to draw a line under the Trump era" should be domesticated as أنَّ عهد ترامب قد ولَّى بلا رجعة rather than يرسمُ يضعُ خطًّا تحت ترامب

(iv) Dynamic equivalence aims for equivalent effect: This translation approach attempts to produce the closest natural equivalent to the SL message, as in the following examples which demonstrate the complete naturalness of expression and equivalent effect.

unmanned aircraft – طائرة بلا طيار

drone – طائرة مُسيرة

NHS (National Health Service) – هيئة الصحة الوطنية

P45 – قسيمة العاطل عن العمل

to parents – الى أولياء الأمور

income support – معونة الدخل المنخفض (المحدود)

income-based jobseekers allowance – مُخصصات حسب الدخل للباحثين عن العمل

tax credit award – مُنحة الإعفاء من الضريبة

meal vouchers – بطاقات وجبات الغداء

I have nothing to do with this matter – لا ناقة لي فيها ولا جَمَل

It is worthwhile to note that in the last example of لا ناقة لي فيها ولا جَمَل, the translator has deleted the source-culture details ناقة/جَمَل which are "female camel/male camel" that have occurred in the ST and has replaced them with target-culture details in the TT "nothing to do with this matter".

Thus, the above examples demonstrate that dynamic equivalence is a translation which attempts to produce equivalence based on "the principle of equivalent effect" (Rieu and Phillips 1954; cf. Nida 1964:166), where the translator is not concerned with matching the

36 *Translation as process and product*

TL message with the SL message, but with the dynamic relationship, which should be substantially the same as that which existed between the SL audience and the message.

Let us consider ST pun and context-based intertextuality with regards to dynamic equivalence. The aim for equivalent effect is extremely difficult to attain by the TT, especially when the ST is hinged upon intertextuality – when the SL message is dependent on an earlier SL message. Such a ST intertextuality is difficult to establish in the TL and the receptor reader may not grasp what the TT is about; thus, the natural equivalent to the SL message is not realized, as in the advert "Mourning in America" which is intertextually related to the earlier advert "Morning in America", where the ST pun between "mourning" and "morning" is impossible to achieve in Arabic, plus the problem of the context-based intertextuality. The ST "Mourning in America" is a political advert criticizing President Donald Trump's response to the coronavirus pandemic and is produced by a dissident group of anti-Trump Republicans. This advert plays on former President Ronald Regan's re-election advert "Morning in America", which was a one-minute commercial where young Americans look happy and positive, get married, are able to buy a home, and raise the American flag. However, the new commercial advert "Mourning in America" shows a decrepit factory, a body wheeled away on a gurney, and unhappy and hopeless Americans lining up in the rain wearing masks to get coronavirus tests. While the translation of "Mourning in America" is الحِداد في أمريكا, the translation of "Morning in America" is الصباح في أُمريكا. Thus, the two adverts that are intertextually related display the stylistic device of oxymoron (contrasting words, phrases, or sentences placed next to each other) in both the ST and the TT. However, the weakest link in the translation is the context-based intertextuality. How would the TL reader figure out the underlying meaning of "Morning in America" without watching the commercial on TV? A translation of the two intertextually related STs without watching the two TV commercials cannot portray lack of leadership and social inequities hitting American society during the coronavirus pandemic. Thus, equivalent effect has not been produced by the TTs.

Another example of ST pun and context-based intertextuality is a TV commercial for a brand of bottled water. The commercial refers to مياهَنا, which means "our water/our water resources" then a picture of a bottled water brand called هَنا, which means "good health, happiness"; a picture of water, then a picture of a bottled water. The pun is achieved through the phonetic trick of mixing the two هاء sounds, one at the end of the word مياه and the other at the beginning of the bottled water brand هَنا. Thus, with the assimilation of the two sounds الهاء, we have مياه + هنا and the result is مياهنا. However, the success of the commercial lies in the phonetic juncture where the successive sounds of هاء are blended together, through the intonation patterns of the speaker, and the variations in pitch. Through the acoustic transition from مياه to هَنا, the commercial has successfully presented the bottled water brand هَنا to viewers. During the translation process of such a case, it is recommended that the translator translates مياهنا to "The bottled water of Hana" based on context and intertextuality.

(v) This dynamic equivalence translation approach provides a translation whose focus of attention is directed, not so much towards the SL emotive message, as towards the TL receptor response, which may say: "That is just the way we would say it". It is a translation more or less similar to that of the ST; it reflects the meaning and the performative intent of the ST. Dynamic equivalence translation is the closest natural equivalent to the source-language message. It is natural because it is TL-oriented in terms of emotional meaning, as in

"The scenes from Afghanistan are gut-wrenching, Biden says", where "gut-wrenching" is emotively charged, and is translated emotively with the meaning of anguish as يَنعَصِرُ ينكَسِرُ لها القلبُ or emotively-neutral as مُؤْلِمة.

It is primarily concerned with equivalence of response – not equivalence of style (form). It must fit the TL, culture, and audience (Nida 1964; cited in Venuti 2000:136), as in (piggy bank), whose dynamic equivalence translation is (حَصَّالة). Another example is

The Iranian government got cold feet about allowing a US military plane into Iran (*The Guardian*, 2 January 2004).

The suggested dynamic equivalence translation is

انتابَ الحكومة الأيرانية الذعر من السماح لطائرة عسكرية أمريكية بالهبوط في أراضيها

where we have the idiomatic expression "to get cold feet" – انتاب الذعر الخوف, which needs to have a natural translation based on ST context and equivalence of response rather than equivalence of style or word form. Also, the TT fits in well in the TL stylistic norms through the adaptation procedure where the noun (Iran) is transferred to Arabic as أراضيها, whose back-translation is: "its 'Iran's' soil". Thus, a natural translation is guaranteed.

Newmark (1981:38–39) reproduces Nida's dynamic equivalence translation and calls it "communicative translation", which attempts to produce on its readers an effect as close as possible to that obtained on the TL readers. He (ibid) also reproduces Nida's formal equivalence translation and calls it "semantic translation", which attempts to render, as closely as the semantic and syntactic structures of the second language allow, the exact contextual meaning of the original.

Therefore, we can conclude that dynamic equivalence translation and localization translation are both TL-reader-oriented approaches.

On the drawbacks of the equivalence approach, see Nord (1997:44), who considers the equivalence model as inadequate to the needs of professional translation in a modern society (ibid:45).

10 **Natural translation approach**: The major characteristics of this translation approach are as follows.

(i) Adaptation in grammar and lexicon: In general, the grammatical modifications can be made the more readily, since many grammatical changes are dictated by the obligatory structures of the TL; the translator is obliged to make such adjustments like shifting word order, using verbs in place of nouns, and substituting nouns for pronouns (Nida, Principles 1964; cited in Venuti 2000:129).

An example of a natural translation approach where we find grammatical modifications and obligatory changes dictated by the TL grammatical norms is the SL plural active participle noun, which is substituted for a demonstrative pronoun "those" + a relative pronoun "who" + a verb: الآمرون بالمعروف والناهون عن المنكر (Those who bid to honour and forbid dishonour, Q9:112 (Arberry 1955:88), where the ST plural active participle الآمرون and الناهون are substituted for the TL "those" + "who" + verbs "bid" and "forbid" respectively.

38 *Translation as process and product*

The same natural translation approach is adopted by Saheeh International (2005:265) "Those who enjoin what is right and forbid what is wrong".

An example of a natural translation approach where a SL adjective is substituted for a TL verb is إِنِّي لَغَفَّارٌ لِمَنْ تَابَ "I forgive him who repents", Q20:82 (Ahmad 2010:417), where the ST hyperbole adjective غَفَّارٌ is substituted for the TL verb "forgive", which violates the intended meaning of the ST and its performative intent of "most forgiving" of all sins.

An example of a natural translation approach where a SL noun is substituted for a TL adjective is:

"تم استئناف العلاقات الدبلوماسية بين العراق وأمريكا على مستوى السفراء Diplomatic rela-tions between Iraq and the United States has been resumed at ambassadorial level", where the SL plural definite noun السفراء is rendered into the TT as an adjective, "ambassadorial".

Also, the TL plural noun is rendered as a singular noun into the TL through the natural translation approach:

"A car with diplomatic number plates". – سيارة تحمل رقماً دبلوماسياً

where the ST plural noun "plates" is translated as a singular noun in the TT رقماً.

Arabic absolute object (cognate object) is an example of a translation problem which requires adaptation in the SL grammar and where we can apply the natural translation approach to provide a naturalized TT through the grammatical modification of the SL absolute object, which is a lexico-grammatical void (it is absent in the TL), as in

نَزَّلْنَا عَلَيْكَ الْقُرْآنَ تَنزِيلاً (الأنسان 23)

It is We who have sent down to you the Qur'an progressively (Saheeh International 1997:849).

We have sent down this Qur'an to you in gradual revelation (Abdel Haleem 2005:402).

where the ST absolute object تَنزِيلاً has undergone the translation procedure of adaptation through which an adverb, "progressively", or a prepositional phrase, "in gradual revelation", is employed in the TT. Thus, a change in grammatical category in the TT has taken place.

Although Arberry (1955:267) has attempted to mimic the SL absolute object, he has provided a gerund, "a sending down":

We have sent down the Koran on thee, a sending down (Arberry 1955:267).

كَلَّمَ اللهُ موسَى تَكْلِيماً (النساء 164)

Allah spoke to Moses with direct speech (Saheeh International 1997:131).
Unto Moses God spoke directly (Arberry 1955:45).

where the ST absolute object تَكْلِيماً has undergone the translation procedure of adaptation through which a noun phrase "direct speech" or an adverb "directly" is employed in the TT. Thus, a change in grammatical category in the TT has taken place.

(رتِّل القرآن ترتيلاً (المزمل 4) (Q73:4)

Recite the Quran with measured recitation (Saheeh International 1997:836).
Chant the Koran very distinctly (Arberry 1955:264).

where the ST absolute object ترتيلاً has undergone the translation procedure of adaptation
through which a prepositional phrase "with measured recitation" or an adverb "very distinctly"
is employed in the TT. Thus, a change in grammatical category in the TT has taken place.

(ii) Naturalness of SL expression in the TT: The naturalization of a SL expression is
essentially a problem; to make the SL expression appropriate to the TL culture.
When the SL and the TL represent very different cultures, we encounter many cultural notions which cannot be naturalized in the TT. For example, the Jivaro Indians
of Ecuador certainly do not understand 1 Corinthians 11:14, "Does not nature teach
us that for a man to wear long hair is a dishonor to him?" – for in general, Jivaro
men let their hair grow long, while Jivaro adult women usually cut theirs rather
close. Similarly, in many areas of West Africa the behavior of Jesus' disciples in
spreading leaves and branches on his path as he rode into Jerusalem is regarded as
reprehensible; for in accordance with West African custom, the path to be walked
on or ridden over by a chief is scrupulously cleaned of all litter, and anyone who
throws a branch in such a person's way is guilty of grievous insult. Nevertheless,
these cultural discrepancies offer less difficulty than might be imagined, especially
if footnotes are used to point out the basis for the cultural diversity; for all people
recognize that other people behave differently from themselves (Nida 1964). Thus,
based on natural translation approach, the expression (blue-collar voters) is translated as الناخبون من الطبقات العُمالية.

Therefore, we can argue that natural translation and localization translation are both TL-
reader-oriented approaches.

11 **Naturalization translation approach**: This is a translation approach put forward by
Newmark (1988:82) where a SL word is transferred phonetically (transliterated) and
adapted to the TL morphology, as in "taxi" and "micro-bus", which are transferred to
مايكروباص/مايكروباصات and تكسي/تكسيات. The same applies to the expression "TV
and radio stations", which is naturalized into Arabic as محطات التلفاز والراديو. Most
importantly, the translator needs to be aware of the fact that a SL expression can be
translated effectively without being transliterated. For instance, it is better to provide
a translation to the above English expressions rather than naturalize them in Arabic.
Thus, we can easily translate them as سيارة نقل عام صغيرة ، سيارة أجرة ، محطات الإذاعة
المرئية والمسموعة.

An example of how a SL expression is adapted to the TL morphology is "a televised
interview" whose translation based on the naturalization translation approach is لقاء مُتلفز
where both the ST and the TT have employed a passive participle form – "televised" and
مُتلفز.

Another example is "Brexit", whose naturalization translation is بريكست. However, if we
adopt the paraphrase translation approach, we get خروج بريطانيا من الإتحاد الأوربي, which

40 *Translation as process and product*

is a paraphrase translation of "Brexit". Another example is "parliament" which is given a naturalization translation برلمان.

Thus, in naturalization, the SL terms can be easily translated to the TL without paraphrasing (over-translation). Naturalization is different from cultural borrowing.

12 **Cultural borrowing translation approach**: Through this approach, a SL expression is transferred verbatim into the TL. In other words, through the cultural borrowing translation approach, we can introduce the foreign ST element into the TT. Cultural borrowing involves the rendering of a culturally specific expression by a transliteration (Dickins et al. 2002:32). Although both cultural borrowing and naturalization adopt the transliteration of the SL expression and phonetically introduce it in the TT, there is a difference between the naturalization translation approach and the cultural borrowing translation approach. Examples of cultural borrowing are عِقال، كبسة، طعمية، باجة، عقيقة, which are transferred phonetically to English verbatim as "iqal, kabsah, ta'miyyah, bachah, aqeqah". Semantically, some SL lexical items have innate semantic componential features. When such features are lacking in the TL and cannot be represented through a single TL word, we obtain a lexical void. Thus, the above Arabic examples are lexical voids because English fails to accommodate them by a single word like كتاب and "book". We can therefore claim that there is a direct relationship between lexical voids and cultural borrowing. For more details on lexical voids, see Abdul-Raof (2018, Chapter 6).

However, if the translator opts for paraphrase rather than cultural borrowing, this will lead to over-translation, as in the Islamic culture term أضحية, which can be translated through paraphrase as "a party is given by the parents shortly after the birth of a baby where a lamb is slaughtered and served with rice".

13 **Through translation approach**: "This" is also known as *calque* or *loan translation* which is a type of literal translation introduced by Newmark (1988:84) where TL grammar is observed and the SL-specific features are replaced with TL-specific features. Thus, through translation is similar to cultural transposition offered by Dickins et al. (2002:29), as in "Ladies and gentlemen, . . .", whose through translation is سيداتي وسادتي، . . . ، /أيها السيدات والسادة . . . , and whose back-translation is "My ladies and my gentlemen".

14 **Transposition or shift translation approach**: This is a grammar-based translation approach which involves a change in the grammar from the SL to TL (Newmark 1988:85). The transposition translation approach was introduced by Vinay and Darbelnet (1958) while the "shift" translation approach was introduced by Catford (1965). Such an approach involves a change in SL word order, the active and passive participle in Arabic, the Arabic superlative adjective (the superlative afʿal form صيغة أفعل التفضيل), the active and passive voice, the position of the adjective, and singular to plural or vice versa, as in the following examples.

The Prime Minister was received by the American President.

Grammatically, the main verb is "receive" and the sentence structure is in passive voice. Thus, we need to apply the translation procedure of adaptation. While English prefers the

Translation as process and product   41

passive voice structure, Arabic favors an active voice structure. Thus, a transposition (shift) translation approach is adopted to suit the TT stylistic norms. The ST needs three adaptation operations:

(i)   We use تَمَّ + اسم مصدر استقبال;

(ii) We change the ST verb "receive" to a noun in the TT تَمَّ استقبال. Thus, we get: تَمَّ استقبال;

(iii) We need to change the ST preposition "by" to من قِبَل in the TT to suit the stylistic norms of the TL. The suggested TT is تَمَّ استقبال رئيس الوزراء من قِبَل الرئيس الأمريكي.

In English, we have the word order (SVO) while in Arabic, we must adopt the transposition/ shift translation approach and produce a (VSO) word order. The adjective in English occurs before the noun it modifies. However, this order must change in Arabic where the adjective occurs after the noun. In Arabic, the words أثاث ، أخبار occur in the plural form, but they must be used in English in the singular form (news, furniture), which require an auxiliary verb in the singular form (is, does, has) or a main verb with an (s) as a third-person singular (The news says everything/The furniture smells nice).

A unique feature of transposition or shift translation approach is a change in ST word order which occurs in journalistic Arabic and English texts, as in

"Everybody knows me as the 'gold man' in the whole region. Other rich people spend one crore (10 million rupees) to buy Audis or Mercedes, to buy what they like. What crime have I done? I just love gold", Phuge said in 2013.

"Gold has always been my passion since a young age. I've always worn gold as jewelry in the form of bracelets, rings, chains", he added.

(*The Guardian*, Saturday 16 July 2016)

وذكر فوجي في عام 2013 "كل شخص يعرفني ب "رجل الذهب"، في جميع انحاء الولاية. هناك أغنياء ينفقون كروري (ما يعادل 10 مليون روبية) لشراء سيارات نوع أودي أو مرسيدس أو شراء ما يحبون. أيَّ جريمة اقترفتها أنا؟ أنا مجرد أحب الذهب."

وأضاف قائلاً: "إنَّ الذهبَ منذ شبابي كان وما يزال شغفي (هوايتي)." "كنتُ منذ شبابي وما أزال مشغوفاً بحب الذهب."

where the ST starts with the quoted speech of the speaker and ends with the speaker's name as the subject. However, in Arabic journalistic texts, the opposite word order takes place where a word order change is required. In other words, the Arabic journalistic text starts with the verb + the subject before his/her quoted speech.

Another example of a change in SL word order is

كلَّمَ اللهُ موسَى تَكليماً (النساء/ 164)

Unto Moses God spoke directly (Arberry 1955:45).

where the ST starts with a verb كلَّمَ + a subject الله + object موسى + absolute object تكليماً. However, the TT has the grammatical structure: prepositional "unto" + direct object "Moses" + subject "God" + verb "spoke" + adverb "directly".

42 *Translation as process and product*

Arabic absolute object (cognate object) is an interesting example of a translation problem which can be solved through the application of the transposition or shift translation approach, as in the following examples:

(سَلِّمُوا تسليماً) (الأحزاب 56) (Q33:56)

Ask Allah to grant him (Muhammad) peace (Saheeh International 1997:589).
To pray him peace (Arberry 1955:190).

where the ST absolute object تسليما has undergone the translation procedure of adaptation where a noun "peace" is employed in the TT. Thus, a change in grammatical category in the TT has taken place.

صَبَبْنَا الماءَ صَبًّا. شَقَقْنَا الأرْضَ شَقًّا (عبس 25–26) (Q80:25–26)

We poured down water in torrents. We broke open the earth (Saheeh International 1997:863).
We poured out the rains abundantly, then We split the earth in fissures (Arberry 1955:271).

where the ST absolute objects صَبًّا، شَقًّا have undergone the translation procedure of adaptation in which a prepositional phrase "in torrents", a verb "break open", an adverb "abundantly", or a prepositional phrase "in fissures" are employed in the TT. Thus, a change in grammatical category in the TT has taken place.

لا تبرَّجنَ تبرُّجَ الجاهليةِ الأولى (الأحزاب 33) (Q33:33)

Do not display yourselves as was the display of the former times of ignorance (Saheeh International 1997:584).
Display not your finery, as did the pagans of old (Arberry 1955:189).

where the ST absolute object تبرُّج has undergone the translation procedure of adaptation in which a noun "the display, finery" is used in the TT. Thus, a change in grammatical category in the TT has taken place.

As a grammar-based translation approach which involves a change in the grammar from the SL to TL (Newmark 1988:85), the transposition or shift translation approach involves a change in SL word order, as in

لم يكُن لهُ كُفواً أحَدٌ (الإخلاص 4)

The above ST has a marked (unusual) word order because the noun أحَدٌ "one" is backgrounded (placed at the end of the sentence) and the prepositional phrase لهُ "to Him" is foregrounded (placed in the middle of the sentence). The unmarked (usual) word order is لم يكُن أحَدٌ كُفواً لهُ. The translation offered by Abdel Haleem "No one is comparable to Him". 2005:444) has taken into consideration the re-shuffle in the ST word order. Thus, it is a translation based on the transposition or shift translation approach, which involves a change in the SL word order.

An example of the transposition (shift) translation approach which involves a change from the SL plural to a TL singular or vice versa is

سيارة تحملُ رقماً دبلوماسياً – "A car with diplomatic number plates"

Translation as process and product 43

where the ST plural noun (plates) is translated as a singular noun in the TT رَقَمًا.

Therefore, transposition or shift translation and localization translation are both TL-reader-oriented approaches.

15 **Adequate and acceptable translation approaches**: Toury (1995; cited in Venuti 2000:201) talks about two types of translation approaches: (i) adequate translation, and (ii) acceptable translation. In other words, the translator may subject him/herself either to the norms of the ST or to the norms of the TL culture.

(i) **Adequate translation approach**: In this approach, the translator adopts the linguistic and cultural norms of the ST. This approach attempts to achieve adequate translation, but it may entail some incompatibilities with the TL linguistic and cultural norms. Adherence to SL norms provides an adequate translation in terms of the ST. Adequacy-oriented translation may involve some shifts from the ST. These shifts are a universal feature of translation. Shifts from the SL text are an almost inevitable price.

An example of incompatibility with the TL linguistic norms involving shift from the ST is the translation of Q20:82: إِنِّي لَغَفَّارٌ لِمَن تَابَ "I forgive him who repents" (Ahmad 2010:417), where the TL grammar is not accurately observed, and most importantly, the ST hyperbole adjective غَفَّار is changed to a verb "forgive" which does not provide the ST producer's performative intent of being "most forgiving" for all sins.

Additionally, the last part of وَأَعَدَّ لَهُم جَهَنَّمَ وَسَاءَت مَصِيرًا is given an adequate translation "And He 'God' prepared for them hell, <u>and evil it is as a destination</u>," (Q48:6, Saheeh International) and "He has cursed them and got hell ready for them: and evil is it for a destination" (Q48:6, Yusuf Ali 1934), where the ST linguistic norms are preserved in the TT, which has resulted in a grammatical incompatibility (violation of grammatical norms) with the TL because the adjective "evil", the modifier, is placed sentence-initially and its noun (destination), which it modifies, is placed sentence-finally. The TT also involves a shift from the SL verb سَاءَت to the TL adjective "evil". Such a translation is known as "translationese" (Hatim and Munday 2004:12) since the TT is overtly close and influenced by the ST linguistic norms. Also, the translation of the last part of Q48:6 involves unnecessary processing effort on the part of the TL reader (Gutt 1991; cited in Venuti 2000:376); it does not reflect faithfulness in translation based on interlingual interpretive use.

Another example of adequate translation approach which has led to incompatibilities with the TL linguistic norms is

رَبِّ إِنِّي لِمَا أَنزَلتَ إِلَيَّ مِن خَيرٍ فَقِيرٍ (القصص 24)

My Lord, indeed I am, for whatever good You would send down to me, in need (Q28:24)
(Saheeh International1997:535).

The above TT involves the exact transfer of the SL style into the TT without making any adaptation to the ST. we can observe that the adjective فَقِير is placed at the end of the sentence. However, it should occur immediately after its subject إِنِّي to have a natural SL style. The usual ST word order is

رَبِّ إِنِّي فَقِيرٍ لِمَا أَنزَلتَ إِلَيَّ مِن خَيرٍ

44 *Translation as process and product*

whose acceptable style in the TL is

> My Lord, indeed I am in need for whatever good You would send down to me.

It is worthwhile to note that the ST Q28:24 needs an acceptable translation approach through which we get the following TT:

> My Lord, indeed I am in need for whatever good You would send down to me.

Other examples include كيف حالك؟, whose adequate translation is "How is your state?", and the Iraqi Arabic شلونك؟, whose adequate translation is "What is your colour?". However, if we adopt the second translation approach proposed by Toury (1995), which is "acceptable translation", we will find a different translation.

(ii) **Acceptable translation approach**: In this approach, the translator includes the TL cultural norms in the translation. Adherence to the TL cultural norms provides an acceptable translation to the TL receptors; the translator has produced acceptability-oriented translation (Toury 1995; cited in Venuti 2000:201).

For example, the expressions كيف حالك؟ and the Iraqi Arabic greeting expression شلونك؟ can be given an acceptable translation "How are you?", where the ST cultural norms are transferred to the TT culture and the TL features indigenous to the TL culture are adopted. Similarly, the expressions "hard-nosed policy" and "zero tolerance on immigration" can be given either adequate translation where the linguistic and cultural norms of the ST are preserved تحمل الصفر حول الهجرة and سياسة الأنف المتصلب respectively, or acceptable translation where acceptability-oriented translation is the major aim of the translator; thus, we get سياسة عدم التسامح مع الهجرة and سياسة واقعية وصارمة respectively where the TL cultural norms are introduced in the TT.

Thus, acceptable translation is similar to localization translation since both are TL-reader-oriented approaches.

16 **Documentary and instrumental translation approaches**: Nord (1988, 1991; cited in Munday 2001:81–82) provides two types of translation approaches:

(i) **Documentary translation approach**: This serves as a document of a source culture communication between the author and the ST recipient (Nord 1991:72). In literary translation, for example, the TT allows the TT receiver access to the ideas of the ST but where the reader is well aware that the TT is a translation. Other examples of documentary translation given by Nord are word-for-word, literal translation, and "exoticizing translation" (ibid:73). In the latter, certain culture-specific lexical items in the ST are kept in the TT in order to maintain the colour of the ST.

(ii) **Instrumental translation approach**: This is a function-preserving translation; this type of translation is intended to fulfill its communicative purpose without the TL recipient being conscious of reading or hearing a translated text (ibid). In other words, the TT receivers read the TT as though it were an ST written in their own language. The function may be the same for both ST and TT. For instance, a translated computer manual or software should fulfill the function of instructing the TT receiver in the same way as the ST does for the ST reader.

17 **Transference translation approach**: Transference is the process of transferring a SL word to a TL text through transliteration (Newmark 1988:81). It has been introduced by Catford (1965). After the word has been transferred through transliteration from the SL to the TL, the word has been naturalized in the TL, as in (décor) which is transferred to Arabic as (ديكور). This approach is adopted in the transference of cultural objects, culture-specific foods, concepts, names of institutions, inventions, devices, names of newspapers, and trademarks like (Phillips, Toyota, Mercedes). The transference translation approach is a form of cultural transposition translation approach.

18 **Faithfulness translation approach**: Gutt (1991; cited in Venuti 2000:376) provides relevance-based account of faithfulness in translation; faithfulness in translation based on interlingual interpretive use. In the view of Gutt (1991; cited in Venuti 2000:376), a translation is a receptor language text which interpretively resembles the original without unnecessary processing (analysis, comprehension) effort on the part of the TL reader. The guidance Gutt (ibid:378) provides to translators is that

(i) The translation should be adequately relevant to the TL audience;
(ii) It should be clear and natural in expression in the sense that it should not be unnecessarily difficult to understand; and
(iii) It should preserve the ST implicature to the TL reader.

Let us consider the following example:

The Prime Minister said he agreed to make it easier to do business with our friends across the pond.

The translation problem lies in the noun "the pond" whose literal (denotative) meaning out of context is بُركة where we have the following literal translation:

صرَّحَ رئيسُ الوزراء بأنه وافق على تيسير عقد صفقات تجارية مع أصدقائنا في الجانب الآخر من البُركة.

However, the above TT requires unnecessary processing effort on the part of the TL reader, does not preserve to him/her the ST implicature, and does not offer adequate contextual effects. Faithful translation would provide complete naturalness of the SL expression:

صرَّحَ رئيسُ الوزراء بأنه وافق على تيسير عقد صفقات تجارية مع أصدقائنا في الجانب الآخر من المحيط الأطلسي.

or:

صرَّحَ رئيسُ الوزراء بأنه وافق على تيسير عقد صفقات تجارية مع أصدقائنا في الولايات المتحدة الأمريكية.

In interpretive use, Gutt argues (ibid:377), the principle of relevance comes across as a presumption of optimal resemblance; what the translator intends to convey is to interpretively resemble the ST. Otherwise, the TT would not be an instance of interpretive use, The resemblance the TT shows must be consistent with the presumption of optimal relevance; it must have adequate contextual effects without processing effort on the part of the receptor

46 *Translation as process and product*

audience (TL reader). This notion of optimal resemblance seems to capture well the idea of faithfulness. Sperber and Wilson (1986:137) have stated that in interpretive use, the speaker (the translator) guarantees that his/her utterance (the translation) is a faithful enough representation of the original (ST); the TT resembles the ST closely enough in relevant respects. One may wonder whether the general notion of faithfulness is useful for translation. The answer is that the principle of relevance heavily constrains the translation with regard to both: (i) what it is intended to convey, and (ii) how it is expressed. Thus, if we ask in what respects the intended interpretation of the translation should resemble the original, the answer is, In respects that make it adequately relevant to the TL audience, offering adequate contextual effects. However, if we ask how the translation should be expressed, the answer is, The TT should be expressed in such a manner that it yields the intended interpretation without putting the TL audience through unnecessary processing effort. Since consistency with the principle of relevance is always context-dependent, the relevance constraints are context-determined, too.

With regards to what the ST is intended to convey, we can offer the example (the withdrawal of the army) whose faithful translation should be انسحابُ الجيش, rather than: تقهقر الجيش, meaning "the retreat of the army".

Let us consider the following examples:

The Prime Minister outlined a £24 billion austerity package. – وضَعَ رئيسُ الوزراء خطة تقشف قيمتها 24 مليار جنيه استرليني.

The British economy will grow by one percent in 2020 despite the debt storm tearing through the Euro-zone. – سوف ينمو الإقتصاد البريطاني بنسبة 1% على الرغم من زوبعة الديون التي تعصف بمنطقة اليورو.

where the contextual meaning of the ST expressions "package" خطة and "the debt storm tearing through the euro-zone" زوبعة الديون التي تعصف بمنطقة اليورو is provided and the TTs are faithful representations of the STs. The TTs are expressed in such a manner that they have successfully yielded the STs intended interpretation without putting the TL audience through unnecessary processing effort. In other words, the above TTs resemble the STs closely enough in relevant respects. Thus, the intended interpretation of the TTs resembles the STs and makes it adequately relevant to the TL audience; the TT offers adequate contextual effects.

Also, in Qur'an translation, we encounter the problem of mismatches in grammatical categories between Arabic and English such as the distinction between the obsolete pronoun "thou" and أنتَ/أنتم, where the old English "thou" is not used in contemporary English. However, the translator has used "thou" to achieve special contextual effects by using the less common pronoun, since its meaning, in the view of the translator, is recoverable without unnecessary processing effort on the part of the TL audience.

Whatever decision the translator reaches, Gutt argues (ibid:386), is based on *his/her intuitions or beliefs* about what is relevant to his/her audience. The translator does not have direct access to the cognitive environment of his/her audience; without actually *knowing* the audience, all he/she has are assumptions or beliefs about it. However, these assumptions may be wrong. Thus, failure of communication is likely to arise when the translator's assumptions about the cognitive environment of the TL audience are inaccurate.

For instance, وأعدّ لهم جهنّمَ وساءت مصيرا is given a faithfulness translation approach "And for whom He (God) has prepared Hell, an evil destination, for them hell" (Q48:6,

Translation as process and product 47

Abdel Haleem 2005), where the translator has avoided unnecessary processing effort on the part of the TL reader through changing the grammatical structure of the last part of the sentence (verb + implicit subject + adverb) ساءت مصيراً to a TL noun phrase "an evil destination", modifying the head noun جهنم "hell" and using a comma instead of the additive conjunctive particle (و) so that the TT should not be unnecessarily difficult to understand, the ST intended interpretation is maintained, and the TT interpretively resembles the ST.

19 **Exegetical translation approach**: The major characteristics of this translation approach are as follows:

(i) It is a paraphrase of a SL expression: This is a translation strategy offered by Dickins et al. (2002:9, 41, 235), which is a paraphrase of a SL expression. In other words, exegetical translation adds additional details that are not explicitly conveyed in the ST; it is an explication and expansion of the SL expression. This is because the TL is lexically deficient (lexical void, Abdul-Raof 2018:305) – the TL does not have a conventional lexical equivalent. Thus, exegetical translation explains and elaborates on the SL expression. Such a translation incurs notable translation loss in that it is less economical and semantically less precise than the ST. However, this loss is not as serious as the obscurity of the SL expression. For instance, in Q35:13, we encounter the noun قطمير, which is a lexical void for English. Thus, it has been given an exegetical translation as (the skin of a date stone/the thin cover around the seed of a date).

The exegetical translation approach is similar to the first translation approach "equivalence by modifying a generic word" proposed by Beekman and Callow (1974:191–211) previously, and is also similar to descriptive equivalent approach provided by Newmark (1988:83) where the description and function as essential elements of the SL expression are offered in the TL expression.

Examples of exegetical translation are "Brexit" – خروج بريطانيا من الإتحاد الأوربي – and "Brexiteer" – المؤيد لخروج بريطانيا من الإتحاد الأوربي.

We also find examples of exegetical translation in Qur'an translation, as in كأنَّهُنّ بيضٌ مكنون – "Delicate and pure" as if they were "hidden" eggs (Q37:49) (Ahmad 2010).

An example of how exegetical translation explains and elaborates on the SL expression "Planning Minister" whose exegetical translation is وزيرُ الدولة لشؤون التخطيط, where exegetical translation has added additional details الدولة لشؤون that are not explicitly conveyed in the ST; it is an explication and expansion of the SL expression. The same applies to the expression (conservationists) whose equivalent in Arabic is المُنادون بالحِفاظ على البيئة.

We encounter the culture-based expressions "green paper" and "white paper" which are both lexical voids in Arabic and require exegetical translation. We propose the following exegetical translations:

"green paper": مُسودة قرار يتم مناقشتها في البرلمان ليتم الموافقة عليها لكي تصبح قانوناً جديداً.
"white paper": مشروع حكومي حول سياسة ما وغاليا ما يحدد مقترحات لإجراء تغييرات تشريعية قد يتم مناقشتها قبلَ أن تصبح مشروع قانون ثم تصبح قانوناً ساري الأفعال

(ii) The exegetical translation approach provides within-the-TT additional details: The exegetical translation approach adds additional details that are not explicitly conveyed in the ST – it is a clarification and expansion of a SL expression. Thus,

48 *Translation as process and product*

exegetical translation is less economical (over-translation), semantically less precise than the ST, and provides a commentary on the translation process, as in

من الجِنَّةِ والناس (الناس 6)

"'Those whisperers could be' from jinn or man"
where the additional details are "Those whisperers could be".

لا تبدلَ لخلق اللهَ ذلكَ الدينُ القيّمُ (الروم 30)

Let us first consider different translations of the above ST and their translation approaches:

There is no altering (the laws of) Allah's creation. That is the right religion (Pickthall 1930: no page).
(for,) not to allow any change to corrupt what God has thus created – this is the [purpose of the one] ever true faith (Asad 1980:846).
Do not change what Allah has created (e.g., give proper training to children to follow Islamic religion). That is the Straight religion (to which the natural instinct directs) (Ahmad 2010:539).

where the additional details are added by the translator and are placed between brackets as within-the-TT clarifications of the ST. Thus, the TT has become less economical as it is an over-translation.

Shortly after take-off, we hear the announcement by the air hostess: "In the unlikely event of emergency landing, . . .". However, the TL announcement adds the culture-based additional details لا سامَحَ الله at the end of the TT. Thus, we get: لا اضطراري في حالة الهبوط الأضطراري لا, where the extra culture-bound details لا قَدَّرَ الله are added.

Consider this next instance of exegetical translation which adds additional details not explicitly conveyed in the ST. This example in Q18:1–2 includes an explication and expansion of the SL expression "Allah" and the ST noun (عوجاً) "crookedness", as follows:

الحمدُ للهِ الذي أنزلَ على عبدهِ الكتابَ ولم يجعل لهُ عِوَجاً قيّمَاً . . . (الكهف 1–2)

All form of praise and thanks are for Allah (Alone), who has sent down His slave [Muhammad] the Book which has no crookedness (in its wordings and meanings and no deviation from the middle path). It is a straight forward and firm Book.

(Ahmad 2010:381)

where "Alone" and "in its wordings and meanings and no deviation from the middle path" represent additional details not mentioned in the ST.

20 **Domestication translation approach**: Domestication provides a transparent and fluent TL style in order to make the TT closely conform to the TL culture and minimize the ST strangeness for the TL readers. Venuti (1995:19–20) provides two types of translation approaches which deal with the question of how much a translation assimilates a ST to the TL and culture, and how much the translation signals the differences of ST. Venuti (1995:21) sees domestication as dominating Anglo-American translation culture. Venuti (1995:20) objects strongly to domestication since it involves an ethnocentric reduction of the foreign text to Anglo-American TL values. This entails translating in a

Translation as process and product 49

transparent, fluent, and "invisible" style in order to minimize the foreignness of the TT. Domestication aims to leave the TL reader in peace, as much as possible, and moves the author towards him/her. This translation strategy adheres to domestic literary norms by carefully selecting the texts that are likely to lend themselves to such a translation strategy (Venuti 1997:241). As a translation strategy, domestication is equivalent to the cultural transposition strategy proposed by Dickins et al. (2002:29), and which involves the choice of TL-specific features inherent to the TL and the target culture to reduce the foreignness of the TT.

The major characteristics of domestication are

(i)   The localization (naturalization) of the ST to reduce the foreignness of the TT: The TT should not smell of foreignness. This means the domestication of the cultural, linguistic, and stylistic values (norms) of the ST. The aim of this translation approach is to make the SL message intelligible to the TL audience through the translation process of localization where a ST expression is stripped of its culture-specific features. For instance, the notions of "sin" and "repentance" may be replaced by "spit on the ground in front of", as in Shilluk spoken in the Sudan. This idiom is based upon the requirement that plaintiffs and defendants spit on the ground in front of each other when a case has been finally tried and punishment meted out. The spitting indicates that all is forgiven and that the accusations can never be brought into court again. Similarly, the expression "white as snow" may be rendered as "white as egret feathers" if the TL audience are not familiar with snow but speak of anything very white by this phrase (Nida 1964).

To domesticate a ST is to reduce its foreignness in the TT, as in "to sell coal in Newcastle" whose translation based on domestication is يبيعُ الماءَ في حارة السقائين. This applies also to the expression "the tip of the iceberg", which is wrongly translated literally as قمة الجبل الجليدي, whose domestication-based translation is غيضٌ من فيضٍ.

Domestication also aims for the intelligibility of the SL metaphor, metonymy, and proverb. The translator aims to adapt the ST in order to reduce foreign (SL) features – cultural foreignness – in the TT. Thus, the translator has naturalized the ST into the TL and its cultural setting. Such a translation strategy also involves cultural transposition where a wholesale deletion of source-culture details mentioned in the ST are replaced by target-culture details in the TT, as in رجَعَ بخُفّي حُنَين whose domestication translation is "He came back 'returned' empty handed". Also, بيَّضتَ وجهي should be domesticated as "You made me feel proud" rather than its out-of-context literal meaning "You whitened my face". The domestication of the Iraqi proverb is a prerequisite for intelligibility: نفس الطاسة ونفس الحمَّام whose domestication translation is "Nothing has changed". The domestication of the expression مربط الفرس is "the main point". Thus, the translation of هذا هو مربط الفرس في نقاشنا اليوم is "This is the main point in our discussion today". Literally, however, مربط الفرس means "the place in which a horse is tied up".

Similarly, consider the literal and word-for-word translation of the Arabic expression: لا ناقة لي فيها ولا جَمَل is "Neither a female camel do I have in this matter nor a male one" whose meaning is alien to the TL audience. Through the domestication translation approach, the SL message can be made intelligible to the TL reader: "I have nothing to do with this matter".

50 *Translation as process and product*

Another example of domestication where we replace a SL word by a culturally acceptable TL word is the expression "Guinea pigs". Since the word "pig" has a negative connotative meaning in Arabic, the TL expression has been changed to فئران تجارب where the word "pig" is changed to فئران meaning "mice".

The translation of Q37:49 كأنّهُنّ بيضٌ مكنون (As if they were hidden pearls) by Arberry (1955:200) is an example of the domestication translation approach where a TL expression "hidden pearls" close to the TL culture is employed; it does not translate literally to the SL culture-specific expression بيضٌ مكنون.

Venuti's domestication translation strategy can also be compared to cultural transplantation (adaptation) as described by Dickins et al. (2002:32), where the wholesale deletion of source-culture details have occurred in the ST and are replaced with target-culture details in the TT. Thus, this translation approach leads to the entire ST being rewritten in a native target culture setting – as in قيس وليلى, which is translated as "Romeo and Juliet" (ibid).

Therefore, we can claim that the domestication translation approach is similar to localization translation because both are TL-reader-oriented approaches.

(ii) Similarity to other translation approaches: The domestication translation approach is similar to the communicative, dynamic equivalence, natural, acceptable, instrumental, and faithful translation approaches. These translation approaches allow cultural transposition, are TL culture-based, and context-based; they take into consideration the contextual intended meaning of the ST. The aims of all these translation approaches are (1) to provide a comprehensible TT to its audience with an acceptable natural TL style, and (2) to achieve complete naturalness of the TT; to domesticate the TT and reduce its foreignness.

21 Foreignization translation approach: Foreignization provides a TT which deliberately violates the TL conventions through retaining some of the foreignness of the ST. It is a SL-author-oriented approach. This opens up the foreign work (ST) to us in its utter foreignness (Venuti 2000:286). The major characteristics of foreignization are

(i) Translation out of context to maximize foreignness of the TT and send the TT reader abroad, as in

وأُحِبُّها وتُحِبُّني ويُحِبُّ ناقتها بعيري

This is a verse from the love poem by the poet المُنخّل اليشكري, whose translation based on the foreignization approach is

I love her and she loves me / And her she-camel loves my he-camel

This poem was called القصيدةُ اليتيمةُ, whose translation based on the foreignization approach is "the orphan poem". However, to adopt the domestication translation approach, we get "the outlawed poem" which is a context-based meaning because the ruler at the time placed the poem under a ban and it was illegal to mention it because he thought the poem was about his wife. However, in Arabic, the expression قصيدةٌ يتيمةٌ can be translated based either on the foreignization approach "an orphan poem" or on the domestication (context-based) translation approach "a plagiarized poem" قصيدةٌ مُنتَحَلَةٌ – a poem whose real author (poet) is unknown but is claimed falsely by another poet.

Translation as process and product 51

To maximize foreignness in the TT and attain foreignization, the expression "blue-collar voters" is translated as الناخبون من ذوي الياقات الزرقاء instead of domesticating (localizing) it as الناخبون من الطبقات العمالية.

In Qur'an translation, foreignization is encountered frequently, as in حرثَ الآخرة) الشورى 20) where the noun حرث is foreignized as "tilth, harvest" "the tilth 'harvest' of the hereafter" while its context-based meaning is "reward, deeds which lead to reward". The foreignization of the expression مربطُ الفرس is "the place in which a horse is tied up". Thus, the translation of هذا هو مربطُ الفرس في نقاشنا اليوم is "This is the place in which the horse is tied up in our discussion today".

The out-of-context translations of the expressions بيتُ المال and بيتُ الله as "the house of money" and "the house of God" respectively represent foreignization.

(ii) The verbatim transfer of a SL style into the TT without making any adaptation to the SL style: An example of the foreignization translation approach which involves the transfer of the stylistic (structural) pattern of the ST to the TT is as follows.

الله يعلمُ وأنتم لا تعلمون – Allah knows, while you know not (Q2:216)

where the ST stylistic structure is preserved in the TT. The ST involves the reiteration of the same verb يعلم "to know" and the TT violates its cohesion and structural norms of verbal substitution where the second verb تعلمون should be substituted by the auxiliary verb "do". Thus, we should have "God knows and you <u>do</u> not", which is a domestication translation approach.

Similarly,

لم يكُن له كُفواً أحَدٌ (الإخلاص 4)

where the ST is a marked (unusual, unexpected) word order with a structural ambiguity. However, its unmarked (usual, unambiguous) structure is

لم يكُن أحدٌ كُفواً له – No one is comparable to Him. (Abdel Haleem 2005:444)

which is based on the domestication translation approach. However, Arberry (1955:281) has provided a foreignization translation to Q112:4 "And equal to Him is not any one", where we can see close adherence to the ST structure and syntax, resulting in a non-fluent alienating translation style. Venuti (1995:20) considers the foreignizing method as an ethno-deviant pressure on TL cultural values to register the linguistic and cultural difference of the foreign text, sending the TT reader abroad. This method of translation aims to restrain the ethnocentric violence of translation through the close adherence to the ST structure and syntax.

An interesting example of the foreignization translation approach which involves the verbatim transfer of a SL style into the TT without making any adaptation to the SL style is

ربِّ إنّي لِما أنزلتَ إليَّ من خيرٍ فقيرٍ (القصص 24)
My Lord, indeed I am, for whatever good You would send down to me, in need (Saheeh International 1997:535).

52 *Translation as process and product*

where the foregrounded adjective فقير at the end of the sentence should be immediately after its subject إِني to have a natural SL style. This is a marked (unusual, unexpected) word order in Arabic. The unmarked (usual) word order is

$$ربِّ إِني فقيرٍ لِما أنزلتَ إلِيَّ من خيرٍ$$

whose domesticated and natural style in the TL is

> My Lord, indeed I am in need for whatever good You would send down to me.

We can therefore conclude that the foreignization translation approach is source-reader-oriented, allows the TT to smell of foreignness, and involves the verbatim transfer of a SL style into the TT without making any adaptation to the SL style. This is the opposite of localization translation, which is TL-reader-oriented.

(iii) The verbatim transfer of a ST metaphor, metonymy, proverb content, and form into the TT: Consider this example of the foreignization translation approach in the following Iraqi proverb:

الطول طول النخلة والعقل عقل الصخلة – His height is the height of a date palm and his brain is the brain of a goat.

The utter foreignness of the above ST makes the translator quite visible. The underlying meaning, retrieved through the domestication or dynamic equivalence translation approaches, is "He is childish", meaning "He is silly, immature". Similarly, بيَّضتَ وجهي can be given a foreignization translation "You whitened my face". Also, نفس الطاسة ونفس الحمَّام, whose foreignization translation is "The same bowl and the same bathroom".

أنا رجلٌ محدودُ الدخل لا أريدُ سوى بنت التنُّور على الطاولة – I'm a limited income man. I only want a daughter of the clay oven on the table.

where foreignization lies in the literal translation of the ST metonymy (بنت التنُّور) "the daughter of the clay oven", whose underlying (domestication) meaning is "a loaf of bread". For more examples on metonymy, see Chapter 2, Section 2.7, example 21.

The expression قميصُ عُثمان "'Uthman's shirt" is widely used in Arabic as a metonymy for "pretext (ploy) to deceive others and win their support for his/her personal interests". Muhammad Ashtiyyah محمد أشتية, the Palestinian Prime Minister (17 August 2020) has used this expression as a metonymy: تطبيع العلاقات مع اسرائيل بقميص عُثمان الفلسطيني. This is in reference to the United Arab Emirate's newly established diplomatic relations with Israel. Thus, to foreignize the metonymy expression, we get "The normalization of relations with Israel using a Palestinian 'Uthman's shirt". Thus, we have used the SL cultural value قميص عُثمان in the TT. However, to domesticate the SL-culture-based expression قميص عُثمان is to provide its underlying context-based meaning, which is "to use Palestine as a pretext for the normalization of relations with Israel".

Another example is "Trump abandoned his pledge to drain the swamp", whose foreignization translation approach is ترامب يتخلى عن وعده في تجفيف المستنقع, which sounds unfamiliar to the Arab reader. The domestication approach yields ترامب يتخلى عن وعده في استئصال الفساد.

(iv) The phonetic transfer (transliteration) of ST expressions: The foreignizing translation approach is employed in Q30:30 where the SL Qur'anic expression فطرة is transferred phonetically (transliterated) into the TT as "fitrah" by Saheeh International (1997:562).

This foreignizing translation approach is also called "resistancy" (Venuti 1995:305–306) and "minoritizing" (Venuti 1998:11). For Venuti (ibid), it cultivates a varied and "heterogeneous discourse"; it is a "visible" translating strategy. It is a non-fluent or estranging translation style designed to make visible the presence of the translator by highlighting the foreign identity of the ST and protecting it from the ideological dominance of the TL culture. An example of making visible the presence of the translator is آية، سورة، مُحكمات، مُتشابهات, which have been transferred phonetically as "ayah, surah, muhkamat, mutashabihat" in Qur'an translation.

A unique foreignization translation approach that is phonetically based is depicted by the Sufi Qur'an translators Helminski (2000; cited in Sideeg 2015:215) and Hulusi (2013):

اللهُ لا إلهَ إلاَّ هُو الحيُّ القيُّومُ . . . العليُّ العظيمُ (البقرة 255)

Allah – there is no deity but HU, the Ever-Living, the Self-Subsisting source . . . the Highest and Most Exalted (Helminski 2000).

Allah is HU! There is no God, only HU! The Hayy and the Qayyum . . . He is the Aliy and the Azim (Hulusi 2013:84).

(v) The verbatim transfer of culture-based expressions: The foreignizing method of translating is a strategy which entails the choice of a foreign text and developing a translation method along lines which are excluded by dominant cultural values in the TL (Venuti 1997:242). Venuti's foreignization translation approach is similar to the cultural borrowing approach put forward by Dickins et al. (2002:32). The cultural borrowing translation approach involves the verbatim transfer of a SL expression into the TT without making any adaptation or explanation to the SL expression. For instance, the expressions حجاب and نِقاب are kept in the TT in a transliterated form "hijab" and "niqab" rather than being translated literally as "Islamic dress" and "face cover" respectively. However, the mechanism of cultural borrowing of a ST expression is through the transliteration of the SL expression and the use of italics, as in

اثناء ذروة انتشار وباء كورونا، المُمثّلة الكويتية (حياة الفهد) في يوم الأربعاء 1 أبريل 2020 تقول: (طهِّروا الكويت من الأجانب وارموهم في البر (أي: الصحراء))

The Kuwaiti soap actress Hayat al-Fahad has used the word طهِّروا meaning "to cleanse". This word has been used during the peak of the Covid-19 pandemic and is associated with "cleansing" to get rid of the virus. Thus, the translation "Cleanse Kuwait of the foreigners and throw them away in the desert" fits well into the context of the situation. Thus, the foreignization approach works well in the above example. The domestication approach will not do the performative intent of the ST: "Get the foreigners out of Kuwait and throw them out in the desert". However, the verb طهِّروا has occurred 31 times in the Qur'an with all its morphologically related forms, and is translated as "to purify".

The expression التطهير العرقي occurred for the first time during the Balkan War and was given a foreignization translation approach "ethnic cleansing".

54 *Translation as process and product*

Another example of foreignizing a ST is: لا ناقة لي فيها ولا جَمَل, which is "Neither a female camel do I have in this matter nor a male camel". However, if the ST is domesticated, the TT is: "I have nothing to do with this matter".

In Arabic-Islamic culture, the expressions صدر، قلب occur in Arabic and Qur'anic Arabic. Both expressions can be foreignized when translated literally, as in أعرف ما في قلبك and إِنَّ اللهَ عليمٌ بِذاتِ الصدور (آل عمران 119), whose translations based on the foreignization approach are "I know what is in your heart" and "Indeed, Allah is knowing of that within the breasts", (Q3:119), respectively. However, to adopt a domestication translation approach, we get "I know what is in your mind" and "Indeed, Allah knows what is people's mind", respectively. The same applies to Q94:1, where the TT reader is sent abroad by the foreignization-based translation: "Do We not expand for you your breast?" (Saheeh International 1997:893)/ "Have We not opened your breast for you?" (Ahmad 2010:835). However, we propose a domestication-based translation: "Have We not relieved you?", which is also ST context-based.

Culture-based expressions which constitute lexical voids in the TL need to be transferred through the foreignization translation approach, as in طواف الإفاضة: The act of worship in circumambulating the Kaʿbah in Makkah during Hajj on عيد الأضحى.

22 **Jargon translation approach**: We have put forward eight jargon production approaches: (i) mimicking the function of the SL jargon, (ii) mimicking the event which the SL jargon refers to, (iii) mimicking the shape of the SL jargon, (iv) mimicking the operational method of the SL jargon, (v) mimicking the sound of the SL jargon, (vi) mimicking the semantic features of the jargon, (vii) blending, and (viii) joint approach. This translation approach is primarily concerned with the mimicking mechanisms through which the translator creates a new TL jargon taking into consideration the TL grammatical, lexical, morphological, stylistic, and cultural norms in an attempt to domesticate and remove the smell of foreignness of the TT. Our translation approach looks into the English jargon that have been borrowed by Arabic. This translation approach is concerned with word- and phrase-level translation. We put forward three different types of jargon: (i) one-word jargon – a single-word jargon like (parliament) and (capital); (ii) noun phrase jargon – made up of two or more words which function as a noun phrase like (sky scraper); and (iii) acronyms – a type of jargon made up of the initial letters of two words like (UN – United Nations). For more details on this translation approach, see Chapter 6.

1.6 Translator training and translation practice

This section combines theory and practice and prepares students for the translation industry. Through detailed translation commentary and analysis of several examples, we aim to put theory into practice as well as provide practical translation training exercises with a solution to each question and informative discussion. The discussion and analysis aim to provide students with an insight into the translation process, guide them to achieve a successful translation, and demonstrate to them how and why a particular solution is given. These exercises are of high value to translation commentary assignments required by any translation program. We have also provided many Arabic and English texts as STs together with our proposed translations as a valuable pool of teaching materials for translation teachers. The rainbow of exercises provides the translation student with an insight into both Arabic and English culture.

Translation as process and product 55

1   Give reasons for your translation to the following ST. Explain the translation approach adopted during your translation process.

Have I Got News for You is a long-running BBC comedy panel show. In an episode hosted by Jeremy Clarkson that was broadcast in December 2008, one panelist said: "This is from the widows of the polar bears", whilst making a hand gesture as though he was throwing his shoes at Mr Clarkson.

How would you translate the panelist's sentence above? The suggested TT is

خُذ هذا الحِذاء هدية من أرامل الدُب القُطبي.

We can observe three important matters in this TT:

(i)   Intertextuality between the ST and the Iraqi journalist مُنتظر الزيدي who famously threw his shoes at the US President George W. Bush during a press conference in Baghdad. Whilst throwing his second shoe at President Bush, Mr Al-Zaidi yelled: "This is from the widows and orphans of all those killed in Iraq". Because Mr Al-Zaidi used his Iraqi Arabic, we need to adjust the above translation:

أُخذ هايَ القُندَرة هدية من أرامل الدُب القُطبي.

where we have substituted the standard Arabic خُذ هذا الحذاء by Iraqi Arabic أُخذ هايَ القُندَرة.

(ii) However, in the above ST example, the panelist was referring to the issue of global warming and implying that Jeremy Clarkson   through his love of motoring and his main television program which he hosted at the time on the BBC, *Top Gear* – personally contributed to global warming by causing polar ice caps to melt and polar bears to die as a result. Therefore, intertextual expressions are culture-specific items, and as such the translator needs to master the TL in the context of its culture.

(iii) SL culture and the connotative meaning of the word هدية, which is an addition procedure to the TT. The translation procedure of addition is adopted in the TT where the word هدية is added to highlight sarcasm and intensify the negative connotative meaning of "shoes" in Arabic culture. In some Arabic-speaking countries, especially Iraq, items of footwear (including shoes) and the word حذاء – or rather قُندَرة in Iraqi Arabic – can have negative connotations when utilized to inflict insult or show disrespect. Thus, throwing a shoe, hitting someone with a shoe, or causing a shoe to make contact with another person can be deemed to be a severely insulting gesture of disrespect.

2   In a report on the Arabic version of the Saudi news channel العربية, we hear the following statement. Translate, with commentary, the following sentence:

بعملها هذا، تكون حماس قد أكلت من ثمار الشجرة المُحرّمة.

56 *Translation as process and product*

We propose the TT: (Through its own actions, Hamas has eaten fruits from the forbidden tree).

Here we can make the following observations:

(i) Both the ST and the TT involve the same intertextual reference الشجرة المُحرَّمة –
"the forbidden tree", which is known to both the SL and TL readers; to Jewish, Christian, and Muslim cultures. Thus, this is a literal and formal equivalence translation approach.

(ii) The TT has not unfolded the intended meaning of the expression الشجرة المُحرَّمة;
rather, a literal translation has been provided. To provide a TT that conveys the performative intent (pragmatic, contextual, intended meaning) of the ST's producer, the translation would have been: "Hamas will be punished due to its own actions" or "Through its own actions, Hamas will be punished". The latter TT versions are based on one of the translation approaches such as the communicative, dynamic equivalence, natural, acceptable, instrumental, transposition or shift translation, or faithful. These translation approaches take into consideration the contextual intended meaning of the ST in order to provide a comprehensible TT to its audience with an acceptable natural TL style. These translation approaches aim at complete naturalness of the TT; to naturalize the TT and reduce its foreignness. The above translation interpretively resembles the original without unnecessary processing effort on the part of the TL reader.

A translation with the ST's performative intent relies on the intertextual reference to Q7:22–25 and Q20:121. Adam and Eve have been warned by God not to eat from the "forbidden tree", yet they listened to Satan who misguided them and misled them into defying God's order. Similarly, based on intertextuality and context, Hamas defied Israel's order, obeyed Israel's opponents, and eventually was misled. Thus, like Adam and Eve, Hamas "deserves to be punished".

3   Translate the following text and provide a translation commentary:

هؤلاء هم المُغلّفة قلوبهم بأقفالٍ غليظةٍ فهم يُهددون أمننا الوطني وسنقرأُ على أرواحهم الفاتحة قريباً.

Our suggested TT is either

Those are the ones whose hearts are wrapped up with heavy padlocks. They threaten our national security. We will read (Surah) Al-Fatihah on their souls soon.

Or

Those are the stone-hearted ones who are merciless and who threaten our national security. They will disappear soon.

The first TT adopts one of the translation approaches, such as literal, exoticizing, formal equivalence, adequate, or foreignization, where the same Arabic expression الفاتحة is transferred to the TT out of context in an effort to keep the ST flavor. Such a translation is source

Translation as process and product 57

oriented. However, the TT is not easy to process by the TL audience who is not familiar with the notion of الفاتحة. Based on Islamic culture, الفاتحة refers to the first Qur'anic chapter, which is usually read for the soul of a deceased person. Thus, the second translation adopts a translation approach such as domestication, dynamic equivalence, communicative, natural, faithful, or acceptable, which aims to transfer the SL notion of الفاتحة and maintain the source content and language acceptable and comprehensible to TL readership. This is a target-oriented translation which aims to be appropriate to the TL and culture and which does not require unnecessary processing effort on the part of the TL reader.

4   Translate the following sentence which a policeman in the Iraqi Passport Office told me 45 years ago:

لا تستطيع إنجاز معاملة الجواز إلا إذا دفعت المعلوم.

Some TL expressions are highly local and culture-specific, as in المعلوم in the above example, which is specific to the Iraqi culture then. Thus, one of the translation approaches can be adopted – such as cultural transposition, dynamic equivalence, communicative, natural, acceptable, faithful, or domestication – which are appropriate translation strategies for the above ST.

The suggested TT is: "You will not be able to get your passport unless you pay a bribe".

However, to adopt one of the translation approaches such as literal, exoticizing, formal equivalence, adequate, or foreignization will lead to inappropriate and difficult-to-process TT because it is a source-oriented translation: "You will not be able to get your passport unless you pay what is known".

5   On 12 Saturday December 2009, the 2009 British Comedy Awards were broadcast on the British television channel ITV. During the program, host Jonathan Ross said:

"We mustn't offend anyone. This year's Comedy Awards must be whiter than white; they'll be whiter than Nick Griffin's dream pub".

This statement has an embedded SL culture-specific joke; its underlying sarcastic overtone is quite difficult to translate unless the translator is aware of

(i)   Who Nick Griffin is, what his political leanings were/are and what his political agenda is/was,
(ii) Famous slogans used in British advertising, and
(iii) Drinking culture in the United Kingdom.

In British politics, Nick Griffin was the chairman of the far-right British National Party or "BNP", between 1999 and 2014. The BNP is notorious for being associated with racist ideologies such as white supremacy, and calls for the return of an all-white Britain, which would involve the repatriation/deportation of non-British and non-white citizens and non-citizens. In the United Kingdom, the expression "whiter than white" was popularized by (and is often associated with) the marketing slogan of the laundry detergent Persil, which promoted itself as being able to preserve and further whiten already-white laundry items such as shirts, socks, and t-shirts. Over time and on the back of this marketing slogan, in the

58 *Translation as process and product*

United Kingdom "whiter than white" has garnered a further meaning of being completely upright, moral, and righteous. Ross' sarcasm is generated by stating that the Awards must be "whiter than white". By this, he means that everything at the Awards including the words and actions of the guests must be so inoffensive that the Awards could be deemed to be innocent, virtuous, and angelic. However, Ross goes further and employs a hyperbolic simile to express that the pureness and innocence of the "whiter than white" Awards would actually make them "whiter than Nick Griffin's dream pub". A "pub" in the United Kingdom, Ireland and some Commonwealth countries is an abbreviation of the term "public house" (خمَّارة) – premises for socializing where alcohol may be consumed. They are of importance to drinking culture in the United Kingdom, and much like cafes and restaurants, cater to the various tastes and styles of customers. As Mr Griffin idolizes a return to an all-white Britain, by the same virtue, his ideal pub (i.e., one that he would obviously dream of) would be one at which all its customers were ethnically white British. Ross quips that the Awards would be even whiter than such a scenario, which ordinarily would be the most "white" imaginable.

Our suggested translations:

ستكون الليلة أبيضُ من البياض تماماً مثل خمارة نِك غريفن المثالية.
ستكون الليلة أبيضُ من البياض تماماً كما يحلُم به حزب نك غريفين.

Having produced the translation, do we need a footnote or an addition of a word or two to the TT in the interest of clarity for the TL reader, who is unaware of the cultural setting of the British political landscape as well as marketing and culture? I believe that for an effective communicative approach translation, we need to adopt the addition procedure where the word عُنصري – "racist" is added to the TT:

ستكون الليلة أبيضُ من البياض تماماً كما يحلُم به حزب نك غريفين العنصري.

Taking Arabo-Islamic culture into consideration, we have adopted the communicative translation approach and the adaptation procedure whereby the word "pub" – خمَّارة is deleted and replaced with حزب – "party". Thus, the TT provides the contextual meanings of the SL words, the intended meaning of the ST producer, and a natural TL style. A gloss translation approach is not appropriate where the TT is supplemented with a footnote explaining who Nick Griffin is, his party's political agenda, and what a pub is.

6   Provide a commentary on the translation process of the following text. Compare the ST with the TT and explain the translation strategies adopted by the translator.

وفي ذلكم بلاءٌ من ربكم عظيمٌ (البقرة 49)

whose translation is: "And in that was a great trial from your Lord". (Saheeh International 1997:9), "This was a great trial from your Lord". (Abdel Haleem 2005:8), and "Therein was a tremendous trial from your Lord". (Ali 1934:no page).

Based on our textual and discourse analysis of the ST, we can make an interesting observation about the above three translations. We have a ST word order different from the TT word order. In the ST, the prepositional phrase من ربكم – "from your Lord" is moved from its normal position at the end of the sentence (sentence-final position) and is placed in the

Translation as process and product 59

middle of the sentence after the noun بَلاءٌ – "trial". Thus, on the stylistic level, the ST has achieved the rhetorical feature of hyperbaton because an element is moved from its position and placed elsewhere within the sentence. Hyperbaton is a ST stylistic idiosyncrasy and is a stylistic technique which conveys the perlocutionary force of saliency (focus) given to the displaced prepositional phrase من ربكم. Thus, the adjective عظيم – "great" is displaced and is moved to the end of the sentence. In other words, we expect a word order where the adjective, as a modifier, comes after its noun and the prepositional phrase occurs at the end of the sentence. Thus, we expect

وفي ذلكم بلاءٌ عظيمٌ من ربكم

However, the TL linguistic norms do not allow hyperbaton stylistic device to occur; the TT does not allow us to separate the adjective "great, tremendous" from its noun "trial". For this reason, we generated the previous translations. Due to the word order distinction, we need to apply the natural translation approach where shift in the ST word order is adopted and the Tl structural (grammatical) norms are observed. In other words, we have a naturalized TT. This is also a transposition (shift) translation approach. The وقالوا لولا نُزّلَ هذا القرآن على رجلٍ من القريتين عظيم الزخرف 31 where the adjective عظيم is a hyperbaton taken out from its original position and placed at the end of the sentence. We expect وقالوا لولا نُزّلَ هذا القرآن على رجلٍ عظيم من القريتين الزخرف 31. To observe the TT grammatical norms, we get rid of the stylistic feature of hyperbaton and produce "a great man" – رجلٍ عظيم. For more details on hyperbaton, see Abdul-Raof (2020:94).

7 Discuss the translation process involved in the translation of "to sell coal in Newcastle" and comment on the translation approach adopted by the translator.

(i) During the translation process, the translator needs to consider the ST context so that he/she can provide an accurate rendering of the ST intended meaning to a reader whose culture is not familiar with the sale of coal in the streets.

(ii) Newcastle is a northeast city of the United Kingdom famous for its coal mining industry since Medieval times, and has been a coal-mining centre for 400 years. This city is also very cold and people used to sell coal for heating during the winter and for cooking. Thus, to bring coal to Newcastle to sell it would be something superfluous, pointless, and unnecessary – no one would buy your coal.

(iii) The translator needs to search for an Arabic proverb with a similar effect to that of the TT.

(iv) Based on the above details, the proposed translation for "to sell coal in Newcastle" is يبيعُ الماءَ في حارة السّقائين. The Arabic proverb is also based on a cultural experience where we have an area famous for carrying and selling water in a hot country; water is in abundance in this area, where it would be superfluous, pointless, and unnecessary to bring water from other areas for sale. In Arabic, السقاية means (irrigation, watering) and also means (selling water from the waterskins, traditional watering vessels carried on the shoulder).

(v) We have adopted the translation approaches which aim for complete naturalness of the TT; to reduce the smell of foreignness of the ST. This is a culture-based translation based on one of the translation approaches such as the communicative, dynamic equivalence, natural, acceptable, or faithful. These translation approaches

60 *Translation as process and product*

take into consideration the contextual intended meaning of the ST in order to provide a comprehensible TT to its audience with an acceptable natural TL style. These translation approaches aim at complete naturalness of the TT; to naturalize the TT and reduce its foreignness. The above translation interpretively resembles the original without unnecessary processing effort on the part of the TL reader.

8   What is the translation of the advert: "Vaux: A trademark that speaks for itself?" Discuss the translation process.

The suggested translation is فوكس: علامةٌ تجاريةٌ غنيةٌ عن التعريف

The expression "Vaux" is a car brand in the United Kingdom. Thus, it is source culture-specific and a cultural problem. However, there is no SL cultural equivalent because it is an industrial and commercial trademark (name). It refers to **Vauxhall** Motors – a British automotive company owned by Groupe PSA and headquartered in Bedfordshire, England. This car company was founded by Alex Wilson in 1857 as a pump and marine engine manufacturer, then began manufacturing cars in 1903.

Let us conduct textual and discourse analysis before the translation process:

(i)   A transference translation approach has been adopted which involves the transference of the SL word "Vaux" to the TL text through transliteration. The SL word "Vaux" is transferred phonetically (transliterated) and adapted to the TL morphology and spelling where the initial "V" is written as "ف". Also, based on the transference translation approach, the foreign name "Vaux" is transliterated as فوكس where TL spelling norms are observed.

(ii)   The SL relative pronoun "that" is deleted; thus, the deletion translation procedure is adopted in order to meet the TL linguistic (grammatical) norms.

(iii) The TL main-verb expression "speaks for itself" is translated as adjective + a prepositional phrase: غنية عن التعريف, which involves a dynamic or natural translation approach where we find adaptation in grammar and lexicon. The grammatical modifications are dictated by the obligatory grammatical structure of the TL.

9   What is the translation of the following texts? Discuss the translation process.

يُرجى قراءة التعليمات الموجودة على بطاقة صعود الطائرة قبل الصعود. (أو) قبل الصعود الى الطائرة، يُرجى قراءة التعليمات الموجودة على بطاقة الصعود.
يُرجى حُضُوركم الى بوابة الصعود حسب الوقت الموضح على بطاقة صعود الطائرة.

(i)   We propose the following translation:

Before boarding the airplane, please read the instructions on the boarding card.
Please report to the boarding gate at the time shown.

(ii)   The first TT has adopted the foregrounding (putting at the beginning of the sentence) of the prepositional phrase "Before boarding the airplane" to give it saliency (focus). The ST nominalized noun قراءة is translated as a verb "read". The preposition إلى is taken out because the verb "board" does not need a preposition in English. The preposition على is translated as "on". The noun phrase بطاقة صعود الطائرة is translated as a noun phrase "boarding card" where الطائرة "airplane" is deleted.

Translation as process and product 61

(iii) The second TT has the nominalized noun حُضُور, which literally means (attendance, presence), and is translated as a verb (report). The attached possessive plural pronoun كُم is deleted. The noun حسب is translated as a preposition (at); the noun phrase إسم مفعول where الموضَّح is a passive participle الوقت الموضَّح is translated as a noun phrase (the time shown), where we also have a past participle (shown), which is originally (the time (which is) shown). The prepositional phrase على بطاقة صُعود الطائرة is deleted.

(iv) In such a translation process, we have adopted a TL-culture-based translation (TL-oriented) based on one of the translation approaches, such as communicative, dynamic equivalence, natural, acceptable, instrumental, transposition (shift), or faithful translation. These translation approaches take into consideration the contextual intended meaning of the ST in order to provide a comprehensible TT to its audience with an acceptable natural TL style. These translation approaches aim at complete naturalness of the TT; to naturalize the TT and reduce its foreignness. The above translation interpretively resembles the original without unnecessary processing effort on the part of the TL reader.

10 How would you translate the following expressions? Provide the translation approaches which justify the translation output (TT).

(a) يجب أن تكون سيُارتك خالية, (b) life vest, (c) قسم الأفراد, (d) MOT, (e) خبر عاجل, (f) نبضٌ واحدٌ, (g) meal vouchers, and (h) P45. من العطلات

(i) For the texts in question, we need a TL culture-based translation (TL-oriented) based on one of the translation approaches – such as communicative, dynamic equivalence, natural, acceptable, instrumental, faithful, or domestication – which aim at complete naturalness of the TT. The translator needs to naturalize the TT and reduce its foreignness (cultural transposition). These translation approaches take into consideration the contextual intended meaning of the ST in order to provide a comprehensible TT to its audience with an acceptable natural TL style.

(ii) Based on the above translation approaches, we propose the following translations of the previous expressions:

(a) breaking news, (b) الفحصُ الفني الدوري, (c) "personnel", (d) صدرية النجاة, (e) "Your vehicle (car) must be in a road-worthy condition", للسيارات (f) "hearts beating as one", (g) قسيمة العاطلين عن and (h) بطاقة وجبات الطعام العمل.

(iii) In example (d), the SL abbreviation "MOT" refers to "Ministry of Transport", which designates the vehicle's annual mechanical check-up. In example (g) "Meal Vouchers", we have added the word الغداء – "lunch" based on the ST context, which is the provision of free school meals to students and pupils. In Britain, a free lunch at noon is provided to children whose parents are on low or limited income.

11 Translate the following text and explain the translation procedures and required translation approaches:

أكَّدَ خادمُ الحرمين الشريفين الملك سلمان بن عبد العزيز على أهمية التعاون المُشترك

62 *Translation as process and product*

We propose the following translation:

King Salman Bin Abdul-Aziz of Saudi Arabia stressed the importance of joint cooperation.

(i) We have adopted the following two translation procedures:

(a) The procedure of deletion where the expression خادمُ الحرمين الشريفين is a SL culture-specific honorary title used exclusively in Saudi Arabia. This expression needs to be deleted in the TT because the TL audience are not aware of it, and

(b) The procedure of addition where the expression "of Saudi Arabia" is added in the interest of clarity.

(ii) We have adopted a TL-culture-based translation (TL-oriented) which is based on one of the translation approaches such as the communicative, dynamic equivalence, natural, acceptable, instrumental, transposition (shift), or faithful translation. These translation approaches take into consideration the contextual intended meaning of the ST in order to provide a comprehensible TT to its audience with an acceptable natural TL style. These translation approaches aim at complete naturalness of the TT, i.e., to naturalize the TT and reduce its foreignness.

(iii) Stylistically, the expression خادمُ الحرمين الشريفين is a rhetorical device of metonymy referring to King Salman of Saudi Arabia.

12 What is the translation of "The Prime Minister is following the 'kitchen sink' policy"? Explain why.

Our suggested translation is

يتبع رئيس الوزراء سياسة ''إلقاء اللوم على الخصم''، أو ''إلقاء اللوم على المُعارضة''.

The meaning of the expression "kitchen sink approach" derives from the expression "everything but the kitchen sink", and means "everything that can be conceived of, such that the Prime Minister is utilizing everything available against opponents".

13 A picture of Ian Wright, an Arsenal football player who never gets substituted because he is such an excellent player. He appears in an advert sitting comfortably holding a cup of Nescafé. On the right-hand side of the advert, we read the text "No Substitute". This is an example of intertextuality and culture in translation. Nescafé is well known in Arab countries, but Ian Wright may not be so well known. Thus, this advert about Nescafé cannot be displayed in such countries. The suggested translation is: لا بديل – "No substitute to it" where a direct reference is made to Nescafé coffee, which is a feminine noun; that is why the feminine coreferential pronoun -ها is used. Thus, the addition translation procedure is adopted لا بديلَ لها.

14 We recommend that the whole sentence, the whole paragraph, or the whole text is first read carefully, as a textual and discourse analysis process, before we take any decision about which translation approach or which meaning is selected for specific words. The text meaning always unfolds at the end rather than at the beginning. Let us consider the following examples:

(i) The ultimate word processor for less than the price of a mouse.

Translation as process and product 63

This is an advert about Parker pens in the front page of *The Guardian* (27 March 1997).

(ii) Lose weight instantly

Buy a Metrocard and you won't have to carry tons of loose change around

This is an advert displayed on buses in Leeds and elsewhere by the Metro bus company.
Having read the whole text (i), we can establish the accurate meaning of "mouse" which is
a polyseme through making an intertextual relationship between "mouse" and "word processor". Thus, the suggested translation is

أفضل مُعالِج كلمات بسعر أرخص من الفأرة.

where فأرة can be understood as فأرة الحاسوب.
In text (ii), the suggested translation is

خفُّف وزنك فوراً : احصل على بطاقة حافلات مترو وبهذا لا تحتاج الى حمل أطنان من القطع النقدية
معك.

where the SL culture-specific expression "Metrocard" is explained through the word
حافلات – "buses". Thus, (Metro) is now understood as the name of a bus company.

15 Translate the following advert (taken October 1999):

More BEEF that's
SCARING the GERMANS

On the left-hand side of the poster is a dark silver sports car with "GALANT" as its licence
plate.
Underneath the sports car, we see in pink colour the slogan:

IDENTIFY YOURSELF
Mitsubishi GALANT

Discussion: The Mitsubishi Galant is an automobile which was produced by the Japanese
manufacturer Mitsubishi from 1969 until 2012. The model name "Galant" was derived from
the French word *galant*, which means "chivalrous". We can now make the following textual
and discourse analysis of the advert that appeared in/around October 1999 in the United
Kingdom.

(i) The word "BEEF" appears in capital letters because a high-performance Japanese
     sports car is challenging rival German sports cars.
(ii) The word "BEEF" is polysemous in this advert and designates three distinct meanings: (a) a reference to Bovine Spongiform Encephalopathy (BSE), also known as
     "mad cow disease" – a reference to the BSE crisis in the UK in the 1990s which
     caused widespread concern about the safety of British beef and a temporary ban by
     Germany on imports of British beef; (b) strength/power; and (c) a grudge.

64 *Translation as process and product*

    (iii) The features of "strength/power" refer to the Mitsubishi Galant sports car.

    (iv) The Germans (with their own reputable sports car manufacturers) will – having already been made to fear "BEEF" from British cows due to BSE – now have an additional type of "BEEF" to fear: the sheer power of the Mitsubishi Galant that will outperform and intimidate Germany's sports car manufacturers. The word "BEEF" is also capitalized to emphasise the power of the Mitsubishi Galant against rival German sports cars; more "ENGINE POWER". Equally, "BEEF" is slang for "grudge" or "an unresolved issue with someone", so that this is another score that needs to be settled, which would scare Germany's sports car manufacturers.

    (v) The capitalization of the main words – "BEEF", "SCARING" and "GERMANS" – suggests that it is beef as a meat that is scaring the Germans.

    (vi) Mitsubishi's marketing slogan at the time was "Identify Yourself". This has two meanings: the first stems from the command "identify yourself": when requested to provide identification, your Mitsubishi motor vehicle is your form of identification. The second meaning stems from a person's desire to create an identity for themselves, and they can proudly do this by owning and driving a Mitsubishi motor vehicle. Ergo, Mitsubishi gives one a sense of identity.

Based on the above textual analysis, the suggested translation of the advert "More BEEF that's SCARING the GERMANS. IDENTIFY YOURSELF. Mitsubishi" is

محركٌ أكثر قوة . . . هذا ما يخوِّفُ الألمان . . . بطاقتك الشخصية هي متسوبيشي جالانت.

The back-translation is: "More powerful engine . . . This is what scares the Germans . . . Create an identity for yourself with a Mitsubishi".

16   Let us consider the translation of

   I forgot what an ordeal labour can be (*The Daily Mail*, 22 May 2000).
   Based on textual and discourse analysis, we make the following observations:

    (i)   Texts carry political and cultural overtones. *The Daily Mail* is a right-leaning tabloid newspaper in the United Kingdom and tends to support the Conservative Party. In order to do so, it manipulates texts against the Labour Party. On 21 May 2000, Mrs Cherie Blair, wife of the then British Prime Minister Tony Blair, gave birth to their third son, Leo. The above statement was the caption under a photograph of Mrs Blair after she had left hospital.

    (ii) The two words, (ordeal) and (labour), are placed next to each other. Most importantly, *The Daily Mail*'s performative intent (intended meaning) is to influence the public opinion against the Labour Party. Thus, the above text bears an underlying political overtone: "I forgot that the Labour Party could be an ordeal".

    (iii) The word "labour" is a polyseme: (a) the process of childbirth المخاض, and (b) Labour Party (with a capital L).

    (iv) The word "ordeal" means "a prolonged painful or unpleasant experience" – محنة.

Having said the above, the placement of the words "ordeal, labour" next to each other, which can be understood as "labour is an ordeal", is a perfect political manipulation of discourse, word order, and abuse of semantics. Although the word "labour" appears with an initial small

Translation as process and product 65

letter (l), *The Daily Mail* has successfully managed to manipulate Mrs Blair's statement. The suggested translation is: نسيتُ أنَّ المخاضَ مِحنةٌ.

The back-translation is: "I forgot that giving birth was an ordeal". Thus, the TT has failed to relay *The Daily Mail*'s politically performative intent. This is primarily due to the cultural stylistic gap represented by the initial letters of the word "labour" and "Labour". Thus, it can be related to the fact that "labour" and "Labour" represent a pun in English but not in Arabic. A pun is an SL, phonetically based rhetorical device that cannot be re-produced in the TL; it does not have a lexical equivalent, especially between languages like Arabic and English, which are linguistically and culturally incongruous and whose orthography is different. Thus, puns must be sacrificed in English-Arabic-English translation.

17   Let us consider the translation of

Maternity ward fails to deliver (*BBC Yorkshire Look North*, 28 January 2008).
Textual and discourse analysis of the ST:

(i)   The translation problem in the above text stems from polysemy. The verb "deliver" in this text is polysemous: (a) to provide something promised or expected, and (b) to give birth to a child.

(ii) To adopt a literal translation approach means we have treated the subject noun phrase "maternity ward" as personified where the non-human noun phrase is given the [+ Human] attribute of "giving birth". Also, we have selected the second meaning "to give birth to a baby" of the verb "deliver". The literal translation below is not based on ST context: جناحُ التوليد يفشلُ في تقديم المساعدات في الولادات

(iii) To adopt an acceptable and faithful translation approach that is hinged upon the ST context, we need to provide the following contextually based translation:

جناحُ التوليد يفشلُ في تقديم الخدمات المطلوبة (المتوقعة).

where the first meaning of the verb "deliver" is selected: "to provide something promised or expected".

18   Translate the following texts and explain the translation approaches required:

(a) عُذرُ البليد مسحُ السبورة, (b) Beauty is in the eye of the beholder, (c) Like father like son, and (d) Do not judge a book by its cover.

(i)   We propose the translations:

(a) A bad workman always blames his tools, (b) القرد بعين أمه غزال (c) هذا الشبل من هذا الأسد, and (e) لا تحكم على المظاهر.

(ii) We have adopted a TL-culture-based translation (TL-oriented) based on one of the translation approaches, such as the communicative, dynamic equivalence, natural, acceptable, instrumental, or faithful translation. These translation approaches take into consideration the contextual intended meaning of the ST in order to provide a comprehensible TT to its audience with an acceptable natural TL style. These translation approaches aim at complete naturalness of the TT; to naturalize the TT and reduce its foreignness. The above translation interpretively resembles the original without unnecessary processing effort on the part of the TL reader.

66 *Translation as process and product*

19 Translate the following text:

What is the winning move?

X	0	0
0	X	X
0	X	

Good legal advice is just as easy to get.

The above text was printed on the rear of a First Leeds bus ticket, and was from an advert for the Leeds Community Legal Service. The suggested translation is

ما هي خطوة النجاح؟ إنَّ الحصولَ على نصائح قانونية ناجحة (رابحة) سهلٌ كسهولة هذا اللغز .

20 Provide a commentary on the translation process of the following text. Compare the ST with the TT and explain the translation strategies adopted by the translator.

الى اللهِ مرجِعُكُم (هود 4)

TT: To God is your return (Ali 1934).
To Allah is your return (Saheeh International 1997).
It is to God that you will all return (Abdel Haleem 2005).

وإنّنا لفي شكٍّ مما تدعونا اليه مُريب (هود 62)

TT: But we are really in suspicious (disquieting) doubt as to that which thou invitest us (Ali 1934:no page).
And indeed we are, about that to which you invite us, in disquieting doubt (Saheeh International 1997:298).
We are in grave doubt about what you are asking us to do (Abdel Haleem 2005:140).
We are, indeed, very doubtful (about the religion) to which you are inviting (Ahmad 2010:294).

21 Provide a commentary on the translation process of the following text. Compare the ST with the TT and explain the translation strategies adopted by the translator.

لا يدخلون الجنّة حتى يلجَ الجَملُ في سَمِّ الخياط (الأعراف 40)

TT: they shall not enter into Paradise until a camel shall pass into a needle's eye (Palmer 1880).
. . . nor shall they enter Paradise until the camel passes through the eye of the needle (Arberry 1955:67).
Until the camel can pass through the eye of the needle (Ali 1934:no page).
Until a camel enters into the eye of a needle (i.e., never) (Saheeh International 1997:200).
Even if a thick rope were to pass through the eye of a needle (Abdel Haleem 2005:97).
Until the camel goes through the eye of a needle (which is impossible) (Ahmad 2010:201).

Translation as process and product 67

We can make the following observations about these different translations:

(i)   The foreignization, adequate translation approach and the literal sense have been adopted by Palmer, Arberry, and Ali, where SL cultural values are kept intact in the TT in an attempt to relay the TT to its readers in all its foreignness, to register the linguistic and cultural difference of the foreign text, and to send the TT reader abroad. The SL cultural values include the employment of the noun جَمَلٌ "camel" and the verbal expression يلجَ في سَمِ الخياط "to go through the eye of a needle" whose perlocutionary force is hyperbole – something that will never take place.

(ii) The translations by Saheeh International and Ahmad have adopted a foreignization approach, in addition to exegetical translation – "never" and "which is impossible" – respectively. The exegetical translation approach adds additional details not explicitly conveyed in the ST; the extra details between brackets represent an explication and expansion of the SL subordinate clause يلجَ الجَمَلُ في سَمِ الخياط

(iii) The translation by Abdel Haleem (2005) has provided a different meaning to the cultural item جَمَل. His translation is based on a different Qur'anic mode of reading القراءات القرآنية, where the noun جَمَل is read as جُمَل, meaning (a thick rope which is used in a ship or for climbing a date palm).

(iv) Stylistically, the ST is hypotactic. Hypotaxis is a syntactic mechanism and is a relation between two clauses within the same hypotactic sentence. The features of the hypotactic sentence are:

   (1) It has more than one clause (a clause complex);
   (2) It has clauses which are in an unequal relationship to each other;
   (3) It has a subordination relationship (main clause + subordinate clause);
   (4) The clause order can be reversed – either the main clause occur first or the subordinating clause occurs first; and most importantly,
   (5) It has a subordinating conjunction. The hypotactic relation is that of subordination; we have one of the subordinating conjunctions (حتى، بينما، عندما، (إن)، إذا) (if, when, ((قبل، بعد، مالم، منذ، بسبب (لأن)، حيث، لكي، ولو أن (على الرغم من while, until, before, after, unless, since, because, where, whereas, so that, in order to, although). In the ST we have the subordinating conjunction (حتى).

22 What is the translation of "Jacko surrenders?" Discuss the translation process.

There are two interrelated matters to address:

(i)   Cultural awareness of the SL is a prerequisite of a successful and accurate translation. The above ST involves a SL culture-specific nickname "Jacko". If such a translation problem occurs in a headline, it is recommended to read through the whole ST until the full name is given by the text producer. The nickname "Jacko" refers to the American pop star Michael Jackson.

(ii) We recommend an exegetical translation approach. The translator needs to unlock the nickname and use the full name plus explication and expansion as additional details. Thus, the suggested translation is المُطربُ الأمريكيُ الشهيرُ النجم الغنائي

68 *Translation as process and product*

الأمريكي مايكل جاكسون يستسلم – "The well-known American pop star Michael Jackson surrenders".

23 What is the translation of "shopaholic"? Discuss the translation process.

We can make the following observations:

(i) The translation of neologisms is a translation problem. The dictionary usually provides explication of the term "a person with an uncontrollable urge to go shopping". If the translator relies on the definition of a neologism, the result will be an over-translation.
(ii) We recommend providing a brief descriptive TL expression based on the explication provided by the SL dictionary.
(iii) We recommend the procedure of analogy; when there is a parallel term, we adopt a similar meaning in terms of the general notion of the term. The SL has the term "alcoholic", whose translation is مُدمِن على الخمر, and whose back-translation is "addicted to alcohol". Thus, we recommend the translation by analogy: مُدمِن على التبضُّع, whose back-translation is "addicted to shopping". The general notion is "addiction, addicted to", which establishes the parallelism between the two terms "alcoholic" and "shopaholic".

24 Translate the following advert and discuss the translation process:

Pentel – Four wen new reely knead two Correkt Yor Miztakes

Textual and discourse analysis:

(i) To the left of the above advertisement, there is a corrector pen. To promote sales of the corrector pen, the indispensable function of the pen is given but the advert words are wrongly spelt. Thus, the advert has achieved its goal by attracting the reader to read the advert through in an attempt to make the reader appreciate the need for the corrector pen.
(ii) We recommend providing a TT with spelling errors to promote the SL sale promotion drive. The word "Pentel" is a trademark which must be transliterated in the TT. The suggested translation is بنتل: عنتما دكون فيعلا بيحاجاتن ماصة ليتسحيح أخطو ءاك

25 Translate the following news headline and discuss the translation process:

Tony Blair is blown aside by Hurricane Charlie (BBC news, 19 September 2003).

Let us provide a textual and discourse analysis to arrive at an accurate and effective TT:

(i) The news reporter is reporting on the by-election in the United Kingdom for the Brent East (UK) constituency, in which the Liberal Democrats party candidate Sarah Teather wins a landslide victory.
(ii) For two days, 18 and 19 September 2003, Hurricane Isabel lashed the East Coast of the USA, hitting Virginia and Washington D.C.

Translation as process and product 69

(iii) The news reporter has played on words by using "Hurricane" and "Charlie". Here lies the key to a successful and effective translation. The translator needs to be aware of the overtone and intertextuality in the ST.

(iv) The news reporter makes an intertextual reference through the employment of "hurricane Charlie". In fact, the name "Charlie" refers to "Charles Kennedy" who was the party leader of the Liberal Democrats at the time. Now, the jigsaw is clear.

(v) Based on the above, the translator needs to make a link between "Hurricane Charlie" which is metaphorically used – "the hurricane of Charles Kennedy" – and "Hurricane Isabel", the real hurricane.

(vi) Based on intertextuality and the political metaphor, the suggested translation is

إعصار جارلس كندي يعصف بتوني بلير جانباً. (أو) إعصار جارلس كندي يطرح توني بلير أرضاً.

It is interesting to note that there was a real hurricane called Hurricane Charley that struck the United States and Jamaica in 2004. Thus, we have "Charley" and "Charlie".

26 Provide the translation of the following text and discuss the translation process:

WE WILL NOT LOSE YOUR BAGS.

Based on the context and intertextuality of the above advert, we can make the following observations:

(i) This advertisement was displayed in Leeds Bradford Airport. It was placed on the top of the luggage check-in counters. There is an image of a man with eye-bags (bags underneath his eyes).

(ii) The translator needs to make an intertextual reference between the man's eye-bags and the overtone of the advert.

(iii) The word "bags" in the advert is a pun and a polyseme. It either means "eye-bags" or "travel bags, luggage".

(iv) The bags under the man's eyes are the key to an effective and successful translation. The ST says: "WE WILL NOT LOSE YOUR BAGS", referring to the passengers' travel bags "luggage". This effectively means "YOUR LUGGAGE IS UNDER OUR WATCHFUL EYES".

(v) The suggested translation of the advert becomes fairly straightforward لن تضيع حقائبكَ معنا

27 At Leeds Bradford Airport, on a departures board, we read the text in the following advert:

KLM Cityhopper.
Let us do first the textual and discourse analysis of the ST:

(i) KLM stands for Royal Dutch Airlines. KLM Cityhopper has a total fleet of 49 small planes, operates flights to 73 scheduled European destinations, and its base/main hub is at Amsterdam Airport Schiphol.

(ii) The term "Cityhopper" is intertextually related to "Inter-City train", a type of high-speed train service operating in several countries that starts in, ends in, stops in, and

70 *Translation as process and product*

connects major towns and cities. Being familiar with the contextual meaning of "Inter-City train" is the key to the meaning of "Cityhopper". The same principle of travelling from one city to another and then another applies to the KLM Cityhopper service.

(iii) The meaning of "hopper" is derived from the verb "to hop": to jump along on one foot from one place to another/to leap or bounce – i.e., يَثِبُ ,يقفزُ من مكان الى آخر

(iv) The verb "to hop" was used by American forces during World War II to refer to the military strategy of "hopping" from "landing on" one island to another in their advance against the Japanese forces until they reached the Japanese mainland.

(v) Based on the above analysis, we can recommend the translation خطوط كي أل أم: الرحلات بين المدن الأوربية. In other words, "hopper" designates "inter-city" – i.e., بين المدن من مدينة إلى مدينة.

28 Let us consider the translation of

The world is just a click away.
Let's first do the textual and discourse analysis of the ST:

(i)   The above text is written on the side of a KLM airplane. Thus, it is to do with travelling by air, the overtone of which is "You are able to travel to other parts of the world as quickly and easily as 'a mouse click'"; you can easily and quickly book arrangements and be in another part of the world, as opposed to going to a travel agency or other service for booking a ticket. Thus, the underlying meaning of "click" means a "mouse click" – i.e., convenient online, retail booking. This is just like "Your groceries are a click away".

(ii) We recommend the translation العالمُ يبعد مُجرّد لمحة بصر, whose back-translation is "The world is just a blink of an eye/a twinkling of an eye/a glance of the eye". Based on the analogy translation procedure, the expression لمحة بصر is taken from Qur'an 16:77.

(iii) The ST preposition "away" is transferred to the TL as a main verb يبعد "whose distance is", and the indefinite noun "a click" is transferred as a noun phrase لمحة بصر.

29 Let us consider the translation of

Fasten Seat Belt While Seated
Discuss the translation process.
    We recommend the translation

أربط حزام المقعد ما دُمتَ جالساً

where we have the past participle verb (seated), while in the TT, we have made a shift to the active participle noun جالس, and thus اسم الفاعل, whose illocutionary force is [+ Continuity] – the passenger is still sitting (continuously sitting) in his/her seat. The transposition (shift) translation approach is adopted. This is to provide a comprehensible TT to its audience with an acceptable natural TL style. The translation aims at complete naturalness of the TT; to naturalize the TT and reduce its foreignness.

30 What is the translation of the abbreviation BSE?

The abbreviation "BSE" stands for "Bovine Spongiform Encephalopathy". However, the layman TL reader may not understand the translation of the veterinary medical term and for

Translation as process and product 71

this reason we need to provide a translation based on what is commonly known about this animal disease affecting cows "bovine". BSE is commonly and colloquially known as "mad cow disease" because it is a neurodegenerative disease of cattle whose symptoms include abnormal behavior, trouble walking, and weight loss. Thus, the most common translation of "BSE" is based on the exegetical translation approach, which is مرض جنون البقر, since we have explained to the TL reader what "BSE" is. The ST adjective "mad" is transferred as a nominalized noun جنون and not an adjective مجنون.

31 Translate the following text and discuss the translation process.

التقى فلان وفلان يوم أمس على هامش مؤتمر القمة في لندن لكن سُرعان ما جرت بينهما مُلاسنات خارج حدود الأدب وتراشق فيها بالإهانات والتُهم.

(i)   We recommend the translation "Mr X and Mr Y held a meeting yesterday on the sidelines of the London Summit. No sooner had they met than they had an impolite (rude) heated argument".

(ii) We also recommend an alternative translation: "An impolite, heated argument erupted between Mr X and Mr Y yesterday during a meeting on the sidelines of the London Summit, who traded (exchanged) insults and accusations".

(iii) We also recommend an alternative translation: "Impolite heated argument erupted between Mr X and Mr Y yesterday during a meeting on the sidelines of the London Summit and traded (exchanged) insults and accusations".

(iv) Based on the above details and the TT, we need a culture-based translation based on one of the translation approaches, such as the communicative, dynamic equivalence, natural, acceptable, or faithful. These translation approaches take into consideration the contextual intended meaning of the ST in order to provide a comprehensible TT to its audience with an acceptable natural TL style. These translation approaches aim at complete naturalness of the TT; to naturalize the TT and reduce its foreignness. The above translation interpretively resembles the original without unnecessary processing effort on the part of the TL reader.

(v)   Having examined carefully the TT, we make the following observations:

(a)   To enhance the translation student vocabulary stock, it is worthwhile to note the rendering of the ST jargon: على هامش مؤتمر قمة "on the sidelines of", "summit", مُلاسنات خارج حدود الأدب "had impolite (rude) heated argument", and the verb تراشقَ "to trade, to exchange".

(b)   The translator has also implemented a transposition (shift) translation approach for the SL-specific style لكن سُرعان ما جرت بينهما, whose acceptable natural TL style is "No sooner had they met than they had". This also demonstrates how the translator divided up the ST into two separate TT sentences. The second sentence begins with "No sooner . . .".

(c)   The translator has provided an alternative style in which the transposition (shift) translation approach is adopted where the TT begins from the second part of the ST and the translation of the verb جرت is given a metaphorical expression "erupted". The back-translation of this style is

جرت مُلاسنات خارج حدود الأدب بين فلان وفلان يوم أمس على هامش مؤتمر القمة في لندن وتراشق فيها بالإهانات والتُهم.

72 *Translation as process and product*

32 Translate the following text and discuss the translation process.

> The internet can be employed as a useful resource for checking the meaning and contextual usage of words.

Grammatically, the ST structure is in passive voice. It must be changed to active voice and use the translation procedure of adaptation. Grammatically, the main verb is "employ". However, because of the stylistic norm of Arabic, we need to make the auxiliary verb (can) the main verb in the TT.

Grammatically, the noun phrase (the meaning and contextual usage of words) is made up of two semantic units: (the meaning of words) + (the contextual usage of words). We need to adopt the transposition (shift) translation approach and the translation procedure of adaptation to suit the stylistic norms of Arabic. The suggested TT is

يمكن استخدام الأنترنت كمصدرٍ مفيدٍ للتأكد من معاني الكلمات واستخدامها السياقي.

This is a natural translation approach put forward by Nida (Nida 1964; cited in Venuti 2000:129), which involves adaptation in grammar and lexicon. In general, grammatical modifications can be made more readily since many grammatical changes are dictated by the obligatory structures of the TL; the translator is obliged to make such adjustments.

33 For in-class discussion: Discuss the translation of "yellow journalism/yellow press", explain which translation approach you have adopted, and why.

34 For in-class discussion: Discuss the translation based on managing and monitoring of:

(i) "Palestinian Militants/prisoners/fugitives" in American and British media compared to الأسرى الفلسطينيون in the Arab media.

(ii) سُقوط طائرة مُسيَّرة في جنوب لبنان compared to إسقاط طائرة مُسيَّرة في جنوب لبنان

For more exercises related to this Chapter, see Appendix 1.

Notes

1 i.e., "surrender thy whole being"; the term "face" is often used metonymically in the sense of one's "whole being".
2 For this rendering of hanif, see note 110 on 2:135.
3 The term "fitrah", rendered by me as "natural disposition", connotes in this context man's inborn, intuitive ability to discern between right and wrong, true and false, and, thus, to sense God's existence and oneness. Cf. the famous saying of the Prophet, quoted by Bukhiri and Muslim: "Every child is born in this natural disposition; it is only his parents that later turn him into a 'Jew', a 'Christian', or a 'Magian'". These three religious formulations, best known to the contemporaries of the Prophet, are thus contrasted with the "natural disposition", which, by definition, consists in man's instinctive cognition of God and self-surrender (Islam) to Him.
4 Lit., "no change shall there be [or 'shall be made'] in God's creation خَلْق", i.e., in the natural disposition referred to above. In this context, the term تبديل "change" obviously comprises the concept of "corruption".

2 Stylistics and translator training

2.1 Introduction

The present chapter provides practical training for the translation student and the translation teacher in critical translation quality assessment through contrastive stylistic analysis between the ST and the TT. The major focus of the discussion is on the semantic and stylistic idiosyncrasies of the ST and the TT. In other words, this is an assessment of the translator's stylistic skills in terms of the conscious selection of rhetorical and linguistic devices.

The semantic and stylistic idiosyncrasies of the ST and the TT can be illustrated through the Arabic-specific case-endings (case-markings) حركاتُ الإعراب. A case-ending indicates the grammatical role (function) of the noun, which can function as a subject (مرفوع بالضمة) or object (منصوب بالفتحة). For this reason, stylistically, Arabic is a free word order language thanks to its case-endings where the subject noun can occur at the beginning, middle, or end of the sentence, but it can be easily diagnosed as a subject noun through its nominative case-marking inflection (الضمة) حركة الرفع and the same applies to the object, which has the accusative case-marking inflection (الفتحة) حركةُ النصب. Let us consider the following examples:

أنا صائمُ يوم الخميسِ versus أنا صائمٌ يومَ الخميس

where the active participle صائم has either the nunation صائمٌ التنوين or the nominative case-ending صائمُ الضمة, and the object noun يوم occurs either in the accusative case يومَ منصوبٌ بالفتحة or in the genitive case يوم مجرور بالكسرة. Now, we turn our attention to the semantic distinction between أنا صائمٌ يومَ الخميسِ versus أنا صائمُ يوم الخميسِ and the accurate translation of each sentence. Based on the stylistic idiosyncrasy of Arabic case-ending, the meaning of أنا صائمٌ يومَ الخميس is "I will 'I am going to' fast next Thursday". However, the meaning of أنا صائمُ يوم الخميسِ is "I was fasting 'I fasted' last Thursday".

The stylistically based translation quality assessment is a vital measurement tool that aims:

1 To enhance the translation student's skills in critical translation analysis; and
2 To train him/her in how to employ stylistic analysis in the quality assessment of the translation process and product and the assessment of the ST and the TT.

DOI: 10.4324/9781003268956-3

74 *Stylistics and translator training*

This translation quality assessment approach is of high value to other languages; thus, the universality of our approach where translation students and teachers can apply this approach to their own languages. Our translation quality assessment approach is also of value to the translation projects required for undergraduate and postgraduate translation students. The present chapter provides stylistic and semantic details about Arabic conjunctions.

2.2 Stylistic analysis and translation

The contrastive stylistic analysis is employed in the present discussion as a model for translation quality assessment and is based on the contrastive measurement of the ST and the TT at word, phrase, and sentence levels. This translation assessment approach provides the translation student with an insight into the translation process and translation output. This assessment approach aims to investigate the following salient textual and discourse features of the two texts:

1 The analysis of the different styles of the ST and the TT,
2 The investigation of the word order variation between the ST and the TT,
3 The analysis of the cohesion and punctuation techniques adopted by the translator,
4 An account of the distribution of lexical items in terms of their grammatical functions (verbs, nouns, adjectives, adverbs, prepositional phrases, active participles, hyperbole adjectives, absolute (cognitive) objects),
5 The investigation of sentence structure: paratactic versus hypotactic sentences, passive voice versus active voice sentences,
6 An account of the translation approach adopted by the translator, and
7 An account of the culture-specific expressions and contextual factors.

2.3 Tight texture and loose texture

Halliday and Hasan (1976:295–297) make a distinction between two types of texture: "tight and loose texture". Variation in texture is a general feature we encounter in texts of all kinds. In "tight texture", we find dense clusters of cohesive ties which serve to signal that the meanings of the parts are strongly interdependent and that the whole forms a single unity. We can argue that tight texture is a prototypical stylistic feature of Arabic and Qur'anic Arabic. In other texts, however, we find "loose texture" where fewer cohesive ties are used – perhaps just one or two. This is a stylistic idiosyncrasy of headlines and captions in both English and Arabic journalistic texts.

2.4 Stylistic idiosyncrasies of conjunctions

Arabic conjunctions are characterized by prototypical pragmatic and stylistic functions, such as the attainment of a given illocutionary force, and the delivery of the text producer's performative intent. Among their idiosyncratic features, they are context-sensitive stylistic resources to achieve cohesion in the Arabic text. Most importantly, they are semantically oriented because they have inherent semantic componential features which are missing in English. Therefore, Arabic conjunctions constitute limits of translatability. However, in both Arabic and English, conjunctions occur intra-sententially and inter-sententially.

Stylistics and translator training   75

Let us consider the following examples which illustrate the stylistic idiosyncrasies and undertones of the major conjunctions إذا، إن، لو، فـ، ثَمَّ، و، لمّا:

Example 1: إذا

إذا سألكَ عبادي عنّي فإنّي قريبٌ أُجيبُ دعوة الداعِ إذا دعانِ فليستَجيبوا لي (البقرة 186)

When my servants ask you (O Muhammad) concerning Me, indeed I am near. I respond to the invocation of the supplication when he/she calls upon Me. So let them respond to Me, Q2:186.

The major stylistic idiosyncrasy of the conjunction إذا "when, if" is its innate illocutionary force and the following pragmatic functions:

1   When something is guaranteed to take place, as in

كُتِبَ عليكُم إذا حَضَرَ أَحَدُكُم الموتَ

Prescribed for you when death approaches one of you, Q2:180.

إذا الشمسُ كُوِّرَت وإذا النُّجُومُ إنكَدَرَت

When the sun is wrapped up in darkness and when the stars fall, dispersing, Q81:1–2, where death, the wrapping up of the sun in darkness, and the falling of the stars are inevitable events.

2   When something occurs frequently, i.e., [+ Repetition] and [+ Multitude], as in

وترى الشمسَ إذا طَلَعَت تزاورُ عن كهفهم (الكهف 17)

You would see the sun when it rose, inclining away from their cave, Q18:17.

إذا أُحصِنَّ

When, if they are sheltered, Q4:25.

أُجيبُ دعوةَ الداعِ إذا دعانِ

I respond to the invocation of the supplication when he calls upon Me, Q2:186.

Let us consider the following example which demonstrates how the conjunctions إذا and "in" perform distinct perlocutionary effects:

إذا قُمتُم الى الصلاةِ فاغسِلوا . . . و إن كُنتُم جُنُباً فاطّهَّرُوا (المائدة 6)

When you prepare for prayer, wash . . . If you are in a state of ceremonial impurity, bathe your whole body, Q5:6.

We can observe that the conjunction إذا is selected for actions which are frequently repeated, such as the action of ablution for the five daily prayers. However, the conjunction إن is stylistically employed when we have actions which do not take place frequently, such as جُنُباً "the state of ceremonial impurity" that does not happen frequently.

76 *Stylistics and translator training*

3   When إذا designates a prescribed legal obligation تكليف حتمي, as in Q2:282 and Q5:6 where "the writing down of a loan contract" and "the rise to perform prayer" are considered as obligatory and prescribed legal obligations.

4   When something is desired to take place, as in Q7:131 where إذا collocates with the word الحسنة which means "all the good things bestowed upon mankind such as welfare, good health, prosperity, children, knowledge, etc." Similarly, in Q110:1, إذا collocates with the word نصر "victory".

Through the employment of the conjunctive particle إذا, the ST Q2:186 has attained the following semantic entailments:

(i)   that people will definitely enquire about their Lord,
(ii) that the person is required to supplicate repeatedly, and
(iii) that his/her prayers will definitely be answered.

However, the use of the TL conjunction "when" fails to communicate the SL pragmatic functions.

Example 2: إن

In Arabic, the conjunction إن "when, if" has the following prototypical pragmatic functions and illocutionary force, such as

(i)   The impossibility of something to take place, as in

قُل إن كانَ للرحمان وَلداً (الزخرف 81)

Say: "If the Most Merciful had a son . . . ?" Q43:81.

which semantically entails "monotheism" – its underlying meaning is "it is impossible for God to have a son". Therefore, semantically, the use of إذا instead of the conjunction إن will produce a counter-productive illocutionary force of the ST producer's performative intent of Q43:81. The same applies to Q5:116 إن كُنتُ قُلْتُهُ فقد عَلِمتَهُ – "If I had said it, You would have known it", where the conjunctive particle إن is used by Jesus in his dialogue with God to entail: "It is impossible that I (Jesus) have said such a thing about You (God)".

(ii) The rarity of something to take place, as in

إن آتَينَ بفاحِشَةٍ (النساء 25)

If they commit adultery, Q4:25.

قُل أرأيتُم إن جَعَلَ اللهُ عليكُم النهارَ سَرمَداً (القصص 71)
If God should make for you the night continuous? Q28:71.

(iii) the probability or uncertainty of something to take place, as in

إن طائفتان من المؤمنينَ اقتتلوا (الحجرات 9)

Stylistics and translator training 77

"If two factions among the believers should fight", (Q49:9), and also in Q4:3 which means "probably, we may deal unjustly with orphan girls" – in other words, "we are uncertain whether we will deal justly with orphan girls". The same applies to Q2:271 and Q3:144 where the conjunctive particle إن is employed to designate uncertainty of whether Muhammad will be killed in battle or die a normal death.

(iv) The uncertainty of something to take place, as in

لكن انظُر الى الجبل فإن استقرَّ مكانَهُ فسوفَ تراني (الأعراف 143)

But look at the mountain; if it should remain in place, then you will see Me, Q7:143.

فسألوا أهلَ الذِكر إن كنتُم لا تعلمون (الأنبياء 7)

So ask the people of the message if you do not know, Q21:7.

(v) When something is undesired to take place, as in Q3:140, where "in" collocates with the word قرحٌ "a wound". Similarly, إن collocates with سيئةٌ "affliction, hardship" in Q7:131.

Example 3: لو
The cohesive device لو "if" designates the perlocutionary effect of reproach التوبيخ, i.e., it pragmatically entails that something is impossible to take place, as in لو طار الفيلُ – "if the elephant flies", i.e., "it is impossible for an elephant to have wings to fly". However, if we say إن طار الفيلُ – "if the elephant flies", it means "it is likely that an elephant can have wings to fly".

Let us consider Q35:14 below which illustrates the perlocutionary effect of the conjunction لو:

لو سَمِعُوا ما استجابُوا (فاطر 14)

If they (the idols) heard, they would not respond.

Since the ST is about the idols, the employment of the cohesive device لو censures the polytheists and semantically designates the impossibility for idols to take the action of responding to their worshipper's prayers. Therefore, if we substitute لو by "in", the perlocutionary effect will change dramatically to: "It is possible 'likely' that the idols will respond". Therefore, the translation has failed the ST producer's intentionality (intended meaning and performative intent).

Example 4: فَ, و, ثُمَّ, and لمّا:
Stylistically, the temporal conjunction فـ is an affirmation particle which is employed to achieve an illocutionary "communicative" force that cannot be met by English, as in

ضربها على رأسها فقتلها – He hit her on the head and killed her immediately.

where we have translated the temporal conjunction فـ as "immediately".

78 *Stylistics and translator training*

فادخُلوا أبوابَ جهنّمَ خالدينَ فيها فلبئسَ مثوى المتكبرين (النحل 29)

Hence, enter the gates of hell, therein to abide! And evil, indeed, shall be the state of all who are given to false pride, Q16:29.

فتمتّعُوا فسوفَ تعلمون (النحل 55)

Enjoy, then, your (brief) life: but in time you will come to know (the truth)! Q16:55.

In Q16:29, the use of the affirmation particle ف – "and" prefixed to فادخُلوا "enter" (imperative) and لبئسَ "what an evil" semantically designates "the intensity of torment" and stylistically delivers the rhetorical device of hyperbole of the punishment to this category of disbelievers who are mentioned earlier in Q16:23–24. The conjunctive particle ف, however, performs the perlocutionary effect of a threatening command. Semantically, however, the conjunction و "and" in ولنعمَ دار المتقين "And how excellent is the home of the righteous" (Q16:30) has a distinct meaning which is that of explaining the high level of pleasure and joy for the companions of paradise.

Also, semantically, the conjunction ف designates an action that takes place without delay. Thus, its major semantic componential features are [+ Immediate Action] and [– Delay], as in

إذا قضى أمراً فإنّما يقولُ لهُ كُن فيكون (غافر 68)

When He decrees a matter, He says to it: "Be", and it is, Q40:68.

where we can observe in كُن "be" + فيكون "and it is" the phonetic process of concealment الإخفاء that takes place between the alveolar nasal sound /ن/ and the labio-dental sound /ف/. This concealment is due to the fact that the place of articulation of both consonant sounds /ن/ and /ف/ are adjacent to each other. This phonetic process of concealment semantically designates the meaning that, in terms of time, not even a split second is required by God to create humans or non-humans. Therefore, stylistically, the use of و instead of ف will change the illocutionary force and the ST producer's performative intent dramatically.

While the SL makes a crucial stylistic and semantic distinction between the conjunction ف "and" and its counterpart و "and", the TL stands helpless to negotiate this problem and can only provide the conjunction (and) for (fa). Semantically, the componential features of و are [– Immediate Action] and [+ Delay]. This semantic distinction can be illustrated by Q12 where we encounter the employment of both ف and و. When the context entails [+ Immediate Action] and [– Delay] in the action denoted by the verb, the ف is used, as in Q12:63, 70, 88, and 99. However, when the context involves [– Immediate Action] and [+ Delay] in the action denoted by the verb, the conjunction و in ولمّا "and when" is used, as in Q12:59, 65, 69, and 94.

The order in the occurrence of conjunctions is context-sensitive and semantically oriented. A pragmatic distinction can be made between the temporal cohesive device ثُمّ "then" whose semantic componential features are [– Immediate Action] and [+ Delay] and its counterparts ف. In Q7:195, we encounter ثُمّ followed by ف:

ثُمّ كيدون فلا تُنظرُون (الأعراف 195)

Stylistics and translator training 79

Then conspire against me and give me no respite.

where ثُمَّ occurs first followed by ف. However, in Q11:55, we encounter the opposite order:

فكيدونِ . . . ثُمَّ لا تُنظِرونِ (هود 55) – So, plot against me . . . then do not give me praise

where ف occurs first, followed by ثُمَّ. In Qur'anic discourse, the contextual meaning of the cohesive device needs to be taken into account although it is unlikely that the TL will be able to capture the nuances involved. Q7:195 and Q11:55 provide insight into the complex nature of Arabic conjunctions and their translation:

(i) The marriage of context and meaning: Exegetically, Q7:195 is an implicit reference to Muhammad and his people who are polytheists worshipping idols. The context of Q7 involves a short period of challenge between the two parties. Because the challenge in Q7:195 is less intense than in Q11:55, we do not find the word جميعاً "all of you" in Q7:195, and we find a word-final short vowel /i/ الكسرة in كيدونِ "plot against me". The phonetic feature of the word-final short vowel /i/ signifies the short period of challenge between the two parties. However, in Q11:55, the context involves confrontation, a long period of intense challenge between Prophet Hud and his polytheist people, and an accusation against Hud of sanity inflicted upon him by their gods (Q11:50–58). This has led him to challenge them and their gods and pronounce himself free from whatever they associate with God. Thus, Hud in Q11:55 has challenged the polytheists not to give him any respite. To exaggerate in his perlocutionary effect of challenge, Hud stylistically adds the word جميعاً "all of you" and the word-final long vowel /i/ الياء in كيدوني "plot against me". The phonetic feature of the word-final long vowel /i/ signifies the long period of challenge between the two parties. Unlike Q7:195, the surrounding co-text of Q11: 55 has played a role in the occurrence of the word-final long vowel /i/ in كيدوني where many other words have also occurred with the phonetic feature of a word-final long vowel: إنّي "I am", (Q11:54), أنّي "I am", (Q11:54), إنّي . . . ربّي "I am . . . my Lord", (Q11:56), ربّي "my Lord", Q11:56 (twice), 57 (twice).

(ii) In Q7:195, the temporal conjunction ثُمَّ comes first to express an [– Immediate Action] and [+ Delay] in the verb كيدون, i.e., you can take your time in plotting against me. However, the conjunction "fa" occurs next and is prefixed to the negative particle لا "no", i.e., give me no respite immediately and as soon as you can. The immediate no respite suits well the context of Q7:195, which is marked by a short period of challenge and the immediate punishment that will be imposed on the polytheists during this life. In other words, the ف → "the punishment will be inflicted very soon, unexpectedly". This analysis is intertextually backed up by Q7:4 and Q7:95 "How many cities have We destroyed, and Our punishment came to them at night or while they were sleeping at noon" and "We seized them suddenly". This designates the immediate "sudden" punishment signified by the conjunction "fa", the word-final short vowel /i/ in كيدون "to plot against me" and تُنظِرونِ "to give me no respite" in Q7:195. Thus, فلا تُنظِرونِ "give me no respite", (Q7:195) is synonymous with فأخذناهُم بغتة "We seized them suddenly" (Q7:95).

(iii) In Q11:55, the cohesive device ف occurs first to express [+ Immediate Action] and [– Delay] with regards to the action of plotting. However, ثُمَّ occurs next as a

80 *Stylistics and translator training*

contextual requirement of the delay in the infliction of punishment that will be imposed on the polytheists during this life. In other words, the ثُمَّ → "the punishment will not be inflicted soon". This analysis is intertextually backed up by Q11:3 and Q11:8 "Seek forgiveness from your Lord and repent to Him. He will let you enjoy a good provision for a specified term and give every doer of favor his reward. But if you turn away, then indeed, I fear for you the punishment of a great day" and "If We hold back from them the punishment". Semantically, this entails the delay in punishment signified by the conjunction ثُمَّ in Q11:55.

The temporal conjunction لَمَّا "when" occurs in the subordinated clause, as in: "When I took David to the library, the staff welcomed him". Let us compare this to the following ST:

فلما ذهبوا به وأجمعوا أن يجعلوهُ في غيابتِ الجُبّ وأوحينا اليه لَتُنبّئَنَّهُم بأمرهِم هذا وهم لا يشعُرون

(يوسف 15)

So, when they took him (Joseph) out and agreed to put him into the bottom of the well. But We (God) inspired to him: "You will surely inform them sometime about this affair of theirs while they do not perceive".

Here we find the temporal conjunction لَمَّا translated as "when". This is wrong. The subordinate clause in which لَمَّا "when" occurs has an ellipted main clause فجعلوهُ فيها "they dropped Joseph into the well".

The translation strategies we can adopt are either: (i) to ignore لَمَّا and replace it with "so" or "then" so that you have one TL main clause; or (ii) to add to the translation the ellipted main clause "they dropped Joseph into the well" if we want to use "when".

Stylistic idiosyncratic differences between Arabic and English in terms of collocation of prepositions is another issue in Arabic translation. It demonstrates the linguistic incongruity between the two languages and is an interesting area of contrastive linguistics and translation studies. For instance: the Arabic verb يغفر needs a preposition لـ + an object; the English verb "forgive" does not need a preposition; the verb يعفو requires a preposition عن + an object; the verb "pardon" does not need a preposition; the verb يرحم does not need a preposition; and the verb "have mercy" requires a preposition "on/upon". Thus, we have

> اللهُ يغفِرُ لسالم – (subject + verb + preposition (لـ)+ object) – God forgave Salim (subject + verb + object).
> اللهُ يَعفو عن المُذنِبِ – (subject + verb + preposition (عن)+ object) – God pardons the wrongdoer (subject + verb + object).
> اللهُ يَرحَمُ سالمَ – (subject + verb + object) – God has mercy on Salim (subject + verb + preposition + object).

However, some verbs and adjectives require a preposition in both Arabic and English, as in يعتمد + على "depend on/upon", and فخورٌ بـ "proud of".

2.5 Translation and stylistic variation

There is a yawning gap between Arabic and English in terms of stylistic variation in Arabic. This is attributed to a number of reasons such as hyperbaton, shift الإلتفات, the letter لـ for affirmation, negation particle, interrogative particle, morphological form of the

Stylistics and translator training 81

verb, singular/plural, plural of paucity جمع قلة/جمع plural of multitude جمع الكثرة, masculine/feminine, the detached pronoun ضمير الفصل, synonymy, and stylistic differences that are semantically oriented in Arabic.

It is interesting to note that the translations of such examples cannot reflect the subtle semantic differences between any pair of stylistically different sentences. English cannot capture this unique linguistic phenomenon in Qur'anic Arabic. Throughout history, Brisset (1996; cited in Venuti 2000:343–344) argues that translators have had to contend with the fact that the target language is deficient when it comes to translating the source text into that language. Such deficiencies can be clearly identified as lexical, or morpho-syntactic deficiencies, or as problems of polysemy. The difficulty of translation does not arise from the lack of a specific translation language. It arises, rather, from the absence in the target language of a subcode equivalent to the one used by the source text in its reproduction of the source language. Based on Brisset's claim, we can argue that the Arabic متشابهات uncovers the linguistic deficiency in English since the متشابهات constitutes a linguistic void in English. According to Brisset (ibid:345), translation does not fill a linguistic void.

This is illustrated in the following examples below where the translations of any pair of such sentences are identical but inaccurate.

1   Provide the translations for the following pair of grammatically similar but stylistically different sentences and discuss their semantic distinction.

وما أُهِلَّ بِهِ لغير الله (البقرة 173)
وما أُهِلَّ لغير اللهِ بِهِ (المائدة 3، الأنعام 145، النحل 115)

And that which has been dedicated to other than Allah.

The TT is the same for the above two stylistically and semantically different sentences, although there is a stylistic difference between the two STs in terms of word order. In Q5:3, Q6:145, and Q16:115, we have the rhetorical device of hyperbaton where the prepositional phrase به is moved from its sentence-final position to the middle of the sentence. This is a marked (unusual, unexpected) word order. Q2:173 represents the unmarked (usual, expected) word order where the prepositional phrase به occurs in its normal position, which is the middle of the sentence. On the pragmatic level, the STs producer's performative intent in Q5:3, Q6:145, and Q16:115 is to highlight the object لغير الله "other than Allah" and give it the illocutionary force of polytheism الشرك, as well as bring it to reader's attention. One may wonder whether the translator will be able to capture this subtle semantic distinction between the two different ST word orders. For more details on the rhetorical device of hyperbaton, see Abdul-Raof (2020:94).

2   Provide the translations for the following pair of grammatically similar but stylistically different sentences and discuss their semantic distinction.

لا يقدرون على شيء مما كسبوا (البقرة 264)
لا يقدرون مما كسبوا على شيء (إبراهيم 18)

They are unable (to keep) anything of what they have earned.

The stylistic variation lies in the word order. Q2:264 is the unmarked word order where the prepositional phrase على شيء "anything" occurs first after the verb يقدرون "to be

82 *Stylistics and translator training*

able". Q14:18 is a marked word order where the verb كسبوا "earned" in order to achieve lexical coherence with the earlier noun أعمال "deeds", which are both semantically and intertextually related.

3   Provide translations for the following pair of grammatically similar but stylistically different sentences and discuss their semantic distinction.

وقالوا لن تمسَّنا النارُ إلاَّ أياماً معدودة (البقرة 80)

وقالوا لن تمسَّنا النارُ إلاَّ أياماً معدودات (آل عمران 24)

And they said: "Never will the fire touch us except for a few numbered days".

We have the same noun phrase: plural noun ايام + plural adjective معدودة and plural noun ايام + plural adjective معدودات. There is a semantic distinction between معدودة and معدودات. One may wonder whether the translator will be able to capture this subtle semantic distinction between the two ST conjunctions. The word معدودة is a plural of "multitude" جمع كثرة and means "unspecified in terms of time or number but it is more than 11", but the important thing is that the Jews will get out of hell sooner or later. Thus, the context of Q2:80 refers to the Jews. However, the context of Q3:24 refers to the Muslims who falsely claim that they will be told about the exact number of days they must spend in hell before they will be transferred to paradise. Thus, they know exactly how many days of their residence in hell. Thus, معدودات is a plural of paucity جمع قلة meaning "specified in terms of time and number and less than 11".

4   Provide the translations for the following pair of grammatically similar but stylistically different sentences and discuss their semantic distinction.

ومنهم من يستمعُ اليكَ (الأنعام 25)

ومنهم من يستمعونَ اليكَ (يونس 42)

And among them are those who listen to you.

The stylistic difference lies in the verb سَمَعَ, which occurs in the singular يستمع in Q6:25 but in the plural form يستمعون in Q10:42. The context has brought about the difference in the verb form. In Q6:25, the singular verb form يستمع occurs because it refers to a group of people who are few in number, while the plural verb form يستمعون in Q10:42 refers to a large number of people.

The other stylistic difference is between the singular subject pronoun هو implicit in the verb يستمع "'he' listens", which refers to a group of people who are treated as one person, and the plural subject pronoun هم implicit in the verb يستمعون "'they' listen", which refers to disbelievers.

5   Provide the translations for the following pair of grammatically similar but stylistically different sentences and discuss their semantic distinction.

بالبأساء والضرَّاء لعلَّهُم يتضرَّعُون (الأنعام 42)

بالبأساء والضرَّاء لعلَّهُم يضرَّعُون (الأعراف 94)

Stylistics and translator training 83

With poverty and hardship that perhaps they might humble themselves.

where the stylistic distinction between the two STs lies in the difference in the verb morphological forms يتضرَّع/يضَرَّرع ع "to humble oneself". Co-text "the surrounding linguistic environment" has influenced the occurrence of يتضرَّع ع in Q6:42 because of the occurrence of the same verb in Q6:43. Thus, in terms of coherence, the two sentences Q6:42–43 have achieved lexical symmetry. However, the verb يضَرَّع ع has undergone the phonetic change of assimilation of the letter ت – it is deleted. This means that its original full verb form is also يتضرَّع ع

Let us consider the following pair of sentences:

فكذَّبوهُ فأنجيناهُ (الأعراف 64)

فكذَّبوهُ فنجَّيناهُ (يونس 73)

But they denied him, so We saved him.

The stylistic distinction between the two STs is demonstrated by the difference on the morphological level of the two verbs. Both verbs أنجا and نجَّا "to save" are transitive verbs. However, co-text has influenced the occurrence of أنجا in Q7:64 due to the four occurrences of other derivative verb forms, as in Q7:72, 83, 141, 165. Similarly, co-text has influenced the occurrence of نجَّا in Q10:73 due to the three times of occurrence of other derivative verb forms, as in Q10:86, 92, 103. Thus, on the coherence level, the two STs have achieved lexical symmetry. On the semantic level, however, the verb نجَّا signifies multitude and hyperbole, stylistically.

Another interesting stylistic feature of the ST is the employment of the temporal conjunction ف cliticized onto the two verbs. Stylistically, the context of both sentences requires the conjunction ف, which semantically designates an immediate action taken without any delay. Prophet Noah was sent his people to observe and adhere to monotheism. However, his people rejected his message and disbelieved his prophethood straightaway. Also, God's support to him came immediately when he was in the ship.

In terms of Qur'anic exegesis, the above STs are intertextually related to Q37:75. However, we need to focus on the meaning of the temporal conjunction ف:

ولقد نادانا نوحٌ فلنِعمَ المُجيبون (الصافات 75)

And Noah had certainly called Us, and We are the best of responders, Q37:75.

where the temporal conjunction ف is employed by the ST to signify God's immediate action without delay to save Noah. However, the TT has failed to achieve the ST producer's performative intent and the illocutionary force of the temporal conjunction.

6   Provide the translations for the following pair of grammatically similar but stylistically different sentences and discuss their semantic distinction.

يأتوكَ بكلِّ ساحر عليم (الأعراف 112)

يأتوكَ بكلِّ سحَّار عليم (الشعراء 37)

who will bring you every learned magician, Q7:112.

who will bring you every learned, skilled magician, Q26:37.

84 *Stylistics and translator training*

Stylistically, in Q7:112 we have the object noun ساحِر "magician, sorcerer", which is an active participle on the morphological pattern فاعِل, while in Q26:37 we have the object noun سحَّار "skilled magician", which is also an active participle but on the morphological pattern فعَّال and it also performs the rhetorical device of hyperbole. Lexical co-text has influenced the occurrence of each of these object nouns where the morphological pattern فاعِل occurs in Q7:109, and the morphological pattern فعَّال occurs in Q26:153 and 185. Through lexical and morphological co-text, the text achieves stylistic harmony and symmetry.

7   Provide the translations for the following pair of grammatically similar but stylistically different sentences and discuss their semantic distinction.

إنَّنا لفي شكٍّ مما تدعونا إليه مُريب (هود 62)
إنَّا لفي شكٍّ مما تدعوننا إليه مُريب (إبراهيم 9)

We are in grave doubt about what you are asking us to do.

The stylistic difference is represented by إنَّنا and إنَّا where the first is made up of the affirmation particle إنَّ + the first-person plural pronoun نَا; thus, we get إنَّنا, which is the unmarked (usual) grammatical form of the first-person plural. Stylistically, إنَّنا is more emphatic in terms of affirmation. The verb form تدعونا designates a single addressee who is the Prophet Salih. However, إنَّا is also a first-person plural pronoun but it occurs with the verb form تدعوننا in Q14:9 because it designates more than one addressee; it is an address to more than one Prophet. The lexical co-text has influenced the occurrence of إنَّا because it has already occurred in the same sentence Q14:9; it has occurred twice.

8   Provide the translations for the following pair of grammatically similar but stylistically different sentences and discuss their semantic distinction.

إنَّ هذا لشيءٌ عَجيب (هود 72، ق 2)
إنَّ هذا لشيءٌ عُجاب (ص 5)

That would be a strange thing!

Morphological co-text has played a major role in the stylistic variation between عجيب, which is on the morphological pattern فعِيل, and عُجاب, which is on the morphological pattern فعَّال. In Q11:66, 68, 73, 75, Q50:1, 3, 4, 5, we encounter adjectives with the same morphological pattern فعِيل, such as عصيب، شديد. Also, we encounter adjectives with the same morphological pattern فعَّال, such as شِقاق، مناص. Through lexical and morphological co-text, the text achieves stylistic harmony and symmetry.

9   Provide the translations for the following pair of grammatically similar but stylistically different sentences and discuss their semantic distinction.

وما كانَ ربُّكَ ليُهلكَ القُرى (هود 117)
وما كانَ ربُّكَ مُهلكَ القُرى (القصص 59)

Stylistics and translator training 85

Your Lord would never destroy towns.

Although there is a sharp contrast between the verb يُهلك and the active participle noun مُهلك, the translation is the same for the two sentences. Both contextual and co-textual reasons have led to the shift from the verb in Q11:117 to the active participle in Q28:59. For instance, in sentences Q11:112–117, we find the focus on the theme of morality such as righteousness التقوى, justice العدل, avoiding wrong deeds تجنب الفواحش, establishing regular prayers المحافظة على الصلاة, patience الصبر, and prohibiting mischief عدم الفساد. Therefore, we do not find any mention of God's favors أنعُم الله. Thus, the affirmation letter اللام is employed in Q11:117 to affirm the justice of the Lord through the negation of God's injustice when He inflicts some people with His wrath. In other words, the performative intent of the ST producer is that "God would never do such a thing had people been abiding by morality". However, the focus of the situational context of Q28:59 is on the infinite favors bestowed by God upon people (Q28:57–59) and how people deny God's favors بطرت معيشتها "people exulted in their wanton wealth and ease of life". Thus, stylistically the active participle noun مُهلك is employed to verify God's justice.

10 Provide translations for the following pair of grammatically similar but stylistically different sentences and discuss their semantic distinction.

ليكفُروا بما آتيناهُم فتَمتَّعوا فسوفَ تعلمون (النحل 55، الروم 34)

ليكفُروا بما آتيناهُم وليتَمتَّعوا فسوفَ يعلمون (العنكبوت 66)

So they will deny what We have given them; let them take their enjoyment – soon you (they) will know.

Stylistically, in Q16:55 and Q30:34, we find the use of the temporal conjunction ف and the use of the verb تَمَتَّعُوا in the imperative form. Pragmatically, however, the occurrence of the temporal cohesive device ف is for the illocutionary force of threat. Grammatically, however, the addressee is in second-person plural تمتَّعُوا/تعلمون. Stylistically, however, in Q29:66, we have the additive conjunction و, which grammatically performs coordination العطف between the two verbs يكفروا/يتمتعوا, and the same third-person plural is addressed. Also, the verb ليتمتعوا is not in the imperative form.

11 Provide translations for the following pair of grammatically similar but stylistically different sentences and discuss their semantic distinction.

أنجينا الذينَ آمنوا وكانوا يتَّقون (النمل 53)

نجَّينا الذينَ آمنوا وكانوا يتَّقون (فصلت 18)

We saved those who believed and used to fear God.

Stylistically, the distinction is between the two morphological forms of the verbs أنجى/نجَّى. There is a subtle semantic distinction between these synonymous verbs. However, the use of each depends on the context of situation. The verb نجَّى means that someone has been saved from something bad, like a serious car crash, and he/she has not witnessed the accident when it took place; he/she was supposed to be among the passengers but he/she

86 *Stylistics and translator training*

took a different means of transport for his/her journey. However, the verb أنجى means that someone has been saved from something bad, like a serious car crash, and he/she has witnessed the accident when it took place, but he/she was not harmed by the crash. On the textual level, other verbs of the same morphological form of أنجى have occurred in Q27:53, 56, 57, and 60 أنبت ، أنزل ، أمطر ، أنجى ، أخرجوا. Thus, the employment of the verb form أنجى has achieved morphological lexical symmetry with other verbs of a similar morphological form. Similarly, the morphological form of نجّى has also occurred in Q41:12 and 25 زيّنَ، قيض to achieve lexical symmetry with نجّى in Q41:18.

12   Provide translations for the following pair of grammatically similar but stylistically different sentences and discuss their semantic distinction.

ووصيّنا الإنسانَ بوالديهِ حُسنا (العنكبوت 8)
ووصيّنا الإنسانَ بوالديهِ إحسانا (الأحقاف 15)

We have commanded man to be good to his parents.

The stylistic difference lies in the short form adjective حُسنا in Q29:8 and the long form nominalized noun إحسانا in Q46:15. For contextual reasons, حُسنا occurs because there are less details about parents: "but if they 'either of them' strive 'to force' thee to join with Me 'in worship' anything of which thou hast no knowledge, obey them not" (Q29:8) (Ali 1934:no page). Semantically, حُسن designates "beauty, looking good", which in fact refers to the "command" given by God to man and that this command is "beautiful". This meaning is based on the grammatical fact that there is ellipsis, which is إيصاء ذا حُسن "good, beautiful command". However, in Q46:15, we find more details on parents:

> In pain did his mother bear him, and in pain did she give him birth. The carrying of the (child) to his weaning is (a period of) thirty months. At length, when he reaches the age of full strength and attains forty years, he says, "O my Lord! Grant me that I may be grateful for Thy favor which Thou has bestowed upon me, and upon both my parents", Q46:15

> (ibid)

Semantically, إحسانا designates the highest frequency of doing good acts for someone, and refers to the highest rank of doing good deeds. Thus, it denotes a multitude of good deeds for people. The semantic distinction between the two words حُسنا and إحسانا can be made clear through the antonym of each word, where قبيح "ugly" is the antonym of حُسنا and إساءة "insult, mistreatment" is the antonym of إحسانا.

13   Provide translations for the following pair of grammatically similar but stylistically different sentences and discuss their semantic distinction.

ذلك بما قدَّمت أيديكُم (آل عمران 182، الأنفال 51)
ذلك بما قدَّمت يداكَ (الحج 10)

That is for what your hands have put forth.

Stylistics and translator training 87

In terms of number, English does not differentiate between the plural and the dual. The stylistic difference in the above STs lies in the plural noun أيديكم "your 'second-person plural' hands" and the dual يداك "your 'second-person singular' hands". The second-person plural noun in Q3:182 and Q8:51 occurs in the context of the wealthy who are miserly and do not help the poor (Q3:180–181), and the hypocrites (Q8:49–50). However, the second-person singular in Q22:10 occurs in the context of one person called النَّضَر بن الحارث بن علقمة (Q22:8–9), who was very wealthy but miserly.

14 Provide translations for the following pair of grammatically similar but stylistically different sentences and discuss their semantic distinction.

ذوقُوا عذابَ النّار الذي كنتم به تكذّبُون (السجدة 20)
ذوقُوا عذابَ النّار التي كنتم بها تكذّبُون (سبأ 42)

Taste the punishment of the fire which you used to deny.

The stylistic difference lies in the occurrence of the masculine relative pronoun الذي in Q32:20 and the use of the feminine relative pronoun التي in Q34:42. One may wonder whether the translator will be able to capture this subtle semantic distinction between the two ST relative pronouns. Grammatically, the masculine relative pronoun الذي in Q32:20 refers to the masculine noun عذاب "punishment" and to the masculine coreferential pronoun (ه) of به. However, grammatically, the feminine relative pronoun التي in Q34:42 refers to the feminine noun النّار "the fire" and the feminine coreferential pronoun ها of بها.

15 Provide translations for the following pair of grammatically similar but stylistically different sentences and discuss their semantic distinction.

إنَّ ربَّكَ هو أعلمُ من يضلُّ عن سبيله وهو أعلمُ بالمُهتدين (الأنعام 117)
إنّ ربَّكَ هو أعلمُ بمن ضلَّ عن سبيله وهو أعلمُ بالمُهتدين (النحل 125، القلم 7)

The Lord knows best who strays from His way. He knows best who they are that receive His guidance.

The first stylistic difference lies in the occurrence of the preposition ب which is cliticized onto the relative pronoun من "who" in Q68:7 and its absence in Q6:117. The presence or absence of the preposition ب is also context sensitive. The meaning of Q6:117 is that God is aware of who is going to be guided and believe in the revelation and who is going to be misguided and disbelieve in the revelation. Also, this meaning is based on the context sentence Q6:116 and 119. However, the meaning of Q68:7 is that God knows the circumstances of people who are misguided, why they have gone astray, and whether they will be guided soon or not. This meaning hinges upon the context sentence Q68:5 where we find the verb يُبصر "to see" – to see two groups of people: those who will be guided and those who will continue to be misguided. Thus, semantically, the preposition ب magnifies the faculty of knowing on the part of the subject (God), who knows well those who stray and those who do not.

The other stylistic difference lies in the present tense verb يضلُّ in Q6:117 and the past tense verb ضلَّ in Q16:125 and Q68:7. The past tense ضلَّ is the unmarked (usual,

88　*Stylistics and translator training*

expected) tense in such statements. However, the occurrence of the present tense verb يَضِلُّ in Q6:117 is attributed to the lexical co-text where present tense verbs have occurred in Q6:116 and 119; thus, grammatical symmetry is achieved at the present tense level.

16　Provide translations for the following pair of grammatically similar but stylistically different sentences and discuss their semantic distinction.

> أَأُنزِلَ عليهِ الذِّكرُ مِن بيننا؟ (ص 8)
> أَأُلقِيَ الذِّكرُ عليهِ مِن بيننا؟ (القمر 25)

Has the message been sent down to him out of all of us?

The stylistic difference lies between (i) the two passive voice verbs أُنزِلَ in Q38:8 and أُلقِي in Q54:25, and (ii) the rhetorical device of hyperbaton in Q38:8, where the prepositional phrase عليه is moved from its original position and placed after the verb. Semantically, the verb أُنزِلَ signifies the piecemeal revelation of the Qur'an مُنجَّماً نزول القرآن – the revelation at different phases and places and refers to the Prophet Muhammad. However, the verb أُلقِي means the revelation of the Scripture as a whole scoop النزولُ كامِلاً and refers to the Prophet Salih. The prepositional phrase عليه as a rhetorical device of hyperbaton in Q38:8 is employed for the illocutionary force of affirmation to highlight the notion of the prophethood of Muhammad.

17　Provide translations for the following pair of grammatically similar but stylistically different sentences and discuss their semantic distinction.

> فانفجرت منه اثنتا عشرةَ عيناً (البقرة 60)
> فانبجست منه اثنتا عشرةَ عيناً (الأعراف 160)

There gushed forth from it twelve springs.

There is a semantic distinction between the two verbs إنفجر and إنبجس. However, this is not captured in the translation. The semantic componential features of إنفجر designate the gushing of water in large quantities while the semantic componential features of إنبجس designate the flowing of water in small quantities.

18　Provide translations for the following pair of grammatically similar but stylistically different sentences and discuss their semantic distinction.

> أفلم يسّيروا في الأرضِ فينظرُوا كيفَ كانَ عاقبةُ الذينَ من قبلهم (يوسف 109)
> أوَلَم يسيروا في الأرضِ فينظرُوا كيفَ كانَ عاقبةُ الذينَ من قبلهم (الروم 9)

Do not they travel through the earth and see what was the end of those before them?

This is an example of the marriage between context and time through the stylistic variation between the temporal conjunction ف and the additive conjunction و, which both occur within the interrogative particle ألم. One may wonder whether the translator will be able to capture this subtle semantic distinction between the two ST conjunctions. In Q12:109, the context is about the previous nations who were destroyed due to their arrogance. However,

Stylistics and translator training 89

people take no notice of this moral lesson to become God-fearing. The reader is urged implicitly to take an immediate action without delay in his/her response to such details of destruction. Such an implicit command is performed by the conjunction ف, which semantically signifies taking an action immediately without delay. However, the context of Q30:9 deals with the beautiful creation of God and the reader is implicitly urged to use his/her cognitive skills and ponder the magnificence of all sorts of creation. Therefore, semantically, the conjunction و requires longer time to process; the reader needs time to comprehend God's omnipotence through looking at the different sorts of creation.

19 Provide translations for the following pair of grammatically similar but stylistically different sentences and discuss their semantic distinction.

ومن أظلمُ ممّن ذُكِّرَ بآياتِ ربِّه فأعرضَ عنها (الكهف 57)

ومن أظلمُ ممّن ذُكِّرَ بآياتِ ربِّهِ ثُمَّ أعرضَ عنها (السجدة 22)

Who is more unjust than one who is reminded of the verses of his Lord but turns away from them.

This is another example of the marriage between context and time through stylistic variation between the temporal conjunctions ف and ثم and their subsequent semantic distinction and translation. Semantically, the temporal conjunction ف means "an action is taken immediately without delay" while the conjunction ثم means "an action is taken after a while, i.e., not immediately and with some delay". The context of Q18:57 is about people who are still alive; it is about the reader himself/herself. The reader is told that although people are urged to ponder God's signs آيات الله and are reminded frequently about them, they forget God's command immediately and persist with their arrogance. However, In Q32:22, the cohesive device ثم is employed because the context is different. The reader is told by Q32:12 about the people who died a long time ago; thus, the span of time is longer. The dead people were also reminded of and urged to ponder God's signs, but they used to ignore the reminder. However, it is too late for them to repent because they are now dead. Stylistically and semantically, this long span of time requires the conjunction ثم. One may wonder whether the translator can capture this subtle distinction. A good example of ثم and the meaning of a long span of time is given in Q30:54, which refers to the different stages of one's life starting from childhood through old age.

20 Provide translations for the following pair of grammatically similar but stylistically different sentences and discuss their semantic distinction.

قُل أرأيتم إن كانَ من عند اللهِ ثُمَّ كفرتُم بهِ (فصلت 52)

قُل أرأيتم إن كانَ من عند اللهِ و كفرتُم بهِ (الأحقاف 10)

Say: "Have you considered: if it was from God, and you disbelieved in it".

The stylistic difference between the above STs lies in the change from the temporal conjunction ثم to the additive conjunction و due to the change in context. This change has a semantic bearing on the TTs and needs to be addressed. The context of Q41:52 is about people who are continuously ungrateful to God but have been given sufficient time to repent. However, after a long time, they persisted with their disbelief and wrong deeds, as we are

90   *Stylistics and translator training*

told by Q41:49–51. Stylistically, this long period of respite requires the conjunction ثمَّ. However, the conjunction و also designates the meaning of non-immediate action; some period of time but shorter than that required by ثمَّ. We are told by Q46:9 about the revelation and the prophethood of Muhammad. However, most pagan Arabs disbelieved and rejected both after they were admonished about these concepts.

21   Provide translations for the following pair of grammatically similar but stylistically different sentences and discuss their semantic distinction.

إنَّ الساعة آتية (طه 15)

إنَّ الساعة لآتية (غافر 59)

Although grammatically the two STs are no-main-verb nominal sentences, stylistically they are distinct because of the occurrence in Q40:59 of the affirmation letter اللام, which is cliticized onto the noun آتيةُ. This is another example of the context and the occurrence of conjunctions and their semantic bearing. The context of Q20:15 are sentences 14–16 where we encounter details about the concept of monotheism التوحيد. Thus, enough affirming evidence examples have been provided about monotheism. Therefore, stylistically, there is no need for an affirmation letter اللام. However, Q40:59 has a different context and needs the affirmation letter اللام because the sentence has the illocutionary force of refutation of the sceptics of the day of resurrection يوم البعث/يوم القيامة and affirmation through اللام that resurrection will definitely take place. The context sentence is Q40:56 where reference is made to the people who deny the day of judgement.

22   Provide the translations for the following pair of grammatically similar but stylistically different sentences and discuss their semantic distinction.

إنّا الى ربنا مُنقلبون (الشعراء 50)

وإنّا الى ربنا لمُنقلبون (الزخرف 14)

Indeed, we will return to our Lord.

In Q43:14, we have the additive conjunction و and the affirmation letter اللام. However, Q26:50 does not have these two stylistic features. Sentence Q43:14 is part of the reported speech by the magicians قالوا لا ضيرَ إنا الى ربنا منقلبون "They 'the magicians' said: 'No harm. Indeed, we will return to our Lord'". It is worthwhile to note that the magicians are among the elite of the Pharaoh and believe that their Lord is Pharaoh, too. Thus, their Lord is false and does not require the affirmation letter اللام. Also, grammatically, it does not require the conjunctive element و for coordination العطف at the beginning of the sentence. However, the linguistic environment and context are different in Q43:14. Grammatically, the و is a coordination additive conjunction أداة عطف where Q43:14 is coordinated to معطوفة على Q43:13. Also, Q43:14 refers to the Lord who is Allah and is a statement the Muslim is urged to pronounce before his/her journey. The context of Q43:14 is about the Lord's blessings. Thus, the affirmation letter اللام is stylistically and semantically required to express people's acknowledgement of the infinite blessings bestowed upon them by God.

Stylistics and translator training 91

23 Provide translations for the following pair of grammatically similar but stylistically different sentences and discuss their semantic distinction.

إنَّ ذلكَ مِن عزم الأمور (لقمان 17)
إنَّ ذلكَ لمِن عزم الأمور (الشورى 43)

Indeed, that is of the matters requiring determination.

The STs are stylistically different because they refer to two different contexts of patience. Q31:17 refers to the context of patience which can be successfully achieved by people who lose a beloved one who passes away naturally. This sort of bereavement is easy somehow to come to terms with and there is no injustice and no revenge involved due to the death of the beloved one. Thus, stylistically, sentence Q31:17 does not require the affirmation letter اللام. However, the context of sentence Q42:43 deals with the concept of patience due to the murder of a beloved one. This sentence requires the affirmation letter اللام to urge the bereaved family to be patient, to forgive, and not to listen to the evil whisper of Satan and resort to acts of revenge and murder. The affirmation letter semantically designates admonition.

24 Provide translations for the following pair of grammatically similar but stylistically different sentences and discuss their semantic distinction.

ولن يتمنَّوهُ أبداً بما قدَّمت أيديهم (البقرة 95)
ولا يتمنَّونَهُ أبداً بما قدَّمت أيديهم (الجمعة 7)

They will never/not wish for it, ever, because of what their hands have put forth.

The negation particles لن "never" and لا "not" are stylistically context sensitive. The context of Q2:95 is about people who falsely claim that the garden and the hereafter الجنة والدار الآخرة will be exclusively theirs. Sentence Q2:94 challenges them: إن فتمنوا الموت "Then you should wish for death if what you claim is true". Since their false كنتُم صادقين claim is highly exaggerated, stylistically, the strong negation particle لن "never" is required to match their claim. In other words, there is the stylistic device of hyperbole in both their false claim and in the rebuttal negation particle. However, the context of Q62:7 is sentence Q62:6, which is about a group of people who falsely claim that they are God's friends. Sentence Q62:6 challenges them: فتمنوا الموتَ إن كنتُم صادقين "Then you should wish for death if what you claim is true". Stylistically, a mild negation particle لا "not" is employed in Q62:7 because their false claim is not as extreme and highly exaggerated as that made in Q2:94–95.

25 Provide translations for the following pair of grammatically similar but stylistically different sentences and discuss their semantic distinction.

إذ قالَ لأبيه وقومِهِ ما تعبدون؟ (الشعراء 70)
إذ قالَ لأبيه وقومِهِ ماذا تعبدون؟ (الصافات 85)

An interesting stylistic distinction is made in terms of the different interrogative particles ما "what" and ماذا "what". The response to Q26:70 where the interrogative

92 Stylistics and translator training

particle ما occurs is نَعبُدُ أصناماً "We worship idols" (Q26:71). However, the response to Q37:85 where the interrogative particle ماذا is employed is not available. Therefore, pragmatically, ماذا designates the illocutionary force of rebuke to the people who are worshipping idols. Other rebuke interrogatives are also mentioned in Q37:86 and 87: "Is it falsehood as gods other than Allah you desire? What is your thought about the Lord of the worlds?".

26 Provide the translations for the following pair of grammatically similar but stylistically different sentences and discuss their semantic distinction.

إنَّ ربَّكَ سريعُ العقاب (الأنعام 165)
إنَّ ربَّكَ لسريعُ العقاب (الأعراف 167)

Indeed, your Lord is swift in penalty.

The stylistic variation is represented by the occurrence of the affirmation letter اللام cliticized onto the adjective سريع (swift) in Q7:167 and its absence in Q6:165. In sentence Q7:167, the context is about God's punishment and that he is able to afflict the wrong doers with grievous punishment. Therefore, more focus is given to God's penalty than to His mercy. Stylistically, this meaning requires the employment of the affirmation letter اللام to highlight God's ability to deliver swift punishment to the wrongdoers. However, the context of the sentence Q6:165 refers to people who do good deeds, and that they will have ten times as much to their credit. The major focus of Q6:165 is on God's forgiveness; more weight is given to God's mercy than to His punishment. Stylistically, therefore, there is no need for the use of the affirmation letter اللام.

27 Provide translations for the following pair of grammatically similar but stylistically different sentences and discuss their semantic distinction.

إنَّ اللهَ ربي وربُّكُم فاعبُدُوه (آل عمران 51)
إنَّ اللهَ هو ربي وربُّكُم فاعبُدُوه (الزخرف 64)

Indeed, God is my Lord and your Lord, so worship Him.

The two STs are stylistically distinct because of the use of هو, which is a detached pronoun ضمير فصل in Q43:64 and its absence in Q3:51. The affirmation detached pronoun هو delivers the illocutionary force of affirmation and specificity التخصيص. Grammatically, it denotes that the subject هو is exclusive to the predicate ربي "my Lord" and at the same time the predicate is exclusive to the subject. The role of context is also important in the occurrence of the detached subject pronoun هو because the context sentences Q43:61, 62, 63 refer to the concepts of resurrection (eschatology) البعث، المعاد and polytheism الشرك. Therefore, the pronoun هو has become a stylistic prerequisite for sentence Q43:64. However, the context of Q3:51 is delivered through the sentences Q3:42–50 which provide information about the story of Mary and Jesus, but there is no reference to the concepts of resurrection and polytheism. Therefore, stylistically, the affirmation pronoun هو is not required.

Stylistics and translator training 93

2.6 Translation of hyperbole pattern

Stylistically, there are two categories of hyperbole in Arabic:

1 Semantically based hyperbole: This is a rhetorical device which signifies an exaggerated point of view. There is no morphological relatedness involved in the lexical item which designates semantic hyperbole. Hyperbole means extreme exaggeration; it is a deliberate overstatement. Unlike the Arabic active participle, hyperbole is semantically based. Hyperbole is also used in ordinary speech and writing. However, it is a common expressive means of our everyday speech, as in "I've told you a million times", where the expression "a million times" represents the rhetorical device of hyperbole. It also appears in the Arabic phrase (الأعراف 40 حتى يلجِّ الجَملُ في سَمِّ الخِياط) "until a camel enters into the eye of a needle" (Q7:40). The major perlocutionary effects of hyperbole are

   (i)   To evoke strong feelings,
   (ii) to create a strong impression on the reader/listener,
   (iii) to affirm an idea, and
   (iv) to give colour and depth to a character in a novel or play (Abdul-Raof 2020:99).

In terms of Arabic translation studies, we do not encounter a problem with the semantically based hyperbole.

2 Morphologically based hyperbole: This refers to the hyperbole morphological patterns صيغة المُبالغة, which are nouns and are derived from verbs in order to form morphological hyperbole patterns. Semantically, words which are morphologically related can designate different nuances; they are partial synonyms. Let us consider the following examples of Arabic morphological patterns which have no semantic equivalents and can demonstrate the context-sensitive nature of morphological shift in Qur'anic Arabic, where the TT fails to capture.

The morphologically based hyperbole can be achieved morphologically through five hyperbole forms which all semantically have the componential features [+ Multitude] and [+ Extreme], as in the following examples.

   (i) The hyperbole morphological pattern فعَّال, as in

   إنَّك أنتَ علّامُ الغُيوب – Indeed, it is You who is knower of the unseen, Q5:109.
   إنَّ ربَّكَ فعَّالٌ لما يُريد – Indeed, your Lord is an effecter of what he intends, Q11:107.

where the rhetorical device of hyperbole is represented by the noun علّام "knower" and فعَّال "effecter".

   Also, in Q68:10–12 where we encounter the hyperbole nouns حلّاف "habitual swearer", مشّاء "going about with something malicious", and منّاع "preventer".

   (ii) The hyperbole morphological pattern فعول, as in

94 *Stylistics and translator training*

إنّه كان عبداً شكور – Indeed, he was a grateful servant, Q17:3.

We also encounter the hyperbole pattern فعول in words like شكور "appreciative", (Q64:17), رؤوف "kind", (Q2:143), ودود "affectionate", (Q11:90), صبور "patient", ظلوم "unjust," (Q33:72), هلوع "anxious", (Q70:19), قنوط "despairing", (Q41:49), طهور "pure", (Q25:48), ذلول "tame", (Q67:15), and فخور "boastful", (Q4:36).

(iii) The hyperbole morphological pattern فعيل, as in

اللهُ شكور حليم – God is most appreciative and forbearing, Q64:17.

where the hyperbole pattern فعيل is represented by حليم "forbearing". However, both شكور and حليم are hyperbole expressions for multitude. We also encounter this hyperbole pattern in words like رحيم "especially merciful" (Q1:1), عليم "knowing of all things" (Q2:29), and عزيز حكيم "exalted in might and wise" (Q2:209).

(iv) The hyperbole morphological pattern مفعال, as in

وأرسلنا السماءَ عليهم مدرارا – We sent rain from the sky upon them in showers, Q6:6.
إنَّ جهنّمَ كانت مرصادا – Indeed, hell has been lying in wait, Q78:21.

where both nouns مدرار "in showers" and مرصاد "lying in wait" represent the rhetorical device of hyperbole.

(v) The hyperbole morphological pattern فَعِل, as in

إنَّ اللهَ لا يُحِبُّ الفَرحين – Indeed, God does not like the exultant, Q28:76.
بل هُم قومٌ خَصِمون – But in fact they are a people prone to dispute, Q43:58.

where both nouns فرح "exultant" and خَصِم "prone to dispute" represent the rhetorical device of hyperbole (Abdul-Raof 2020:99).

(vi) The superlative adjective أعلمُ and the superlative صيغة (أفعل) التفضيل (أفعل), as in اللهُ أعلمُ بالظالمين (الأنعام 58) أنا أعلمُ بالفاسدين" "God knows best of the corrupt" and "God knows best who does wrong" or "God is the most knowing of the wrongdoers". The superlative adjective أعلمُ represents an Arabic stylistic idiosyncrasy which designates the illocutionary force of [+ Affirmation] and [+ Rebuttal to Skepticism]. For this reason, we recommend the superlative form (the most + gerund (the most knowing)) to retrieve at least some of the illocutionary force of the ST أعلمُ.

2.6.1 Translation of morphologically based hyperbole

The morphologically based hyperbole is Arabic-specific and, therefore, constitutes a major translation problem as illustrated in the following discussion.

Stylistics and translator training 95

The word يُمَسِّكون in Q7:170 is given the meaning of a different lexical item يَمسِكون that is morphologically related to the first one. The SL verb يُمَسِّكون has the inherent semantic componential features [+ Repetition of Action] and [+ Hyperbole]. However, the TL provides an alternative meaning يَمسِكون "to hold fast", which neither signifies repetition nor does it provide the perlocutionary effect of hyperbole. Thus, the SL intended meaning is lost. The same applies to الخَلاّق (Q15:86), which is a lexical void and has been confused with الخالِق "creator". However, الخَلاّق has a distinct morphological form which semantically designates [+ Repetition of Action] and [+ Hyperbole].

Similarly, the passive participle in Arabic has an additional perlocutionary effect of hyperbole which cannot be captured by the TL, as in

جناتُ عدنٍ مُفتَّحةٌ لهم الأبواب (القصص 50)

Gardens of Eternity, where doors will (ever) be open to them, Q38:50 (Ali 1983:1228).

In this structure, there is a special type of passive participle مُفتَّحةٌ. إسم مفعول Thus, neither the ordinary passive participle form فُتِحَت nor the adjective مفتوحةٌ are employed. Although both verb forms and the adjective mean "be open", there is a subtle underlying semantic difference between these three forms: The ordinary passive form فُتِحَت and the adjective مفتوحةٌ simply mean "be open"; the lexical item مُفتَّحةٌ signifies "the doors get open by order rather than by any form of touch, i.e., automatically open by order of the people of paradise". The expression مُفتَّحةٌ entails that the people of paradise simply say: "Open!" and the doors get open. If the adjective مفتوحةٌ is used instead, it will mean that someone else opens the doors for the people of paradise (al-Qurtubi 1997:15, 193).

Another interesting example is the Qur'anic expression خَوّان, which has a semantically and stylistically motivated morphological form:

إنَّ اللهَ لا يحبُّ من كانَ خوّاناً أثيما (النساء 107)

Allah loveth not anyone who is a traitor, guilty, Q4:107 (Bell 1937:1,83).

Qur'anic genre employs خوّان to express a special emotive signification as well as a perlocutionary effect of hyperbole. Although Arabic has another word خائن, this lexical item neither provides an emotive signification nor does it have any rhetorical purpose. The word خائن simply means "traitor". However, the word خوّان defies the TL since it has the innate semantic feature [+ Hyperbole]. For this reason, its intended meaning has been diluted and betrayed by all Qur'an translators who have simply provided the same meaning of a [– Hyperbole] word خائن "traitor" (al-Zamakhshari 1995:1, 551; al-Qurtubi 1997:5, 360).

Due to the cross-linguistic variations between Arabic and other related or non-related languages, morpho-semantic change, especially in the hyperbole pattern of adjectives, cannot be captured by the TL. Consider the following Qur'anic statement with different hyperbole patterns which echo different degrees of hyperbole and, thus, trigger distinct semantic overtones that cannot be accommodated by the TL:

إنّا هديناهُ السبيلَ إمّا شاكراً وإمّا كفورا (الأنسان 3) – Lo! We have shown him the way, whether he be grateful or disbelieving, Q76:3 (Pickthall 1930:no page).

96 *Stylistics and translator training*

In this structure, we have two distinct hyperbole morphological patterns: one is the pattern فاعل for the adjective and the other pattern is فعول for the adjective كفور. This shift in morphological pattern is not without good semantic and pragmatic reasons. One may wonder why one cannot have the same pattern without this morphological mismatch. We can argue that this morphological shift is semantically motivated. Although both morphological patterns are stylistically employed to express hyperbole, only the pattern كفور → فعول enjoys the innate semantic componential features [+ Great Degree of Hyperbole] and [+ Majority]. The other one شاكر → فاعل does not. This is attributed to the fact that the majority of people are ungrateful to their Lord. Thus, Qur'anic discourse employs the [+ Greater Degree of Hyperbole] pattern كفور → فعول meaning "disbelieving, ungrateful". However, to express the pragmatic function that only a minority of people are grateful to their Lord, a weaker hyperbole pattern شاكر → فاعل meaning "grateful" is selected. The latter morphological form represents the innate semantic componential features: [+ Weak Degree of Hyperbole] and [– Majority].

We can argue that this morpho-semantic change in Q76:3 is justified by the intertextual relationship with Q34:13 where the morphological pattern فعول for the word شكور is employed:

وقليلٌ من عباديَ الشكور (سبأ 13)

Few of My servants are grateful, Q34:13 (Ali 1983:1137).

However, to weaken the greater degree of hyperbole of the pattern فعول, Qur'anic genre opts for the employment of the word قليل "few" as a stylistic mechanism negating the componential semantic features: [+ Great Degree of Hyperbole] and [+ Majority]. Thus, the use of قليل "few" has weakened the hyperbole nature of the pattern فعول which can now only designate [+ Weak Degree of Hyperbole] and [– Majority], meaning only few people are شكور "grateful".

We can also argue that the morphological change in the word form is semantically oriented. Some Qur'anic expressions appear in different morphological forms with two distinct meanings. Qur'an translators cannot capture the semantic subtleties involved because they form morphological voids in the TL. Instead, they provide the same translation to the stylistically and semantically different sentences, as in

لا جَرَمَ أنَّهُم في الآخرةِ هُم الأخسرون (هود 22)

Assuredly, it is they in the hereafter who will be the greatest losers, Q11:22.

لا جَرَمَ أنَّهُم في الآخرةِ هُم الخاسرون (النحل 109)

Assuredly, it is they in the hereafter who will be the greatest losers (Q16:109),
which have both the same translation. However, the two morphologically related words الخاسرون and الأخسرون signify distinct semantic significations. The hyperbole words on the morphological pattern فعّال are morphological voids in English. The adjectives الخاسرون and الأخسرون express the same pragmatic function of hyperbole, but express different meanings. For example, semantically, الأخسرون, (Q11:22) refers to a double action

Stylistics and translator training   97

by people who have misled themselves but have also misled others. However, الخاسرون, (Q16:109) signifies a single action by people who have misled themselves only. The TT has provided an identical meaning for the two semantically and pragmatically different adjectives; The TT has failed to represent the semantic distinction between the two morphologically distinct lexical items. This is because the hyperbole adjective الأخسرون constitutes a de-lexicalized item in English – a lexical gap in the English lexicon.

The translator must consider three important facts: (i) the adjectives الأخسرون and الخاسرون are semantically distinct; (ii) they are partial synonyms; and (iii) pragmatically, they express the same illocutionary force of hyperbole.

Let us consider other morphologically related words which are partial synonyms and express different meanings.

1   The verbs أنزلَ and نزّلَ are morphologically related: The verb نزّلَ has the morphological pattern فعّلَ which signifies that something is repeatedly taking place for some time. For this reason, the Qur'an is called تنزيل because its revelation took 23 years; it was revealed piecemeal at different stages over many years. The semantic distinction between أنزلَ, whose morphological pattern is أفعلَ, and نزّلَ, whose morphological pattern is فعّلَ, is illustrated by the following sentence:

نزّلَ عليكَ الكتابَ . . . أنزلَ التوراةَ والإنجيلَ (آل عمران 3)

He (God) has sent down upon you the Book (the Qur'an), and He revealed the Torah and the Gospel, Q3:3.

الكتابَ الذي نزّلَ على رسولِهِ والكتابَ الذي أنزلَ من قبلِ (النساء 136)
The Book that He sent down upon His messenger and the Scripture which He sent down before, Q4:136.

where نزّلَ in Q3:3 and Q4:136 signifies multitude in terms of quantity and recurrence of the revelation to highlight the fact that it was not revealed as one piece, while أنزلَ in Q4:136 denotes the revelation of a divine scripture as one piece. Therefore, the verb نزّلَ enjoys the semantic componential features [+ Recurrence] and [+ Multitude], while the verb أنزلَ has the semantic componential features [– Recurrence] and [– Multitude]. Based on context-based meaning, نزّلَ and أنزلَ are partially synonymous. The TL lacks the morphological mechanism to generate the semantic distinction made in Qur'anic Arabic. This is another example of linguistic incongruity between Arabic and English.

2   The hyperbole morphological patterns: فعّال + فعِل, as in كفّار أثيم "a sinning disbeliever", (Q2:276); خوّان أثيم "a habitually sinful deceiver", (Q4:107); أفّاك أثيم "a sinful liar," (Q26:222); or فعّال repeated twice, as in سمّاعون . . . أكّالون "listeners . . . devourers," (Q5:42). Also, we encounter the hyperbole morphological pattern recurrently used in the same surah, as in أوّاب "one who repeatedly turns back to God," (Q38:17, 30, and 44) and حلّاف مهين . . . همّاز . . . منّاع . . . أثيم "a worthless habitual swearer . . . a scorner . . . a preventer . . .," (Q68:10–12).

98 *Stylistics and translator training*

The hyperbole morphological pattern semantically signifies hyperbole and persistence to carry on doing the same action which generates the same outcome. An interesting example of a translation problem related to the hyperbole morphological patterns is as follows.

3 The partially synonymous adjectives خالِق and خلّاق:

لا إلهَ إلَّا هُو خالقُ كُلِّ شيء – There is no deity except Him, the Creator of all things, Q6:102.

إنَّ ربَّكَ هُو الخلّاقُ العليم – Indeed, your Lord, He is the Knowing Creator, Q15:86.

4 The translator should be aware of the semantic distinction between the following adjectives which are partial synonyms and have different meanings:

   (i) The hyperbole adjective علّام, (Q5:109, 116, Q9:78, and Q34:48) does not mean "know, knower" and is semantically different from the adjective عليم → فعيل.
   (ii) The hyperbole adjective ظلوم جهول, (Q33:72) does not have the same meaning of the adjective ظالِم جاهل → فاعِل.
   (iii) The hyperbole adjective كفّار, (Q14:34) does not have the same meaning as the adjective كافر.
   (iv) The hyperbole adjective صبّار (Q14:5, Q31:31, Q34:19, and Q42:33) is semantically different from the adjective صبُور → فعُول.
   (v) The hyperbole adjective غفّار (Q20:82, Q38:66, Q39:5, Q40:42, and Q71:10) is semantically different from the adjective غفور → فعول and غافر → فاعِل. The same applies to يتضرَّعُون (Q6:42) and يضرَّعُون (Q7:94) which are both translated as "to humble themselves".

We recommend that the translator take into account the semantic componential features of the hyperbole adjectives and provide a periphrastic translation because there are no word-for-word equivalents in English for such morphological voids.

In terms of voids, one may have to contend with Levý's (1969:103; cited in Venuti 2000:382) fragile claim that in translation there are situations which do not allow one to capture all values of the original. Then the translator must decide which qualities of the original are the most important and which ones one could miss out.

2.7 Translator training and translation practice

This section combines theory and practice and prepares students for the translation industry. The present section aims to develop the translation student's stylistic critical assessment through the contrastive analysis of the idiosyncrasies represented by the ST and the TT. The stylistic analysis should involve the search for both the rhetorical and linguistic devices, and what translation approaches the translator has adopted. This training exercise is of high value for promoting student skills in writing a translation commentary on any text type.

1 Translate the following literary text and discuss the stylistic idiosyncrasies involved in the ST and the TT.

Stylistics and translator training   99

Disclaimer: The information contained in this message is intended for the addressee only and may contain classified information. If you are not the addressee, please delete this message and notify the sender; you should not copy or distribute this message or disclose its contents to anyone. Any views or opinions expressed in this message are those of the individual(s) and not necessarily of the university. No reliance may be placed on this message without written confirmation from an authorized representative of its contents. No guarantee is implied that this message or any attachment is virus free or has not been intercepted and amended.

The TT is

إخلاءُ مسؤلية: ان جميع المعلومات المتضمنة في هذه الرسالة تخص المُستلم، وربما تتضمن معلومات سرية، واذا لم تكن انت المستلم فالرجاء الغاء الرسالة وإشعار المُرسِل، كما يُمنع نسخ او توزيع هذه الرسالة او افشاء محتوياتها لآخرين. ويجدرُ بالعلم انَّ جميع الآراء ووجهات النظر الواردة في هذه الرسالة تعتبر شخصية وليست بالضرورة منسوبة للجامعة. كما لا يمكن ان يُعتمد على هذه الرسالة ما لم تحصل على موافقة خطية من المسؤول عن محتوياتها. كما لا يوجد ضمان بان هذه الرسالة أو مرفقاتها خالية من الفيروسات أو انها لم يتم اعتراضها وتعديلها.

(i)   Having read thoroughly the ST and the TT for textual and discourse analysis, we can safely claim that the TT represents a grammar-based translation which involves many cases of a change in the grammar from the SL to TL because the translator has relied on the transposition (shift) translation approach.

(ii)   The ST is made up of six sentences. Full-stops and a semi-colon are used. Sentences five and six begin with the negation particle (No + a passive voice sentence structure), i.e., (No reliance may be placed/No guarantee is implied).

(iii)   Two of the TT sentences begin with the affirmation particle اِنَّ. The first ST sentence is a coordinated sentence through the conjunction "and" linking two grammatical sentences: "The information contained in this message is intended for the addressee only **and** may contain classified information". The ST has deleted the word "only" and the passive voice sentence structure "is intended" is rendered as an active voice sentence structure تخص المستلم فقط –.

(iv)   The TT has joined up the first three ST sentences. The TT uses commas instead of full-stops as markers between sentences. However, the comma in the second sentence "please . . ." is translated as ف فالرجاء.

(v)   The ST noun phrase "classified information" has been preserved as a noun phrase معلومات سرية.

(vi)   The ST verbs "delete, notify" have been changed to nominalized nouns مصدر الغاء، اشعار. The translator has adopted the transposition (shift) translation approach.

(vii)   The third ST sentence "you should not copy or distribute this message or disclose its contents to anyone" is in the active voice and does not have an initial conjunction. The TT employs a passive voice sentence structure through the verb يُمنع + nominalized nouns توزيع، نسخ، انشاء instead of the ST verb forms "copy, distribute, disclose".

(viii) The ST singular "anyone" is changed to plural الآخرين "others".

100 *Stylistics and translator training*

(ix)   Exegetical details are added at the beginning of the fourth ST sentence "Any views . . ." ويُجدر بالعلم + the use of the affirmation particle إنَّ, the change of "any" to the plural جميع, the auxiliary "are" in "are those of" is translated as a TT main verb تُعتبر, the definite plural noun "the individuals" is translated as an adjective شخصية, the preposition "of" is translated as a full lexical item منسوب.

(x)   ST sentence five "No reliance . . ." is a negated passive voice sentence and is preserved as a negated passive voice sentence in the TT. However, the TT uses the additive conjunction كما at the beginning of the sentence.

(xi)   The exegetical translation approach is adopted through the addition of ما لم تحصل على "without you get", i.e., it is the translation of "without".

(xii)   The additive conjunction كما is used at the beginning of the sixth ST sentence. This is a passive voice sentence "No guarantee is implied", which has been changed to an active voice sentence in Arabic.

(xiii)   The ST singular noun "attachment" is changed to the plural noun مرفقات. Also, the last part of the sixth ST sentence ". . . has not been intercepted . . ." is in the passive voice while the TT has provided an active voice sentence structure لم يتم اعتراضها وتعديلها.

(xiv)   The ST has six main verbs "contain, delete, notify, copy, distribute, disclose", ten past participles "contained, intended, classified, expressed, placed, written, authorized, implied, intercepted, amended", and 24 nouns "disclaimer, information, message, addressee, information, addressee, message, sender, message, contents, views, opinions, message, individuals, university, reliance, message, confirmation, representative, contents, guarantee, message, attachment, virus".

(xv)   The TT has ten main verbs تخص، تتضمن، يمنع، يجدر، تعتبر، يمكن، يعتمد، تحصل، two auxiliary verbs, ليست تكن ناقص فعل 15 wnominalized nouns مصدر يتم، يوجد، إخلاء، مسؤولية، الرجاء، إلغاء، إشعار، نسخ، توزيع، إفشاء، العلم، النظر، الضرورة، 28 nouns جميع، معلومات، هذه، رسالة، مستلم، موافقة، ضمان، اعتراض، تعديل معلومات، أنت، مستلم، رسالة، مرسل، هذه، رسالة، محتويات، آخرين، جميع، آراء، وجهات، هذه، رسالة، جامعة، هذه، رسالة، مسؤول، محتويات، هذه، الرسالة، مرفقات، seven adjectives المتضمنة، سرية، الواردة، شخصية، منسوبة، خطية، الفيروسات, and خالية five active participles اسم فاعل المستلم، المرسل، المستلم، الواردة، خالية، seven passive participles اسم مفعول المعلومات، معلومات، محتويات، المسؤول، محتويات، مرفقات، المتضمنة.

(xvi)   Inter-sentential cohesion: This is concerned with the employment of conjunctions between consecutive sentences. Stylistically, the ST is asyndetic, i.e., there are no conjunctions (cohesive devices) linking the sentences. Each sentence ends with a full-stop. The following sentence starts without a conjunction. However, the TT is fully polysyndetic where we find the Arabic sentences linked by conjunctions like و "and", and كما "also".

(xvii)   Intra-sentential cohesion: This is concerned with the employment of conjunctions within the same sentence. The ST employs the conjunctions "and" and "or"

Stylistics and translator training 101

to link two main-verb sentences. Similarly, the TT has employed intra-sentential conjunctions ف "and", أو "or", and و "and" to link two main-verb sentences.

(xviii) We can also observe that tight texture is the stylistic idiosyncrasy of the ST through the dense clusters of 16 conjunctions, such as و، إذا، ف، كما، أو، مالم.

2 Provide a textual and discourse analysis of Q28:24, compare different translations, and provide a commentary on the stylistic differences.

إنَّ اللهَ لسميعٌ عليمٌ (الأنفال 42)

This is a unique example of: (a) translation loss, and (b) stylistic void in English. The translator stands helpless and cannot provide any remedy to these two translation problems. This is because English does not have the same stylistic mechanisms available as Arabic at the grammatical and morphological levels. In both Arabic and English, syntax and morphology are semantically oriented, and both feed into stylistic variations, through, for instance, word order re-shuffle and morphological derivations. Hence, the relationship between stylistics and translation.

Let us consider the different Qur'an translations:

Lo! Allah in truth is Hearer, Knower (Pickthall 1930:no page).
Verily Allah is He Who heareth and knoweth (all things) (Ali 1934:no page).
Surely God is All-hearing, All-knowing (Arberry 1955:79).
Behold, God is indeed all-hearing, all-knowing (Asad 1980:340).
Indeed, Allah is Hearing and Knowing (Saheeh International 1997:236).
God is all hearing and all seeing (Abdel Haleem 2005:113).
Indeed, Allah is All-hearer, All-Knower (Ahmad 2010:235).

Let us consider the following observations based on the stylistic differences among the different TTs and on the textual and discourse analysis:

(i) In Q2:181, we encounter the same sentence structure but without the affirmation letter (ل).

إنَّ اللهَ سميعٌ عليمٌ (البقرة 181)

Strangely, however, we have exactly the same translation as that provided to Q8:42 above:

Indeed, Allah is Hearing and Knowing (Saheeh International 1997:34).

This is attributed to the fact that the affirmation letter ل is a stylistic void "unavailable" in English, leading to a translation loss at the pragmatic level.

(ii) All the above TTs have demonstrated a translation loss, and have illustrated the yawning gap between Arabic and English at the grammatical and the stylistic levels.
(iii) The striking stylistic features of Q8:42 include:

(a) On the grammatical level, the ST is a no-main-verb nominal sentence.
(b) It has five affirmation mechanisms which, pragmatically speaking, mirror the ST producer's performative intent of monotheism التوحيد and omnipotence قُدرة الله. The English equivalent has the no-main-verb nominal sentence

102 *Stylistics and translator training*

"John is kind", where the auxiliary verb "is" is not a main verb. However, such a grammatical structure does not have the pragmatic functions of [+ Permanency] and [+ Continuity] as it is in Arabic. Thus, the performative intent expressed by the Arabic and the English no-main-verb nominal sentences is neither equivalent nor the same.

(c) In semantic discourse analysis, sentences like Q8:42 are categorized as discursive structures which designate ideological (theological) connotative meanings specific to Islamic culture.

(d) The five affirmation mechanisms in the ST are: (a) the nominal status of the sentence because, grammatically, it is a no-main-verb nominal sentence and it starts with a subject noun الله, (b) the affirmation particle إنَّ, (c) the affirmation letter اللام, (d) the occurrence of the active participles سميع/عليم, and (e) asyndeton (the absence of conjunctions (cohesive devices) between words).

(iv) The TTs have attempted to capture the meaning of the affirmation particle إنَّ through the synonyms (indeed/verily), which semantically designate that something is true, i.e., they are used for affirmation of a topic. The TTs have also attempted to translate the active participles سميع/عليم through the expressions "Hearer, Knower/All-hearing, All-knowing/Hearing and Knowing/All-hearer, All-Knower". However, the TTs have not been able to find a translation for the affirmation letter اللام.

(v) Why do the above TTs have translation loss? Pragmatically, the illocutionary force of the active participle includes [– Renewability], [+ Repetition], [+ Continuity] and [+ Permanency] of the features of being سميع/عليم (being able to hear and being able to know). Semantically, the active participle is not restricted by time, i.e., it is not limited by one of the tenses (present, past, or future). However, the main verb is limited by time. Thus, the verb cannot signify continuity and repetition; the characteristics of being able to hear and being able to know continuously. For this reason, the ST (Q8:42) has not occurred in the main verb form: إنَّ اللهَ يسمعُ ويعلمُ. For instance, the person who يكتب "writes" can do so for a limited period of time but cannot carry on writing for several days or years without a stop. However, the person who is a كاتب "writer, author", i.e., an active participle, can do so for several years and can produce several works. Thus, the active participle is not restricted by time. For this reason, the active participle has the illocutionary force of [+ Repetition] and [+ Continuity] without being restricted by a specific temporal limitation. Through the affirmation mechanisms and especially the pragmatic functions of the active participle, God's omnipotence (in terms of being able to hear and being able to know) has been successfully achieved in the ST. In terms of contrastive linguistics, the TL expressions (hearer/knower) are not active participles.

(vi) Stylistically, the ST has the linguistic device of asyndeton where the two active participles سميع/عليم are not linked by the additive conjunction و. In the TTs, however, this stylistic device has been achieved through the use of the comma as in the translations of Pickthall, Arberry, Asad, and Ahmad. However, Ali, Saheeh International, and Abdel Haleem have employed the linguistic device of polysyndeton through the use of the additive conjunction "and" which is not used in the ST.

Stylistics and translator training 103

(vii) The anachronism translation approach has been adopted by Ali "heareth and knoweth" as well as the exegetical translation approach, where we have explication and addition of details "all things" that are not explicitly mentioned by the ST.

(viii) Assonance in the ST is achieved through the nunation التنوين at the end of the active participle words سميعٌ/عليمٌ. However, assonance in the TTs is attained through the "-er" of "hearer/knower", the "-eth" of "heareth/knoweth", and the "-ing" of "hearing/knowing".

(ix) The occurrence of the ST active participles سميع/عليم are context-based – i.e., in the Battle of Badr, the Muslim fighters were outnumbered by the well-equipped Quraish army. They used to implore God and appeal for Him to support them and gain victory over Quraish. Thus, affirmation is made that God is سميع/عليم "God can hear them and is aware of their plea". The battle of Badr took place on the 17th of Ramadan of the second year of the Hijri calendar, i.e., 13 March 624.

3 Translate the following sentences and discuss the stylistic differences involved in the ST and the TT:

(i) (a) Although John was ill, he came to the party.
(b) John came to the party although he was ill.

(أ) على الرغم من (ولو) أنَّ جون كان مريضاً إلاَّ أنَّهُ جاء الى الحفلة.
(ب) جاء جون الى الحفلة على الرغم من (ولو) أنَّهُ كان مريضاً.

Discussion: In English, when the subordinating conjunction (although) occurs at the beginning of the subordinate clause, there must be a comma before the main clause, as in (a) sentence. However, the comma is not required if (although) occurs in the middle of the sentence, as in (b) sentence. In Arabic, however, (although) is translated either as ولو أن or على الرغم من. However, the important stylistic different is the stylistic requirement of having إلاَّ أن + الضمير, i.e., إلاَّ + أنه/أنها/أنهم in the middle of the sentence when we start the Arabic sentence with على الرغم من (ولو) أنَّ. It is worthwhile to note that whether we encounter sentence (a) or (b), stylistically, we are allowed to choose any style – either أ or ب.

(ii) It is too cold to go to school.

الجو باردٌ جداً بحيث لا أستطيع الذهاب (أن أذهبَ) الى المدرسة.

Discussion: The underlying grammatical structure of the ST is
It is so cold that I cannot go to school.

What we translate is the underlying (original) sentence structure. Thus, the translation of (too + adjective + to + main verb) semantically entails a negation. Therefore, the meaning in Arabic is) بحيث لا أستطيع + المصدر أو أن + الفعل.

4 Translate the following sentence and discuss the stylistic differences involved in the ST and the TT.

يصارع سالمٌ الموتَ

104 *Stylistics and translator training*

We can propose two TT styles:

(a) Salim is clinging to life.
(b) Salim is fighting for his life.

(i) The ST employs the rhetorical device of metaphor through the present tense verb يُصارع. However, the TTs have employed the present continuous tense and employed the stylistic device of imagery in (a) and metaphor in (b).

(ii) The ST employs the object noun الموت "death" while the TTs have employed the transposition translation approach and used instead the object noun "life", which is the opposite of "death".

(iii) The TTs have adopted a culture-based translation which is based on one of the translation approaches such as the communicative, dynamic equivalence, natural, acceptable, or faithful. These translation approaches take into consideration the contextual intended meaning of the ST in order to provide a comprehensible TT to its audience with an acceptable natural TL style. These translation approaches aim at complete naturalness of the TT, i.e., to naturalize the TT and reduce its foreignness. The above translation interpretively resembles the original without unnecessary processing effort on the part of the TL reader.

(iv) The literal translation of the ST is "Salim is wrestling with death", i.e., metaphor.

(v) The back-translation of the TTs are سالمٌ يتشبّث بالحياة and سالمٌ يقاتلُ من أجل حياته.

(vi) If we want to foreignize the TT, the translation will be "Salim is wrestling with death", i.e., to preserve the ST metaphor in the TT.

5 Translate the following sentence and discuss the stylistic differences involved in the ST and the TT.

You know where the door is.

(i) The ST expresses the perlocutionary force of rebuke and the speaker's performative intent is to tell the addressee "Get lost and leave the room now". Thus, the literal translation أنت تعرف أين هي الباب. However, we need a culture-based translation which is based on one of the translation approaches such as the communicative, dynamic equivalence, natural, acceptable, or faithful. These translation approaches take into consideration the contextual intended meaning of the ST in order to provide a comprehensible TT to its audience with an acceptable natural TL style. These translation approaches aim at complete naturalness of the TT, i.e., to naturalize the TT and reduce its foreignness. The above translation interpretively resembles the original without unnecessary processing effort on the part of the TL reader.

(ii) The translator needs to naturalize the TT and reduce its foreignness. We propose the TT الباب توسع جمل. However, the literal translation of the Arabic is "The door is wide enough for a camel", whose performative intent and illocutionary force is exactly the same as "You know where the door is".

(iii) Both the ST and TT employ the rhetorical device of sarcasm السُخرية.

Stylistics and translator training 105

6   Translate the following literary text and discuss the stylistic differences involved in the ST and the TT.

Troilus: The Greeks are strong and skillful to their strength,
Fierce to their skill and to their fierceness valiant;
But I am weaker than a woman's tear,
Tamer than sleep, fonder than ignorance,
Less valiant than the virgin in the night,
And skilless as unpractised infancy.

(William Shakespeare, *Troilus and Cressida*)

(i)   The ST is a unique example of ellipsis. To facilitate the translation process, next is the new version of the ST without ellipsis. The ellipted elements are in brackets. Word order change has also been done:

Troilus: The Greeks are strong and skillful to their strength,
(They are) Fierce to their skill and (they are valiant) to their fierceness;
But I am weaker than a woman's tear,
(And I am) Tamer than sleep, (I am) fonder than ignorance,
(I am) Less valiant than the virgin in the night,
And (I am as) skilless as unpractised infancy.

(ii)   The proposed translation is:

تريليوس: اليونانيون أقوياءٌ وبارعون في قوتهم،
إنّهم شرسون في مهارتهم، وأنّهم شجعانٌ في شراستهم،
بيد أنّي أضعفُ من دمعةِ امرأةٍ،
وأرقُّ من النوم وأسذجُ من الجهلِ،
وأجبَنُ من العذراء ليلاً،
وأقلُّ مهارةً من طفولةٍ غيرُ مُتمرِّسَةٍ.
(وليام شكسبير، مسرحية ترولِيوس وكراسيدا)

(iii) We can observe that the major ST stylistic features are preserved in the TT such as

(a)   polyptoton (the change of grammatical category in the text of the same word) as in adjective to noun "strong/strength", "skillful/skill", and "fierce/fierceness";
(b)   hyperbole "I am weaker than a woman's tear" – as well as the rest of the text; and
(c)   ellipsis where the subject pronoun + the auxiliary verb are taken out. The same applies to the TT where أنّي is also taken out (ellipted). The TT without ellipsis is

و(أني)   أرقُّ من النوم و(أني) أسذجُ من الجهلِ،
و(أني)   أجبَنُ من العذراء ليلاً،
و(أني)   أقلُّ مهارةً من طفولةٍ غيرُ مُتمرِّسَةٍ.

106 *Stylistics and translator training*

(iv)   A change in ST word order in "to their fierceness valiant", which has become "valiant to their fierceness" in the TT.

(v)   We can also observe that while the ST has employed the comparative adjectives "weaker, tamer, fonder, less valiant", the TT has employed the superlative adjective known as the التفضيل صيغة (أفعل) as in أضعفُ، أرقُّ، أسذجُ، أجبنُ، أقلُّ.

(vi)   In terms of sentence structure, both the ST and the TT have employed no-main-verb nominal sentences.

(vii)   It is worthwhile to discuss the translation of the Arabic superlative form adjective to English: If the Arabic text employs the superlative adjective referring to anyone other than God, it must be translated as a comparative adjective, as in سالمٌ أكبر وأرحم من أحمد and الأسدُ أقوى من الأرنب, whose translations are "Salim is older and more merciful than Ahmad" and "The lion is stronger than the rabbit", where the superlative adjectives أكبر/أرحم/أقوى are rendered as "older/more merciful/stronger" in the comparative form. However, in Qur'anic Arabic, the same superlative form adjectives must be translated in the superlative form الله أكبرُ/أللهُ أرحم "God is the greatest/God is the most merciful". This applies only to any Qur'anic superlative form adjective which semantically designates an epithet of God صفة من صفات الله. An epithet is an attribute of someone, something, or God, i.e., of God or His creatures. In translation, if the superlative form adjective occurs to describe someone or something – i.e., a creature – it is translated in the comparative form. However, if it occurs with the definite article, it is translated in the superlative form, as in سالم هو الأكبر والأرحم, i.e., "Salim is the eldest and the most merciful".

(viii)   We can also observe that both the ST and TT are marked by tight texture as a stylistic idiosyncrasy of both texts through the dense clusters of four conjunctions "and, but" and six conjunctions و، بيد أنَّ.

7   The following ST is translated by a student. Discuss the translation errors in terms of stylistic structure and accuracy.

ST:
A Muslim man who punched a nurse for trying to remove his wife's burqa during childbirth has been jailed in France.

Student's translation:

الرجلُ المسلم الذي ودع السجنَ في فرنسا وذلك جراء ضربه ممرضة عندما حاولت إزالة غطاء الوجه الخاص بزوجته أثناء عملية الولادة.

(i)   Stylistically, the ST is a passive voice whose subject is "a Muslim man" + a relative clause "who punched a nurse for trying to remove his wife's burqa during childbirth" modifying the noun phrase subject "a Muslim man" + the main verb phrase "has been jailed".

(ii)   Since it is a passive voice structure, it is recommended to employ the active voice style in Arabic الفعل الأصلي. Thus, we get تمَّ + مصدر سجنُ تم, whose subject is implicitly known which is "the police", i.e., the police put the Muslim man in jail.

(iii) What has taken place during the translation process? What is required are the following translation steps:

Stylistics and translator training 107

(a) To start from the ST main verb (jailed) سُجِنَ, change it to a nominalized noun سِجنُ, then move up to the subject noun phrase "A Muslim man", then move down to the prepositional phrase "in France". Thus, we get تم سِجنُ رجُلٍ مسلم في فرنسا.

(b) We change the relative pronoun "who" to لأنّه, i.e., the relative pronoun clause is the cause of the sending the man to jail. Thus, "who" is translated as "because" in Arabic.

(c) The translation of "for trying" is كانت تحاول, the infinitive "to remove" is translated as a nominalized noun نَزع.

(d) The suggested translation is

تَمَ سِجنُ مسلم في فرنسا لأنه لكم ممرضة كانت تحاول نزع نقاب زوجته اثناء الولادة.

(iv) The reason why the translation provided by the translation student is wrong is due the structural fault he has made:

(a) The student has translated "who" as الذي and not لأنّه; and

(b) The student has provided a long subject noun phrase which is grammatically a مبتدأ, whose خبر is missing.

(c) If we want to correct the student's translation, we can adjust it stylistically to:

الرجلُ المسلم الذي **ضُرب** ممرضة عندما حاولت إزالة غطاء الوجه الخاص بزوجته أثناء الولادة **أودِعَ السجنَ في فرنسا.**

or:

الرجلُ المسلم الذي أُدِعَ السجنَ في فرنسا **هو لأنه ضُرب** ممرضة عندما حاولت إزالة غطاء الوجه الخاص بزوجته أثناء الولادة.

8 Consider the grammatical ambiguity involved in the following ST, consult different Qur'an translations, and provide your stylistic analysis and commentary:

وكذلكَ زَيَّنَ لكثيرٍ من المشركينَ قتلَ أولادِهم شُرَكاوُهُم لِيُردُوهُم (الأنعام 137)

The ST refers to infanticide practiced by the pagan Arabs. We have considered the following Qur'an translations:

Thus have their (so-called) partners (of Allah) made the killing of their children to seem fair unto many of the idolaters, that they may ruin them (Pickthall 1930:no page).
Even so, in the eyes of most of the pagans, their "partners" made alluring the slaughter of their children, in order to lead them to their own destruction (Ali 1934:no page),
Thus those associates of theirs have decked out fair to many idolaters to slay their children, to destroy them (Arberry 1955:63).
And, likewise, their belief in beings or powers that are supposed to have a share in God's divinity makes [even] the slaying of their children seem goodly to many of those who ascribe divinity to aught beside God, thus bringing them to ruin (Asad 1980:274).

108 *Stylistics and translator training*

> In the same way, their idols have induced many of the pagans to kill their own children, bringing them ruin (Abdel Haleem 2005:90).
>
> And likewise, to many of the polytheists their partners have made (to seem) pleasing the killing of their children in order to bring about their destruction (Saheeh International 1997:186).

Based on the above different translations, we can make the following observations:

(i) The above ST Q6:137 involves a syntactic (structural) ambiguity where the subject شُرَكاؤُهُم "their partners 'idols'" is backgrounded, whose verb is زَيَّنَ "to induce, to make something 'to someone' pleasing 'fair'". There are two objects: its first object is the prepositional phrase لكثيرٍ من المشركين "to many of the pagans 'polytheists'", and the second object is the construct noun phrase قَتْلَ أولادِهم "the killing of their children", which are both foregrounded.

(ii) To solve a syntactic ambiguity, we recommend ST word re-ordering to produce a simple ST grammatical structure which is an unmarked (usual) word order.

(iii) Pickthall has provided within-the-text exegetical details. However, in Asad's translation, structural ambiguity is solved through exegetical translation based on paraphrase and additional details which are not conveyed explicitly by the ST. Asad, Abdel Haleem, and Saheeh International provide footnotes.

(iii) Saheeh International (1997:186) has opted for keeping the ST structural ambiguity and marked (unusual) word order. Thus, the translation has produced a syntactically ambiguous sentence structure.

(iv) In Pickthall's translation, we recommend removing "their 'so-called' partners 'of Allah'" and using "the idols" instead. The same applies to Ali's translation where "their 'partners'" be replaced with "the idols". The same goes for Arberry that "those associates of theirs" be replaced with "the idols". In Abdel-Haleem's version (2005:90), we recommend that the pronoun "their" of "their idols" be changed to a definite article "the" → "the idols".

(v) It is worthwhile to note that Q6:137 is intertextually related to Q6:140, which helps reduce the grammatical ambiguity of Q6:137:

قد خَسِرَ الذين قَتَلُوا أولادَهُم سَفَهاً بغيرِ علم (الأنعام 140)

Lost indeed are those who kill their own children out of folly (Abdel Haleem 2005:91).

8   Discuss the translation process involved in the translation of المفعول المطلق, the absolute object (cognate object). Compare and comment on the stylistics of the following Qur'an translations:

فَدَمَّرْنَاهَا تَدْمِيرًا. (الأسراء 16)
إِذَا دُكَّتِ الأَرْضُ دَكًّا دَكًّا. (الفجر 21)
يَكِيدُوا لَكَ كَيْدًا. (يوسف 5)
إِنَّا فَتَحْنَا لَكَ فَتْحًا مُبِينًا. (الفتح 1)

(i) Let us first discuss the absolute object in Arabic:

(a) The absolute object (cognate object) is a nominalized noun which is morphologically derived from its root verb and occurs in the accusative case (a short vowel /a/ + nunation /n/ = /an/) as in دَكَّ – دَكّاً, كِيد – كيداً.

Stylistics and translator training 109

(b) The major illocutionary force of the absolute object is affirmation, i.e., to affirm the action denoted by the verb. The absolute object also occurs to explain the type of action denoted by the verb, or to specify the number of instances of an action denoted by the verb.

(c) The absolute object represents a grammatical void in English.

(d) Through the absolute object, Arabic achieves the rhetorical device of polyptoton (change from one grammatical category to another (e.g., from a verb to a noun or a noun to an adjective, etc.). Stylistically, English also has the rhetorical device of polyptoton, but not through the absolute object.

(ii) Let us now provide different Qur'an translations for the four examples above:

(a) Translations of Q17:16 are as follows:

We annihilate it with complete annihilation (Pickthall 1930:no page).
We destroy it utterly (Arberry 1955:123).
We destroyed it with complete destruction (Saheeh International 1997:375).
We destroyed them utterly (Abdel Haleem 2005:176).

(b) The translations of Q89:21 are as follows:

When the earth is ground to powder (Arberry 1955:276).
When the earth is ground to atoms, grinding, grinding (Pickthall 1930:no page).
When the earth has been levelled – pounded and crushed (Saheeh International 1997:884).
When the earth is pounded to dust (Abdel Haleem 2005:421).

(c) The translations of Q12:5 are as follows:

They plot a plot against thee (Pickthall 1930:no page).
They devise against thee some guile (Arberry 1955:101).
They will contrive against you a plan (Saheeh International 1997:308).
They may plot to harm you (Abdel Haleem 2005:145).

(d) The translations of Q48:1 are as follows:

We have given thee a signal victory (Pickthall 1930:no page).
Surely We have given thee a manifest victory (Arberry 1955:231).
Indeed We have given you a clear conquest (Saheeh International 1997:724).
We have opened up a path to clear triumph for you (Abdel Haleem 2005:334).

(iii) Having considered the different TTs whose STs involve an absolute object, we can make the following observations:

(a) All the translations above have followed the adaptation procedure where the grammatical category of the ST absolute object has been modified to suit the TL grammar, lexicon, and style.

(b) The translators have adopted the natural, transposition (shift) translation approaches. These are TL-oriented grammar-based translation approaches which involve a change in the grammar from the SL to TL. The grammatical modification (substitution) can be made the more readily since such a grammatical change is dictated by the obligatory structure of the TL, i.e., the translator is obliged to make such an adjustment to the SL absolute object.

110 *Stylistics and translator training*

(c) Most importantly, the SL absolute object is a lexico-grammatical void which is absent in the TL. Thus, the translator has provided the semantic componential features of the SL absolute object and transferred them to the TT.

(d) We have the following translations based on the semantic componential features of the SL absolute object:

دَمَّرَ تَدْمِيرًا – destroyed utterly.

دُكَّتِ دَكًّا دَكًّا – levelled – pounded and crushed, pounded to dust, pounded to powder.

يَكِيدُ كَيْدًا – to contrive a plan, plot to harm, devise some guile.

فَتَحَ فَتْحًا – a clear conquest, opened up a clear triumph, a manifest victory, a signal victory.

(e) We have the following translations based on mimicking the SL absolute object. These translations are provided by (Saheeh International 1997:375) of Q17:16 and Pickthall 1930:no page) of Q17:16, Q89:21, and Q12:5, as demonstrated below:

دَمَّرَ تَدْمِيرًا – annihilate with complete annihilation (Pickthall 1930:no page).

دُكَّتِ دَكًّا دَكًّا – is ground to atoms, grinding, grinding (Pickthall 1930:no page).

يَكِيدُ كَيْدًا – to plot a plot (Pickthall 1930:no page).
destroyed with complete destruction (Saheeh International 1997:375).

(f) All the STs have demonstrated the rhetorical device of assonance through the nunation التنوين of the word-final short vowel /an/ الفتحة. However, Pickthall has achieved assonance in Q89:21 through the final words "grinding". Saheeh International has achieved assonance through the /-ed/ in "levelled, pounded, crushed".

(g) Most STs have alliteration through the repetition of the same initial sound, such as the initial /d/ consonant in دُكَّتِ دَكًّا دَكًّا. However, some TTs have demonstrated the rhetorical device of alliteration as in the sound /p/ in "pounded to powder".

9   Provide a textual and discourse analysis of Q112:4, compare different translations, and provide a commentary on the stylistic differences.

لم يكُن لهُ كُفوًا أحَدٌ (الإخلاص 4)

Let us first provide different translations of the above ST:

And there is none comparable unto Him (Pickthall 1930:no page).
And there is none like unto Him (Ali 1934:no page).
And equal to Him is not anyone (Arberry 1955:281).
And there is nothing that could be compared with Him (Asad 1980:1315).
Nor is there to Him any equivalent (Saheeh International 1997:913).
No one is comparable to Him (Abdel Haleem 2005:444).

Let us first provide a textual and discourse analysis of the ST:

(i)   The ST involves a word order change. Thus, the ST is a marked (unusual, unexpected) word order. The unmarked (usual, expected) word order is:

لم يكُن أحدٌ كُفوًا لهُ

Stylistics and translator training 111

(ii)   Stylistically, Q112:4 is an example of hyperbaton where an element is moved from its normal (expected) position to another position (but not to the beginning of the sentence). For more details on hyperbaton in English and Arabic, see Abdul-Raof 2020, Chapter 2.

(iii)   In order to provide a word order reshuffle where the noun أَحَدٌ "one" is backgrounded (placed at the end of the sentence) and the prepositional phrase لهُ "to Him" is foregrounded (placed in the middle of the sentence).

(iv)   Through the mechanism of hyperbaton, the ST producer's performative intent is delivered. The marked (unusual) word order through hyperbaton has the illocutionary force of saliency (focus) of the Islamic culture-based notion of monotheism, i.e., "nothing is equivalent to God". In other words, this notion, through hyperbaton, has attained saliency and focus, and has been made a God-specific feature.

(v)   The unmarked (usual) word order: لم يكن أحدٌ كفواً لهُ does not involve saliency of the notion of monotheism. Thus, this unmarked word order does not mirror the text producer's performative intent. However, we can observe that two processes of word order change have taken place in the marked word order (Q112:4). These processes are

(a)   The change of كفواً (equivalent), which is the predicate خبر of the auxiliary verb يكن. The subject اسم of يكن is أحدٌ "one", which is backgrounded مؤخر (placed sentence-finally).

(b)   The change of place of the prepositional phrase لهُ "to him", which is placed before the word كفواً. Thus, the prepositional phrase له is made salient (given discourse focus).

(vi)   The illocutionary force of moving له is to make the notion of "nothing is equivalent to God" more salient and focused, as well as making this notion a God-specific feature.

(vii)   The translator is challenged by the ST structural ambiguity. In order to provide a TT that observes the TL grammatical (structural) norms, the ST should undergo a word order re-shuffle, i.e., to provide an unmarked (usual) ST word order to make the translation process possible and to achieve a translation that is TL culture-based, naturalizes the TT, and reduces its foreignness.

(viii) We recommend the following translation approaches: communicative, dynamic equivalence, acceptable, cultural transposition, and domestication. These translation approaches provide a comprehensible TT to the audience with an acceptable natural TL style. These translation approaches aim at complete naturalness of the TT.

(ix)   The translations offered by Pickthall, Ali, Asad, and Abdel Haleem have taken into consideration the re-shuffle in the ST word order. Thus, they are based on the communicative, dynamic equivalence, acceptable, cultural transposition, and domestication. Also, these translations are based on the transposition or shift translation approach, which involves a change in the SL word order; their translations are based on the ST unmarked (usual) word order, which involves no hyperbaton. Their TTs are based on the transposition (shift) approach.

(x)   Arberry (1955:281) has provided a foreignization translation to Q112:4 "And equal to Him is not any one". He has made close adherence to the ST structure and syntax to preserve the flavor of the unusual ST style and give the TT a touch of foreignness through keeping the hyperbaton word أَحَدٌ "any one" at the end of the sentence.

(xi)   Saheeh International has also adopted the transposition (shift) approach but the TT has been foregrounded (placed at sentence-initial position) أَحَدٌ.

112 *Stylistics and translator training*

10 Provide a textual and discourse analysis of Q28:24, compare different translations, and
provide a commentary on the stylistic differences.

ربِّ إنِّي لِما أنزلتَ إليَّ من خيرٍ فقيرٌ (القصص 24)

Let us first provide different translations of the above ST:

My Lord! I am needy of whatever good Thou sendest down for me (Pickthall 1930:no
page).
O my Lord! truly am I in (desperate) need of any good that Thou dost send me! (Ali
1934:no page).
O my Lord, surly I have need of whatever good Thou shalt have sent down upon me
(Arberry 1955:174).
O my Sustainer! Verily, in dire need am I of any good which Thou mayest bestow upon
me! (Asad 1980:808).
My Lord, indeed I am, for whatever good You would send down to me, in need (Saheeh
International 1997:535).
My Lord, indeed I am in dire need for whatever good You would send down to me
(Abdel Haleem 2005:246).

(i) This is an example of the foreignization translation approach, which involves the verbatim transfer of a SL style into the TT without making any change to the ST.

where the adjective فقير is foregrounded مؤخر; placed at the end of the sentence. However,
it should be immediately after its subject أني to have a natural SL style. The above example
is a marked (unusual, unexpected) word order in Arabic. Stylistically, the ST involves the
rhetorical device of hyperbaton (moving a word from its normal position to another position
but not to the front of the sentence). The unmarked (usual) word order is

ربِّ إنِّي فقيرٍ لِما أنزلتَ إليَّ من خيرٍ

whose domesticated and natural style in the TL is
My Lord, indeed I am in need for whatever good You would send down to me.

(ii) It is worthwhile to note that we have two lexical items, خير "good" and فقير "need",
which both end with the same consonant /r/. This is evidence that had hyperbaton
been employed for the purpose of rhyme, Q28:24 could have ended with the lexical
item خير and the other lexical item فقير placed after the subject pronoun إني (I). Thus,
we get

ربّ إنِّي فقيرٍ لِما أنزلتَ إليَّ من خيرٍ

(iii) The rhetorical device of hyperbaton has placed فقير at the end of the sentence for a
pragmatic function to establish the illocutionary force of attracting the attention of the
reader. In other words, this lexical behavior resulting in word order change in the ST
structure is employed for the perlocutionary effects of focus, saliency, affirmation, and
vivid depiction of the idea portrayed by the word فقير.

Stylistics and translator training 113

This lexical behavior is for focusing the notion of لِمَا أنزلتَ إلِيَّ مِن خيرٍ "for whatever good You would send down to me" and giving it communicative prominence.

(iv) Based on the previous discussion, the translator needs to adopt the transposition (shift) translation approach, which allows for ST word order re-shuffle in order to provide a receptor (TL reader)-oriented translation based on one of the translation approaches, such as the communicative, dynamic equivalence, natural, acceptable, or faithful. These translation approaches take into consideration the contextual intended meaning of the ST to provide a comprehensible TT to the audience with an acceptable natural TL style. These translation approaches aim at complete naturalness of the TT; to naturalize the TT and reduce its foreignness. The translation "My Lord, indeed I am in need for whatever good You would send down to me" does not involve unnecessary processing effort on the part of the TL reader.

(v) The only translation that has preserved the ST marked (unusual) style is that by Saheeh International (1997:535). The translator has adopted the adequate translation approach which allows for keeping the ST linguistic and cultural norms, but the disadvantage of the adequate translation approach is that it may entail some incompatibilities with TL linguistic and cultural norms. However, the other translators have done a word order reshuffle to the ST style; they have moved فقير from its position at the end of the sentence and put it back in its original position next to its subject إنّي.

(vi) The TTs provided by Pickthall, Ali, and Arberry have adopted both the anachronism translation approach (using old-fashioned language) plus the transposition (shift), natural, and domesticated translation approaches. Saheeh International and Asad have adopted an unnatural style because their translations have been based on formal equivalence and foreignization. Asad has also used anachronism in his translation. However, the style by Abdel Haleem demonstrates a transposition (shift), natural, and domesticated translation approaches.

11 Provide a textual and discourse analysis of Q18:1–2, compare different translations, and provide a commentary on the translation process.

الحمدُ للّهِ الذي أنزلَ على عبدهِ الكتابَ ولم يجعل لهُ عِوَجًا قيّمًا . . . (الكهف 1–2)

Let us first provide different translations of the above ST. The following TTs are source-oriented grammatical structure:

Praise belongs to God who has sent down upon His servant the Book and has not assigned unto it any crookedness; **right**, . . . (Arberry 1955:127).
All praise is due to Allah, who has sent down upon His servant (Muhammad) the Book and has not made therein any deviance. [He has made it] **straight** . . . (Saheeh International 1997:391).
ALL PRAISE is due to God, who has bestowed. this divine writ from on high upon His servant, and has not allowed any deviousness to obscure its meaning: 1 (18:2) [a divine writ] unerringly **straight**, . . . (Asad 1980:601).
Praise be to Allah Who hath revealed the Scripture unto His slave, and hath not placed therein any crookedness, (But hath made it) **straight** . . . (Pickthall 1930:no page).

114　*Stylistics and translator training*

However, we encounter target-oriented grammatical structure translations:

> Praise be to God, who sent down the Scripture to His servant and made it unerringly straight (Abdel Haleem 2005:183).
> All form of praise and thanks are for Allah (Alone), who has sent down His slave [Muhammad] the Book which has no crookedness (in its wordings and meanings and no deviation from the middle path). It is a straight forward and firm Book . . . (Ahmad 2010:381).

Let us first provide a textual and discourse analysis of the ST:

(i)　The ST involves a structural (grammatical) ambiguity. It involves a word order change. Thus, the above ST is a marked (unusual, unexpected) word order because the adjective قيماً "straight" has occurred at the end of the sentence (a backgrounded adjective). The unmarked (usual, expected) word order is

الحمدُ للّهِ الذي أنزلَ على عبدهِ الكتابَ **قيماً** ولم يجعل لهُ عِوَجَاً

All praise is due to God who has sent down upon His servant (Muhammad) the Book **straight** and has not made therein any deviance.

where the adjective قيّماً "straight" has occurred after the object noun الكتابَ "the Book".

(ii)　Stylistically, Q18:1–2 are examples of hyperbaton, where an element is moved from its normal (expected) position to another position (but not to the beginning of the sentence).

(iii)　In order to provide a TT that observes the structural norms of the TL, we need a word order reshuffle where the adjective قيّماً "straight" is placed after the object noun الكتابَ "the Book":

الحمدُ للّهِ الذي أنزلَ على عبدهِ الكتابَ **قيماً** ولم يجعل لهُ عِوَجَاً

(iv)　The mechanism of hyperbaton through which the adjective قيّماً is moved to the end of the sentence has given it focus (saliency). In other words, the reshuffling of the adjective's position to the end of the sentence has given pragmatic focus to the adjective through the cognitive effect of alerting the reader/hearer to such a prominence-oriented reshuffle.

(v)　The word-order re-shuffle in the ST is a ST-specific stylistic technique which is absent in English. Thus, the translator needs to be aware of this linguistic difference between Arabic and English. During the translation process, the translator needs to bring back the foregrounded adjective (bring the adjective from its position at the end of the sentence) to its normal position after the object noun الكتابَ which the adjective describes.

(vi)　The translations by Arberry, Saheeh International, Asad, and Pickthall involve source-oriented grammatical structure;ِ the translators have preserved the ST grammatical structure where the adjective قيّماً has been kept at the end of the TT. Thus, a literal, formal equivalence translation approach has been adopted.

(vii)Grammatically, the translations by Abdel Haleem (2005) and Ahmad (2010) have adopted the communicative, dynamic equivalence, and transposition (shift) translation approaches. Abdel-Haleem has overcome the ST grammatical ambiguity by starting a

Stylistics and translator training 115

new sentence beginning with providing a verb "made" followed by its object "it the Scripture" and then by the adjective "straight". Abdel Haleem also got rid of the negation particle "lam – not" and instead used the adverb "unerringly". However, Ahmad has provided two separate sentences. In order to overcome the structural ambiguity of the ST, the translator has started a new sentence whose subject is "It", belonging to the object noun "the Book" followed by the foregrounded adjective "straight forward".

12   Discuss the translations of the following texts and provide a textual and discourse analysis of the ST:

اللهُ يشهدُ إنَّهم لكاذبون. (التوبة 107، الحشر 11)

اللهُ يشهدُ إنَّ المنافقينَ لكاذبون (المنافقون 1)

We can make the following textual and discourse analysis of the STs:

(i)   Grammatically (in terms of word order), the STs (Q9:107, Q59:11, and Q63:1) are main-verb nominal sentences; the ST has a main verb يشهدُ but the sentence starts with a noun as subject.

(ii) The STs are about the hypocrites and involve three semantically oriented affirmation mechanisms: (a) the sentence-initial noun اللهُ, (b) the affirmation particle إنَّ, and (c) the affirmation particle لِ, which is referred to as لام التوكيد. These affirmation mechanisms are employed in argumentation الجدل for the purpose of rebutting the opponent's thesis and for substantiating the text producer's point of view.

(iii) The TTs involve the employment of the active participle اسم الفاعل, which is a stylistically and semantically powerful expression with specific illocutionary force useful for rebutting and substantiation. The illocutionary force of the active participle in Arabic includes the attributes of [+ Continuity], [+ Permanency]. This means that "lying" الكذب is practiced continually by the hypocrites and that this is a permanent character trait of each hypocritical person. The لام التوكيد means "continually, permanently".

(iv) Based on the above details, we can argue that the TTs suffer from loss of meaning with regards to the performative intent of the STs. Let us consider the following sample translations of the above STs:

Allah testifies that they are liars, Q9:107, Q59:11.
Allah testifies that the hypocrites are liars, Q63:1 (Saheeh International 1997:264, 789, 801).
God testifies they are truly liars, Q9:107, Q59:11.
God bears witness that the hypocrites are truly liars, Q63:1 (Arberry 1955:87, 253).
God bears witness that they are liars, Q9:107, Q59:11.
God bears witness that they are liars, Q63:1 (Abdel Haleem 2005:125, 374).
Allah beareth witness that they verily are liars, Q9:107, Q59:11.
Allah beareth witness that the hypocrites indeed are speaking falsely, Q63:1 (Pickthall 1930:no page).

(v)   The translators have relied heavily on the employment of the auxiliary "are", which is a requirement for the employment of the noun "liars". Thus, the ST active participle is rendered as a noun "liars". However, the TT noun does not have the illocutionary force or the semantic componential features of the ST active participle.

116 *Stylistics and translator training*

(vi) English is a SVO language; the initial subject noun is not an affirmation mechanism used for rebutting and substantiation of the performative intent of the TT.

(vii) The pragmatically based affirmation particles إِنَّ and لَ are lost because the TL does not possess such an affirmation technique.

(viii) The above STs have employed the three affirmation mechanisms to semantically signify the meaning: "The hypocrites are liars. The hypocrites are liars. The hypocrites are liars". Thus, such a stylistic technique has served the rhetorical and semantic functions of succinctness الأيجاز.

13 Provide a textual and discourse analysis of Q112:4, compare different translations, and provide a commentary on the stylistic differences.

ما مِن دابَّةٍ إلاَّ هو آخِذٌ بناصِيَتِها (هود 56)

Not an animal but He doth grasp it by the forelock! (Pickthall 1930:no page).
There is not a moving creature, but He hath grasp of its forelock (Ali 1934:no page).
There is no creature that crawls, but He takes it by the forelock (Arberry 1955:98).
For there is no living creature which He does not hold by its forelock (Asad 1980:444).
There is no creature but that He holds its forelock (i.e., controls it) (Saheeh International 1997:297).
There is no moving creature which He does not control (Abdel Haleem 2005:140).
There is not a (living) creature but He is holding its forelock (i.e., He has full control over it) (Ahmad 2010:293).

(i) The ST includes a SL culture-specific expression ناصِية meaning "forelock: a lock of hair growing just above the forehead" شَعَر مُقدَّم الرأس and which occurs in the idiom سالمٌ يأخذُ بناصية أحمدَ, meaning "Salim holds Ahmad's forelock", i.e., "Salim is in full control of Ahmad".

(ii) The SL culture-specific expression ناصِية has been foreignized and preserved in the TTs with the meaning "forelock", i.e., God holds every creature by its forelock, which is a foreign concept to the TT readers. This is a foreignization and literal translation approach "He doth grasp it by the forelock, He hath grasp of its forelock, He takes it by the forelock, holds by its forelock, He holds its forelock, He is holding its forelock".

(iii) The TTs which have used "forelock" are Pickthall, Ali, Arberry, Asad, Saheeh International, and Ahmad.

(iv) The only TT which has provided a context-based meaning is that by Abdel Haleem where he employed a culture-based translation based on one of the translation approaches such as the communicative, dynamic equivalence, natural, acceptable, or faithful. These translation approaches take into consideration the contextual intended meaning of the ST to provide a comprehensible TT to its audience with an acceptable natural TL style. These translation approaches aim at complete naturalness of the TT; to naturalize the TT and reduce its foreignness. The above translation interpretively resembles the original without unnecessary processing effort on the part of the TL reader.

(v) The TTs that have adopted the exegetical translation approach are Asad, Saheeh International, and Ahmad.

(vi) The TTs by Abdel Haleem and Asad have used a footnote explaining what a forelock is.

Stylistics and translator training 117

(vii) The TTs by Pickthall and Ali have employed the anachronism translation approach through the use of archaic words "doth, hath".

(viii) The negation expression ما مِن has been translated as "not, there is not, there is no". The noun دابة has been translated as "animal, a moving creature, creature that crawls, living creature, creature". Thus, "animal" is a literal translation which is not accurate since دابة can be best translated communicatively as "creature". As for "a moving creature, creature that crawls, living creature" – they are over-translations.

(ix) The ST exception particle إلّا is kept as "not/no . . . but + the subject 'He'".

(x) The ST is a no-main-verb nominal sentence; it does not have a main verb. The word آخِذٌ is an active participle noun acting as a predicate of the subject هو. The nominal status of the ST signifies the perlocutionary force of God's omnipotence. In other words, the no-main-verb nominal status through the active participle fulfills the ST producer's performative intent that God is in control of every creature "any animate being". However, all TTs have used main verbs as a grammatical requirement "grasp, move, crawl, take, hold". Had the ST used a verb يأخذ, neither the perlocutionary force of the ST nor the performative intent of the ST producer would have been achieved.

(xi) The ST active participle آخِذٌ is translated as a verb "grasp, take, hold".

14 Provide a translation of the following texts and a commentary on the stylistic differences between the STs and the TTs.

    (a) a care home
    (b) a nursing home
    (c) جليسة مُسنين

We propose the following translations for the above expressions:

(a) دار المُسنين/دار رعاية المُسنين
(b) دار المُسنين ذوي الأحتياجات الطبية
(c) a social carer (social care provider/care provider)

(i) The TL expressions (a) and (b) are more available in the United Kingdom than in the Arab countries. Usually, in the UK, such homes are separate – each for a special category of the elderly. However, we still find "care homes" in some Arab countries but not "nursing homes". This is because in Arab countries, "a care home" accommodates both the elderly who need only live-in housing and care but do not require skilled medical staff, as well as the elderly who need live-in housing, care, and skilled medical staff. As for (c), this is available in some Arab countries such as Saudi Arabia where "a social carer" attends to an elderly person while he/she still lives with his/her family.

(ii) On the stylistic level, the English expressions "a care home" and "a nursing home" employ euphemism and avoid any mention of age "elderly". However, the Arabic expression دار المُسنين/دار المُسنين ذوي الأحتياجات الطبية/جليسة مُسنين employs the "age" label مُسنين, meaning "elderly".

(iii) We have noun phrases in both the STs and the TTs. However, the translation of "a nursing home" to دار المُسنين ذوي الأحتياجات الطبية demonstrates an example of exegetical

118 *Stylistics and translator training*

and paraphrase translation approaches; over-translation which has relied on the semantic componential features of the ST expression. The back-translation of the ST (c) is (a nursing home for the elderly with special medical needs).

15 Provide a translation of the following text and a commentary on the stylistic differences between the ST and the TT.

The callous neglect of older people in nursing homes is a national scandal, but it is the predictable result of the long-term neglect of the care sector, compounded by the cuts to local authorities under Tory austerity (Professor Chris Phillipson, University of Manchester, *The Guardian*, 13 April 2020).

The proposed translation is

إنَّ إهمال كبار السن بلا شفقة في دور رعاية المُسنين ذوي الأحتياجات الطبية هو فضيحة وطنية، لكنه نتيجة حتمية يمكن التنبؤ بها جراء الإهمال منذ أمدٍ طويل لقطاع رعاية المُسنين اضافة الى تخفيض نفقات السلطات المحلية في ظل سياسة تقشف حزب المحافظين.

We can make the following observations on both texts:

(i) Both the ST and the TT have employed emotive expressions in support of a moral cause. These are "callous neglect" إهمال بلا شفقة, "long-term neglect" إهمال منذ أمد طويل, and "austerity" (سياسة تقشف).

(ii) The rhetorical device of hyperbole expression "compounded by" has a negative connotative meaning. Its translation to اضافة الى fails to deliver this rhetorical device in Arabic.

(iii) The TT has employed the affirmation particle إنَّ at the beginning of the sentence as a translation of the ST auxiliary verb "is".

(iv) The ST adjective "callous" is translated as بلا شفقة, the noun phrases "older people/national disaster/long-term neglect/care sector/local authorities/Tory austerity" are translated as noun phrases كبار السن/فضيحة وطنية/الإهمال منذ أمدٍ طويل/قطاع رعاية المُسنين/السلطات المحلية/سياسة تقشف حزب المحافظين. However, the plural noun "cuts" is rendered as a noun phrase تخفيض نفقات, the preposition "under" is translated as a prepositional phrase في ظل, which is a metaphor, and "the predictable result" and "Tory austerity" are examples of over-translation transferred through the exegetical and paraphrase translation approaches as نتيجة حتمية يمكن التنبؤ بها and سياسة تقشف حزب المحافظين, where, in the interest of clarity, we find additional details – يمكن التنبؤ بها and سياسة/حزب – not explicitly mentioned in the ST.

16 Provide a translation of the following text and a commentary on the stylistic differences between the ST and the TT.

Temporary and short-duration face-offs between border-guarding Indian and Chinese troops occurred yesterday. Indian and Chinese troops were throwing punches and stones which resulted in minor injuries to troops.

The proposed translation is

وقعت يوم أمس مُصادمات مؤقتة ولمدة قصيرة بين قوات حرس الحدود الهندية والصينية . وكان الجنود الهنود والصينيون يتبادلون اللكمات ويرمرون الحِجارة على بعضهم الآخر مما أدى إلى وقوع إصابات طفيفة في صفوفهم.

The ST is journalistic and involves some grammatical features:

(i)   The ST has a long noun phrase acting as the subject "Temporary and short-duration face-offs between border-guarding Indian and Chinese troops" whose main verb is "occurred", which has occurred at the end of the sentence.

(ii) The TT also has a long noun phrase subject "Temporary and short-duration face-offs between border-guarding Indian and Chinese troops", whose main verb is وقعت, which has occurred at the beginning of the sentence. Thus, a transposition (shift) translation approach has been adopted.

(iii) The ST has long noun phrases "Temporary and short-duration face-offs) and (border-guarding Indian and Chinese troops", whose translations are also long noun phrases:

(مُصادمات مؤقتة ولمدة قصيرة) and (قوات حرس الحدود الهندية والصينية).

(iv) In the ST, we have one verb "throw" with two object nouns "punches" and "stones". This is because in English we have "to throw a punch at someone" and "to throw a stone at someone". Putting the two objects together, we need one verb only: "throw". However, in Arabic, we need two verbs: تبادل, whose object is اللكمات, and يرمي whose object is الحِجارة.

(v)   The verb "resulted in" is rendered as أدى إلى وقوع, the preposition "to" is translated as في, and "troops" is translated as صفوفهم, whose back-translation is "their lines".

(vi) It is worthwhile to note that prepositions constitute a translation problem. For instance, the preposition "under" is translated as بـ in the idiom "under the pretext of" بِحُجَّة, as in "The US attacked China under the pretext of the coronavirus" هاجمت الولايات المتحدة الصين بحُجَّة فيروس كورونا. The preposition "under" is translated as أثناء, as in "Life under quarantine in London" الحياة أثناء الحجر المنزلي في لندن.

Another interesting example of a long noun phrase is

We need to investigate the disproportionate impact of coronavirus on people of Black, Asian and minority ethnic backgrounds.

The proposed translation is

نحتاج الى أن نُحقق في التأثير غير المتكافيء لفيروس كورونا على الأشخاص من الخلفيات السوداء والأسيوية والأقليات العرقية.

17   Provide a translation of the following text and a commentary on the stylistic differences between the ST and the TT.

120 *Stylistics and translator training*

أخبري ناقتَكِ الشّقراء أنَّ بعيريَ الأسمَر لم يعُد مشغولاً بها ، فقد شغلته الحَربُ عن الحُب، والاشتغال بالسّعي في السوق عن الجري وراء النُوق، وجلَّ همه هو إطعامُ أحورَتهُ زغبُ الحواصل.

The proposed translation is

> Inform your blond she-camel that my black he-camel is no longer preoccupied with her. He is more preoccupied with war than love, more preoccupied with carrying goods in the market than running after she-camels. His major concern is to feed his baby camels whose giblets are empty.

Based on the textual and discourse analysis of the ST, we can make the following observations:

(i)   The translator has adopted the foreignization translation approach through which the TT reader is sent abroad, the TT is opened up in its full foreignness, and in which the translator's presence has been made visible by highlighting the foreign identity of the ST.

(ii) The translator has divided the ST into two segments to facilitate the translation process and has taken out the comma and the cohesive device فقد:

أخبري ناقتكِ الشّقراء أنَّ بعيريَ الأسمَر لم يعُد مشغولا بها/شغلته الحَربُ عن الحُب، والاشتغال بالسّعي في السوق عن الجري وراء النُوق/وجلَّ همه هو اطعامُ أحورَتهُ زغبُ الحواصل.

(iii) The translator has preserved the ST culture-based expressions in the TT to foreignize it. These include ناقتكِ الشقراء، بعيري الأسمر، النوق، أحورة، الحواصل.

(iv) The ST producer is talking implicitly to his beloved عشيقته. He has employed أحورة "baby camels", whose singular is حُوار, but he used implicit simile in which the baby camels are likened to chicks, which have "giblets". Thus, the ST producer has not used مِعدة "stomach".

(v)   An alternative translation based on domestication is proposed: "I would like to let you know that I'm no longer interested in you because I'm quite busy with the military service, too busy with my work, and my major goal is to feed my children."

(vi) We can also observe that, unlike the TT, the ST is marked by tight texture as a stylistic idiosyncrasy through the dense clusters of three conjunctions فقد، و.

18   Provide a translation of the following text and a commentary on the stylistic differences between the ST and the TT.

قامت وزارةُ الأوقاف المصرية بسحب تراخيص خطابة من ثلاثة أئمة لأنهم يحرضون على الفتنة الطائفية ووجدنا في خطبهم أشياء يندى لها الجبين.

The proposed translation is

> The Egyptian Ministry of Endowments has withdrawn the sermon licenses of three *imams* because they incite sectarian strife and found in their sermons things which the forehead dews.

Stylistics and translator training 121

Let us consider the following observations based on textual and discourse analysis and translation approaches:

(i)   The TT reader is not aware of these two Islamic culture-specific expressions: الأوقاف and إمام. Thus, for الأوقاف, we need to adopt dynamic equivalence and domestication translation approaches to produce faithful and context-based meaning and provide a comprehensible TT with an acceptable natural TL style. These translation approaches aim at complete naturalness of the TT; to naturalize the TT and reduce its foreignness. Thus, we propose the translation (religious affairs). However, the second culture-based expression إمام needs the naturalization translation approach through which the SL word is transferred phonetically (transliterated) and adapted to the TL morphology. Thus, we get "imams" with the "s" plural. This ST expression cannot be translated as "priest" or "saint". Theologically and religiously, these expressions are not compatible with the semantic componential features of إمام.

(ii) Out-of-context translation of the verb يندى has been given a literal and foreignization translation as "to dew", meaning "to moisture a surface and minute droplets of water appear". Thus, the ST reflects the rhetorical device of imagery and hyperbole. Having read the sermons, the forehead of the investigating person has been covered with droplets of water. The expression يندى لها الجبين is an emotive one conveying shock and dismay at the contents of the hate sermons. However, the TT reader is unaware of the ST emotive expression and the translator must adopt a context-based meaning and a translation in which we employ one of the translation approaches such as the communicative, dynamic equivalence, natural, acceptable, or faithful. These translation approaches take into consideration the contextual intended meaning of the ST to provide a comprehensible TT with an acceptable natural TL style. These translation approaches aim at complete naturalness and domestication of the TT; to naturalize the TT and reduce its foreignness.

19   Provide context-based translations for the following proverbs and a commentary on the stylistic differences between the STs and the TTs:

"'Never trust a crocodile', 'A fox is not taken twice in the same snare', 'Charity begins at home', 'Cleanliness is next to godliness', 'Familiarity breeds contempt', 'God's mill grinds slow but sure', 'Dog does not eat dog', 'Let sleeping dogs lie', 'When the cat is away, the mice play', 'Kill two birds with one stone', 'Deeds not words', 'History repeats itself', 'Love is blind', 'Necessity is the mother of invention', 'Walls have ears', 'Life is a journey', and 'East or west, home is best'".

(i)   General comments on the translation of proverbs: Proverbs are culture-specific – they present a translation problem and should not be translated literally. To achieve an SL culture-based translation is the best translation approach adopted for the translation. The translation of proverbs needs a culture-based translation based on one of the following translation approaches: communicative, dynamic equivalence, natural, acceptable, or faithful. These translation approaches take into consideration the contextual intended meaning of the ST to provide a comprehensible TT to the audience with an acceptable natural TL style. These translation approaches aim at complete naturalness of the TT; to naturalize the TT and reduce its foreignness. The above translation interpretively

122 *Stylistics and translator training*

resembles the original without unnecessary processing effort on the part of the TL reader.

(ii) Proverbs and the context of culture: To achieve an accurate translation of proverbs, we need to understand the SL context of culture. Let us consider the English proverb "Never trust a crocodile". If this proverb is translated literally to Arabic لا تأمن التمساح, the Arab reader will not understand the intended meaning of the SL message because the "crocodile" is not part of the Arabic culture.

In order to domesticate the TT, we need to provide a cultural equivalent for the SL proverb "Never trust a crocodile". The SL culture-specific word "crocodile" should be changed to the TL culture-specific word عقرب "scorpion" in Arabic. The translation should be لا تأمن العقرب "Do not trust a scorpion".

(iii) Proverbs and the context of religious culture: The context of religious culture is also important in the translation of proverbs. For instance, the proverb "A fox is not taken twice in the same snare" is best given an Islamic culture-specific overtone. We need to translate the word "snare" to the TL culture-specific word جُحر "a hole". Thus, we get the SL proverb لا يُلدَغُ المُؤمنُ من جُحرٍ مرتين, whose back-translation is: "The believer is not stung from the same hole twice". We can observe the usage of يُلدَغُ "to be stung" and جُحر "a hole" in this Islamic culture-based proverb. This confirms that the "scorpion" is known in the Arab culture and that it lives in holes and it stings.

The context of religious culture also applies to the translation of English proverbs like "Charity begins at home", which can be translated as الأقرباءُ أولى بالمعروف, whose back-translation is "Relatives deserve charity before others". Similarly, the proverb "Cleanliness is next to godliness" is rendered to Arabic as النظافةُ من الإيمان, the proverb "Familiarity breeds contempt" is translated as المُزاحة تُذيب المحبَّة where the SL word "familiarity" is translated to Arabic as المُزاحة "too much joking and laughing". We can observe that the verb "breed" is translated as تُذيب "it causes something to dissolve, disappear", and the noun "contempt" is not translated but is replaced by المحبة "respect". Thus, the back-translation of the Arabic translation is "Too much joking makes 'one's' respect disappear".

An interesting example of a religious, culture-specific proverb is "God's mill grinds slow but sure", which is best translated to Arabic as إن الله يُمهلُ ولا يُهملُ, and whose back-translation is "God delays 'the punishment of evil people' but does not ignore 'their evil actions'". Thus, the TT is naturalized (domesticated) to achieve equivalent effect on the TL readers.

(iv) Translation and taboo culture-specific words: Some SL proverbs may have words which are acceptable to the SL culture and speakers but are rejected by the TL culture and speakers, as in "Dog does not eat dog". Animal words like "dog" and "pig" or sexual words which may be found in colloquial proverbs are taboo words in Arabic.

The cultural taboo word "dog" should be avoided in the TT and needs to be replaced by a culturally acceptable TL word so that the translation achieves an effective cultural equivalence and equivalent response. Because "dog" is not favorable in the Arabic or Islamic

Stylistics and translator training   123

culture and has a negative connotation, the SL proverb should be translated as اللصُّ لا يَسرقُ لِصَّاً, whose back-translation is "A thief does not burgle a thief", where the word "dog" is changed to اللص "thief". Similarly, the proverb "Every dog has its day" should be translated as يومٌ لكَ ويومٌ عليكَ whose literal translation is either "One day you are at the top and another day you are at the bottom", or "A day for you and a day against you", where the word "dog" is changed to يومٌ "a day". The same applies to the word "dog" in the proverb "Let sleeping dogs lie", whose context-based meaning is الفتنةُ نائمةٌ لَعَنَ اللهُ من أيقظها. The back-translation of the TT is "Evil is sleeping, may God curse whoever wakes it up".

(v)   Literally translated proverbs: There some proverbs which are shared by different cultures; some proverbs are not culture-specific, such as "When the cat is away, the mice play" and "Kill two birds with one stone".

In order to achieve an accurate translation of such proverbs shared by different cultures, we recommend the literal translation but with a natural TL style. The literal translation of "When the cat is away, the mice play" is غاب القط فالعب يا فار; the literal translation of the proverb "Kill two birds with one stone" is يضرب عصفورين بحجر; the literal translation of "Deeds not words" is أعمال لا أقوال; the literal translation of the proverb "History repeats itself" is التأريخ يُعيدُ نفسهُ; the literal translation of "Love is blind" is الحُبُ أعمى; the literal translation of "Necessity is the mother of invention" is الحاجة أم الإختراع; the literal translation of the proverb "Walls have ears" is للجدران آذان; and the literal translation of the proverb "Life is a journey" is الحياة رحلة.

However, the Inuit culture may reject the literal translation of proverbs like "When the cat is away, the mice play" and "Kill two birds with one stone". This is because their ecological environment does not have cats, mice, and birds. The word "bird" can be changed to "seal" and the word "stone" is changed to "spear". Thus, we can have "Kill two seals with one spear", which suits the Inuit culture, as the "seal" is part of the Inuit culture and the "spear" is used for hunting by the Inuit people.

Paraphrase and the translation of proverbs: We may find SL proverbs which are not culture-specific and can be understood when modified slightly by the TL speakers, as in "East or west, home is best".

In order to achieve an accurate translation of such non-culture-specific proverbs, the translator must adopt the paraphrase, exegetical, minor adjustment, natural (shifting of word order, using verbs/nouns instead of nouns/verbs) translation approaches. Thus, the translation of the proverb "East or west, home is best" is مهما شرَّقتَ أو غَربتَ فلن تَجدَ خيراً من الوطن, where we find additional words (explications) added to the TT not explicitly mentioned in the ST. For instance, we find that an additional word is added "whatever", the word "east" is translated as شرَّقتَ "you went to the eastern part of the world", "west" is translated as غرَّبتَ "you went to the western part of the world", the phrase فلن تجدَ "you will never find" is added, and the word "home" is translated as الوطن "country". If we do back-translation of the TT, we get "Whatever eastern part or western part of the world you went to, you would never find a better 'place' than 'your' country".

20   Provide culture-based translations for the following metaphors and a commentary on the stylistic differences between the STs and the TTs:

124 *Stylistics and translator training*

"heavy heart", سالِمٌ ثَعلبٌ, " 'Poverty encouraged John to do this act', 'The Pound is out of intensive care', 'heavy sorrow', 'heavy traffic', 'heavy meal', 'heavy industry', 'heavy labor or heavy task', 'John is a loyal friend. You can bank on him', and 'heavy offense'".

(i) Definition of metaphor and general comments on the translation of metaphor: A metaphor is a direct comparison of two different things without using the words "like" or "as". Thus, when we use a metaphor, our statement does not make sense literally. In English, polysemous words – such as "heavy" in "heavy heart" – can also function as a metaphor. In the view of Newmark (1988:104), the purpose of metaphor is twofold: its referential purpose is to describe a mental process or state, a concept, a person, an object, a quality or an action more comprehensively and concisely than is possible in literal or physical language. Its pragmatic purpose is to appeal to the senses, to interest, to clarify, to please, to delight, to surprise. Because the metaphor is false, it violates Grice's Maxim of Quality, which requires one to say the truth, i.e., be truthful, where one tries to be truthful, and does not give information that is false (Abdul-Raof 2020:112).

(ii) How to translate the metaphor: We propose four translation methods to choose from:

(1) Translate the image of the metaphor: We can keep the ST metaphor as metaphor in the TT: سالِمٌ ثَعلبٌ "Salim is a fox".

(2) Change the metaphor to a simile: We can use the simile particles كـ/مثل "as, like" and keep the metaphorical word. Thus, we can change the metaphor to a simile: سالم مثلَ الثعلب "Salim is like a fox".

(3) Translate the meaning of the metaphor: We can translate the ST metaphor as non-metaphor in the TT. Thus, we can open the metaphor and provide its contextual meaning in the TT:

سالِمٌ يمكرُ بمهارة "Salim plots skillfully".

(4) Translate both the image and the meaning of the metaphor: We can translate both the image of the metaphor and its contextual meaning. Thus, we can say سالِمُ يمكرُ بمهارةٍ مثلَ الثعلبِ "Salim plots skillfully like the fox".

(iii) A metaphor can be the personification of an abstract noun, as in "Poverty encouraged John to do this act", where "poverty" is an abstract noun but behaves like a person. Also, let us consider this headline in a British newspaper: "The Pound is out of intensive care", where the word "Pound", which is the currency in Britain, is given the features of a patient in the intensive care unit in hospital.

(iv) How can we translate personification? We propose two translation methods to choose from:

(a) Translate the image of the personification (metaphor): We can keep the ST personification as personification in the TT: الفقرُ شجعَ جون على أن يقومَ بهذا العمل "Poverty encouraged John to do this act". Also, خرجَ الجنيه الإسترليني من العناية المركزة "The Pound is out of intensive care".

(b) Translate the meaning of the personification (metaphor): We can translate the ST metaphor as non-metaphor. Thus, we can open the metaphor and provide its contextual meaning in the TT: الحالة المالية السيئة جعلت جون يقوم بهذا العمل "The bad financial situation made John do this act",

Stylistics and translator training 125

"The Pound's monetary value has improved" تحسَّنت القيمة النقدية للجُنيه الإسترليني.

For more on personification, see Abdul-Raof (2020:145).

(v) A metaphor can be a polyseme (a word which has more than one meaning): As in "John is a loyal friend. You can bank on him", where "bank" is a polysemous word and is used metaphorically meaning "depend on". Also, the word "heavy" is a polyseme and can be used as a metaphor, as in "I have a heavy heart" meaning "dull and lacks energy", "heavy sorrow" meaning "sorrow which is grievous and hard to bear", "heavy traffic" meaning "unusually large number of vehicles on the road", "heavy meal" meaning "a meal which is difficult to digest", "heavy industry" meaning "industry which produces steel and cars", "heavy labor or heavy task" meaning "very difficult labor or very difficult task".

(vi) How to translate the above metaphors: We propose the following two methods:

(1) Translate the image of the metaphor: We can keep the ST metaphor as metaphor in the TT, as in Arabic صناعة ثقيلة "heavy industry", قلب مُكتئب كئيب "heavy heart", وجبة ثقيلة "heavy meal". "heavy traffic" ازدحام كثيف, "heavy sorrow" حُزْن عميق.

(2) Translate the meaning of the metaphor: We can translate the ST metaphor as non-metaphor. Thus, we can open the metaphor and provide its contextual meaning in the TT, as in Arabic جون صديقٌ وفيٌّ يُمكن أن تَعتمِدَ عليه "John is a loyal friend. You can bank on him", where the metaphor "bank" is translated as يعتمدُ على "depend on". This translation approach also applies to the metaphor "heavy" in Arabic مُهمَّة "heavy task", in Arabic جريمةٌ خطيرةٌ "heavy offense", in Arabic صعبة ازدحام مرور "heavy traffic". سيارات كثيف.

21 Provide a definition of metonymy, culture-based translations for the following metonymy expressions and explain briefly what each metonymy is:

(i) Metonymy is referred to in Arabic as الكناية. It is a figure of speech in which a thing or concept is not called by its own name but by the name of something intimately associated with that thing or concept. In other words, metonymy is the replacement of an underlying meaning by another expression (Abdul-Raof 2020:118). Metonymy in translation studies is culture-specific.

He stressed that the Prime Minister's spin doctor Jonathan White destroyed democracy, where the metonymy expression "spin doctor" has the underlying meaning "a public relations advisor to a head of state" مُستشار العلاقات العامة لرئيس الدولة.

The king's guns were aimed at the enemy.

قوات المشاة/القوات البرية "The metonymy word is "guns", which means "infantry.

The word "Crown" may be used metonymically to refer to "the King or 'the Queen', and at times to 'the law of the land'" الملك، الملكة، القانون قانون البلد. The expression "the red caps" is used as a metonymy for "the Royal Military Police of the British army" الشرطة العسكرية الملكية.

A famous metonymy is "the pen is mightier than the sword", which was introduced by the British politician and author Edward George Bulwer-Lytton in his play (*Richelieu* (i.e., *The Conspiracy*)) in 1839 الكلمة أقوى من القوة العسكرية.

126 *Stylistics and translator training*

The noun phrase "the White House" is used as a metonymy for the US presidential administration الحكومة الأمريكية/الرئيس الأمريكي. "Washington" is a metonymy for "the United States government" الحكومة الأمريكية/الرئيس الأمريكي. "The Pentagon" is a metonymy for "the American Ministry of Defence" وزارة الدفاع الأمريكية. "Wall Street" is a metonymy for "the New York Stock Exchange" السوق المالية الأمريكية البورصة الأمريكية. The word "Hollywood" is used as a metonymy for "American cinema" السينما الأمريكية. The word "hand" is used as a metonymy for "help" مُساعَدة.

Metonymy can also represent an event of reality, as in: "to earn one's bread" and "to keep one's mouth shut" يحصل على قوته/يغلق فمه

The expression "yellow journalism" or "the yellow press" الصحافة الصفراء is a US term which is a metonymy for a type of journalism that is based on distortion of facts, which presents little or no legitimate well-researched news, and which uses eye-catching headlines to sell more newspapers. "Tabloid journalism" الصحافة الشعبية is a British term which is a metonymy for any journalism geared towards sensationalism and scandal-mongering in an unprofessional way. The expression "top brass" كبار المسؤولين is also a metonymy meaning: "people in authority, the most important persons in a governing body". "10 Downing Street" is a metonymy for "the British Government" الحكومة البريطانية/رئيس الوزراء. "Whitehall" is a metonymy for "the British Government" الحكومة البريطانية/رئيس الوزراء. "The Treasury" is a metonymy for "the British Ministry of Finance" وزير المالية البريطاني. "The City" is the metonymy for "UK Foreign Exchange Market" السوق المالية البريطانية. "Brussels" is a metonymy for "leaders of the EU nations" البورصة البريطانية. رؤساء قادة "Capitol Hill" is a metonymy for "the US Congress" – i.e., the US دول الإتحاد الأوربي Congress assembles in the Capitol Building which is on Capitol Hill مجلس الشيوخ الأمريكي. الإمام الأكبر is the metonymy for the Grand Imam of al-Azhar in Egypt. الهلال الخصيب, literally meaning "the fertile crescent", is the metonymy for the countries Iraq, Syria, and Lebanon.

(ii) Examples of metonymy in Qur'anic Arabic:

We encounter an example of metonymy in Q2:177 where metonymy is represented by the expression أبن السبيل, literally meaning "the son of the road, i.e., the traveler". We also encounter metonymy in "هُنَّ لباسٌ لكم وأنتم لباسن لهُنَّ" "They are clothing for you and you are clothing for them" (Q2:187), whose underlying meaning is "to have sexual intercourse", and in باشروهُنَّ "to approach them" (Q2:187), whose underlying meaning is "to have sexual intercourse", in Q2:222 فأتوهُنَّ "to come to the wife" whose underlying meaning is "to have sexual intercourse through the vagina", in Q4:21 أفضى "go in unto each other" and in Q4:23 دَخَلْتُم بهنَّ "unto whom you have gone in", whose underlying meaning is "to have sexual intercourse", in Q2:243 الموت "death", which refers to الطاعُون "the plague", and in Q2:268 where الفحشاء literally meaning "immorality" means البُخل "to be a miser". It is worthwhile to note that the word الفحشاء has occurred several times in the Qur'an with the meaning "immorality, foul deeds, adultery" الزنى. However, the only time where الفحشاء

Stylistics and translator training   127

occurs with the underlying (metonymy) meaning "to be a miser" البُخْل is in Q2:268. Thus, semantically, الفحشاء is a polyseme which leads to semantic ambiguity.

In Q3:119, the expression عضُّوا عليكم الأناملَ "They bite their fingertips" represents metonymy because it is a performative speech act whose underlying meaning is "rage". We also find metonymy in Q3:123 أذِلّة "weak", which signifies "weakness", in Q4:124 نقير "the speck on a date seed", whose underlying meaning is "scarcity", and in Q6:25 through the nouns أكِنّة "coverings" and وقرا "deafness".

In Q5:64 and Q17: 29, we encounter metonymy expressions like "تجعل يدَكَ مغلولة to make your hand chained to your neck", يدُ اللهِ مغلولة "The hand of God is chained", and in Q9:67 يقبضون أيديَهُم "They close their hands", whose underlying "intended" meaning is "being a miser". However, the metonymy expression يبسُط اليد "stretch the hand" designates the underlying meaning of "extreme generosity".

In Q5:66, metonymy is represented by the verbal sentence لأكلوا من فوقِهم ومن تحتِ أرجلِهم "They would have consumed provision from above and from beneath their feet", whose underlying meaning is "expansion in provision" البسط في الرزق. The expression سَقَط في "Regret overcame them" in Q7:149 is metonymy whose underlying meaning reflects أيديهم the perlocutionary effect of regret الندَم. The expression يُقلِبُ كفيهِ "began to turn his hands about" in Q18:42 is metonymy for "regret", خُشّعًا أبصارُهُم, "their eyes humbled" in Q54:7 and Q79:9 designate the underlying meaning of "humility, weakness" الذُل, which is the same meaning reflected by the metonymy expression نَكِسُوا رووسِهم "hanging their heads" in Q32:12.

(iii) Metonymy in the Qur'an can be expressed through a whole sentence, as in Q33:11 هُنالِكَ ابتُلِيَ المؤمنونَ وزُلْزِلُوا زِلزالًا شديدا "There the believers were tested and shaken with a severe shaking", whose underlying meaning is "fear" الخوف.

Another example of a sentence-metonymy is Q43:18 أوَمن يُنَشّوَ في الحِليةِ وهو في الخِصام غيرُ مُبين "So is one brought up in ornaments while being during conflict unevident?" whose underlying meaning is "woman" المرأة.

It is also interesting to note that the imagery depicted by Q22:2 is sentence-metonymy whose underlying meaning is "the fear, panic, and terror which people are experiencing during the convulsion of the final hour" فزَعُ الناس عند زلزلة الساعة. In Q44:29, we have sentence-metonymy in "فما بكَت عليهم السماءُ والأرضُ وما كانوا مُنذرين The heaven and earth did not weep for them, and they were not reprieved", whose underlying meaning is "indifference towards the destruction of the misguided" عدَم الأكتراث بهلاك الضالين. In Q38:23, metonymy is introduced by the noun نعجة, literally meaning "ewe" but whose underlying meaning is "woman". We also have phrase-metonymy in أولي الأيدي والأبصار, literally meaning "those of hands and vision" (Q38:45), but whose intended meaning is "righteous, good deed". In Q49:4, metonymy is introduced by the noun الحُجُرات "chambers", whose underlying meaning is "place of rest".

128 *Stylistics and translator training*

Below are some of the common Arabic metonymy expressions:

Metonymy Expressions	Literal Meaning (foreignization)	Non-Literal Meaning (domestication)
بنت الشفة	The daughter of the lip	The word
بنت العين	The daughter of the eye	The tear
بنت العقل	The daughter of the brain	The idea
بنت اليمن	The daughter of Yemen	Coffee
بنت اليم	The daughter of water	The ship
بنات الليل	The daughters of the night	The dreams
بنات التنانير	The daughters of clay ovens	The loaves of bread
بنات الصدور	The daughters of the chests	The worries
ابن الليل	The son of the night	The thief
ابن الغبراء	The son of the dust	The poor
ابن الحرب	The son of war	The brave
ابن سمير	The son of Sameer	The night
ابن الليالي	The son of the nights	The moon
ابن الغمد	The son of the sheath	The sword
أبو الصخب	The father of noise	The oboe
أبو أيوب	The father of Aiyub (Job)	The camel
أم الكتاب	The mother of the book	Chapter 1 of the Qur'an
أم القرى	The mother of the villages	Makkah
أم الفضائل	The mother of virtues	Knowledge
أم الرذائل	The mother vice	Ignorance
أم الخبائث	The mother of all sins	Alcohol
أم الندامة	The mother of regret	Haste
أم الطعام	The mother of food	Wheat

22 Provide a translation of the following text and a commentary on the stylistic differences between the ST and the TT.

ألم يعلمُوا أنَّ اللهَ هو يقبلُ التوبة عن عباده ويأخُذُ الصدَقاتِ وأنَّ اللهَ هُو التوَّابُ الرحيمُ (التوبة 104)

(i) Available translations:

Know they not that Allah is He Who accepteth repentance from His bondmen and taketh the alms, and that Allah is He Who is the Relenting, the Merciful (Pickthall (1930:no page).
Do they not know that God is He who accepts repentance from His servants, and takes the freewill offerings, and that God – He turns, and is All-compassionate? (Arberry 1955:87).

Stylistics and translator training 129

Do they not know that it is God alone who can accept the repentance of His servants and is the [true] recipient of whatever is offered for His sake – and that God alone is an acceptor of repentance, a dispenser of grace? (Asad 1980:386).

Do they not know that it is Allah who accepts repentance from His servants and receives charities and that it is God who is the Accepting of repentance, the Merciful? (Saheeh International 1997:263).

Do they not know that it is God Himself who accepts repentance from His servants and receives what is given freely for His sake? He is always ready to accept repentance, most merciful (Abdel Haleem 2005:125),

Don't you know that Allah accepts repentance from His slaves, and also accepts the alms, and, indeed, Allah is Most Forgiving, Most Merciful? (Ahmad 2010:260).

(ii) Having read the ST, we can observe the employment of different stylistic mechanisms for a given illocutionary force set up by the text producer. However, the dominant illocutionary force of this sentence is affirmation, which is achieved through different stylistic mechanisms:

(1) The use of the auxiliary verb أَنَّ;

(2) The noun-initial nominal sentence with a main verb اللهُ هُو يقبلُ التوبة "It is God who accepts repentance". The stylistic mechanism of affirmation is achieved through the nominal sentence. The nominal status of the sentence can be achieved through either a no-main-verb sentence or a noun-initial sentence with a main verb;

(3) The use of restriction القصر through the employment of the pronoun هو "He", which is a detached pronoun ضمير الفصل, in order to designate the meaning: الله لا غيره "God only and no one else (who accepts repentance", i.e., accepting repentance is restricted to God only; and

(4) The use of the adjective الرحيم "the Merciful", whose pragmatic function is glorification of God and praising Him. This adjective has a similar function to that of the active participle.

(iii) The employment of four stylistic affirmation devices is to achieve the illocutionary force of rebuttal of any denier مُنكِر. Also, Q9:104 has employed the rhetorical feature of metaphor through the word يأخذ, literally meaning "take", whose underlying meaning is يقبل "accept". The sentence has employed the word الصدقات (charities) instead of the expected word الزكاة. This style has the performative intent of encouraging people to give charity since giving charity is a voluntary action, rather than using الزكاة, which entails a compulsory Islamic legal action.

(iv) The interrogative ألم يعلموا is translated as "Do they not know" by Arberry, Asad, Saheeh International, and Abdel Haleem. However, Pickthall has employed an unnatural TL interrogative style "Know they not that Allah is He Who" and has also employed anachronism through the words "accepteth, taketh". Ahmad has made a serious translation error in his use of the second-person plural "you" "Don't you know" instead of the third-person plural pronoun "they" يعلموا, i.e., هُم "Do they not know".

(v) Mimicking the ST style: This means the employment of stylistic literalness of إنَّ اللهَ هُوَ "that Allah is He Who". Other TTs have employed the dummy subject "it", styled "it is Allah who". English employs a dummy subject in sentences like "It is hot", "It is John who broke the window".

130 *Stylistics and translator training*

(vi) In an attempt to preserve the detached pronoun هو "He" ضمير الفصل, some TTs have employed "Allah is He" for هو الله.

23 Provide different translations for the following texts and a commentary on the stylistic differences between the ST and the TT.

أنزل لكُم من الأنعام ثمانية أزواج (الزمر 6)
أنزلنا عليكم لباساً (الأعراف 26)
ليستعفف الذين لا يجدون نكاحاً (النور 33)

(i) The translation of الأنعام:

Pickthall (1930:no page) → "cattle", Ali (1934:no page) → "cattle", Arberry (1955:207) → "cattle", Asad (1980:957) → "cattle", Saheeh International (1997:645) → "grazing livestock", Abdel Haleem (2005:295) → "livestock", Ahmad (2010:614) → "cattle" + exegetical details.

(ii) The translation of لباس:

Pickthall (1930:no page) → "raiment", Ali (1934:no page) → "raiment", Arberry (1955:66) → "garment", Asad (1980:288) → "garments", Saheeh International (1997:197) → "clothing", Abdel Haleem (2005:95) → "garments", Ahmad (2010:198) → "clothing".

(iii) The translation of نكاح:

Pickthall (1930:no page) → "a match", Ali (1934:no page) → "the wherewithal for marriage", Arberry (1955:207) → "means to marry", Asad (1980:739) → "marry", Saheeh International (1997:483) → "the means for marriage", Abdel Haleem (2005:223) → "marry", Ahmad (2010:467) → "marry".

(iv) Textual and discourse analysis: Polysemes abound in Qur'anic Arabic and this makes Qur'an translation a challenge. The major translation problem in the above STs is polysemy (polyseme), which refers to a word with different meanings. Polysemy is also called lexical ambiguity. Although semantic ambiguity (lexical ambiguity) can result from polysemy, context plays a major role in the clarification of ambiguity and the understanding of the intended meaning. Thus, polysemy is context-sensitive. The TTs are literal translations.

(v) The polysemous words are الأنعام/لباس/نكاح. For instance, أنزل لكُم من الأنعام ثمانية أزواج, the verb أنزلَ "to send down" and its object الأنعام "livestock", should not be understood such that different types of livestock are sent down from the sky. In this context, the ST is semantically ambiguous, and the accurate meaning is that الماء "water/rain" is sent down to water the plants which are the food for all types of livestock. Thus, the verb أنزلَ means "to produce" → "He 'God' produced 'i.e., created' for you the livestock". Thus, we have the semantic relation of cause and effect where God sent down "the water, rain" as a cause for causing the plants to grow, from which the livestock feeds, and the result is to have livestock, which – without the cause "water, rain" – cannot survive.

Similarly, let us consider أنزلَ عليكم لباس, literally meaning: "We (God) have sent down upon you clothing" (Q7:26), where the context-based intended meaning is (الماء) "water/rain", which is the source for cultivating cotton from which clothes are made and is also the source

Stylistics and translator training 131

for plants which sheep, for instance, eat – and that wool is taken from the sheep. Thus, Q7:26 is semantically ambiguous, and to disambiguate it, we need to paraphrase it → "We (God) have sent down upon you water to cultivate cotton for clothing".

The same applies to ليستعفف اللذينَ لا يجدونَ نِكاحاً "Let them who do not find marriage abstain from sexual relations", (Q24:33), where نِكاح "marriage" is not something that can be found. Thus, the intended meaning is that نِكاح means المال "money" that can be used to get married → "Let them who do not have money to get married abstain from sexual relations".

(vi) The understanding of polysemy should not be mixed up with metaphorical meaning – only denotative (dictionary, surface structure) meaning. Also, polysemy is related to homonymy. Homonymy (homonym) refers to two or more words which have the same form (graphic and phonological form) but differ in meaning, such as the English word (bank): (a) a financial institution, (b) edge of a river or a lake), and (c) to rely on.

24   Check different Qur'an translations and make sure that the following polysemes in the Qur'an are translated accurately:

   الآخرة which has different meanings: (1) القيامة "hereafter", (Q2:102, Q23:74, Q92:13), (2) الجنة "paradise", (Q43:35), (3) جهنم "hellfire", (Q39:9), and (4) القبر "the grave", (Q14:27).

   السوء which has different meanings: (1) الشدَة "affliction", (Q2:49 and Q7:141), (2) العقر "to harm, wound", (Q7:73), (3) السوء "evil", (Q12:25, 51 and Q19:28), (4) البرص "leprosy", (Q20:22 and Q27:12), (5) العذاب "punishment", (Q13:11, Q16:27 and Q39:61), (6) الشرك "polytheism", (Q16:28 and Q30:8), (7) الشتم "foul words, swearing", (Q4:148 and Q60:2), (8) البأس "wretched, worse", (Q13:25 and Q40:52), (9) الذنب "sin", (Q4:17 and Q6:54), (10) الضرر "harm", (Q7:188 and Q27:62), and (11) القتل والهزيمة "getting killed and defeated", (Q33:17).

25   Provide and discuss a number of metaphors from Qur'anic Arabic.

   Metaphor is referred to as استعارة/مجاز. In Q1:6, we encounter an explicit metaphor استعارة تصريحية represented by the noun phrase الصراط المستقيم "the straight path", where a simile relationship is established between the expression الدين الحق "the true religion" and الصراط المستقيم. The notion of الختم "sealing" is likened to الصراط المستقيم; الدين الحق is attributed to القلوب "hearts" in Q2:7. Thus, the rhetorical feature of proverbial metaphor استعارة تمثيلية is introduced through which an image of a sealed heart is depicted. We can visualize vividly an image of a device or substance used to prevent any message passing to the heart, which is the pivotal center of recognition and emotion. Q2:7 can also be an example of cognitive allegory مجاز عقلي.

   In Q2:10, we have explicit metaphor استعارة تصريحية, where مرض "disease" is borrowed and used to describe the heart. The word مرض means فُتُور عن الحق "laxity or lack of interest in accepting the truth". In Q2:18, we have explicit metaphor in صُمٌّ "deaf", بُكمٌ "dumb", and عُميٌ "blind"; in Q2:86 and 174 يشترون "to buy"; and in Q2:138, the explicit metaphor is صِبغة الله "literally meaning 'the dye or paint of God'".

   In Q3:106, 181, 185, Q4:56, Q5:95, Q6:30, 65, 148, Q8:14, Q10:52, Q16:94, Q22:9, 25, Q29:55, Q30:41, 46, Q38:8, Q54:37, 39, 48, Q59:15, Q64:5, and Q65:9, the verb ذوقوا

132 *Stylistics and translator training*

"taste" is a metaphor, and in Q3:118, the noun البطانة "intimates" is a metaphor, because it literally means "lining" and usually collocates with dresses that need a lining like a jacket. In Q4:2, the expression تأكُلوا أموالهم "consume their properties" is a metaphor. The expression مُسفِحٌ in Q4:24 signifies "a person who is practicing adultery excessively". Thus, it is a metaphor.

Another of metaphor is represented by the verb أقرضتم "give a loan" in Q5:12. In Q5:16, we have a metaphor in الظُلمات "darkness" and النور "light", whose underlying meanings are "misguidance" and "guidance" respectively. Metaphors are also introduced in Q7:26 لباس مُبصِرَة, "the clothing of righteousness", in Q9:111 اشترى "to buy", and in Q17:12 التقوى literally meaning "is able to see, has been given sight".

Metaphors are also encountered in the sentence واخفض لهُما جناحَ الذُلِّ من الرحمةِ "Lower to them the wing of humility out of mercy", (Q17:24), which is metaphorical through the employment of the noun جَناح "wing". In Q18:11 and 14, metaphor is realized through the verbs ضربنا, literally meaning "to hit" and ربطنا, literally meaning "to tie up with a rope" respectively.

Metaphor is also introduced in Q19:4 اشتعلَ الرأسُ شيباً (My hair is ashen grey); in Q21:18 بل نقذفُ بالحقِّ على الباطل فيدمغُهُ "We dash the truth upon falsehood, and it destroys it" through the words نقذفُ "dash" and يدمغُهُ "destroy"; in Q22:19 قُطعَت لهم ثيابٌ من نارٍ "cut out for them garments of fire", which literally means "clothes made of fire have been tailored for them"; in Q22:55 يوم عقيم "a sterile day", literally meaning "a day that cannot produce children"; in Q23:13 قرار مكين "a firm lodging 'a safe place'", where the word قرار refers to the womb; in Q27:86 النهار مُبصراً "the day has sight, literally: it can see"; and in فارغاً "empty" in أصبحَ فُؤادُ أُم مُوسى فارغاً "The heart of Moses' mother has become empty", (Q28:10); as well as in الأرضَ خاشِعة (Q41:39), literally meaning "The earth is humble to God".

26 Translate the following legal text and discuss the process of translating the ST stylistic idiosyncrasies, the full-stop, and other translation problems.

> Criminal law is the body of law that relates to crime. It proscribes conduct perceived as threatening, harmful, or otherwise endangering to the property, health, safety, and moral welfare of people inclusive of oneself. Most criminal law is established by statute, which is to say that the laws are enacted by a legislature. Criminal law includes the punishment and rehabilitation of people who violate such laws. Criminal law varies according to jurisdiction, and differs from civil law, where emphasis is more on dispute resolution and victim compensation, rather than on punishment or rehabilitation. Criminal procedure is a formalized official activity that authenticates the fact of commission of a crime and authorizes punitive or rehabilitative treatment of the offender.
>
> (*Wikipedia, the free encyclopedia*, accessed on 5 June 2020)

(i) We propose the following translation:

إنَّ القانونَ الجنائيَ هو عبارةٌ عن مجموعة القوانين التي تتعلق بالجريمة وهو الذي يُحرِّم (يحظر) السلوك الذي نعتبرهُ (نراه) بأنه تهديد أو ضار أو يعرضُ للخطر بشكل آخر الممتلكات والصحة والسلامة والرفاهية المعنوية للأشخاص بما في ذلك الذات. ويتم وضع معظم القانون الجنائي بموجب

Stylistics and translator training 133

القانون، وهذا يعني أن القوانين يتم سنها من قبل هيئة تشريعية. ويشمل القانون الجنائي معاقبة وإعادة تأهيل الأشخاص الذين ينتهكون هذه القوانين. ويختلف القانون الجنائي وفقاً للسلطة القضائية كما يختلف عن القانون المدني الذي يركز بشكل أكبر على حل النزاعات وتعويض الضحايا أكثر مما يركز على (أكثر من/أكثر من تكيزه على) العقاب أو إعادة التأهيل. وتُعتبر الإجراءات الجنائية نشاطاً رسمياً يُثبت حقيقة ارتكاب جريمة ما ويُجيز العمل العقابي (المعاملة العقابية) أو التأهيلي للجاني.

(ii) Translation of punctuation analysis:

   We can observe that the ST, in terms of the occurrence of the full-stop and texture, enjoys loose texture because of the lack of conjunctions. However, the TT is characterized by tight texture due to the employment of dense conjunctions such as the و.

(iii)   In terms of clause relations, the ST is asyndetic while the TT is polysyndetic.
(iv)   In terms of stylistic idiosyncrasies, we observe the following stylistic features:

   (a) The use of the affirmation particle إنَّ at the beginning of the initial sentence of the TT followed by the nominal sentence. This is a stylistic signal of a legal genre.
   (b) Stylistically, both the ST and the TT are void of rhetorical devices because legal texts are serious discourses and avoid stylistic devices like metaphor, metonymy, and personification.
   (c) Syntactically, the passive voice has occurred twice in "Most criminal law is <u>is estab-lished</u> by statute, which is to say that the laws <u>are enacted</u> by a legislature". Stylistically, the English passive voice pattern should be translated as an active voice in Arabic. Thus, we use the active voice pattern (pseudo-passive) يتم + المصدر يتم Arabic. Thus, we use the active voice pattern (pseudo-passive) . . . . وضع . . . يتم سن.

(v)   The second sentence "It proscribes conduct perceived as . . ." involves the ellipsis of the relative pronoun "which": "It proscribes conduct 'which is' perceived as . . .". However, in the TT, we need to retrieve it and add it as الذي.
(vi)   In the sentence ". . . where emphasis is more on dispute resolution and victim com-pensation, rather than on punishment or rehabilitation . . .", the expression "rather than on" is related to the earlier expression "is more on". Thus, we have "is more on . . . than on". Therefore, we need to translate "rather than on" as a verb أكثر مما يُركزُ على. Also, the noun "emphasis" in "where emphasis is" is translated as a verb يركز على and the conjunction "where" is translated as a relative pronoun الذي.
(vii)   In the sentence "Most criminal law is established by statute . . . the laws are enacted by a legislature", the preposition "by" occurs twice and is translated as من and بموجب قِبَل respectively.
(viii) In terms of texture, the ST is asyndetic with regards to inter-sentential cohesion, i.e., it is marked by loose texture. However, the TT is polysyndetic, i.e., it is characterized by tight texture. On texture and polysyndetic sentences, see Abdul-Raof (2019:17 and 2020:247 respectively).

For more exercises, see Appendix 2.

3 Stylistic literalness in Qur'an translation

3.1 Introduction

The chapter accounts for the foreignization of Qur'anic style by some Qur'an translations where we encounter a greater focus of attention upon SL stylistic features (form). Such translations are unique examples of foreignizing the SL style and syntactic patterns. Different Qur'an translations are given distinct considerations to content and form. As a Qur'an translation strategy, the foreignization of Qur'anic style (stylistic literalness) favors form over content, giving style (stylistic features) a higher priority in the TT. For such Qur'an translations, the importance of TL form far exceeds the consideration of the content of the SL message. There is abundance of evidence of such a translation approach with regards to the Qur'anic stylistic features of hyperbaton, foregrounding, the absolute object, verbal substitution, the detached pronoun, and Arabic-specific stylistic structures which have been sources of stylistic literalness that tend to alienate the TL audience.

3.2 What is stylistic literalness?

Stylistic literalness is an unnatural TL style which aims to imitate the ST stylistic structure with disregard to TT linguistic norms, as represented by Saheeh International Qur'an translation. Stylistic literalness completely typifies the structural equivalence with the ST. Stylistic literalness is structural equivalence, also known as "gloss translation", in which the translator attempts to reproduce as literally and meaningfully as possible the form and content of the original. Like Cicero, Qur'an translators who have adopted stylistic literalness have "sought to preserve the general style and force of the language". Similarly, Yusuf Ali's Qur'an translation is an example of anachronism, which produces unsmooth translation – using old-fashioned English language (the receptor language), hence giving an impression of unreality. Stylistic literalness is not related to word level literal translation; it does not deal with lexical void, as in أصلح, which is given the literal meaning (to amend, Q21:90) by Saheeh International (1997:448) while its context-based meaning is (to cure). For more details on lexical void (word level literal translation), see Abdul-Raof (2018:305).

The landscape of Qur'an translation reflects the contrast in translation strategies between the literalist and spiritualist translations. We find the Yusuf Ali and Saheeh International translations as examples of stylistic literalness. Ali's style is different from that of Saheeh. This reflects the universal fact that live languages are constantly changing, and stylistic

DOI: 10.4324/9781003268956-4

Stylistic literalness in Qur'an translation 135

preferences undergo continual modification. Thus, "a translation acceptable in one period is often quite unacceptable at a later time" (Nida 1964 Principles of Correspondence).

Stylistic literalness seeks to provide the truest possible finish (feel) of the original; to reflect the mind and heart of Qur'anic Arabic with the result that the translation lacks the original feel. Stylistic literalness translation provides more SL form and obscure sense. In an attempt to convey the spirit and manner of the SL, stylistic literalness renders Qur'anic style as far as possible violating TL stylistic and grammatical norms.

Closely related to the requirement of sensitivity to Qur'anic style is the need for a "natural and easy" form of expression in English (Campbell 1789:445 ff.; cited in Nida 1964). Stylistic literalness is, thus, a failure to be natural in expression because the translator makes the reader "acutely conscious that the work is a translation. For the most part, the translator's ingenuity consists in finding phrases that could not possibly be used by the average Englishman (Max Beerbohm 1903:75). For Goodspeed (1945:8), "the best translation is not one that keeps forever before the reader's mind the fact that this is a translation, not an original English composition, but one that makes the reader forget that it is a translation at all" (cited in Nida 1964).

A translation based on stylistic literalness adopts the formal equivalence (structural equivalence, gloss translation) approach, which focuses attention on the message itself, in both form and content (Nida 1964; cited in Venuti 2000:129). The translator is concerned that the TL message should match as closely as possible the different elements in the SL. The type of translation which most completely typifies this structural equivalence might be called a gloss translation, in which the translator attempts to reproduce as literally and meaningfully as possible the form and content of the original. Such a translation requires:

1   a relatively close approximation to the structure of the ST in form (syntax and idioms) and content (themes and concepts), and
2   numerous footnotes in order to make the TT fully comprehensible.

A stylistically literal translation is designed to permit the reader to identify as fully as possible with a person in the source-language context, and to understand as much as he/she can of the customs, manner of thought, and means of expression.

Although strictly literal translation is not common among languages which are linguistically and culturally incongruous like Arabic and English, stylistic literalness in Qur'an translation is so closely influenced by the ST that the translation turns to be a "translationese": an awkward translation due to overtly literal translation of ST form in terms of grammar and style. A literal, word-for-word translation was and has been the appropriate translation approach for the translation of sensitive texts like the Bible and the Qur'an, which are considered as the word of God. A translator who did not remain "true" to the "official" interpretation of that word often ran a considerable risk. Sometimes, as in the case of the 16th-century English Bible translator William Tyndale, it was the mere act of translation into the vernacular that led to persecution and execution (Hatim and Munday 2004:11). In the case of the Qur'an, the translator must use "interpretation" or "translation" of the meanings of the Qur'an. Our position towards stylistic literalness runs counter to that made by Savory (1957:49) who supports stylistic literalness and proposes that "a translation should read like a translation and should reflect the style of the original". We are in agreement with the view made by de Waard and Nida (1986:37–38) who argue rightly that "changes of form can and should be made in translation when a formal correspondence involves a serious obscurity in meaning".

136 *Stylistic literalness in Qur'an translation*

3.3 Natural and easy style

This is a discussion regarding whether meaning or style should have priority. For Tancock (1958:29), meaning must have priority over style (Tancock 1958:29). However, in the view of Nida (1964), the translation must be an effective blend of matter and manner. Adherence to content (meaning), without consideration of form (style), usually results in stylistic weakness (uneven style), with nothing of the sparkle and charm of the stylistically sublime ST. However, sacrifice of meaning for the sake of reproducing the SL style may produce only an impression, but fail to communicate the message. The SL style can be changed more radically than the content and can still be substantially equivalent in its effect (response) upon the SL receptor. Therefore, correspondence in meaning must have priority over correspondence in style.

The call for a natural and easy TL style represents a rejection of the literalist views on TL style, such as that of Newman (1861:xiv). For instance, Nida (1964) has called for equivalent (similar) response in the TL and argued that it is not easy to produce a completely natural translation, especially if the original writing is good literature, precisely because truly good writing intimately reflects and effectively exploits the total idiomatic capacities and special genius of the language in which the writing is done. A translator must therefore not only contend with the special difficulties resulting from such an effective exploitation of the total resources of the source language, but also seek to produce something relatively equivalent in the receptor language. An easy and natural style in translating, Nida (ibid) adds, despite the extreme difficulties of producing it – especially when translating an original of high quality – is essential to producing in the TL audience a response similar to that of the SL audience. This principle of "similar response" has been widely held and effectively stated by a number of specialists in the field of translating. Similarly, Matthew Arnold (1861, as quoted in Savory 1957:45) also referred to the principle of "similar response" and declares that: "A translation should affect us in the same way as the original may be supposed to have affected its first hearers".

Campbell (1789:445ff; cited in Nida 1964) refers to the requirement of sensitivity to the SL style and calls for the need for a "natural and easy" form of expression in the TL. Max Beerbohm (1903:75; cited in Nida 1964) warns of the failure to be natural in expression in the TL. He (ibid) argues that the translator should not make the reader "acutely conscious that their work is a translation. . . . For the most part, their ingenuity consists in finding phrases that could not possibly be used by the average Englishman". Goodspeed (1945:8) echoes the same sentiment:

> The best translation is not one that keeps forever before the reader's mind the fact that this is a translation, not an original English composition, but one that makes the reader forget that it is a translation at all and makes him feel that he is looking into the ancient writer's (SL text producer's) mind, as he would into that of a contemporary. This is the task of any serious translator.

Phillips (1953:53) confirms the same viewpoint when he declares: "The test of a real translation is that it should not read like translation at all". Similarly, Jowett (1891, as quoted in Savory 1957) also supports the notion of "similar response", and states that the translator should seek to produce on his/her TL reader an impression similar or nearly similar to that produced by the ST on its audience. Also, Nida (1964) expresses the same view and states the ideal translation should aim to produce on the minds of TL readers as nearly as

Stylistic literalness in Qur'an translation 137

possible the same effect as was produced by the original on its readers. Similarly, Knox (1957:5) insists that a translation should be "read with the same interest and enjoyment which a reading of the original would have afforded". The support for a natural and easy TL style also comes from Procházka (in Garvin 1955) who re-enforces this translation strategy and claims that "the translation should make the same resultant impression on the TL reader as the original does on its SL reader".

The lack of easy and natural style is often encountered in Qur'an translation, where stylistic literalness has led to confusing TTs, as in Q20:78 and Q35:28 provided below:

فَأَتَبَعَهُم فِرعَونُ بِجُنودِهِ فَغَشِيَهُم مِن اليَمِ ما غَشِيَهُم (طه 78) – So Pharaoh pursued them with his soldiers, and there covered them from the sea that which covered them, Q20:78.

إِنَّما يَخشى اللهَ مِن عِبادِهِ العُلَماءُ (فاطر 28) – Only those fear Allah, from among His servants, who have knowledge, Q35:28.

3.4 Sources of stylistic literalness

There are six major sources that lead to stylistic literalness in Arabic translation. These are (i) hyperbaton, (ii) foregrounding, (iii) the absolute object, (iv) verbal substitution, and (v) the detached pronoun.

1. Hyperbaton: Grammatically, this is concerned with word order. Hyperbaton is a marked (unusual) word order in Arabic. In terms of discourse semantics and discourse pragmatics, hyperbaton is a discursive structure; a sentence which involves hyperbaton entails an ideological connotative meaning. The TTs are based on Saheeh International (1997).

Example 1:
When Abraham was raising the foundations of the hose and with him Ishmael.

وَإِذ يَرفَعُ إِبراهيمُ القَواعِدَ مِن البيتِ وَإسماعيلُ (البقرة 127)

where the second subject noun إسماعيلُ "Ishmael" is placed at the end of the sentence while it should have been placed after the first subject noun إبراهيمُ "Abraham". The unmarked (usual) word order is

وَإِذ يَرفَعُ إِبراهيمُ وَإسماعيلُ القَواعِدَ مِن البيتِ

Example 2:
يَمحُو اللهُ ما يَشاءُ وَيُثبِتُ (الرعد 39) – God erases whatever He will or confirms.

where the second verb يُثبِتُ "to confirm" should have been placed next to the first verb يمحُو "to erase". The unmarked word order is

يمحو وَيُثبِتُ اللهُ ما يَشاءُ

Example 3:
فَأوجَسَ في نفسِهِ خيفةً موسى (طه 67) – He (Moses) sensed within himself apprehension

138 *Stylistic literalness in Qur'an translation*

In this type of hyperbaton, the marked word order is employed for the perlocutionary effect of rhythmic effects; stylistically, to achieve the rhetorical device (assonance) through the re-shuffle of lexical items. The unmarked (usual) word order is فأوجَسَ موسى خيفةً في نفسِهِ

The backgrounding (placement at the end of the sentence) of the subject noun موسى "Moses" is for a stylistic reason: to achieve assonance, since the macro text is characterized by the rhythmic effect through the long vowel /-a/ (ى) at the end of ayah-final words. However, the placement of the prepositional phrase في نفسِهِ "within himself" is for the pragmatic function of focus and saliency.

> Example 4:
> جَعَلوا للهِ شُركاءَ الجنَّ (الأنعام 100) – They have attributed to God partners – the jinn.

This is a marked (unusual) word order with three objects. The main verb is جَعَلوا "they 'the polytheists'" attributed, whose first direct object is الجنَّ "the jinn"; its second direct object is شُركاءَ "partners"; and its third object is للهِ "to God". However, the first direct object الجنَّ is not placed next to the prepositional phrase للهِ "to God". This stylistic pattern is employed for a dogmatic performative intent (communicative purpose). The text producer has avoided the placement of الجنَّ next to the prepositional phrase (the third direct object) للهِ to achieve the illocutionary force of glorification to الله "God" because, theologically, الجن are of lower status than God and are created by Him. Therefore, a lexical re-shuffle in word order is required to preserve the Qur'anic notion of monotheism and de-anthropomorphism التنزيه. The unmarked (usual) word order is جَعَلوا الجنَّ شُركاءَ للهِ وخَلَقهُم, where the third object للهِ "to God" appears at the end of the sentence. Thus, focus (saliency), which has a high communicative value, has been given to الجنَّ, while الله has appeared with zero focus. The same applies to Q37:126.

2. Foregrounding: Stylistically, foregrounding is a linguistic device. However, grammatically, foregrounding is concerned with word order. It is a marked (unusual) word order in Arabic because a word or an expression is moved from its usual position and placed at the beginning of the sentence for the perlocutionary effect of saliency (focus). Thus, foregrounding is "prominence that is motivated" (Halliday 1971:339). In terms of discourse semantics and discourse pragmatics, foregrounding represents a discursive structure; a sentence that involves foregrounding entails an ideological connotative meaning. However, in Arabic, foregrounding can also be employed to maintain the rhythmic effects of assonance; it is a stylistic mechanism, as illustrated through the following examples that demonstrate stylistic literalness. The TTs are based on Saheeh International (1997:167, 176, 462, 485):

> الموتى يبعَثُهُم اللهُ (الأنعام 36) – The dead, God will resurrect them
> نوحاً هدينا من قبلُ (الأنعام 84) – Noah, We guided before
> النارُ وعَدَها اللهُ الذين كفروا (الحج 72) – It is the fire which God has promised those who disbelieve.
> للهِ مُلكُ السماواتِ والأرضِ والى اللهِ المصيرُ (النور 42) – To Allah belongs the dominion of the heavens and the earth, and to Allah is the return.

Stylistic literalness in Qur'an translation   139

In the above examples, foregrounding is represented by the plural noun الموتى "the dead", نوحاً "Noah", النارُ "the fire", لله "to Allah", and الى اللهِ "to Allah", which have been made salient by their initial positions. The above examples are marked (unusual) word orders. Their unmarked (expected, usual) word orders are

يبعثُ اللهُ الموتى
هدينا نوحاً من قبلُ
وعدَ اللهُ الذين كفروا النار
مُلكُ السماواتِ والأرض للهِ/المصيرُ الى اللهِ

The foregrounded elements include (i) the direct object, as in القمرَ "the moon" and الأرضَ "the Earth" in Q36:39 and Q79:30 respectively; (ii) المبتدأ, as in السارقُ "the male thief" and الزانية "the unmarried woman found guilty of sexual intercourse" in Q5:38 and Q24:2 respectively; and (iii) the prepositional phrase, as in بالنجم "by the stars" in Q16:16.

3. The absolute object: This is also a source of stylistic literalness, as in

إنَّهُم يكيدونَ كيداً. وأكيدُ كيداً. (الطارق 15–16)

Stylistic literalness has been adopted by most Qur'an translators:
Lo! they plot a plot (against thee, O Muhammad)
And I plot a plot (against them) (Pickthall 1930:no page).
As for them, they are but plotting a scheme, And I am planning a scheme (Ali 1934:no page).
They are devising guile, and I am devising guile (Arberry 1955:275).
Behold, they [who refuse to accept it] devise many a false argument [to disprove its truth]; but I shall bring all their scheming to nought (Asad 1980:1276).
Indeed, they are planning. But I am planning a plan (Saheeh International 1997:878).

However, a TT which observes cohesion can provide the following TT:

They plot and scheme, but so do I (Abdel Haleem 2005:417).

where verbal substitution is provided through the replacement of the verb (to plan) with the verb (do).

Other examples based on Saheeh International (1997:586, 830, 831, 884):

Remember Allah with much remembrance – (الأحزاب 41) اذكروا اللهَ ذِكراً كثيراً
Extract you extraction – (18 نوح) يُخرِجُكُم إخراجاً
They conspired a conspiracy – (22 نوح) مكروا مكراً
You love wealth with immense love – (الفجر 20) تُحبُّونَ المالَ حُبّاً جمّاً

4. Verbal substitution: Substitution is the replacement of one item (a verb or a noun/noun phrase) by another to avoid repetition. English has verbal substitution through the verbal substitutes (do, be, have). However, Arabic does not have verbal substitution but prefers to reiterate (repeat) the main verb. Stylistic literalness takes place when the translator ignores the English stylistic/grammatical norm of verbal substitution and repeats the same Arabic

140 *Stylistic literalness in Qur'an translation*

verb in English, as in Q20:69 where the translator ignores verbal substitution and repeats the same verb صَنَعَ, which should be "what they have done":

الله يعلمُ وأنتم لا تعلمون (البقرة 216) – Allah knows, while you know not

And throw what is in your right hand; it will swallow up what they have crafted. What they have crafted is but the trick of a magician – وألقِ ما في يمينِك تَلقَف ما صنعوا إنَّما صنعوا كيدُ ساحر (طه 69)

The above TTs involve stylistic literalness due to the repetition of the verbs يعلمُ "know" and صَنَعُوا "crafted". However, to avoid stylistic literalness, the translator needs to observe verbal substitution:

Allah knows, while you do not.
    And throw what is in your right hand; it will swallow up what they have crafted. What they have done is but the trick of a magician.

For more details on verbal substitution, see Chapter 5, Section 5.6.1.1.

5. The detached pronoun ضمير الفصل: The detached pronoun occurs in Arabic as an affirmation mechanism to the subject noun. However, English does not have this stylistic feature and the TT does not need to have an extra pronoun, which does not provide the TT with affirmation, as in the following examples:

إنَّ ربَّكَ هو أعلمُ بالمعتدين (الأنعام 119)
Thy Lord, He is Best Aware of the transgressors, Q6:119 (Pickthall 1930:no page).
Indeed, your Lord – He is most knowing of the transgressors, Q6:119 (Saheeh International 1997:183).

إنَّ ربَّكَ هو الخلاّقُ العليم (الحجر 86)
Thy Lord! He is the All-Wise Creator, Q15:86 (Pickthall 1930:no page).
Surely thy Lord, He is the All-creator, the All-knowing, Q15:86 (Arberry 1955:115).
Indeed, your Lord – He is the knowing creator, Q15:86 (Saheeh International 1997:151).

إنَّ ربَّكَ لهو العزيزُ الرحيم (الشعراء 9، 68، 104، 122، 140، 175، 191)
Thy Lord! He is indeed the Mighty, the Merciful, Q26:9, 68, 104, 122, 140, 175, 191 (Pickthall 1930:no page).
Surely thy Lord, He is the All-mighty, the All-compassionate, Q26:9, 68, 104, 122, 140, 175, 191 (Arberry 1955:163).
And verily, thy Lord is He, the Exalted in Might, Most Merciful, Q26:9, 68, 104, 122, 140, 175, 191 (Ali 1934:no page).
Verily, thy Sustainer – He alone – is almighty, a dispenser of grace!, Q26:9, 68, 104, 122, 140, 175, 191 (Asad 1980:765).
Your Lord – He is the exalted in might, the merciful, Q26:9, 68, 104, 122, 140, 175, 191 (Saheeh International 1997:502).

Throughout the above TTs, stylistic literalness of the Arabic detached pronoun is represented by either the addition of the dash (–) after the subject noun followed by the pronoun

Stylistic literalness in Qur'an translation 141

"He" + "is the" or the repetition of the ST detached pronoun "He". Below are samples of translations without stylistic literalness:

> Thy Lord knows very well the transgressors, Q6:119 (Arberry 1955:62).
> Your Lord knows best who oversteps the limit, Q6:119 (Abdel Haleem 2005:89).
> Indeed, your creator knows best the transgressors, Q6:119 (Ahmad 2010:185).
> For verily it is thy Lord who is the Master-Creator, knowing all things, Q15:86 (Ali 1934:no page).
> Verily, thy Sustainer is the all-knowing Creator of all things! Q15:86 (Asad 1980: 536).
> Your Lord is the all-knowing creator, Q15:86 (Abdel Haleem 2005:164).
> Indeed, your creator is the all-knowing creator, Q15:86 (Ahmad 2010:344).
> Your Lord alone is the almighty, the merciful, Q26:6, 68, 104, 122, 140, 175, 191 (Abdel Haleem 2005:232).
> Indeed, your creator is all-mighty, the most merciful, Q26:6, 68, 104, 122, 140, 175, 191 (Ahmad 2010:484).

6. Arabic-specific stylistic structure: There are three Arabic stylistic structures which lead to stylistic literalness in English:

(i) third-person masculine singular pronoun هو "he" + relative pronoun الذي "who" + main verb, as in

> It is He who made for you the night to rest therein and the day – هو الذي جَعَلَ لكم الليلَ لتسكنُوا فيه والنهارَ مُبصِرا (يونس 67)
> It is He who begins creation; then He repeats it – (27 هو الذي يبدأ الخلقَ ثُمَّ يُعيدُهُ (الروم

where stylistic literal translation is achieved through the TL cleft sentence stylistic structure "It is He who" + main verb . . . .

(ii) third-person masculine singular pronoun هو "he" + noun الله "God" + relative pronoun الذي "who" + no-main-verb nominal sentence, as in

> He is God; there is no god but He – (22 هو اللهُ الذي لا إلهَ إلاَّ هُو (الحشر

where the third-person pronoun هو is a cataphoric reference because it has occurred before its antecedent noun الله. Stylistic literalness is achieved through adherence to the ST stylistic word order.

(iii) noun "Allahu" "God" or cataphoric pronoun هو "he" + relative pronoun + main verb, as in

> It is Allah who sent down the Book in truth. – (الشورى 17) اللهُ الذي أنزلَ الكتابَ بالحق
> It is He who forms you . . . It is He who had sent down to you the Book – هو الذي يُصوِّرُكُم . . . هو الذي أنزلَ عليكَ الكتابَ (آل عمران 6–7)

where the above ST-specific stylistic structure are translated literally through the TL cleft sentence stylistic structure (It is He who . . .).

142 *Stylistic literalness in Qur'an translation*

3.5 Translator training and translation practice

This section combines theory and practice and prepares students for the translation industry. These exercises aim to put theory into practice and provide practical translation training exercises with a solution to each question. The discussion and analysis aim to provide students with what has taken place during the translation process and guide them to achieve a successful translation of sensitive texts. The exercises provide valuable insight into translations which adopt stylistic literalness, typifying the structural equivalence with the ST, as well as gloss and formal equivalence translation approaches, concerned with equivalence of style – comparing these approaches with translations which adopt transposition, dynamic equivalence, and natural translation approaches, which allow for the shifting of ST word order, aim for minimizing the foreignness of the TT and the complete stylistic naturalness of the TT based on the TL grammatical norms.

1 Compare the ST and the TT in terms of textual and discourse features and provide a translation commentary based on the TT stylistic literalness:

أُولَئِكَ عِند اللّه هُم الكَاذبون (النور 13)

The above ST is a marked (unusual) word order because the prepositional phrase عندَ الله is moved from its position at the end of the sentence and placed after the subject demonstrative pronoun أُولَئِك "those". The source of stylistic literalness is the rhetorical feature of hyperbaton represented by the prepositional phrase عند الله "in the sight of God", whose original position is at the end of the sentence: أُولَئِكَ هُم الكَاذبونَ عند الله. We have encountered the following TTs with stylistic literalness, and which employ the gloss translation approach, where the translator attempts to reproduce the ST form and content as literally and meaningfully as possible:

> Such men, **in the sight of Allah**, (stand forth) themselves as liars! (Ali 1934:no page).
> It is those [accusers] who, **in the sight of God**, are liars indeed! (Asad 1980:733).
> It is they, **in the sight of Allah**, who are the liars (Saheeh International 1997:479).

In contrast, let us consider the following TTs which have adopted the transposition (shift) and dynamic equivalence translation approaches, and abandoned ST hyperbaton:

> They verily are liars in the sight of Allah (Pickthall 1930:no page).
> In God´s sight they are the liars (Arberry 1955:155).
> They are the liars in God's eyes (Abdel Haleem 2005:221).

2 Compare the ST and the TT in terms of textual and discourse features and provide a translation commentary based on the TT stylistic literalness:

. . . ولا يُشركْ بعبادةِ ربِّه أَحَدا (الكهف 110)

This is a marked (unusual, unexpected) word order and involves hyperbaton through the occurrence of the object noun أَحَداً at the end of the sentence, when it should have occurred after the verb يُشرك "associate". The unmarked (ordinary) word order that does not involve hyperbaton is ولا يُشركُ أَحَداً بعبادةِ ربِّه. Among the TTs which have maintained ST hyperbaton and provided stylistically literal translations are

Stylistic literalness in Qur'an translation 143

not associate with his Lord's service **anyone** (Arberry 1955:133).
and not associate in the worship of his Lord **anyone** (Saheeh International 1997:407).

Other TTs have ignored the ST hyperbaton and provided a natural TT style, as in

make **none** sharer of the worship due unto his Lord (Pickthall 1930:no page).
in the worship of his Lord, admit **no one** as partner (Ali 1934:no page).
and let him not ascribe unto **anyone** or anything a share in the worship due to his Sustainer! (Asad 1980:627).
and give no one a share in the worship due to his Lord (Abdel Haleem 2005:190).

3 Compare the ST and the TT in terms of textual and discourse features and provide a
   translation commentary based on the TT stylistic literalness:

لا جَرَمَ أَنَّهُم في الآخِرَةِ هُم الخاسِرون (النحل 109)

Stylistically, the ST is a marked (unusual) word order because it involves the rhetorical device of hyperbaton through the active participle noun الخاسِرون "the losers", which has been taken from its normal position after the subject هُم (they) and is placed at the end of the sentence: لا جَرَمَ أَنَّهُم الخاسِرون في الآخِرَة. The following translations have maintained the same ST style and word order – stylistic literalness – and applied the gloss and formal equivalence translation approaches that are concerned with equivalence with the ST style:

Assuredly in the Hereafter they are **the losers** (Pickthall 1930:no page).
Without doubt, in the Hereafter they will **perish** (Ali 1934:no page).
Without a doubt, in the world to come they will be **the losers** (Arberry 1955:121).
Truly it is they, they who in the life to come shall be **the losers**! (Asad 1980:567).
Assuredly, it is they, in the hereafter, who will be the **losers** (Saheeh International 1997:369).

Let us consider the following translation, which has adopted the transposition (shift) and dynamic equivalence translation approaches, and abandoned ST hyperbaton. The following TTs aim to minimize the foreignness of the TT and to achieve complete stylistic naturalness of the TT based on the TL grammatical norms:

There is no doubt that they will be the **losers** in the hereafter (Abdel Haleem 2005:173).
No doubt, they will be the **losers** in the hereafter (Ahmad 2010:361).

It is worthwhile to note that the translator needs to maintain the TT grammatical norms even when the ST involves hyperbaton, as in in: حَضَرَ يعقوبَ الموتُ البقرة 133 "Death approached Jacob", where hyperbaton is introduced by the object noun يعقوبَ which has been taken out of its ordinary position after the verb, and is placed before the subject الموتُ. This is a marked (unusual) word order whose unmarked (usual) word order is حَضَرَ الموتُ يعقوبَ. Due to TT grammatical requirement, we need to provide a translation based on the unmarked word order: "Death approached Jacob", Q2:133.

4 Compare the ST and the TT in terms of textual and discourse features and provide a
   translation commentary based on the TT stylistic literalness:

واللهُ جَعَلَ لكُم مِمّا خَلَقَ ظِلالًا (النحل 81)

144 *Stylistic literalness in Qur'an translation*

The ST involves the rhetorical device of hyperbaton through the plural noun ظِلَالَ "shadows", which is placed at the end of the sentence while its expected position is after the prepositional phrase لكم "for you": وَاللهُ جَعَلَ لكم ظِلالاً ممَّا خَلَقَ. Having adopted the gloss and formal equivalence translation approaches, the following TTs have favored stylistic literalness, kept the ST hyperbaton, and have produced equivalence with the ST style:

> Allah hath given you, of that which He hath created, **shelter from the sun** (Pickthall 1930:no page).
> It is Allah Who made out of the things He created, some things to give you **shade** (Ali 1934:no page).
> And among the many objects of His creation,95 God has appointed for you [various] **means of protection** (Asad 1980:559).
> And Allah has made for you, from that which He created, **shadows** (Saheeh International 1997:365).
> Among the creations of Allah are **shades** (Ahmad 2010:357).

Also, the TT by Saheeh International has translated the plural noun ظِلالاً as "shadows" literally and out of context, while its accurate context-based meaning is "shade". However, Pickthall and Asad have provided exegetical (paraphrastic) translation for the noun ظِلالا. For more stylistic literalness, Ahmad has kept the ST plural noun ظِلالا as plural in English, although it violates TT grammatical norms.

To follow are the translations which have adopted the transposition (shift) and dynamic equivalence translation approaches and abandoned ST hyperbaton. The following TTs attempt to minimize the foreignness of the TT and achieve complete stylistic naturalness of the TT based on the TL grammatical norms:

> It is God who has appointed for you **coverings** of the things He created (Arberry 1955:120).
> It is God who has given you **shade** from what He has created (Abdel Haleem 2005:171).

5   Compare the ST and the TT in terms of textual and discourse features and provide a translation commentary based on the TT stylistic literalness:

إنَّ الذين أجرموا كانوا من الذين آمنوا **يضحكون** . . . فاليومَ الذينَ آمنوا من الكُفّار **يضحكون** (المطففين 29، 34)

The above ST involves the repetition of the same masculine plural verb يضحكون "'they' laugh". In other words, the previous STs involve one source of stylistic literalness: hyperbaton. The two ST sentences represent a marked (unexpected) word order; they involve hyperbaton where the main verb يضحكون is moved from its normal position and placed at the end of the sentence. The unmarked (expected, normal) word order is below:

إنَّ الذين أجرموا كانوا **يضحكون** من الذينَ آمنوا . . . فاليومَ الذينَ آمنوا **يضحكون** من الكُفّار

However, the above stylistic structure (the unmarked word order) does not involve hyperbaton and has led to the loss of the stylistic (rhetorical) feature of assonance (السجع) achieved

Stylistic literalness in Qur'an translation 145

through the word-final sound ون, which is the major phonetically based stylistic feature of Q83. Let us consider the following TTs:

> The guilty used to **laugh** at those who believed . . . This day it is those who believe who have the **laugh** of disbelievers (Pickthall 1930:no page).
> Those in sin used to **laugh** at those who believed . . . But on this Day the Believers will **laugh** at the Unbelievers (Ali 1934:no page).
> Behold, the sinners were **laughing** at the believers . . . So today the believers are **laughing** at the unbelievers (Arberry 1955:273).
> BEHOLD, those who have abandoned themselves to sin are wont to **laugh** at such as have attained to faith . . . But on the Day [of Judgment], they who had attained to faith will [be able to] **laugh** at the [erstwhile] deniers of the truth (Asad 1980:1269).
> Indeed, those who committed crimes used to **laugh** at those who believed . . . So today those who believed are **laughing** at the disbelievers (Saheeh International 1997:872).
> The wicked used to **laugh** at the believers . . . So today the believers are **laughing** at the disbelievers (Abdel Haleem 2005:414).

Based on the above TTs, we can safely argue that the TT grammatical norms have not allowed stylistic literalness where the main verb "laugh" must occur after the subject and before its object. Thus, the transposition (shift) and natural translation approaches have been adopted. These are grammar-based translation approaches that involve a change in the grammar from the SL to TL. Although the ST involves the repetition of the same verb يضحكون this does not constitute a source of stylistic literalness in the TT where verbal substitution can be employed.

6   Compare the ST and the TT in terms of textual and discourse features and provide a translation commentary based on the TT stylistic literalness:

وفي ذلكم بلاءٌ من ربّكم عظيم (البقرة 49)

The above ST involves the stylistic feature of hyperbaton represented by the adjective عظيم "great, tremendous", which has been taken from its original position after the noun بلاءٌ and is placed at the end of the sentence. This is regarded as a marked word order because the adjective عظيم "great" has been moved from its normal position. However, as a grammatical requirement by English, the adjective must occur before the noun it modifies. Let us consider the following TTs, which do not employ stylistic literalness. The following TTs have adopted transposition, dynamic equivalence, and natural translation approaches, allowing for the shifting of ST word order and aiming to minimize the foreignness of the TT, as well as to achieve complete stylistic naturalness of the TT based on the TL grammatical norms.

> That was a **tremendous** trial from your Lord (Pickthall 1930:no page).
> Therein was a **tremendous** trial from your Lord (Ali 1934:no page).
> In that was a **grievous** trial from your Lord (Arberry 1955:6).
> Which was an **awesome** trial from your Sustainer (Asad 1980:36).
> And in that was a **great** trial from your Lord, Q2:49 (Saheeh International 1997:9).
> That was a **great** trial from your Lord (Abdel Haleem 2005:8).

146 *Stylistic literalness in Qur'an translation*

7 Compare the ST and the TT in terms of textual and discourse features and provide a translation commentary based on the TT stylistic literalness:

إنّهُم عن ربِّهم يومئذٍ لمحجوبون (المطففين 15)

The TTs that preserve the ST hyperbaton and provided marked (unusual) word order are

> Verily, from (the Light of) their Lord, that Day, will they **be veiled** (Ali 1934:no page).
> Verily, from [the grace of] their Sustainer shall they on that Day **be debarred** (Asad 1980:1267).
> Indeed, from their Lord, that day, they will be **partitioned** (Saheeh International 1997:871).

In these translations, both the ST and the TTs stylistically represent marked (unusual) word orders. The TTs involve stylistic literalness because the ST involves hyperbaton where the plural passive participle اسم المفعول محجوبون "be partitioned" is placed at the end of the sentence. The ST unmarked (usual) word order is إنّهُم لمحجوبون عن ربّهم يومئذٍ "Indeed, they will be partitioned from their Lord that day". The latter stylistic structure of both the ST and the TT does not involve hyperbaton and has led to the loss of the rhetorical feature of assonance and the absence of stylistic literalness. Thus, the above TTs have adopted transposition, dynamic equivalence, and natural translation approaches, which allow for the shifting of ST word order, aim to minimize the foreignness of the TT as well as to achieve complete stylistic naturalness of the TT based on the TL grammatical norms.

However, other TTs have abandoned stylistic literalness and adopted transposition, dynamic equivalence, and natural translation approaches:

> But surely on that day they will **be covered** from (the mercy of) their Lord (Pickthall 1930:no page).
> Indeed; but upon that day they shall **be veiled** from their Lord Arberry 1955:273).
> On that day they will **be screened off** from their Lord (Abdel Haleem 2005:413).
> They (the disbelievers) will, indeed, **be kept behind a barrier to prevent them from seeing their Creator** that day (Ahmad 2010:818).

8 Homework assignment: The following examples involve verbal substitution. You are told about the verbal substitution for each sentence. Compare each ST with various TTs in terms of textual and discourse features and provide a translation commentary based on the TT stylistic literalness:

(i) (بل كذّبوا بالساعة وأعتدنا لِمَن كذَّبَ بالساعة سعيرا (الفرقان 11

where the verb كذَّبَ "to deny" is repeated in Q25:11 but in English it should be substituted by the verb (to do).

(ii) (ربنا هاؤلاء الذين أغوينا أغويناهُم كما غوينا (القصص 63

where the verb أغوى/غَوى "to deviate" is repeated in Q28:63 but in English it should be substituted by the verb "to do".

Stylistic literalness in Qur'an translation 147

(iii) (إِن تَدعُوهُم لا يسمعُوا دُعاءَكُم ولو سَمِعُوا ما استجابُوا لَكُم (فاطر 14

where the verb يسمعُ "to hear" is reiterated while in English it should be substituted by the auxiliary verb "could".

(iv) (من تزكَّى فإِنَّما يتزكَّى لنفسِهِ (فاطر 18

where the verb يَتزكَّى "to purify" is reiterated while in English it should be substituted by the auxiliary verb "do".

9 Homework assignment: The following example involves verbal substitution and the deletion of the absolute object المفعول المطلق كيداً in order to avoid stylistic literalness. You are told about the verbal substitution for each sentence. Compare each ST with various TTs in terms of textual and discourse features and provide a translation commentary based on the TT stylistic literalness:

إِنَّهُم يكيدونَ كيداً وأَكيدُ كيدا (الطارق 15–16)

where the verb أَكيدُ + the absolute object كيداً are repeated in Arabic but they are substituted by the verb (to do) in English. In order to avoid stylistic literalness, the translation process should involve two steps: (i) verbal substitution through the verb (to do), and (ii) the deletion of the ST absolute object.

10 Homework assignment and in-class discussion: Compare different translations of the following STs and provide a translation commentary for each ST based on the different translation processes and the cohesion systems of both the ST and the TTs. The following STs involve either verbal or nominal substitution. The TT that avoids the TL cohesion system is providing stylistic literalness. Discuss in detail.

(i) (فإِن آمنوا بمِثلِ ما آمنتُم بهِ فقد اهتَدَوا (البقرة 137
(ii) (هوَ ربُّنا وربُّكُم ولنا أعمالُنا ولكُم أعمالُكُم (البقرة 139

ولَئن أَتيتَ الذينَ أُوتُوا الكتابَ بكُلِّ آيةٍ ما تَبِعُوا قِبلَتَكَ وما أنتَ بتابِعٍ قِبلَتَهُم وما بعضُهُم بتابِعٍ قِبلَةَ بعضٍ (البقرة 145)

11 Homework assignment: The following ST constitutes a source of stylistic literalness. Discuss the ST stylistic structure, compare the ST with various TTs in terms of the TL cleft sentence stylistic structure, and provide a translation commentary based on the TT stylistic literalness:

هو الذي أنزلَ من السماء ماءً (الأنعام 99)

12 Homework assignment: The following ST constitutes a source of stylistic literalness. Provide sentence demarcation, discuss the ST stylistic structure, compare the ST with various TTs, and provide a translation commentary based on TT stylistic literalness:

إِذ قالَ يوسُفُ لأبيهِ يا أبتِ إني رأيتُ أَحَدَ عَشَرَ كوكباً والشمسَ والقمَرَ رأيتُهُم لي ساجدين (يوسف 4)

148 *Stylistic literalness in Qur'an translation*

13 Homework assignment: Compare different translations for the following text and provide a translation quality assessment. Specify the sentence grammatical structure (i.e., passive or active), the subject, the object or objects, and the meaning of the verb:

أحضِرَت الأنفسُ الشُّحَّ (النساء 128)

14 Faced with ST-based stylistic idiosyncrasies, Qur'an translators struggle between the stylistic literalness translation approach and other approaches like communicative, dynamic equivalence or domestication translation approaches. Provide a translation commentary based on different Qur'an translations of Q12:103 and 108. Discuss the major Qur'an-specific stylistic features that have led to the translation problems involved:

وما أكثرُ الناس ولو حرصتَ بمؤمنين (يوسف 103)
قُل هذهِ سبيلي أدعوا إلى اللهِ على بصيرةٍ أنا ومن اتبعني (يوسف 108)

4 Translation beyond the full-stop

4.1 Introduction

The current chapter accounts for the translation of punctuation as a stylistic idiosyncrasy of English, and how punctuation plays a major role in ST and TT textual continuity and coherence. This chapter is concerned with the flow of information intra-sententially (within the same sentence) and inter-sententially (among different sentences) by looking at the linguistic features of the text like text cohesion and texture. Thus, it provides insight into the textual geography of the ST and the TT through investigating the sequence of sentences, their word order re-shuffle, and rearranging them according to a coherent and cohesive TL sentence/paragraph structure with the main idea reproduced in a fresh form with equivalent effect. The aim is to rid the TT of the ST clumsiness and structural complexity in order to enhance clarity and meaning. The examples discussed provide valuable insight into how the textual geography of Arabic is distinct from that of English.

4.2 Punctuation and translation

Any written text such as a sentence, a paragraph, or a whole text should be correctly punctuated. Wrong punctuation leads to ambiguity and incorrect translation. Punctuation is semantically oriented; two differently punctuated sentences have different meanings, as "No, don't stop!", meaning "Do not stop and you should continue moving/driving/walking/doing something", and "No! Don't! Stop!", meaning "Stop now. Do not continue moving/driving/walking/doing something and you should stop immediately".

The discussion and examples provide an insight into ST sentence demarcation; to create the sentence boundaries, underline the ST conjunction, and classify whether conjunctions are inter-sentential or intra-sentential. Sentence delineation is mainly concerned with Arabic texts because Arabic is a polysyndetic language, while English is asyndetic. Thus, English does not need as many conjunctions as Arabic does. However, English punctuation marks like the full-stop, comma, colon, semi-colon, and the dash are all semantically oriented; they are meaningful and should be translated to Arabic. However, Arabic renders the English punctuation marks to conjunctions. This is attributed to the fact that punctuation marks are alien to Arabic, are stylistically misused, and are English-specific.

Arabic and English depict two distinct linguistic and textual systems. Thus, different SL and TL punctuation and cohesive systems designate distinct stylistic preferences in the two languages and may reflect different illocutionary force and different text producer's performative intent. Thus, different SL and TL punctuation and cohesive systems designate distinct stylistic preferences in the two languages.

DOI: 10.4324/9781003268956-5

150 *Translation beyond the full-stop*

Taking punctuation into consideration, it is worthwhile to keep in mind the following observations on Arabic translation:

1   Check whether you need a full-stop at the end of the sentence you are translating. Since Arabic and English are linguistically different, the punctuation system of the SL and the TL is different, too. Therefore, you may need to join two or more English sentences into one Arabic sentence because you must follow the Arabic stylistic norms. However, when you translate into English, you need to drop the Arabic conjunctions. In other words, apply inter-sentential Arabic cohesive devices. The first Arabic sentence in any text does not need a conjunction. Arabic needs a conjunction at the beginning of the second sentence onwards. You also need to apply inter-paragraph Arabic cohesive devices.
2   Be careful with the style of journalistic English text. Let us consider the following newspaper report: "The suspect was arrested in his London home yesterday evening", the police said.

Notice that the phrase "the police said" is placed at the end of the sentence. If we translate this to Arabic, the journalistic stylistic structure needs to place "the police said" at the beginning of the sentence. Thus, we allow adjustment of the ST form of the message in order to satisfy the requirements of Arabic stylistic norms:

ومن الجديرُ بالذكر أنَّ الشرطة ذكرت بأنَّه تم اعتقال المشتبه به في منزله بلندن يوم أمس.

where we have used the journalistic conjunction ومن الجديرُ بالذكر + أنَّ, which is not employed in the ST. Also, we have started from the end of the ST and put the reported speech at the end of the TT.

3   Postpone translating the headlines and begin first with the text: In the translation of journalistic texts, we must leave the news headline until we have finished the translation of the whole news report. The details in the news report will provide valuable information about the intended meaning of the headline. Let us consider the following headlines, which are difficult to translate before we read the full newspaper report:

"Hiccup Not Headache": This is a metaphorical newspaper headline. The newspaper report talks about Britain's inflation and its effect on the value of the Sterling Pound. The report then explains that this problem is not very serious and the economy will recover soon. Thus, the present economic problem is like a "hiccup" which only lasts for a short period of time and is not serious: أزمة بسيطة, meaning "a simple crisis" or to keep the metaphorical style, we say غمامة زائلة عابرة meaning "an ephemeral cloud".

"The House is Not Your Home" has appeared as a newspaper headline about MPs "Members of Parliament" in the British House of Commons who stay late in their offices forgetting about their wives and family duties. The report reminds MPs that the "House (of Commons) is not your family home". MPs are told to go home once they have finished their office hours: مجلس العُموم ليس منزلك, where we have unlocked the ambiguous ST headline.

Similarly, "A Day for Day" is a newspaper headline about Mr Day, who works as a BBC radio and TV program presenter. The report appears one day before Mr Day retires. The report tells us that Mr Day has got one "day" left before he retires tomorrow: يومٌ واحدٌ للسيد دَي, where ambiguity is removed in the TT.

Translation beyond the full-stop   151

4.3   Translation of punctuation

This is an account of translation as text where the full-stop separating individual ST sentences in a text are not taken into account, and the translation strategy is to go beyond the ST full-stop and link the following sentence with the preceding one in order to achieve a cohesive TL statement. Punctuation is a stylistic idiosyncrasy of English and is a translation problem which requires a subtle translation strategy in Arabic-English-Arabic translation. As linguistically incongruent languages, Arabic and English employ the full-stop differently. However, English employs more punctuation marks than Arabic because punctuation is not a stylistic idiosyncrasy of Arabic. On the stylistic and cohesion levels, we can make the following observations:

1   The full-stop occurs more in English than in Arabic,
2   Arabic is generally polysyndetic through the employment of the conjunctive particle و "and",
3   English is asyndetic through the employment of the full-stop separating individual sentences, and
4   In the journalistic genre, Arabic employs a punctuation distinct from that employed in English journalism.

4.4   Conjunctions in Arabic and English

Conjunctions are cohesive devices that occur at the beginning of the sentence or at the beginning of a new paragraph. However, stylistically, some Arabic conjunctions do not occur in English. These should be deleted in the translation from Arabic to English. Also, stylistically, English does not tend to employ certain conjunctions at the beginning of the sentence or the paragraph, such as "and, or, on his/her part, it is worth mentioning", whereas Arabic employs these conjunctions at both the beginning of the sentence and the paragraph. The major cohesive devices are:

1. Additive conjunctions: These are و "and", أو "or", إضافة الى ذلك/علاوة على ذلك "moreover, besides", جديرٌ بالذكر من جانبه/من جهته "on his/her part", "it is worth mentioning", وبطبيعة الحال من ناحية ثانية/من جهة أخرى/على صعيد آخر "naturally, actually", أمّا . . . أو "on the other hand", كما أنَّ/أيضاً/كذلك للسبب نفسه "also", "by the same token", لا . . . و لا "either . . . or", مثلاً/على سبيل المثال "neither . . . nor", بعبارة "for instance", and أخرى/وبتعبير آخر "in other words".

The most recurrent additive conjunction in Qur'anic Arabic is أو "and", which joins between the following sentence elements:

(i)   The additive conjunction و links between nouns, as in السماواتِ والأرض والجبال "the heavens and the earth and the mountains" (Q33:72).
(ii)   The additive conjunction و links between pronouns, as in إنكَ ميّتٌ وإنّهُم ميّتون "Indeed, you are to die, and indeed, they are to die" (Q39:30) and سخَّرَ الشمسَ والقمرَ "He subjected the sun and the moon" (Q36:78).
(iii) The additive conjunction و links between relative pronouns, as in من كان يُريدُ حرثَ الآخرةِ نَزد له في حرثِهِ ومن كان يُريدُ حرثَ الدنيا نُؤتِهِ منها "Whoever desires the reward of the hereafter – We increase for him in his reward. Whoever desires the benefits of this world – We give him thereof" (Q42:20).

152 *Translation beyond the full-stop*

(iv)   The additive conjunction و links between verbs, as in يُكوِّر الليلَ على النهار ويُكوِّر النهارَ
على الليل وسَخَّرَ الشمس والقمرَ "He wraps the night over the day and wraps the day over
the night and has subjected the sun and the moon" (Q39:5); وضَرَبَ لنا مثلاً ونَسِيَ خَلْقَهُ
"And he presented for Us an example and forgot his own creation" (Q36:78).

(v)   The additive conjunction و links between adjectives, as in الصابرينَ والصَّادقينَ والقانتينَ
والمُنفقينَ والمُستغفرينَ "The patient, the true, the obedient, those who spend in the way
of God, and those who seek forgiveness" (Q3:17).

(vi)   The additive conjunction و links between prepositional phrases, as in عليه توكلتُ وإليهِ
أنيب "Upon Him I have relied and to Him I return" (Q11:88).

(vii) The additive conjunction و links between nominalized nouns مصدر, as in قياماً وقُعُوداً
"standing and sitting" (Q4:103).

The conjunctive elements و "and", أو "or", and فَ "so" also express a relation of coordination. While Arabic abounds with the sentence-initial coordination conjunct و "and", written
English employs it in the middle of the sentence. The coordination relation through the
conjunctive و "and" appears between a pair of nouns, nominal groups, verbs, verbal groups,
clauses, adverbs, adverbial groups, prepositions, or prepositional groups. We also encounter the conjunctive element و before other conjuncts like ولمّا "and when" (Q43:30, 57, 63)
and ولو لا "and if" (Q43:33) occurring in sentence-initial position. It is worthwhile to point
out that the two together function as a single conjunctive element but taking into consideration that the second element is the major one; for instance, لمّا "when" and لو لا "if".

Qur'anic Arabic also employs double additive conjunctive elements, such as ما . . . و "not
. . . and", لا . . . و لا "neither . . . nor", أما . . . وأمَا "either . . . or", ما . . . وما "neither . . .
nor", and فَ . . . أمَا . . . "as for . . .".

ما يستوي الأعمى والبصير (فاطر 19)

<u>Not</u> equal are the blind <u>and</u> the seeing, Q35:19.

و لا الظُّلماتُ ولا النورُ ولا الظِّلُّ ولا الحَرورُ (فاطر 20–21)

<u>Nor</u> equal are the darkness and the light, <u>nor</u> are equal the shade and the heat, Q35:20–21.

لا الشمسُ ينبغي لها أن تُدركَ القمرَ ولا الليلُ سابقُ النهار (يس 40)

<u>It is not</u> possible for the sun to reach the moon, <u>nor</u> does the night overtake the day,
Q36:40.

ما أنزلنا على قومهِ من بعده من جُندٍ من السماء وما كُنَّا مُنزلين (يس 28)

And We <u>neither</u> sent down upon his people after him any soldiers from the heaven, <u>nor</u>
would We have done so, Q36:28.

ما علمناهُ الشعرَ وما ينبغي لهُ (يس 69)

We <u>neither</u> gave him (Muhammad) knowledge of poetry, <u>nor</u> is it befitting for him,
Q36:69.

Translation beyond the full-stop 153

لا يُقضى عليهم فيموتوا ولا يُخقَّفُ عنهم من عذابها (فاطر 36)

(Death) is <u>neither</u> decreed for them so they may die, <u>nor</u> will its fire torment be lightened, Q35:36.

The conjunctive element أو "or" expresses the relation of alternative, as in:

قالَ لبثتُ يوماً أو بعضَ يوم (البقرة 259)

He (the man) said: "I have remained a day <u>or</u> part of a day", Q2:259.

The other additive conjunctive elements are أما . . . ف "as for . . .", as in

ف أمّا اليتيمَ فلا تقهر وأمّا السائلَ فلا تنهر وأمّا بنعمة ربك فحدّث (الضحى 9–11)

So <u>as for</u> the orphan, do not oppress him, and <u>as for</u> the petitioner, do not repel him, but <u>as for</u> the favor of your Lord, report it, Q93:9–11.

The conditional conjunctive element إن "if" expresses an additive relation, as in

إن تمسسكم حسنة تسؤهم وإن تُصِبكم سيئةٌ يفرحوا بها وإن تصبروا وتتقوا لا يضُرُّكُم كيدُهُم شيئا (آل عمران 120)

If good touches you, it distresses them, and if harm strikes you, they rejoice at it. And if you are patient and fear God, their plot will not harm you at all, Q3:120.

The conditional conjunctive elements لَ . . . لو "if . . .", فَ . . . إذا "if . . .", and فَ . . . إن "if . . ." are also additive, as in

لو أنهم صبروا . . . لكانَ خيراً لهم (النساء 46، الحجرات 5)

If they had been patient . . . it would have been better for them, Q49:5, Q4:46.

ف إذا قضيتُم الصلاةَ فاذكروا اللهَ قياماً وقُعوداً (النساء 103)

When you have completed the prayer, remember God standing and sitting, Q4:103.

ف إن لم تفعلوا ولن تفعلوا فاتّقوا النارَ . . . (البقرة 24)

But <u>if</u> you do not – and you will never be able to – then fear the fire, Q2:24.

إن يمسسكَ اللهُ بضُرٍّ فلا كاشِفَ لهُ إلاَّ هُو وإن يُردكَ بخيرٍ فلا رادَّ لفضلهِ (يونس 107)

If God should touch you with adversity, there is no remover of it except Him; and if He intends for you good, then there is no repeller of His bounty, Q10:107.

The negative form of the additive relation is expressed in the Qur'an as ما/لا . . . ولا "neither . . . nor", as in

ما يستوي الأعمى والبصير ولا الظُّلمات ولا النور (فاطر 19–20)

Neither the blind nor the seeing are equal, and neither the darkness nor the light are equal, Q35:19–20.

154 *Translation beyond the full-stop*

ما يستوي الأحياءُ و لا الأمواتُ (فاطر 22)

Neither the living nor the dead are equal, Q35:22.

Let us also consider لا ... و لا "neither . . . nor", as in

و إن تُبتُم فلكُم رُؤوسُ أموالِكُم لا تظلِموْنَ ولا تُظلمون (البقرة 279)

If you repent, you may have your capital – thus, you do no wrong, nor are you wronged, Q2:279.

ف   لا يستطيعونَ توصيةً ولا إلى أهلِهم يرجِعُون (يس 50)

They will neither be able to give any instruction, nor to their people can they return, Q36:50.

Other examples of the comparative additive relation include Q2:171, 261, 264, 265, Q3:117, Q11:24, Q14:18, 26, Q18:45, Q29:41, Q57:20, Q59:16, and Q62:5.

2. Adversative conjunctions: An adversative relation means contrary to expectation (Halliday and Hasan 1976:250). These include لكن/بيد أنَّ/على نقيض ذلك "but, however, yet", في نفس "on the contrary, by contrast", مع ذلك/بالرغم من ذلك "nevertheless, in spite of this", في الحقيقة/في الواقع "although", رغمَ أنَّ/مع أنَّ "at the same time", الوقت/في الوقت نفسه "in fact, as a matter of fact", and على أية حال "anyhow, in any case". It is interesting to note that the conjunction ثمَّ which we have classified as a temporal conjunction in point (iv) below can also occur at times, though very rarely, as an adversative conjunction as in Q6:1–2. Let us consider the following examples:

وما ظلمونا ولكن كانوا أنفُسَهُم يظلمون (البقرة 57)

They <u>did not</u> wrong Us <u>but</u> they were wronging themselves, Q2:57.

و ما كان اللهُ ليظلِمَهُم ولكن كانوا أنفُسَهُم يظلمون (العنكبوت 40، الروم 9)

God <u>would</u> <u>not</u> have wronged them <u>but</u> it was they who were wronging themselves, Q29:40, Q30:9.

Thus, the conjunctive element لكن (but) expresses an adversative relation. Most frequently, however, لكن is preceded by the additive conjunctive element (wa – and), which does not affect the adversative relation.

The adversative conjunction element لكن (but) occurs with an initial negative element ما (no) or لا (no); thus, we have ما ... ولكن (not . . . but) or لا ... ولكن (not . . . but) as in

و ما ظلمناهُم ولكن ظلموا أنفُسَهم (هود 101)

We <u>did not</u> wrong them <u>but</u> they wronged themselves, Q11:101.

إنَّ اللهَ لا يظلِمُ الناسَ شيئاً ولكنَّ الناسَ أنفُسَهُم يظلمون (يونس 44)

God does not wrong people at all but it is people who are wronging themselves, Q10:44.

3. Causal conjunctions: These are لهذا "so, therefore", أن/لكي لا/لكي "so that, in order that", إذ/حيثُ/فَ "lest, in order not to", بسبب/جرّاء "because of", ب "because", إذن "thus, therefore", لهذا السبب/لهذا الغرض/نتيجة لذلك "for this reason, consequently", "because, since, for",

156 *Translation beyond the full-stop*

اذكروا ما فيه لعلّكُم تَتَّقُون (الأعراف 171)

Remember what is in it <u>so that</u> you may fear God, Q7:171.

It is worthwhile to note that the causal conjunction أنْ – "lest, in order not to" is wrongly translated as "because" in Q16:92 by Saheeh International (1997:366).

(فأغرقناهُم في اليمِّ بأنّهم كذّبوا بآياتنا (الأعراف 136 – We drowned them in the sea <u>because</u> they denied Our signs, Q7:136.

(بأنّهُم قومٌ لا يفقهون (الأنفال 65 – . . . <u>because</u> they are a people who do not understand, Q8:65.

4. Temporal conjunctions: These include ثُمَّ/ف/و/ومن ثُمَّ/بعد ذلك "then, next", بعد "after", في نفس الوقت/في الوقت نفسه "at the same time", في هذا الأثناء/في غُضُون ذلك "before", قبل "meanwhile, in the meantime", خلال "during", بينما/ما دامَ "while", في حينها "at that time", باختصار/خُلاصة الأمر/خُلاصة القول/ختاماً/وفي الختام "in conclusion, finally", أخيراً "finally", "to sum up, briefly" أولاً "first, firstly", ثانياً "second, secondly", ثالثاً "third, thirdly", مُنذُ "since", لمّا "when", إذا "when", متى ما/كلّما "whenever", من الآن فصاعداً "henceforth, from now on", لحد الآن "up to now", and سابقاً "previously".

Qur'anic Arabic temporal conjunction is realized through the cohesive devices ثُمَّ/بعدئذٍ/بعد "then", قبل/بعد "before/after", كلّما "whenever, every time", الآن "now", أن "before", and إذا/إذا "when", as in

<u>كلّما</u> نضجت جُلودُهُم بدّلناهم جُلُوداً غيرها (النساء 56)

<u>Every time</u> their skins are roasted through We will replace them with other skins, Q4:56.

<u>كلّما</u> دخلَ عليها زكريا المحرابَ وجدَ عندها رزقاً (آل عمران 37)

<u>Every time</u> Zachariah entered upon her in the prayer chamber, he found with her provision, Q3:37.

<u>الآنَ</u> وقد عصيتَ قبلُ وكنتَ من المُفسدين (يونس 91)

<u>Now</u>? And you had disobeyed before and were of the corrupters?, Q10:91.

من نُطفةٍ خلقهُ . . . <u>ثُمَّ</u> السبيلَ يسّرهُ <u>ثُمَّ</u> أماتهُ . . . <u>ثُمَّ</u> إذا شاءَ أنشرَهُ (عبس 19–22)

From a sperm-drop He (God) created him (man) . . . <u>Then</u> He eased the way for him . . . <u>Then</u> He causes his death . . . <u>Then</u> when He wills, He will resurrect him, Q80:19–22.

For more examples on ثُمَّ "then", see Q23:13–16, Q30:20, 25, 27, and Q40:67.

<u>إذا</u> الشمسُ كُوِّرَت و <u>إذا</u> النُجُومُ انكدرت و <u>إذا</u> الجبالُ سُيِّرت و <u>إذا</u> العشارُ عُطِّلَت (التكوير 1–4)

<u>When</u> the sun is wrapped up, and <u>when</u> the stars fell dispersing, and <u>when</u> the mountains are removed, and <u>when</u> full-term she-camels are neglected, Q81:1–4.

For more examples on إذا "when", see Q81:1–8.

The other temporal conjunctive element is أن "before" meaning قبل "before", as in

ولا تأكُلوها إسرافاً وبداراً <u>أن</u> يكبُروا (النساء 6)

And do not consume it wastefully and in haste <u>before</u> they grow up, Q4:6.

Translation beyond the full-stop 155

وبالتالي "thus", ولذا "therefore", وإلّا "otherwise", and وهكذا "thus". There is a limited number of causal conjunctions in Qur'anic Arabic. These include أن "lest, in order not to", من أجل هذا "because of that", بما "because of", لعلّ "so that", and the letter /f/, i.e., فَ "so, because", as in the following examples:

مِن أجلِ ذلكَ كتبنا على بني إسرائيلَ أنّهُ من قتلَ نفساً بغير نفسٍ . . . (المائدة 32)
Because of that, We (God) decreed upon the Children of Israel that whoever kills a soul unless for a soul . . ., Q5:32.

لن يتمنوهُ أبداً بما قدَّمت أيديهم (البقرة 95)
They will never wish for it <u>because of</u> what their hands have put forth, Q2:95.

فكيفَ إذا أصابتهم مُصيبة بما قدَّمت أيديهم (النساء 62)
So how will it be when disaster strikes them <u>because of</u> what their hands have put forth, Q4:62.

يُبيّنُ اللهُ لكم أنْ تَضِلّوا (النساء 176)
God Makes clear to you (His law) <u>lest</u> (<u>in order not to</u>) go astray, Q4:176.
(ذلكَ بما قدَّمت يداكَ 10 – 10 الحج) That is <u>because of</u> what your hands have put forth, Q22:10.

إنْ تُصيبهُم سيئة بما قدَّمت أيديهم إذا هم يقنطون (الروم 36)
<u>If</u> evil afflicts them for what their hands have put forth, they despair immediately, Q30:36.

The letter /f/ فَ "so, because" is a causal conjunction meaning (so, for this reason), which usually occurs sentence-initially, as in

فَعَقروا الناقة . . . فَأخَذَتهُم الرجفةُ . . . (الأعراف 77–78)
<u>So</u>, they hamstrung the she-camel . . . So the earthquake seized them . . ., Q7:77–78.

فَفَررتُ منكُم لمّا خِفتُكم . . . (الشعراء 21)
<u>So</u> I fled from you when I feared you, Q26:21.

The causal conjunction (fa) also means (therefore), as in

فلمّا نَسُوا ما ذُكِّروا بهِ فتحنا عليهم أبوابَ كُلّ شيءٍ . . . (الأنعام 44)
<u>Therefore</u>, when they forgot that by which they had been reminded, We opened to them the doors of everything . . ., Q6:44.

فحقَّ علينا قولُ ربّنا (الصافات 31)
<u>Therefore</u>, the decree of our Lord has come into effect upon us, Q37:31.

فإنّهُم يومئذٍ في العذابِ مُشتركون (الصافات 33)
<u>Therefore</u>, on that day, they will be sharing in the punishment, Q37:33.

. . . لعلَّكُم تتَّقون (البقرة 21، 183، الأنعام 153)
. . . <u>so that</u> you may fear God, Q2:21, 183, Q6:153.

Translation beyond the full-stop 157

4.5 Punctuation, texture, and translation

During any translation process, it is worthwhile to consider the following textual features:

1 For Halliday and Hasan (1976:9), the conjunctions (cohesive devices) أدوات الربط between sentences in the text stand out more clearly because they are the only source of texture. A text should be unified whose units – words and sentences – are connected together in a cohesive manner through cohesive devices – such as ولو أنَّ "although", ثُمَّ "then", و "and", لأن "because", قبْل "before" – that make the ST and the TT hang together and create unique texture and total unity.

2 We find variation in texture from one text type to another in both Arabic and English. Different conjunctions occur in different text types. Therefore, the translator must be aware of the fact that conjunctions are not employed haphazardly neither in the ST nor in the TT.

3 The translator needs to be aware of the distinction between the two types of texture: "tight and loose texture" (Halliday and Hasan 1976:295–297).

4 While Arabic favors tight (dense) texture, English favors loose texture. Therefore, in terms of texture, tight texture is a prototypical stylistic feature of Arabic. During the translation from Arabic into English, we must delete many Arabic conjunctions. However, in the translation from English into Arabic, we must employ several context-based conjunctions.

5 However, both languages favour loose texture in their paratext. The paratext represents the additional elements such as the titles, media headlines, sub-headlines, captions, headings, and footnotes. In terms of punctuation, the titles, media headlines, sub-headlines, the captions, and headings do not end with a full-stop; only footnotes do. These are considered as additional elements to the main body of the text (Hatim and Munday 2004:345). It is worthwhile to note that the Qur'an does not have any paratext, as in:

Headlines:

Hundreds of thousands march against racial injustice (*The Guardian*, 7 June 2020).
مئاتُ الآلاف في مسيرات احتجاجية مُناهِضة للظلم العنصري
شُعبة المُستلزمات الطبية تكشف مزايا الكمامة القماش (صحيفة الأهرام، 7 يونيو 2020)

Medical equipment unit unveils the features of the cloth mask.

Captions:

Peaceful protestors near Lafayette Park in Washington on Saturday (*The Guardian*, 7 June 2020).
مُتظاهرون سلميون قرب متنزه لافايت في واشنطن يوم السبت
الكمامة القماش

The cloth mask.

6 Stylistically in Arabic, the first sentence of any text type does not start with a conjunction at the beginning of the sentence. The first sentence of any Arabic text begins with a verb without a conjunction. Conjunctions in Arabic are employed within the first

158 *Translation beyond the full-stop*

sentence (inter-sententially) in any text type and at the beginning of every sentence starting from the second sentence in any text type. However, we may encounter the affirmation particle اِنَّ at the beginning of the first sentence and at the beginning of subsequent sentences in the text.

7   Texture is the semantic interdependence within text. A text which lacks texture is a non-text because its sentences have no relationship to each other. Each sentence in any ST or TT should be linked coherently to the previous sentence. Thus, we have sequentiality – linear sequence – among the constituent sentences of a text. The internal ties within the text are semantic in nature and lead to cohesion. The texture of the ST and the TT can be produced if cohesion is preserved. Thus, conjunctions give the ST and the TT a text texture (Halliday and Hasan 1976:23). For Halliday and Hasan (ibid:7), sentences, clauses, and words are structured because they are internally "cohesive"; thus, structure is one means of expressing texture. Texture, in the view of Halliday and Hasan (ibid:2), is also created through co-referentiality, which is a cohesive agency, as in: (I saw Janet and told her about the book), where co-referentiality holds between (Janet) and the anaphoric item (her). Therefore, texture is achieved through cohesion as a linguistic means.

8   For Halliday and Hasan (1976:9), the cohesive devices أدوات الربط between sentences in the ST and the TT stand out more clearly because they are the only source of texture. A text should be unified whose units – words and sentences – are connected together in a cohesive manner through cohesive devices, such as ولو أنَّ "although", فَ "and", ثُمَّ "then", و "and", لأَنَّ "because", قبل "before", that make the text gel together and create its unique texture and total unity.

4.6   Learning objectives

The learning objectives of the following exercises are as follows:

1   To highlight the importance of punctuation in the translation process;
2   To demonstrate ST sentence demarcation, i.e., to create the sentence boundaries, underline the ST conjunction, and classify them whether they are inter-sentential or intra-sentential conjunctions;
3   To provide an insight into the textual and discourse features of punctuation, texture, and cohesion in translation studies based on the fact that the translation process is not simply a sentence-by-sentence process;
4   To enhance the student's translation skills in dealing with STs that require special attention in cohesion and texture;
5   To highlight the fact that the full-stop which separates two ST consecutive sentences may not be required in the TT and, therefore, a translation for the ST full-stop should be provided;
6   To demonstrate how punctuation (full-stop, comma, colon, semi-colon, and the dash) are meaningful and translatable; and most importantly,
7   To demonstrate that the dictionary is helpless in the translation of punctuation.

Before we begin the exercise, it is useful to be aware of some theoretical notions which will help us in our translation commentary and translation quality assessment.

Translation beyond the full-stop   159

Our analysis of the ST and the TT should be based on the understanding of clauses and how they relate to each other (McCabe 2011:128–129). We need to look for two types of clause relations: parataxis and hypotaxis (Halliday and Hasan 1976:222–224). These are syntactic mechanism through which clause relations can be established. While English is mostly asyndetic, Arabic is generally polysyndetic. Both Arabic and English have paratactic and hypotactic sentences.

1   A paratactic sentence has one clause (a clause simplex). Clauses that can be combined as equals, express different kinds of meaning, and are related to each other in this way are in a paratactic relationship. The paratactic relation is that of coordination, i.e., we have coordinating conjunctions "and, or, but, so".
2   A hypotactic sentence has more than one clause (a clause complex). Clauses which are in an unequal relationship to each other, have a subordination relationship (main clause/ subordinate clause), and have a clause order that can be reversed are in a hypotactic relationship. The hypotactic relation is that of subordination; for instance, the subordinating conjunctions إذا إن، عندما، بينما، حتى، قبل، بعد، مالم، منذ، بسبب لأن، حيث، لكي، ولو أن على الرغم من "if, when, while, until, before, after, unless, since, because, where, whereas, so that, in order to, although".

Both Arabic and English involve texture. Halliday and Hasan (1976:295–297) make a distinction between two types of texture: "tight and loose texture". In "tight texture", we find dense clusters of conjunctions which serve to signal that the meanings of the parts are strongly interdependent and that the whole forms a single unity. However, in other texts, we find "loose texture", where fewer conjunctions are used, perhaps just one or two. Loose texture is a feature of subtexts which occur within a text.

It is worthwhile to note that the procedure of demarcation of Arabic sentences we have recommended can also be applicable to a single English expression. In this case, phonetic juncture is crucial in deciding the meaning of the expression based on which point we should pause at, as in "cheap quality tyres". I've read this in a tyre service place in Leeds 6 and wondered how it can be of value to translation studies. Thus, like semantic ambiguity represented by polysemy, grammatical ambiguity is also of value to translation students. We can have two different readings leading to two distinct meanings:

(i)   cheap/quality tyres
(ii)   cheap quality/tyres

The meaning of the first reading where there is a juncture after the adjective "cheap" means that the shop has "quality tyres" that are cheap in price. However, the second reading where we have a juncture after the adjectival word "quality" means that the shop has "tyres" which are "of cheap quality" – the quality of the tyres is not certified, is inferior, and does not meet necessary standards. Based on this semantic analysis, we have two possible TTs:

(i)   إطارات رخيصة ذات جودة عالية, and
(ii)   إطارات رديئة الجودة.

The example "cheap quality tyres" demonstrates the importance of reading the ST at a sentence level.

160 *Translation beyond the full-stop*

4.7 **Translator training and translation practice**

This section combines theory and practice and prepares students for the translation industry. Through detailed translation commentary and analysis of several examples, we aim to put theory into practice as well as provide practical translation training exercises with a solution to each question and informative discussion. The exercises aim to provide students with insight into the translation process, guide them to achieve a successful translation, and demonstrate to them how and why a given solution is given. We have also provided many Arabic and English texts as STs together with our proposed translations as a valuable pool of teaching materials for translation teachers. Thorough analysis of examples and their translations provides insight into the cohesion process and texture of the TT, as well as the distinction between the mechanisms of asyndeton and polysyndeton in Arabic and English. The exercises provide a variety of SL texts whose consecutive sentences are, at times, asyndetic while the TT needs to be polysyndetic. Thus, a contrastive and a critical assessment of the ST is required to specify the conjunction suitable for the linking process of the consecutive sentences in the TT.

1. Translate the following text and discuss the process of translating the ST full-stop.

When Sarah was very young, she lived in Leeds with her parents. Her father was a farmer. He grew wheat and vegetables in Golden Acre, a beautiful village that was well known for agriculture.

(i)   We propose the following translation:

عندما كانت سارة صغيرةً كانت تسكن مع والديها في مدينة ليدز وكان والدها مُزارعاً يزرعُ الحنطةَ والخضروات في جولدن أيكر وهي قرية جميلةٌ مشهورةٌ بالزراعة.

(ii) Translation of punctuation analysis: The ST is asyndetic because it has no conjunctions linking the three sentences. It has two commas and two full-stops. However, the TT is polysyndetic through the employment of conjunctions linking the three ST sentences together. The first comma is translated as كانت "was"; the first full-stop is translated as و "and"; the second full-stop is deleted; the verb "grow" is translated as يزرعُ which has the third-person singular pronoun "he"; and the second comma is translated as هي + و. Thus, in terms of clause relations, we can observe that the ST is asyndetic while the TT is polysyndetic.

2. Translate the following text, then discuss the translation process and the mechanisms of translating the ST punctuation:

This is why we say responsive rather than conscious: we cannot always know whether a person is conscious or unconscious.

(i)   Our proposed translation is

لهذا السبب نقول مُستجيب وليس واع إذ (لانهُ) لا يمكننا دائماً معرفة ما إذا كان الشخصُ واعياً أو فاقداً للوعي.

(ii) Translation of punctuation analysis: The ST is asyndetic and involves a colon (:) separating the two sentences. However, the ST is polyseyndetic through the employment of the causal conjunction إذ/لأنهُ "because" for linking the two sentences.

Translation beyond the full-stop   161

3. Translate the following medical text, then discuss the translation process and the mechanisms of translating the ST punctuation:

> This medicine has been prescribed for you. Do not pass it on to others. It may harm them, even if their symptoms are the same as yours.
> Possible side effects: The most common side effects is sedation, varying from slight drowsiness to deep sleep, and including dizziness.

(i)   We propose the following translation:

إنَّ هذا الدواء قد تمَّ وصفُهُ لك خصيصاً بموجب وصفةٍ طبيةٍ. لهذا يجب عليك عدمُ اعطائه لأشخاص آخرين لأنَّ ذلك قد يؤذيهم حتى وإن كانوا يعانون من نفس الأعراض التي سبقَ وإن عانيت أنت منهًا.

الآثار الجانبية المُحتملة: انَّ الأثرَ الجانبي الأكثر شيوعاً هو التسكين الذي يتراوح بين النُعاس الخفيف والنوم العميق أو الدوار.

(ii)   Translation of punctuation analysis: Within the text, we encounter three full-stops, a semi-colon, and a comma. We have kept the first full-stop but used the TL conjunction لهذا "therefore". We have taken out the second full-stop and used the conjunction لأن "because". The semi-colon is kept in the TT and the comma is translated as a relative pronoun الذي "which".

We have translated the present tense verb "has been prescribed" as قد تمَّ وصفُ . . . بموجبِ وصفةٍ طبيةٍ, whose back-translation is "has been prescribed . . . according to a medical prescription". The use of the demonstrative pronoun ذلك represents verbal clause substitution; the verbal clause "pass it on to others" is replaced by the ST demonstrative pronoun ذلكَ. The subordinate clause "even if their symptoms are the same as yours" has no main verb. However, it is translated to a main-verb clause حتى وإن كانوا يُعانونَ من نفس الأعراضِ التي سَبقَ وإن عانيتَ أنتَ منها.

4. Translate the following journalistic text, then discuss the translation process and the mechanisms of translating the ST punctuation:

> The hefty garment earned Phuge – a money lender from Pune in Maharashtra state – the moniker "gold man", a title he cherished (*The Guardian*, 16 July 2016).

(i)   We propose the following translation on which we establish our translation commentary and the translation of punctuation:

ويُذكر أنَّ هذا القميص ثقيل الوزن (الثقيل) قد أكسب فوجي وهو مقرض أموال من مدينة بوني بولاية مهارشترا لقب "رجل الذهب"، وهو لقب طالما اعتز به.

(ii)   Translation of punctuation analysis: As a journalistic text, we have employed a journalistic conjunction ويُذكر أن "it is worthwhile to mention, to report that" at the beginning of the sentence. The dash is translated as an additive conjunction + a pronoun و + هو "and he". The comma is translated as an additive pronoun + a pronoun و + هو "and it", where the "it" is a masculine pronoun referring to the masculine noun "shirt" قميص.

162   *Translation beyond the full-stop*

5. Translate the following text, then discuss the translation process and the mechanisms of translating the ST punctuation:

> Police said Phuge, believed to be in his mid-40s, was attacked and killed by 12 assailants brandishing stones and sharp weapons on Thursday night after one of the suspects had invited him for a party, according to the Press Trust of India news agency (*The Guardian*, 16 July 2016).

(i)   We propose the following translation:

ووفقا لوكالة الأخبار الهندية فإن الشرطة ذكرت بان السيد فوجي الذي يتراوح عمره مُنتصف الأربعينات قد تمَّ مُهاجمته وقتلهُ على يد 12 مهاجماً مستخدمين الحجارة والأسلحة الحادة ليلة يوم الخميس بعد ان دعاه أحد المهاجمين لحفلة

(ii) Translation of punctuation analysis: The first comma is translated as الذي يتراوحُ عُمرُهُ "whose age is in the". The second comma is taken out, and the TT starts from the end of the ST after the second comma. The TT journalistic style requires the additive conjunction و "and" + the reporting source which is "the Press Trust of India news agency" + the conjunction فإنَّ "that" and بأنَّ "that".

> India is the world's biggest consumer of gold, with purchases an essential part of religious festivals and weddings (*The Guardian*, 16 July 2016).

(iii) We propose the following translation:

ومن الجديرُ بالذكر أنَّ الهند هي (تُعتبر) أكبرُ مُستهلكٍ للذهب في العالم حيثُ تُعتبر مشترياته جزءا أساسيا للأحتفالات الدينية وللأعراس.

(iv) Translation of punctuation analysis: As a journalistic text, Arabic requires the journalistic conjunction ومن الجديرُ بالذكر "it is worthwhile to mention" + anna "that". The comma is translated as حيثُ, which is an affirmation conjunction substantiating the previous statement. Thus, in terms of clause relations, we can observe that the ST is asyndetic while the TT is polysyndetic.

6. Translate the following text, then discuss the translation process and the mechanisms of translating the ST punctuation:

> Nestle faces the wrath of chocolate lovers after it refuses to permanently reinstate the much-loved Toffee Deluxe to Quality Street. Britons were in uproar when the confectionery giant decided to ditch the sweet from its iconic Quality Street boxes back in September. Nestle swapped the Toffee Deluxe for its new Honeycomb Crunch treat, making its first change to the Quality Street line-up since 2007. Nestle has decided to reinstate the Toffee Deluxe in time for the Christmas period – but unfortunately, its stay will be short lived. A spokesperson for Quality Street told the Sun: "We're incredibly excited to welcome the new Honeycomb Crunch, and were amazed by the response on social media when the cat was let out of the 'purple' bag, and people heard it would be replacing Toffee Deluxe in the standard tub". "We hope people enjoy the new Honeycomb Crunch sweet and want to reassure Toffee Deluxe lovers that they can still find their favourite Quality Street sweet this Christmas". The Deluxe was created in 1919 as

Translation beyond the full-stop   163

a sweet in its own right and was included in one of the first ever boxes of Quality Street, after it was invented in 1936.

(*The Daily Mail*, 21 November 2016)

(i)   We propose the following translation on which we establish our translation commentary and the translation of punctuation:

تواجه شركة نسلة للحلويات غضب عشاق الشوكولاتة بعد ان رفضت إرجاع قطعة الحلوى (توفي ديلوكس) المحبوبة جدا الى علبة كواليتي ستريت بشكل دائم اذ غضب البريطانيون عندما قررت شركة الحلويات العملاقة التخلي عن قطعة الحلوى هذه من علبة الحلويات المشهورة في سبتمبر الماضي. ويذكر ان شركة نسلة استبدلت قطعة الحلويات هذه بقطعة حلويات جديدة تسمى (هوني كومب كرانش) وبهذا تكون اول تغيير لحلويات كواليتي ستريت في إنتاجها منذ عام 2007. وقد قررت شركة نسلة إعادة قطعة الحلوى القديمة في الوقت المناسب لفترة أعياد الميلاد لكن للأسف سوف يكون بقائها لفترة قصيرة. وقد اخبر المتحدث الرسمي من كواليتي ستريت لصحيفة الصن البريطانية: (نحن متحمسون بشكل لا يصدق للترحيب بقطعة الحلوى الجديدة ومتعجبون من ردة فعل وسائل التواصل الاجتماعي عندما تم إفشاء السر وسمع الناس انها ستحل محل قطعة الحلوى (توفي ديلوكس) في العلبة الاعتيادية ونأمل ان يستمتع الناس بقطعة الحلوى الجديدة ونود ان نطمئن عشاق قطعة الحلوى القديمة أن باستطاعتهم ان يجدوا قطعة حلواهم المفضلة في أعياد الميلاد القادمة). ويذكر ان قطعة الحلوى القديمة (توفي ديلوكس) قد تم صناعتها في ١٩١٨ كحلوى قائمة بذاتها وقد أضيفت الى أول علبة من علب كواليتي ستريت بعد ان تم صنعها في عام 1936. (من مراسلنا ألكس ماثيوز لصحيفة الديلي ميل البريطانية)

(ii) Translation of punctuation analysis: The ST is asyndetic where full-stops are employed instead. The TT, however, has employed many conjunctions linking consecutive sentences together. After the first full-stop, the affirmation conjunction "idh" is used; after the second full-stop, the journalistic conjunction يُذكرُ أن + و it is worthwhile to report that) is used; the comma after the word "treat" is translated as وبهذا + و "by this"; the third full-stop is translated as an additive conjunction و; the fourth full-stop is translated as قد + وِ; the fifth full-stop is taken out and is translated as an additive conjunction و "and" the sixth full-stop is kept and the journalistic conjunction يُذكرُ أن + و is added; and the last comma is taken out. Thus, in terms of clause relations, we can observe that the ST is asyndetic while the TT is polysyndetic.

7. Translate the following text, then discuss the translation process and the mechanisms of translating the ST punctuation:

The Report showed shortages in key areas, such as providing care to elderly in their own homes. Only a third of local authorities said they had enough nursing homes with specialist dementia support. The report, from the Family and Childcare Trust, included Freedom of Information data from around 150 local authorities and health and social care trusts across the UK. Claire Harding, head of research at the Family and Childcare Trust, said: "It is inexcusable that vulnerable people are left unable to find the care that they need". "Without these steps, families will continue to struggle to find care and to meet the numerous care costs on their shoulders ". The Local Government Association

164 *Translation beyond the full-stop*

(LGA), which represents councils, said money is being diverted away from road repairs, leisure centres and local bus routes in order to maintain the struggling social care sector. It warned that the system is "in crisis" and called on the Government to invest in social care in the Autumn Statement.

(*The Daily Mail*, 21 November 2016)

(i) We propose the following translation on which we establish our translation commentary and the translation of punctuation:

أشار التقرير الى وجود نقص في مناطق حيوية كتأمين الرعاية لكبار السن في منازلهم اذ ان ثلث مجالس البلديات ذكرت ان لديها رعاية طبية متخصصة بمرض الخرف. ويذكر ان هذا التقرير الصادر من هيئة الاسرة ورعاية الطفل يتضمن تفاصيل من مؤسسة حرية المعلومات من حوالي ١٥٠ مجلس بلدية وهيئات الرعاية الاجتماعية والصحية في جميع ارجاء المملكة المتحدة. وقد ذكرت السيدة كلير هاردنق مديرة قسم البحوث في هيئة الاسرة ورعاية الطفل " انه لا يمكن تبرير ان يترك المسنون وهم غير قادرين على إيجاد الرعاية التي يحتاجونها فمن دون هذه الخطوات سوف تستمر العوائل في معاناتها لإيجاد الرعاية وتحمل أوزار تكاليفها." ومن جهتها ذكرت هيئة المجالس البلدية التي تمثل جميع مجالس البلديات أن الأموال ما زال يتم تحويل مسارها لإصلاح الطرق ومراكز ترفيه وطرق الحافلات المحلية الى دعم قطاع الرعاية الاجتماعية المترنح. وحذرت هيئة المجالس البلدية ان نظام الرعاية الاجتماعية في (أزمة) و ناشدت الحكومة ان تستثمر في الرعاية الاجتماعية في بيان وزير المالية .

(ii) Translation of punctuation analysis: Within the ST, there are 7 full-stops. The first full-stop is translated as an affirmation conjunction اذ "where", which substantiates the previous statement; the second full-stop is kept but we have used the journalistic conjunction و + يُذكرُ أن "it is worthwhile to report that"; the third full-stop is kept but we have used the conjunction و + قد; the fourth full-stop is translated as . . . هذا دون فمن ف "because without these . . ."; the fifth full-stop is kept but we have added the journalistic conjunction و + من + جهتها "on its part, according to"; and the sixth full-stop is kept but we have used the additive conjunction و. Thus, in terms of clause relations, we can observe that the ST is asyndetic while the TT is polysyndetic.

8. Translate the following text, discuss the translation process, and the mechanisms of translating the ST punctuation:

Wealthy Chinese tourists are to benefit from a relaxation of the visa system, in an effort to boost Britain's retail trade. Tourism bosses estimate the UK misses out £1.2billion from Chinese visitors each year as a result of its "over-zealous" visa system. France, for example, receives eight times more Chinese visitors than Britain.

(*The Daily Mail*, 13 October 2013)

(i) We propose the following translation on which we establish our translation commentary and the translation of punctuation:

سوف يستفيد السياحُ الصينيون الأثرياء من تيسير نظام تأشيرة الدخول في محاولة لتعزيز تجارة ا التجزئة في بريطانيا حيث (إذ) قدَّرت مكاتب السياحة الكبرى بأن بريطانيا تخسر 1.2 بليون جنيه أسترليني من السياح الصينيين سنويًا نتيجة للنظام المتشدد لتأشيرة الدخول. ففرنسا مثلا (على سبيل المثال) ، تستقبل سياح صينيون أكثر مما تستقبل بريطانيا بثمانية أضعاف .

Translation beyond the full-stop 165

(ii) Translation of punctuation analysis: Within the ST, we have two full-stops. The comma after (the visa system) is dropped; the first full-stop is translated as حيثُ/إذ substantiating the previous statement; and the second full-stop is kept but we have used the conjunction ف "and". Thus, in terms of clause relations, we can observe that the ST is asyndetic while the TT is polysyndetic.

9. Translate the following text, then discuss the translation process and the mechanisms of translating the ST punctuation:

Many animals produce chemicals called pheromones which send "smell messages" to other animals of the same species. These odors have different meanings. One odor attracts a mate. Another sends a warning. Another marks a territory. A honeybee, for example, makes over thirty-six different pheromones to communicate such information as where to find good flowers. An ant that has found food will take a bit of it and then head back "home" to the anthill.

(i) We propose the following translation on which we establish our translation commentary and the translation of punctuation:

تفرز العديد من الحيوانات مواد كيماوية تسمى بالفيرومونز التي ترسل رسائل على شكل روائح إلى حيوانات أخرى من نفس جنسها (فصيلتها) وهذه الروائح لها معان مختلفة إذ إن رائحة واحده تَجذِبُ صديقاً ما و أخرى نُرسل تهديداً وأخرى تُحدد بها أرضها، فالنحلةُ مثلاً تُفرزُ أكثر من 36 نوعاً مختلفاً من مادة الفيرومون لنقل معلومات تتعلق بأنواع جيده للزهور، أما النملة التي وجدت طعاماً فتأخذ منه قطعه ومن ثم تتجه به إلى منزلها.

(ii) Translation of punctuation analysis: The ST involves six full-stops. The first full-stop is translated as an additive conjunction و; the second full-stop is taken out and is translated as إذ substantiating the previous statement; the third full-stop is taken out and is translated as an additive conjunction و; the fourth full-stop is taken out and is translated as و; the fifth full-stop is translated as an additive conjunction ف "and" preceded by a comma; and the sixth full-stop is taken out and is translated as أمّا . . . ف "... as for ... the ..." preceded by a comma.

10. Translate the following text, then discuss the translation process and the mechanisms of translating the ST punctuation:

In frantic, work-obsessed modern Britain, where fast-food is king, the cabbage has become one of the kitchen-table causalities. Traditional root vegetables and greens – once integral to the Sunday lunch – have made way for ready-made alternatives and three-minute-in-the-microwave food.

(i) We suggest the following translation:

في بريطانيا العصرية المسعورة التي يستبد بها حُبَّ العمل وحيث أصبحت الوجبات السريعة مَلِكٌ يتربع على عرشها أصبح الملفوفُ أحد ضحايا مائدة الطعام. وحيثما كانت الخضروات الجذرية والخُضار الطازجة التقليدية جزءاً أساسياً من غداء يوم الأحد إلاّ أنها قد تراجعت لتفسحَ الطريق لأطعمةٍ أخرى جاهزة وأكلاتٍ سريعةٍ يمكنُ تجهيزها في المايكرويف في غضون ثلاث دقائق.

166 *Translation beyond the full-stop*

(ii) Translation of punctuation analysis: In terms of clause relations, the ST is heavily punctuated and is asyndetic. However, the TT involves no punctuation and is polysyndetic where the additive conjunction و "and" is employed instead of the commas, and the dashes are taken out.

11. In Q6:1–3, we encounter the conjunction ثُمَّ used three times. Discuss the meaning of each time this conjunction occurs and provide an accurate translation for the ST based on the different meanings of this conjunction.

(i) The TT is below:

الحمدُ للهِ الذي خَلَقَ السماواتِ والأرضَ وجَعَلَ الظُّلماتِ والنُّورَ ثُمَّ الذينَ كَفَروا بربِّهم يَعدِلُون. هو الذي خَلَقَكُم من طينٍ ثُمَّ قضى أجَلاً وأجَلٌ مُسَمَّى عندهُ ثُمَّ أنتم تَمترون. وهو اللهُ في السماواتِ وفي الأرضِ يعلمُ سِرَّكم وجَهرَكم ويعلمُ ما تكسبون (الأنعام 1–3).

(ii) Translation of punctuation analysis:

(a) The first step is to do the ST sentence demarcation, i.e., to create the sentence boundaries, underline the ST conjunction, and classify them whether they are inter-sentential or intra-sentential conjunctions. There are 11 conjunctions و/ثُمَّ in the above ST.

(b) Let us do the sentence demarcation (delineation of sentences):

الحمدُ للهِ الذي خَلَقَ السماواتِ (و) الأرضَ (و) جَعَلَ الظُّلماتِ (و) النُّورَ // (ثُمَّ) الذينَ كَفَروا بربِّهم يَعدِلُون // هو الذي خَلَقَكُم من طينٍ (ثُمَّ) قضى أجَلاً (و) أجَلٌ مُسَمَّى عندهُ // (ثُمَّ) أنتم تَمترون. (و) هو اللهُ في السماواتِ (و) في الأرضِ // يعلمُ سِرَّكم (و) جَهرَكم (و) يعلمُ ما تكسبون (الأنعام 1–3).

(c) Analysis of conjunctions: The first و is a coordinating additive conjunction used to link two nouns السماواتِ والأرضَ "the heavens and the earth". The second و is a coordinating conjunction linking two main verbs خَلَقَ "created" and جَعَلَ "made". Thus, it is an intra-sentential conjunction. This is because it is within (intra) the same sentence that is hypotactic whose subject noun الله "God" is the same, though the same sentence has two main verbs. The third و is a coordinating additive conjunction used to link two nouns الظُّلماتِ والنُّور "the darkness and the light". The fourth conjunction is ثُمَّ, which is an inter-sentential (between two separate sentences) conjunction. The fifth conjunction ثُمَّ is a temporal conjunction meaning "then". It is an intra-sentential conjunction because it is within the same sentence that is hypotactic, whose subject noun هو "He" is the same, though the same sentence has two main verbs: خَلَقَ "created" and قضى "decreed". The sixth conjunction is و, which is intra-sentential resumptive article أداة استئناف starting a new no-main-verb sentence أجَلٌ مُسَمَّى عندهُ. The seventh conjunction ثُمَّ is adversative and inter-sentential. The eighth conjunction و is inter-sentential. The ninth conjunction و is a coordinating additive conjunction employed to link two prepositional phrases في السماواتِ "in the heavens" and في الأرض "in the earth". The tenth conjunction و is a coordinating additive conjunction used to link two

Translation beyond the full-stop 167

nominalized nouns سِرّ "the secret" and جَهَر "made public". The eleventh conjunction و is additive and intra-sentential. It is an intra-sentential conjunction because it is within the same hypotactic sentence whose subject is an implicit pronoun هو "He" referring to اللـه "God"; the larger sentence is hypotactic and has two main verbs: يَعلَمُ "know" and يَعلَمُ "know".

(d) We must understand the following translation strategies:

   (1) The inter-sentential conjunctions should be retained in the TT,
   (2) Some inter-sentential conjunctions like the additive conjunction و "and" should not be used in the TT,
   (3) Some intra-sentential conjunctions like the additive conjunction و "and" should be retained in the TT, and
   (4) Additive conjunctions grammatically coordinating (linking) nouns or noun phrases should be retained in the TT.

(e) Based on the above delineation of ST sentences, the grammatical construction of the TT sentences can be set up. Also, based on the previous punctuation translation rules and our textual and discourse analysis, we can propose the following accurate translation:

All praise is (due) to Allah, who created the heavens and the earth and made the darkness and the light. However, those who disbelieve equate (others) with their Lord. He is the one who created you from clay and then decreed a term and a specified time (known) to Him. However, you are in dispute. He is the only God in the heavens and the earth. He knows your secret and what you make public, and He knows that which you earn, Q6:1–3.

Now, let us compare our translation with what is available in most Qur'an translations, which have missed the distinction between inter-sentential temporal and adversative conjunctions, and whose ST sentence demarcation is inaccurate:

All praise is (due) to Allah, who created the heavens and the earth and made the darkness and the light. Then those who disbelieve equate (others) with their Lord. It is He who created you from clay and then decreed a term and a specified time (known) to Him; then (still) you are in dispute. And He is Allah (the only deity) in the heavens and the earth. He knows your secret and what you make public, and He knows that which you earn, Q6:1–3.

(f) We established in Section 3.5 that the conjunction ثُمَّ is a temporal conjunction meaning "then, next". However, the above ST has demonstrated that ثُمَّ can also function as an adversative conjunction meaning "however, but, yet", as the TT has shown based on the meaning of adjacent sentences.

(g) The conjunction ثُمَّ in the above ST has occurred three times. The meaning of the first ثُمَّ in the first sentence (Q6:1) is for contrast. Thus, it should be translated as an adversative conjunction meaning "however, but". This is because the meaning signifies a contrast between the first and the second notion: "God created you from . . . However, the disbelievers do not believe . . . ", i.e., in spite of these clear

168 *Translation beyond the full-stop*

signs which demonstrate God's omnipotence in creation, they still do not believe in God. Thus, ثُمَّ designates contrast and is an inter-sentential adversative conjunction. However, the second ثُمَّ in Q6:2 signifies a temporal conjunction and means "then, and". This is because it designates time, i.e., from one phase to another "from the time of creation from clay to the time of death". The third time the conjunction ثُمَّ is used designates the adversative meaning and should be translated as "however, but" because it signifies contrast between the two notions: the first notion of God's omnipotence of creation and causing death to His creation, but the second notion is about people's disbelief and dispute (skepticism) about creation, death, and resurrection.

(h) The fourth and seventh conjunction ثُمَّ, which is inter-sentential (between two separate sentences) should be translated as an adversative conjunction meaning "however, but, yet". The fifth conjunction ثُمَّ is a temporal conjunction translated as "then".

(i) The eighth conjunction وهو الله في ... و is inter-sentential and should not be translated (to be deleted). However, the eleventh coordinating conjunction و is an intra-sentential (within the same hypotactic sentence) conjunction which must be retained in the TT.

12. Translate the following text and discuss the process of translating the ST full-stop.

سيرةُ حياةٍ: كان وفاةُ عمر بن الخطاب (رضي الله عنه) نكبةً حقيقيةً للإسلام فقد كان صارماً كما كان يتمتعُ ببُعدِ الأفق في تفكيره ويفهمُ تماماً شخصية قومهِ، ولهذا كان مُؤهلاً حقاً لقيادة العرب الذين يصعُبُ حُكمهُم. لقد تمكن من تأسيس الديوان أو ما نطلقُ عليه اليوم وزارة المالية والذي كان مسؤولاً عن إدارة العوائد المالية، كما قام بتشريع القوانين الثابتة لإدارة الأقاليم.

(i) Let us do the sentence demarcation (delineation of sentences):

سيرةُ حياةٍ: // كان وفاة عمر بن الخطاب (رضي الله عنه) نكبة حقيقية للأسلام // كان صارماً كما كان يتمتعُ ببُعدِ الأفق في تفكيره ويفهمُ تماماً شخصية قومه، ولهذا كان مُؤهلاً حقاً لقيادة العرب الذين يصعُبُ حُكمهُم. // تمكن من تأسيس الديوان أو ما نطلقُ عليه اليوم وزارة المالية والذي كان مسؤولاً عن إدارة العوائد المالية، // قام بتشريع القوانين الثابتة لإدارة الأقاليم.

where we have also taken out all the Arabic conjunctions which English does not need: (فقد, (لقد, كما).

(ii) We propose the following translation:

Biography: The death of Omar Ibn al-Khattab was a real calamity to Islam. Stern but just, far-sighted and thoroughly versed in the character of his people, he was especially fitted for the leadership of the unruly Arabs. Omar had established the *Diwan*, or what is known today as the Ministry of Finance, which was entrusted with the administration of the revenues. He also introduced fixed rules for governing the provinces.

(iii) Having read the ST and TT, we can conclude that the translation strategy has been to provide a demarcation of the sentence boundaries in the ST; in other words – to provide

Translation beyond the full-stop 169

short meaningful TL sentences without the ST conjunctions (cohesive devices). This will facilitate the translation process since Arabic tends to employ longer sentences joined up by different conjunctions which English (TT) does not need. Thus, we recommend to take out the ST conjunctions فقد، كما، ولهذا، لقد، كما.

(iv) Questions on the translation process:

(1) In your textual and discourse analysis of the ST, comment on the ST double cohesive devices ف + قد.

(2) The TT starts a new sentence beginning with "Stern but . . .". What has been omitted and why?

(3) What has happened to the ST cohesive device كما and the comma before it? Explain why.

(4) What has happened to the ST double cohesive devices ولهذا + و، ولهذا and the comma before them? Explain why.

13. Provide a translation and a translation commentary based on the translation process, punctuation, and the stylistic idiosyncrasies and the textual and discourse features of the following ST and TT:

An overweight woman is more likely to require a caesarean because either she or the baby is too big. My doctor explained that exercise helps to strengthen the baby's heart as it increases blood flow. It also helps prepare the body for labor, and if you're fit while pregnant, you're likely to have fewer complications at birth, plus a speedier delivery and recovery. Exercising during pregnancy has brought huge health benefits to me. At seven months pregnant, I was exercising in a gym one morning. It was a huge shock when people began to stop and stare at me blatantly as I ran in the park.

(*The Daily Mail*, 14 May 2015)

(i) We propose the following translation on which we establish our translation commentary and the translation of punctuation:

من المحتمل أن (قد) تحتاج المرأة البدينة الى عملية قيصرية إما لأنها أو لأن الجنين (الطفل) كبير جداً. وقد أوضح لي طبيبي بأن التمارين الرياضية تساعد على تقوية قلب الجنين لأنها تزيد من جريان (تدفق) الدم وتساعد أيضا على تهيأة الجسم للولادة، ثم أنه إذا كنتِ لائقة بدنياً (ذو لياقة بدنية) أثناء حملكِ فإنه من المحتمل أن تتعرضي لتعقيدات أقل عند الولادة اضافة الى سرعة الوضع (الولادة) والتماثل للشفاء. لقد منحتني التمارين الرياضية أثناء الحمل فوائد صحية جمّة حيث كنت أمارس الرياضة في النادي الرياضيِ مرة صباحا (في الصباح) وأنا حامل في الشهر السابع. إلّا أنها كانت صدمة كبيرة جداً لي عندما كان الناس يتوقفون ويحدقون عليّ بحماقة بينما كنت أركض في المُنتزه.

(ii) We can make the following observations about the translation process, translation commentary, and stylistic idiosyncrasies of the ST and the TT:

(a) We have started the TT with the prepositional phrase من المحتمل + أن, which is for "is more likely to". The verb "require" does not need a preposition in English, but it needs a preposition in Arabic تحتاجُ الى. The indefinite singular object noun phrase "a caesarean" is translated to a definite singular noun phrase عملية قيصرية.

170 *Translation beyond the full-stop*

The double conjunctions "because either . . . or . . ." are translated as . . . إمّا لأنها أو لأنَّ . . . , i.e., we repeat "because" in Arabic.

(b) We have used the full-stop in Arabic after the first sentence and starting the second sentence. We can observe that, stylistically, the second sentence is hypotactic because it involves three subjects "my doctor, exercise, it" and three verbs "explained, helps, increases". The same stylistic idiosyncrasy applies to the TT where we have three subjects ها, التمارين الرياضية, طبيبي and three verbs أوضَحَ, تُساعد, تزيد. We have started the second Arabic sentence with a double conjunction قد + و. We have adopted the translation strategy of addition where we have added the prepositional phrase لي "to me". This is an exegetical translation approach.

(c) Syntactically, the verbal clause "that exercise helps to strengthen the baby's heart as it increases blood flow" is an embedded clause in the main clause "my doctor explained". We have the complementizer "that", which begins the embedded sentence, whose subject is "exercise" and whose verb is "help".

The second subject indefinite noun "exercise" is translated as a subject definite plural noun phrase التمارين الرياضية. The causal conjunction "as" remains as a causal conjunction لأنها where the anaphor ها refers to its antecedent التمارين الرياضية. We have the verb "help" + infinitive "to strengthen", which is translated as تُساعدُ على + nominalized noun تقوية. The indefinite noun phrase "blood flow" is translated as an indefinite noun phrase جريان تدفُق الدم.

(d) We do not need the full-stop at the end of the second ST sentence. Thus, we use the additive conjunction و to join up the third TT sentence with the second sentence. The anaphor "it" refers to the antecedent "exercise". The same applies to Arabic. The verb "help" does not need a preposition in English, but in Arabic the verb يساعد needs the preposition على and, stylistically, is followed by a nominalized noun. Thus, the verb "prepare" is translated as a nominalized noun تهيأة. The adjective "fit" is translated as لائقة بدنياً ذو لياقة بدنية. The ST "while pregnant" involves ellipsis of "you are", i.e., originally, it is "while you are pregnant" إذا كُنتِ لائقة بدنياً. The ST double conjunction "and if" is translated as a double conjunction ثمَّ أنه preceded by a comma in order to start a new ST sentence beginning with ثمَّ إنه. The ST noun "labor" has the synonyms "birth" and "delivery" ولادة. The expression "plus" is translated as إضافة الى with no need for the comma before it in the TT. The noun phrase "a speedier delivery and recovery" is translated as سرعة الوضع الولادة والتماثل للشفاء.

(e) We use a full-stop after the third ST sentence and we employ the double affirmation conjunction لقد, i.e., لام التوكيد + قد at the beginning of the TT sentence. The subject "Exercising during pregnancy" involves the nominalizaion "gerund" "exercising", which is translated as التمارين الرياضية أثناء الحمل, and the verb "brought" is translated as مَنَحَ. The prepositional phrase "to me" at the end of the sentence is attached to the Arabic verb منحتني, and the object noun phrase "huge health benefits" is translated as object noun phrase فوائد صحية جمَّة.

Translation beyond the full-stop   171

(f) The full-stop at the end of the fourth ST sentence is not required for the TT where the full-stop is replaced by the affirmation causal conjunction حيثُ to affirm the value of exercise. For more details on causal conjunctions, see Abdul-Raof (2001:79). There is a subtle translation process involved in the translation of the sentence "At seven months pregnant, I was exercising in a gym one morning". This involves a foregrounded (placed at the beginning) prepositional phrase. This is translated as حيث كنت أمارس الرياضة في النادي الرياضي مرة صباحا في الصباح followed by the prepositional phrase "at seven months pregnant", which is translated as وأنا حامل في الشهر السابع, where we have used the additive conjunction و and have repeated the subject pronoun أنا. Note that the prepositional phrase "at seven months pregnant" is placed at the end of the Arabic sentence.

(g) We need the full-stop at the end of the fifth ST sentence, i.e., we keep it in the TT. After the full-stop, we begin the last TT sentence with an adversative conjunction like لكن, إلاَّ أنَّ, بيدَ أنَّ. Thus, the ST "It was a huge shock" is translated as إلاَّ أنها كانت صدمة كبيرة جداً لي. For more details on adversative conjunctions in Arabic, see Abdul-Raof (2001:77).

14. Translate the following legal text and discuss the process of translating the ST punctuation.

Family law is a legal practice area that focuses on issues involving family relationships, such as adoption, divorce, and child custody, among others. Attorneys practicing family law can represent clients in family court proceedings or in related negotiations and can also draft important legal documents such as court petitions or property agreements. Some family law attorneys even specialize in adoption, paternity, emancipation, or other matters not usually related to divorce. States have the right to determine "reasonable formal requirements" for marriage, including age and legal capacity, as well as the rules and procedures for divorce and other family law matters.

(FindLaw's team of legal writers and editors, 10 October 2018)

(i) We propose the following translation:

إنَّ قانونَ الأسرةِ هو مجالُ الممارسة القانونية التي تركز على القضايا التي تنطوي على العلاقات الأسرية مثل التبني والطلاق والوصاية على الأطفال (حَجر الأطفال قضائيا/الحجر القضائي للأطفال)، من بين أمور أخرى. ويمكن للمحامين الذين يمارسون قانون الأسرة تمثيل العملاء (الزبائن) في إجراءات محكمة الأسرة أو في المفاوضات ذات الصلة ويمكنهم أيضًا صياغة وثائق قانونية مهمة مثل التماسات المحكمة أو اتفاقيات الملكية (الممتلكات). ويتخصص بعض محامي قانون الأسرة في التبني أو الأبوة أو التحرر أو أية مسائل أخرى لا تتعلق عادةً (لا علاقة لها) بالطلاق. وللدول الحق في تحديد «المتطلبات الرسمية المعقولة (المناسبة)، للزواج بما في ذلك العُمر والأهلية القانونية فضلاً عن (و) قواعد وإجراءات الطلاق ومسائل أخرى تتعلق بقانون الأسرة. (فريق فيند لو من الكتاب والمحررين القانونيين، العشر من أكتوبر 2018)

(ii) Translation of punctuation analysis and a commentary on the stylistic idiosyncrasies of the ST and the TT:

(a) Both the ST and the TT are composed of three sentences which are void of any rhetorical devices because the ST represents a legal genre. The ST full-stop has been

172 *Translation beyond the full-stop*

kept in the TT due to the legal genre status of the ST. However, after the full-stop, the second and third TT sentences start with the additive conjunction و.

(b) The TT starts with the affirmation particle إنّ to comply with the legal status of the text. The first ST sentence is hypotactic and polysyndetic through the employment of the subordinating relative pronoun conjunction "that", and involves listing, which requires commas. The first TT sentence is also hypotactic and polysyndetic through the employment of the subordinating relative pronoun conjunction التي, and involves listing with the employment of the additive conjunction و. We have used و among the listed items because the ST employs "and" in the last listed item "and child custody".

(c) The second ST sentence is hypotactic and polysyndetic through the additive conjunction "and", which is an intra-sentential (within the same sentence) conjunction. The subject "Attorneys" involves an ellipted relative pronoun "who" + an auxiliary (are), i.e., we have "Attorneys who are". Thus, this is translated in full as المحامين الذين. The second TT sentence is hypotactic and polysyndetic through the additive conjunction "and", which is an intra-sentential (within the same sentence) conjunction. The verbs "represent, draft" in the second ST sentence are translated as nominalized nouns تمثيل، صياغة. The modal verb "can" has occurred twice in the ST "can represent, can also draft" where there is no subject before the second "can". However, in the TT, we must repeat the subject with the verb يمكن, i.e., يمكنهم where the plural subject pronoun هم is used.

(d) The third ST and TT sentence is paratactic. However, the commas employed in the ST are taken out in the TT.

15. Translate the following text, discuss the translation process, and the mechanisms of translating the ST punctuation as a stylistic idiosyncrasy of English:

Theresa May, broken at last: how the steeliest person in politics was reduced to tears

As she announced her resignation, Theresa May broke down and wept. It hurt to watch. You could see in her face the battle she was fighting. Fighting to keep her composure. Fighting to maintain her dignity.

Fighting to show that, despite it all, she was going out with her head held high. Sadly, it was yet another battle that Theresa May just couldn't win. For six minutes – almost the whole of her speech – she'd managed to stand firm. She'd sounded calm. Steady. In the circumstances, heroic. But then she glanced down at the closing lines of her script. "I will shortly leave the job", read Mrs May, "that it has been the honour of my life to hold". Then she gulped. Audibly gulped.

(The Daily Telegraph, 24 May 2019)

(i) We propose the following translation on which we establish our translation commentary and the translation of punctuation:

رئيسة الوزراء البريطانية تاريزا مي تنهار أخيرا. هكذا تغرقُ في دموعها أكثرُ النساء صلابة في السياسة

انهارت رئيسة الوزراء البريطانية السيدة تاريزا مي وبكت عندما أعلنت استقالتها. إنه لمن المؤلم مشاهدة رئيسة الوزراء بهذا الحال. يمكنك أن ترى في وجهها المعركة التي ستخوضها. القتال من أجل الحفاظ على رباطة جأشها. القتال من أجل المحافظة على كرامتها والقتال من

Translation beyond the full-stop 173

أجل أن تبرهن أنه على الرغم من تخليها عن المنصب فإنها ستبقى شاهقة القامة (مرفوعة الرأس). لكن للأسف هذه معركة خاسرة أخرى لتاريزا مِي. وطيلة خطابها الذي دام ست دقائق، تمكنت من الوقوف بثبات وكان صوتها هادئاً ومتزناً، وفي خضم هذه الظروف أثبتت بطولتها. لكن فجأةً، نظرت الى السطور الأخيرة من خطابها وقالت: "سأترك عملي قريباً الذي تشرفت به في حياتي". ثم ابتلعت ريقها بصوت مسموع.

(ii) Translation of punctuation analysis: Having compared the ST with the TT, we can make the following observations:

(a) Halliday and Hasan (1976:295–297) make a distinction between two types of texture: "tight and loose texture". In "tight texture", we find dense clusters of conjunctions which serve to signal that the meanings of the parts are strongly interdependent and that the whole forms a single unity. However, in other texts, we find "loose texture", where fewer conjunctions are used – perhaps just one or two. Loose texture is a feature of subtexts which occur within a text. However, though the above ST headline is a subtext, it enjoys tight texture where we can observe the use of the comma and a semi-colon. Constrastingly, in Arabic, the headline involves a full-stop only. The ST is made up of 15 sentences and employs five different conjunctions: two adversative conjunctions "sadly, but" and three temporal conjunctions "for six minutes, in the circumstances, then". The TT, however, employs a double conjunction لكن للأسف for "sadly", لكن for "but", the additive conjunction و and ثُم for "then". The ST also employs a temporal conjunction "For six minutes" followed by a dash (–) where a parenthetical phrase "almost the whole of her speech" is kept in the TT but without the dash.

(2) Among the stylistic and linguistic idiosyncrasies involved in the ST and TT headline are:

(a) The ST employs a comma after the subject "Theresa May" + a past participle "broken". This is a passive voice construction which is originally "Theresa May is broken at last". This is translated as an active voice followed by a full-stop رئيسة الوزراء البريطانية تاريزا مي تنهار أخيرا.

(b) The word "how" is an adverb meaning "the way in which", i.e., it is not an interrogative word. The second part of the ST headline "how the steeliest person in politics is reduced to tears" is a passive voice structure. A shift is required in ST word order where we start from the end of the sentence "was reduced to tears", which is translated as a metaphor + an imagery تغرقُ في دموعها. The adverb "how" is translated as هكذا; the noun phrase "the steeliest person in politics" is placed at the end of the TT headline and is translated as أكثرُ النساء صلابة في السياسة.

(c) The first ST sentence employs cataphora "she" (a pronoun that occurs before its antecedent تاريزا مي). However, in the TT, we start with the main clause "Theresa May broke down and wept" إنهارت . . . وبكت, followed by the subordinate clause عندما أعلنت استقالتها وبكت. Thus, we have the Arabic anaphora ها (a pronoun that occurs after its antecedent). A full-stop is employed after the first, second, and third TT sentences.

(d) The first ten sentences of the ST are asyndetic, i.e., without conjunctions at the beginning of each sentence. The 11th sentence employs the temporal conjunction "in the circumstances" and the 12th sentence uses the adversative conjunction "but".

174　*Translation beyond the full-stop*

The TT employs the same conjunctions و, + لكن و and و + في خضم هذه الضروف respectively.

(e) Stylistically, the ST employs the rhetorical device of anaphora, which means the repetition of the same word or phrase at the beginning of neighboring sentences. The rhetorical device of anaphora is represented through the initial gerund "fighting", which is followed by an infinitive "to" + main verb. In the TT, the rhetorical device of anaphora is maintained, preceded by the additive conjunction و and the ST infinitive is translated as a nominalized noun: "Fighting to keep . . . Fighting to . . . Fighting to show" القتال من أجل الحفاظ . . . القتال من أجل المحافظة . . . القتال من أجل أن تبرهن It is worthwhile to note that أن + تبرهن is also a type of nominalization in Arabic.

(f) Stylistically, paratactic (short sentences with a simple syntactic structure) and asyndetic sentences are employed in the ST "It hurt to watch . . . Fighting to keep her composure. Fighting to maintain her dignity . . . She'd sounded calm. Steady. In the circumstances, heroic". There is ellipsis involved in "Steady. In the circumstances, heroic". The original sentences without ellipsis are "She sounded 'was' steady. In the circumstances, she was heroic". The TT adopts the original ST sentence structure, i.e., without ellipsis, where we get و. + في خضم هذه الظروف أثبتب بطولتها + a comma + ومتّزنا

(g) Mood, as a literary element, is employed in the ST to conjure specific feelings through particular words and description, such as "broken, steeliest, reduced to tears, resignation, broke down and wept, hurt to watch, fighting, firm, calm, steady, heroic, gulped". The same mood is preserved in the TT where the text atmosphere remains tense and charged with emotion. The ST and TT employ asyndeton to fit in well in the text mood. Thus, many full-stops are employed in the TT. Also, for this reason, the second, third, and fourth TT sentences begin without a conjunction.

(h) For sentences 12–13 "But then she glanced . . ." "I will shortly leave . . . " the TT employs a comma after the adversative conjunction لكن فجأةً, . . . and the quotation commas are used. The last two ST sentences are joined up without a full-stop in the TT ثمَّ ابتلعت ريقها بصوتٍ مسموع.

16. Translate the following text, then discuss the translation process and the mechanisms of translating the ST punctuation:

Indian businessman famed for $240,000 gold shirt "beaten to death"
　　Datta Phuge, who ordered a shirt made from 14,000 pieces of 22-carat gold in 2013, was reportedly attacked by 12 assailants.
　　An Indian businessman who made headlines in 2013 for purchasing a shirt made entirely of gold has been beaten to death in western India, according to a report on Friday. Datta Phuge gained fame when he ordered a customized gold shirt worth 12.7 million rupees, around $240,000 at the time. It was made up of 14,000 pieces of 22-carat gold, weighed 3.32 kilograms (7.3 pounds) and was put together by 15 craftsmen over 16 days. The hefty garment earned Phuge – a money lender from Pune in Maharashtra state – the moniker "gold man", a title he cherished. Police said Phuge, believed to be in his mid-40s, was attacked and killed by 12 assailants brandishing stones and sharp weapons on Thursday night after one of the suspects had invited him for a party, according to the Press Trust of India news agency. Phuge's 22-year-old son witnessed his father being murdered and had been spared by the alleged killers. The police suspected the motive could have been a dispute over a money transaction. Four suspects have

been detained. "Everybody knows me as the 'gold man' in the whole region. Other rich people spend one crore (10 million rupees) to buy Audis or Mercedes, to buy what they like. What crime have I done? I just love gold", Phuge said in 2013. "Gold has always been my passion since a young age. I've always worn gold as jewelry in the form of bracelets, rings, chains", he added. India is the world's biggest consumer of gold, with purchases an essential part of religious festivals and weddings.

(*The Guardian*, 16 July 2016)

(i)   We propose the following translation on which we establish our translation commentary and the translation of punctuation as a stylistic idiosyncrasy of English:

(a)   Useful expressions:

(in the headline) beaten to death: مقتل

(within the ST) beaten to death: القتل ضربا (يضربه حتى الموت)

. . . has reportedly been killed (was reportedly attacked): ذكرت التقارير مقتل. . .

garment: كسوة

the Ka'bah garment: كسوة الكعبة

who made headlines: الذي تصدَّر عناوين الصُحُف

(b)   We propose the following translation:

مقتل رجل الأعمال الهندي ضربا بقميصه المشهور من الذهب بقيمة 240000 دولار أمريكي تقارير تفيد بأن 12 شخصاً هاجموا السيد دتا فوجي الذي طلب خياطة قميص من 14000 قطعة ذهب من عيار 22 في 2013

وفقا لتقرير يوم الجمعة فإن رجل الأعمال الذي تصدر عناوين الصحف في 2013 إثر شرائه قميص مصنوع من الذهب بالكامل قد تم ضربه حتى الموت (قد لقي حتفه ضربا حتى الموت) في غرب الهند. وقد اشتهر السيد دتا فوجي عندما طلب خياطة قميص مفصل قيمته 12.7 مليون ربية أي ما يعادل (أي ما قيمته) 240000 دولاراً أمريكياً. ويتكون هذا القميص من 14000 قطعة ذهب من عيار 22 ويزن 3.32 كيلوغراماً (7.3 رطل) وتم خياطته من قبل 15 حرفي واستغرق 16 يوما. ويذكر أن هذا القميص ثقيل الوزن (الثقيل) قد أكسب فوجي وهو مقرض أموال من مدينة بوني بولاية مهارشترا لقب "رجل الذهب" وهو لقب طالما اعتز به. ووفقا لوكالة الأخبار الهندية فإن الشرطة ذكرت بان السيد فوجي الذي يتراوح عمره منتصف الاربعينات قد تم مهاجمته وقتله على يد 12 مهاجماً مستخدمين الحجارة والأسلحة الحادة ليلة يوم الخميس بعد ان دعاه أحد المهاجمين لحفلة. ويذكر أن ابن فوجي البالغ من العمر 22 عاما قد شهد مقتل والده لكن القتلة المزعومين استثنوه من القتل. وتظن الشرطة بأن الدافع (وراء هذه الجريمة) هو احتمال حدوث خلاف حول صفقة مالية. وقد تم اعتقال أربعة من المشتبه بهم. وقد ذكر فوجي في عام 2013 "كل شخص يعرفني ب "رجل الذهب" في جميع انحاء الولاية. هناك أغنياء ينفقون كروري (ما يعادل 10 مليون روبية) لشراء سيارات نوع أودي أو مرسيدس أو شراء ما يحبون. أي جريمة اقترفتها أنا؟ أنا مجرد أحب الذهب." وأضاف قائلا: "إن الذهب منذ شبابي كان وما يزال شغفي (هوايتي)." "كنت منذ شبابي وما أزال مشغوفا بحب الذهب." ومن الجدير بالذكر أن الهند هي (تعتبر) أكبر مستهلك للذهب في العالم حيث تعتبر مشترياته جزءا أساسيا للأحتفالات الدينية وللأعراس. (عن صحيفة الغارديان البريطانية الصادرة في 16 يوليو (تموز) 2016)

(c)   The major punctuation marks of the ST are the full-stop, the reported speech inverted commas, and the dash. We can make the following observations:

176 *Translation beyond the full-stop*

(1) The ST and the TT headline as a subtext is marked by loose texture, i.e., the absence of conjunctions. The ST headline also involves a missing relative pronoun + an auxiliary "who + was", i.e., "Indian businessman who was famed for . . . ". The ST and the TT sub-headlines are also subtexts and represent loose texture, but have both employed the conjunction "who" الذي as a grammatical requirement. Both the ST and the TT sub-headlines are marked loose texture.

(2) In the major headline, the translation of the passive voice "beaten to death" as مقتل is a nominalized noun without using commas. In the sub-headline, the passive voice "was reportedly attacked" is translated as تقارير تُفيد. The passive voice "has been beaten to death" is translated as تم ضربه حتى الموت. The passive voice forms "it was made up of . . . 'was' weighed . . . was put together . . . was attacked and killed . . . being murdered and had been spared . . . have been detained . . ." are translated as يتكون من . . . يزنُ . . . تمَّ خياطته . . . تم مهاجمته فقتله . . . استثنوهُ من القتل . . . . تم اعتقال

(3) The ST reported speech is followed by a comma. The reporting agent occurs after the comma, i.e., after the ST reported speech. The reporting agents are "according to a report on Friday", "according to the Press Trust of India news agency", "Phuge said in 2013", and "he added". These are placed at the beginning of the TT and are translated as وفقاً لتقرير يوم الجمعة/وفقاً لوكالة الأخبار الهندية/وقد ذكر فوجي/و أضاف قائلاً respectively.

(4) The first full-stop of the ST is maintained in the TT followed by the double conjunction و + ق. The comma after "rupees" is translated as أي. The full-stop after "the time" is kept in the TT and the additive conjunction و is employed. The comma after "gold" is translated as و. The full-stop after "16 days" is translated as an additive compound journalistic conjunction و + يُذكر + أن. The first dash ". . . earned Phuge – a money lender . . ." represents a deleted relative pronoun + auxiliary "was", i.e., ". . . earned Phuge who was a money lender . . .". Thus, "who was" is translated as وهو. The second dash "state – the moniker" is not translated. The comma after "gold man" is translated as "which was" and is translated as وهو. The full-stop after ". . . he cherished" is kept in the TT and the following TT sentence starts with و. The comma after ". . . Phuge, . . ." represents "who was" and is translated as الذي. The full-stop after ". . . news agency" is translated as a journalistic compound conjunction و + يُذكرُ + أنَّ. The full-stop after ". . . the alleged killers" is translated as و. The full-stop after ". . . a money transaction" is translated as و + قد. The full-stop after "have been detained" is translated as و + قد. The full-stops are kept after each reported speech. The full-stop after ". . . he added. India . . ." is translated as a compound journalistic conjunction و + من الجديرُ بالذِكر + أن. The comma after ". . . of gold," is translated as حيثُ تُعتبر.

17. Translate the following text, then discuss the translation process and the mechanisms of translating the ST punctuation:

ذهبَ رجلٌ الى قريةٍ ومعه كلب ثمين لكنه أضاع الكلبَ في القرية فاتصل بجريدة مسائية وطلب نشر إعلان بأوصاف الكلب، وأنه سيدفع مبلغ مائة جنيه استرليني لمن يعثر عليه. وفي المساء لم يجد

Translation beyond the full-stop 177

الجريدة معروضة للبيع في سوق القرية. فذهب الى إدارة الجريدة، وهناك وجدَ الحارس على الباب، فسألهُ عن موعد صدور الصحيفة. فقال الحارس: لا أعتقد أنَّ العدد سيصدر هذه الليلة. ولما سألَ الحارس عن السبب، قال: أنَّ المحررين جميعُهُم قد خرجوا بحثاً عن الكلب.

We suggest the following translation:

> A man went to a village and had a special breed of dog with him. The dog got lost in the village. The man contacted an evening newspaper and requested (asked them) to put a notice about the description of the dog (of the lost dog, of his dog) and the £100 reward that he would pay to whoever found it. However, that evening he did not see the newspaper on sale in the village. He went to the newspaper's offices to meet the editor-in-chief. There, he met the porter and asked him about the time when the newspaper would be out. The porter responded: "I believe the issue will not be out tonight". When the man asked the porter about the reason, the porter said: "All the editors have gone out looking for the dog".

Having read the ST, we can make the following recommendations:

(i) We do the demarcation of the Arabic text sentence boundaries. The Arabic text reads now as below:

ذهبَ رجلٌ الى قريةٍ ومعه كلب ثمين // أضاع (الرجلُ) الكلبَ في القرية // اتصل الرجلُ بجريدة مسائية وطلب نشر إعلان بأوصاف الكلب وأنه سيدفع مبلغ مائة جنيه استرليني لمن يعثر عليه // في المساء لم يجد الجريدة معروضة للبيع في سوق القرية // ذهب (الرجلُ) الى إدارة الجريدة // هناك وجدَ الحارس // سألَ (الرجلُ الحارسَ) عن موعد صدور الصحيفة // قال الحارس: لا أعتقد أنَّ العدد سيصدر هذه الليلة // لما سألَ (الرجلُ) الحارسَ عن السبب، قال (الحارسُ): أنَّ المحررين جميعُهُم قد خرجوا بحثاً عن الكلب.

(ii) We recommend removing the ST conjunctions لكن، ف، و، ف، و، ف.

(iii) We have taken out the prepositional phrase, على الباب because the word الحارس "the porter" is understood to be "at the front door of the building". Thus, the ST prepositional phrase is semantically redundant.

(iv) Based on the ST context, the translation of لم يجد الجريدة معروضة للبيع في سوق القرية is "he did not see the newspaper on sale"; the translation of إدارة الجريدة is "the editor-in-chief"; the translation of موعد صُدور الصحيفة is "the time when the newspaper would be out"; and the translation of لا أعتقد أنَّ العدد سيصدر هذه الليلة is "I believe the issue will not be out tonight".

(v) Most importantly, we recommend to replace the difficult Arabic word with a simpler synonym to facilitate the translation process; as in إندهَشَ is replaced by its simpler synonym تَعَجَّبَ.

18. Translate the following text, then discuss the translation process and the mechanisms of translating the ST punctuation:

> Dawn is a magical time to experience the natural world. It's an opportunity to notice nature awakening, to see and listen to what's around us, as night passes into day. The break of day is "a special moment to witness" that is both precious and fleeting.
>
> (The Guardian, 24 April 2020)

178 Translation beyond the full-stop

We propose the following translation:

يُعتبرُ الفجرُ وقتاً سِحرياً لاكتشاف عالم الطبيعة فهو (إنَّه) فرصةٌ لمراقبة استيقاظ الطبيعة ومشاهدة ما يُحيط بنا والإستماع اليه بينما يُولجُ الليلُ في النهار (بينما ينسلخُ الليلُ من النهار). إنَّ الفجرَ 'لحظةٌ متميزةٌ تستحقُ المشاهدة حيث (إذ) أنها نفيسةٌ وزائلة في آنٍ واحدٍ.

(i) We recommend the translation of the auxiliary verb "is" in such syntactic patterns as the passive voice expression يُعتَبر or as an affirmation particle. However, in the second sentence, we can either use the conjunction ف + هو referring to الفجر or use the affirmation particle إنَّ.

(ii) The translation of the expression "as night passes into day" harks back to Qur'anic style يولجُ الليلَ في النهار (آل عمران 27، فاطر 13، and has adopted the Qur'anic expression الحديد 6. Our translation also offers another style ينسلخُ الليلُ من النهار which is stylistically a metaphor. However, the expression "that is" is translated as an affirmation particle حيثُ أنها/إذ أنها, and the word "both" is rendered as a temporal expression في آنٍ واحدٍ.

19. Translate the following text, discuss the translation process, and the mechanisms of translating the ST punctuation:

المُثابرةُ على الدرس
كان رجلٌ يطلب العلمَ فلم يقدر عليه فعزم على تركه، فمرَّ بماء ينحدر من رأس جبل على صخرة قد أثر فيها. فقال: "الماءُ على لطافته قد أثر في صخرة على كثافتها، والله لأطلبنّ العلم فطلبَ فأدركَ.

We suggest the following translation:
Perseverance (endurance, determination) for knowledge

A man was seeking knowledge but he could not continue and decided to give up. He passed by a mountain spring falling on a rock which was marked by the water (The water made an impression (a mark) on the rock). The man said: "In spite of the gentleness of water, it has made an impression (a mark) on the rock. By God, I'll seek knowledge". He sought knowledge and mastered it (he got what he was looking for).

Having read the ST, we can make the following recommendations:

(i) We demarcate the Arabic text sentence boundaries. The Arabic text reads now as below:
المُثابرة على الدرس
كان رجلٌ يطلب العلمَ (لكنه) لم يقدر عليه (و) عزم على تركه // مرَّ (الرجلُ) بماء ينحدر من رأس جبل على صخرة قد أثر فيها // قال (الرجلُ): "الماءُ على لطافته قد أثر في صخرة على كثافتها ، والله لأطلبنّ العلم // طلب الرجلُ) (و) أدرك (أي نال كان يتمنى).

(ii) We recommend to take out the ST conjunctions ف. We replace the conjunctions ف with simpler conjunctions لكن، و to facilitate the translation process. This applies to كان رجلٌ يطلب العلمَ فلم يقدر عليه فعزم على تركه. Based on the ST context, the

Based on the above discussion of punctuation, we can argue that, in terms of clause relations, we can observe that the ST is polysyndetic while the TT is asyndetic.

translation of الدرس is "knowledge"; the translation of يَطلب is "seek"; the translation of عزم على is "decided to"; and the translation of مرَّ بـ is "passed by"; the translation of ماء ينحدر من رأس جبل is "a mountain spring falling on"; the translation of قد أثَّر في is "to mark, to leave an impression on"; and the translation of أدركَ is "to master".

(iii) Based on the above discussion of punctuation, we can argue that, in terms of clause relations, we can observe that the ST is polysyndetic while the TT is asyndetic.

20. Translate the following narrative text, discuss the translation process, and the mechanisms of translating the ST punctuation:

ذهب رجلٌ الى حلاق ليحلق له رأسه فكان كلما حلق موضعاً جرحه وغطى الجرح بالقطن حتى امتلأ نصف رأس الرجل قطناً. فعندها قال للحلاق: "أرجوك أن تترك نصف رأسي الباقي كما هو". فقال الحلاق متعجباً : "ولماذا يا سيدي؟". فأجاب الرجل: "يكفي أنك زرعت النصف الأول قطناً. إنني أريد أزرع الباقي كتاناً".

Our suggested translation is:

A man went to a hairdresser (barber) to have his hair cut. However, whenever the hairdresser cut (shaved) a section of the man's (client's) hair, he would inadvertently injure the man and cover the injury with a piece of cotton until half of the man's head was covered with cotton. The man then told the barber: "Will you please leave the other half of my head as it is?" The hairdresser was surprised and responded: "Why Sir?!" The man replied: "You have grown cotton on half of my head. I would like to grow flax on the other half".

Having read the ST, we can make the following recommendations:

(i) We demarcate the Arabic text sentence boundaries. The Arabic text reads now as below:

ذهب رجلٌ الى حلاق ليحلق له رأسه (الحلاق) كان // كلما حَلَقَ موضعاً جرحَهُ وغطّى الجرحَ بالقطن حتى امتلأ نصفُ رأس الرجل قُطناً // عندها قال (الرجلُ) للحلاق: "أرجوك أن تترك نصف رأسي الباقي كما هو" // قال الحلاق متعجباً : "لماذا يا سيدي؟" // أجاب الرجل: "أنك زرعت النصف الأول قطناً // إنني أريد أزرع الباقي كتاناً ".

(ii) We recommend to remove the ST conjunctions فكان، ف، ف، و ، ف. We also take out the verb يكفي. Based on the ST context, the translation of the noun حلاق is "hairdresser"; the translation of ليحلق رأسه is "to have his hair cut"; the translation of the verb حَلَقَ is "to shave, to cut"; the translation of موضعاً is "a section"; and the translation of the verb جَرَحَ is "to injure"; the translation of بالقطن is "with a piece of cotton"; and the translation of امتلأ is "covered with". We replace the difficult Arabic word موضع with a simpler synonym جُزء to facilitate the translation process. Thus, we have "section".

(iii) Based on the above discussion of punctuation, we can argue that, in terms of clause relations, the ST is polysyndetic while the TT is asyndetic.

180　*Translation beyond the full-stop*

21. Translate the following biography text, then discuss the translation process and the mechanisms of translating the ST punctuation:

My childhood was a queer and not altogether happy one. Circumstances conspired to make me shy and solitary. My father and mother died before I was capable of remembering them. I was an only child, entrusted to the care of an unmarried aunt who lived quietly in the country. My aunt was no longer young when I began to live in her comfortable, old-fashioned house with its large, untidy garden. She had settled down to her local interests, seldom had anyone to stay with her, and rarely left home. She was fond of her two Persian cats, busied herself sensibly with her garden.

(i) Our proposed translation is below:

كانت طفولتي غريبة ولم تتسم بالسعادة إذ (حيثُ) تآمرت الظروفُ عليَّ وجعلتني خجولة ومنعزلة عن الآخرين. فقد توفي والديَّ قبل أن أتمكن من أن أتذكر هما. وكنتُ طفلة وحيدة وتمَّ توكيل رعايتي الى عمة غير متزوجة تعيش بهدوء في منزلها بالريف. ولم تكن عمتي في شبابها عندما بدأت العيش في منزلها المريح ذي الطراز القديم والحديقة الشاسعة غير المُرتبة. ولقد تعودت عمتي على اهتماماتها بالأمور المحيطة بها، وكان نادراً ما يزورها أحدٌ ليبقى معها ونادراً ما كانت تغادر منزلها. وكانت مولعة بقطتيها الفارسيتين وتشغل نفسها لحد معقول بحديقتها.

(ii) Translation of punctuation analysis: The ST involves six full-stops. The first full-stop is taken out and is translated as a substantiation conjunction إذ/حيثُ; the second fll-stop is kept but we have added the conjunction فقد; the third full-stop is kept but we have employed the additive conjunction و; the fourth full-stop is kept but we have employed the additive conjunction و; the fifth full-stop is kept but we have employed the conjunction و + لقد; and the sixth full-stop is kept but we have employed the additive conjunction و.

(iii) Based on the above discussion of punctuation, we can argue that, in terms of clause relations, the ST is asyndetic while the TT is polysyndetic.

22. Translate the following text, then discuss the translation process and the mechanisms of translating the ST punctuation:

Scientific Medical Instructional Text

As described in Chapter 2, after you recognize the emergency and check the scene for safety, you then check the victim to see what problems may need first aid.

This check, called an assessment, has two primary steps:

1. In the initial assessment, check for immediate life-threatening conditions. Check for responsiveness and breathing.

2. In the secondary assessment, get the victim's history (find out what happened and what may have contributed to the emergency), and perform a physical examination of a responsive victim to check for any injuries or other signs of sudden illness. Then while giving first aid for any injuries you find, and while waiting for help to arrive, continue with a third step:

3. Monitor the victim for any changes.

Always perform these steps in this order. If you find a life-threatening problem, such as the absence of breathing, the victim needs immediate help. This victim could die if

Translation beyond the full-stop 181

you first spend time looking for broken bones or asking bystanders what happened. Always remember to do the initial assessment first.

(*Freshman Engineering*, p. 12, KSA, Taibah University 2011/2012)

(i) We propose the following translation:

نص علمي طبي إرشادي

كما شرحنا في الفصل الثاني وبعد أن عرفتَ الحالة الطارئة **وتأكدت** من سلامة مكان الحادث، بعدها **افحص** المصاب لمعرفة أية إصابات تحتاج إلى إسعافات اولية. وهذا **الفحص** الذي يسمى بالتقييم له خطوتان أساسيتان:

١- خلال التقييم الأولى، **ابحثٍ** عن الحالات الخطرة جداً **وتأكد** من استجابة المصاب وتنفسه.

٢- خلال التقييم الثاني، **تأكد** مما حدث للمصاب (معرفة ما حدث وما ساهم في هذه الحالة الطارئة) ثم قوم بأجراء فحص بدني لمريض مُستجيب من أجل **التأكد** من أي جروح او علامات مرض مفاجأة ثم أثناء تقديم الإسعافات الأولية لأي إصابات وجدتها، وبينما تنتظر وصول مساعده أخرى، استمر في (تابع) الخطوة الثالثة.

٣- راقب المصاب عن كثب توقعاً لأية تغييرات قد تحدث له.

دائما نفذ هذه الخطوات بهذا الترتيب وإذا وجدت مشكلة خطرة مثل انقطاع التنفس **فإن** المصاب بحاجة إلى مساعدة فورية **إذ** قد يموت المصاب إذا استمريت في البحث عن عظام مكسورة أو استمريت في سؤال المتفرجين (المارة) عما حدث للمصاب وتذكر دائماً بأن تقوم بالتقييم الأولي في بداية الأمر.

(ii) The word "check" has occurred six times, with different grammatical functions and contextual meanings:

(1) "check" in "check the scene" is a verb whose meaning is تأكد من.

(2) "check" in "check the victim" is a verb whose meaning is أفحص.

(3) "check" in "this check" is a noun whose meaning is الفحص.

(4) "check" in "check for" is a verb whose meaning is إبحث عن.

(5) "check" in "check for" is a verb whose meaning is تأكد من.

(6) "check" in "check for any injuries" is a verb whose meaning is التأكُد من.

(iii) The contextual meaning of the verb "see" in ". . . the victim to see what . . ." is لكي تتأكد من.

(iv) The expression "As described" is originally "As we described" and is translated as كما شرحنا; the expression "check the scene for safety" is translated as تأكد من سلامة المكان; the expression "victims history" is translated as ما حدث للمصاب الأمور التي تعرضَ لها المصاب; the expression "immediate life-threatening conditions" is translated as الحالات الخطرة جداً; and the expression "responsiveness and breathing" is translated as استجابة المصاب وتنفسه, where we have adopted the addition translation procedure where an exegetical translation approach is adopted and the word المصاب is added.

(v) The first comma in the first sentence is left out while the second one ". . . safety, you then . . ." is kept in the TT. The full-stop at the end of the first line is kept in the TT. The comma in "This check, called . . ." is translated as الذي, while the comma after

182   *Translation beyond the full-stop*

"an assessment," is left out. The commas in points (1) and (2) are kept in the TT. The first comma in "Then while . . ., and while . . .," is removed while the second is kept, and a third comma is added to the TT مساعدة أخرى ، استمر في . . . In the sentences "Always perform these steps in this order. If you find a life-threatening problem, such as the absence of breathing, the victim needs immediate help. This victim could die", we have two full-stops and two commas. The first full-stop is translated as an additive conjunction و; the first comma is taken out; the second comma is translated as a conjunction ف + إن; and the second full-stop is translated as إذ. The full-stop before the last sentence is translated as a conjunction و. It is worthwhile to note that the conjunction إذ is employed for affirmation of an opinion as in "Air is vital for life. Without it, we cannot survive", where we have the full-stop translated as إذ and the comma removed الهواءُ ضروريٌّ للحياة إذ لو لاهُ لما استطعنا البقاء.

23. Translate the following texts, then discuss the translation process and the mechanisms of translating the ST punctuation:

Text one: Job cuts are already hitting staff in London, where adult education is under particular threat, Manchester, Cardiff, Derbyshire, Hampshire, and Lancashire.
Translation:

بدأ التقليص في الوظائف يؤثر سلباً على (يضربُ) المعلمينَ في لندن التي يعاني تعليم الكبار فيها من تهديد مُحدق كما بدأ يضرب مدناً أخرى مثل مانشستر وكاردف وداربيشر وهامشر ولانكاشر.

Discussion: The ST constitutes a translation problem due to the listing of many nouns "cities" and, in particular, the use of the comma after "London", which is followed by a parenthetical clause "where adult education is under particular threat", followed by the resumption of listing other cities. Such a style is not possible to achieve in Arabic. Therefore, we need to repeat the first main verb بدأ يضربُ + the addition of the expression مُدناً أخرى مثل. Therefore, the comma after "London" is taken out.

Text two: The Liberal Democrats leader has agreed to compromise over voting reform, the issue being considered by a commission headed by Lord Jenkins, and settle for a system which would fall short of his party's previous demands.
Translation:

وافق زعيم الديمقراطيين الليبراليين على حل وسط بشأن إصلاح التصويت وهي القضية التي تنظر فيها لجنة برئاسة اللورد جينكنز ، وقبول نظام لا يفي بمطالب حزبه السابقة.

Discussion: The ST constitutes a translation problem due to (i) having two infinitive verbs – "compromise" and "settle for" – which, grammatically, occur after the main verb "agreed", whose subject noun is "the Liberal Democrats leader": "The Liberal Democrats leader has agreed (1) to improve, (2) has agreed to settle for", and due to (ii) the comma after "voting reform" and the comma after "Lord Jenkins". The comma must be taken out and translated as a relative pronoun و + هي. Then, we must keep the comma after "Lord Jenkins" + the coordinating conjunction و + the use of the nominalized noun قبول. Thus, grammatically and stylistically, we have the structure وافقَ . . . على حل . . . و + قبول.

Translation beyond the full-stop 183

24. For in-class discussion: The following sentences involve grammatical (structural) ambiguity. You need to (i) provide the phonetic juncture for each sentence, and (ii) provide two translations for each sentence based on each reading:

(i)   Young mothers appeal to the manager.
(ii) We saw her duck.
(iii) The teacher killed the farmer with the knife.
(iv) Visiting relatives can be boring.
(iv) The thing that bothered Bill was crouching under the table.
(v)   I gave a few olives to my friend that I stabbed with a fork.

25. For in-class discussion: The ST (Q3:18) below is a one-sentence hypotactic (structurally complex) text without any punctuation. However, we encounter some translations such as that by Pickthall, which have resorted to the sentence demarcation procedure and divided the TT into two or three sentences. Discuss the ST structure, whether you can produce an alternative ST after you have provided a word order re-shuffle, and provide an alternative smooth style one-sentence TT:

شَهِدَ اللهُ أَنّهُ لا إِلهَ إِلاَّ هُوَ والملائكةُ وأُلوا العلم قائماً بالقِسطِ (آل عمران 18)

Allah (Himself) is Witness that there is no God save Him. And the angels and the men of learning (too are witness). Maintaining His creation in justice (Pickthall 1930:no page). God bears witness that there is no god but He, as do the angels and those who have knowledge. He upholds justice (Abdel Haleem 2005:35).

26. For in-class discussion: Compare the ST and the TT in terms of punctuation, sentence demarcation, the stylistic linguistic devices of asyndeton and polysyndeton, and the notions of loose and tight texture; then provide a translation quality assessment.

Happiness is where you are now, or nowhere at all: It's not a new relationship, it's not a new job, it's not a completed goal, and it's not a new car. Until you give up on the idea that happiness is somewhere else, it will never be where you are.

السعادةُ هي في مكانك الحالي، أو أنها ليست موجودة على الإطلاق: إنها ليست علاقة جديدة، إنها ليست وظيفة جديدة، إنها ليست هدفاً مكتملاً، و(هي ، وأنها ، كما أنها) ليست سيارة جديدة. وحتى تتخلى (ومتى ما تخليت) عن فكرة أنَّ السعادة في مكان آخر، فلن تكون السعادة أبدًا في مكانك (في المكان الذي أنت فيه).

27. For in-class discussion: Compare the ST and the TT in terms of punctuation. The ST is a newspaper caption:

Shannon Mulcahy of Whitestown, Indiana, voted for Trump in the last election. This time his rival Joe Biden will get her vote (*The Guardian*, 16 October 2020).

We propose the following translation:

شانون مولكا هي من وايتستاون بولاية إنديانا كانت قد صوتت لصالح ترامب في الانتخابات الأخيرة ولكن هذه المرة سيحصل منافسه جو بايدن على صوت شانون. (عن صحيفة الجارديان البريطانية، الصادرة في 16 أكتوبر (تشرين الأول) 2020)

184 *Translation beyond the full-stop*

Discussion:

(i) The translation of newspaper headlines and captions should always be مبتدأ وخبر. Since it is a caption تعليقٌ على شرحُ الصورة جملة, stylistically we need a noun-first sentence مُبتدأ وخبر. Therefore, we start with the noun شانون مولكا as the مبتدا وخبر.

(ii) The full-stop should be translated as an adversative conjunction ولكن because of the semantic contrast between the first sentence and the second. In other words, first Shannon Mulcahy voted for the Republicans, but now she has changed her mind and will vote for the Democrats "Joe Biden".

28. For in-class discussion: Compare the ST and the TT in terms of sentence structure and punctuation. The ST is a newspaper caption:

"I didn't back down from my promises – and I've kept every single one", Donald Trump told the Republican national convention in August as he campaigned for a second term (*The Guardian*, 16 October 2020).

We propose the following translation:

دونالد ترامب أمام المؤتمر الوطني للحزب الجمهوري في أغسطس أثناء حملته الانتخابية لولاية ثانية: "لم أتراجع عن وعودي – وقد احتفظت بكل واحدة منها". (عن صحيفة الجارديان البريطانية، الصادرة في 16 أكتوبر (تشرين الأول) 2020)

Discussion:

(i) Since it is a newspaper caption, we cannot say قال, i.e., we must delete the ST verb (told). Thus, we start the caption with a noun دونالد ترامب, add the preposition أمام, and use the colon (:) to be followed by the quotation.

29. For homework: Mark the ST sentence boundary based on the text geography, translate the following text, and then discuss the translation process and the mechanisms of translating the ST punctuation:

دورُ المرأةِ في المُجتمع

إنَّ دَورَ المرأةِ البارز لا يظهرُ للعيان إلاَّ إذا تذكَّرنا أيامَ طُفولَتِنا كيفَ أنها كانت تسهرُ الليالي حُبّاً منها علينا لتسقينا من لبَنِها في أيَّةِ لحظةٍ نشاءُ سواءاً في أعماق الليلِ أو في وسطِ النهار دون ملَلٍ ولا ضجَرٍ بل تقومُ بذلكَ طوعاً وحُبّاً وشفقةً لا تُضاهى. كم مِن مرَّةٍ أرضَعَتك أمُّك؟ وكم مَن مرَّةٍ سَهِرت الليلَ عند مَرَضك؟ هل تتذكَّر كم من مرَّةٍ بكت عليك عند تعثُّر صحَّتك؟ هل تتذكر كم من مرَّةٍ نظَّفتك؟ فالرجلُ مهما كان لا يستطيع أن يقدم هذه الخدمات الجليلة لطفله بل لا يتحمل مُقاطعة نومه مِرارا في ليلةٍ واحدةٍ لرعاية طفله. وهذا ما يُطلقُ عليه بالأمومة وهي الغريزةُ التي أنبتها الله سُبحانه وتعالى في قلبِ المرأةِ وأصبحت غريزة في دمها وسلوكِها. هل يُمكِن أن نتصور إذا وجودَ مجتمع يتربى الأطفالُ في ظل آبائهم فقط دون رعاية الأمُّ؟ كلاَّ وألف كلاّ فلا يوجد بديلٌ للأمِ في تربية الأطفال. بيد أنَّ دور المرأةِ لا ينحصرُ في تربية الأطفال فحسب بل يتعداهُ الى مُساهماتِها الفعالة في التعليم والطب والتضميد والخدمات الإجتماعية الأخرى. كم مِنّا يُقدِّرُ مكانة المرأة وينظرُ اليها نظرة اعتزاز

Translation beyond the full-stop 185

وتفاخُر مُعطَّرةً بالإحترام والتقدير دونَ المساس بكرامتها وعِزِّها ودونَ النظر اليها بأنَّ دورَها ثانويٌّ أو مجرد سلعة للرجل إذَ لا يستغني المُجتمعُ عَن مُساهمة المرأة في بناءه بناءاً فعالاً وستبقى المرأةُ العمود الفقري للرجل كما سيبقى الرجلُ عمودها الفقري. (حسين عبدالرؤوف ، ليدز ، المملكة المتحدة ، فبراير (شباط) 1996)

Discussion:

(i) Let us consider the ST's geography and then mark the sentence boundary:

دورُ المرأةِ في المجتمع

إنَّ دَورَ المرأة البارز لا يظهرُ للعيان إلاّ إذا تذكرنا أيامَ طُفولتَنا // كيفَ أنها كانت تسهرُ الليالي حُبًّا منها علينا لتسقينا من لبَنِها في أيَّةِ لحظةٍ نشاءُ سواءاً في أعماق الليل أو في وسطِ النهار دون مللٍ ولا ضجَرٍ // بل تقومُ بذلكَ طوعاً وحُبًّا وشفقة لا نُضاهى. // كم من مرَّةٍ أرضَعَتْك أمُّك؟ // وكم من مرَّةٍ سهرت الليلَ عند مَرَضِك؟ // هل تتذكر كم من مرَّةٍ بكت عليك عند تعثُر صحَّتك؟ // هل تتذكر كم من مرَّةٍ نظَفتك؟ // فالرجلُ مهما كان لا يستطيع أن يقدم هذه الخدمات الجليلة لطفله بل لا يتحمل مُقاطعة نومه مراراً في ليلةٍ واحدةٍ لرعاية طفله. // وهذا ما يُطلق عليه بالأمومة وهي الغريزة التي أنبتها الله سُبحانه وتعالى في قلب المرأة وأصبحت غريزة في دمها وسلوكها. // هل يُمكِن أن نتصور إذا وجودَ مجتمع يتربى الأطفالُ في ظلِّ آبائهم فقط دون رعاية الأم؟ // كلاّ وألف كلاّ فلا يوجد بديلٌ للأمّ في تربية الأطفال. // بيد أنَّ دور المرأة لا ينحصرُ في تربية الأطفال فحسب بل يتعداهُ الى مُساهماتها الفعالة في التعليم والطب والتضميد والخدمات الإجتماعية الأخرى. // كم منّا يُقدِّرُ مكانة المرأة وينظرُ اليها نظرة اعتزاز وتفاخُر مُعطرةً بالإحترام والتقدير دون المساس بكرامتها وعِزِّها ودونَ النظر اليها بأنَّ دورها ثانويٌّ أو مجرد سلعة للرجل // اَذ لا يستغني المُجتمعُ عن مساهمة المرأة في بناءه بناءاً فعالاً // وستبقى المرأةُ العمود الفقري للرجل كما سيبقى الرجلُ عمودها الفقري. (حسين عبدالرؤوف، ليدز ، المملكة المتحدة ، فبراير (شباط) 1996)

(ii) Consider whether we need the full-stop in the Arabic text.

(iii) Consider the conjunctions like بل فسب ، ف ، كما ، إذ ، بيد أنَّ ، بل ، و ، إنَّ.

(iv) Consider the synonyms ضجر ، ملل ِ، طوعاً، حباً، شفقةِ، إعتزاز وتفاخُر and وعِزِّها وكرامتها.

(v) Consider the absolute object المفعول المُطلق بناءه بناءاً.

(vi) Consider the metaphor العمود الفقري. Do we translate the metaphor as a metaphor or as a non-metaphor?

(vii) Are there ST conjunctions which English does not need?

30. For homework assignment regarding text geography analysis and demarcation of sentence boundaries: The following text does not include a full-stop. Demarcate the sentence boundaries, using full-stops at the end of each meaningful sentence, and provide a translation.

القطن المصرى يتعافى . . بعد زيادة الطلب عليه

يكتسب محصول القطن أهمية خاصة، فهو محصول استراتيجى يُشكل المادة الخام التى تقوم عليها صناعات الغزل والنسيج والصباغة والتجهيز والملابس فى مصر، والتى تعد منذ عقود صناعات رائدة وكانت فى بعض الفترات قاطرة للاقتصاد المصرى، تراجعت تلك الصناعات كثيرا بتراجع القطن المصرى بعد تحرير تجارة القطن بالقانون رقم 210 لسنة 1994، وأصبح الاعتماد الكلى على

186 *Translation beyond the full-stop*

التجارة الحرة فى تسويق الأقطان وإلغاء نظام التسويق التعاونى بعد أن كانت الدولة مسئولة عن القطن المصرى من حيث الجمع والتصنيع والتصدير، مما أدى لظهور عدد كبير من المشاكل أهمها انخفاض انتاج القطن لتراجع المساحة المزروعة من 1.9 مليون فدان فى منتصف الستينيات إلى 884 ألف فدان فى موسم 1994، بالإضافة لذلك ظهرت مشكلة الخلط فى القطن والتى لم تكن موجودة من قبل نظرا لوجود الدولة كراعية وضامنة لتسويقه، إضافة إلى ذلك تقادم المغازل المحلية مما جعلها غير قادرة على المنافسة والاستفادة من ميزة مواصفات القطن المصرى واعتمادها على أقطان رخيصة الثمن. (الأهرام، 19 أغسطس (آب) 2021)

5 Translation of cohesion

5.1 Introduction

The present chapter is concerned with the flow of information intra-sententially (within the same sentence) and inter-sententially (among different sentences) by looking at the linguistic features of the text like text cohesion and texture. In other words, it is a sentence-level investigation of cohesive relationships within and between consecutive Arabic sentences. It examines the different types of cohesive mechanisms like reference, ellipsis, substitution, conjunction, and lexical cohesion. The chapter examines tight (dense) texture and loose texture in both the ST and the TT, and questions whether overrepresented SL additive conjunctions like و are necessary in the TL or whether textual continuity and TL lexical cohesive system are undermined. Thus, the present discussion provides an insight into the linguistic phenomenon that Arabic and English have their own exclusive inherent cohesion system; the cohesion system is language-based. The discussion of examples illustrates how dense texture is an idiosyncratic stylistic feature of Arabic, where some of its elements like nominalization, the active participle, the no-main-verb nominal sentence, and the subject noun-initial sentences with a main verb have innate performative intent that may not be possible to reproduce in English.

The chapter accounts for the unnatural TT style and why the TL audience is alienated by the TT which has violated the TL cohesion system. The examples will also demonstrate how Arabic, at times, does not observe the cohesion system, and how the translator has opted for literal translation and preserved the ST violation of the cohesion system. Thus, the discussion will provide an acute discernment of how the literal translation of Arabic at the cohesion system level leads to an unnatural English style – the TT is semantically meaningful but stylistically sluggish.

5.2 Translation and cohesion

At both the micro and macro levels, cohesion is a text-centred, grammatically based, and a major mechanism of effective communication, sublime style, and eloquence. Cohesion plays a pivotal role in the attainment of the ST and TT texture (the connectedness of the micro text – word, noun phrase, clause, sentence – and the macro text – a paragraph or a whole running text). There are five different grammatically based textual cohesive devices (cohesion elements, cohesion mechanisms) which lead to texture and indicate how sentences relate to each other: reference, ellipsis, substitution, conjunction, and lexical cohesion. Through cohesion:

DOI: 10.4324/9781003268956-6

188 *Translation of cohesion*

1   The ST and the TT components (words, phrases, clauses, sentences, paragraphs) become associated semantically and grammatically; and

2   The sentences and the paragraphs become linked together into a semantically and grammatically unified text.

For Halliday and Hasan (1976:18, 274), cohesion makes the text hang together. Based on the problems encountered by the translator in Arabic translation practice and translator training, our discussion will hinge upon two major aspects: (i) textual contrastive analysis, and (ii) translation problems projected through examples which unveil Arabic and English incongruent stylistic and textual idiosyncrasies of the five cohesive devices. The critical analysis of translation examples aims to equip the translation student with an insight into the following:

1   How Arabic, at times, flouts the employment of textual cohesive devices,

2   How the TT accommodates the ST textual cohesive devices, and

3   How the TT violates the employment of the textual cohesive devices required by the TT textual norms, and

4   How the translator opts for stylistic literalness to please the ST at the expense of an unnatural TL style.

The five different types of grammatical cohesion are defined briefly:

1   reference (endophoric and exophoric),

2   ellipsis (verbal, nominal, and clausal),

3   substitution (nominal and clausal),

4   conjunction (additive, adversative, causal, and temporal), and

5   lexical cohesion (the general noun, reiteration, synonymy, antonymy, collocation, hyponymy, and meronymy).

For more details on textual cohesive devices, see Halliday and Hasan (1976) and Abdul-Raof (2001, 2019).

It is necessary to remind the translation student of the distinction between the two types of cohesive elements:

1   The intra-sentential and inter-sentential cohesive devices: These are micro cohesion devices which are the conjunctions employed to link between words, phrases, clauses, sentences, and paragraphs. In both Arabic and English, we have four different types of micro cohesion devices: additive, adversative, causal, and temporal conjunctions, and

2   The textual cohesive devices: These are macro textual cohesion devices, such as reference, ellipsis, substitution, conjunction, and lexical cohesion.

5.3 Translation of reference

Reference is a relationship between a lexical item and its pronoun. Therefore, reference words are pronouns which refer to persons, things, and places; a word is linked to its pronoun. They do not have a full meaning in their own right but their meaning is determined through their context. Thus, pronouns create cohesion in the ST and the TT.

Translation of cohesion 189

In Arabic, reference words refer to nouns, determiners, adverbs, personal and demonstrative pronouns, and implicit pronouns within a verb, as in

الذين يُنفقونَ أموالهُم في سبيل اللهِ . . . لهم أجرُهُم عند ربِّهم ولا خوفٌ عليهم ولا هم يحزنون
(البقرة 262)

Those who spend their wealth in the way of God . . . will have their reward with their Lord, and there will be no fear concerning them, nor will they grieve, Q2:262.

where the implicit plural subject pronoun ون "they" of the verb يُنفقُونَ "they spend", the possessive plural pronoun (-hum) "their", the plural pronoun هُم "them" of لهُم, the plural possessive pronoun هُم "their" of أجرُهُم "their reward" and ربِّهم "their Lord", the plural object pronoun هم "them" of عَليهِم "upon them", the pronoun هُم "they", and the implicit plural subject pronoun ون "they" of the verb يحزنون "they grieve" refer to the same subject plural relative pronoun الَّذين "who".

5.3.1 Types of reference

The major types of reference are: (i) personal reference, (ii) anaphoric reference, (iii) cataphoric reference, (iv) demonstrative reference, and (v) comparative reference.

1 Personal reference refers to the following pronouns:

(i) The detached personal pronouns ضمير منفصل, such as إنِّي "I", أنا "I", هو "he", هي "she", هُنَّ "they" (feminine, plural), أنتَ "you" (singular, masculine), أنتم "you" (masculine, plural), as in

هي الممرضة – She is the nurse.
إنَّني أنا اللهُ لا إلهَ إلاَّ أنا (طه 14) – Indeed, I am God. There is no deity except Me, Q20:14, where (أنا) (I) is the personal pronoun.

(ii) The attached personal pronouns ضمير متصل which can be attached either to a verb, a noun, or a preposition, or which can be an implicit pronoun within a verb, as in

هذا كتابهم – This is their book.
سمر كتبت له – Samar wrote to him.

where the attached personal pronouns are هم، ه.

(iii) Possessive pronouns which are referred to as "determiners", such as ي "my" كتابي "my book", ه his كتابهُ "his book", ها "her" كتابها "her book".

إقرأ كتابَكَ كفى بنفسِكَ اليومَ عليكَ حسيبا (الإسراء 14)

Read your record. Today your own soul is enough to calculate your account, Q17:14.

where the determiner possessive pronoun كَ "your" (second-person singular masculine) of كتابَكَ "your book" is the personal reference.

190 *Translation of cohesion*

2 Anaphoric reference: This takes place when a noun (the antecedent) occurs first, then followed by its reference pronoun (anaphor), as in

سلمى طالبة مُجتهدةٌ. هي من مواليد بغداد – Salma is a hard-working student. She was born in Baghdad, where the antecedent is سلمى and its anaphor is هي.

نسائكُم هُنَّ لباسٌ لكم (البقرة 187) – Your wives, they are clothing for you, where the antecedent noun نساء (wives) is mentioned first then followed by its anaphoric reference pronoun هُنَّ (they).

3 Cataphoric reference: This takes place when a reference pronoun occurs first, then followed by the noun it refers to, as in

هُوَ اللهُ الذي لا إلهَ إلاَّ هُوَ (الحشر 22) – He is God, other than whom there is no deity.

where the pronoun هُوَ is cataphoric reference referring forward to its noun الله.

وفي خطابه يوم أمس أكّد الرئيسُ على أهمية التعاون الأقتصادي – In his speech yesterday, the President stressed the importance of economic cooperation.

where the pronoun ه refers forward to its noun الرئيس.

4 Demonstrative reference: This refers to demonstrative pronouns which refer to something either nearby or further away, such as هذا "this 'masculine, singular'", هذه "this 'feminine, singular'", ذلك "this, that", أوْلئك "those", and هؤلاء "those 'masculine, plural'", as in

هذا ربي هذا أكبر (الأنعام 78) – This is my lord, this is bigger, Q6:78.
هؤلاء أصدقائي – Those are my friends.

5 Comparative reference: Comparative reference is concerned with reference words such as أكبر "bigger, greater", (Q6:78), كبير "big, large", (Q2:282), أصغر "smaller", (Q10:61), صغير "small, little", (Q2:282), أقل "fewer, less", (Q18:39), قليل "little", (Q9:82), كثير "many, much", (Q9:82), أكثر "more, most", (Q18:34), كَثُرَ "become large, much", (Q4:7), أسوأ "worse", (Q39:35), and أقل "smaller, less", (Q72:24).

5.4 Translation and conjunctions

In Arabic translation studies, we need to consider the following:

1 The translator needs to distinguish between conjunctions (cohesive devices) أدوات الربط and texture devices أدوات حِبكة النص. There are different intra- and inter-sentential texture cohesive ties in the ST and the TT, such as (i) reference (endophoric reference and exophoric reference), (ii) substitution, (iii) ellipsis, (iv) conjunction, and (v) lexical cohesion (Halliday and Hasan 1976:4).
2 The translator should be aware of the fact that during the translation process from Arabic into English, we encounter translation problems with only two texture cohesive ties in Arabic – substitution and ellipsis.

Conjunction is a cohesive semantic relation and is a process that keeps words and sentences semantically connected (Halliday and Hasan 1976:226, 228, 320). For Salkie (1995:xi), conjunctive (cohesive) devices make the text coherent.

Translation of cohesion 191

In Arabic, we encounter two kinds of conjunctive adjuncts:

1 simple adverbs (coordinating conjunctions) like ولكن "but", لهذا "so", ثُمَّ "then", and
2 compound adverbs (prepositional expressions) like لهذا/عليه "therefore, thereupon", من علاوة على "whereat, because of that", (Q5:32), بسبب "because of", أجل ذلك/بسبب ذلك "furthermore", على الرغم من ذلك "in spite of that", مع ذلك "nevertheless", على كل حال "anyway", بدلاً من ذلك "instead of that", إضافة الى ذلك "besides, in addition to that", and على العكس من ذلك "on the contrary".

There are four major types of conjunctions:

1 additive conjunction و "and",
2 adversative conjunction لكن "but, however",
3 causal conjunction من أجل ذلك "because of that", and
4 temporal conjunction ثُمَّ/بعد إذن/بعد ذلك "then", قبل/بعد "before/after".

For more details on Arabic conjunctions, see Chapter 4, Section 4.4, and Abdul-Raof (2001:74–80).

5.5 Translation of ellipsis

Ellipsis indicate something left unsaid. For Beaugrande and Dressler (1981:66), an ellipsis is a cohesive device that contributes to the text's compactness and efficiency. There are three types of ellipses:

1 nominal ellipsis, as in John and Peter are students. Both came to the party, where we have nominal ellipsis because the nouns John and Peter are ellipted in the second sentence, and instead both is employed.
2 verbal ellipsis, as in John came to the party. Peter did not where verbal ellipsis is represented by the missing verb (come) in the second sentence.
3 clausal ellipsis, as in Have you finished your essay? Yes where clausal ellipsis is represented by the missing clause have finished the essay in the second sentence.

It is worthwhile to note that ellipses in Arabic have the pragmatic functions of (i) warning, (ii) specification, (iii) rebuke, and (iv) glorification.

An ellipsis is a cohesive device entailing a lexico-grammatical relation in which a word or a phrase is specified through the use of a grammatical signal indicating that this word or phrase is to be recovered from what has gone before – to be retrieved from the preceding text (Halliday and Hasan 1976:308, Salkie 1995:57). In other words, ellipsis indicates the leaving out of a word or a phrase instead of repeating the same word or phrase. Thus, there is a gap, but as readers, we can make sense of the ellipted (left out) items through the background information, which we derive from the previous or subsequent text. Therefore, ellipsis is a form of anaphoric and cataphoric cohesion where we presuppose something by means of what is implied or unsaid (Abdul-Raof 2019:150–154). Ellipsis contributes to the semantic structure of the ST and the TT. Ellipsis in Arabic can be both anaphoric and cataphoric. Anaphoric ellipsis refers to what has already been mentioned in the previous sentence. Cataphoric ellipsis refers to someone or something that is mentioned in the following sentence; the reader can recover the ellipted elements from the following sentence

192 *Translation of cohesion*

or from intertextuality. Ellipsis is also related to presupposition; it refers to what is known to the ST or TT reader.

It is worthwhile to note that ellipsis is somewhat similar to the cohesive tie of substitution because both involve referring back to someone/something that has been mentioned earlier in the previous text. Whereas in substitution a particular word refers back, in ellipsis there is a "gap" in the text. It is this "gap" that refers back to someone/something in the previous text (Salkie 1995:57). For Beaugrande and Dressler (1981:66), ellipsis is a cohesive device that contributes to the text's compactness and efficiency.

5.5.1 *Translation of anaphoric ellipsis*

In anaphoric ellipsis, we do not translate the ST ellipted elements although we know their specific ellipted words and their meanings. In other words, Arabic anaphoric ellipsis remains as anaphoric ellipsis in English. Anaphoric ellipsis occurs in both the ST and the TT and takes place when the context sentence occurs first followed by the elliptical sentence (a sentence which involves ellipsis). The context sentence is the sentence from which the translator can retrieve his/her presupposed meaning of the ellipted element. In terms of Arabic translation, the translator should not include the ellipted element(s), as in the following examples:

(A) لو كتبت الواجب ثانية هل ستقبلهُ؟

If I re-write the assignment, will you accept it?

(B) نعم

Yes

where the answer in (B) involves the ellipsis and the ellipted verb is سأقبلهُ "'I will' accept 'it'", which comes after the response word نعم.

أَئِذا مِتنا وكُنّا تُراباً وعِظاماً أَئِنّا لمبعُوثُونَ أَوَ آباؤُنا الأولون؟ قُل نَعَم (الصافات 16–18)
When we have died and become dust and bones, are we indeed to be resurrected? And our forefathers as well? Say: "Yes", Q37:16–18.

where the context sentence is أَئِذا مِتنا وكُنّا تُراباً وعِظاماً أَئِنّا لمبعُوثُونَ أَوَ آباؤُنا الأولون؟. This is followed by the sentence which has ellipsis: قُل نَعَم (. . .) – "Say: 'Yes (. . .)'". The ellipted verb تُبعثُون "you will be resurrected" comes after the response word (نَعم – yes), which the translator can retrieve from the passive participle مبعوثون "resurrected", (Q37:16) that has occurred in the previous context sentence.

We can now re-write the elliptical sentence (the sentence which involves ellipsis) Q37:18 and provide a sentence without ellipsis:

(أَئِذا مِتنا وكُنّا تُراباً وعِظاماً أَئِنّا لمبعُوثُونَ أَوَ آباؤُنا الأولون؟ قُل نَعَم (تُبعَثُون))
When we have died and become dust and bones, are we indeed to be resurrected? And our forefathers as well? Say: "Yes, (you will be resurrected)", Q37:16–18).

أَيَحسَبُ الإنسانُ أَلّن نجمَعَ عِظامَهُ؟ بَلى قادرينَ على أن نُسَوِّيَ بنانهُ (القيامة 3)
Does man think that We will not assemble his bones? Yes, we are able to proportion his fingertips, Q75:3–4.

Translation of cohesion 193

The context sentence is أَيَحسَبُ الإنسانُ ألَّن نجمعَ عِظامَهُ؟, from which the translator can retrieve his/her presupposed ellipted element that occurred in the elliptical sentence (the sentence which involves ellipsis) Q75:4 as explained below:

أَيَحسَبُ الإنسانُ ألَّن نجمعَ عِظامه؟ بَلى (نجمعُها) قادرينَ على أن نُسوِّيَ بنانه (القيامة 3–4)

Does man think that We will not assemble his bones? Yes, we are able to proportion his fingertips, Q75:3–4.

Through the context sentence (Q75:3), the translator can retrieve the presupposed ellipted element نجمعُها "to assemble them 'i.e., the bones'". The position of the ellipted element in the elliptical sentence Q75:4 is after the response word بَلى "yes", which signals an ellipted verb. The verb نجمعُ "to assemble" that occurred in the context sentence has made possible for the translator to provide the meaning of the ellipted element.

We can now re-write the elliptical sentence Q75:4 to get a sentence without ellipsis:

(بَلى (نجمَعُها) قادرينَ على أن نُسوِّيَ بنانهُ) – Yes, (We will assemble them (the bones)) and we are able to proportion his fingertips).

5.5.2 *Translation of cataphoric ellipsis*

Cataphoric ellipsis occurs when the elliptical sentence (a sentence which involves ellipsis) occurs first, followed by a sentence which is either immediately after the elliptical sentence or somewhere else in the same macro text. Therefore, the subsequent sentence that comes after the elliptical sentence acts as the context from which the translator can retrieve the presupposed meaning of the ellipted element. We have two types of cataphoric ellipsis:

1   Personal pronouns: We translate the ST ellipted personal pronoun. In the next example, we have ellipted personal pronouns which are preserved in the TT:

كريمٌ وشجاع – He is generous and brave.

where the ellipted pronoun هو is translated as "he".

صُمٌّ بُكمٌ عُميٌ (البقرة 18) They are deaf, dumb and blind, Q2:18
(هُم) صُمٌّ بُكمٌ عُميٌ) – They are deaf, dumb and blind.

ولا تحسبنَّ الذين قُتِلوا في سبيلِ اللهِ أمواتاً بل أحياءٌ عند ربِّهم يُرزَقُون (آل عمران 169)
And never think of those who have been killed in the cause of God as dead. Rather, they are alive with their Lord, receiving provision, Q3:169.

(ولا تحسبنَّ الذين قُتِلوا في سبيلِ اللهِ أمواتاً بل (هُم) أحياءٌ عند ربِّهم يُرزَقُون)
where the ellipted pronoun هم is translated as "they".

وقالوا اتَّخذَ الرحمانُ ولدا سبحانهُ بل عبادٌ مُكرمون (الأنبياء 26)
(وقالوا اتَّخذَ الرحمانُ ولدا سبحانهُ بل (هُم) عبادٌ مُكرمون)
And they say: "The Most Merciful has taken a son" Exalted is He. Rather they are honored servants.

where the ellipted pronoun هم is translated as "they".

194 *Translation of cohesion*

وقالت عجوزٌ عقيمٌ (الذاريات 29)

(وقالت (أنا) عجوزٌ عقيمٌ)

And said: (I) am a barren old woman, Q51:29

where the ellipted pronoun (أنا) is translated as (I).

يومٌ طويلٌ – It is a long day.

where the ellipted pronoun (هو) referring to the masculine noun يوم "a day" is kept in the TT as "it".

نارٌ حامية (القارعة 11)

((هي) نارٌ حامية)

(It) is a fire, intensely hot, Q101:11.

نارُ اللهِ الموقدة (الهُمزة 6)

((هي) نارُ اللهِ الموقدة)

(It) is the fire of God, fueled, Q104:6.

في سِدرٍ مخضُود (الواقعة 28)

((أصحابُ اليمين/هم) في سِدرٍ مخضُود)

"The companions of the right/They" are among lote trees with thorns removed, Q56:28.

where either the noun phrase أصحابُ اليمين "the companions of the right" or its pronoun هم "they" is mentioned in the TT.

They accuse him of corruption. Rather <u>he</u> is an honest man – مونه بالفساد، بل رجلٌ نزيه

2 Cataphoric ellipsis through the deletion of the verb اذكر "remember" (imperative, second-person masculine) in the ST: This represents verbal ellipsis and the ellipted verb should have occurred sentence-initially, i.e., if we re-write the ellipted sentence. The particle إذ "when" signals this form of ellipsis. However, the ellipted verb إذكر occurs neither in the ST nor in the TT; the ellipted verb إذكر should not be recovered and translated. Thus, both the ST and the TT remain elliptical – we do not recover the verb اذكر and translate it, as in the following examples:

إذ قالَ ربُّكَ للملائكةِ (البقرة 30)

((إذكر) إذ قالَ ربُّكَ للملائكةِ)

When your Lord said to the angels, Q2:30, but not "Mention, Remember" When your Lord said to the angels.

إذ يمكُرُ بكَ (الأنفال 30)

((إذكر) إذ يمكُرُ بكَ)

When plotted against you, Q8:30, but not "Mention, Remember" When plotted against you.

إذ يحكمان في الحرث (الأنبياء 78)

((إذكر) إذ يحكمان في الحرث)

When they judged concerning the field, Q21:78, but not "Mention, Remember" When they judged concerning the field.

5.5.3 Translation of nominal ellipsis

Nominal ellipsis includes the deletion of either (i) a personal pronoun, (ii) a noun, or (iii) an adjective.

(A) Can all birds fly?
(B) They all can; and most do. (Meaning (All (birds) can; and most (birds) do).

(A) You need to have a car.
(B) OK, I'll get one. (Meaning (OK, I'll get a (car)).

If you want to know how to polish your shoes, just ask Janet. Hers sparkle.
Take these pills three times a day. And you'd better have some more of those, too.
Your shoes are dirty. Smith's (mine/hers/my father's) sparkle.

(A) Which shirt will you wear?
(B) The best. (Meaning (The best (of the shirts)).

(A) I hope no bags are stolen.
(B) None to speak of. (Meaning (No (bags) to speak of).

(A) I've cooked a very nice chocolate cake.
(B) May I give you some? (Meaning (May I give you some (very nice chocolate cake)?)

(A) Have some orange juice.
(B) I don't see any. There isn't any.

(A) There is some in the fridge.
(B) There is none. (Meaning (I don't see any (orange juice)/There isn't any (orange juice)/ There is some (orange juice) in the fridge/There is no (orange juice)).

1　Examples of ellipsis of a personal pronoun (this also applies to all the examples discussed in section 5.5.2):

أغبياء – Stupid!
where the ellipted personal pronoun is هم "they"; "They are stupid".

(البقرة 18) Q2:18 ,صُمٌّ بُكمٌ عُميٌ – Deaf, dumb and blind
(هُم) صُمٌّ بُكمٌ عُميٌ – (They) are deaf, dumb and blind.

ولا تحسبنَّ الذين قُتِلوا في سبيلِ اللهِ أمواتاً بل أحياءٌ عند ربِّهم يُرزَقُون (آل عمران 169)
And never think of those who have been killed in the cause of God as dead. Rather, (they) are alive with their Lord, receiving provision, Q3:169.

(ولا تحسبنَّ الذين قُتِلوا في سبيلِ اللهِ أمواتاً بل (هُم) أحياءٌ عند ربِّهم يُرزَقُون)
where the ellipted pronoun هم is translated as "they".

وقالوا اتَّخذَ الرحمانُ ولدا سبحانهُ بل عِبادٌ مُكرمون (الأنبياء 26)
And they say: "The Most Merciful has taken a son" Exalted is He. Rather (they) are honored servants.

196 *Translation of cohesion*

(وقالوا اتَّخذ الرحمانُ ولدا سبحانهُ بل (هُم) عِبادٌ مُكرمون)

where the ellipted pronoun هم is translated as "they".

And said: (I) am a barren old woman, Q51:29 – وقالت عجوزٌ عقيمٌ (الذاريات 29)

(وقالت (أنا) عجوزٌ عقيمٌ)

where the ellipted pronoun أنا is translated as "I".

نارٌ حامية (القارعة 11)

((هي) نارٌ حامية)

(It) is a fire, intensely hot, Q101:11.

نارُ اللهِ الموقدة (الهُمزة 6)

((هي) نارُ اللهِ الموقدة)

(It) is the fire of God, fueled, Q104:6.

2   Examples of ellipsis of a noun or a noun phrase: The ellipted noun or the noun phrase should not be translated, as in the following examples:

اسأل المدرسة عني – Ask the school about me.

where the ellipted noun phrase is (إدارة المدرسة/مدير المدرسة) (the school administration/the school headteacher).

أوَكُلَّما عاهدُوا عَهداً نبَذَهُ فريقٌ منهم (البقرة 100)

(أوَكُلَّما عاهدُوا (اللهَ) عَهداً نبَذَهُ فريقٌ منهم)

Is it not that every time they took a covenant (with God) a party of them threw it away?

وسئل القرية (يوسف 82)

And ask (the people of) the city.

كلاً إذا بلَغَت التراقي (القيامة 26)

(كلاً إذا بلَغَت (الروحُ/النفسُ التراقي)

No! When (the spirit/the soul) has reached the collar bones.

حتى توارت بالحِجاب (ص 32)

(حتى توارت (الشمسُ) بالحِجاب)

Until it (the sun) disappeared into the curtain of darkness.

وجَعلَ لكم سرابيلَ تقيكُم الحرَّ (النحل 81)

(وجَعلَ لكم سرابيلَ تقيكُم الحرَّ (والبردَ))

And He has made for you garments which protect you from the heat (and the cold).

قالَ فمن ربُّكُما يا مُوسى (طه 49)

(قالَ فمن ربُّكُما يا مُوسى (وهارون))

He said: "So who is the Lord of you two, O Moses (and Aaron)?"

والراسخونَ في العِلم يقُولونَ آمنّا بهِ (آل عمران 7)

(والراسخونَ في العِلم يقُولونَ (ربَّنا) آمنّا بهِ)

But those firm in knowledge say: (Our Lord) "We believe in it."

في سِدر مخضودٍ (الواقعة 28)

((أصحابُ اليمين) في سِدر مخضودٍ)

(The companions of the right) Among lote trees with thorns removed.

Translation of cohesion 197

فَأَتاهُم اللهُ مِن حيثُ لم يحتسِبوا (الحشر 2)

(فَأَتاهُم (أمرُ) اللهُ مِن حيثُ لم يحتسِبوا)

(The decree) of God came upon them from where they had not expected.

مِن عَمِلَ صالِحاً فلِنَفسِهِ ومن أساءَ فعَليها (فصلت 46)

مِن عَمِلَ صالِحاً ف (عملُهُ) لِنَفسِهِ ومن أساءَ فعَليها)

Whoever does righteousness, (his work) is for his soul, and whoever does evil does so against it.

إذا قيلَ لهُم ماذا أنزلَ ربُّكُم قالوا أساطيرُ الأولين (النحل 24)

(إذا قيلَ لهُم ماذا أنزلَ ربُّكُم قالوا (هو) أساطيرُ الأولين)

When it is said to them "What has your Lord sent down?" They say: "(It, i.e., the Qur'an) legends of the former people."

3   Example of ellipsis of a nominal sentence without a main verb: The ellipted nominal sentence without a main verb should be translated, as in the following example:

ولو أنَّ قُرآناً سُيِّرت بهِ الجبالُ أو قُطِّعَت به الأرضُ أو كُلِّمَ به الموتى (الرعد 31)

Had it been possible for a Lecture to cause the mountains to move, or the earth to be torn asunder, or the dead to speak, (this Qur'an would have done so) (Pickthall 1930:no page).

If there were a Qur'an with which mountains were moved, or the earth were cloven asunder, or the dead were made to speak, (this would be the one!) (Ali 1934:no page).

If only a Koran whereby the mountains were set in motion, or the earth were cleft, or the dead were spoken to (Arberry 1955:109).

Yet even if [they should listen to] a [divine] discourse by which mountains could be moved, or the earth cleft asunder, or the dead made to speak – [they who are bent on denying the truth would still refuse to believe in it]! (Asad 1980:501).

If there were a Qur'an with which mountains were moved, or the earth were cloven asunder, or the dead were made to speak, (this would be the one) (Mushaf Al-Madinah An-Nabawiyah 1990:683).

And if there was any Qur'an by which the mountains would be removed or the earth would be broken apart or the dead would be made to speak, (it would be this Qur'an) (Saheeh International 1997:332).

If there were ever to be a Qur'an with which mountains could be moved, the earth shattered, or the dead made to speak (it would have been this one) (Abdel Haleem 2005:155).

where the ellipted information placed between brackets in the above TTs is necessary for the meaning and the grammatical structure of the TT. This is because the ellipted details represent the main clause of the conditional sentence. However, the only translation which has left out the ellipted nominal sentence is Arberry's. In Arabic, the ellipted no-main-verb nominal sentence is placed back in its position below:

ولو أنَّ قُرآناً سُيِّرت بهِ الجبالُ أو قُطِّعَت به الأرضُ أو كُلِّمَ به الموتى (لكانَ هذا القرآن).

The nominal ellipsis which involves the ellipsis of a nominal sentence without a main verb is rare in Arabic. The Arabic conditional sentence usually involves the subordinate and the main clauses. Also, we encounter in Qur'anic Arabic the subordinate clause with a main verb, as in

198 *Translation of cohesion*

لو كانَ البحرُ مِداداً لكلماتِ ربي لنفدَ البحرُ قبل أن تنفدَ كلماتُ ربي (الكهف 109)

If the whole ocean were ink for writing the words of my Lord, it would run dry before those words were exhausted, Q18:109.

where the conditional subordinate clause is لو كانَ البحرُ مِداداً لكلماتِ ربي, followed by the main-verb subordinate clause لنفدَ البحرُ ....

4   Examples of ellipsis of an adjective: This includes examples like

How many things we have witnessed.

where the adjective سيِّئةٍ "bad" is ellipted.

كم من أمورٍ سيِّئةٍ شهدنا

How many bad things we have witnessed.

And how many {} cities have we destroyed, Q7:4.

وكم من قرية أهلكناها
هو الذي جعلَ لكم الليلَ لِتسكُنوا فيه والنهارَ مُبصِرا (يونس 67)

It is He who made for you the night {} to rest therein and the day giving sight, Q10:67.

وكان ورائَهم ملكٌ يأخُذُ كُلَّ سفينةٍ غصبا (الكهف 79)

There was after them a {} king who seized every ship by force, Q18:79.

The ellipted adjectives in the above elliptical sentences are

And how many (unjust) cities have we destroyed, Q7:4

وكم من قرية (ظالمةٍ) أهلكناها
هو الذي جعلَ لكم الليلَ (مُظلِماً) لِتسكُنوا فيه والنهارَ مُبصِرا

It is He who made for you the night (dark) to rest therein and the day giving sight, Q10:67.

وكان ورائهم ملكٌ (ظالمٌ) يأخُذُ كُلَّ سفينةٍ غصبا

There was after them an (unjust) king who seized every ship by force, Q18:79.

5.5.4   *Translation of verbal ellipsis*

Verbal ellipsis involves the deletion of a main verb. However, the translator must be aware of the fact that the Arabic verb includes an implicit subject, such as كتَبَ "He wrote", and that we may encounter a verbal construction including an object, like سألَهُم "He asked them". Thus, in Arabic translation, we must consider such grammatical structures as examples of verbal ellipsis. Thus, verbal ellipsis in Arabic should be distinguished from clausal substitution which will be discussed in Section 5.6.1.3 next. Let us consider the following examples of verbal ellipsis:

(A) **Would you like to have** a boiled egg or a cheese sandwich?
(B) A cheese sandwich, please.

Translation of cohesion   199

where the ellipted component is a verbal clause: "**I would like to have** 'a cheese sandwich'".

(A) Is Janet going to resign?
(B) She might.

  She may not.
  She should.

where the ellipted component is a verb: "She might **resign**/She may not **resign**/She should **resign**".

(A) Had you been reading?
(A) Yes, I have.

where the ellipted element is a verb: "Yes, I have 'been reading'".

(A) What have you been doing?
(B) Reading.

where the ellipted element is a verbal clause: "I have been 'reading'".

وإذ استسقى موسى لقومهِ فقُلنا أضرب بعصاكَ الحَجَرَ فانفَجَرَت منهُ إثنتى عشرةَ عيناً (البقرة 60)
(وإذ استسقى موسى لقومهِ فقُلنا أضرب بعصاكَ الحَجَرَ (فَضَرَبَ) فانفَجَرَت منهُ إثنتى عشرةَ عيناً)
When Moses prayed for water for his people, so We said: "Strike the stone with your staff. (And he struck) And there gushed forth from it twelve springs".

وإذ يَضَعُ إبراهيمُ القواعِدَ من البيتِ وإسماعيلُ ربنا تقبَّل منَّا (البقرة 127)
(وإذ يَضَعُ إبراهيمُ القواعِدَ من البيتِ وإسماعيلُ (قائلاً) ربنا تقبَّل منَّا)
And when Abraham was raising the foundations of the house and Ishmael. (Saying:) "Our Lord accept this from us".

الذينَ يذكُرونَ اللهَ قياماً وقُعُوداً . . . ربَّنا ما خَلَقتَ هذا باطلاً (آل عمران 191)
(الذينَ يذكُرونَ اللهَ قياماً وقُعُودا . . . (يقُولونَ) ربَّنا ما خَلَقتَ هذا باطلاً)
Who remember God while standing or sitting . . . (They say:) "Our Lord, You did not create this aimlessly".

والملائِكَةُ يدخُلونَ عليهم من كلِّ بابٍ سلامٌ عليكم (الرعد 23–24)
(والملائِكَةُ يدخُلونَ عليهم من كل بابٍ (قائلينَ) سلامٌ عليكم)
And the angels will enter upon them from every gate (saying): "Peace be upon you".

قيلَ للذينَ اتقوا ماذا أنزلَ ربُّكم قالوا خيراً (النحل 30)
(قيلَ للذينَ اتقوا ماذا أنزلَ ربُّكم قالوا (أنزلَ) خيراً)
It will be said to those who feared God: "What did your Lord send down?" They will say: "Good (was sent down)".

200 *Translation of cohesion*

فأقِم وجهَكَ للدين حنيفاً فِطرتَ اللهِ التي فَطرَ الناسَ عليها (الروم 30)

(فأقِم وجهَكَ للدين حنيفاً (ألزمو ا/إتّبعو ا) فِطرتَ اللهِ التي فطرَ الناسَ عليها)

So, direct your face toward the religion inclining to truth. (Follow/adhere to) the natural disposition of God which He has instilled in people.

فإذا لقيتُم الذينَ كفرو ا فضَربَ الرقاب (محمد 4) – So when you meet those who disbelieve, (strike) necks.

(فإذا لقيتُم الذينَ كفرو ا فَ (أضربو ا) ضَربَ الرقاب)

إنّا زيّنّا السماءَ الدُنيا بزينةِ الكواكب وحِفظاً من كلِّ شيطانٍ مارد (الصافات 6–7) – Indeed, We have adorned the nearest heaven with an adornment of stars. And (protected it) as protection against every rebellious devil.

(إنّا زيّنّا السماءَ الدُنيا بزينةِ الكواكب و (حَفَظناها) حِفظاً من كلِّ شيطانٍ مارد)

However, at times, verbal ellipsis takes place in the TT because the Arabic sentence is stylistically a hypotactic (complex structure) sentence that does not repeat the same verb, and the second and third subject do not have a verb. Thus, we have the following translation based on verbal ellipsis to overcome the ST complex structure problem:

شهِدَ اللهُ أنّهُ لا إلهَ إلاّ هوَ والملائكةُ وأولو ا العلم قائماً بالقسطِ (آل عمران 18)

Allah witnesses that there is no deity except Him and so **do** the angels and those of knowledge and that He is maintaining creation in justice, Q3:18.

However, to make the translation process simple, we recommend to simplify the ST complex structure to the student as illustrated here:

شهِدَ + اللهُ + و الملائكةُ + و أولو ا العلم + أنّهُ لا إلهَ إلاّ هوَ + قائماً بالقسطِ

where we have the main verb شَهِدَ + three subjects اللهُ/الملائكةُ/أولو ا العلم + the complement. Thus, we can produce a straightforward translation with a smooth style as

Allah, the angels and those of knowledge witness that there is no deity except Him and that He is maintaining creation in justice.

where we have the three subjects "Allah, the angels, and those of knowledge" + main verb "witness" + the complement "that there is no . . .". Thus, we have avoided the translation based on verbal ellipsis.

Also, in

(أ)   لم أرى في حياتي مثل هذا قط.

(ب)   ولا أنا.

(A) I did not see anything like this in my life at all.

(B) Neither did I.

where, in both Arabic and English, we have verbal ellipsis instead of repeating the same verb أرى "see". Verbal ellipsis is represented by the pronoun أنا, which is also an implicit subject pronoun أنا in the main verb أرى. Thus, in English, we have employed verbal ellipsis through "did" to replace the ellipted main verb "see". Without verbal ellipsis, the Arabic sentence should read as ولم أرى أنا كذلك.

5.6 Translation of substitution

Substitution is the replacement of one item (a word or phrase) by another to avoid repetition and is a cohesive and textual relation between words or phrases. It is a cohesive tie in both the ST and the TT whose function is to cohere one piece of text to another (Halliday and Hasan 1976:226). In substitution, a word is specified through the use of a grammatical signal indicating that it is to be recovered from what has gone before.

5.6.1 Types of substitution

Substitution is a lexico-grammatical relation – a relation in the wording rather than in the meaning. Therefore, the different types of substitution are defined grammatically rather than semantically (Halliday and Hasan 1976:90). The substitute may function either as a noun, a verb, or as a clause. There are three types of substitution:

1   nominal substitution: This is represented by "one" or "ones", as in "I gave you red, green, and yellow colouring pencils. Give back the green ones only" where substitution is represented by the word "ones" that stands for the noun "colouring pencils". The word "same" also functions as a nominal substitute, as in:

(A): I will buy a new red car. سأشتري سيارة حمراء جديدة
(B): I will buy the same. سأشتري نفس الشيء

2   verbal substitution: This is realized by "do", as in:

(A): I hope you understood my point. أتمنّى أنّك فهمتني
(B): I did. فهمتُ

where "did" used by the second speaker (B) is employed in English but it does not exist in Arabic, which requires the repetition of the same verb فهمتُ used by the second speaker (B), substituting the verb فهِمَ.

3   clausal substitution: This refers to the substitution of an entire clause through the word (so), as in

(A): Did John pass his driving test? هل إجتازَ جون اختبار السياقة؟
(B): I was told so. أخبَروني بذلكَ

Thus, in both the ST and the TT, we have (i) nominal substitution, and (ii) clausal substitution.

5.6.1.1 Translation of verbal substitution

In Arabic to English translation, the translator must be aware of the fact that English has verbal substitution through the verbal substitutes "do, be, have"; however, Arabic does not have

202 *Translation of cohesion*

this type of verbal substitution. Instead, Arabic favors to reiterate (repeat) the main verb, as illustrated in the following examples:

There many facts. I know them but you <u>do</u> not. – لا انتم و أعرفها أنا. كثيرة حقائق هناك
تعرفونها

The child did not break the window. Janet <u>did</u>. – كسرته جانيت. الشباك الطفلُ يكسر لم

لا أمتلكُ هذا المبلغ الكبير من المال. أنت تمتلكه

I do not have this large amount of money. You <u>have</u>.

You are not lying. He <u>is</u> – دائما يكذبُ هو. تكذب لا أنت

I will work as hard for those who didn't vote for me as those who did (Joe Biden, the president-elect, 8 November 2020).

سأعملُ بجدٍ من أجل أولئك الذين لم يصوّتوا لي ولأولئك الذين صوّتوا لي (جو بايدن، الرئيس الأمريكي المُنتخب، 8 نوفمبر 2020)

where we have verbal substitution through the verbal substitutes "do, did, have, is", which each substitutes a whole verbal clause كَسَرَتهُ "She broke it", تَملِكُهُ "you have it", الكاذبُ "the liar", and "did vote for me" الذين صوَّتُوا لي, respectively.

اللهُ يعلمُ وأنتم لا <u>تعلمون</u> (البقرة 216)

God knows and you <u>do</u> not, Q2:216.

وما كفرَ سليمانُ ولكنَّ الشياطينَ <u>كفروا</u> (البقرة 102)

It was not Solomon who disbelieved but the devils <u>did</u>, Q2:102.

where the verb كفرَ "disbelieved" is repeated at the end of the sentence, while English employs the linguistic mechanism of verbal substitution through the verbal substitute "did". The same applies to the English verbal substitute "be 'am, is, are, was, were'" and "have 'has, have, had'". An alternative translation of Q2:102 is to have the verb كفرَ translated to "has disbelieved" or to a noun "disbeliever":

It is not Solomon who has disbelieved but the devils <u>have</u>, Q2:102.
It was not Solomon who was a disbeliever but the devils <u>were</u>, Q2:102.

This is an interesting observation in contrastive linguistics surrounding Arabic translation: English has the linguistic mechanism of verbal substitution through the verbs "have" and "were" at the end of the sentence. However, Arabic reiterates the first verb كفرَ. Thus, we can claim that the linguistic verbal element كفرَ "disbelieved, has disbelieved" or the linguistic nominal element كافرٌ "disbeliever" is not repeated in English but is replaced by a substitution item "do", "has", or "be".

Similarly,

أولائِكَ يلعنُهُم اللهُ ويلعنُهُم اللّاعِنُون (البقرة 159)

God rejects them, and so <u>do</u> others, Q2:159.

Translation of cohesion 203

where the verb يَلْعَن "to curse" is reiterated.

فاقض ما أنتَ قاض إنَّما تقض هذه الحياةَ الدنيا (طه 72)

So decide whatever you will. You can only <u>do</u> so for the matters of this present life, Q20:72.

where the verb أقضِ "to decide" is repeated in Q20:72 but is substituted in English by the verb (do).

إنَّهُم يكيدونَ كيداً. وأكيدُ كيداً. (الطارق 15–16)

They plot and scheme, but so do I (Abdel Haleem 2005:417).

where the verb أكيدُ "to plot" is replaced by the verb "do".

5.6.1.2 *Translation of nominal substitution*

Nominal substitution occurs when a noun or noun phrase is replaced by another noun. Both Arabic and English have nominal substitution. The nominal substitutes in Arabic include (i) the noun غير, "نفس الشيء الأمر, الشخص "the same 'thing, matter, person'", واحِد/واحِدة "one", آخر/أخرى "another", (ii) demonstrative pronoun هذا "this", (iii) personal pronoun هو "he", (iv) demonstrative pronoun أولئك "those", (v) a general word, and (vi) the pronoun هُم- "they" attached to the auxiliary verb إنَّ. Let us consider the following examples of nominal substitution in Arabic to English translation:

My car is old. I want to buy a new <u>one</u>.

سيارتي قديمة. أريد أن أشتري واحِدة جديدة
(أ)   ما هو رأيك؟ أظن أن الأمر فيه مبالغة. وما رأي أخيك؟
(ب)   نفس الشيء

(A) What is your opinion? I believe there is exaggeration. And what about your brother's opinion?
(B) The <u>same</u>.

هذا مكاني. كلاّ هذا لي – This is my place. No. This is <u>mine</u>.
إنكسر هاتفي. أحتاج أن أشتري غيره. – My mobile has broken. I need to buy <u>another one</u>.
يجب أن نحترم أحمد. هو صديقي – We have to respect Ahmad. He is my friend and yours
وصديقكم
جنّات عدنٍ مُفتَّحة لهُم الأبواب . . . عندهُم قاصِراتُ الطرفِ أتراب. هذا ما تُوعدونَ ليوم الحساب (ص 50–53)

Gardens of perpetual residence whose doors will be opened to them. With them will be women limiting their glances and of equal age . . . <u>This</u> is what you are promised for the day of account, Q38:50–53.

where the demonstrative pronoun هذا "this" substitutes for the no-main-verb nominal sentences جنّاتُ عدنٍ مُفتَّحة لهُم الأبواب "Gardens of perpetual residence whose doors will be

204   *Translation of cohesion*

opened to them" and أتراب قاصراتُ الطرفِ عندهُم "With them will be women limiting their glances and of equal age".

إنَّ للطاغينَ لشرَّ مآبٍ . . . جهنَّمَ يصلونها (ص 55–56)
> Indeed, for the transgressors is an evil place of return – <u>hell</u>, in which they will burn, Q38:55–56).

where the general word جهنَّمَ "hell" substitutes for the noun phrase شرَّ مآبٍ "an evil place of return".

والقُرآن ذي الذكر . . . هو نبأٌ عظيم . . . إن هو إلاَّ ذكرٌ للعالمين (ص 1، 67 و 87)
> By the Qur'an containing reminder . . . <u>It</u> is great news . . . <u>It</u> is but a reminder to the world, Q38:1, 67 and 87.

The above text includes nominal substitution where the pronoun هو "it" substitutes for the noun phrase القُرآن ذي الذِكر "the Qur'an containing reminder". If we bring back what the pronoun هو has substituted, the alternative sentence will not hang together because it lacks cohesion:

والقُرآن ذي الذكر . . . القُرآن ذي الذكر نبأً عظيم . . . إن القُرآن ذي الذكر إلاَّ ذكرٌ للعالمين

By the Qur'an containing reminder . . . The Qur'an containing reminder is great news . . . The Qur'an containing reminder is but a reminder to the world.

السابقون السابقون. أُولئِكَ المُقرَّبون (الواقعة 10–11)
> The forerunners, the forerunners. <u>Those</u> are the ones brought near to God, Q56:10–11.

This is a cohesive sentence where nominal substitution in Q56:10–11 is achieved through the demonstrative pronoun أُولئِكَ "those", which substitutes the noun phrase السابقون السابقون "the forerunners, the forerunners". Without substitution, the sentence will lack cohesion as can be observed in the following alternative grammatical and stylistic pattern:

السابقون السابقون. السابقون السابقون المُقرَّبون

The forerunners, the forerunners. The forerunners, the forerunners are the ones brought near to God.

أصحابُ الشمال ما أصحابُ الشمال. في سموم وحميم. وظلٍ من يحموم. لا باردٍ ولا كريم. إنَّهُم كانوا قبلَ ذلكَ مُترفين (الواقعة 41–45)
> The companions of the left – what are the companions of the left? They will be in scorching fire and scalding water, and a shade of black smoke, neither cool nor beneficial. Indeed, <u>they</u> were, before that, indulging in affluence, Q56:41–45.

where nominal substitution is achieved through the masculine third-person plural pronoun هُم "they" attached to إنَّ and substitutes for the noun phrase أصحابُ الشمال "the companions of the left".

Translation of cohesion 205

مَثَلُ الجَنَّةِ التي وُعِدَ المُتَّقُونَ تجري من تحتها الأنهارُ أُكُلُها دائِمٌ وظِلُّها تِلْكَ عُقبى الذينَ اتَّقوا (الرعد 35)

> The example of paradise which the righteous have been promised is that beneath it riv-
> ers flow. Its fruit is lasting, and its shade. That is the consequence for the righteous,
> Q13:35).

where the demonstrative pronoun تِلْكَ "that" substitutes for the noun الجَنَّةِ "paradise".

5.6.1.3 *Translation of clausal substitution*

In clausal substitution, the presupposed is a whole clause with a main verb. The clausal substitutes are like the expressions نفس الشيء/نفس الشيء/كذلك "the same/the same thing", إن صحَّ "if so", the demonstrative pronoun ذلك "that", ذلك/إن كان الأمرُ كذلك/إن كان هذا صحيحاً the personal pronoun أولئكَ "those", the demonstrative pronoun هذا "this", the pronoun هو "he", and the pronoun هاؤلاء "these". In terms of Arabic translation, there is no problem involved in the translation of clausal substitution, as we can observe from the following examples:

أُريد ساندوج جبنة رجاءً – I want a cheese sandwich, please.
(وأنا كذلك (أنا نفس الشيء – And so do I (The same for me),
where (كذلك/نفس الشيء – do/the same) substitutes the verbal clause (أُريدُ – I want).
كسرت جانيت الباب وأطفأت جميع الأضوية. إن صحَّ ذلك (إن كان هذا صحيحا) فيجب محاسبتها – Janet broke the window and switched off all lights. If so, she much be held accountable.
where (if so) has substituted the two verbal clauses (كَسَرَت . . . أطفأت . .).
يقولون أنَّ الأقتصاد سوف يتحسن. أنا شخصياً لا أُصدّق ذلك أبداً – They say that the economy will improve. I, personally, do not believe this at all.
الناس الذين يساعدون المحتاج والذين يعملون بإخلاص والذين لا يسرقون أموال الناس، هؤلاء يستحقون الثناء – People who help the needy, who work sincerely, and who do not steal people's money; these are the ones who deserve to be praised.
زُيِّنَ للناسِ حُبُّ الشهواتِ من النساءِ والبنينَ والقناطيرَ المُقنطرةِ من الذهب والفضَّةِ والخيلِ المُسوَّمةِ والأنعام والحرثِ ذلكَ متاعُ الحياةِ الدنيا (آل عمران 14 – (Beautified for people is the love of that which they desire – of women and sons, heaped-up sums of gold and silver, fine branded horses, and cattle and tilled land. That is the enjoyment of worldly life, Q3:14.

where the demonstrative pronoun ذلكَ "that" substitutes for the clause:
حُبُّ الشهواتِ من) النساءِ والبنينَ والقناطيرَ المُقنطرةِ من الذهبِ والفضَّةِ والخيلِ المُسوَّمةِ والأنعامِ والحرثِ – the love of that which they desire – of women and sons, heaped-up sums of gold and silver, fine branded horses, and cattle and tilled land.

الذين يستحبُّونَ الحياةَ الدنيا على الآخرةِ ويصُدّونَ عن سبيلِ اللهِ ويبغُونها عِوجاً أولئكَ في ضلالٍ بعيد (إبراهيم 3)

> The ones who prefer the worldly life over the hereafter and avert people from the way
> of God, trying to make it crooked. Those are in extreme error, Q14:3.

206 *Translation of cohesion*

where the demonstrative pronoun أُولَئِكَ "those" substitutes the clause الَّذِينَ يَسْتَحِبُّونَ الْحَيَاةَ الدُّنْيَا عَلَى الآخِرَةِ وَيَصُدُّونَ عَن سَبِيلِ اللهِ وَيَبْغُونَهَا عِوَجَا "The ones who prefer the worldly life over the hereafter and avert people from the way of God, trying to make it crooked".

الَّذِينَ آمَنُوا وَعَمِلُوا الصَّالِحَاتِ فِي رَوْضَاتِ الْجَنَّةِ لَهُم مَّا يَشَاؤُونَ عِندَ رَبِّهِمْ ذَلِكَ هُوَ الْفَضْلُ الْكَبِيرُ (الشورى 22)

Those who have believed and done righteous deeds will be in lush regions of paradise having whatever they will in the presence of their Lord. <u>That</u> is what is the great bounty, Q42:22.

where ذَلِكَ "that" substitutes for the clause فِي رَوْضَاتِ الْجَنَّةِ لَهُم مَّا يَشَاؤُونَ عِندَ رَبِّهِمْ "in lush regions of paradise having whatever they will in the presence of their Lord."

وَهُوَ الَّذِي يَبْدَأُ الْخَلْقَ ثُمَّ يُعِيدُهُ وَهُوَ أَهْوَنُ عَلَيْهِ (الروم 27)

It is He who begins creation; then He repeats it, and that is easier for Him, Q30:27.

where هُوَ "this, that" substitutes for the clause يَبْدَأُ الْخَلْقَ ثُمَّ يُعِيدُهُ "He begins creation then He repeats it".

Other examples of clausal substitution are encountered in Q63:9 where the demonstrative pronoun ذَلِكَ "that" substitutes for the clause لَا تُلْهِكُمْ أَمْوَالُكُمْ وَلَا أَوْلَادُكُمْ عَن ذِكْرِ اللهِ "let not your wealth and your children divert you from the remembrance of God". In Q17:22–39, the demonstrative pronoun ذَلِكَ "that" substitutes for all the clauses that have been said before. In Q18:96–98, the demonstrative pronoun هَذَا "this" substitutes for the clauses آتُونِي زُبَرَ الْحَدِيدِ حَتَّى إِذَا سَاوَى بَيْنَ الصَّدَفَيْنِ قَالَ انفُخُوا حَتَّى إِذَا جَعَلَهُ نَاراً قَالَ آتُونِي أُفْرِغْ عَلَيْهِ قِطْراً "Bring me sheets of iron" until, when he had leveled them between the two mountain walls, he said: "Blow with bellows' until when he had made it like fire, he said: 'Bring me, that I may pour over it molten copper", فَمَا اسْطَاعُوا أَن يَظْهَرُوهُ "were unable to pass over it", and وَمَا اسْتَطَاعُوا لَهُ نَقْبا "nor were they able to effect in it any penetration". In Q5:59–60, the demonstrative pronoun ذَلِكَ "that" substitutes for the clause آمَنَّا بِاللهِ وَمَا أُنزِلَ إِلَيْنَا وَمَا أُنزِلَ مِن قَبْلُ "we have believed in God and what was revealed to us and what was revealed before". However, the pronoun أُولَئِكَ "those" substitutes for the clauses مَن لَعَنَهُ اللهُ "those whom God has cursed" and وَغَضِبَ عَلَيْهِ وَجَعَلَ مِنْهُمُ الْقِرَدَةَ وَالْخَنَازِيرَ وَعَبَدَ الطَّاغُوتَ "with whom He became angry and made of them apes and pigs and slaves of ṭāghūt". In Q56:52–56, the demonstrative pronoun هَذَا "this" substitutes for the clauses لَآكِلُونَ مِن شَجَرٍ مِّن زَقُّومٍ "You will be eating from trees of zaqqum", فَمَالِئُونَ مِنْهَا الْبُطُونَ "filling with it your bellies", فَشَارِبُونَ عَلَيْهِ مِنَ الْحَمِيمِ "drinking on top of it from scalding water", and شُرْبَ الْهِيمِ "and will drink as the drinking of thirsty camels". In Q30:38, the demonstrative pronoun ذَلِكَ "that" substitutes for the clause فَآتِ ذَا الْقُرْبَى حَقَّهُ وَالْمِسْكِينَ وَابْنَ السَّبِيلِ "So, give the relative his right, as well as the needy and the traveler" and the demonstrative pronoun أُولَئِكَ "those" and the detached pronoun هم "they" substitute for الَّذِينَ يُرِيدُونَ وَجْهَ اللهِ "who desire the countenance of God". The same applies to مَا آتَيْتُم مِّن زَكَاةٍ تُرِيدُونَ وَجْهَ اللهِ "What you give in zakat desiring the countenance of God", (Q30:39). In Q36:38, the demonstrative pronoun ذَلِكَ "that" substitutes for the main-verb nominal sentence الشَّمْسُ تَجْرِي لِمُسْتَقَرٍّ لَّهَا "the sun runs on course towards its stopping point".

Translation of cohesion 207

5.7 Lexical cohesion

Lexical cohesion refers to lexical ties in a macro text where the related items produce a semantic chain which links the semantically related words. In both the ST and the TT, lexical cohesion is achieved by the selection of vocabulary through one of the seven lexical mechanisms: (i) the general noun, (ii) reiteration, (iii) synonymy, (iv) antonymy, (v) collocation, (vi) hyponymy, and (vii) meronymy. These are cohesive mechanisms which enable the ST and the TT hang together and make words refer back to another; words operating anaphorically. For Halliday and Hasan (1976:282), lexical cohesion is the reiteration of a lexical item in a context of grammatical cohesion, the cohesion being simply a matter of reference; lexical cohesion is lexical reiteration. The seven mechanisms of lexical cohesion are discussed below.

5.7.1 *General noun*

Lexical cohesion is attained through the repetition of the replacement (substitute) general noun, which is anaphoric to the noun, noun phrase, or whole clause mentioned earlier. The general noun is a form of reiteration. Examples include (i) concrete human nouns إنسان/إنسانة "a human being", ولد/بنت "boy, girl", رجُل/زوج/مرأة "man, husband, woman", مخلوق/عائلة/قوم/أقلِّيَّة ناس/شَعَب/العرب "people, nation, ethnic minority", "a creature, a family, the Arabs"; (ii) abstract nouns إنسانية/بشرية/إسلام/مسيحية/يهودية/ديانة/حضارة/ عادات/تقاليد/زواج/صداقة/محبة/عِداء "humanity, Islam, Christianity, Judaism, religion, civilization, traditions or customs, marriage, friendship, relationship, enmity"; and (iii) concrete animate non-human nouns حشرة/سمك/ديدان/حيوانات "an insect, fish, worms, animals". Let us consider the following examples:

> أعرفُ أحمد جيدا فهو إنسانٌ طيبٌ جدا – I know <u>Ahmad</u> very well. He is a nice <u>human being</u> (<u>person</u>).
>
> الغربيون يحبون الحيوانات كثيرا ولديهم هذه العادات منذ زمن طويل – **The Europeans love animals. These traditions have been held for a long time.**
>
> الإسلامُ ينادي بالوسطية فهو دين متسامح – <u>Islam</u> calls for moderation. It is the <u>religion</u> of tolerance.
>
> حتى إذا جاءَ أحَدُهُم الموتُ قالَ ربي أرجعني لعلّي أعمل صالحاً فيما تركتُ. كلاّ إنّها كلمة هو قائلُها (المؤمنون 99–100)

When death comes to one of them, he cries, my Lord, let me return so as to make amends for the things I neglected. Never! This will not go beyond his words, (Q23:99–100).

where lexical cohesion is achieved by the general noun كلمة "a word, a saying", which is anaphoric, referring back to ربي أرجعني لعلّي أعمل صالحاً فيما تركتُ "my Lord, let me return so as to make amends for the things I neglected".

> إنَّ في خلق السماواتِ والأرضِ واختلافِ الليلِ والنهارِ والفُلكِ التي تجري في البحرِ بما ينفعُ الناسَ وما أنزلَ اللهُ من السماءِ من ماءٍ فأحيا الأرضَ بعدَ موتها وبثَّ فيها من كلِّ دابةٍ وتصريفِ الرياحِ والسحابِ المُسخَّرِ بينَ السماءِ والأرضِ لآياتٍ لقومٍ يعقلون (البقرة 164)

Indeed, in the creation of the heavens and the earth, and the alternation of the night and the day, and the ships which sail through the sea with that which benefits people, and

208 *Translation of cohesion*

what God has sent down from the heavens of rain, giving life thereby to the earth after its lifelessness and dispersing therein every kind of moving creature, and His directing of the winds and the clouds controlled between the heaven and earth are signs for a people who use reason, Q2:164.

where lexical cohesion is achieved through the general noun آيات "signs", which is anaphoric and refers back to

(إنَّ في خلق السماواتِ والأرضِ واختلافِ الليلِ والنهارِ والفُلكِ التي تجري في البحرِ بما ينفعُ الناسَ وما أنزلَ الله من السماءِ من ماءٍ فأحيا به الأرضَ بعدَ موتِها وبثَّ فيها من كلِّ دابَّةٍ وتصريفِ الرياحِ والسحابِ المُسخَّرِ بينَ السماءِ والأرضِ)

Indeed, in the creation of the heavens and the earth, and the alternation of the night and the day, and the ships which sail through the sea with that which benefits people, and what God has sent down from the heavens of rain, giving life thereby to the earth after its lifelessness and dispersing therein every kind of moving creature, and His directing of the winds and the clouds controlled between the heaven and earth.

من وراءِه جهنَّمُ ويُسقى من ماءٍ صديد. يتجرَّعُهُ ولا يكادُ يُسيغُهُ ويأتيه الموتُ من كلِّ مكان ((إبراهيم 16–17 –Hell is before him and he will be given a drink of purulent water. He will gulp it but will hardly be able to swallow it. Death will come to him from every place, Q14:16–17.

where lexical cohesion is achieved through the general noun مكان "place" which is anaphoric to the place noun جهنَّم "hell".

وقالوا لن يدخُلَ الجنَّةَ إلاَّ من كانَ هُوداً أو نصارى تلكَ أمانيُّهُم (البقرة 111)
They say: "None will enter paradise except one who is a Jew or a Christian". That is merely their wishful thinking, Q2:111.

where lexical cohesion is achieved through the general noun أمانيُّهُم "their wishful thinking", which is anaphoric and harks back to لن يدخُلَ الجنَّةَ إلاَّ من كانَ هُوداً أو نصارى "None will enter paradise except one who is a Jew or a Christian".

وقالت اليهودُ ليست النصارى على شيءٍ وقالت النصارى ليست اليهودُ على شيءٍ وهُم يتلونَ الكتابَ كذلكَ قالَ الذين لا يعلمونَ مثلَ قولِهِم (البقرة 113)
The Jews say: "The Christians have nothing true to stand on", and the Christians say: "The Jews have nothing to stand on", although they both recite the Scripture. Thus, do those who do not know speak the same as their words, Q2:113).

where lexical cohesion is achieved through the general noun قول "words 'i.e., speech'" which refers back to وقالت اليهودُ ليست النصارى على شيءٍ وقالت النصارى ليست اليهودُ على شيءٍ وهم يتلونَ الكتابَ "The Jews say: 'The Christians have nothing true to stand on', and the Christians say: 'The Jews have nothing to stand on', although they both recite the Scripture".

5.7.2 Reiteration

Reiteration means the repetition of the same word, phrase, or clause (sentence) many times in the same sentence or in consecutive sentences of the ST or TT. It is a means of making the text cohesive through linking the different parts of the text (Halliday and Hasan 1976:278, 318; Crystal 2003:394). The repeated lexical items have the same referent; there is identity of reference between the lexeme and its repeated form. It is worthwhile to note that repetition is not restricted to the same morphological form. The verb and its morphologically related forms (nouns, adjectives) are considered as reiteration, as in the following sentence which is an example of the reiteration of the same word:

> – (وقد مكروا مكرَهُم وعند اللهِ مكرُهُم وإن كان مكرُهُم لتزولَ منه الجبال (إبراهيم 46 – They had planned their plan, but with God their plan is recorded, even if their plan had been sufficient to do away with the mountains, Q14:46.

where the verb *makara* "to plan" is repeated in a different morphological form, which is a nominalized noun مصدر مكرٌ "plan". Stylistically, this is called polyptoton.

> – يُريدُ اللهُ أن يُحِقَّ الحقَّ بكلماته ويقطعَ دابرَ الكافرينَ لِيُحِقَّ الحقَّ ويُبطِلَ الباطِلَ (الأنفال 7–8) God intended to establish the truth by His words and to eliminate the disbelievers. That He should establish the truth and abolish falsehood, even if the criminals disliked it, Q8:7–8.

An example of the reiteration of the same word is the superlative adjective صيغة أفعَلُ التفضيل أعلمُ "most knowing", which is repeated four times in Q18:19, 21, 22, 26. At the macro level, we also encounter the reiteration of words: اللهُ "God" has occurred 980 times in the Qur'an, the noun ربّ "Lord" has occurred 84 times, the singular noun إله "God/god" has occurred 80 times, and the plural noun آلهة "gods" has occurred 18 times. Similarly, the noun الأرض "the earth" has occurred 451 times, the singular noun السماء "heaven" has occurred 120 times, and the plural noun السماوات "heavens" has occurred 190 times.

An example of reiterating the same phrase is

> (الشعراء) إنَّ ربَّكَ لهو العزيزُ الرحيمُ – And indeed, your Lord – He is the exalted in might, the merciful.

which is reiterated eight times in Q26:9, 68, 104, 122, 140, 159, 175, and 191.

An example of reiterating the same sentence or clause is

> – قُل هل من شُركائكم من يبدأ الخلقَ ثُمَّ يُعيدُه قُل اللهُ يبدأ الخلقَ ثُمَّ يُعيدُه (يونس 34) – Say: "Are there of your partners any who begins creation and then repeats it? Say: 'God begins creation and then repeats it'", Q10:34.

where we have reiteration of the same sentence يبدأ الخلقَ ثُمَّ يُعيدُه "He begins creation and then repeats it". This also applies to Q55, where the interrogative sentence فبأيِّ آلاءِ ربّكما تُكذّبان "So which of the favors of your Lord would you deny?" (Q55) is reiterated 31 times.

210 *Translation of cohesion*

قُل هل من شُركائكُم من يهدي الى الحقّ قُل الله يهدي للحقّ (يونس 35) – Say: "Are there of your partners any who guides to the truth?" say: "God guides to the truth", Q10:35.

5.7.3 *Synonymy*

Reiteration through synonymy is an Arabic translation problem. Unlike English, Arabic favors the employment of a synonym (verb, noun, adjective, adverb), which can be classified in Arabic translation studies as a semantic redundancy, and for this reason, we recommend that it should not be translated, as in

إنَّ هذا القرار خاطيء وغير صحيح ويجب التخلي عنه فورا – This decision is **wrong** and is **incorrect** and should be abandoned immediately.

where we have the adjective خاطيء "wrong" and its synonym غير صحيح "incorrect", which have led to a translation marked by semantic redundancy. Semantically, the use of synonymy in Arabic is a form of tautology إطناب – unnecessarily saying the same thing twice with different words – as in ضبابية/عدم وضوح meaning "unclarity", الوقوف على/مناقشة meaning "discuss", يتّكِلُ على/يعتمدُ على meaning "depend on", and يعترفُ/يقرُ meaning "acknowledge, admit".

We advise that the synonym غير صحيح should be left out. Thus, we get
This decision is wrong and should be abandoned immediately.

Synonymy (semantic redundancy) can also occur through one of the following grammatical categories:

1 a verb, as in يجب أن يدرس ويُذاكر كلَّ يوم "He must <u>study</u> and <u>revise</u> every day → He must study every day".
2 a noun كدأيهم وعادَتِهم فإنَّهُم يكذِبون "As their <u>habit</u> and <u>habit</u>, they lie → As their habit, they lie", يكثُرُ الفسادُ في هذه الحِقبة والمدة الزمنية "Corruption abounds during <u>this time</u> and <u>this time</u> → Corruption abounds during this time".
3 a nominalized noun يجب أن تسوق بهدوء وبُطيئ "You must drive <u>slowly</u> and <u>slowly</u> → You must drive slowly". It is interesting to note that the Arabic nominalized nouns هدوء، بُطء، are translated as an adverb "slowly".

Synonymy and near-synonymy (partial synonymy) are forms of reiteration that occur when have the same referent. As Halliday and Hasan (1976:282) put it, "There must be identity of reference between the two, i.e., between the word and its synonym or near-synonym". Synonym is a major type of meaning relation between lexical items that can occur when these items are close enough in their meaning (Salkie 1995:9; Crystal 2003:450), as in سنة "year" and عام "year"; بحر "sea" and يم "sea"; يخاف "to fear" and يخشى "to fear"; تفجر "to break open" and تُفجّرُ "to gush forth"; واق "protector" and ولي "protector". At times, we encounter synonymy as a noun phrase like النهج الصحيح والطريقة السليمة "The right method and the sound method → The right method".

Complete synonymy is very rare in language and can only take place when two words have exactly the same meaning and we have the choice to use any of them without making

Translation of cohesion 211

any difference in the sentence meaning, as in "I sleep at 11pm" or "I go to bed at 11pm". However, partial (near) synonyms are not very similar in meaning. We cannot substitute one synonym for the other in different contexts. Near synonyms have different shades of meaning and different connotations. Although "brave/courageous" are synonyms, we can say, "Liz does not want to go to the dentist. She is not brave". However, we cannot say, "Liz does not want to go to the dentist. She is not courageous". Partial synonyms are like "big → large", "almost → nearly", "brave → courageous". Therefore, formal and informal style and different contexts create partial synonyms (Abdul-Raof 2015:79). In Q2:249, we encounter lexical cohesion through the verbs شَرِبَ "to drink" → طَعَمَ "to taste" → شَرِبَ "to drink". However, طَعَمَ "to taste" is classified as a contextual synonym of شَرِبَ "to drink", since the context of the statement is that of liquid where the نَهَر "river" occurs.

5.7.4 *Antonymy*

Antonymy is a form of reiteration and is part of the study of oppositeness of meaning (Crystal 2003:27), as in غيب "the unseen" and شَهَدَ "the witnessed"; نعيم "pleasure" and جحيم "hell"; حسنة "good" and سيئة "evil"; حقّ "truth" and باطلٌ "falsehood"; يضِلّ "misguide" and يهدي "guide"; مؤمِن "believer" and كافر "disbeliever"; جنة "garden" and نار "fire"; and نور "light" and ظلمات "darkness".

5.7.5 *Collocation*

Collocation produces cohesive chains because of the lexical relations between words. Collocation is concerned with the co-occurrence of individual lexical items (Crystal 2003:82) – lexical items that regularly co-occur (Halliday and Hasan 1976:284). Lexical cohesion takes place through the occurrence of a different lexical item related to the first one, as a synonym or superordinate of it (ibid). Examples of words which have collocational cohesion are جامعة "university", which collocates with طالب "student"; كلب "dog", which collocates with the verb ينبح "to bark"; سحابة "a cloud", which collocates with مطر "rain"; and مريض "ill", which collocates with طبيب "doctor". The occurrence of such pairs generates a cohesive effect in the ST and the TT. In Qur'anic Arabic نذير "warner" collocates with مبين "clear", عذاب "punishment" collocates with أليم "painful" or مبين "clear", and يغفر "forgive" collocates with ذنب "sin".

5.7.6 *Hyponymy*

Hyponymy (hyponym) refers to the relationship between specific and general words. When the meaning of one word is included in the meaning of another, the relationship is called hyponymy. For instance, the word "horse" is a specific word but the word "animal" is a general word because there are many other types of animals; the word "horse" is included in the word "animal". Other words such as "camel, cat, lion, tiger, cow, calf, bull, sheep, lamb, ram, ewe, stallion, mare, horse, donkey, dog, pig", are all animals, and are thus called cohyponyms of the superordinate word "animal".

Hyponymy occurs in Arabic as in جان "a snake", which is included in (part of) the word ثُعبان "a serpent". Semantically, ثُعبان is the superordinate (it has the generic meaning),

212 *Translation of cohesion*

while جان is a co-hyponym (it has a specific meaning). The semantic componential features of ثُعبان include [+Big], [+ Male], [+ Adult], [+ Long], and [– Fast]. However, the semantic componential features of جان are [– Big], [± Male], [– Adult], [– Long], and [+ Fast]. Context plays a major role in the occurrence of a hyponym. For instance, the word ثُعبان occurs in Q7:107 to entail its enormous size and to depict an image of horror to the people involved in the scene. However, the word جان is used in Q27:10 to indicate its tiny size, speed, and agility. The major semantic distinction in the lexical shift from ثُعبان to جان is the fear generated by the size of each reptile; the componential features of each word. We also encounter the super-ordinate noun إنسان "human being" and its co-hyponyms: رجُل "a man", مؤمن "a he-believer", إمرأة "a woman", طفل "a child", مؤمنة "a she-believer", حواريون "the disciples", منافق "a hypocrite", كافر "a he-disbeliever", الكافرون "the disbelievers", نبي "a prophet", رسول "messenger", قوم "people", أهل الكتاب "the People of the Book", بني إسرائيل "the Children of Israel", and مَلِك "King".

5.7.7 *Meronymy*

Meronymy is something which is a part of something else, or something which has something else. Meronymy is a form of lexical cohesion that refers to the whole-part relationship between words, such as "hand-finger" where the "hand" is the whole and the "finger" is the part. In other words, the "hand" is bigger than the "finger". Also, the word "tree" represents the whole, but the words that are part of the whole are "trunk, branch, leaf". Other examples of meronymy are "car-engine", "house-room", "telescope-lens", "door-handle". This also applies to شجرة "tree", which designates the whole, and its related parts include the جذع "trunk" and ورق "leaves". Similarly, we have the whole صدر "chest" whose part is قلب "heart".

5.8 Translator training and translation practice

This section combines theory and practice and prepares students for the translation industry. The training exercises will focus on the cohesion system in Arabic translation. The exercises and the translation commentary will provide insight into the flow of information intra-sententially (within the same sentence) and inter-sententially (among different sentences). The discussion will also account for text cohesion and texture, how they are achieved, and, in terms of this matter, the contrast between the ST and the TT. The discussion will also examine the different cohesive mechanisms (reference, ellipsis, substitution, conjunction, and lexical cohesion). The student will be made aware of the violation of either the ST or the TT cohesion system, the flouting of textual cohesive devices, and how the TT accommodates the ST textual cohesive devices.

1. Provide a translation for the following ST and a critical translation quality assessment of the cohesion system of both the ST and the TT. British Rail displays the advert "Be Patient Before You Become One".

(i) Context analysis: An increase in injuries on the platforms due to passengers standing on the edge of the platform too close to the running trains.
(ii) In terms of the cohesion system of the ST, we have the cohesive device of nominal substitution where the noun "one" replaces the word "patient". Thus, the underlying (without substitution) sentence is "Be Patient Before You Become a Patient".

Translation of cohesion 213

(iii) Taking the performative intent of the ST producer, we can produce an unambiguous sentence: "Be Patient and Keep Away From The Platform". However, in Arabic, preserving the ST nominal substitution will lead to an inaccurate and literal translation:

كُن صبوراً قبل أن تصبح واحداً

which does not make sense in Arabic. Thus, being an advert, the translator needs to take into account the localization of the advert in Arabic and should aim for a target-reader-oriented translation. Based on the above details and the above literal translation, we need a culture-based translation employing one of the following translation approaches: communicative, dynamic equivalence, natural, acceptable, instrumental, transposition (shift) translation, or faithful. These translation approaches take into consideration the contextual intended meaning of the ST in order to provide a comprehensible TT to its audience with an acceptable natural TL style.

(iv) The best translation approach is to provide a translation that is based on the underlying meaning and has no substitution. Thus, we can obtain an accurate and context-based translation:

(كُن صبوراً قبل أن تصبحَ مريضاً)

Although the ST requires some processing (analysis and comprehension) effort on the part of the reader, the translator can save the unaware TT reader this inconvenience of processing effort through the faithful translation approach, where "one" or "patient" can be translated as رصيف:

(كُن صبوراً وابتعد عن الرصيف)

2. Provide a translation for the following ST and a translation commentary on the cohesion system of both the ST and the TT:

الصلاةُ : مُجلبةٌ للرزق، حافظةٌ للصحة، دافعةٌ للأذى، طاردةٌ للأدواء، مقويةٌ للقلب، مُبيضةٌ للوجه، مُفرحةٌ للنفس، مُذهبةٌ للكسل، مُنشِّطةٌ للجوارح، مُمدةٌ للقوى، شارحةٌ للصدر، مُغذيةٌ للروح، مُنورةٌ للقلب، حافظةٌ للنعمة، دافعةٌ للنقمة، جالبةٌ للبركة، مُبعدةٌ من الشيطان، مُقربةٌ من الرحمن. (إبن قيم الجوزي، أنوار الإسلام)

We propose the following TT:

> Prayer brings sustenance, keeps good health, fends off harm, repels medicines, strengthens the heart, whitens the face, brings to the soul, keeps laziness away, stimulates the body's major parts, promotes the body's strength, pleases the heart, nourishes the soul, enlightens the heart, preserves the blessing, keeps away indignation (of God), brings blessing, keeps you away from Satan, and brings closer to the merciful (God).
> (Ibn Qaiyyim al-Jawziyyah, Anwar al-Islam)

(i) The ST and the TT are marked by the stylistic linguistic feature of asyndeton where there are no conjunctions used because it is a listing of the virtues of prayers. Thus, this is a unique example of a loose texture text in both Arabic and English.

214 *Translation of cohesion*

(ii) The ST is dominated by the active participle which has occurred 18 times. However, the TT has employed the verb to stand for the ST active participle, as in مُجلِبة "bring", حافِظة "keep".

3. Provide different translations for the following ST and a translation commentary on the different translation processes and the cohesion system of both the ST and the TTs:

وألق ما في يمينِكَ تلقف ما صنَعوا إنَّما صنَعوا كيدُ ساحِر (طه 69)

Throw that which is in thy right hand! It will eat up that which they have made. Lo! that which they have <u>made</u> is but a wizard's artifice (Pickthall 1930:no page).

Throw that which is in thy right hand: Quickly will it swallow up that which they have faked what they have <u>faked</u> is but a magician's trick (Ali 1934:no page).

Cast down what is in thy right hand, and it shall swallow what they have fashioned; for they have <u>fashioned</u> only the guile of a sorcerer (Arberry 1955:139).

And [now] throw that [staff] which is in thy right hand – it shall swallow up all that they have wrought: [for] they have <u>wrought</u> only a sorcerer's artifice (Asad 1980:654).

And throw what is in your right hand; it will swallow up what they have crafted. What they have <u>crafted</u> is but the trick of a magician (Saheeh International 1997:426).

Throw down what is in your right hand; it will swallow up what they have produced. They have only <u>produced</u> the tricks of a sorcerer (Abdel Haleem 2005:198).

And throw that which is in your right hand. It will swallow that which they have made. Indeed, what they have <u>made</u> is just a magician's trick (Ahmad 2010:415).

(i) The ST involves the cohesive tie of reiteration where the verb صنَعوا "to produce" is repeated in Q20:69. However, all the TTs have adopted the cohesive tie of reiteration. This has led to stylistic literalness due to the keeping of the same verb repeated. Thus, no TT has adopted the cohesive tie of verbal substitution where the verb صنَعوا can be substituted in English by the verb "to do".

(ii) All the above TTs have adopted the literal translation approach. They should have adopted the transposition (shift) or dynamic equivalence translation approach to meet the TT grammatical norms in terms of verbal substitution.

(iii) Our proposed translation for Q20:69 is

Throw down what is in your right hand; it will swallow up what they have produced. They have only <u>done</u> the tricks of a sorcerer.

where the cohesive tie of verbal substitution is attained through the substitution of the second verb صنَعوا by the verb "do".

4. Provide different translations for the following ST and a critical translation quality assessment of the different translation processes and the cohesion system of both the ST and the TTs:

فاستمتعُوا بخلاقِهم فاستمتعتُم بخلاقِكُم كما استمتعَ الذينَ من قبلِكُم بخلاقِهم وخُضتُم كالذي خاضُوا (التوبة 69)

Translation of cohesion 215

(i) The TTs of Q9:69 are:

> They enjoyed their lot a while, so ye enjoy your lot awhile even as those before you did enjoy their lot a while. And ye prate even as they prated (Pickthall 1930:no page).
>
> They had their enjoyment of their portion: and ye have of yours, as did those before you; and ye indulge in idle talk as they did (Ali 1934:no page).
>
> They took enjoyment in their share; so do you take enjoyment in your share, as those before you took enjoyment in their share. You have plunged as they plunged (Arberry 1955:85).
>
> And they enjoyed their share [of happiness]. And you have been enjoying your share – just as those who preceded you enjoyed their share; and you have been indulging in scurrilous talk – just as they indulged in it (Asad 1980:376).
>
> They have enjoyed their portion (of worldly enjoyment) and you have enjoyed your portion as those before you enjoyed their portion, and you have engaged (in vanities) like that in which they engaged (Saheeh International 1997:256).
>
> They enjoyed their share in this life as you have enjoyed yours; like them, you have indulged in idle talk (Abdel Haleem 2005:122).
>
> So they derived their benefits from the worldly life. So you have also derived your benefits from this life as did people before you. And you did vain discussions as they did (or, you are lost in the enjoyment of worldly life as they did) (Ahmad 2010:253).

(ii) We can observe that in order to achieve texture and textual cohesion, Arabic adopts the cohesive tie of reiteration through the repetition of the verbs with their objects فاستمتعوا بخلاقهم "they have enjoyed their portion" → فاستمتعتم بخلاقِكم "you have enjoyed your portion" → استمتعَ الذينَ من قبلِكم بخلاقِهم "those before you have enjoyed their portion" and وخُضتُم "you have engaged" → خاضُوا "they have engaged".

(iii) The only TT that has involved the cohesive tie of both nominal and verbal substitution and has met the TL grammatical norms is that of Ali (1934:no page), which has provided a smooth TL style based on the transposition, shift or dynamic equivalence translation approaches:

They had their enjoyment of their portion: and ye have of yours, as did those before you; and ye indulge in idle talk as they did (Ali 1934:no page).

(iv) The above TT enjoys TL texture and cohesion because it has observed TT nominal and verbal substitution: The verb "had" is substituted by the verbs "have" and "did", the noun phrase "their portion" is substituted by the possessive pronoun "yours", the verb "indulge" is substituted by the verb "did".

(v) Pickthall has adopted the anachronism translation approach through the employment of the old-fashioned pronoun "ye", which has produced unsmooth translation.

(vi) The TTs provided by Pickthall, Arberry, and Saheeh International have employed the cohesive tie of reiteration, repeating the verbs and nouns, stylistically and grammatically mimicking the ST.

(vii) Abdel Haleem and Ahmad are straddling on two lanes: They employ reiteration (repeating the same verbs) as well as verbal substitution.

5. Provide different translations for the following ST and a translation commentary on the different translation processes and the cohesion system of both the ST and the TTs:

216 *Translation of cohesion*

بل كذّبوا بالساعةِ وأعتدنا لمن كذّبَ بالساعةِ سعيرا (الفرقان 11)

(i) Based on the translation of cohesion, the verb (كذّبَ – to deny) is repeated in Q25:11. Therefore, in English the same repeated verb should be substituted by the verb (do): (We have prepared for those who <u>have done so</u> a blaze). Let us see which of the following TTs has adopted verbal substitution:

> Nay, but they deny (the coming of) the Hour, and for those who <u>deny (the coming of) the Hour</u> We have prepared a flame (Pickthall 1930:no page).
> Nay they deny the hour (of the judgment to come): but We have prepared a blazing fire for such as <u>deny the hour</u> (Ali 1934:no page).
> Nay, but they cry lies to the Hour; and We have prepared for him <u>who cries lies to the Hour</u> a Blaze (Arberry 1955:159).
> But nay! It is (the very coming of] the Last Hour to which they give the lie! (Asad 1980:753).
> But they have denied the hour and We (God) have prepared for <u>those who deny the hour</u> a blaze (Saheeh International 1997:492).
> It is actually the coming of the hour that they reject; We have prepared a blazing fire for <u>those who reject the hour</u> (Abdel Haleem 2005:227).
> In fact, they deny the hereafter, and We have prepared a flaming fire for <u>those who deny the hereafter</u> (Ahmad 2010:475).

(ii) The ST violates the cohesion mechanism of clausal (verbal) substitution. Similarly, none of the above TTs has observed verbal substitution. We propose the TT, which observes the cohesion mechanism of clausal (verbal) substitution: (however, they have denied the hour and We have prepared for those who do a blaze), where the verb (do) substitutes the verbal clause (those who deny the hour).

6. Provide different translations for the following ST and a translation commentary on the different translation processes and the cohesion system of both the ST and the TTs:

فإن آمنوا بمثلِ ما آمنتُم بهِ فقد اهتدوا (البقرة 137)

(i) We propose a translation which adopts verbal substitution: (And if they believe in the same way you do, they are indeed rightly guided). However, let us consider the other translations below:

> And if they believe in the like of that which ye believe, then are they rightly guided (Pickthall 1930:no page).
> So if they believe as ye believe, they are indeed on the right path. (Ali 1934:no page)
> And if they believe in the like of that you believe in, then they are truly guided (Arberry 1955:11).
> And if [others] come to believe in the way you believe, they will indeed find themselves on the right path (Asad 1980:60).
> So if they believe like you do, they will be rightly guided (Abdel Haleem 2005:16).
> So if they believe in the same as you believe in, they have been (rightly) guided (Saheeh International 1997:26).
> Hence if they believe similarly as you believe, then they are rightly guided (Ahmad 2010:37).

Translation of cohesion 217

(ii) The ST is an example of flouting verbal substitution because of the textual fact that it repeats the same verb آمنَ "to believe". Thus, stylistically, the ST displays the rhetorical device of epizeuxis (repetition of a linguistic expression such as a verb, noun, an adjective, an adverb, or a preposition). However, the TT should be based on verbal substitution through the deletion of the second verb آمنَ, which should be replaced by the auxiliary verb "do" to provide a stylistically natural TT.

(iii) Six out of the above seven TTs have adopted stylistic literalness. Like the ST, the translations by Pickthall, Ali, Arberry, Asad, Saheeh International, and Ahmad have flouted the English cohesion system. The translation by Abdel Haleem has observed the cohesion system through the employment of verbal substitution where the second verb آمنَ is substituted by the auxiliary verb "do".

7. For homework assignment: Provide a translation for each of the following STs and a translation commentary on the major conjunction in the STs:

Lest you not be just . . . Lest you go astray, Q4:135, 176.

أن تعولوا . . . أن تضلُّوا (النساء 135، 176)

Lest a soul be given up to destruction . . . Lest you say . . ., Q6:70, 156.

أن تُبسلَ نفسٌ . . . أن تقولوا (الأنعام 70، 156)

Lest you say . . ., Q7:172.

أن تقولوا (الأعراف 172)

Lest they understand it, Q18:57.

أن يفقهُوهُ (الكهف 57)

The major translation problem of the above STs is the conjunction "an", which is a causal conjunction for purpose whose meaning is لكي لا "lest, so that you may not, in order not to". Originally, the ST conjunction أن is لا أن, but it has orthographically assimilated to ألا, as in Q4:3 ألاَّ تعُولوا "so that you may not incline to injustice".

8. Provide a translation for each of the following STs and a translation commentary on the major cohesion problem in the STs:

Our lord, these are the ones we caused to deviate. We caused them to deviate as we ourselves did, Q28:63.

ربَّنا هؤلاءِ الذينَ أغوينا أغويناهُم كما غَوينا (القصص 63)

where the verb أغوى/غوى "to deviate" is repeated in Q28:63, but in English it is substituted by the verb "to do".

If you call them, they cannot hear you. If they could, they wouldn't answer you, Q35:14.

إن تدعُوهُم لا يسمعوا دُعائكُم ولو سَمِعُوا ما استجابوا لكم (فاطر 14)

where the verb يسمع "to hear" is reiterated, while in English it is substituted by the auxiliary verb "could".

218 *Translation of cohesion*

Whoever purifies himself does so for his own benefit, Q35:18.

من تزكّى فإنّما يتزكّى لنفسهِ (فاطر 18)

where the verb يتزكّى "to purify" is reiterated, while in English it is substituted by the aux-iliary verb "do".

The translation problem in the above STs is represented by the major cohesion mechanism of verbal substitution, which is a syntactic and cohesion requirement by the TT. The ST verbs أغوى/غوى "to deviate", سَمَعَ/سَمَعَ, and تزكّى/يتزكّى are repeated in Q28:63, Q35:14, and Q35:18. However, in English, these verbs are substituted by the verbs "do", "can", and "do" respectively. Thus, Arabic does not have verbal substitution, while in English it is a cohesion and a syntactic prerequisite for a grammatically acceptable TT.

9. Homework assignment: Provide different translations for the following STs and a transla-tion commentary on the different translation processes, the major cohesion problem, and the cohesion system of both the STs and the TTs:

يا معشرَ الجنّ والإنس إن استطعتُم أن تنفُذوا من أقطار السماواتِ والأرضِ فانفُذوا لا تنفُذُونَ إلاَّ بسلطانٍ (الرحمان 33)

كما قالَ عيسى ابنُ مريمَ للحواريينَ من أنصاري الى اللهِ قالَ الحواريونَ نحنُ أنصارُ اللهِ (الصف 14)

10. Homework assignment: Provide a detailed critical translation quality assessment of the following hypotactic (complex structure) Qur'anic Arabic text:

شهدَ اللهُ أنّهُ لا إلَهَ إلاّ هوَ والملائكة وأولوا العلم قائماً بالقسطِ (آل عمران 18)

(i)   provide a paratactic (simple structure) Arabic sentence and a sentence demarcation (sentence boundaries), (ii) compare the following translations in terms of the cohesion system:

Our proposed translation:
Allah, the angels and those of knowledge witness that there is no deity except Him and that He is maintaining creation in justice.
   Other Qur'an translations:

> God bears witness that there is no god but He – and the angels, and men possessed of knowledge – upholding justice (Arberry 1955:24).
> There is no god but He: That is the witness of Allah, His angels, and those endued with knowledge, standing firm on justice (Ali 1934:no page).
> Other translations:
> God bears witness that there is no god but Him, as do the angels and those who have knowledge. He upholds justice (Abdel Haleem 2005:35).
> Allah (Himself) bears witness (in all Scriptures) that none has the right to be worshipped except Him alone, so do the angels (in their remembrance of Allah) and the people with knowledge (in their speeches and books) (Ahmad 2010:74).

11. For in-class discussion: Provide a critical translation assessment of إنَّ اللهَ ربي وربُّكُم فاعبُدُوه آل عمران 51 and comment on the cohesion problem involved and stylistic literalness.

Translation of cohesion 219

12. For in-class discussion: Provide a critical translation assessment of

لا تُدرِكُهُ الأبصارُ وهوَ يُدرِكُ الأبصارَ (الأنعام 103)

and comment on the cohesion problem involved and the ST stylistic idiosyncrasy. In the above ST, we notice the repetition of the same noun الأبصار instead of having an anaphoric reference pronoun ها, i.e., . . . وهو يدرِكُها – the attached personal pronoun should have occurred لا تُدرِكُهُ الأبصارُ وهوَ يُدرِكُها. Provide a translation commentary on different translations and explain why the same noun الأبصار is employed instead of the personal pronoun (anaphoric reference pronoun) ها.

13. For in-class discussion: Provide a critical translation assessment of

"We learn more by looking for the answer and not finding it than we do from learning the answer itself" (Lloyd Alexander, American author).

Discuss the translation problem involved in the ST cohesion system. What is the textual cohesive device used in the ST? Does Arabic require the same cohesive device and why?

We propose the following translation so that we can establish our assessment of the cohesion problem:

نتعلمُ أكثر من خلالِ البحثِ عن الجواب وعدم العثور عليهِ مما نتعلمهُ من تعلُّم الجوابِ نفسه. (لويد الكسندر ، كاتب أمريكي)

Brief points: (i) The translation problem lies in the fact that the ST has verbal substitution represented by the verbal substitute "do" as a textual cohesive device which substitutes the main verb "learn"; (ii) Arabic favors to repeat the main verb "learn"; (iii) Arabic uses نتعلمه; (iv) the word "than" is translated as مما; and (v) we have employed in the TT the same textual cohesive device of reference used in the ST. These are the anaphoric reference cohesive devices "it, itself", which are translated as ه in عليه and نفسه which refer to "answer" الجواب.

6 Jargon translation

6.1 Introduction

The study of jargon in the present chapter is primarily concerned with the borrowing through a translation approach of a foreign expression (a lexical item or a noun phrase). The current chapter accounts for the creation of a jargon, as a notion, in Arabic and provides a detailed analysis, with numerous examples, of the different linguistic approaches through which SL jargon (terminology) is produced in a given TL; how a jargon is born in the TL. We have proposed eight TL jargon-generation approaches that can be universal mechanisms of high value to other languages through which an account can be made on how a given jargon is generated. The semantic relationship between the SL and the TL jargon is also explained. The discussion deals with whether the literal (foreignization) translation approach, through phonetic borrowing (transliteration), can always be adopted in the birth (production) of new jargon, or whether the naturalization (domestication) translation approach, through semantic borrowing, is an option for the translator to deliver new jargon. The chapter also provides many recommendations for the creation of new Arabic jargon and how newly adopted lexical items (jargon) can be disseminated in the Arab countries. This chapter has provided more than 70 SL jargon with their translations and a thorough analysis of how a new jargon is born and, most importantly, which type of jargon production approach is employed and why.

6.2 The birth of a jargon

A jargon is defined here as any foreign expression that is non-existent in Arabic and that has been borrowed through a given jargon production approach. Thus, words like (cloud, pen) are not considered as jargon because Arabic has already got them (سحابة, قلم). Thus, a jargon is a TL word or a noun phrase.

A jargon is referred to as علمُ المُصطلح/المُصطلحية/إصطلاح/مُصطلح – a specialized terminology which designates a specific notion of any field of knowledge (science or human sciences) and may not be understood well without a context. Jargon is a universal lexical phenomenon, and languages have always borrowed different jargon from each other. The borrowing of a SL jargon by a TL is attained through different linguistic approaches which mimic the SL jargon in an attempt to preserve the semantic componential features of the original jargon and naturalize (domesticate) it in the receptive language, taking into consideration the TL linguistic and cultural norms and values. The newly born jargon can be a lexical item, a morpheme, or a noun phrase. The creation – or rather, the borrowing – of jargon from other languages represents the inter-cultural fertilization among both linguistically and culturally related or unrelated languages.

DOI: 10.4324/9781003268956-7

Jargon translation 221

Seven linguistic approaches are proposed for the creation of a jargon in the TL. Throughout the discussion, several examples are provided to illustrate the seven linguistic mechanisms which can be employed to create a new jargon in science or human sciences. The semantic relationship between the SL jargon and the jargon borrowed by Arabic is explained. Among the most common linguistic approaches (mechanisms) used in the creation of a new jargon and loan words in Arabic are phraseological calque, borrowing, and blending. It also deals with phonetic imitation (transliteration) and semantic matching between the foreign jargon and the newly coined Arabic jargon.

According to Jakobson (1959), terminology is translated through loan-words or loan-translations, neologisms or semantic shifts, and finally, by circumlocutions. Thus, in the newborn literary language of the Northeast Siberian Chukchees, "screw" is rendered as "rotating nail", "steel" as "hard iron", "tin" as "thin iron", "chalk" as "writing soap".

As imported linguistic items from different languages, the borrowed literary and scientific jargon enrich the lexical asset of the borrowing language and contribute effectively in the cultural and linguistic inter-fertilization among languages. The birth of a jargon in any language represents the linguistic vigor of the borrowing language, the efficiency of its morphological mechanism, and its readiness to borrow different jargon to match the cultural, literary, and scientific developments worldwide especially during globalization.

The study of jargon and how it is produced in the TL is also related to the creation of new jargon within the same language (SL). In other words, in both Arabic and English, we encounter many novel words that have been formed from within the same language; this category of same-language jargon (as opposed to borrowed jargon from other languages) also have certain production mechanisms. This is referred to as word formation processes which have been dealt with by George Yule (2006). However, this is not our concern in the present chapter since we are primarily concerned with borrowed jargon from other languages through a specific translation approach.

To enhance our understanding of jargon production mechanisms in Arabic, which are the focus of the present chapter, it is worthwhile to account briefly for the word formation processes in English.

6.3   Word formation processes

This is an account of the production mechanisms which lead to the creation of new words in English. In other words, we are dealing with how a new word (a lexical item or a phrase) is created in English. There are ten word-formation processes:

1   Derivation: English can create new words through affixes or suffixes. We can add prefixes to the beginning of a word, as in "en-", which can be added to "able" to produce "enable". We can add the prefix "mis-" to "lead" to derive "mislead". We can also add the prefix "pro-" to "long" to derive "prolong". Also, we can add the prefix "un-" to "happy" to produce "unhappy". We can also add suffixes to the end of a word, as in "-ly", which can be added to "nice" to derive "nicely". We can add the suffix "ful-" to "hope" to derive "hopeful". We can add the suffix "-ness" to "happy" to derive "happiness".

2   Acronyms: In English, we can make an acronym from the initial letters of a group of words, as in (PC) from (personal computer), (CD) from (compact disk), (UN) from (United Nations), (NATO) from (North Atlantic Treaty Organisation), (SAM) from (Surface to Air Missile), and (radar) from (radio detecting and ranging).

222 *Jargon translation*

3 Backformation: English can create a new word by removing an affix from another word. For example, through the process of backformation, we produce new words like "resurrect", which was originally "resurrection", the new word (donate), which was originally "donation", and "housekeep", which was originally "housekeeper". Also, through the process of backformation, we produce new verbs like "edit" which was originally "editor", the word "babysit" which was originally "babysitter", and the new word "self-destruct" which was originally "self-destruction".

4 Blending: We produce a new word by joining the beginning of one word to the end of another word. For example, the new word "smog" is produced by blending the beginning of the word "smoke" with the end of the word "fog". The same process occurs with blended words like "brunch" which is taken from "breakfast + lunch", and "motel" which is a blend from "motor + hotel". Also, the new expression "Reaganomics" is created through joining the name "Reagan", who was an American President to the economic policy he adopted, which became known as "Reaganomics".

5 Borrowing: Languages borrow words from each other. Japanese, for example, borrowed the English words "supermarket" and "radio". Arabic borrowed the English word "parliament". English borrowed "alcohol" from Arabic, "piano" from Italian, and "yogurt" from Turkish.

6 Calque: This is also called "loan translation", which means the literal translation of a foreign word to another language. A calque is an expression introduced into a TL by translating it from a SL. For example, we have the English word "skyscraper". This word is borrowed by other languages and is translated literally as ناطحة سحاب, meaning "the building which butts the clouds", "wolkenkratzer" in German meaning "cloud scraper", and "un gratteciel" in French meaning "a scrape sky". In terms of translation studies, a calque is a form of cultural transposition (the deletion of SL cultural details and replacing them with TL cultural details) whereby a TL expression is closely modelled on the grammatical structure of the corresponding SL expression; the TL expression respects the TL syntax (Dickins et al. 2002:31, 233, 235).

7 Clipping: In English, long words can be shortened. If the word has more than one syllable, it can be reduced to a shorter form, as in "Professor", which is reduced to a shorter form "Prof"; "Doctor" is reduced to "Dr"; "laboratory" is reduced to "lab"; "facsimile" is reduced to "fax"; "influenza" is reduced to "flu"; and "hamburger" is reduced to "burger". Long names can also be shortened, like "Elizabeth" is reduced to "Liz", and "Robert" is reduced to "Rob".

8 Coinage: Trade names of products can be used to create new words, as in (Aspirin, Nylon, Kleenex, Xerox).

9 Compounding: In English, we can join two words together to create a new word. For instance, we combine "wall + paper" to get "wallpaper", "text + book" to get "textbook", "finger + print" to get "fingerprint", "sun + burn" to get "sunburn", and "door + knob" to get "doorknob".

10 Conversion: In English, we get conversion when there is a change in the grammatical function of a word, as in the following cases:

(i) when a noun is used as a verb: For example, words like "paper, bottle, butter, ship" are nouns. However, through the process of conversion, we can also use these nouns as verbs, as in "I want to paper my sitting-room walls", "She bottled the milk", "Sam buttered the bread", "I shipped the goods to China".

Jargon translation 223

(ii) when a verb is used as a noun: For example, words like "report, walk" are verbs. However, through the process of conversion, these verbs are also used as nouns, as in "She wrote a good report", "I take a long walk every morning".

(iii) when an adjective is used as a verb: For example, words like "empty, open, dry" are adjectives. However, through the process of conversion, these adjectives can also be used as verbs, as in "Mary emptied the bags", "Liz opened the book", and "James dried his shirt".

(iv) when a preposition is used as a verb: For example, the prepositions "down, up" can be used as verbs "down → to drink" and "up → to increase". For instance, we say: "Peter downed three cans of coke" and "They upped petrol prices".

6.4 Important observations

In the study of jargon, we need to take into consideration the following matters:

1   Consultation with discipline-based experts: Before the translation of any borrowed SL target and its dissemination to readers, experts of different fields in science and literature should be consulted. Some jargon cannot be left to the translator alone, and the translator needs expert advice about the semantic componential features of some SL jargon – especially scientific and medical jargon. The translator also needs to be fully aware of the SL culture.

2   The dissemination and unification of the newly born jargon: It is the sole responsibility of the Arab academies مجمعُ اللغة العربية to disseminate the newly borrowed jargon in science and literature and to inform all outlets of media, the ministries of information, the ministries of education, and universities in the Arab countries of any newly produced jargon in Arabic. This policy will help establish consistent usage of the same jargon all over the Arab countries and will put an end to the different translations for the same SL jargon. For instance, the SL jargon "parliament" has found its way into Arabic with many different translations in different Arab countries, such as برلمان, مجلس الأمة, مجلس الشورى and مجلس الشعب, مجلس النواب.

3   Related SL jargon with different concepts: The translator must be well aware of some SL jargon which designate distinct concepts. In other words, the translator needs to be fully aware of the distinction between deceptively similar SL concepts represented by distinct SL jargon. For instance, the jargon "supermarket" is different from the jargon "department store". A translation of context-based meaning provides us with two distinct jargon in Arabic: متجر ملابس and أسواق غذائية.

4   Change in some SL jargon: The translator must be aware of the fact that some SL jargon have changed and acquired different labels due to technological or scientific developments. However, the concepts and componential semantic features of such jargon have remained almost the same. For instance, the jargon "bicycle/bike" has acquired a novel label and a different mechanical operational method, as in "motorcycle/motor-bike". Then, during the third phase of engineering development, we get the jargon "pushbike", "scooter", and more recently we encounter the new jargon "e-scooter".

5   Semantically oriented prefixes and suffixes: The translator must be fully aware of the SL prefixes and suffixes and their impact on the meaning of the SL jargon. The translator also needs to know the morphological derivation processes of Arabic. The meanings of prefixes and suffixes are listed below:

224 *Jargon translation*

(i) The prefix "inter-" as in "inter-continental missile": The meaning of this prefix is عابر and therefore we can produce a new Arabic jargon صاروخ عابر للقارات, based on the semantic componential features of the SL jargon, which means a missile that can be launched from one continent and can reach other continents.

(ii) The prefix "inter-" meaning بين as in "inter-city train", whose meaning, based on analogy with the above first prefix meaning, is بين; thus, we get قطار بين المدن – travelling to different cities "it travels from one city to another".

(iii) The prefix "inter-" meaning بين, as in "inter-sentential coherence", whose translation is الترابط بين الجمل, meaning the concepts among different sentences that occur consecutively one after another.

(iv) The prefix "inter-" meaning الوسيط as in "inter-language", whose translation is اللغة الوسيطة – in applied linguistics اللغة الوسيطة بين اللغة الأم واللغة المكتسبة meaning "the intermediary language between the mother language and the acquired 'second' language".

(v) The prefix "extra-" meaning غير ، أَلّا "not, other than", as in "extra-curricular activities", whose translation is الأنشطة اللاصفية, and whose back-translation is "the activities which are not 'other than' those taken in the classroom". It is important to note that the prefix "extra-" should be hyphenated.

(vi) The suffix "-less" as in the jargon "wireless", whose translation is لاسلكي; the meaning of the suffix "-less" is "no/without".

6.5 Types of jargon

Based on our empirical investigation of the SL jargon that have been borrowed by Arabic, we can claim that there are three different types of jargon:

1 One-word jargon: This is a single-word jargon like "parliament" and "capital".
2 Noun phrase jargon: This is made up of two or more words which function as a noun phrase like "skyscraper".
3 Acronyms: This type of jargon is made up of the initial letters of words, like (UN – United Nations) or (NATO – North Atlantic Treaty Organization).

6.6 Jargon production approaches

This section is concerned with the mimicking mechanisms through which the translator creates a new TL jargon, taking into consideration the TL grammatical, lexical, morphological, stylistic, and cultural norms in an attempt to domesticate and remove the smell of foreignness of the TT.

We have designed eight jargon production approaches: (i) mimicking the function of the SL jargon, (ii) mimicking the event to which the SL jargon refers, (iii) mimicking the shape of the SL jargon, (iv) mimicking the operational method of the SL jargon, (v) mimicking the sound of the SL jargon, (vi) mimicking the semantic features of the jargon, (vii) blending, and (viii) joint approach. These are discussed below.

1. Mimicking the function of the SL jargon: The Arabic word formation process of derivation الإشتقاق has been employed in the production of the TL jargon. This jargon production approach is concerned with the accurate transfer of the SL jargon function; what

Jargon translation   225

the jargon does, as in "cash machine/cash point", which are transferred to Arabic as صرّاف based on the morphology of the verb صَرَفَ and on its function of giving cash to the customer. Similarly, the Arabic word formation process of derivation الإشتقاق has been employed in the production of the TL jargon غسّالة, ثلّاجة, مُجمدة which are morphologically related to and derived from the verbs جَمَدَ, ثلّج, and غَسَلَ, respectively. Thus, we have Arabic jargon which perform the functions of غسيل, تثليج, تجميد.

Also, the jargon "car", which is transferred to Arabic as سيارة based on the morphology of the verb سار since السيارة performs the function of moving fast السير بسرعة and moving people. Based on mimicking the function of the SL jargon "facsimile, fax", which perform the photocopying of documents, the Jordanian Academy has adopted the jargon ناسوخ rather than mimicking their sounds (transliteration) الفاكسيمسلس، فاكس. Morphologically, the TT jargon الناسوخ is based on the morphological pattern فاعول, which designates the name of a machine أسم الآلة and stylistically designates the rhetorical device of hyperbole. However, the TL jargon الفاكس is more commonly used in the Arab countries than الناسوخ. The operational function of the SL jargon "photocopier" is translated to Arabic as ماكنة جهاز تصوير، جهاز نسخ الوثائق. The transfer of the SL jargon "ice cream" to Arabic as مُرطّبات is also based on the function performed by the "ice cream", which is to make the consumer feel cool (literally, to moisten the body from the heat). Thus, morphologically, it is related to the verb رطّبَ "to moisturize", and grammatically it is an active participle which semantically designates something is the Agent "doer" of the action of ترطيب "moisturizing" the body. However, the jargon "ice cream" is at times translated as مُثلّجات, which literally means "to something has become like ice" – morphologically derived from ثلّجَ "ice". Also, "ice cream" has been transferred to Arabic through the mimicking of its constituent sounds (transliteration) as آيس كريم.

The jargon "computer" is a unique example of how its alternative function-based Arabic jargon حاسوب، حاسب has been molded on Arabic morphology, where we have the verb يُحوسِب "to computerize", and the passive participle اسم مفعول مُحوسَب "computerized". On the mimicking of the sounds of "computer", see point (v) below.

Awareness of the SL culture is a prerequisite for the accurate translation of some SL jargon, as in "social benefits" and "child benefits". In the United Kingdom, "social benefits" are paid to the unemployed or to people who are on low pay. Thus, their function is "to help the needy by the state". To apply the mimicking of the function of the SL jargon, we get الضمان الإجتماعي، المعونة الحكومية. The same applies to "child benefits", which is a four-weekly salary to the child from the date of birth till he/she is under 16 years old. Thus, the TL jargon is مُرتّب الطفل، مُخصَّصات الطفل. Similarly, there is the SL jargon "zebra crossing", which is a type of pedestrian crossing marked with black and white stripes on the road surface, resembling the coat of a zebra, to warn drivers that there may be pedestrians crossing or waiting to cross the road. Having understood the function of these stripes, we can produce the TL jargon based on mimicking the function of the SL jargon. Thus, we propose منطقة عبور مشاة. This is a translation based on one of the following translation approaches: communicative, dynamic equivalence, natural, acceptable, instrumental, or faithful. These translation approaches take into consideration the contextual intended meaning of the ST in order to provide a comprehensible TT to its audience with an acceptable natural TL style. These translation approaches aim at complete naturalness of the TT; to naturalize the TT and

226 *Jargon translation*

reduce its foreignness. The above translation interpretively resembles the original without unnecessary processing effort on the part of the TL reader.

One may wonder why we have not produced the TL jargon based on mimicking the shape of the SL jargon. The black and white stripes on the road surface do not help produce an accurate translation of "zebra crossing". We may end up getting translations like العبور من منطقة المُخطَّطة or من منطقة الحمار الوحشي, which are over-translations, out of context and are based on one of the translation approaches like literal, formal equivalence (source-oriented), paraphrase, and exegetical.

Mimicking the function of the SL jargon approach is also adopted in the production of the SL jargon "thermal camera", whose function is to gauge the person's temperature حرارة during the Covid-19 pandemic. We have taken the same function and proposed the translation الكاميرا الحرارية. Similarly, the SL jargon "warship, destroyer" are translated as سفينة حربية، مُدمِّرة حربية, which is based on mimicking the military function each jargon performs.

The military jargon "surrogate aircraft" appeared in *The Daily Express* on 14 July 2019. We recommend the translation الطائرة المقاتلة البديلة. Because this is a drone, I have taken into consideration the mimicking function of the SL jargon approach. Its model is Skyborg, and it will replace fighter jets. Therefore, having understood what the drone's military function is, I can continue with translating the full name of the drone. Thus, I must add المقاتلة البديلة. Because the word "drone" is not used in the ST, I cannot use the expression طائرة مُسيَّرة. However, we can also recommend an over-translation الطائرة المُسيَّرة المُقاتلة البديلة of the jargon "surrogate aircraft" after we have read the full news report about this drone. The reason why we have adopted mimicking the function of the SL jargon approach in the production of a new jargon in Arabic is due to the fact that we have considered the drone's military function, which is "fighting". The reason for our choice of the word البديلة is based on the procedure of analogy. Let us also consider the SL jargon "surrogate mother", which appeared in 1985–1986 in Britain when a woman got pregnant through the fertilization of the egg taken from another woman. When the pregnant woman gave birth, the second woman took the baby as her own baby and was considered as its real mother. As for the first woman, she was a "surrogate mother" – she only carried the egg in her womb for nine months and after she gave birth, she passed on the baby to the other woman. Thus, the jargon "surrogate mother" is translated as الأم البديلة. By analogy, we can claim that the jargon "surrogate aircraft" is translated as الطائرة المقاتلة البديلة, because it has undertaken the same military function of the other ordinary aircraft fighter.

The SL jargon "seatbelt" is another example of mimicking the function of the SL jargon approach in the production of a new jargon in Arabic. Through the function of the SL jargon and the word-for-word literal translation, the new TL jargon حزام الأمان has been produced.

Additionally, we encounter the SL jargon "Chief Whip" in the UK House of Commons, which is SL-culture-based. The Chief Whip in the parliament undertakes the role of coordination. Each party in the House of Commons has a Chief Whip whose role is to coordinate among the party members he/she belongs to, to make sure that a large number of Members of Parliament (MPs) vote for their own party on a given bill after it has been discussed, and to send to his/her MPs the parliament agenda within the same week. Having considered the above roles of the Chief Whip, we can propose the TL jargon المُنسِّق البرلماني للحزب.

Jargon translation 227

Similarly, the SL jargon "radio" has been produced in Arabic as مذياع based on mimicking the function of the broadcasting machine. The radio's function is to tell the news. See point (iv) for the other approach used for this jargon.

The SL jargon "food processor, blender" are kitchen equipment whose purpose (function) is mixing, grinding, chopping, and liquidizing fruits and vegetables (food). Thus, we benefit from the words "mixing" and "liquidizing" to mimic the operational method of the SL jargon "food processor, blender", and can produce the TL jargon خَلَّاط/خَلَّاطة and خَفَّاقة, respectively.

Also, the SL military jargon "pre-emptive attack" is transferred to Arabic as هُجوم استباقي، هُجوم إجهاضي، إحباطي or ، هُجوم إحباطي, where a touch of imagery is involved. This translation is based on the mimicking of the function (purpose) of such an attack – to pre-empt, to abort the attack being planned by the enemy.

Other SL jargon whose translation has been based on mimicking their function are the SL jargon "fridge" and "freezer". It is worthwhile to note that the Arabic word formation process of derivation الإشتقاق has been employed in the production of the TL jargon ثَلَّاجة and مُجمِّدة, which are morphologically related to and derived from the verbs ثَلَجَ and جَمَدَ, respectively. Thus, the new Arabic jargon reflect the function of each machine.

2. Mimicking the event to which the SL jargon refers: This jargon production approach is concerned with studying the semantic componential features of the SL jargon, as in "ethnic cleansing", which appeared during the Bosnia and Herzegovina conflict in 1992–1995. The semantic analysis of the jargon reflects a racist connotative meaning because the Serbian army was trying to eliminate any ethnic existence from Bosnia and Herzegovina. For the Serbian army, the operation was highlighted by "cleansing" the Muslims from Bosnia and Herzegovina who were considered as "unwanted". Thus, the expression "cleansing" has the connotative meaning of "cleaning from germs", just like Dettol is used domestically to cleanse the germs from kitchen surfaces. Thus, the people from Bosnia and Herzegovina were labelled by the Serbian army as similar to "germs". The SL jargon has been wrongly used by European and Arab media until the present time without realizing its racist connotative undertone. The accurate translation should be based on the jargon's innate semantic features and the event during which it was formed. Thus, we propose the translation of the synonym of the jargon, which is "genocide". Therefore, the SL jargon "ethnic cleansing" should be produced in Arabic as الإبادة الجماعية.

Similarly, the SL jargon "colonization/colonizer" was translated wrongly until the present time to Arabic as إستعمار/مُستعمِر and مُبشِّر/تبشير, which are false friends. For more details on false friends, see Chapter One, Section 1.4, Example 4.

British and the French colonizers introduced the idea that they were not occupiers of the Arab countries but rather were there to develop and re-build these countries. The jargon إستعمار/مُستعمِر were based on Qur'anic intertextuality:

هو أنشأكم من الأرض واستعمرَكُم فيها

He has produced you from the earth and made you settle down in it, Q11:61.

where the verb إستعمرَ "to enable someone settle down somewhere" is employed in the Qur'an with a positive connotative meaning. Thus, based on the innate semantic features of the jargon and the event during which the SL jargon was formed, the accurate translation should be إحتلال/مُحتَل.

228 *Jargon translation*

Additionally, the jargon "demonstration/demonstrator" designates an event during which people march in the street or gather in major squares in either support of or in protest against someone or something. To mimic this event in Arabic, we can produce the TL jargon مُضاهِرة/مُتضاهِر. Similarly, the scientific SL jargon "moonshot" also designates an event. The translation should be based on the semantic componential features of the jargon. The SL jargon refers to a spacecraft mission to the moon and most importantly the moment the taking-off of the spacecraft event takes place after the spacecraft has just left the launching pad منصّة الإطلاق, leaving behind a thick cloud of smoke. Having understood the SL event and its semantic features, we are now able to produce a TL jargon لحظة إطلاق مركبة فضائية since the SL jargon focuses on the moment of the taking-off of the spacecraft. For this reason, we use لحظة "the moment".

The Covid-19 pandemic which began in December 2019, introduced to the broader public new SL medical jargon – the disease "coronavirus". However, at the beginning, the TL jargon was based on the place where the virus lives – which parts of the body are attacked by the virus. Since the coronavirus attacks the human respiratory system, the TL jargon has been produced as مرض الجهاز التنفسي, whose back-translation justifies the mimicking of the event which the SL jargon refers to "the disease of the respiratory system"; the place where the disease takes place. However, the latter TL jargon has quickly been replaced in the Arab media by mimicking the sounds (transliteration) of the SL jargon فيروس كورونا.

Similarly, the jargon "global warming" designates an event during which there is rapid increase in Earth's average surface temperature due to the greenhouse gases emitted by people burning fossil fuels that pump carbon dioxide (CO2). Thus, based on the semantic componential features of the jargon, "global warming" has been translated as الإحتباس الحراري.

3. Mimicking the shape of the SL jargon: This jargon production approach is concerned with the accurate transfer of the SL jargon shape, as in the military jargon "mortar", whose semantic componential features are "a portable muzzle-loading weapon having a tube short in relation to its caliber that is used to throw bombs at high angles". However, in Arabic, we have a kitchen device called هاون, whose semantic componential features are a sturdy portable vessel in which seeds (material) are crushed with a pestle. The shape of this seed-crushing mortar is round and has a tube-shape. In terms of the TL jargon production approach based on mimicking the shape of the SL jargon, we consider the expressions that have occurred in the definition of the two devices (the military device and the kitchen device). These shape-based words include "muzzle, tube, caliber". If we consider the shape-based words in the kitchen device, we are concerned with "vessel, round, tube-shaped".

Also, in terms of shape, we can observe close similarity between the semantic features of the military device and those of the kitchen device. Thus, Arabic has produced military jargon هاون based on mimicking the shape of the SL military device. Sometimes, we find مدفع هاون, where the expression مدفع "cannon" is added to the TL military jargon.

Similarly, the SL jargon (skyscraper) is defined as "a high-rise building that has over 40 floors and is taller than approximately 150m '492ft'". Having considered the semantic componential features of the jargon "skyscraper", we need to focus on the words "high-rise building, 150m high". Having looked at pictures of skyscrapers and their major features, we can mimic the shape of the jargon – not what it is used for. Since the building is extremely high, stylistically, we can employ the rhetorical device of imagery to mimic the shape of the SL jargon. Thus, we employ the TL jargon production approach of shape and produce ناطِحة سحاب. Our decision is based on the above semantic details on the SL jargon.

It is worthwhile to note that the literal word-for-word translation of "skyscraper" is
كاشِطةُ سماء. However, the back-translation of the TL jargon ناطِحةُ سحاب is "the butter
of clouds", where the active participle noun ناطِحة derived from the verb "to butt, i.e., to
ram" is employed plus the object plural noun سحاب meaning "clouds". Therefore, we can
observe that the TL jargon has deleted all the SL jargon elements. Thus, in the production
of the TL jargon ناطِحةُ سحاب, we have adopted the through translation approach known
as *calque* or *loan translation*, which is a type of literal translation where TL grammar is
observed and the SL-specific features are replaced with TL-specific features. Thus, through
translation is similar to cultural transposition where the SL "sky" is replaced with TL سحاب
"clouds", and SL "scraper" is replaced with TL ناطِحة "butter (from the verb 'to butt') ram-
mer". These translation approaches also aim at complete naturalness of the TL jargon; to
naturalize and domesticate the TL jargon and reduce its foreignness. The new TL jargon
interpretively resembles the original without unnecessary processing effort on the part of
the TL reader.

Another example of mimicking the shape of the TL jargon is "tongue". Let us consider
the semantic details of this jargon: The seat belt has a buckle and a "tongue" which is made
of metal and which fits into the buckle to secure the seat belt. The "tongue" at the end of
the seat belt goes into the buckle, which secures and releases the metal tongue. Having seen
the picture of the seat belt "tongue" and read its semantic details, we are now in a position to
produce the TL jargon لسانٌ معدني based on mimicking the shape of the SL jargon.

Let us consider the SL jargon related to road traffic system adopted in Britain: (i) "dual
carriageway/divided highway", and (ii) "single carriageway/undivided highway". Having
considered the semantic details of the above SL road traffic system jargon, we can propose
the translation and the new TL jargon: (i) طريق بإتجاه واحد and (ii) طريق مُتعاكس الإتجاه,
whose back-translations are: (i) "a road with opposite directions" and (ii) "a road with a single direction". The production of the TL jargon is based on the shape of the road. Based on the
above semantic componential details on the SL jargon, we need the translation approaches
such as the communicative, dynamic equivalence, cultural transplantation, natural, acceptable, instrumental, or faithful. These translation approaches take into consideration the contextual intended meaning of the SL jargon in order to provide a comprehensible TL jargon to
its audience. These translation approaches aim at complete naturalness of the TL jargon; to
naturalize and domesticate the TL jargon, reduce its foreignness, and resemble the original
without unnecessary processing effort on the part of the TL reader. However, it is worthwhile
to note that in our production of the TL jargon, we have missed significant details which
distinguish between the two types of roads: (i) "dual carriageway/divided highway" and
(ii) "single carriageway/undivided highway". In the UK, these two types of road are dif-
ferentiated through the middle island separating the two roads, the speed limit of each road,
the type of street lightening on the side of each road, and the height of the street light posts.
Such road system features do not exist in the Arab countries. Thus, these features are SL
culture-specific.

Some SL-shape-based jargon have overlaps in Arabic. Thus, Arabic needs to adopt the
exegetical translation approach, where an additional word is added to TL jargon to differentiate between the two TL jargon, as in "airplane" and "aircraft". Based on mimicking the
shape of the SL jargon, Arabic has طائرة. However, the semantic distinction between "airplane" and "aircraft" has not been captured by the TL jargon طائرة. Thus, we need to use the
exegetical translation approach to produce طائرة حربية and طائرة نقل.

230 *Jargon translation*

4. Mimicking the operational method of the SL jargon: This jargon production approach is concerned with the accurate transfer of the operational mechanism of an expression, as in the SL jargon "blending", whose translation to Arabic is based on how this expression works in language – as a word formation process. Thus, we have the TL jargon النحت.

Other SL jargon whose translation has been based on mimicking their operational method are "satellite", "drone", and "submarine", which are transferred to Arabic as قمرٌ صناعي, غوَّاصة, and مُسيَّرة, respectively. However, we need to make the following observations:

(i) The TL jargon قمرٌ صناعي is based on mimicking the operational method of the SL jargon "satellite", which rotates around the Earth. However, the TL jargon قمرٌ صناعي mimics both "satellite" and the "moon", which both rotate around the Earth. In other words, it is the semantic feature of rotating around the Earth that is taken into consideration in the production of the Arabic jargon.

(ii) The Arabic word formation process of derivation الإشتقاق has been employed in the production of the TL jargon غوَّاصة "submarine", which is morphologically related to and derived from the verb غاصَ "to dive". The SL military jargon "radio" has also been produced in Arabic as جهاز لاسلكي ، جهاز إرسال واستقبال لاسلكي based on mimicking the operational method of the communication equipment. The back-translation explains this "equipment without wires/equipment for sending and receiving without wires". See the first jargon production approach (function) used for the translation of the jargon "radio".

Over time, some SL jargon change their names and, thus, their semantic componential features – although, technically speaking, they remain having the same method of operation, as in "bicycle, bike". We next encountered the SL jargon "motorcycle, motor-bike", then the jargon "pushbike", then "scooter", and then very recently the jargon "e-scooter". Through mimicking the mechanism operating these jargon, the TL jargon have been produced as درَّاجة ، درَّاجة هوائية for "bicycle". Since it does not have an engine, we find the exegetical translation approach where an additional expression هوائية appears in the TL jargon. Since "motorcycle, motor-bike" have an engine which operates by petrol and smoke is generated, Arabic uses the jargon درَّاجة نارية بُخارية, which is an exegetical translation approach where the additional expression نارية بُخارية appears in the TL jargon. The smoke from exhaust of the "motorcycle, motor-bike" has misled the translator who inadvertently provided بُخارية wrongly taking the smoke for "steam" بُخار. As for the SL jargon "pushbike", we can propose the translation درَّاجة الرجل للأطفال, since it is specifically for children who use one of their legs to push the bike. Thus, we have employed the exegetical translation approach and added the details الرجل للأطفال. However, the novel equipment is "e-scooter", which we translate as الدرَّاجة الألكترونية where the initial "e" stands for "electronic". Thus, the SL jargon has been produced through a combination of two jargon production approaches: the mimicking of the operational method (in this case, an electronic method of operation) and the mimicking of the sounds (transliteration) of the SL jargon الألكترونية.

Similarly, we have encountered the TL jargon الحافلة المفصَّلية for the new SL jargon "bendy bus/articulated bus", based on the fact that this type of public transport bus is long and characterized by its method of operation comprising two or more rigid sections linked by a pivoting joint (articulation). The short wheelbase of the front half of the vehicle gives good maneuverability in tight spaces, allowing the large articulated bus to negotiate narrow roads. See the picture below.

الصورة أعلاه للمصطلح "articulated 'bendy' bus" الذي يقابلهُ في العربية المُصطلح (الحافِلة المِفصَلية).

5. Mimicking the sound of the SL jargon: This jargon production approach is concerned with how a SL jargon is transferred phonetically (transliterated) and adapted to the TL morphology. This SL jargon production approach is related to the cultural borrowing, naturalization, and and transference translation approaches, where the SL jargon is transferred phonetically (transliterated) and adapted to the TL morphology, and where the SL expression is transferred verbatim into the TL by a transliteration; phonetically introduced in the TL. We encounter a large number of phonetically based jargon used in Arabic, as in "computer" and the novel jargon "selfie". However, the jargon "computer" has also been produced according to mimicking its function, as discussed in point (i) above. We can observe two types of phonetically based Arabic jargon:

(i) onomatopoeic TL jargon: For instance, when the "missile" is fired, it produces a shrieking "whistling" sound which Arabic has turned into a TL jargon صاروخ. This TL jargon is based on the Arabic word formation process of derivation الإشتِقاق, and is morphologically related to the verb root صَرَخَ "to shout loudly, to shriek". Another sound-based TL jargon can be found in "twitter/tweet", which have been translated as ، تغريد تغريدة مُغرِد using the jargon production approach of mimicking the onomatopoeic bird's intrinsic sounds of tweeting "singing", rather than the intrinsic sounds (transliteration) of the SL jargon. The same applies to the Iraqi jargon شِخّاطة for the SL jargon "a box of matches", whose standard Arabic translation is عِلبة كبريت. However, شِخّاطة is an onomatopoeic Iraqi TL jargon due to the noise the stick of matches makes when you strike it against the coarse surface of the box.

(ii) mimicking the intrinsic sounds of the SL jargon (transliteration): There are many SL jargon which have been borrowed by Arabic through their intrinsic sounds, such as

232 *Jargon translation*

"computer", "selfie", "twitter", "WhatsApp", "oxygen", "corona", "virus", "chlorophyll", "radar", "aluminum", "sodium", and "cholesterol". This jargon approach is based on the naturalization translation approach, where a SL word is transferred phonetically (transliterated) and adapted to the TL morphology. For more details on this translation approach, see Chapter 1, Section 1.5, point 11.

Acceptability by the Arab reader plays a major role in the proliferation of some of the above sound-based TL jargon borrowed from English. For instance, the jargon "radar" is more acceptable and more widely used than its accurately translated form نِظامُ الكشفِ وتحديد المدى, which is produced through mimicking the method of operation jargon approach. The same applies to "television", which is transliterated as تلفزيون and has been accepted, instead of المرأي, whose back-translation is "what can be seen". More examples include "chlorophyll", which is accepted in its transliterated form كلوروفيل instead of its translated as الصيغة الخضراء، طائرة مروحية; "helicopter", which is widely used as هليكوبتر instead of طوافة ، عمودية ، سمتية; and also the SL jargon "ice cream", which has been transferred to Arabic through the mimicking of its constituent sounds (transliteration) – آيس كريم instead of مُرطّبات ، مُثلّجات, based on mimicking the function of the SL jargon.

6. Mimicking the semantic features of the SL jargon: This jargon production approach is concerned with the accurate transfer of the SL jargon semantic features المكونات الدلالية, as in "Reaganomics", which has been created in English through the word formation process of blending. This jargon is created by joining the American President's name "Reagan" with his economic policy he adopted; thus, we get "Reaganomics". However, having considered the semantic features of the SL jargon, we can mimic the same semantic features and translate it as السياسة الإقتصادية للرئيس ريجن or سياسة الرئيس ريجن الإقتصادية. Similarly, we have the SL jargon "module", which is transferred as مادة دراسية or مُقرّر based on the semantic componential features of the SL jargon. The same applies to the novel SL jargon "selfie", to which I propose the translation "صورة ذاتية". The translation of the jargon "cornerstone" as حجر الزاوية has also been based on the jargon's semantic features "the stone that forms the basis of a corner of a building".

A unique example of mimicking the semantic features of the SL jargon is the Arabic jargon المُتشابهات, which is a Qur'an-specific jargon. This Arabic jargon has been incorrectly transferred to English as "ambiguous". Based on the Qur'anic semantic features of the jargon, we recommend that the translation of المُتشابهات should be "the stylistically distinct but grammatically similar expressions", since we are dealing with expressions and sentences which are theologically oriented and stylistically different, but are similar on the grammatical level. Thus, the translation needs to be based on the exegetical and paraphrastic translation approach (over-translation). The jargon المُتشابهات does not have a one-to-one correspondence in English. Also, the scientific jargon "a crewed spaceship" is based on the semantic componential features of the word "crewed", which means "a spaceship which is manned by astronauts, i.e., it has a crew" who are human beings who can inhabit a place. Thus, we produce the TL jargon as مركبة فضاء مأهولة, whose back-translation is "a spaceship which is populated".

Another example of mimicking the semantic features of the SL jargon is the English jargon "monogenesis theory", which has been rendered as نظرية الأصل الواحد. The translation is based on the semantic componential features of the ST jargon: "the theory of development from a single source", whose word-for-word literal translation is نظرية النشوء من أصلٍ واحدٍ.

Jargon translation 233

7. Blending: This is a word formation process through which we produce a new jargon by joining the beginning of a word to the end of another. For instance, the new word "smog" is produced in English by blending the beginning of the word "smoke" with the end of the word "fog". The same applies to other blended words like "brunch" which is taken from "breakfast + lunch", "motel" which is a blend from "motor + hotel", and the new expression "Reaganomics", created through joining the American President's name "Reagan" with the economic policy he adopted, giving us "Reaganomics". The SL jargon "electromagnetic" is blended from "electricity + magnetism". The TL jargon كهرومغناطيسي is also blended from كهرباء + مغناطيس. The Arabic jargon برمائي is blended from ماء + بَر, meaning "land + water". This Arabic jargon is the translation of the SL jargon "amphibious", which is a single-word adjective meaning "living or able to live both on land and in water". We also encounter the novel SL jargon "burqini 'burkini'" and "veilkini" which are blended jargon from بُرقُع + بكِيني and "veil + bikini" as swimming costumes. However, Arabic cannot produce TL jargon based on the blending of such expressions. Arabic can mimic the function (purpose) of these SL jargon. We recommend the TL jargon ثوبُ سباحةٍ اسلامي, whose back-translation is "an Islamic swimming costume".

Similarly, we have seen the SL jargon "Brexit, Brexiteer" in 2016 made through the word formation process of blending in English "Britain + exit 'from the European Union'" and "a British person wanting to + exit 'from the European Union'". However, we cannot use blending in Arabic for these jargon. We recommend a different jargon production approach based on mimicking the event of the SL jargon. Thus, we get خروج بريطانيا من الإتحاد الأوروبي and الشخص الذي يؤيد خروج بريطانيا من الإتحاد الأوربي, which are based on the exegetical translation approach.

Blending has also been used in the translation of the jargon "smog", which is transferred to Arabic as ضباب + دُخان, or the less commonly used jargon الدخان, where الضبابُ الدخَاني are blended.

8. Joint approach: At times, we encounter a joint approach in the production of a new Arabic jargon where the translator adopts two approaches, as in "air-borne firebomb/incendiary balloon" whose translations are طائرة حارقة and whose back-translation is "burning kite" – where "kite" is also translated as طائرة in Arabic, mimicking the shape of the SL jargon "kite". Thus, we have a joint approach in the production of the ST jargon, which are translated as طائرة حارقة, based on mimicking both the shape طائرة and the function حارقة. In other words, the function is to "burn or cause fire". It is also translated as بالونات حارقة, meaning (burning balloon), which is based on mimicking both the sound "balloon" + the function حارقة "to burn".

Similarly, the jargon "frigate" is transferred to Arabic as سفينةٌ حربيةٌ مُتوسطةُ الحجم, where we have mimicked the military function of the jargon + the shape of the jargon. Our translation is based on mimicking the military function of the "frigate" and its shape. It is worthwhile to note that the "frigate" is much smaller in size than the "warship, destroyer". Thus, we have chosen the exegetical translation approach and added مُتوسطةُ الحجم, adopting both the function and the shape of the SL jargon.

The translation of the jargon "drone" is at times translated as طائرةٌ مُسَيَّرةٌ. Thus, it is based on mimicking the shape and the operational method of the jargon. Similarly, we have the jargon "breeches buoy", whose translation involves a joint approach to produce the Arabic jargon ينطال إنقاذ, where ينطال mimics the shape of the ST "breeches" and the function

234 *Jargon translation*

الإنقاذ, mimicking the function of "buoy". The same applies to the jargon "nimbus". This is discussed in detail in Section 6.8, exercise number 2.

6.7 Proliferation of jargon

Although some SL jargon have been produced in a transliterated form, translated literally, or wrongly transferred to Arabic, they are still widely used in Arabic. For instance, the SL jargon "chlorophyll" is transferred phonetically as كلوروفيل instead of its translation as اليخضور, due to its dominant green colour characteristic. Also, the SL jargon "virus" is transferred phonetically as فيروس instead of its translation as الحُمى; "fax" is transferred phonetically as فاكس instead of its translation as ناسوخ; "sandwich" is transferred phonetically as ساندويج instead of its translation as شطيرة or تصبيرة; "iPad" is transferred phonetically as آيباد instead of its translation as الحاسوب اللوحي; "mouse" is transferred phonetically as ماوس instead of its translation as مُؤشِّر ، مُؤشِّر الشاشة; "mobile" is transferred phonetically as موبايل instead of its translation as نقّال ، جوّال ، محمول; "electronics/electronic" are transferred phonetically as الكترونيات ، الكتروني instead of their translations as الكُهيربيات or الكُهيربي; "e-mail" is transferred phonetically as إيميل instead of its translation as بريد الكتروني or رسالة الكترونية; and "Instagram" is transferred phonetically as الألستغرام instead of its translation as تبادُل الصور والأفلام على شبكات التواصُل الإجتماعي. However, the SL jargon "Adam's apple" is literally translated as تُفاحة آدم and has been widely used instead of its alternative accurate translation, القُردوحة. Some SL jargon acronyms are widely used in Arabic although some of them are wrong – as in "SAM", which is wrongly transferred phonetically (transliteration) to Arabic as صاروخ سام. However, its correct translation is صاروخ أرض‒جو, based on the acronym's words (surface-to-air missile). Similarly, the acronym "radar" is widely used as رادار, instead of its translation as نظام الكشف وتحديد المدى, based on the acronym's words "radio detection and ranging".

6.8 Translator training and translation practice

This section combines theory and practice and prepares students for the translation industry. The commentary and analysis of the following examples aim to put the previous theoretical discussion of the seven jargon production approaches into practice, and to show translation students how and why a given solution is given to each jargon borrowed by Arabic. Thus, it is aimed at providing the translation students practical translation training with a solution to each question and a discussion to aid translation students and guide them to achieve a successful translation of newly borrowed jargon into Arabic.

1. Give reasons for the translation of the jargon "parliament", "capital" and "module". Discuss the jargon production approaches together with the translation approach adopted in your translation and explain why.

We can make the following observations:

(i) The translator has adopted the jargon production mechanism of mimicking the function of the SL jargon "parliament", i.e., the SL and TL jargon perform the same function of debating national political matters, consulting each other, and voting on political decisions. This is based on the first jargon production mechanism.

Jargon translation 235

(ii) Based on the types of jargon in Section 7.4, we can claim that "parliament" is a one-word jargon whose production and translation in Arabic are based on intertextuality with Q42:38, which has led to the birth of different noun phrase Arabic jargon: مجلس النواب and مجلس الشورى, مجلس الأمة. The translator has adopted a culture-based translation based on one of the following translation approaches: communicative, dynamic equivalence, natural, acceptable, domestication, or faithful. These translation approaches take into consideration the contextual intended meaning of the ST in order to provide a comprehensible TT to its audience with an acceptable natural TL style. These translation approaches aim at complete naturalness of the TT; to naturalize the TT and reduce its foreignness. The above translation interpretively resembles the original without unnecessary processing effort on the part of the TL reader.

(iii) However, the other type of jargon produced in Arabic for the SL jargon "parliament" is a one-word Arabic jargon: يرلمان. The translator has adopted the foreignization, naturalization, cultural borrowing, or transference translation approaches where the SL jargon is transferred phonetically (transliterated), transferred verbatim into the TL, and adapted to the TL morphology. This is based on the fifth jargon production mechanism, which is mimicking the sound of the SL jargon. This is also related to the cultural borrowing, naturalization, and transference translation approaches where the SL jargon is phonetically transferred to Arabic and adapted to its morphology.

(iv) We can observe that a single-word SL jargon can be produced in Arabic either as a noun phrase jargon or a single-word jargon.

(v) However, the translator has produced a one-word TL jargon, عاصمة, for the single-word SL jargon "capital". The birth of the TL jargon is based on the denotative lexical meaning أنها القاعدة الإدارية الأساسية للبلد أو للإقليم, i.e., قاعدة القطر أو الإقليم.

(vi) The translator has adopted the jargon production mechanism of mimicking the semantic componential features of the jargon, i.e., the SL and TL jargon have the same semantic features. This is based on the sixth jargon production approach.

(vii) As for the translation of the SL jargon "module", the translator has adopted the jargon production mechanism of mimicking the semantic componential features of the jargon "module", i.e., the SL and TL jargon have the same semantic features. This is based on the sixth jargon production approach. The TL jargon is مقرر ، مادة دراسية, which is based on the SL and TL jargon's denotative lexical meaning ("module" refers to an instructional unit that focuses on a particular topic).

2. Give reasons for the translation of the jargon "nimbus". Discuss the jargon production approach together with the translation approach adopted in your translation and explain why.
   We can make the following observations:

(i) The translator has adopted a joint approach, i.e., the translation is based on the jargon production approach of mimicking the function of the SL jargon "nimbus"; the SL and TL jargon perform the same function of producing rain. This is based on the first jargon production approach of the jargon's function. Additionally, the translation of "nimbus" into Arabic is based on the semantic componential features of "nimbus", which are "a large grey rain cloud". The SL jargon "nimbus" is based on intertextuality with Q78:14, which has led to the birth of the Arabic jargon مُعصِرات – a noun in the plural form, while it is in the singular form in English. This Arabic plural form is due to the reliance of the translator on intertextuality with the Qur'anic statement: Q78:14 أنزلنا من

المُعصِرات ماءأ ثجَّاجا "We sent down pouring rain from the rain clouds". Arabic provides exactly the same semantic componential features of المُعصِرة, which are: هي السحابة المُنخَفِضة المُمطِرةُ سوداءُ اللون. This is based on the seventh jargon production mechanism (joint approach). Thus, the translation of "nimbus" is based on function + componential semantic features.

(ii) The alternative translation of "nimbus" is سحابة مُمطِرةٌ, which is also based on mimicking the function of the SL jargon "nimbus" and its semantic componential features. However, the Arabic jargon مُعصِرة، مُعصِرات is, stylistically, more succinct, and succinctness is the pivotal feature of eloquence and a requirement of Arabic rhetoric.

(iii) The translator has adopted a culture-based translation based on one of the following translation approaches: the communicative, dynamic equivalence, natural, acceptable, domestication, or faithful translation approach.

3. Give reasons for the translation of the jargon "Instagram". Discuss the jargon production approach together with the translation approach adopted in your translation and explain why.
We can make the following observations:

(i) The translation of the jargon "Instagram" is based on exegetical and paraphrase translation approaches. Thus, we get تبادُل الصور والأفلام على شبكات التواصل الإجتماعي (the exchange of photos and films on social media). In terms of jargon production mechanisms, the translator has mimicked the semantic componential features of the SL jargon (Instagram).

(ii) The translator has adopted the foreignization, naturalization, cultural borrowing, or transference translation approaches, where the SL jargon is transferred phonetically (transliterated), transferred verbatim into the TL, and adapted to the TL morphology. This is based on the fifth jargon production mechanism, which is mimicking the sound of the SL jargon. This is also related to the cultural borrowing, naturalization, and transference translation approaches, where the SL jargon is phonetically transferred to Arabic and adapted to its morphology.

4. Give reasons for the translation of the jargon "SAM, radar, NATO". Discuss the jargon production approach together with the translation approach adopted in your translation and explain why.

(i) The above SL jargon are acronyms, i.e., each jargon is made up of the initial letters of a group of words. The jargon "SAM" is the acronym of "surface-to-air-missile", "radar" is the acronym of "radio detection and ranging", and "NATO" is the acronym of "North Atlantic Treaty Organization". Thus, they are all abbreviations.

(ii) The transfer of the above SL jargon has been based on the mimicking of their sounds. In other words, in Arabic, the TL jargon are all transliterated, i.e., the transfer of the SL jargon is based on the naturalization and transference translation approaches where the SL jargon is transferred phonetically (transliterated) and adapted to the TL morphology.

(iii) There has been a common mistake in Arabic with regards to the translation of the jargon "SAM", where it has been wrongly translated as صاروخ سام. In fact, "SAM" is not a missile model. Rather, it is an acronym for "surface-to-air missile". Thus, we need to change the translation to صاروخ أرض-جو. Therefore, we have adopted the

Jargon translation 237

mimicking of the SL jargon function approach, i.e., its function is to attack air targets الأهداف الجوية. In other words, the missile's purpose is to be launched from the surface to attack an aircraft. However, the SL military jargon "SS" has two meanings, and the translator needs to capture the semantic distinction between the "SS" fired by the land force and the "SS" fired by the naval force. An "SS" is an acronym which stands for "surface-to-surface" missile. If it is fired by the army, it is translated as صاروخ أرض- أرض. However, if it fired by a warship, a submarine, or a frigate – i.e., it is fired by the naval force – it should be translated as صاروخ سطح-سطح, where the expression سطح refers to the "surface of water" سطحُ الماء. We have adopted the approach of mimicking the SL jargon function.

(iv) The transfer of the SL jargon "radar" has been based on the mimicking of its sounds (transliteration). The jargon "radar" is an acronym for "radio detection and ranging", whose translation is نظامُ الكشفِ وتحديد المدى. Our translation is based on mimicking the function of the SL jargon – its function is to detect targets.

5. Give reasons for the translation of the following jargon. Discuss the jargon production approach together with the translation approaches adopted in your translation and explain why: "burqini, veilkini, piggy bank".

(i) Having considered the semantic componential features of the above SL jargon, we are in a position to claim that we need to mimic the function of the SL jargon. The purpose of the ST jargon "burqini, veilkini" is to indicate use on the beach and for swimming. The purpose of the ST jargon "piggy bank" is for saving money for children until they are adults and are able to open a bank account.

(ii) The SL jargon have SL culture-specific features alien to the Arabic or Islamic culture. Thus, we need to employ the cultural transplantation or domestication translation approaches, which allow the translator to remove the SL culture features and replace them with TL culture details. The SL culture-specific details are represented by the suffix "-ini" which is taken from "bikini". Thus, in terms of word formation processes discussed above in Section 7.3, we have blending, which produces in the SL a new jargon by joining the beginning of one word to the end of another word. Thus, we have blended "veil + bikini" to get "veilkini" and we have blended "burqu' + bikini" to get "burqini". Therefore, "veilkini" and "burqini" are formed through the blending word process in English. However, the SL expression "bikini" is not suitable for Arabic culture since (1) it does not designate decorum الحِشمة, and most importantly, (2) there is a contrast between the two words constituting the SL expression "veil", which designates decorum and modesty + "bikini" which does not designate decorum and modesty. In other words, stylistically, the SL jargon has the rhetorical device of oxymoron (contrasting words placed next to each other). Since the purpose (function) of the jargon is for beaches and swimming, we need to produce a TL Arab culture-specific jargon based on the cultural transplantation translation. We propose ثوب سباحة اسلامي, where we have replaced the word "bikini" with TL culture-specific words ثوب اسلامي + the function of the dress سباحة, whose back-translation is "an Islamic dress for swimming". Thus, the oxymoron (contrast) has been taken out from the TT jargon.

(iii) The ST jargon "piggy bank": Although the purpose of the ST jargon "piggy bank" is for saving money for children until they are adults and are able to open a bank account, we

238 *Jargon translation*

cannot produce the same jargon literally in Arabic because of the SL culture-specific word "piggy, i.e., pig" خنزير. We have a similar purpose in Arabic but we must adopt the cultural transplantation translation approach through which we delete the SL culture word "piggy" and replace it with a TL culture word. Thus, we propose حَصَّالة حصَّالة أطفال, whose back-translation is "saving box/children's saving box". However, the literal translation of "piggy bank" is مصرف الخنزير، حصَّالة الخنزير, and both are incompatible with the TL culture.

6. Give reasons for the translation of the jargon "airbed". Discuss the jargon production approach and provide the translation.

(i)   First, we need to consider the semantic componential features of the SL jargon "airbed". This is an inflatable mattress used for sleeping. Based on these details and especially the noun phrase "an inflatable mattress", the jargon production approach for the SL jargon "airbed" should be based on the mimicking of the shape of the SL jargon.

(ii) The shape of this kind of bed is similar to the shape of a "mattress" but it is made of plastic and is filled with air. Thus, we can produce the TL jargon مرتبة منفوخة، مرتبة هوائية. This is a cultural transplantation approach translation because we have deleted the SL expression "air" and replaced it with a TL expression منفوخة، هوائية based on "inflatable", which is a shape. Thus, the reason why we have employed منفوخة، هوائية is because it is based on the semantic componential features of the SL jargon "air", i.e., "inflatable". Therefore, we have adopted the shape approach based on mimicking the shape of the SL jargon "inflatable".

(iii) The SL jargon includes the word "bed", which we have replaced with مرتبة, i.e., "mattress". Because the shape of a "bed/mattress", we need to mimic the shape and produce the shape-based TL jargon, مرتبة. Thus, the translation of the SL jargon "airbed" is مرتبة منفوخة، مرتبة هوائية.

(iv) Based on the lexical details of the above SL jargon, we need the translation approaches such as the communicative, dynamic equivalence, cultural transplantation, natural, acceptable, instrumental, or faithful. These translation approaches take into consideration the contextual intended meaning of the SL jargon in order to provide a comprehensible TL jargon to their audience. These translation approaches aim at complete naturalness of the above TL jargon; to naturalize and domesticate it, reduce its foreignness, and make the new TL jargon interpretively resemble the SL jargon without unnecessary processing effort on the part of the TL reader.

7. Give reasons for the translation of the jargon "electronic tag 'tag'", "ventilator", and "eye bag". Discuss the jargon production approach together with the translation approach adopted in your translation and explain why.

(i)   The translation of "electronic tag 'tag'" is خَلخال الكترونى. This is a literal translation based on mimicking the shape of the SL jargon. The tag is an electronic device of surveillance used to enforce a curfew or house arrest. It is fitted to the person above his/her ankle as part of his/her bail or probation conditions. It is also called "electronic monitoring" or "tagging", and is used in England and Wales. The reason why we have adopted the shape approach is because the tag's shape is round and is placed above the ankle of the person. Thus, it is likened to a "bangle, wrist-band" worn by ladies. The reason why

Jargon translation 239

we have used خَلْخال is because it is worn above the ankle. If it is worn on the wrist, it would have been سِوار. Through cultural transplantation, we have managed to delete the SL expression "tag" and replace it with a TL expression خَلْخال.

(ii) The translation of the SL jargon "eye bag" is انتفاخ تحت العين/هالة سوداء تحت العين. This is a cultural transplantation approach translation because we have deleted the SL expression "bag" and replaced it with a TL expression انتفاخ/هالة سوداء تحت. An "eye bag" is a mild swelling or puffiness under the eyes. Thus, the reason why we have employed انتفاخ is because it is based on the semantic componential features of the SL jargon "swelling or puffiness under the eyes". Therefore, we have adopted the shape approach based on mimicking the shape of the SL jargon.

As for the second alternative translation which we have suggested, it is TL stylistically based translation where the rhetorical device of imagery is employed هالة.

(iii) During the coronavirus pandemic (December 2019), the medical SL jargon "ventilator" was widely used in the media. First, we need to consider the semantic componential features of "ventilator". A ventilator takes over the critically ill Covid-19 patient's breathing process when the disease has caused the lungs to fail. Thus, the ventilator's function is to provide artificial respiration التنفس الإصطناعي. Based on the semantic componential features of the SL jargon and its medical purpose in hospitals treating coronavirus patients, we have proposed the TL jargon جهاز التنفس الإصطناعي. Therefore, we have adopted the function approach, which is based on mimicking the operational function of the SL jargon.

(iv) Based on the lexical details of each of the above SL jargon, we need the translation approaches such as the communicative, dynamic equivalence, cultural transplantation, natural, acceptable, instrumental, or faithful. These translation approaches take into consideration the contextual intended meaning of each of the three SL jargon in order to provide comprehensible TL jargon to their audience. These translation approaches aim at complete naturalness of the previous TL jargon; to naturalize and domesticate them, reduce their foreignness, and make each of the new TL jargon interpretively resemble the SL jargon without unnecessary processing effort on the part of the TL reader.

8. Give reasons for the translation of the jargon "jackknife", "tailback", and "double-decker". Discuss the jargon production approach together with the translation approach adopted in your translation and explain why.

We can make the following observations:

(i) The jargon "jackknife" has been left out in monolingual and bilingual dictionaries. The noun "jackknife" collocates with large articulated tools which can fold and resemble the acute angle of a folding pocket knife. Based on mimicking the operational method of the tool, we can propose the jargon شاحنة مُفصّلة قادرة على الإنحناء "an articulated vehicle than can bend". This is the fourth jargon production approach, which is concerned with the operational mechanism of the jargon.

(ii) For the jargon "tailback" and "double-decker", we propose the jargon طابور سيارات and حافلة بطابقين ، حافلة ذات طابقين, where we have mimicked the shape of the SL jargon. This jargon production approach is concerned with the accurate transfer of the SL jargon shape.

240 *Jargon translation*

الصورة أعلاه للمُصطلح "double-decker" الذي يقابله في العربية المُصطلح (حافلة بطابقين، حافلة ذات طابقين).

9. Give reasons for the translation of the jargon "helicopter", "drone", "blade", "fan", "ventilator", and "extractor". Discuss the jargon generation approach together with the translation approach adopted in your translation and explain why.

It is interesting to note that, in terms of Arabic morphology and translation studies, the five SL jargon "helicopter", "drone", "blade", "fan", "ventilator", and "extractor" are inter-related in terms of derivation الإشتقاق, concept, shape, or function jargon production approaches.

- (i) It is worthwhile to note that the SL jargon "helicopter" has different names, each generated in Arabic through a different approach. The jargon "helicopter" is transferred to Arabic through the following jargon production approaches:

  - (a) Through mimicking the operational method of the SL jargon "helicopter": In terms of the SL jargon mechanism of taking-off, the TL jargon طائرة مروحية, طائرة عمودية and طائرة سمتية are employed since we are told by its semantic features that the "helicopter" uses rotating or spinning wings called blades to fly. Through this approach, we have got the above three Arabic jargon based on how this equipment works in terms of taking-off and landing. As for the Arabic word سمتية, this is related to the "azimuth, zenith, vertex". Thus, there is a relationship between the way how the helicopter takes off "vertical take-off" and the concept of vertex or zenith. Based on this semantic relationship, we have the TL jargon سمتية for "helicopter" since it can move straight up or down and can take off or land without a runway.

Jargon translation 241

Similarly, due to the mechanism of operating the "drone" by someone in terms of taking off, course of action, and landing, we can claim that the Arabic jargon مُسَيَّرة is based on mimicking the operational method of the SL jargon.

(ii) However, the translation of the SL jargon "blade" has been based on mimicking its shape, which is translated to Arabic as ورقة نبات ، ورقة عِشب, i.e., the "blade" is something that is similar in shape to نصل النبات – especially trees with longitudinal leaves which look like blades.

(iii) In the translation of the SL jargon "fan" and "ventilator", Arabic has employed the Arabic word formation process of derivation الإشتقاق through which we have مروحة and مهوات مروحة تهوية, respectively. This morphologically based translation has relied on the Arabic verb root راحَ، رَوَّحَ "to fan", meaning "to fan air to refresh and cause relaxation", where the "fan" مروحة is fixed to the ceiling of a room, and where the "ventilator" is fixed to the wall of a room or building to cause air to enter and circulate freely. Thus, the TL jargon production has been based on mimicking the function of the SL jargon "fan" and "ventilator".

During the Covid-19 pandemic period in the early months of 2020, the jargon "ventilator" was used widely on the news. The jargon "ventilator" is medical equipment used in hospitals to take over the body's breathing process when disease has caused the lungs to fail. Thus, based on the function of the machine, we can mimic the medical function of the equipment and translate it as جهاز تنفس اصطناعي.

(iv) In the translation of the SL jargon "extractor", Arabic has also employed the Arabic formation process of derivation, which has produced the TL jargon شافِطة، ساحِبة, i.e., شافطة هواء، ساحِبة هواء. Although the "extractor" has "blades" in its operational mechanism to extract fresh air, Arabic has preferred to resort to mimicking the function of "extracting" شافِطة، ساحِبة. Thus, we have سحب، شفط.

10. Provide a context-based translation for the IT jargon "log off" and "screen", and provide a commentary.

(i) The translator is unable to provide an accurate translation without an insight into the context in which the ST jargon or sentence occurs. Let us assume that the ST expressions have occurred in the sentence: "She logged off and turned off the screen of her computer". In this case, we are in a position to provide the translation: قامت بتسجيل الخروج وإغلاق شاشة جهاز الكمبيوتر الخاص بها.

(ii) However, the ST jargon "log off" and "screen" have occurred in a different context. On Friday 16 June 2006, we are informed by the TV news reporter that Bill Gates, the founder of Microsoft company, has stepped down from the day-to-day running of his company: "Bill Gates has decided to <u>log off</u> and disappeared from the <u>screen</u>". The news reporter has employed IT jargon as metonymy كِناية. Thus, the translator is advised not to translate "log off/screen" literally in order to provide a context-based translation which aims at complete naturalness of the TL jargon; to naturalize and domesticate the TL jargon, and reduce its foreignness, without unnecessary processing effort on the part of the TL reader. Thus, the translator needs to employ translation approaches such as

242   *Jargon translation*

the communicative, dynamic equivalence, cultural transplantation, natural, acceptable, instrumental, or faithful: "Bill Gates has decided to <u>log off</u> and disappeared from the <u>screen</u>". We can propose this translation:

قرر بيل غيتس ترك إدارة شركته والإبتعاد عنها

11. Give reasons for the translation of the jargon "shuttle diplomacy", "space shuttle", "spaceship", and "probe". Discuss the production approach together with the translation approach adopted in your translation and explain why.

(i)   The SL diplomatic jargon "shuttle diplomacy" appeared in the 1970s during the US Secretary of State Henry Kissinger's shuttle diplomacy peace mission between Egypt and Israel during which he made several visits to the Middle East. Thus, we have the action of going there and back many times.

(ii)   The production of the TL jargon is based on the word "spindle" مِغزل ، مكُوك, which is "a straight rode or spike which revolves and is usually made of wood for spinning, twisting fibers such as wool, flax cotton into yarn". Thus, the translator has adopted the mimicking of the operational method (method of action) jargon production approach.

(iii)   Stylistically, this represents the rhetorical device of imagery, where going to the Middle East and back to his country the USA many times, i.e., revolving to make peace, is likened to a spindle, which also revolves to make yarn.

(iv)   Lexically, the translator has favored the word مكُوك over مِغزل, and produced the TL jargon جولة مكوكية ، دبلوماسية مكوكية rather than جولة مِغزلية ، دبلوماسية مِغزلية.

(v)   This takes us to the translation of the SL jargon "space shuttle", where the translator has adopted the same method of mimicking the operational method jargon production approach and produced the TL jargon مكوك فضاء because it revolves the Earth many times.

(vi)   However, the SL jargon "spaceship" requires a different jargon production approach. The translator has adopted the mimicking of the shape jargon production approach and produced the TL jargon كبسولة الفضاء ، مركبة الفضاء because of the similarity between the capsule and the "spaceship". However, "capsule" is a SL jargon which has been retained phonetically in Arabic; the translator has adopted the mimicking of the sounds of the SL jargon. Thus, a naturalization or transference translation approach is adopted where a SL word is transferred phonetically (transliterated) and adapted to the TL morphology. However, had we adopted a jargon production approach based on the mimicking of the shape of the capsule, we would have produced the TL jargon عُلّيبة "a tiny container" or الجُرو "a puppy". Morphologically, the Arabic jargon عُلّيبة is the diminutive form اسم التصغير of عُلبة "container", which seems more acceptable than الجُرو because of its negative denotative meaning. The semantic componential features of "capsule" are "a tough sheath or membrane that encloses something in the body".

(vii)   The TL jargon مركبة فضاء for the SL jargon "spacecraft" is based on the mimicking of the shape jargon production approach. The translator has mimicked the shape of the "spaceship", which looks like a "boat" مركب (masculine) ، مركبة (feminine).

Jargon translation 243

(viii) The SL jargon "probe" is translated as مِسبار derived from the verb سَبَرَ meaning to find out about the secrets of something. Thus, we have mimicked the function of the "probe", as in "China sends a probe to the moon".

(ix) In terms of translation approaches, we need the communicative, dynamic equivalence, cultural transplantation, natural, acceptable, instrumental, or faithful. These translation approaches take into consideration the contextual intended meaning of the SL jargon in order to provide a comprehensible TL jargon to its audience. These translation approaches aim at complete naturalness of the TL jargon; to naturalize and domesticate the TL jargon and reduce its foreignness. The new TL jargon interpretively resembles the original without unnecessary processing effort on the part of the TL reader.

12. Provide the translation and the jargon production approach of the jargon "breakwater", "balloon", "ball-and-socket joint", "TV dish", "bookend", and "buggy".

(i) The translation of "breakwater" is حائل الأمواج, which is based on mimicking the function of the SL jargon.

(ii) The translation of "balloon" is مُنطاد, which is based on mimicking the operational method of the SL jargon. It is a passive participle noun اسم مفعول derived from the root verb إنطادَ, meaning to rise up and go high into the sky.

(iii) The translation of "ball-and-socket joint" is مِفصَل كُروي, which is based on mimicking the shape of the SL jargon. Similarly, the translation of "TV dish" is صَحَن/طَبَق, which is based on mimicking the shape of the SL jargon.

(iv) The translation of "bookend" is مِسنَد كُتُب, which is based on mimicking the function of the SL jargon.

(v) The translation of "buggy" is البوجية, which is based on mimicking the sound of the SL jargon.

13. Provide the translation and the jargon production approach of the jargon "wheelchair". We have encountered three different translations for "wheelchair":

(i) كرسي مُتحرك, whose back-translation is "moving chair". This translation is based on mimicking the operational method approach since it refers to someone who moves the chair,

(ii) كُرسي مُدولب, whose back-translation is "a chair with wheels". This translation is based on mimicking the operational method approach since it refers to مُدولب "having wheels to make the chair move", and

(iii) كُرسي مُعوَّقين, whose back-translation is "chair of the handicapped". This is based on mimicking the function of the jargon since it refers to the service it provides to "handicapped, disabled" people. Due to the negative connotative meaning of the word مُعوَّق "handicapped, with physical disability", we recommend abandoning the former translation and adopt كُرسي ذوي الإحتياجات الخاصة "chair of special needs people". However, the best translation for "wheelchair" is كُرسي مُتحرِّك mentioned in (i) above.

244 *Jargon translation*

14. Homework assignment: Discuss the translation and the jargon translation approach of the expressions: (i) أخ بالرضاعة, to which we suggest "a brother by nursing"; (ii) برنامج ماجستير عابر للحدود, to which we suggest "MA trans-national program"; (iii) "MRI" جهاز الرنين المغناطيسي; (iv) "caricature" الرسوم المتحركة; (v) the Japanese word "omamuri", to which we suggest تعويذة since it signifies charm and is believed to provide protection and good luck; (vi) "despatch box" in the British House of Commons "the Commons Chamber", to which we propose الحقيبة البرلمانية; and "to drain the swamp" in American politics, to which we propose القضاء على إستئصال الفساد.

15. Provide the translation and the jargon production approach of the jargon "vacuum cleaner".

16. Provide the translation and the jargon production approach of the jargon "Seaglider". Below are useful details for your translation process:

> The sea lanes along any country's east and west coasts can be turned into high-speed transit corridors without road traffic or airport hassle. The *Seaglider* can run a regular and reliable commercial service. The *Seaglider* is a "flying ship", i.e., it is a "boat-plane".
> What is the translation of *Seaglider*?

17. Provide the translation and the jargon production approach of the jargon "cluster bomb".

Appendix 1

Translation as process and product

Appendix 1 aims to promote a sharp insight into translation strategies and enable students more understanding and knowledge of the translation process and the translation approach required for a given translation problem at word, phrase, sentence, and text levels.

The following practice-based exercises are for training translation students and translators. The texts are analyzed and critically assessed. Translation problems are provided with proposed solutions through a comprehensive translation commentary.

Translator training and translation practice

1. For in-class discussion of the translation process, stylistic, grammatical, and semantic translation problems, and translation strategies:

الجُزُر الإماراتية الثلاث

طُنَب الكُبرى وطُنَب الصُغرى وأبو موسى، تحتلها إيران منذ 1971، ومنذ ذلك الحين تحتل القضية بُعداً استراتيجياً، فعلى الرغم من صُغر هذه الجُزر فإنها ذات أهمية استراتيجية بالغة، إذ أنها تقعُ على امتداد الطريق الضيق الذي يعبُر الخليج العربي نحو مضيق هُرمُز ومنه إلى خليج عُمان.

The Greater Tunnab, the Lesser Tunnab and Abu Musa, have been occupied by Iran since 1971, and since then the issue has occupied a strategic dimension. Although these islands are small, they are of vital strategic importance as they are located (situated) along the narrow road that crosses the Arabian Gulf towards the Strait of Hormuz and from there to the Gulf of Oman.

Consider during the translation process the following:

فإنها . . . من الرغم فعلى . . . . : Although . . . + a comma (,) + the subject "they", i.e., as below:

Although . . ., they . . .

كما أنَّ مُعظم صادرات الخليج النفطية ووارداته غير النفطية تمر عبر هذا الطريق. وعلاوةً على ذلك، فإن عدداً من حقول النفط والغاز البحرية تقع على مقربة من الجزر الثلاث ، مما يعطي هذه الجُزُر أهمية استثنائية بالنسبة إلى أي قوة تسعى إلى حماية الملاحة البحرية والحقول البحرية في هذه المنطقة أو مهاجمتها.

246 *Appendix 1*

Most of the Gulf's oil exports and non-oil imports pass through this route. Moreover, a number of offshore oil and gas fields are located in close proximity to the three islands. This gives these islands exceptional importance for any country seeking to protect or attack maritime navigation and offshore fields in this area.

Consider during the translation process the following:

We have taken out the initial conjunction كما + أنَّ which is not required by the TT. The comma (,) in ... من الجزر الثلاث ، مما يعطي هذه ... is removed and replaced by a full-stop in English, and we have started with the subject "This" + يعطي – "gives".

قوة : This is given a context-based meaning as "country".

حماية الملاحة البحرية والحقول البحرية في هذه المنطقة أو مهاجمتها: We can observe the distance between the two nominalized nouns حماية ... مهاجمة. However, in English, we must change these nouns to verbs "protect and attack" + their objects الملاحة البحرية والحقول البحرية "maritime navigation and offshore fields".

The adjective البحرية of الحقول البحرية is given a context-based meaning "offshore". Thus, we have "offshore fields". However, for البحرية of الملاحة البحرية is given "maritime navigation".

Note Below: The adjective البحرية in الأكلات المأكولات البحرية is translated as "seafood".

كيفية احتلال الجُزُر :

وحول كيفية احتلالها، وبحسب دراسة قديمة نشرتها صحيفة الإتحاد الإماراتية، عندما أعلنت بريطانيا عن نيتها للإنسحاب من الخليج في عام 1968، صمَّم شاه إيران محمد رضا بهلوي على أن يضعَ يدهُ على جُزُر طنب الكبرى وطنب الصغرى وأبو موسى.

How the islands were occupied

According to an old study published by the Emirati newspaper *Al-Ittihad*, when Britain announced its intention to withdraw from the Gulf in 1968, the Shah of Iran, Muhammad Reza Pahlavi, decided to occupy the islands of Greater Tunnab, Lesser Tunnab, and Abu Musa.

Consider during the translation process the following:

We have taken out the initial conjunction و which is not required by the TT.

صمَّمَ على أن يضعَ يدهُ على : This is translated as "decided to occupy".

وتحت وطأة التهديدات الإيرانية باحتلال الجزر بالقوة، خضعت إمارة الشارقة للظروف السائدة في حينه ووقعت مُذكرة تفاهُم بشأن جزيرة أبو موسى مع إيران بالإكراه في نوفمبر 1971.

Under the pressure of Iranian threats to occupy the islands by force, the Emirate of Sharjah accepted the status quo and signed, under duress, with Iran a memorandum of understanding in November 1971 regarding Abu Musa Island.

Appendix 1 247

Consider during the translation process the following:

We have taken out the initial conjunction و which is not required by the TT.
الظروف السائدة في حينه: This is translated as "the status quo".
بالإكراه : This is translated as "under duress".
Note Below: We have changed the word order of the Arabic text with regards to
(بالإكراه), (مع إيران), (في نوفمبر 1971).

وفي مُذكرة التفاهُم، لم تتنازل الشارقة أو إيران عن مطالبها بالسيادة على جزيرة أبو موسى كما
لم تعترف أي منهما بسيادة الأخرى على الجزيرة. *(اليوم السابع، 29 أبريل (نيسان) 2020)*
In the memorandum of understanding, neither Sharjah nor Iran relinquished their claims
to Abu Musa Island, nor did either of them recognize the other's sovereignty over the
Island (*Al-Yawm Al-Sabi'*, 29 April 2020).

Consider during the translation process the following:

We have taken out the initial conjunction و which is not required by the TT.
لم . . . أو . . . : neither . . . nor . . .

2. Consider the translations of Q37:49 below and discuss the translation process of the following translations:
كأنهُن بيضٌ مكنون is translated as "Pure" as they were hidden eggs "of the ostrich" by
Marmaduke Pickthall (1993:no page), as "As free as if they were hidden ostrich eggs" by
Asad (1980:928), as "Like protected eggs" + a footnote by Abdel Haleem (2005:286), and as
"As if they were hidden pearls" by Arthur Arberry (1955:200). What translation approaches
have the translators adopted?
We can make the following observations:

(i)   On the lexical on the lexical level, Qur'an translation is marked by over-translation
        even when lexical voids are not involved. Over-translation is also evident in the trans-
        lation of the simile particle "ka – like" which is over-translated as "as free . . . as if".
(ii)   The word مكنون, which is a passive participle, is over-translated to "free of faults . . .
        hidden ostrich" without realizing that the ST does not refer to the ostrich which may
        even be an alien concept to the TL reader who does not know the fact that this bird
        looks well after its eggs.
(iii)   Abdel Haleem has added a footnote: "Arabs described beautiful women as being as
        precious as the ostrich eggs. Ostriches protect their eggs from the dust with their feath-
        ers". Thus, he has adopted the gloss translation and formal equivalence approaches,
        which both license the use of footnotes.
(iv)   Arthur Arberry has adopted the dynamic equivalence, communicative, and domestica-
        tion translation approaches.

3. Provide some Arabic-Islamic culture-based words and comment on their translations
in terms of cultural borrowing, exegetical (paraphrase) and foreignization translation
approaches.

248 *Appendix 1*

(i) We can provide the following SL culture-specific expressions:

أُضحية، ظِهار، عُمرة، السعي، تيمُم، عِدَّة، تراويح، أيام التشريق، طواف الإفاضة، الجمرة الصُغرى، الجمرة الكُبرى، أذان، حجاب، نقاب، خِمار، عباية.

(ii) The above SL culture-specific terms represent lexical voids where the TL lacks the semantic componential features of each SL word. Due to this argument, we can claim that the above Arabic expressions are examples of cultural borrowing (foreignization) through which a ST expression is transferred verbatim into the TT. In other words, through the cultural borrowing approach we can introduce the foreign element into the TT (Dickins et al. 2002:32), because there is no word-for-word correspondence. However, in the interest of clarity, the translator may be able to provide exegetical translation, though the disadvantage is that each of these Arabic expressions require paraphrastic (over-translation) and long details.

(iii) Based on what we have said in point (ii) above, we must distinguish between cultural borrowing and naturalization translation approaches. Because the above Arabic terms represent lexical voids in English, we should adopt the cultural borrowing translation approach where each term is transferred phonetically (transliterated) to English. This translation approach also helps the translator to avoid over-translation because there is no TL single-word correspondence, like مدرسة, whose single-word correspondence is "school".

(iv) Based on what we said in (iii) above, we cannot adopt the naturalization translation approach to the above Arabic expressions. This is due to the fact that such a translation approach applies to a SL term which can be easily translated, but the translator opts for transliteration. For instance, "taxi" is naturalized in Arabic as تاكسي. However, there is a word-for-word correspondence in Arabic for the English word "taxi", which is سيارة أجرة.

(v) Based on the above details, we can adopt the cultural borrowing (foreignization) translation approach to the above Arabic terms as below:

(أُضحية، ظِهار، عُمرة، سعي، تيمُم، عِدَّة، تراويح، أيام التشريق، طواف الإفاضة، الجمرة الصُغرى، الجمرة الكُبرى، أذان، حِجاب، نِقاب، خِمار، عباية)

(vi) To illuminate the TT reader with what each ST expression semantically stands for, we propose the following exegetical (paraphrase) translations:

أُضحية: The slaughter of animal for the Eid al-Adha celebration.

ظِهار: The evil statement of saying to one's wife that she is prohibited for him by saying "you are like the back of my mother".

عُمرة: The lesser pilgrimage to Makkah.

سعي: Part of the pilgrimage walking between the two mounts Safa and Marwah signifying the wife of Prophet Abraham whilst she was looking for water in desert conditions.

تيمُم: Purification with earth when water is not available or due to an illness where using water may cause harm.

عِدَّة: The period lasting three months for a divorced woman where she does not marry and prepares herself for marriage.

تراويح: Night prayers in the month of Ramadan.

أيام التشريق: The 11th, 12th, and 13th day of the Islamic month Dhu al-Hijjah during the days of Hajj.

Appendix 1 249

طواف الإفاضة: The act of worship in circumambulating the Kaʿbah in Makkah during Hajj on the Eid al-Adha day.

الجمرة الصُّغرى: The first of the three stones signifying where Satan tried to misguide Prophet Abraham.

الجمرة الكُبرى: The third of the three stones signifying where Satan tried to misguide Prophet Abraham.

أذان: The call to prayer.

حجاب: The state of modesty of the heart, tongue and limbs, which includes dressing in a modest way such as the head covering for women.

نقاب: The face veil.

خِمار: The head covering that covers head and shoulders.

عباية: The covering that veils a woman from the head and loosely fitting the body down to the feet.

(vii) The Arabic culture-based expressions above represent cultural untranslatability, which is a situational feature that is functionally relevant and ad hoc to the SL culture but is absent in TL culture. Culture-specific words constitute cultural voids, especially those such as the above which are specific to Arabic-Islamic culture and have a connotative meaning. Larson (1984:132) warns the translator of the problem of the SL connotative meaning. Cultural voids also include articles of clothing like الخِمار, which occurs in the plural in Q24:31. In the view of Catford (1965:100), articles of clothing provide examples of material culture which differ from one culture to another and may lead to translation difficulties. Larson (1984:180) admits that terms which deal with the religious aspects of a culture are usually the most difficult, both in analysis of the source vocabulary and in finding the best receptor language equivalents. This is because the TL reader "is not conscious of meaning involved". For instance, the Muslim culture-specific expression السلامُ عليكم "Hello", literally meaning "Peace upon you" has a Qur'anic connotative meaning, as it is an Islamic obligation to great each other, as we are informed by Q24:61 فسلموا على أنفسِكُم – "give greetings of peace upon each other" and the prophetic tradition (hadith) which also urges people to do this: أفشوا السلام – "Spread greetings among you".

Similarly, while the words مزرعة/بيت/حفلة زواج/صيام and "farm/house/wedding party/fasting" are functionally identical, such words require a different taxonomy in Arabic and English cultures.

The discussion above also applies to Islamic culture-specific words like الجن ، آية ، سورة, which should be introduced to English through the cultural borrowing approach via transliteration: "jinn, ayah, surah".

4. Comment on the Arabic-Islamic culture-bound words in Qur'anic discourse (مكة, 48:24) and بَكَّة, Q3:96.

The word مكة is a name of a city which has special cultural significance in Islam. Thus, its transliteration in Q48:24 has solved the problem. However, in Q3:97, we have the word بَكَّة, which is a metonymy for مكة, i.e., it can be used as a name for the same city مكة. Thus, we have either

250 *Appendix 1*

(i)   to foreignize the metonymy and transliterate it,

(ii)   to paraphrase the metonymy and explain the denotative meaning of بكَّ as a verb, or

(iii) to foreignize the metonymy, transliterate it, and provide a footnote with an intertextual reference to the other name of the city مكَّة in Q48:24.

The meaning of the noun بكَّة in Q3:97 is context-based. Since reference is made to حجُّ البيت "pilgrimage to Ka'bah", the use of بكَّة is stylistically more appropriate. The noun بَكَّة is morphologically derived from the verb بكَّ [b + k + k] and whose nominalised noun مصدر is البك "overcrowdedness". This is due to the fact that during the pilgrimage season, Muslims in huge numbers perform pilgrimage. Thus, we need a word which can portray the extremely busy place. Semantically, the noun بكَّة means "overcrowdedness". Thus, this noun successfully depicts the semantic context of the very busy season of pilgrimage because يبكِ الناسُ بعضهم بعضا "people jostle 'mill about'". The noun مكَّة is another name for بكَّة. Since there is no need for the depiction of overcrowdedness, the noun مكَّة is employed in Q48:24.

5. Discuss, through reference to different Qur'an translations, the foreignization and domestication translation approaches through the translation of Arabic-Islamic culture-specific words that have occurred in Q43:48 أُخت, Q35:13 نقير, قطمير in Q4:53 and 124, and صدرُه in Q39:22.

ما نُريهم من آيةٍ إلاَّ هي أكبرُ من أُختِها (الزخرف 48)

> TT: We showed them not a sign except that it was greater than its sister (Saheeh International 1997:693).
>
> Even though each sign We showed them was greater than the previous one (Abdel Haleem 2005:318).
>
> Although each sign that We showed them was weightier than the preceding one (Asad 1980:1026).

Although cultural transplantation (Dickins et al. 2002:32) may work for ordinary cultural expressions like قيس وليلى "Romeo and Juliet", this type of cultural adaptation is unlikely to satisfy Qur'an-specific cultural expressions which are non-existent in the TL culture. For Venuti (1992), however, the translator should not be forced to alter the ST in order to conform to the TL cultural norms and ideas. In other words, the translator should not be subservient to the ST author. For Venuti (ibid), the SL cultural and linguistic norms should be carried over into the TL. One may wonder whether this would work for Q43:48 above where SL linguistic norms "style and lexis أُختِها 'sister'" are carried over into the TL → (literal) versus أُختِها – "previous" as adapted and domesticated to suit the TL norms → (communicative). However, Venuti's approach in Qur'an translation will alienate the TL audience due to the linguistic and cultural incongruity between Qur'anic Arabic and English. The foreignization translation approach has been used in Qur'an translation in Q35:13 قطمير, which is rendered as "the membrane 'skin' of a date seed" instead of the domesticating translation approach through which the SL metonymy قطمير is translated as "nothing, anything" → "They possess nothing/They do not possess anything". The same applies to نقير in Q4:53 and 124, which is foreignized as "the speck on 'groove of/the speck on' a date seed 'stone'" instead of adopting the domesticating translation approach through which the SL metonymy نقير is translated as "nothing, anything" → "They would give people nothing/They would not give the people anything".

Appendix 1 251

The same applies to the translation of Q39:22: أَفَمَن شَرَحَ اللهُ صَدْرَهُ لِلإِسلام

The expression شرح صدره للإسلام is Arabic-Islamic culture-specific. We have encountered Qur'an translations by Arberry, Asad, Pickthall, Al-Hilali and Khan, Saheeh International, and Ahmad which have provided a source-oriented translation; they have adopted a foreignization translation approach and have given "So is the one whose breast/heart/bosom Allah has expanded to Islam . . . ". However, Abdel Haleem has provided a target-oriented translation – a domestication translation approach: "What about the one whose heart God has opened in devotion to Him . . . ". Thus, we have two translations:

(i)   source-oriented translation (foreignization): God has expanded the breast/heart/bosom of X to Islam, and

(ii)   target-oriented translation (domestication): God has opened the heart of X in devotion to Him.

6. Discuss the translation approaches of cultural transplantation, domestication, cultural transposition, and foreignization after you have considered the translations of Q4:147 and Q8:7 below:

ما يفعل اللهُ بعذابِكم إن شكرتم وآمنتُم (النساء 147)
وتَوَدُّون أنَّ غيرَ ذاتِ الشوكةِ تكونُ لكم (الأنفال 7)

(i)   We have encountered different translations to the above two Qur'anic statements:

The translations of Q4:147 are
   What would Allah do with (i.e., gain from) your punishment if you are grateful and believed? (Saheeh International 1997:128).
   Why should God make you suffer torment if you are thankful and believe in Him? (Abdel Haleem 2005:64).
   What will Allah gain by punishing you if you have thanked Him and have believed (in Him)? (Ahmad 2010:136).
   What would God do with chastising you if you are thankful, and believe? (Arberry 1955:44).
   What concern hath Allah for your punishment if ye are thankful (for His mercies) and believe (in Him)? (Pickthall 1930:no page).
   Why would God cause you to suffer [for your past sins] if you are grateful and attain to belief? (Asad 1980:330) + a footnote: (literally: while you would have liked the one which was not powerful to be yours" – i.e., the caravan coming from Syria, which was accompanied by only forty armed men and could therefore, be attacked without great danger).

(ii)   The translations of Q8:7 (وتَوَدُّون أنَّ غيرَ ذاتِ الشوكةِ تكونُ لكم) are

   You wished that the unarmed one would be yours (Saheeh International 1997:230).
   You wanted the unarmed group to be yours (Abdel Haleem 2005:110).
   You wished that the unarmed (the caravan) should be yours (Ahmad 2010:229).
   Ye longed that other than the armed one might be yours (Pickthall 1930:no page).
   You would have liked to seize the less powerful one (Asad 1980:330) + a footnote: (while you would have liked the one which was not powerful to be yours" – i.e., the caravan coming from Syria, which was accompanied by only forty armed men and could therefore, be attacked without great danger).

252 *Appendix 1*

(iii) We can provide the following translation commentary based on the translation processes involved in each of the previous translations:

Language behaves under the influence of its own culture. This universal fact is demonstrated through translation studies. To this effect, verbatim rendering should be avoided and cultural transplantation – domestication and cultural transposition, of the source text (ST) – must be applied. Our claim can be brought into line with Nida's (1945:194) argument that almost all would recognize that language is best described as a part of culture when dealing with many types of semantic problems – particularly those in which the culture under consideration is quite different from one's own. The expression "brother-in-law", for instance, loses its signification when translated literally into Arabic أخ في القانون "a brother in the law". Based on context, English applies the hyphenated expression "brother-in-law" to the brother of your husband, the brother of your wife, the husband of your sister, the husband of your husband's sister, and the husband of your wife's sister. However, Arabic expresses itself differently with regards to the same expression: the brother of your husband أخ زوجي, the brother of your wife أخ زوجتي, the husband of your sister زوج أختي, the husband of your husband's sister زوج أخت زوجي, and the husband of your wife's sister زوج أخت زوجتي.

According to Beaugrande (2003:2), the priority of the translator is to invest a well-developed bilingual sensitivity and bicultural sensitivity in weighing the complex factors of the translation process, such as the multiplex relations between word-meanings and text-meanings in light of cultural differences (Abdul-Raof 2018:264).

Cultural transplantation (Dickins et al. 2002:32) seems to be a useful translation technique in the translation of proverbial expressions, such as لا ناقة لي فيها و لا جَمل "I have nothing to do with this", the verbatim counterpart of which is "neither a female camel do I have in this matter nor a male camel", which is misleading to the target text (TT) audience. Cultural transplantation can be of value to sensitive texts as in ما يفعل الله بعذابكم إن شكرتم وآمنتم, (Q4:147), which can be domesticated to New Guinea's readers with luxuriant imagery "God does not hang up jaw bones" since this relates to their custom of hanging jaw bones of the enemies. However, in Qur'an translation, we get "What would Allah do with your punishment if you are grateful and believe?" (Saheeh International 1997:128). Cultural transplantation in Qur'an translation is ruled out entirely due to the objection by Muslim scholars. The opposite to cultural transplantation (domestication) is "foreignization", introduced by Venuti (1995), which preserves the ST cultural values and is ST's author-oriented:

وتَودَّون أنَّ غيرَ ذاتِ الشوكةِ تكونُ لكم (الأنفال 7)

Domestication: You wished that <u>the unarmed one</u> (unarmed group, unarmed enemy party) would be yours.

Foreignization: You wished that <u>the one that has no thorn</u> would be yours.

where غير ذات الشوكة is a metonymy for "an unarmed enemy group which have wealth". Thus, defeating such a group is both easy and financially beneficial (Abdul-Raof 2018:264).

7. Consider the translation of الفحشاء in Q2:268. Compare different Qur'an translations and discuss the major semantic problem the translator encounters in such a word.

Appendix 1 253

We have considered the following Qur'an translations:

الشيطانُ يعِدُكُم الفقرَ ويأمُرُكُم بالفحشاء (البقرة 268)

The devil promiseth you destitution and enjoineth on you **lewdness** (Pickthall 1930:no page).

The Evil one threatens you with poverty and bids you to **conduct unseemly** (Ali 1934:no page).

Satan promises you poverty, and bids you unto **indecency** (Arberry 1955:22).

Satan threatens you with the prospect of poverty and bids you to be **niggardly** (Asad 1980:102).

Satan threatens you with poverty and orders you to **immorality** (Saheeh International 1997:56).

Satan threatens you with the prospect of poverty and commands you to do **foul deeds** (Abdel Haleem 2005:31).

Satan threatens you with poverty and tempts you to indulge in **obscene activities** (Ahmad 2010:66).

Based on the above different translations, we can make the following observations:

(i)   Semantically, the word الفحشاء is a noun and a polyseme, which leads to semantic ambiguity. Polysemy is a major translation hurdle facing the translator. According to Welch (1990:273), many Arabic words which are central to the teachings of the Qur'an are rich in their connotations and require a variety of English renderings in different contexts. This is true with regards to polysemy.

(ii) The noun الفحشاء, literally meaning "immorality" is polysemous, which has led to the inaccurate translations mentioned above, such as Pickthall, Ali, Arberry, Saheeh International, Abdel Haleem, and Ahmad. Asad's is the only translation that has taken polysemy into account and provides the accurate meaning of الفحشاء as البُخل, i.e., "to be a miser".

(iii) Stylistically, the noun الفحشاء is employed as a metonymy كناية whose underlying and accurate (intended) meaning is البُخل "to be a miser".

(iv) Since the word الفحشاء is a polyseme, it has occurred several times in the Qur'an with different meanings like "immorality", "foul deeds", and "adultery" الزنى. However, the only time where الفحشاء occurs with the underlying (metonymy) meaning "to be a miser" بخيل is in Q2:268.

(v)   Polysemy is a major problem in Arabic translation. Qur'an translation suffers from polysemy problems, as in the polyseme الهدى, which has 17 different meanings, such as

(a) "to explain" as in Q20:128, Q41:17, (b) "religion" as in Q2:120, Q3:73, Q22:67, (c) "belief" as in Q18:13, Q19:76, Q34:32, (d) "to call upon someone" as in Q37:23, (e) "to know, to find out" as in Q16:16, Q20:82, Q21:31, (f) "prophets" as in Q2:38, Q20:123, (g) "the Qur'an" as in Q17:94, Q53:23, (h) "monotheism" as in Q9:33, Q28:57, Q48:28, (i) "inspiration" as in Q20:50, Q87:3, (j) "to repent" as in Q7:156.

8. Consider the translation of اسم الفاعل, the active participle noun صافَّات "outspread wings", and the verb يقبضن "occasionally folded in wings" in Q67:19.

254 *Appendix 1*

أوَلَم يرَوا إلى الطير فوقهُم صافاتٍ ويقبضنَ. (المُلْك 19)

Compare different Qur'an translations and discuss the major semantic and grammatical (structural) problems the translator encounters. Discuss the illocutionary force of the present tense verb and the active participle in Arabic. Which translation approach can the translator adopt?

We have considered the following Qur'an translations:

Have they not seen the birds above them spreading out their wings and closing them? (Pickthall 1930:no page).

Do they not observe the birds above them, spreading their wings and folding them in? (Ali 1934:no page).

Have they not regarded the birds above them spreading their wings, and closing them? (Arberry 1955:257).

Have they, then, never beheld the birds above them, spreading their wings and drawing them in? (Asad 1980:1192).

Do they not observe the birds above them, spreading their wings and folding them in? (Mushaf al-Madinah an-Nabawiyyah 1990:1787).

Do they not see the birds above them with wings outspread and (sometimes) folded in? (Saheeh International 1997:814).

Do they not see the birds above them spreading and closing their wings? (Abdel Haleem 2005:383).

And don't you see the birds, flying over you with their wings spread out and (at times) folded in? (Ahmad 2010:772).

Based on these various translations, we can make the following observations:

(i) Q67:19 is an example of syntactic shift – a change from one grammatical function of a word to another grammatical function – a grammatical change from the noun, to a verb, to an adjective, or vice versa. It also includes a syntactic change from the active participle to an active participle, or from a past tense to a present tense. This syntactic shift is a major stylistic feature of Qur'anic Arabic.

(ii) The active participle noun صافات "outspread wings" occurs first, then next to it a verb occurs, which is يقبضن "occasionally folded in winds". This is a syntactic shift from the noun to a verb. This shift in grammatical function is not without a performative intent (illocutionary force).

(iii) The active participle noun designates [+ Permanency] and [+ Continuity] (الثُبوت). However, the verb designates [+ Renewability] (التجدد) and [+ Action] (الحُدوث).

(iv) Based on the different translations above, Q67:19 is an example of the inability of the TL to convey the illocutionary (communicative) force of the active participle in Qur'anic Arabic. The TL can only provide past participle verbs: "outspread" and "folded in".

(v) The ST (Q67:19) could have provided either: (active participle + active participle → يصفُفنَ + يقبضنَ), i.e.,: or (verb + verb → صافاتٍ + قابضات)

Appendix 1   255

أَوَلَمْ يَرَوْا إِلَى الطَّيْرِ فَوْقَهُمْ صَافَّاتٍ وَقَابِضَاتٍ.
أَوَلَمْ يَرَوْا إِلَى الطَّيْرِ فَوْقَهُمْ يَصْفُفْنَ وَيَقْبِضْنَ.

During flying, the birds' permanent physical characteristic is to outspread their wings throughout their flying process.

This intended meaning is safely relayed through the active participle صَافَّاتٍ. However, birds occasionally fold their wings in. This intended meaning is conveyed through the verb يَقْبِضْنَ. Thus, the verb is required to demonstrate that the occasional folding-in of wings is renewed every now and then but not continually. However, the outspreading of the wings is a normal permanent flying procedure. This illocutionary force is conveyed through the active participle noun صَافَّاتٍ.

(vi)   The TT fails to deliver the ST illocutionary force and performative intent.
(vii) Discussion of the illocutionary force of the present tense verb and the active participle in Arabic:

   (1) The verb:

      (a) The verb designates short duration of an action [– Continuity]. For instance, the act of eating designated by a verb lasts for a few minutes, and other actions represented by verbs like "talk, read" last for a limited period of time, like an hour or more.

      (b) The verb does not designate the continuity or a repetition of an action. In other words, any action comes to an end, as in "live, die". One lives and dies once; living and death do not continue forever. Both come to an end. Based on Islamic culture, death ends with the beginning of the day of judgement where eternal life begins either in paradise or the hellfire.

   (2) The active participle noun:

      (a) The active participle noun designates [+ Continuity] in doing an action and [+ Permanency] of a given character trait (feature) or of a given state, such as being generous, brave, merciful, knowledgeable, and being a writer (author), or a state (habit) like white, black, soft, dead.

(كَرِيم، شُجَاع، رَؤُوف، عَالِم، كَاتِب/أَبْيَض، أَسْوَد، نَاعِم، مَيِّت)

      (b) The active participle designates the illocutionary force of [+ Definiteness/ Necessity] الحتمية, as in إِنَّكَ مَيِّتٌ وَإِنَّهُم مَيِّتُون "Indeed, you are to die, and indeed, they are to die" (Q39:30), i.e., definitely, you and they will die. (However, the translation of Q39:30 demonstrates that the SL active participle noun must be changed to a verb in the TT, i.e., the TL can neither accommodate nor convey the SL active participle noun). The active participle noun صَافَّاتٍ designates the illocutionary force of [+ Necessity], i.e., it is absolutely necessary for birds to outspread their wings while flying and that

256 *Appendix 1*

this is a habit (state, feature) [+ Continuity]. However, when they are tired, they can "stop for a short period of time", i.e., the verb يَقبِضن is required to demonstrate that the occasional folding-in of wings is renewed every now and then [– Continuity].

(c) The active participle noun designates the illocutionary force of [+ Something is absolutely necessary to take place], as in Q29:33 إِنَّا مُنجَّوُك "We will save you". However, the translation of Q29:33 demonstrates that the SL active participle noun must be changed to a verb in the TT; the TL can neither accommodate nor convey the SL active participle noun.

(viii) The translators of Q67:19 have adopted the transposition (shift), natural, and dynamic equivalence translation approaches, which are TT-oriented. These translation approaches involve adaptation in grammar and lexicon. Grammatical modifications can be made the more readily, since many grammatical changes are dictated by the obligatory structure of the TL. In other words, the translator must make such grammatical adjustments to make the TT compatible with the TL syntactic norms. Such translation approaches aim to provide a comprehensible TT to the audience with an acceptable natural TL style. These translation approaches aim at complete naturalness of the TT; to naturalize the TT and reduce its foreignness. The above translations interpretively resemble the original without unnecessary processing effort on the part of the TL reader. They are grammar-based translations and involve a change in the grammar from the SL to TL.

9. In Arabic, we say: فلان دمه خفيف and فلان دمَّهُ ثقيل. Provide a literal and a non-literal translation and comment on the translation approach that is more normal than the other.

The literal translation of فلان دمه خفيف is "X has light blood" and of فلان دمه ثقيل is "X has heavy blood", which both seem unnatural TTs. However, the non-literal translations of the above culture-based sentences employ translation approaches such as the communicative, dynamic equivalence, acceptable, cultural transposition, and domestication approaches, taking into consideration the contextual intended meaning of the ST in order to provide a comprehensible TT to its readers with an acceptable natural TL style. Any one of these translation approaches aims at complete naturalness of the TT; to naturalize the TT and reduce its foreignness. Thus, we recommend a translation based on the approaches mentioned previously, that accounts for TL meaning and style. Thus, the proposed translations of the above examples are "X is a merry 'cheerful' person" and "X is a dull 'gloomy' person" respectively. Such a translation is a mode of free translation. The translation of such culturally conventional clichés is produced, when, in a given situation, the ST uses an SL expression which is standard for that situation, and the TT uses a TL expression which is standard for an equivalent target culture situation (Dickins et al. 2002:17, 35, 234).

10. Consider the translation of the SL culture-specific expressions يعَضُّ الأنامل and على يديه in Q3:119 and Q25:27. Compare different Qur'an translations and provide and discuss suggested translations.

The SL culture-specific expressions يعَضُّ على يديه and يعَضُّ الأنامل in Q3:119 and Q25:27 have been foreignized in Qur'an translations; they have been rendered literally in the TL as "to bite at one's fingertip" and "to bite on one's hand", respectively. These are SL-oriented translations provided by Arberry (1955:30, 160), Pickthall (1930:no page), Asad (1980:136, 756), Saheeh International (1997:82, 494), and Abdel Haleem (2005:43, 228). A TL-oriented

Appendix 1 257

translation based on the communicative, dynamic equivalence, acceptable, cultural transposition, and domestication approaches takes into consideration the contextual intended meaning of the ST in order to provide a comprehensible TT to its readers, and aims at complete naturalness of the TT; to naturalize the TT and reduce its foreignness. The context-based translation of Q3:119 يَعَض الأنامل is "He/She is enraged out of envy" and the context-based translation of Q25:27 يَعَضُ على يديه is "He/She regrets deeply".

11. Provide a translation of the following journalistic text:

"I did not yet receive the required political assurances from the lenders of the Greek coalition parties on the implementation of the program", Jean-Claude Juncker, chairman of the Eurogroup, said (*The Times*, 15 February 2012).

We propose the following translation:

وذكرت السيدة جين كلود جانكر، رئيسة المجموعة الأوربية، بأنها لم تستلم بعد الضمانات السياسية المطلوبة من قادة الأحزاب السياسية اليونانية حول تنفيذ البرنامج.

Having done the textual and discourse analysis of the ST, we can make the following observations:

(i)   The ST starts with the quoted speech of the speaker "Jean-Claude Juncker, chairman of the Eurogroup" and ends with her name as the subject. However, in Arabic journalistic texts, the opposite word order takes place, where a word order change is required. In other words, the Arabic journalistic text starts with the verb + the subject before his/her quoted speech.
(ii)   A transposition or shift translation approach is adopted where a change in ST word order should be implemented in the journalistic TT.
(iii) While the journalistic ST employs quoted speech where the quoted speech of the speaker is place between inverted commas, the TT employs indirect speech where the inverted commas are not used.
(iv)   Stylistically, it is also possible to use the direct speech of the speaker and put it within inverted commas, as in

وذكرت السيدة جين كلود جانكر، رئيسة المجموعة الأوربية: "لم أستلم بعد الضمانات السياسية المطلوبة من قادة الأحزاب السياسية اليونانية حول تنفيذ البرنامج."

12. Translate and comment on the following text:

It brings out the woman in you.
Having done the textual and discourse analysis, we can make the following comments:

(i)   The above TT is an advert on maternity bras (brassiers). There is a picture of a woman wearing a bra.
(ii)   In its attempt to promote the sale of these maternity bras, the text producer employs the definite article "the" before the noun "woman". After giving birth, some women may have problems with the size of their breasts due to breast-feeding. The definite article performs the illocutionary force of convincing this category of women to buy these bras.

258   *Appendix 1*

(iii)   The definite article contributes in the performative intent and perlocutionary force of the SL message (advert). It highlights the intended meaning of the ST which is "femininity". The ST reassures the woman that she does not need to worry about her femininity, which can be brought back to her through the wearing of these bras. In other words, wearing such bras *can* bring out in her the femininity she used to enjoy before her pregnancy.

(iv)   Based on the above details, we suggest the following translations:

تبعثُ فيكِ الإنوثة or حمالة النهد الصدر التي تبعثُ فيكِ الإنوثة.

13. Translate and comment on the following text:

Only balls bounce.
We can provide the following textual and discourse features of the above ST:

(i)   The genre of the text is an advertisement. It is an advert on bras حمالة الصدر, and there is a picture of a woman wearing a bra.

(ii)   The ST is paratactic (simple structure) and starts with an affirmation word "only" to reiterate the fact that nothing else should bounce; thus, alerting the lady who has such a problem.

(iii)   The advert is directed to a category of women who have big breasts. Having big breasts can be a problem to the lady because they bounce when walking. Big bouncing breasts can inconvenience the lady.

(iv)   The advert makes an implicit comparison between footballs and big breasts. In other words, there is an implicit simile involved in the ST: "Big breasts bounce like footballs". Through the picture, the ST reassures the woman with big breasts that she does not need to worry about this inconvenience, which can be resolved through the wearing of these bras. In other words, wearing such bras *can* hold firmly to her breasts and the inconvenience of bouncing will come to a comfortable end. Thus, the implicit simile of the ST is maintained in the TT.

(v)   Having done the textual and discourse analysis, we can provide our suggested translation: الكرات فقط تنطّ تقفز. Thus, the implicit simile of the TT is transferred to the TT.

14. Translate and comment on the expression "blog".

(i)   We need to undertake a lexical search first. We have "a blog is an on-line journal or diary of an individual".

(ii)   The above definition constitutes a semantic componential analysis of the expression.

(iii)   Based on the semantic componential analysis of the expression, we can suggest the translation صحيفة الكترونية شخصية. However, our suggested translation of "blogger" is below:

الشخص الذي يملك صحيفة الكترونية خاصة به/بها.

(iv)   Our translation put forward above has adopted paraphrase translation approach – a translation with freedom where the author is kept in view by the translator, but his/her words are not so strictly followed as his/her sense. This involves changing whole phrases and more or less corresponds to faithful or sense-for-sense translation.

Appendix 1   259

15. Translate and comment on the expression أمّ الخبائث.
    We can make the following observations on the above ST:

(i)   This is a metonymy كناية whose context-based (intended, underlying) meaning refers
        to alcohol الخمر.
(ii)   The literal (verbatim) translation of the above ST is "The mother of evil 'malice'".
(iii)   The context-based translation which takes into consideration the TL culture and aims
        to make the ST intelligible to the TL audience is "alcohol".
(iv)   The TT has adopted a culture-based approach based on one of the following translation
        approaches: communicative, dynamic equivalence, acceptable, cultural transposition,
        and domestication. These translation approaches take into consideration the contextual
        (intended) meaning of the ST (the performative intent of the ST's producer) in order
        to provide a comprehensible TT to the audience with an acceptable natural TL style.
        These translation approaches aim at complete naturalness of the TT; to naturalize the
        TT and reduce its foreignness.

16. Translate the following STs and comment on the translation process:

(a) Bill will take the law into his own hands.
(b) However, Robert will go to law against Bill.

Let us provide the following details based on our textual and discourse analysis:

(i)   In literal translation, according to Newmark (1988:46), the SL grammatical structures
        are converted to their nearest TL equivalents, but the words are translated singly out
        of context. Thus, we can add that when the translator gives the meaning of a SL word
        out of context, he/she has failed to transfer accurately the ST producer's performative
        intent. In other words, in literal translation, according to Dickins et al. (2002:16), the
        denotative meaning of words is taken as if straight from the dictionary, i.e., out of
        context, but TL grammar is preserved.
(ii)   The literal (verbatim) translation of the above ST (a) is

سوف يأخُذ بيل القانونَ بيديه

(iii)   The literal translation of the above ST (b) is

بيد أنّ إلاّ أن روبرت سوف يذهبُ الى القانون ضد بيل

(iv)   The non-literal translation of the above ST (a) is

سوفَ يثأرُ بيل لنفسه سوف يأخُذ بيل حقَّهُ بالقوة

(v)   The non-literal translation of the above ST (b) is

بيد أنّ إلاّ أن روبرت سوف يُقيمُ دعوى ضد بيل

(vi)   The non-literal translations above are context-based translations which have taken into
        consideration the TL culture and aim to make the ST intelligible to the TL audience.
(vii)   The TT has adopted a culture-based approach based on one of the following translation
        approaches: communicative, dynamic equivalence, acceptable, cultural transposition,
        and domestication. These translation approaches take into consideration the contextual

260 *Appendix 1*

(intended) meaning of the ST (the performative intent of the ST's producer) in order to provide a comprehensible TT to the audience with an acceptable natural TL style. These translation approaches aim at complete naturalness of the TT; to naturalize the TT and reduce its foreignness.

In terms of the details above, and especially in point (vii), the same applies to the expression "my sister-in-law", whose literal translation is اختي في القانون. However, its non-literal translation involves three different meanings in Arabic: أخت زوجتي/أخت زوجي/زوجة أخي. The back-translations of the latter non-literal translations are "the sister of my wife/the sister of my husband/the wife of my brother", respectively.

17. Provide a textual and discourse analysis of Q30:30, compare different translations, and provide a critical translation quality assessment.

فأقِم وجهكَ للدين حنيفاً فِطرَتَ اللهِ التي فطرَ الناسَ عليها (الروم 30)

Let us first consider different translations of the above ST and their translation approaches:

(i)   The following TTs are source-oriented, i.e., they have preserved the ST expression فطرة and transferred phonetically (transliterated) to the ST:

So direct your face toward the religion, inclining to truth. Adhere to the fitrah of Allah upon which He has created all people (Saheeh International 1997:562).

(ii)   The above translation is an estranging translation because it has adopted the foreignization translation approach where the SL expression فطرة is made visible and its foreign identity has been highlighted via foreignizing it; thus, the translator has sent his/her readers abroad. Such an approach is similar to the cultural borrowing approach offered by Dickins et al. (2002:32), which also involves the verbatim transfer of a SL expression into the TT without making any adaptation to or explanation for the SL expression.

(iii)   However, the following TTs are receptor-oriented; the translator has provided a meaning for the ST expression فطرة as "original, natural instinct, natural disposition, handiwork, nature":

So set thy purpose (O Muhammad) for religion as a man by nature upright – the nature (framed) of Allah, in which He hath created man (Pickthall 1930:no page).
So set thou thy face steadily and truly to the Faith: (establish) Allah's handiwork according to the pattern on which He has made mankind (Ali 1934:no page).
So set thy face to the religion, a man of pure faith – God's original upon which He originated mankind (Arberry 1955:182).
AND SO, set thy face steadfastly towards the [one ever-true] faith, turning away from all that is false, in accordance with the natural disposition which God has instilled into man (Asad 1980:846).
So as a man of pure faith, stand firm and true in your devotion to the religion. This is the natural disposition God instilled in mankind (Abdel Haleem 2005:258).
So set your face exclusively for the (Islamic) religion which is the natural instinct on which Allah has created mankind (Ahmad 2010:539).

Appendix 1 261

(iv)   The above translations interpretively resemble the ST without unnecessary processing effort on the part of the TL reader and have provided culture-based TTs based translation approaches such as the communicative, dynamic equivalence, natural, acceptable, or faithful approaches. These translation approaches take into consideration the contextual intended meaning of the ST in order to provide a comprehensible TT to the audience with an acceptable natural TL style. These translation approaches aim at complete naturalness of the TT; to naturalize the TT and reduce its foreignness.

18. Provide a textual and discourse analysis of Q30:30, compare different translations, and provide a commentary on the translation process.

لا تبديلَ لخلق اللهَ ذلكَ الدينُ القيّمُ (الروم 30)

Let us first consider different translations of the above ST and their translation approaches:

There is no altering (the laws of) Allah's creation. That is the right religion (Pickthall 1930:no page).
No change (let there be) in the work (wrought) by Allah. that is the standard Religion (Ali 1934:no page).
[For,] not to allow any change to corrupt what God has thus created – this is the [purpose of the one] ever true faith (Asad 1980:846).
Do not change what Allah has created (e.g., give proper training to children to follow Islamic religion). That is the Straight religion (to which the natural instinct directs) (Ahmad 2010:539).

Having considered the above translations, we can observe that the translator has employed the exegetical translation approach in which the TT explains and elaborates on the SL expression and provides additional details (within-the-TT details) that are not explicitly mentioned in the ST; an explication and expansion of the SL expression.

However, other translations such as those by Arberry and Abdel Haleem, have not adopted the exegetical translation approach:

There is no changing God's creation. That is the right religion (Arberry 1955:182).

There is no altering God's creation – and this is the right religion (Abdel Haleem 2005:259).

19. We encounter the two expressions أصحاب اليمين and أصحاب الشمال in Q56:27, 90 and Q56:41 lacking either in-text details or a footnote to tell the TL reader what these expressions stand for in the SL culture. Explain why.

We make the following observations:

(i)   The translation of the two expressions أصحاب اليمين and أصحاب الشمال are "the companions of the right" and "the companions of the left", respectively. This is based on the exotic translation approach which is similar to the literal and adequate translation approaches. In the exotic translation approach, the linguistic and cultural features of the ST are imported into the TT. Exoticism signals cultural foreignness in the TT and maintains the local colour of the ST.
(ii)   The reason why we do not need the exegetical translation approach, which allows the use of within-the-text details, or the gloss translation approach, which allows the

262   *Appendix 1*

use of footnotes, is because the ST elaborates immediately on the two expressions أصحاب الشمال and أصحاب اليمين and tells the reader who they are. We are told about who the companions of the right are in Q56:28–40. Similarly, we are told about who the companions of the left are in Q56:42–56.

20. We encounter the two expressions الخلّاق in Q15:86 and Q36:81, and الخالق in Q6:102 and Q39:62, lacking either within-the-text details or a footnote to tell the TL reader how these two expressions are semantically, stylistically, and pragmatically different in the TT. Explain this translation problem. Provide a textual and discourse analysis based on the context in which the above two expressions have occurred.

Let us provide the following critical translation quality assessment:

(i)   This is a translation problem related to stylistics, pragmatics, and semantics.

We can make the following observations based on the following sample translations:

الخلّاق "all-creator" Arberry (1955:115), الخالق "creator" Arberry (1955:61).
الخلّاق "creator" Abdel Haleem (2005:164), الخالق "creator" Abdel Haleem (2005:88).
These examples are in addition to other Qur'an translations which use "creator" for the two semantically, stylistically, and pragmatically different expressions above.

(ii)   The translations of الخلّاق and الخالق have applied the formal equivalence translation approach, typifying structural equivalence in which the translator attempts to reproduce as literally and meaningfully as possible the grammatical and stylistic patterns (form) and the meaning (content) of the ST. In other words, the translator aims to achieve a relatively close approximation to the structure and content of the ST and also attempts to reproduce consistency in word usage because he/she usually aims at concordance of terminology; the translator always renders a particular term, such as the ST hyperbole form الخلّاق by a corresponding term (noun) in the TT.

(iii)   It is worthwhile to note that the TL does not have such a hyperbole form because the hyperbole form الخلّاق is a lexical void in the TL. We must provide a relatively close approximation to the content (meaning) of الخلّاق. However, the result is a TT that does not convey the performative intent and the illocutionary force of the ST.

(iv)   The above translations of the expression الخلّاق are only approximations because there is no word-for-word equivalence between Arabic and English with regards to this particular expression.

(v)   We can provide a text and discourse analysis based on the context in which the above two expressions have occurred. The hyperbole form الخلّاق has occurred twice only in the whole Qur'an (Q15:86 and Q36:81) in the context in which the performative intent of the text producer requires the perlocutionary force of affirmation to rebut the denier of God's omnipotence جحود نكران قدرة الله. Thus, God's omnipotence with regards to the creation of the heavens and earth is highlighted in the ST. When the ST refers to such a performative intent, the expression الخلّاق becomes a semantic, stylistic, and pragmatic prerequisite to deliver the perlocutionary effect of the omnipotence of the Lord. The ST also involves other linguistic mechanisms of affirmation to rebut the denier of God's omnipotence, such as the affirmation particle إنّ and the interrogative

Appendix 1 263

affirmation particle أوَلَيس "is not 'He'", plus the affirmation positive answer particle بلى "Yes". Thus, there are three affirmation mechanisms involved in the ST, where الخلّاق is one of them. English lacks such innate linguistic affirmation techniques directly linked to a given notion (concept) that is pragmatically based and dogmatically (theologically) oriented. Thus, خلّاق befits well the context and the substantiation of God's ability to create. The alternative active participle خالق, which has occurred in Q6:102 and Q39:62, has been given the same translation as that for الخلّاق and *is not* suitable stylistically, semantically, and pragmatically.

21. Translate the following legal text, comment on the translation process, and provide a critical translation quality assessment.

Criminal law is the body of law that relates to crime. Criminal procedure is a formalized official activity that authenticates the fact of commission of a crime and authorizes punitive or rehabilitative treatment of the offender (Wikipedia, the free encyclopedia, accessed on 5 June 2020).

We propose the following translation:

إنَّ القانون الجنائي هو عبارة عن مجموعة القوانين التي تتعلق بالجريمة ... وتُعتبر الإجراءات الجنائية نشاطاً رسمياً يُثبتُ حقيقة ارتكاب جريمة ما ويُجيزُ العمل العقابي (المعاملة العقابية) أو التأهيلي للجاني.

(i)   The striking feature of the ST is the occurrence of the auxiliary verb "is" as the pivotal verb of the sentence. We recommend the translation of "is" in such syntactic patterns as an affirmation particle إنَّ + هو عبارة عن, or the passive voice expression يُعتَبر. However, in descriptive texts, the auxiliary verb "be" should be translated as يقعُ as in "My house is next to the library" يقع منزلي بجنب المكتبة – although you can still say إنّ منزلي بجنب المكتبة.

(ii)   The noun "body" is translated as مجموعة/مجموعة من, the singular indefinite noun "law" is translated as a plural definite noun القوانين, and the indefinite noun "crime" is changed to a definite noun الجريمة.

(iii)   The second occurrence of the auxiliary "is" is translated as a passive voice expression يُعتَبر preceded by the sentence-initial conjunction و, and the indefinite singular noun phrase "punitive or rehabilitative treatment" is translated as a definite singular noun phrase العمل العقابي التأهيلي.

(iv)   We have adopted the transposition or shift translation approach which is grammar-based and involves a change in the grammar from the SL to TL as well as a change in SL word order. Our translation is also culture-based; it is based on translation approaches such as the communicative, dynamic equivalence, natural, acceptable, instrumental, or faithful. These translation approaches take into consideration the contextual intended meaning of the ST in order to provide a comprehensible TT to the audience with an acceptable natural TL style. They also aim at complete naturalness of the TT; to naturalize the TT and reduce its foreignness. Our translation interpretively resembles the ST without unnecessary processing effort on the part of the TL reader.

22. Translate the following text, comment on the translation process, and provide a critical translation quality assessment.

264　*Appendix 1*

> The wagons travelled at a painfully slow pace covering just 15 miles a day; they were
> pulled by oxen, horses or mules across difficult terrain.

> The wagons travelled <u>at a painfully slow pace</u> جداً بطيئة بسرعة covering قاطعة just
> 15 miles a day; they were pulled by oxen, horses or mules across difficult terrain.

23. Translate the following text, comment on the translation process, and provide a critical translation quality assessment.

> This medicine has been prescribed for you. Do not pass it on to others. It may harm
> them, even if their symptoms are the same as yours.
> Warning: Mentex is a decongestant cough syrup which may give some side-effects such
> as sedation, varying from slight drowsiness to deep sleep, and including dizziness.

The suggested translation is

> أنَّ هذا الدواء قد تم وصفه خصيصاً لك بناءاً على وصفة طبية. لهذا يجب عليك عدم اعطائِه
> لشخصٍ آخر لأن ذلك قد يؤذيه حتى وإن كان يعاني من نفس الأعراض التي سبق وأن عانيت
> منها.

> تنبيه: إنَّ منتكس هو شرابٌ للسُعال ومُزيلٌ للإحتقان وقد يُسبب بعض الأعراض الجانبية مثل
> السكون بدرجاتٍ مختلفة مثل النعاس الخفيف والنوم العميق والدوار.
> In-class translation training: Questions on the translation process:

(i)　　The ST first sentence is a passive voice "This medicine has been prescribed for you".
　　　However, the translation of this sentence is in the active voice. Explain why?

(ii)　　The ST employs "as yours". However, the TT provides التي سبق وأن عانيت منها.
　　　Explain what the translator has done?

(iii)　　What is the translation of "varying from" as provided by the TT?

(iv)　　In the last sentence, the translator has used the additive conjunction (cohesive device)
　　　و. Explain why.

24. Translate the following texts and provide a commentary on the translation process of each text. Compare the ST and the TT and explain the translation approaches adopted by the translator.

(i)　　This orange juice is free from preservatives – عصير البرتقال هذا خالٍ من المواد الحافظة

(ii)　　No preservatives – خالٍ من المواد الحافظة

(iii)　　No artificial sweeteners – خالٍ من المواد المُحَلِّية الإصطناعية

(iv)　　No artificial flavorings – خالٍ من المواد المُنَكِّهة الإصطناعية

(v)　　No artificial colours – خالٍ من الألوان الإصطناعية

25. Provide a commentary on the translation process of the following text. Compare the ST with the TT and explain the translation approaches adopted by the translator.

وقالت وكالة الأنباء المغربية بأن العاهل المغربي الملك محمد الخامس عبَّر عن أمله بأنَّ هذه العلاقات
سوف تساهم في ترسيخ أسس السلام العادل والدائم والشامل في المنطقة وتخدم الشعبين المغربي
والفرنسي.

Appendix 1 265

The suggested translation is

"King Mohammad V of Morocco hopes that these relations would contribute in establishing the foundation of just, permanent, and comprehensive peace in the region and would serve the Moroccan and French nations (the two nations) (the Moroccan and French peoples)", the Moroccan News Agency said.

Having read the ST, we can make the following recommendations:

(i)   We demarcate the Arabic text sentence boundaries and do word order alteration because it is a journalistic text. To achieve equivalent effect as a journalistic text, the Arabic journalistic text needs a word order re-shuffle, and reads now as follows:

"العاهل المغربي الملك محمد الخامس يأملُ أنَّ هذه العلاقات سوف تساهم في ترسيخ أسس السلام العادل الدائم والشامل في المنطقة و سوف تخدم الشعبين المغربي والفرنسي"قالت وكالة الأنباء المغربية.

(ii)   We take out the conjunction و.

(iii)   We do word order modification (re-shuffle) because in Arabic journalism, the speaker وكالة الأنباء المغربية is preceded by the verb قالت/قال, occurring first, followed by the reported speech, which is a quotation. However, in English journalistic texts, the word order is the other way round: the reported speech occurs first, followed by the reporter (the speaker) – in this case, قالت وكالة الأنباء المغربية – which should occur at the end of the ST.

(iv)   Based on the ST context, the translation of the noun العاهل المغربي الملك محمد الخامس is "King Mohammad V of Morocco"; the adjective المغربي is translated as "of Morocco". Notice we have changed the adjective المغربي to a noun "Morocco" plus the addition of the preposition "of". The translation of عبَّر عن أمله is "hoped".

(v)   We replace the difficult Arabic word العاهل with a simpler synonym المَلِك to facilitate the translation process. Thus, we have "King". We replace the difficult Arabic expression عبَّر عن أمله with a simpler synonym يأملُ to facilitate the translation process. Thus, we have "hopes".

(vi)   We have adopted the transposition or shift translation approach, which is grammar-based and involves a change in the grammar from the SL to TL as well as a change in SL word order; the translation should aim at complete naturalness of the TT and reduce its foreignness. We need a culture-based translation based on translation approaches such as the communicative, dynamic equivalence, natural, acceptable, instrumental, transposition or shift translation, or faithful approach. These translation approaches take into consideration the contextual intended meaning of the ST in order to provide a comprehensible TT to its audience with an acceptable natural TL style. The translation interpretively resembles the original without unnecessary processing effort on the part of the TL reader.

26. Provide a translation for the following ST:

Course description:
Applied Translation provides practical translation training in English into Arabic and Arabic into English. The major aim of this course is to develop the student's practical

translation skills from and into English. *Applied Translation* will deal with English texts taken from English newspapers and other text types such as English instructional and scientific texts. *Applied Translation* will also deal with Arabic texts taken from Saudi newspapers and other Arabic text types, including Arabic Islamic texts and Arabic literary texts. The course will discuss many theoretical translation notions that are useful for the development of the student's practical English-Arabic-English translation skills. Different approaches relevant to different English and Arabic genres will also be dealt with throughout the course.

Course objectives:

Applied Translation aims to achieve the following objectives:

1. To enable the student acquire sound practical English-into-Arabic and Arabic-into-English translation skills.

2. To make the student aware of different English and Arabic genres and their major discourse features.

3. To make the student aware of different translation approaches relevant to different English and Arabic genres.

4. To enable the student to understand the linguistic, stylistic, and cultural differences between English and Arabic.

5. To enable the student to understand core theoretical notions about translation studies.

6. To enable the student to understand different types of meaning that are relevant to English and Arabic translation studies.

7. To enable the student to ascertain appropriate meanings from dictionaries.

8. To show the student that dictionaries do not always help in finding accurate meanings.

9. To enable the student to understand the role of the context of situation and the context of culture.

10. To enable the student to understand the cultural differences between English and Arabic and the importance of cultural meaning in translation.

By the end of the course:

1. The student will have acquired sound understanding of major notions in theoretical translation.

2. The student will have acquired sound practical translation skills from English into Arabic and from Arabic into English.

3. The student will have increased his/her stock of English vocabulary, which will be valuable for improving his/her communication skills.

4. The student will have increased his/her stock of English vocabulary, which will be valuable for improving his/her Arabic into English translation skills.

5. The student will have acquired a good understanding of the British culture through classroom discussion of the English texts taken from British media.

We propose the following translation:

يقدّمُ مُقرر (الترجمة التطبيقية) تمارين عملية للترجمة سن الانجليزية الى العربية ومن العربية الى الانجليزية. ويعتبر الهدف الرئيسي من هذا المقرر هو تطوير مهارات الطالب في الترجمة التطبيقية من و إلى الإنجليزية. ويُركز مُقرر (الترجمة التطبيقية) على نصوص انجليزية مقتبسة من الصحف الناطقة باللغة الإنجليزية ونصوص اخرى مثل النصوص الإرشادية والعلمية. كما يُركز مُقرر (الترجمة التطبيقية) ايضاً على النصوص العربية المقتبسة من الصحف السعودية ونصوص عربية

Appendix 1 267

اخرى مثل النصوص الإسلامية والأدبية . وسيركز المقرر على عدة مفاهيم الترجمة النظرية المفيدة لتطوير مهارات الطالب التطبيقية في الترجمة من وإلى الإنجليزية . كما يتطرق المقرر إلى طرق ترجمة مختلفة تتناسب مع نصوص انجليزية وعربية مختلفة طيلة فترة تدريس هذا المقرر .

يهدفُ هذا المقرر (الترجمة التطبيقية) الى تحقيق الأهداف التالية:

١ – تمكين الطالب من اكتساب مهارات عملية سليمة في الترجمة من الإنجليزية الى العربية ومن العربية الى الإنجليزية.

٢ – جَعل الطالبِ يعي بالأساليب المختلفة في اللغة الإنجليزية والعربية وخصائصها النصية المختلفة .

٣ – تمكينُ الطالبِ من إدراك أنواع الترجمة المختلفة المتعلقة بأساليب مختلفة في العربية والإنجليزية .

٤ – تمكينُ الطالب من فهم الاختلافات اللغوية والأسلوبية والثقافية بين الإنجليزية والعربية .

٥ – تمكينُ الطالبِ من فهم المفاهيم النظرية الأساسية المتعلقة بدراسات علم الترجمة .

٦ – تمكينُ الطالبِ من فهم أنواع المعاني المختلفة ذات الصلة بالدراسات العربية والإنجليزية في الترجمة .

٧ – تمكينُ الطالبِ من معرفة الطريقة الصحيحة لاستخراج المعنى المناسب من القاموس .

٨ – التوضيحُ للطالبِ بأن القاموس لا يساعد دائماً في ايجاد المعنى الدقيق .

٩ – تمكينُ الطالب من فهم دور السياق والسياق الثقافي .

١٠ – تمكينُ الطالبِ من فهم الإختلافات الثقافية بين اللغة الإنجليزية والعربية وأهمية المعنى الثقافي في الترجمة .

عند الإنتهاء من المُقرر :

١ – يكون الطالبُ قد اكتسب فهماً جيداً للمفاهيم الأساسية في الترجمة النظرية .

٢ – يكون الطالبُ قد اكتسب مهارات عملية جيدة في الترجمة من الإنجليزية الى العربية وبالعكس.

٣ – يكون الطالبُ قد أثرى (زاد) مخزونه من المفردات الإنجليزية التي تكون لها قيمة لتحسين مهارات تواصله.

٤ – يكون الطالبُ قد زاد مخزونه من المفردات الإنجليزية ذات القيمة لتحسين مهاراته في الترجمة من العربية الى الإنجليزية.

٥ – يكون الطالبُ قد اكتسب فهماً جيداً للثقافة البريطانية من خلال المناقشات الصفية للنصوص الإنجليزية المقتبسة (المأخوذة) من وسائل الإعلام البريطانية.

27. Provide a translation for the following ST:

Brazilian police have arrested five people in an investigation into the causes of the Brumadinho dam disaster. The dam break on Friday at an iron ore mining complex operated by the minerals firm Vale killed at least 65 people, and a further 279 are missing. Federal and state prosecutors said 30-day arrest warrants had been issued "aiming to establish criminal responsibility for the rupture of dams at the Córrego de Feijão mine maintained by Vale". Arrests were carried out in São Paulo and Belo Horizonte on Tuesday morning, prosecutors said. Searches were carried out at a Vale building in Nova Lima and a subcontracted company in São Paulo that provided services and consultancy to Vale. "Three Vale employees directly employed and responsible were arrested. In addition, subcontracted engineers who recently attested to the stability of the dam were arrested", the prosecutors said. Last Friday, after the dam broke, Vale said

268   *Appendix 1*

it had "declarations of the condition of stability" from TÜV SÜD, a German company with headquarters in São Paulo, given on 13 June and 26 September last year. Three years ago, a similar disaster in the same state, Minas Gerais, at a mine run by Samarco, a joint-venture between Vale and BHP Billiton, killed 19 people, poisoned the drinking water of hundreds of thousands and sent mining waste down the river Doce to the sea. Brazil's regional development minister, Gustavo Canuto, said on Tuesday that nearly 4,000 dams in Brazil were classified as having "high damage potential" or being at high risk. He added that 205 of those dams contained mineral waste.

(*The Guardian*, 29 January 2019)

We propose the following translation:

انهيار سد في البرازيل: اعتقال خمسة منهم ثلاثة من موظفي شركة التعدين

اعتقلت الشرطة البرازيلية خمسة أشخاص للتحقيق في أسباب كارثة سد برومادينهو. وأدى انهيار السد يوم الجمعة في مجمع تعدين خام الحديد الذي تديره شركة المعادن فالي الى مقتل 65 شخصا على الاقل وفقدان 279 آخرين. وقال ممثلو الادعاء الاتحاديون والحكوميون إنه تمَّ إصدار مذكرات (قرارات) توقيف مدتها 30 يوماً "تهدف إلى إثبات المسؤولية الجنائية عن انهيار السدود في منجم كوجريغو دي فيجاو الذي تتولى شركة فالي مسؤولية الحفاظ عليها". وقال ممثلو الإدعاء انَّ الإعتقالات نفذت في ساو باولو وبيلو هوريزونتي صباح الثلاثاء. وأجريت عمليات البحث في مبنى فالي في نوفا ليما وشركة متعاقدة من الباطن في ساو باولو قدمت خدمات واستشارات إلى شركة فالي. وقال المدعون العامون أنه "تم إلقاء القبض على ثلاثة موظفين من Vale يعملون بشكل مباشر ومسؤولون في الشركة. بالإضافة إلى ذلك، تمَّ إلقاء القبض على مهندسين تم التعاقد معهم من الباطن الذين شهدوا في الآونة الأخيرة على استقرار السد". وبعد انهيار السد يوم الجمعة الماضي، صرحت شركت فالي إنه كان لديها "بيانات تؤكد حالة استقرار السد" صادرة من شركة تووف سود ، وهي شركة ألمانية مقرها في ساو باولو ، قدمت (تم تقديمها) في 13 يونيو و 26 سبتمبر من العام الماضي. ومن الجدير بالذكر أنه قبل ثلاث سنوات، أدت كارثة مماثلة في نفس الولاية، ميناس جيرايس، في منجم تديره شركة ساماركو، وهي مشروع مشترك بين شركة فالي وشركة بي إتش بي بيليتون، إلى مقتل 19 شخصًا، وتسمم مياه الشرب لمئات الآلاف، وأرسلت نفايات التعدين إلى نهر دوسي ومن ثم الى البحر الذي يصب فيه. وقال وزير التنمية الإقليمي في البرازيل، جوستافو كانوتو، يوم الثلاثاء أن ما يقرب من 4000 سداً في البرازيل صنفت على أنها "تنطوي على أضرار (تصدعات) كبيرة"، أو أنها معرَّضة لخطر كبير. وأضاف أن 205 من هذه السدود تحتوي على نفايات معدنية. (عن صحيفة الغارديان البريطانية ، الثلاثاء 29 يناير (كانون الثاني) 2019)

28. Provide a translation for the following ST:

What are the health benefits of honey?

   Honey is a sweet liquid produced by honeybees using nectar from flowers through a process of regurgitation and evaporation. This Medical News Today information article includes a brief history of honey in traditional medicine and explains some of its potential health benefits. The possible health benefits of consuming honey have been documented in early Greek, Roman, Vedic, and Islamic texts and the healing qualities of honey were referred to by philosophers and scientists all the way back to ancient times, such as Aristotle (384–322 BC) and Aristoxenus (320 BC). Honey has high levels of monosaccharides, fructose and glucose, containing about 70 to 80 percent sugar, which gives it its sweet taste – minerals and water make up the rest of its composition. Honey also possesses antiseptic and antibacterial properties. In modern science we have managed to find useful applications of honey in chronic wound management. However, it should be noted that many of honey's health claims still require further rigorous scientific studies to confirm them. The Quran also praises honey's healing ability:

"And thy Lord taught the Bee to build its cells in hills, on trees, and in (men's) habitations; Then to eat of all the produce (of the earth), and find with skill the spacious paths of its Lord: there issues from within their bodies a drink of varying colors, wherein is healing for men: verily in this is a Sign for those who give thought." (Q16:68–69). Properties of honey: Honey is made up of glucose, fructose, and minerals such as iron, calcium, phosphate, sodium chlorine, potassium, magnesium.

(10 August 2013. *Health Professionals*)

We propose the following translation:

ماهي الفوائد الصحية للعسل؟

العسلُ هو السائلُ الحلو الذي ينتجه نحل العسل باستخدام رحيق الزهور من خلال عمليتي القيء والتبخر. تتضمن الأخبار الطبية اليوم معلومات حول مختصر تاريخ العسل في الطب التقليدي ويشرح بعض من فوائدها الصحية المحتملة. وقد تم توثيق الفوائد الصحية المحتملة لاستهلاك العسل في اليونانية الأولى والفيدية والرومانية والنصوص الإسلامية, كما أشيرت إلى خاصية الشفاء بالعسل من قبل الفلاسفة والعلماء منذ العصور القديمة، مثل أرسطو (384–322) قبل الميلاد) و أربستوكسينوس (320) قبل الميلاد). ويحتوي العسل على مستويات عالية من السكريات الأحادية وسكر الفواكه والجلوكوز و تحتوي على حوالي 70–80 في المائة من السكر، وهو ما يعطيها الطعم الحلو ــ كما تشكل المعادن والمياه بقية تكوينها. إنّ العسل يمتلك أيضا خصائص مطهرة ومضادة للجراثيم. لقد استطعنا أن نجد في العلم الحديث تطبيقات مفيدة من العسل في علاج الجروح المزمنة. ومع ذلك، تجدر الإشارة إلى أنّ العديد من تداعيات صحية العسل لا تزال بحاجة إلى مزيد من الدراسات العلمية الجادة للتأكد منها. والقرآن أيضا يشيد بقدرة العسل على الشفاء (سورة النحل 68–69).

مكوّنات العسل: يتكون العسل من الجلوكوز، والفركتوز، والمعادن مثل الحديد والكالسيوم والفوسفات والكلور الصوديوم والبوتاسيوم والمغنيسيوم. (عن مجلة المتخصصون في الصحة، السبت 10 أغسطس (آب) 2013، الساعة 12 ظهرا).

29. Provide a translation for the following ST:

Nestle faces the wrath of chocolate lovers after it refuses to permanently reinstate the much-loved Toffee Deluxe to Quality Street. Britons were in uproar when the confectionery giant decided to ditch the sweet from its iconic Quality Street boxes back in September. Nestle swapped the Toffee Deluxe for its new Honeycomb Crunch treat, making its first change to the Quality Street line-up since 2007. Nestle has decided to reinstate the Toffee Deluxe in time for the Christmas period – but unfortunately, its stay will be short lived. A spokesperson for Quality Street told the Sun: "We're incredibly excited to welcome the new Honeycomb Crunch, and were amazed by the response on social media when the cat was let out of the 'purple' bag, and people heard it would be replacing Toffee Deluxe in the standard tub". "We hope people enjoy the new Honeycomb Crunch sweet and want to reassure Toffee Deluxe lovers that they can still find their favorite Quality Street sweet this Christmas". The Deluxe was created in 1919 as a sweet in its own right and was included in one of the first ever boxes of Quality Street, after it was invented in 1936.

(By Alex Matthews for *The Daily Mail*, 21 November 2016)

270 *Appendix 1*

We propose the following translation:

تواجهُ شركة نسلة للحلويات غضب عشاق الشوكولاتة بعد ان رفضت إرجاع قطعة الحلوى (توفي ديلوكس) المحبوبة جدا الى علبة كوليتي ستريت بشكل دائم اذ غضب البريطانيون عندما قررت شركة الحلويات العملاقة التخلي عن قطعة الحلوى هذه من علبة الحلويات المشهورة في سبتمبر الماضي. ويذكر ان شركة نسلة استبدلت قطعة الحلويات هذه بقطعة حلويات جديدة تسمى (هوني كومب كرانش) وبهذا تكون اول تغيير لحلويات كوليتي ستريت في إنتاجها منذ عام ٢٠٠٧. وقد قررت شركة نسلة إعادة قطعة الحلوى القديمة في الوقت المناسب لفترة أعياد الميلاد لكن للأسف سوف يكون بقائها لفترة قصيرة. وقد اخبر المتحدث الرسمي من كوليتي ستريت لصحيفة ذي صن البريطانية: (نحن مُتحمسون بشكل لا يُصدَّق للترحيب بقطعة الحلوى الجديدة ومتعجبون من ردة فعل وسائل التواصل الاجتماعي عندما تم إفشاء السر وسمع الناس انها ستحل محل قطعة الحلوى (توفي ديلوكس) في العلبة الاعتيادية ونأمل ان يستمتع الناس بقطعة الحلوى الجديدة ونودُ ان نُطمئن عشاق قطعة الحلوى القديمة أنَّ باستطاعتهم ان يجدوا قطعة حلواهم المفضلة في أعياد الميلاد القادمة. ويُذكر أنَّ قطعة الحلوى القديمة (توفي ديلوكس) قد تمَّ صناعتها في ١٩١٨ كحلوى قائمة بذاتها وقد أضيفت الى أول علبة من علب كوليتي ستريت بعد ان تمّ صنعها في عام 1936. (من مراسلنا ألكس ماثيوز لصحيفة ذي ديلي ميل البريطانية.)

30. Provide a translation for the following ST:

> The Report showed shortages in key areas, such as providing care to elderly in their own homes. Only a third of local authorities said they had enough nursing homes with specialist dementia support. The report, from the Family and Childcare Trust, included Freedom of Information data from around 150 local authorities and health and social care trusts across the UK. Only a third (32%) of local authorities said they had enough nursing homes with specialist dementia support. The figures also varied by region, with 57% of councils in the North East having enough older people's care to meet demand in their area, dropping to just 7% in outer London.
>
> Claire Harding, head of research at the Family and Childcare Trust, said: "It is inexcusable that vulnerable people are left unable to find the care that they need". "Without these steps, families will continue to struggle to find care and to meet the numerous care costs on their shoulders". The Local Government Association (LGA), which represents councils, said money is being diverted away from road repairs, leisure centres and local bus routes in order to maintain the struggling social care sector. It warned that the system is "in crisis" and called on the Government to invest in social care in the Autumn Statement.
>
> (*The Daily Mail*, 21 November 2016)

We propose the following translation:

أشار التقريرُ الى وجودِ نقص في مناطق حيوية كتأمين الرعاية لكبار السن في منازلهم اذ أنَّ ثلث مجالس البلديات ذكرت أنَّ لديها رعاية طبية متخصصة بمرض الخرف. ويذكر أنَّ هذا التقرير الصادر من هيئة الأسرة ورعاية الطفل يتضمن تفاصيل من مؤسسة حرية المعلومات من حوالي ١٥٠ مجلس بلدية وهيئات الرعاية الاجتماعية والصحية في جميع ارجاء المملكة المتحدة. وقد ذكرت السيدة كلير هاردنق مديرة قسم البحوث في هيئة الأسرة ورعاية الطفل " أنه لا يمكن تبرير ان يترك المسنون وهم غير قادرين على إيجاد الرعاية التي يحتاجونها فمن دون هذه الخطوات سوف تستمرُ العوائلُ في معاناتها لإيجاد الرعاية وتحمل أوزار تكاليفها." ومن جهتها ذكرت هيئة المجالس البلدية التي تمثل جميع مجالس البلديات أنَّ الأموال ما زال يتم تحويل مسارها المُخصص لإصلاح الطرق ومراكز ترفيه وطرق الحافلات المحلية وتحويلهُ الى دعم قطاع الرعاية الإجتماعية المُتعثّر مالياً.

Appendix 1   271

وحذّرت هيئةُ المجالس البلدية أنّ نظام الرعاية الإجتماعية في «أزمة»، و ناشدت الحكومة أن تستثمر في الرعاية الإجتماعية في بيان وزير المالية في الخريف. (عن صحيفة ذي ديلي ميل البريطانية ، 21 نوفمبر (تشرين الثاني) 2016)

31. Provide a translation for the following ST:

Migrants Increase Housing Crisis

- Figures suggest 100,000 new homes a year is needed to house immigrants
- Less immigration and more house-building to make Britain "civilized" says Planning Minister Nick Boles

High demand: Planning Minister Nick Boles warned 100,000 new homes will be built to accommodate the expanding British population.

Vast swathes of the countryside will have to be sacrificed to build new homes for immigrants, the Planning Minister warned last night.

Earlier this week, Mr Boles alarmed conservationists by saying up to two million acres of green fields may have to be concreted over to deal with the housing shortage. Now he has become the first government minister to draw a clear link between housing demand and the legacy of Labour's open-door immigration policy. Mr Boles said: "The fact is we allowed the population of this country to expand dramatically. The population of England has gone up by two million in the last ten years. These people now live here, these people are now British and they need homes just like other British people. We need to have less immigration and more house-building and we might then have a civilized country". Deputy Prime Minister Nick Clegg said last month that the number of households was forecast to expand at the rate of 230,000 a year. Mr Clegg said total house building amounted to just 117,000 last year. Sir Andrew Green, founder of the think-tank Migration Watch, said the public would be shocked by the figures, which are significantly higher than the Government's previous estimate on the issue.

(By Jason Groves, *The Daily Mail*, 30 November 2012)

We propose the following translation:

المُهاجرون يؤجّجون الحاجة الي بيوت في منطقة الحزام الأخضر : إعترافٌ صريحٌ لوزير التخطيط عن أزمة السكن

- تشيرُ الأرقامُ إلى الحاجة إلى بناء 100,000 منزلٍ جديدٍ سنوياً لإيواء المُهاجرين.
- يقول وزير التخطيط السيد نيك بولس: الحد من الهجرة وبناء منازل أكثر يجعل بريطانيا دولة «متحضرة»

إرتفاعُ الطلبِ: حدَّر وزيرُ الدولة لشؤون التخطيط السيد نيك بولس من بناء 100,000 وحدة سكنية جديدة لاستيعاب الزيادة السكانية في بريطانيا.

لقد حذر وزيرُ التخطيط ليلة أمس من أنّ مساحات شاسعة من الريف سيتم التضحية بها من أجل بناء بيوت جديدة للمهاجرين. ويُذكر أنّ السيد بويلز قد أثار قلق (أقلق) في مطلع هذا الأسبوع المُنادين بالحفاظ على البيئة بقوله أنه ربما ينبغي بناء مليونين فدان من الحقول الزراعية لحل أزمة السكن .

272 _Appendix 1_

ولهذا قد أصبح أول وزير بالحكومة يرسم علاقة واضحة بين الحاجة إلى المنازل "وترك السياسة والسماح بدخول المهاجرين بأعداد كبيرة التي تبناها حزب العمال". وذكر السيد بولس بولز أنّ الحقيقة هي أننا سمحنا لسكان هذا البلد بالتوسع على نطاق واسع فقد ازداد سكان انكلترة إلى مليونين في خلال السنوات العشرة الماضية. إنّ هؤلاء الناس يعيشون هنا وهم بريطانيون يحتاجون إلى منازل مثل بقيه الشعب البريطاني لكن ينبغي علينا تقليل الهجرة وبناء منازل أكثر ومن ثمّ ربما يكون لدينا بلد "متحضر". ومن جانبه قال نائب رئيس الوزراء السيد نيك كليك الشهر الماضي أنه من المتوقع ارتفاع عدد السكان إلى (بمعدل) 230,000 سنويا وأضاف قائلاً أن العدد الإجمالي للوحدات السكنية التي تم بناؤها العام الماضي بلغ 117,000 منزل. وذكر السيد أندرو جرين مؤسس هيئة مراقبة المهاجرين التي لا تتمتع بسلطات تنفيذية ذكر بأن الناس سوف ينصدمون لو عرفوا الأرقام التي تزيد بكثرة عن الأرقام السابقة للحكومة حول هذه المشكلة. (عن صحيفة ذي ديلي ميل البريطانية ، 30 نوفمبر (تشرين الثاني) 2012)

32. Provide a translation for the following ST:

British tourist is gored to death by a rampaging elephant

- The 36-year-old victim was trekking on the elephant when it turned violent
- It first attacked its handler before trampling and stabbing the tourist
- Incident took place on tropical island of Ko Samui in Thailand
- Eilidh Hughes, 16, was taken to hospital to be treated for minor injuries

A British tourist has been killed by an elephant in front of his teenage daughter in Thailand. Gareth Crowe, aged 36, was trekking on the elephant with Eilidh Hughes, the 16-year-old daughter of his partner and a local guide on the tropical island of Ko Samui when it turned violent. Witnesses said the mahout – the elephant's handler – climbed down to take photos of the tourists when it hit him with its trunk and stabbed him in his body with a tusk. The elephant is then said to have rampaged, throwing the father and daughter off his back before trampling the man and stabbing him in the chest with a tusk, killing him instantly. The teenage girl escaped with minor injuries in the fall as the elephant ran off into the forest. Witnesses said just before the attack the elephant – known as Golf – had appeared upset and refused to follow the instructions of the mahout who hit him several times with a hook. Another local report suggested the elephant was being teased with a banana before it became unsettled and attacked. The girl was initially treated at Samui International Hospital before being moved to Bangkok International Hospital on the island. A hospital spokeswoman confirmed the teenager was being treated there for minor injuries.

(By Joseph Curtis, _The Daily Mail_, 1 February 2016)

We propose the following translation:

فيلٌ هائجٌ يطعنُ سائحاً بريطانياً حتى الموت
من مُراسلنا جوزيف كورتيس
أو (بقلم) فلان بن فلان (إذا كان مقالا علميا)
عن صحيفة ذي ديلي ميل البريطانية ، 1 فبراير (شباط) 2016)

- كان السائح البالغ من العمر 36 عاماً يتنزه على ظهر الفيل
- الفيل يهاجم المدرب قبل أن يدوس ويطعن السائح

Appendix 1 273

- وقعت الحادثة في جزيرة كوسامو الأستوائية التايلندية
- أديث البالغة من العمر 16 عاما يتم نقلها إلى المستشفى لمعالجتها من جروح طفيفة

(لقي سائح بريطاني حتفه) . . . قتل فيل سائحاً بريطانياً على مرأى من ابنته المراهقة في تايلند. وكان السيد جارث كراو البالغ من العمر 36 عاماً يتنزه على ظهر الفيل مع إليد هيوز البالغة من العمر 16 عاماً وهي ابنة صديقته وبصحبة المرشد السياحي المحلي في جزيرة كوسامو الأستوائية التايلندية عندما أصبح الفيل غاضباً. وذكر شهود عيان بأنّ مُدرب الفيل قد نزل من الفيل ليلتقط صوراً للسواح عندما ضربه بخرطومه وطعنه في جسمه بنابه. ويذكر أن الفيل قد هاج مما تسبب في إلقاء (إسقاط) الأب وابنته من على ظهره قبل أن يدوس الرجل ويطعنه بنابه في صدره مما أدى الى مقتله فوراً (في الحال). أما الفتاة المراهقة فقد تعرضت لجروح بسيطة جرّاء سقوطها عندما هرب الفيل الى وسط الغابة. وقد ذكر شهود عيان بأنه قبيل هجوم الفيل الذي يُعرف باسم غولف فإنه كان يبدو منزعجاً ورافضاً لتعليمات مُدربه الذي ضربه عدة مرات بالعصى. ومن جهة أخرى يفيد تقرير محلي بأن الفيل قد تعرض للأثارة بموزة قبل أن يفقد استقراره ويبدأ بهجومه. (جراء : in the fall)

33. Provide a translation for the following ST:

Chinese get "Shop Visa"

Wealthy Chinese tourists are to benefit from a relaxation of the visa system, in an effort to boost Britain's retail trade. Tourism bosses estimate the UK misses out on £1.2 billion from Chinese visitors each year as a result of its "over-zealous" visa system. France, for example, receives eight times more Chinese visitors than Britain. Home Secretary Theresa May has agreed to ease bureaucracy for Chinese tourists who want to come for periods of a fort-night or less, but restrictions on longer-term visitors will remain, amid fears of state-sponsored Chinese espionage and cyber-crime.

(*The Daily Mail*, 4 December 2012)

We propose the following translation:

الصينيون يحصلون على تأشيرة تسوُّق

سوف يستفيدُ السياحُ الصينيون الأثرياء من تيسير نظام تأشيرة الدخول في محاولة لتعزيز تجارة التجزئة في بريطانيا (البريطانية) ، حيث قدَّرت مكاتب السياحة الكبرى بأن بريطانيا تخسر 1.2 بليون جنيه أسترليني من السياح الصينيين سنوياً نتيجة للنظام المتشدد لتأشيرة الدخول. ففرنسا مثلا (على سبيل المثال) ، تستقبل سياحاً صينيين أكثر مما تستقبل بريطانيا بثمانية أضعاف. وقد وافقت وزيرة الداخلية البريطانية تيريزا ماي على تخفيف الإجراءات الإدارية المعقدة للسياح الصينيين الراغبين في المجيء والمكوث في بريطانيا لمدة أسبوعين أو أقل ، لكن (بيد أنَّ) القيود المفروضة على السياح الراغبين في المكوث لمدة أطول ستبقى كما هي وسط مخاوف من أعمالِ تجسسِ الصينيين وجرائمهم الإلكترونية التي تشرفُ عليها الحكومةُ الصينية.

34. Provide a translation for the following ST:

A Muslim man who punched a nurse for trying to remove his wife's burqa during childbirth has been jailed in France. Nassim Mimoune, 24, had already been expelled from the delivery room for branding the midwife a "rapist" as she carried out an intimate examination of his wife. Then through a window he spotted the nurse taking off his wife's burqa as she prepared to give birth. He smashed open the locked door and hit the woman in the face, demanding she replace the full Islamic face veil. As she delivered a

274   *Appendix 1*

baby boy, Mimoune was ejected from the building by security men from the hospital in Marseille and arrested for assault. A judge in the southern French port jailed Mimoune for six months on Wednesday, telling him: "Your religious values are not superior to the laws of the republic."

(*The Daily Mail*, 23 December 2011)

We propose the following translation:

تمَّ سجنُ مُسلم في فرنسا لأنه لكَمَ مُمرّضة كانت تُحاول نزع نقاب زوجته اثناء الولادة. ويذكر انَّ نسيم ميمون البالغ من العمر ٢٤ عاماً قد تمَّ طرده مُسبقاً من غرفة الولادة لوصفه الممرضة بالمغتصبة جنسياً عندما أجرت فحصاً داخليا لزوجته. وبعد ذلك، لمح من خلال الشباك الممرضة تزيل نقاب زوجته عندما كانت تستعد للولادة، بعدها كسر الباب المقفل وضرب الممرضة على وجهها طالباً منها إرجاع النقاب. و بينما ولدت زوجته طفلاً قام رجال الأمن بطرد ميمون من المستشفى الواقعة في مرسيليا واعتقاله بتهمة الإعتداء. وقد قام قاض في ميناء جنوب فرنسا بسجن ميمون لستة أشهر يوم الأربعاء قائلا له: "أنَّ قيمكَ الدينية ليست أعلى من قوانين الجمهورية." (عن صحيفة ذي ديلي ميل البريطانية ، 23 ديسمبر (كانون الأول) 2011)

35. Provide a translation for the following ST:

A judge yesterday said he had no choice but to give a short prison sentence to a driver who horrifically injured a 55-year-old policeman. Mr Coetzee was thrown 24ft from his bicycle in the hit and run. Ten months on, he is still in hospital and has had to end his remarkable career. Mr Coetzee suffered a fractured skull and bleeding to the brain. He is being cared for at a specialist hospital in Northampton. The driver, Mitchel Graham, sped from the scene, leaving the constable lying in the road. But Judge Jonathan Teare said Parliament had decided he could give Graham no more than 15 months behind bars. The maximum sentence for dangerous driving is two years but a shorter term is given to offenders who plead guilty. Graham admitted dangerous driving and failing to stop. The court heard he knew his car was in a highly dangerous condition when he ran into Mr Coetzee who was off duty and cycling to an exercise class in Blidworth, Nottingham-shire, at 6pm on November 25. The 26-year-old pig farmer hid the damaged Volkswagen Corrado in his brother's garage and only gave himself up four days later. Mr Graham admitted drinking alcohol and fleeing the scene. Mr Coetzee has developed a personality disorder, has restricted movement, and needs help with walking and completing simple tasks. He can no longer stand unaided and is able to spend only weekends with his family.

We propose the following translation:

ذكرَ قاض يوم أمس بأنه لم يكن عنده أيَّ خيار اخر سوى إصدار حكم بالسجن لمدة قصيرة لسائق تسبب في إصابة شرطي عمره (55)عاماً بجروح مروعة (فظيعة) ويذكرَ أنَّ الشرطي كوتسي قد ألقي من على دراجته لمسافة 24 قدماً عندما صدمه السائق وهرب وبعد مضي عشرة اشهر على اصابته، مازال الشرطي راقداً في المستشفى مما توجب عليه ترك وظيفته الرائعة بسبب (جراء) أصابته بكسر في الجُمجمة ونزيفٍ في الدماغ. وهو مازال راقداً يتلقى العلاج في مستشفى متخصصة في نوثما مْتنْ. وقد هرب السائق ميتشل جراهم بسيارته من مكان الحادث تاركاً الشرطيَ مطروحاً على الطريق. ومن جانبه ، ذكر الحاكم جوناثان تير أنَّ البرلمان كان قد قرر بأنه لا يستطيع أن يحكم عليه بمده سجن تزيد عن 15 شهراً. ويذكر أنَّ العقوبة القصوى للقيادة المتهورة هي سنتين بيد أنه يتم اعطاء

Appendix 1   275

مدة أقصر للمجرمين الذين يقرون (يعترفون) بذنبهم حيث أنَّ السيد جراهام اعترف بسياقته المُتهورة وعدم الوقوف. وقد استمعت المحكمة اليه قائلاً انه كان على علم بانَّ سيارته كانت في حالةٍ خطرةٍ جداً عندما صدم السيد كوتسي الذي كان خارج ساعات عمله راكباً دراجته الهوائية متجهاً إلى أحد الدروس الرياضية في مدينة بلِيد ورث بمقاطعة نوتينغهامشير وذلِك في الساعة السادسة مساءاً في 25 نوفمبر (تشرين الثاني) وقد خبأ جراهام الذي يعمل فلاح تربيه الخنازير خبأ سيارته من نوع فوكسوا جن كورود في مأرب أخيه ولم يُسلم نفسه للشرطة إلاَّ بعد أربعة أيام كما اعترف بأنه تعاطي الكحول وفرَّ من موقع الحادث. ويُذكر أنَّ السيد كوتزي يُعاني من اضطراب في الشخصية وقلة الحركة وهو بحاجةٍ إلى المساعدة أثناء المشي ولا يستطيع إكمال المهام البسيطة كما أنهُ لا يستطيع الوقوف دون مُساعدة ولا يستطيع زيارة أسرته إلاَّ في عطلة نهاية الإسبوع.

36. Provide a translation for the following ST:

Mr Hollande is France's first Socialist president since Mr Mitterrand in the 1980s. He outlined a £24 billion austerity package خطة تقشف in the harshest budget for 30 years and a 75% tax rise on incomes over £800,000 a year. But business leaders are disappointed. They fear a migration of top business talent and an exodus of the most talented French workers to London. Critics said this financial plan risked driving businessmen and the wealthy overseas and warned that Mr Hollande is doing <u>untold</u> damage أضرار جسيمة "untold = indescribable, numberless" to the economy. They also voiced alarm over the decision to impose £16 billion of tax rises and just £8 billion of spending cuts. They claimed that the government was impeding investment and blocking innovation. Economists are also <u>skeptical</u> يشكك في about the government's ability to meet the target يحقق الهدف particularly as it is based on the <u>assumption</u> إفتراض ، تخمين that the French economy will grow by 0.8 per cent in 2013 and 2 per cent in 2014 <u>despite the debt storm tearing through the euro-zone</u>.

(By Hugo Duncan, *The Daily Mail*, 29 September 2012)

(على الرغم من زوبعة الديون التي تعصف بمنطقة اليورو)

The French Prime Minister Jean-Marc Ayrault insisted it was "a fighting budget <u>to get the country back on the rails</u> لوضع البلاد على الطريق الصحيح ثانية" He said: "It is a budget which aims to bring back confidence and to break this spiral of debt that gets bigger and bigger. Big companies pay less than the small companies and sometimes don't pay at all. So, we're asking them to help the economy, too".

Confirmation of the 75 percent super-tax – the highest rate anywhere in the world, which by the government's own figures <u>will raise</u> (£160) ستوفر million next year – is likely to cause a <u>stir</u> عدم ارتياح in Downing Street. In June, David Cameron promised to "roll out the red carpet and welcome more French businesses to Britain" if the tax hike went ahead. The comments sparked a furious reaction in France.

Mr Hollande swept to power on an anti-austerity and pro-growth ticket but his approval rating has plummeted (fell, tumbled) since he took office in the summer.

Finance minister Pierre Moscovici said the "unprecedented" budget was needed to cut the deficit from nearly £70 billion or 4.5 percent of national income this year to 3 percent next year. "The 3 per cent target is vital for the credibility of the country", he said.

276   *Appendix 1*

We propose the following translation:

يعتبرُ السيد أولاند اول رئيس اشتراكي لفرنسا منذ تولي الرئيس ميتران السلطة في الثمانيناتِ. وقد وضع خطة التقشف التي تبلغ قيمتها 24 مليار جنيه استرليني في أقسى ميزانيته منذ 30 عاماً وزيادة في الضرائب بنسبه 75% على كل من يكون دخله أكثر من 800000 جنيه استرليني سنوياً مما ادى الي إحباط كبار رجال الأعمال الذين يخشون هجرة أفضل رجال الأعمال الموهوبين وتدفق العمال الفرنسيين الأكثر موهبة إلى لندن.

وعلى صعيد اخر، ذكر النقاد أن هذه الخطة المالية سوف تُسببُ في هجرة رجال الأعمال والأثرياء الى خارج الوطن كما حذروا أن السيد أولاند قد تسبب في اضرار جسيمة (لا توصف) للاقتصاد كما أنهم عبروا عن قلقهم إزاء قرار فرض زيادة الضرائب البالغه 16 مليار جنيه استرليني وتخفيف النفقات الى 8 مليار جنيه استرليتي. وزعموا كذلك أن الحكومة تعرقل الاستثمار وتقتل (توقف) الابداع. ويُشكك الاقتصاديون ايضاً في قدرة (مقدرة) الحكومة على تحقيق الهدف لاسيما انه يستند على افتراض أنَّ الإقتصاد الفرنسي سينمو بنسبة 8% في عام 2013 و 2% في 2014 على الرغم من عاصفة الديون التي تمزق منطقه اليورو.

وقد أصرَّ رئيس الوزراء الفرنسي السيد جان مارك أرولت بأن هذه الميزانية هي "ميزانية تحاول إرجاع البلاد إلى وضعها الصحيح" وأضاف قائلاً : "أنها تهدف إلى استرجاع الثقة وكسر دوامة الديون التي تزداد يوماً بعد آخر (باستمرار). فالشركات الكبرى تدفع أقل من الشركات الصغرى وأحياناً لاتدفع على الإطلاق لهذا نطلب من الشركات الكبرى ان يدعموا الإقتصاد".

ومن المحتمل أن يسبب تأكيد ارتفاع الضريبة الي 75% وهوا أعلى نسبة في العالم والتي ستوفر حسب أرقام الحكومة 160 مليون جنيه استرليني العام القادم سيسبب عدم ارتياح لدى الحكومة البريطانية.

ومن جانبه (وعلى صعيدٍ آخر) وعدَ ديفيد كاميرون في شهر يونيو "ببسط السجادة الحمراء والترحيب بالمزيد من الشركات الفرنسية إلى بريطانيا إذا ما تمَّ تبني ارتفاع الضرائب."

37. Provide a translation for the following ST. Consider the Arabic conjunctions and whether they are required in the English translation:

(ومن الجديرُ بالذِكر ، ومن جانبها):

وصفَ مُستشارُ الأمن القومي الأميركي جون بولتون، اليوم، توقيف ناقلة نفط إيرانية يُشتبه بأنها تنقل نفطاً خاماً إلى سوريا قبالة جبل طارق، بـ"النبأ الممتاز".

ومن الجدير بالذِكر أنَّ (ويُجدرُ أنَّ) بريطانيا اعترضت ناقلة النفط العملاقة غريس 1، المحمّلة بالنفط الإيراني إلَى سوريا وهذا هو انتهاك لعقوبات الاتحاد الأوروبي.

ومن جانبها استدعت إيران الخميس سفير بريطانيا في طهران تعبيراً عن استيائها من توقيف الناقلة التي ترفع علم بنما. (صحيفة الشرق الأوسط، 4 يوليو (تموز) 2019)

We suggest the following translation. For in-class translation training, discuss what has taken place during the translation process.

US National Security Adviser John Bolton described as brilliant the news of the seizure (interception) of an Iranian oil supertanker suspected of carrying crude oil to Syria off-shore Gibraltar.

Britain has intercepted the giant oil tanker Grace 1, loaded with Iranian oil to Syria and this is a violation of EU sanctions.

Appendix 1 277

Iran on Thursday summoned Britain's ambassador to Tehran to express its displeasure at the (interception) seizure of the supertanker carrying the Panama flag.

38. Provide a translation for the following ST:

The language of smell

Many animals produce chemicals called pheromones which send "smell messages" to other animals of the same species. These odors have different meanings. One odor attracts a mate. Another sends a warning. Another marks a territory. A honeybee, for example, makes over thirty-six different pheromones to communicate such information as where to find good flowers. An ant that has found food will take a bit of it and then head back "home" to the anthill. As it carries the food, it wipes its stomach on the ground. This leaves a chemical trail or path so that other ants will know where to go for more food. Recent research in animal communication focuses on how animals communicate and how some of these communication patterns are similar to those of humans. Scientists have wondered if animals actually have language. It seems clear to anyone who has a dog or cat or who closely observes animals that there is certainly communication going on. But how do animals communicate? What do they say? And is it truly language? Recent research into everything from ants to chimpanzees is shedding light on animal communication. Benjamin Lee Whorf, an American linguist (1897–1914) says: "Language shapes the way we think and determines what we can think about".

We suggest the following translation. For in-class translation training, discuss what has taken place during the translation process.

لغة الروائح

تفرزُ العديدُ من الحيوانات مواد كيماويةً تُسمى بالفيرومونز التي ترسل رسائل على شكل روائح إلى حيوانات أخرى من نفس جنسها (فصيلتها) وهذه الروائح لها معانٍ مختلفة إذ أن رائحة واحده تَجذِبُ صديقاً ما وأخرى تُرسل تهديداً وأخرى تُحدد بها أرضها ، فالنحلة مثلاً تُفرز أكثر من 36 نوعاً مختلفاً من مادة الفيرومون لنقل معلومات تتعلق بأنواع جيدة للزهور ، أما النملة التي وجدت طعاماً فتأخذ منه قطعة ثم تتجهُ به إلى منزلها. وتقوم النملة بمسح معدتها على الأرض بينما تقوم بنقل الطعام، وهذا يترك اثراً كيماوياً أو مساراً بحيث تتعرف النملات الأخريات على مكان الطعام. وتركز الأبحاث في مجال اتصالات الحيوان على كيفية أتصال الحيوانات وعلى كيفية أنَّ بعض أنماط الأتصال مُشابه لأنماط أتصال التفاهم عند البشر. وقد تسائل العلماء ما إذا كان للحيوانات لغة ويبدو واضحاً لأي شخص لديه قطة أو كلب أو يراقب عن كثب الحيوانات أنَّ هناك أتصالاً مستمراً لكن يا تُرى كيف تتواصل الحيوانات؟ وعن ماذا تتحدث؟ وهل هذه لغه فعلاً؟ وتُسلط البحوث الحديثة التي أجريت على كلِّ شيءٍ من النمل إلى الشمبانزي الأضواء على اتصال الحيوانات. ويقول العالم اللغوي الأمريكي بنجمين لي وورف (1897–1914) "أنَّ اللغة تشكل طريقة تفكيرنا وتحدد ما نفكر به."

39. Provide a translation for the following ST:

Side-effects

Some antibiotics are not prescribed as widely as they used to be because of serious side-effects. For example, tetracycline has been found to discolour children's teeth and affect growing bones. Another kind of side-effects of antibiotics is that while combating one infection, they can also make you vulnerable to others. Antibiotics attack all the

278   *Appendix 1*

bacteria in your body. But some of these bacteria are useful to you, helping to maintain a balance of micro-organisms like yeast and fungi in your body. Antibiotics can upset this balance, leading to an overgrowth of certain groups of micro-organisms, and leaving the body vulnerable to infections like thrush. Some antibiotics side-effects are allergic reactions. One of the more common signs of an allergic reaction is a rash – although this could also be an ordinary, non-allergic side-effect of the drug. Other signs include fever, joint pain, and difficulty in breathing. You should consult your doctor if you suspect you are having an allergic reaction.

We suggest the following translation. For in-class translation training, discuss what has taken place during the translation process.

الأعراضُ الجانبية

لم تعد تُوصف (تُعطى) بعض المضادات الحيوية بكثرة كما كان سابقاً وذلك بسبب الأعراض الجانبية الخطيرة. فلقد وُجد مثلاً أنّ التتراسايكلين يُغير لون أسنان الأطفال ويؤثر على نمو عظامهم. وهناك نوع آخر من الأعراض الجانبية للمضادات الحيوية وهو أنه أثناء مقاومتها لحالة مرضية فهي تعمل على جعل المريض معرّضاً لحالة مرضية أخرى. بيد أنّ بعض هذه البكتريا مفيدة للإنسان إذ تساعد على المحافظة على توازن الكائنات العضوية الدقيقة كالخميرة والفطريات في جسم الأنسان. إلاّ أنّ هذه المضادات الحيوية بإمكانها أن تخل بهذا التوازن مما يؤدي الى إفراط في نمو بعض الكائنات العضوية الدقيقة ، تاركة الجسم مُعرّضاً لبعض الأمراض كالتهابات الفم والحلق عند الأطفال. وبعض الأعراض الجانبية للمضادات الحيوية هي الحساسية. ومن علاماتها المشهورة (المعروفة) هي البهق (الطفح الجلدي) ولو أنّ ذلك قد يكون عرضاً جانبياً اعتيادياً للدواء لاعلاقة له بالحساسية. وهناك علامات أخرى مثل الحُمى وآلام المفاصل وصعوبة التنفس وعليك مراجعة الطبيب إذا شعرت بالحساسية.

40. Provide a translation for the following ST:

Lifeline screening

* Normal artery allows blood to flow through easily.
* As you age, arteries can become narrower or partially blocked.
* Plaque build-up reduces your blood flow and could be dangerous if left untreated.

Your doctor can actually see inside your arteries. Now it is possible with a simple ultrasound screening that can reveal dangerous plaque build-up or blockage. Plaque build-up can lead to stroke, aneurysm and vascular disease. In little over ten minutes, one of our scans can help determine your risks for cardiovascular disease, the UK's number one killer. As you age, fatty deposits known as plaque can build-up in your arteries however you may not notice any symptoms. This could be a sign of underlying risks, often referred to by doctors as "silent killers" because you are not aware until it's too late. While checkups with your doctor are valuable, it is a fact that ultrasound is a superior and more accurate approach to screening potential victims of aortic aneurysms and can visualize the build-up of deposits that can trigger a stroke.

We suggest the following translation. For in-class translation training, discuss what has taken place during the translation process.

Appendix 1 279

الفحصُ بالموجات فوق الصوتية حبل سلامتك

يسمحُ الشريان الإعتيادي للدم بالتدفق (بالجريان/بالسيلان) بسهولة. ومع تقدمك في السن (وبمرور الزمن) فإنه من المحتمل أن تصبح الشرايين ضيقة أو أن تنسد جزئيا. إنّ تراكم (استفحال/تكدس) الترسبات يقلل من تدفق الدم وقد يكون خطيراً إذا لم يتم معالجته. وباستطاعة الطبيب أن ينظر في داخل شرايينك حيث أنه من الممكن اليوم أن نكتشف تراكم الترسبات أو الإنسداد بواسطة الفحص بالموجات فوق الصوتية. وقد يؤدي تراكم الترسبات الى السكتة الدماغية أو تمدد الأوعية الدموية أو أمراض الأوعية الدموية. وبأقل من 10 دقائق ، تتمكن أحد الفحوصات بالأشعة فوق الصوتية أن تُحدد (تحديد) مخاطر اصابتك (تعرضك ل) بأمراض القلب والأوعية الدموية ، وهو المرض الفتاك (القاتل) رقم واحد في بريطانيا. ومع تقدمك في السن، تتراكم الترسبات (التراكمات الدهنية المعروفة بالترسبات) في شرايينك (ولكن) دون أن تشعر (تلاحظ) بأية أعراض. وهذه تمثّل (تكون بمثابة) علامة (ناقوس خطر ، دليل) لمخاطر كامنة يشير اليها الأطباء بمصطلح "القاتل الصامت"، لأنك لم تكن على علم حتى فوات الأوان. ولو أنّ الفحوصات مع الطبيب مهمة جداً إلاّ أنّ الحقيقة هي أنّ الموجات فوق الصوتية هي طريقة متفوقة وأكثر دقة في فحص المرضى المحتملين بتمدد الأوعية الدموية الأبهرية وبإمكانها رؤية تراكم الرواسب التي يمكن أن تؤدي الى السكتة الدماغية.

41. Provide a translation for the following ST:

Inflated by his wondrous success in Spain, Musa Ibn Nusair planned a magnificent campaign, which, had he carried it out, would have given quite a different phase to subsequent European history. He was determined to make his way back to Damascus by way of Constantinople, thus possessing himself of Europe from the West to the East, surrounding the Mediterranean with a connected series of Muslim allies, and arranging the entire ancient world under the standard of the Prophet (peace and blessings and peace be upon him). But just as this grand idea had been conceived, Al-Walid Ibn Abdul Malik sent an order recalling both Tariq Ibn Ziyad and Musa Ibn Nusair.

We suggest the following translation. For in-class translation training, discuss what has taken place during the translation process:

نتيجةً للنجاح الرائع الذي أحرزهُ في أسبانيا، فقد خطط موسى ابن نصير لحملة رائعة التي لو تمكن من تنفيذها لأعطت لأعطت التأريخ الأوربي فيما بعد صفحة مختلفة تماماً. إذ قرر موسى أبن نصير أن يشق طريقه عائداً الى دمشق عن طريق القسطنطينية وبهذا يكون قد سيطر على أوربا من الغرب الى الشرق وكذلك يكون قد طوّق البحر المتوسط بسلسلة متصلة من الحلفاء المسلمين ويكون أيضا قد أخضع العالم القديم برمته تحت راية سنة النبي صلى الله عليه وسلم. لكن حالما اختمرت هذه الفكرة الرائعة في باله، أرسل الوليد أبن عبد الملك أمراً يستدعي فيه كل من طارق أبن زياد وموسى أبن نصير.

42. Provide a translation for the following ST:

The great French philosopher, Voltaire, wrote the following to Mr de Sideville – 1733.

For the last five days, my dear friend, I have been dangerously ill; I had not the strength either to think or write. I have just received your letter and the first part of your "Allegory". In the name of God, do not go beyond your first subject, do not smother it under a mass of foreign flowers; let your meaning be clearly seen; too much brilliance often detracts from clearness. If I might venture to give you a word of advice it would be this: "Make simplicity your object, order your work in a manner perfectly clear,

280   *Appendix 1*

which demands no strained attention from the mind of your reader. Don't attempt to be brilliant, but paint with the brush of truth and your work will be delightful. Go straight to your point without saying more than necessary. You will still be more brilliant than others, even after you have removed what is superfluous. Good-bye, I am too ill to write more".

We suggest the following translation. For in-class translation training, discuss what has taken place during the translation process.

كتب الفيلسوف الفرنسي العظيم فولتير ما يلي للسيد دي سيدفيل في عام 1733:

صديقي العزيز، طيلة الأيام الخمس الماضية كانت صحتي سيئة لدرجة خطيرة بحيث لم أمتلك القوة على الأكل أو الشرب. وقد استلمت رسالتك تواً والجزء الأول من كتابك (المجاز). فبسم الله انصحك بعدم تخطي موضوعك الأول، ولا تكتم أنفاسه بكثير من الأوراد، وأجعل معانيك واضحة تماماً، لأن كثرة البريق يُفسد الوضوح. وإذا تجرأت بتقديم النصيحة لك، فأود أن أقول لك: "اجعل البساطة هدفك، واجعل عملك واضحاً تمام الوضوح بحيث لا يتطلب جهدا كبيرا لفهمه من قبل قراءك، ولا تحاول أبدا أن تكون نجما لامعاً، بل اكتب بقلم الحقيقة وسيكون عملك ممتعاً. وعليك أن تخوض في صلب الموضوع فوراً دون القول بأكثر مما هو ضروري. بل وسيكون نجمك لامعاً أكثر من الآخرين عندما تتخلص من كل ما هو زائد عن الحاجة. مع السلامة، فأني مريض جدا بحيث لا أتمكن من الكتابة أكثر من ذلك.

43. Provide a translation for the following ST:

All around the world, there are international students at institutions of higher education. International students leave their home countries and go to university abroad. Probably, the country with the most students from abroad is the United States. Canada, Great Britain, and some other European countries also have a lot of students from other countries. Often, undergraduates want the experience of life in new cultures. May be they want to learn another language well. Many students want degrees in business, engineering, or technology. These subjects are not always available in their home countries. Some governments and companies send their best graduate students and workers to other countries for new knowledge and skills. And some international students from expensive private schools at home save money through study abroad programs, especially in developing nations. Students from other countries and cultures bring internationalism to the classroom and campus. They bring different languages, customs, ideas, and opinions from many places. Also, educational institutions need money. Tuition is the fee or charge for instruction. Private universities are not supported by government money. They charge high tuition. International students are not citizens or immigrants. All students away from home have to spend money for housing, food, recreation, and other things. For these reasons, many universities want students from other countries.

We suggest the following translation. For in-class translation training, discuss what has taken place during the translation process.

يوجد في جميع أنحاء العالم طلاب أجانب يدرسون في مؤسسات التعليم العالي. حيث يغادر الطلاب الأجانب بلدانهم ليلتحقوا بالجامعات في الخارج (الأجنبية). ومن المحتمل (ومن المرجح) أن تكون الولايات المتحدة الأمريكية الدولة الأكثر استقبالا (استقطابًا) للطلاب الأجانب يليها كندا وبريطانيا وبعض الدول (البلدان) الأوروبية (يليها بعض الدول (البلدان) الأوروبية أبرزها كندا وبريطانيا). فغالبًا

Appendix 1   281

ما يطمح (يود) الطلبة الجامعيون لاكتساب خبرة حياتية في ثقافات جديدة وربما يودون إتقان لغة أجنبية جديدة. بيد أن (لكن) العديد منهم يرغبون في الحصول على شهادات في الأعمال والهندسة أو التقنية (الصناعة) لأن هذه (حيث أنّ هذه) التخصصات غير متاحة (متوفرة) في بلدانهم. وترسل بعض الحكومات والشركات أفضل خريجيها وعمالها إلى بلدان أخرى لاكتساب المعرفة الجديدة والمهارات. ويوفر (يُدخر) بعض الطلبة الأجانب من المدارس الخاصة باهظة التكاليف في بلدانهم أموالاً عن طريق برامج الدراسة في الخارج خصوصاً في البلدان النامية. وغالباً ما يجلب الطلاب القادمين من بلدان وثقافات أخرى تعددية الجنسيات وعادات وأفكار وآراء ولغات مختلفة إلى قاعة المحاضرات (الصف) وإلى (و) الحرم الجامعي. وتحتاج المؤسسات التربوية إلى المال، فرسوم الدراسة تُمثل تكلفة التعليم لأن الجامعات الخاصة لا تتلقى دعماً مالياً من الحكومة ولهذا تفرض أجوراً دراسية عالية. ولا يعتبر الأجانب مواطنون ولا مهاجرون. ويتحتم على الطلبة الأجانب إنفاق أموالهم على الإيجار والأكل والإستجمام وبعض الأمور الأخرى، ولهذا السبب تود (ترغب) العديد من الجامعات قدوم الطلبة الأجانب إليها.

44. Provide a translation for the following ST:

Three rhino horns worth tens of thousands of pounds have been stolen تمّ سرقة from a British museum. Thieves broke into the secure storage area مخزن محكم الأغلاق at Leicester's New Walk Museum and made off هربوا with the valuable pieces القرون.

Experts fear the items القرون الثلاثة may have been taken تم سرقتها by an organised crime gang عصابة الجريمة المنظمة who plan to sell them on the black market. Rhino horns and elephant tusks can fetch tens of thousands of pounds in some Asian countries where they are used as ingredients for traditional medicines. Museum staff are unsure about when الزمن the horns were taken, but the theft is believed to have happened in the past few months. Leicestershire Police were informed وقد تم إعلام of the theft in September, when staff were sure the horns, which were kept in a storage area, had been stolen. Officers have now launched an investigation into the incident and recently arrested a 57-year-old man on suspicion of the theft. He has been released on police bail while officers continue their investigation. A city council spokesman said: "We can confirm that three rhino horns went missing اختفت from the museum stores in September".

(*The Daily Mail*, 30 November 2012)

We suggest the following translation. For in-class translation training, discuss what has taken place during the translation process.

تمّ سرقة ثلاثة قرون لحيوان وحيد القرن تقدر قيمتها بعشرات الآلاف من الجنيهات الأسترلينية من متحف بريطاني. حيث اقتحم لصوصٌ مخزناً محكم الإغلاق في متحف نيو وِلك الواقع بمحافظة ليستر وهربوا بهذه القطع الثمينة. وقد أبدى الخبراء قلقهم من أن عصابة منظمة من المجرمين قد سرقت هذه القرون والتي تنوي بيعها في السوق السوداء. ومن الممكن أن تجلب قرون وحيد القرن وأنياب الفيل عشرات الآلاف من الجنيهات الأسترلينية في بعض الدول الآسيوية حيث تستخدم كمكونات للأدوية التقليدية. ولم يكن موظفو المتحف متأكدين من تأريخ سرقة القرون ، بيد أنه يُعتقد أن السرقة قد وقعت في غضون الأشهر القليلة الماضية. وقد تم إعلام شرطة محافظة ليستر بهذه السرقة في شهر سبتمبر عندما أصبح موظفو المتحف متأكدين من أنّ هذه القرون الموضوعة في مخزن مُحكم الإغلاق قد سُرقت. ونتيجة لذلك بدأ ضباط الشرطة بالتحقيق في هذا الحادث وتمكنوا مؤخرًا باعتقال

282   *Appendix 1*

(بإلقاء القبض) على رجل يبلغ من العمر 57 عاماً بتهمة السرقة. بيد أنه تم إطلاق سراحهُ بكفالة شرطة في حين يواصل ضباط الشرطة تحرياتهم. وعلى صعيد آخر ذكر متحدث باسم مجلس بلدية محافظة ليستر: "بإمكاننا أن نؤكد من أنّ ثلاثة قرون لحيوان وحيد القرن قد اختفت (فُقدت) (سُرقت) من مخازن المتحف في شهر سبتمبر (أيلول).

Note: For lexical cohesion, we find the ST employs different expressions having the same meaning, such as "horns, pieces, items", which all mean قرون, and "taken, stolen", which both mean تم سرقتُها.

45. Provide a translation for the following ST:

How can a teacher make use of the internet in teaching and training?

Every one of us needs to invest in the internet and should be able to employ it effectively in our work. The answer to the question above is as big as the Net itself. Here is a brief reference to some of the benefits of the Net:

1. Vocabulary: The internet can be employed as a useful resource for checking the meaning and contextual usage of words. For instance, if a teacher plans to teach the word (housing), he can select different websites that can provide an insight into the various semantic aspects of this word as well as the different types of housing used by different nations in different places worldwide. The website also provides illustrations of different housing, such as the housing of the Eskimos, of people living in towns, villages, or in the desert. This method of teaching will encourage students to visit different websites searching for meanings of words. Thus, it will enable students to learn new vocabulary.

2. Online language games: These are another source of improving language skills. Language games can be played individually or with someone in any part of the world. They provide useful information about grammar, such as the imperative, conditional, and passive voice grammatical structures. There are also useful websites for reading, writing, and listening language skills.

We suggest the following translation. For in-class translation training, discuss what has taken place during the translation process.

كيف يستطيع المُعلم الإستفادة من الإنترنت في التدريس والتدريب

يحتاج كلُ واحدٍ منا أن يستثمر في الإنترنت وأن يكون قادراً على استخدامه بشكل فعال في عمله. والجواب على السؤال أعلاه كبير كحجم الإنترنت نفسه، وفيما يلي معلومات موجزة لبعض فوائد الإنترنت:

1ـ المُفردات: يمكن تسخير الانترنت كمصدر (كمرجع) مفيد للتأكد من معاني الكلمات واستخدامها السياقي. فمثلا إذا أراد معلم أن يدرّس كلمة (إسكان أو سكن) فبإمكانه اختيار مواقع إلكترونية مختلفة تؤمن له معلومات دقيقة عن الخواص الدلالية المختلفة لهذه الكلمة والأنواع المختلفة للإسكان الذي تستخدمه شعوب مختلفة حول العالم. كما يوفر لك الموقع الإلكتروني صوراً توضيحية عن أنواع سكن مختلفة مثل سكن الأسكيمو وسكن القاطنين في المدن والقرى والصحراء. وتشجع طريقة التدريس هذه الطلاب على زيارة مواقع إلكترونية مختلفة بحثاً عن معاني الكلمات. وبهذا تمكنهم من تعلم مُفردات جديدة.

2ـ ألعاب لغة عن طريق الإنترنت: تُعتبر هذه مصدراً آخر من مصادر تحسين مهارات اللغة. وبإمكان المتعلم (الفرد) أن يلعب ألعاب اللغة لوحده أو مع شخص آخر في أي مكان في العالم. وتوفر هذه

Appendix 1 283

الألعاب معلومات مفيدة عن القواعد (النحو) كالجملة الأمرية والشرطية والمبني للمجهول ، وهناك أيضًا مواقع إلكترونية مفيدة عن مهارات القراءة والكتابة والإستماع.

46. Provide a translation for the following ST:

The Greedy Man and the Shrewd Millionaire

John Wilson was a rich man but very greedy. When he was riding home through the forest, he thought of a plan: "I will give the millionaire my best stallion, then he will give me a better and bigger house with a massive garden".

When he got home, he cooked himself a simple meal, had his coffee, and read the business news in the newspaper looking for shares and properties to buy. He was preoccupied by his silly thought and his mind was dominated by his greediness. He went to bed late but could not fall to sleep. As soon as he woke up the next day, he went to see a shrewd millionaire called Mr Peter Dennison who lived in a big palace on the outskirt of town. He asked the guard whether he could see Mr Peter Dennison. The guard immediately took him to the millionaire. Mr Wilson said: "I have the best horses in the land and you must have the best of my horses. This horse is big and wonderful. It's yours. Please accept it as a gift".

The shrewd millionaire knew the greedy man was not honest. Mr Dennison wanted to play a trick with the greedy man. He accepted the offer and said: "That bushel of potatoes is the best and most expensive in the land. Take it. It's my gift to you".

What could the greedy man do? He had no choice in this awkward situation he had put himself in. He had brought trouble to himself. The millionaire took the horse from the greedy man, and the latter carried the heavy bushel of potatoes and left sadly while the millionaire was laughing.

We suggest the following translation. For in-class translation training, discuss what has taken place during the translation process.

الرجلُ الطمَّاعُ والمليونير الداهية

كان جون ويلسون رجلاً غنياً لكنه شديدُ الطمع. وبينما كان مُمتطياً حصانه عائداً إلى منزله عبر الغابة خطرت في باله فكرة : "سوف أعطي المليونير أفضل خيولي وعندها سيعطيني بيتًا أكبر وأفضل ذو حديقة شاسعة". وعندما وصل منزله طبخ لنفسه وجبة خفيفة وشرب قهوته وقرأ الأخبار الاقتصادية في الصحيفة باحثًا عن أسهم وعقارات لشرائها. بيد أنه لا زال (لكنه كان) مشغول البال (شارد البال) بفكرته التافهة (الساذجة) والجشع مهيمنًا على ذهنه. وذهب إلى فراشه متأخرًا لكنه لم يستطع النوم وبمجرد أن (وحالما) (وعندما) استيقظ في اليوم التالي ذهب لمقابلة مليونير ذكي يُدعى بيتر دينيسون الذي يعيش في قصر كبير في ضواحي المدينة. وطلب من الحارس أن يقابل (مقابلة) السيد بيتر دينيسون ، فأخذه الحارس إلى المليونير. وحينها قال جون ويلسون : "لديّ أفضل الخيول في هذه البلاد ويجب (ويجدر بك) أن تحظى بأفضلها. وهذا الحصان ضخم ورائع ، فهو لك. وأرجوا أن تقبله كهدية". بيد أن المليونير بيتر دينيسون أدرك بأن الرجل الطماع كان كاذبًا (لم يكن صادقًا) ولهذا أراد أن يختبره ، فقبل الهدية وقال : "إنّ هذا الكوم من البطاطس هو الأفضل والأغلى في هذه البلاد فخذه (إنه) هدية لك". وما كان بوسع الرجل الجشع أن يعمل شيئًا؟ فلم يكن أمامه أي خيار في هذا الوضع الحرج الذي وضع نفسه فيه. فقد جلب لنفسه (هذه) المتاعب. حيث أخذ المليونير الحصان منه وأخذ هو بدوره كوم البطاطس الثقيل وغادر المكان حزينًا بينما كان يضحك المليونير.

284   *Appendix 1*

47. Provide a translation for the following ST:

قياس مستوى جودة الأداء للخدمات المقدمة للحُجاج وزوار المدينة المنورة

تمهيد:

شهدت المدينة المنورة ولا تزال، تغيرات هائلة تمثلت في تطوير المواقع الدينية، التاريخية والتجارية، ونجد بأن المنطقة المركزية المحيطة بالمسجد النبوي الشريف قد أصبحت رمزا حضاريا، كل ذلك جعل من شد الرحال للصلاة في المسجد النبوي الشريف وزيارة المواقع الدينية والتاريخية بالمدينة المنورة وجهة ومقصد لملايين المسلمين من أقطار المعمورة لطلب الراحة النفسية والطمأنينة لتتعايش وعبق تاريخ التراث الإسلامي.

وللحاجة الماسة التي رصدتها فرق التنسيق والمتابعة الميدانية التابعة للجنة الحج بالمدينة المنورة لتطوير الخدمات المقدمة في أماكن الزيارة الدينية والسياحية بالمدينة المنورة، يقوم فريق بحثي من جامعة طيبة وبالتعاون مع إمارة المدينة المنورة بدراسة آراء المستفيدين من الحجاج والزوار لأماكن الزيارة الدينية والسياحية بالمدينة المنورة. ويعتبر هذا الاستبيان الأداة الرئيسة لجمع البيانات حول هذه الدراسة.

نشكر لكم تعاونكم في تطوير الخدمات المقدمة لكم في مدينة رسول الله (صلى الله عليه وسلم)

We suggest the following translation. For in-class translation training, discuss what has taken place during the translation process.

> Measuring quality performance of the services provided to pilgrims and visitors to Al-Madinah
>
> Preface:
>
> Al-Madinah has been witnessing significant changes in the development of religious, historical, and commercial sites. The central area surrounding the mosque of the Prophet Mohammad (*peace be upon him*) has become a symbol of civilization. Every year, millions of pilgrims and visitors come to Madinah, pray in the Prophet's Mosque, visiting religious and historical sites, and seek psychological comfort, peace and tranquility in this blessed city which is the symbol of Islamic heritage.
>
> Follow-up field and coordination teams of the Hajj Committee in Al-Madinah have diagnosed some urgent needs for the development of services provided in the religious and tourist sites. Based on these needs, a research team from Taibah University in Al-Madinah, in cooperation with the Emirate of Al-Madinah, has carried out this field study entitled "Measuring the performance quality of the services provided to pilgrims and visitors to Al-Madinah".
>
> The attached questionnaire is a tool for collecting the required data for this study.
>
> Thank you for your cooperation in filling out the questionnaire. The information provided will be used for research purposes only.

48. Provide a translation for the following ST:

داعش وأردوغان يستغلان مجزرة المسجدين.

- ونيوزيلندا تحذر من خطورة تسييس الهجوم

افتتح البرلمان النيوزيلندى جلساته أمس بتلاوة آيات من القرآن الكريم؛ وذلك تكريما لضحايا الحادث الإرهابى الذى وقع الجمعة الماضى فى كرايست تشيرش، وأسفر عن مقتل 51 مصليا على يد إرهابى من اليمين المتطرف.

Appendix 1   285

ووقف جميع أعضاء البرلمان، خلال قراءة القرآن داخل القاعة، وأثنت جاسيندا أرديرن رئيسة وزراء نيوزيلندا، التي اتشحت بالسواد، على شجاعة وجسارة المصلين الذين كانوا فى مسجدي كرايست تشيرش، قائلة إن البلاد تقف إلى جانب الجالية المسلمة المكلومة في أحلك الأيام. (*الأهرام المصرية* ، 20 مارس 2019)

We suggest the following translation. For in-class translation training, discuss what has taken place during the translation process.

> ISIS and Erdogan exploit the mosques' massacre
> New Zealand warns of politicization of attack (atrocity)
> The New Zealand parliament opened its sessions yesterday by reciting verses from the Qur'an in honor of the victims of last Friday's terrorist attack in Christ Church that killed 51 worshipers at the hands of a far-right terrorist.
> All parliamentarians stood while the Qur'an was recited. New Zealand Prime Minister Jacinda Ardern, who was dressed in black, praised the courage and boldness of the worshipers who were in Christ Church's mosques, saying the country stood with the grieving Muslim community in the darkest days.

49. Provide a translation for the following ST:

الشروط والاحكام للدخول في السحب:

1 لا يُشترط الشراء للاشتراك في المسابقة والدخول في السحب.
2 الاجابة على السؤال بطريقة صحيحة وكتابة الاسم الثلاثي ورقم الجوال بخط واضح.
3 التأكد من تسجيل بياناتك بطريقة صحيحة حيث سيتم إلغاء الجائزة وإعادة السحب في حالة الاختلاف بين البيانات المسجلة والوثائق الرسمية.
4 سيتم السحب اسبوعيا بمشاركة الغرفة التجارية على الجوائز التالية:

‒ سيارات هوندا عدد 2
‒ جوالات آيفون 7 / 32 جيجا عدد 4
‒ آيباد 2 / 64 جيجا عدد 4
‒ بلاي ستيشن فور / 1 تيرابايت عدد 4
‒ شاشات سامسونغ يو أتش سمارت 66 أتش عدد 4
‒ بطاقات كارفور الشرائية بقيمة 100 ريال عدد 40

5 في حال تكرار الفوز تعتمد الجائزة الاولى فقط ويعاد السحب.
6 سيتم تسليم السيارات في معارض هوندا ‒ عبدالله هاشم بتأريخ 30 نوفمبر 2019
7 لون السيارة حسب ما هو متوفر في معارض هوندا ‒ شركة عبدالله هاشم المحدودة.
8 لا يحق لأي من موظفي كارفور أو لأحد من أقاربهم المشاركة في المسابقة وفي حال الفوز سيتم إلغاء الجائزة وإعادة السحب.

رقم تصريح الغرفة التجارية: 3807

We suggest the following translation. For in-class translation training, discuss what has taken place during the translation process.

> Terms (Rules) and Conditions (Regulations) of Entering the Draw:

286   *Appendix 1*

1. No purchase necessary to participate in the competition and enter the prize draw.

2. Answer the question correctly and clearly write your full name and contact number.

3. Ensure that the information you provide matches your formal ID. In the event of any discrepancy, the winner will be denied and the draw will be repeated.

4. The draw will be held weekly in coordination with the Chamber of Commerce for the following prizes:

– 2 Honda cars
– 4 Apple iPhones 7/32GB
– 4 Sony PlayStations 4/1TB
– 4 Samsung UHD Smart 55" televisions
– 40 Carrefour Gift Cards worth SAR1000–00

5. In the event a participant wins more than once, only the first prize will be counted, and the draw will be repeated.

6. Cars should be collected from Honda – Abdullah Hashim Company Ltd – on 30 November 2019.

7. Car colour is subject to availability.

8. Carrefour employees and their immediate relatives are not eligible to participate in the competition. Should any such individuals win, the prize will be revoked and the draw will be repeated.

(CoC: 3807)

50. Provide a translation for the following ST:

غسيل أو تبييض الأموال جريمة اقتصادية تهدف إلى إضفاء شرعية قانونية على أموال مُحرمة، لغرض حيازتها أو التصرف فيها أو إدارتها أو حفظها أو استبدالها أو إيداعها أو استثمارها أو تحويلها أو نقلها أو التلاعب في قيمتها إذا كانت متحصلة من جرائم مثل زراعة وتصنيع النباتات المخدرة أو الجواهر والمواد المخدرة وجلبها وتصديرها والاتجار بها.

We suggest the following translation. For in-class translation training, discuss what has taken place during the translation process.

Money laundering is an economic crime aimed at legitimizing illicit funds for the purpose of possession, disposal, management, preservation, replacement, deposit, investment, transfer to another place, exchange to another currency, or manipulation of its value if it is gained (obtained, derived) from offenses such as the cultivation and manufacture of narcotic plants, jewelry, or narcotics, and importing, exporting, and trafficking them.

51. Provide a translation for the following ST:

حاولت زوارقُ حربية إيرانية الأربعاء احتجاز ناقلة نفط بريطانية أثناء إبحارها في مياه الخليج لكنّ فرقاطة تابعة للبحرية الملكية البريطانية تصدّت لها ومنعتها من ذلك، بحسب ما أفادت شبكة "سي إن إن" الإخبارية الأميركية. ونقلت الشبكة عن مسؤولَين في الإدارة الأميركية لم تذكر اسميهما قولهما إنّ الإيرانيين أسروا ناقلة النفط البريطانية "بريتش هيريتدج"، التي كانت تبحر في مضيق هرمز، بتغيير مسارها للتوقف في المياه الإيرانية القريبة. وأوضحت "سي أن أن" أن الواقعة التي صوّرتها طائرة أميركية، انتهت عندما قامت الفرقاطة البريطانية "إتش إم إس مونتروز" – التي كانت ترافق الناقلة – بتوجيه أسلحتها إلى الزوارق الإيرانية فأجبرتها على المغادرة. (*صحيفة الرياض*، 11 يوليو (تموز) 2019).

Appendix 1   287

We suggest the following translation. For in-class translation training, discuss what has taken place during the translation process.

> Iranian gunboats tried on Wednesday to detain (seize) a British oil tanker whilst sailing in the Gulf, but a frigate belonging to the British Royal Navy intercepted and prevented it from doing so, CNN reported.
>
> CNN reported unnamed administration officials as saying: "The Iranians ordered the British tanker British Heritage, which was sailing in the Strait of Hormuz, to change course to stop in nearby Iranian waters".
>
> The incident, which was filmed by an American aircraft, ended when the British frigate "HMS Montrose" – which was accompanying the tanker – directed its weapons to (trained its guns on) the Iranian boats and forced them to leave.

(Al-Riyadh, 11 July 2019)

52. Provide a translation for the following ST:

استغل أحد المواطنين والغريب عن المنطقة فرصة إقامة الصلاة في احد مساجد كفرسوم في لواء بني كنانه للقيام بسرقة المصلين بطرق احتيالية جديدة لا تخطر على بال أحدٍ ، وأنه لاذ بالفرار من مكان الحادثة لجهة غير معلومة. وتشير التفاصيل وفق شهود عيان إلى أنَّ هذا الشخص وبعد إقامة الصلاة ادعى بأنه قد ألمَّ به مرضٌ وجرى له مكروه عارض، وقام بطلب طبيب كي يقوم على علاجه من هذه الحالة التي أصابته. فقام أحد الحضور الذي لم يتم ذكر اسمه، ومعه عدد من المصلين لإنقاذه. وقد ذكر الشهود بأنه وبعد لحظة ادعى ذات الشخص بأن اموره الصحية قد تحسنت، وقام بمغادرة المكان لوجهة غير معروفة إلاّ أنَّ المفاجأة كانت حينما اكتشفوا بان المشهد التمثيلي الذي كان جيد الإخراج والتمثيل كان عبارة عن عملية سرقة لهم حيث تبين بأن الشخص قد سرق أربعة أشخاص دون معرفة منهم أو دراية. ومن الجدير بالذكر أنَّ أحد أئمة المساجد في المنطقة قد أعلن عن سرقة المسجد الذي يؤم فيه وقد تعرض في وقت سابق للسرقة مرتين وطالبَ بإيجاد حلول سريعة وفاعلة لهذه المشكلة.
(*صحيفة الدستور الأردنية*، 20 يوليو (تموز) 2019)

We suggest the following translation. For in-class translation training, discuss what has taken place during the translation process.

> A Jordanian citizen who is an outsider of the region has taken advantage of prayer opportunities at a mosque in Kufrsum in the Bani Kananah area by stealing from the worshipers in previously unheard of new and fraudulent ways. He escaped from the scene to an unknown destination.
>
> According to eyewitnesses, after praying at the mosque, the man claimed that he was suffering from an illness and had had an adverse reaction. He asked for a doctor to treat him for his condition. An unnamed attendant, along with a number of worshipers, tended to him.
>
> The eyewitnesses said that after a moment, the man claimed that he felt better before leaving to an unknown destination. However, the surprise came when the mosque-goers discovered that the incident had been a well-acted theft they were victims of. It turned out that the man had stolen items from four other people without them knowing or realizing.
>
> An imam of a mosque in the area has warned about thefts in the mosque he is in charge of and that he had been previously pickpocketed twice, and demanded a quick and an effective solution to this problem.

288   *Appendix 1*

53. As a translation exercise for in-class discussion: (i) Discuss the translation of the headline, (ii) What translation approach is adopted? (iii) Discuss the semantic, syntactic, stylistic, and cultural problems. Discuss the suggested translation of the headline and the sub-headlines.

Criminal who stole neighbour's flooring before relaying it in own home is jailed for a year

السجن لمدة عام لمجرم سرق سجادة جاره وفرشها في منزله

- Robber took (£726) سرق carpet 726 جنيه استرليني سجادة قيمتها from neighbour's house and had accomplice re-fit it in his home
- Shaine Preston stole the entire carpet and underlay from his neighbour's conservatory غرفة زجاجية
- Ipswich Crown Court jails 26-year-old Shaine Preston for 12 months
- Accomplice لم تتم محاكمة شريكه في الجريمة الذي ساعده في فرش السجادة who helped re-lay carpet not prosecuted

A burglar was jailed yesterday after he stole a neighbour's carpet and re-laid it in his home five doors away على بُعد خمسة بيوت. Shaine Preston, 26 البالغ من العمر 26 عاماً, was arrested after DNA was found on a glove he left behind at the bungalow بيت من طابق واحد. The carpet – worth £726 – and underlay in the conservatory had been pulled up and stolen, along with a television, a remote control and other items أشياء. The remote alone cost almost £194 to replace, the prosecution المحكمة/القضاء said. Jobless Preston, of Carlton Colville near Lowestoft, Suffolk, was jailed for 12 months at Ipswich Crown Court after he admitted burglary. He has 13 aliases هوية مزيفة and a string of سلسلة من convictions for dishonesty إدانات سابقة بالغش والأحتيال. The family were away إجازة when Preston broke in just before 9pm on June 18. A neighbour heard a suspicious noise ضوضاء غير اعتيادي at the home and contacted the owner, who alerted police. A bathroom window had been smashed, apparently with a brick which was lying in the bath, police said وقد ذكرت الشرطة بأنّ الأسرة كانت في إجازة . . . . Preston claimed he was asked to "move an old carpet" and named another man – not prosecuted – as an accomplice شريك في الجريمة وقد. The court heard that استمعت المحكمة الى أنّ the other man had laid the carpet on the stairs and landing منطقة أعلى السلم في الدور الأول of Preston's home, while the burglar himself dumped تخلص the TV in a field. Andrew Thompson, defending, said Preston had been drinking on the night he was asked to help. He was approached by an acquaintance صديق he knew moderately well يعرفه جيداً لحد ما who indicated he needed help to move property from a building. The defendant's address and this address were fairly close. He did go and get a glove from home in order to assist his acquaintance in carrying it [the carpet] out. Judge Rupert Overbury told Preston that he had caused serious damage to the house during the raid السرقة. He said: "Breaking into other people's homes أنّ السطوَ على بيوت whether they are unoccupied or not سواءاً كانت هذه البيوت مسكونة أم غير مسكونة الناس is a serious offence جريمة against the community المجتمع. It affects other people's lives. It affected the owner's life in this case".

(*The Daily Mail*, 28 August 2013)

Appendix 1 289

   It is of value to the translation commentary to provide insight into the notion of texture in the ST and the TT. Halliday and Hasan (1976:295–297) make a distinction between two types of texture: "tight and loose texture". In "tight texture", we find dense clusters of conjunctions which serve to signal that the meanings of the parts are strongly interdependent and that the whole forms a single unity. However, in other texts, we find "loose texture" where fewer conjunctions are used – perhaps just one or two. Loose texture is a feature of subtexts. In the above ST, the subtexts are the headline (Criminal who stole neighbour's flooring before relaying it in own home is jailed for a year) and the sub-headlines (Robber took £726 carpet from neighbour's house and had accomplice re-fit it in his home; Shaine Preston stole the entire carpet and underlay from his neighbour's conservatory; Ipswich Crown Court jails 26-year-old Shaine Preston for 12 months; Accomplice who helped re-lay carpet not prosecuted).

54. Provide a commentary on the translation process of the following texts:

(i)   Israel had strongly opposed the Palestinian bid for recognition at the UN of <u>Palestine to be a non-member observer state</u> منح فلسطين صفة دولة مراقب غير عضو, saying that the tactic was a blow for peace negotiations.
(ii)   <u>Israel had secured strong and vocal</u> ضمنت اسرائيل دعماً قوياً وشفوياً <u>support</u> from the US.
(iii) Palestinian politicians reacted to the new settlement decision with <u>dismay</u> خيبة أمل.
(iv)   The <u>firm</u> US and British <u>line</u> موقف سياسي ثابت on the Israeli decision is unlikely to mark any real shift in <u>allegiances</u> الولاء لأسرائيل or policy.
(v)   President Mahmoud Abbas <u>took a step</u> اتخذ قراراً in the wrong direction this week, <u>to say the least</u> هذا أقل ما أريد أن أقوله.
(vi)   Fresh trouble أعمال شغب/مشاكل جديدة continues to <u>break out</u> يندلع in Gaza, after Hamas and Israel spent eight days <u>trading</u> يتبادل rocket and missile fire earlier this month. The <u>conflict</u> المواجهات العسكرية ended with <u>an Egyptian-brokered truce</u> هدنة بوساطة مصرية <u>but there have been repeated flare-ups since</u> بيد أنَّ المواجهات العسكرية قد تجددت عدة مرات منذ ذلك الحين منذ اعلان الهدنة. The aim was <u>to freeze settlement construction</u> تجميد بناء المستوطنات <u>under</u> بموجب the Roadmap For Peace plan in 2002 خطة خارطة الطريق من أجل السلام المبرمة في عام 2002.
(vii) Translation and context-based meaning: What is the translation of the word "contents" when it appears in (a) a book, and in (b) drink products?

55. The following text is characterized by a long noun phrase. Provide a translation and a commentary on the translation process:
   Yellow-billed hornbills live in the dry savannahs of southern Africa. They feed on <u>creepy crawlies</u> الزواحف من الحشرات, and are characterized by their large, downwardly curved yellow beaks, <u>which is why</u> ولهذا السبب they are sometimes known as "flying bananas".

56. Provide a translation for the following ST:

مؤتمر قمة الدول العشرين

وصل يوم أمس بحفظ الله ورعايته الى أرض الوطن خادم الحرمين الشريفين الملك سلمان بن عبدالعزيز قادماً من تركيا بعد اختتام أعمال مؤتمر القمة للدول العشرين. وفي مؤتمر صحفي قال

290   *Appendix 1*

سعادة السفير السعودي في تركيا بأن المملكة العربية السعودية قد أصبحت من الدول الكبرى العشرين وهذا انجاز رائع تتفرد به المملكة من بين دول المنطقة. وأضاف سعادته قائلاً بأن عضوية المملكة العربية السعودية في مجموعة الدول العشرين يمثل السياسة الحكيمة التي تنتهجها المملكة على الصعيدين الأقليمي والعالمي ويمثل التقدم الأقتصادي الذي أحرزته المملكة. وأكد سعادة السفير بأن من أولويات المملكة العربية السعودية هي مكافحة الأرهاب والتطرف اللذان يهددان أمن وسلامة المجتمع الدولي ويتنافيان وتعاليم الشريعة الأسلامية.

We suggest the following translation. For in-class translation training, discuss what has taken place during the translation process.

2015 G20 Turkey Summit

King Salman of Saudi Arabia arrived back home yesterday following the conclusion of this year's G20 summit in Antalya.

Speaking at a press conference, the Saudi Ambassador to Turkey, [NAME], said: "Saudi Arabia is now a G20 country. This is a superb achievement for the Kingdom amongst other counties in the region".

"The inclusion of the Kingdom of Saudi Arabia as a G20 country is a reflection of the wise policies adopted by the Kingdom at regional and international levels, and shows the economic progress that the Kingdom has achieved", he added.

The Saudi Ambassador also highlighted that amongst Saudi Arabia's priorities was the fight against terrorism and extremism which, he explained, threatened global peace and security, and contradicted Islamic law and teachings.

57. Provide a translation for each of the following STs:

ST: ليسَ اليتيمُ الذي قد ماتَ والدهُ بل   اليتيمُ يتيمُ العلم والأدبِ

TT: The orphan is not the one whose father passed away (who lost his father). But the one who is orphaned by science and literature.

ST: French Prime Minister insisted that the budget was to get the country back on the rails.

TT: أكّد رئيس الوزراء الفرنسي بأنّ الميزانية الجديدة تهدف الى وضع البلاد على الطريق الصحيح ثانية.

ST: شتم رجل خالد بن الوليد، فالتفت اليه وقال: (هي صحيفتك، إملأها بما شئت)

TT: A man swore at Khalid Bin Al-Waleed. Khalid Bin Al-Waleed looked at the man and said: "It is your record of deeds. Fill it in with whatever you wish".

ST: Earlier this week, the Housing Minister Mr X <u>alarmed</u> (أقلق) <u>conservationists</u> المنادون بالحفاظ على البيئة when he said one million acres of green fields may have to be <u>concreted over</u> سيتم بناءها to deal with the housing shortage. He drew a clear link between housing demand and <u>the legacy of Labor's open-door immigration policy</u>.

TT: أقلق وزير الدولة لشؤون الأسكان في مطلع هذا الأسبوع المنادين بالحفاظ على البيئة عندما قال أنه من المحتمل بناء الدور على مساحة مليون فدان من الحقول الخضراء وذلك في سبيل التعامل مع النقص في توفير السكن. وقد أقام العلاقة بين الطلب على السكن وتركة سياسة السماح بدخول المهاجرين بأعداد كبيرة التي تبناها حزب العمال.

Appendix 1   291

58. Provide a commentary on the translation process of the following instructional texts. Compare the ST with the TT and explain the translation approaches adopted by the translator.

Turn left when you see a roundabout.

Cross the junction and keep going for about 2 miles.

Turn right at the end of the road and my house is number 17 Kenworthy Gate.

Take the third road on the right and you will see the office on the left.

59. Provide a commentary on the translation process of the ST (Bike to basics) (*York News & Times*, February 2008). Discuss the textual and discourse analysis of the ST, compare the ST with the TT, and explain the translation strategies adopted by the translator.

(i)   The TT is a news headline in a local newspaper issued in York, UK. The proposed translation is دورات أساسية في تصليح الدراجات الهوائية.

(ii)   The translation problem lies in the initial word "bike", which does not collocate with the prepositional phrase "to basics". However, it is recommended that the translator reads the full text to understand the undertone of the headline and the performative intent of the news reporter.

(iii) Reading the full news report will facilitate the translation process since it will reveal the link between intertextuality and translation. Source language intertextual linkage represents one of the factors in pragmatic failure between Arabic and English. Failure to decode the intertextual links that bind two STs leads to a breakdown in cross-cultural communication. Texts, at times, employ expressions that are intertextually related and harken back to each other. In order to get the message across forcefully, the writer/speaker employs expressions that strike a chord to the reader/listener. Thus, perlocutionary impact is achieved. The news headline "Bike to basics" is a case in point (*York News & Times*, February 2008, p. 5). When the Conservatives were in office during the early 1990s, the Prime Minister John Major launched his moral crusade "Back to Basics" encouraging the British people to go back to basic moral matters to enhance good citizenship. Although there is a play on words between the two expressions, the significant issue for pragmatic success lies in the interpretation of the initial word "Bike" as "Back". This is not the end of the problem, however. The context gives useful clues to achieve an effective TL headline: "A bike training and community workshop have recently begun bike maintenance courses".

(iv)   To solve the jigsaw of the ST headline news report, the translation process has entirely relied on the explications provided within the news report itself, i.e., on the key sentence: "A bike training and community workshop have recently begun bike maintenance courses". Thus, in such cases when the headline news report is semantically or grammatically ambiguous, we recommend reading the full text first to get a clue of what the context (the story) is all about.

(v)   The TT has adopted the exegetical and faithful translation approach and provided a context-based meaning. This demonstrates that the intertextual link between the ST headline and its intertextual link "Back to Basics" – John Major's moral crusade – is not useful in the translation process. The only value of the link is the word (basics), which designates "basic things", but they are to do with "bike maintenance" rather than "moral issues".

60. Provide a commentary on the translation process of the following texts. Compare the ST with the TT and explain the translation strategies adopted by the translator.

292 *Appendix 1*

وأصحابُ اليمينِ ما أصحابُ اليمينِ . . . وأصحابُ الشمالِ ما أصحابُ الشمالِ . . . (سورة الواقعة)

61. Provide a commentary on the translation process and a critical translation quality assessment of the following text. Compare the ST with the TTs and explain the translation approaches adopted by the translators.

من شرِّ الوسواسِ الخنَّاسِ. الذي يوسوسُ في صُدُور الناسِ (الناس 4–5)

From the evil of the sneaking whisperer, who whispereth in the hearts of mankind (Pickthall 1930:no page).

From the mischief of the Whisperer (of Evil), who withdraws (after his whisper), (The same) who whispers into the hearts of Mankind (Ali 1934:no page).

From the evil of the slinking whisperer who whispers in the breasts of men (Arberry 1955:282).

From the evil of the whispering, elusive tempter who whispers in the hearts of men (Asad 1980:1316).

From the evil of the retreating whisperer who whispers (evil) into the breasts of mankind (Saheeh International 1997:915).

Against the harm of the slinking whisperer who whispers into the hearts of people (Abdel Haleem 2005:446).

From the evil of the whisperer (i.e., devil) who runs away (when the remembrance of Allah is made). Who (i.e., devil) whispers in the breasts of mankind (Ahmad 2010:850).

(i) The semantic componential features of the verb "to whisper" are "to make sibilant sounds and speak very softly using one's breath rather than one's throat, especially for the sake of secrecy". Semantically, the verb يوسوس collocates with the nouns شيطان "Satan" and النفس "the self", which both have negative denotative meanings. For instance, we encounter . . . الشيطان فإنهُ يأمُرُ بالفحشاء "Satan enjoins immorality", (Q24:21) and إنَّ النفسَ لأمَّرةٌ بالسوء "Indeed, the soul incites to evil", (Q12:53).

(ii) The anachronism translation approach is used by Pickthall "whispereth", which has led to unsmooth translation due to using old-fashioned language.

(iii) The literal translation approach is used by Arberry, Saheeh International, and Ahmad, where "sudoor" is translated literally as "breasts". This is a word-for-word translation and sticks very closely to the ST lexis and syntax.

(iv) The above translations are not TL culture-based with regards to "الذي يُوسوِسُ في صُدورِ الناس".

(v) We can observe an explication and expansion of SL expressions. This is an exegetical translation approach based on the paraphrase of the SL expression, i.e., some TTs have provided additional details that are not explicitly conveyed in the ST. The TTs are those by Ali, Saheeh International, and Ahmad.

(vi) Based on the above details and the translations provided, we can claim that the translations are not accurate. We need a TL culture-based translation employing on one of the following translation approaches: communicative, dynamic equivalence, natural, acceptable, instrumental, or faithful. These translation approaches take into consideration the contextual intended meaning of the ST in order to provide a comprehensible TT to the audience with an acceptable natural TL style. These translation approaches aim at complete naturalness of the TT; to naturalize and domesticate the TT and reduce its foreignness. We propose the following translation to Q114:4–5,

Appendix 1 293

which interpretively resembles the ST without unnecessary processing effort on the part of the TL reader: الذي يُوسوسُ في صُدور الناس should be translated as (who plays with people's minds).

62. I have found the following Arabic text with its translation displayed in a hotel room in Muscat, Oman. There are translation errors in the TT. Correct the errors, produce an accurate translation, and compare the two TTs:

ST:

الى ضيوفنا الكرام

رجاءاً التكرم بالأحاطة بالعلم بأنه قد تمَّ تزويد سقف جميع الغرف بإنذار حسَّاس جداً ضد أي نوع من الدخان.

لهذا نرجو من جميع ضيوفنا عدم إحراق ''البخور'' أو تدخين ''الشيشة'' بالغرف أو استخدام أية مواد تسبب الدخان. هذه التعليمات لسلامتكم وسلامة جميع النزلاء بالغرف الأخرى وفي حالة الإصرار على استخدام تلك المواد فإن اية خسائر تحدث بسبب ذلك سوف يتم اضافتها على حسابكم.

نشكركم ونتمنى لكم إقامة سعيدة

الإدارة

TT:

To All Our Beloved Guests

Please be informed that all our rooms are equipped with smoke detector at the ceiling which very sensitive to any type of smoke.

So, we are requested to refrain from burning Bhukhoor or Shisha or any thing emits smoke inside your room.

This instruction is for your safety and other guests staying with us and if damage done by you will be charged to you accordingly.

Thanking you and have a nice stay with us.

Management

We have corrected the translation errors of the above TT. Our proposed translation is as follows:

To All Our Beloved Guests

Please be informed that all our rooms are equipped with smoke detectors on the ceilings and which are very sensitive to any type of smoke.

You are therefore requested to refrain from lighting Bhukhoor or Shisha (or anything that emits smoke) inside your room.

This instruction is for your safety and that of other guests staying at this hotel.

In the event that any damage is caused, you will be liable for the cost of repair.

Thank you and have a nice stay with us.

The Management

63. Translate the noun phrase "football widows", comment on the translation process, and provide a critical translation quality assessment.

294 *Appendix 1*

(i)   The translator is unable to provide an accurate translation unless he/she has an insight into the context in which the ST has occurred. Without such awareness of the context and background of the ST, we can propose the TT: أرامل كُرة القدم.

(ii)   The noun phrase "football widows" appeared on 9 June 2006. This noun phrase was said the reporter on Sky-news on Friday 9 June 2006 "Football widows have set up a website which has attracted thousands of women of the same problem". The ST means "women who have football-mad husbands. These women were neglected by their husbands during the three-week world-cup tournament in June 2006".

(iii) In the interest of clarity, we need an additional word – مُشجِّعي – within the TL noun phrase. Thus, we have adopted the paraphrase and exegetical translation approaches, which allow the translator to explicate and add some details not mentioned in the ST.

(iv)   Based on the above details and the TT, we need a culture-based translation based on one of the following translation approaches: communicative, dynamic equivalence, natural, acceptable, instrumental, or faithful. These translation approaches take into consideration the contextual intended meaning of the ST in order to provide a comprehensible TT to its audience with an acceptable natural TL style. These translation approaches aim at complete naturalness of the TT; to naturalize the TT and reduce its foreignness. The above translation interpretively resembles the original without unnecessary processing effort on the part of the TL reader. Thus, we can propose the translation: أرامل مُشجعي كُرة القدم.

64. Provide a translation commentary on the impact of ST context and intertextuality on translation. Provide an assessment of different TTs of the following STs:

يمشون في مساكنهم (السجدة 26)

إن أرادَ النبيُّ أن يستنكِحَها (الأحزاب 50)

(i) Let us consider the first ST (Q32:26):

Amid whose dwelling places they do walk (Pickthall 1930:no page).
In whose dwellings they (now) go to and fro (Ali 1934:no page).
In whose dwelling-places they walk (Arberry 1955:186).
[People] in whose dwelling-places they [themselves now] walk about (Asad 1980:864).
They walk among their dwellings (Saheeh International 1997:576).
In whose homes they now walk (Abdel Haleem 2005:265).

(1)   In terms of context and intertextuality, we are concerned with the preposition في, whose meaning is entirely based on context and intertextuality, and should be translated as "among, amid". This meaning is backed up by the intertextual relationship with other sentences in Q7:92, Q19:98, Q22:45, 56, and Q27:52.

(2)   Only Pickthall and Saheeh International have produced the context-based meaning of the preposition في, which is "amid, among", because people did not live in the destroyed homes of the past unbelieving people whose towns were destroyed. Rather, they only passed by or went between the destroyed homes. The other TTs have provided a literal translation of the preposition في "in".

Appendix 1 295

(ii) Let us consider the second ST (Q33:50):

> The Prophet desires to ask her in marriage (Pickthall 1930:no page).
> If the Prophet wishes to wed her (Ali 1934:no page).
> If the Prophet desires to take her in marriage (Arberry 1955:190).
> The Prophet might be willing to wed (Asad 1980:879).
> If the Prophet wishes to marry her (Saheeh International 1997:587).
> Whom the Prophet wishes to wed (Abdel Haleem 2005:270).

In terms of context and intertextuality, we are concerned with the transitive verb يستنكِح which is semantically distinct from its counterpart partial synonym, ينكح. The context-based meaning of the verb يستنكِح is "a man asks the lady's permission to marry him". Thus, it does not involve just a desire or a wish on the part of the man to marry a lady. The major semantic componential feature of the verb يستنكِح is "seeking the lady's permission and approval of the man's proposal". However, the above TTs have failed to provide the ST's informative intent.

65. Polysemy is a translation problem, such as the verb قضى. Consider the following different meanings of the verb قضى in Qur'an translations to make sure that the translators have taken polysemy into consideration. Among the different meanings of قضى are

(i)   "to advise" as in Q17:23, Q28:44,
(ii)   "to inform" as in Q17:4, Q15:66,
(iii)   "to have completed" as in Q2:200, Q4:103,
(iv)   "to do" as in Q20:72, Q8:42, Q33:36,
(v)   "to send down" as in Q43:77, Q35:36,
(vi)   "to kill" as in Q28:15,
(vii)   "to write" as in Q19:21, Q28:28,
(viii) "has been decided" as in Q6:8, Q10:47, and
(ix)   "to create" as in Q41:12.

66. Provide a translation for the following descriptive text:

جامعة طيبة في سطور

نشأة جامعة طيبة

تأسست الجامعة عام 1424 هجري الموافق 2003 ميلادي

موقعها الجغرافي: المدينة المنورة/طريق الجامعات

الرؤية: جامعة حكومية شاملة تلتزم بالتميز في نشر المعرفة وانتاجها وخدمة المجتمع للارتقاء لمصاف الجامعات المتقدمة محليا واقليميا وعالميا.

الرسالة: تقدم جامعة طيبة برامج اكاديمية عالية الجودة في مختلف فروع المعرفة، وتقوم بتطوير ودعم البحوث بما يسهم في اثراء المعرفة وتحقيق اهداف التنمية، وتلبي احتياجات التنمية الوطنية ومتطلبات سوق العمل المتجدد بتخريج الكوادر البشرية القادرة على المنافسة في ظل الاقتصاد

296 *Appendix 1*

المعرفي والعولمة، وتهدف الجامعة الى تعزيز دورها في خدمة المجتمع وبناء مجتمع المعرفة، وتقوم بتهيئة بيئة جامعية داعمة الانتاج والتميز.

We propose the following translation. For in-class translation training, students are asked to discuss what has taken place during the translation process:

> Taibah University in Brief
> Establishment
> Taibah University was founded (established) in 2003.
> **Location**: Madinah/University Road.
> **Vision**: Taibah University is a comprehensive state University dedicated (committed) to excellence in producing and spreading knowledge and community service in order to reach the level of advanced universities nationally, regionally, and internationally.
> **Mission**: Taibah University provides high quality (top) academic programs in various (different) disciplines. It develops and supports research that contributes to the enrichment of knowledge and the achievement of national development goals. The University meets national development and changing market needs through graduating highly qualified graduates capable of competition in today's knowledge economy and globalization. Taibah University also aims to reinforce its role in serving the community, build a knowledge-oriented (based) society, and create an academic environment supportive of productivity and excellence.

67. Provide an effective style translation to each of the following texts and explain the translation process:

(i)   social media applications (venues/platforms)
(ii)   every aspect of life
(iii)   extraordinary jubilation
(iv)   dirty linen
(v)   bloodshed
(vi)   bloodletting
(vii)   to prevent bloodshed

We propose the following translations:

(i)   وسائل التواصُل الإجتماعي
(ii)   جميع مفاصل الحياة
(iii) فرحة عارمة
(iv)   نشر غسيل الماضي
(v)   سفك الدماء
(vi)   إراقة الدماء
(vii) حقنًا للدماء

Discussion: The translation process has aimed for complete naturalness of the TT; to reduce the TT foreignness. It is a TL culture-based translation based on one of the following translation approaches: communicative, dynamic equivalence, natural, acceptable, instrumental, or faithful translation. These translation approaches take into consideration the contextual

Appendix 1 297

intended meaning of the ST in order to provide a comprehensible TT to the audience with an acceptable natural TL style.

68. Translate شجرة الزقوم and discuss the translation process.

The Qur'anic expression شجرة الزقوم (Q37:62) is translated as "the Zaqqum tree 'an extremely distasteful tree in hell'" or "the Tree of Ez-Zakkoum". Discuss what has taken place in the translation process.

(i) In the TT "the Zaqqum tree 'an extremely distasteful tree in hell'", the translator has adopted two translation approaches:

    (a) The exegetical translation approach which is a paraphrase of a SL expression الزقوم. This approach allows additional details that are not explicitly conveyed in the ST, i.e., it is an explication and expansion of the SL expression, and

    (b) The translator has adopted a cultural borrowing translation approach through which a culturally specific SL expression الزقوم is transferred verbatim phonetically into the TL via transliteration.

(ii) In the TT "the Tree of Ez-Zakkoum", the translator has adopted a cultural borrowing translation approach through which a culturally specific SL expression الزقوم is transferred verbatim phonetically into the TL via transliteration.

(iii) Semantically, some SL lexical items have innate semantic componential features. When such features are lacking in the TL and cannot be represented through a single TL word, we obtain a lexical void. Thus, the above Arabic examples are lexical voids because English fails to accommodate them by a single word like مدرسة and "school". Thus, we can observe a direct relationship between lexical voids and cultural borrowing. For more details on lexical voids, see Abdul-Raof (2018, Chapter 6).

69. The following ST is for in-class discussion of the translation process, stylistic, grammatical, and semantic translation problems, as well as translation strategies:

قيام دولة الإمارات العربية المتحدة

منذ الإعلان رسمياً عن قيام دولة الإمارات العربية المتحدة في 2 ديسمبر 1971 ، أكدت دولة الإمارات مراراً وتكراراً حقها في ملكية الجُزر الثلاث طنب الكُبرى وطنب الصُغرى وأبو موسى ، كما أكدت دولة الإمارات العربية المتحدة رغبتها في تسوية الخلاف مع إيران بالسُبُل السلمية وبما يتفق مع القوانين والأعراف الدولية.

    The establishment of the United Arab Emirates

    Since the official establishment of the United Arab Emirates on 2 December 1971, the UAE has repeatedly affirmed its right of sovereignty over the three islands of Greater Tunnab, Lesser Tunnab, and Abu Musa.

    The UAE also affirmed its desire to settle the dispute with Iran by peaceful means and in accordance with the international laws and norms.

    Consider during the translation process the following:

قيام: establishment

مراراً وتكراراً: repeatedly

298 *Appendix 1*

مِلكِيَّة: This is given a context-based meaning, which is "sovereignty".

وفي 9 ديسمبر 1971 عندما نظر مجلس الأمن التابع للأمم المتحدة في القضية، أكد ممثل دولة الإمارات العربية المتحدة حقَّ دولته في الجُزُر واحتجَّ على احتلال إيران لها.

On December 9, 1971, when the United Nations Security Council considered the case, the representative of the United Arab Emirates asserted his country's right to the islands and protested against Iran's occupation of the islands.

Consider during the translation process the following:

We have taken out the initial conjunction و which is not required by the TT.

لها: This is given a context-based meaning of "the islands", i.e., we have replaced the prepositional phrase لها by the noun phrase "the islands".

وفي الأعوام التالية، واصلت دولة الإمارات العربية المتحدة في المذكرات والبيانات المُقَدَّمة إلى مجلس الأمن والجمعية العامة للأمم المتحدة أنَّ الجُزُرَ تَقَعُ ضمنَ أراضي دولة الإمارات العربية المتحدة.

In the following years, the United Arab Emirates continued in notes and statements to the Security Council and the General Assembly of the United Nations that the islands are within the territory of the United Arab Emirates.

Consider during the translation process the following:

We have taken out the initial conjunction و which is not required by the TT.

تَقَعُ: This is translated as an auxiliary "are" referring to the plural noun "islands"

كما سعت إلى استصدار قرار بشأن قضية الجُزُر مبنيٌّ على المفاوضات الثنائية والوساطة الدولية أو بإحالة القضية إلى محكمة العدل الدولية.

The UAE also sought to obtain a resolution on the islands based on bilateral negotiations and international mediation, or by referring the case to the International Court of Justice.

Consider during the translation process the following:

استصدار قرار: This is translated as "to obtain a resolution".

بشأن: "on"

قضية: This noun needs to be deleted because it is not required by the TT.

ولقيت دولة الإمارات العربية المتحدة ضمن مساعيها إلى اقتراح تسوية سلمية للنزاع على الجُزُر، دعماً واسعاً من الدول العربية والمجتمع الدولي على حدٍّ سواء.

As part of its efforts to propose a peaceful settlement of the dispute over the islands, the UAE has received broad support from both Arab countries and the international community.

Consider during the translation process the following:

We have taken out the initial conjunction و which is not required by the TT.

We must consider the grammatical structure of the sentence:

لقيت دولة الإمارات العربية المتحدة ضمن مساعيها إلى اقتراح تسوية سلمية للنزاع على الجُزُر، دعماً واسعاً

where we have the verb لقيت "to receive" + the subject noun phrase دولة الإمارات العربية المتحدة + the direct object دعماً واسعاً "broad support". This is an Arabic-specific stylistic idiosyncrasy which does not suit English stylistic and grammatical norms. English needs the object "broad support" to be next to the verb "received". The translation strategy we need is to start with the parenthetical clause الجملة الإعتراضية which is ضمن مساعيها إلى اقتراح

Appendix 1   299

تسوية سلمية للنزاع على الجُزُر and take out the comma ، after the noun الجزر. Thus, we have achieved a smooth TL style acceptable to the TL audience.

على حدٍّ سواء: This expression is translated as (both). Thus, as a translation strategy, we provide the synonym of على حدٍّ سواء which is كُلٌّ من, i.e., "both", i.e.,

من الدول العربية والمجتمع الدولي على حدٍّ سواء ← من كُلٍّ من الدول العربية والمجتمع الدولي

ضمن: This is given a context-based meaning "as part of".

ويُشكِّل احتلال إيران بالقوة لجزيرتي طُنب الكبرى وطُنب الصغرى انتهاكاً للمبدأ القانوني الذي ساد القرن العشرين، الذي يدعو الدول إلى تجنب استخدام القوة أو التهديد باستخدامها للإستيلاء على أراضٍ معينة. ويتضمن ذلك انتهاكاً لميثاق الأمم المتحدة. (*اليوم السابع* ، 29 أبريل (نيسان) 2020)

> Iran's forcible occupation of the Greater Tunnab and Lesser Tunnab islands constitutes a violation of the legal principle that prevailed in the twentieth century, which calls on states to avoid using or threatening to use force to seize certain territories. This entails the violation of the United Nations' Charter.
>
> (*Al-Yawm Al-Sabi'*, 29 April 2020)

Consider during the translation process the following:

We have taken out the initial conjunction و which is not required by the TT.

أراض: This is given a context-based meaning, which is "territories".

يتضمن: This is given a context-based meaning, which is "entail".

70. On the Al-Jazeera TV channel, there is a program called يكسر التاء. Provide a translation for the title of the program and comment on the translation process. You need to take three steps: (i) Conduct a search online to find out what the program is about, (ii) Consider how the grammar-based title يكسر التاء can be rendered to English, and (iii) Explain the translation approach you have adopted.

Appendix 2
Stylistics and translator training

Appendix 2 aims to promote sharp insight into translation strategies and enable students again more understanding and knowledge of the translation process and the translation approach required for a given translation problem at word, phrase, sentence, and text levels.

The following practice-based exercises are for training translation students and translators. The texts are analyzed and critically assessed. Translation problems are provided with proposed solutions through a comprehensive translation commentary.

Translator training and translation practice

1 Provide a translation for the following text and a commentary on the stylistic differences between the ST and the TT.

ذلكَ من أنباء القُرى نَقصُّهُ عليكَ منها قائمٌ وحصيدٌ (هود 100)

Let us consider the following translations. Based on the textual and discourse analysis of these translations, we can provide our critical stylistic assessment, contrastive analysis, and translation approaches:

That is (something) of the tidings of the townships (which were destroyed of old). We relate it unto thee (Muhammad). Some of them are standing and some (already) reaped (Pickthall 1930:no page).

These are some of the stories of communities which We relate unto thee: of them some are standing, and some have been mown down (by the sickle of time) (Ali 1934:no page).

That is of the tidings of the cities We relate to thee; some of them are standing and some stubble (Arberry 1955:100).

THIS ACCOUNT of the [fate of those ancient] communities – some of them still remaining, and some [extinct like] a field mown-down – We convey unto thee [as a lesson for mankind] + a footnote (Asad 1980:456).

That is from the news of the cities, which We relate to you; of them, some are (still) standing and some are (as) a harvest (mowed down) + a footnote (Saheeh International 1997:304).

We relate to you (Muhammad) such accounts of earlier towns: some of them are still standing; some have been mown down + a footnote (Abdel Haleem 2005:143).

These are the stories of certain towns which We have related to you (O Muhammad), some of them are still standing (on their feet) and others are totally destroyed (Ahmad 2010:299).

Appendix 2 301

(i) Based on the above translations, we are in a position to claim that the gloss translation approach has been adopted where ST form and content are reproduced in the TT as literally and meaningfully as possible, plus the use of footnotes (Asad, Saheeh International, Abdel Haleem) to explicate the performative intent of the ST producer. The TTs are also based on the formal equivalence translation approach where marginal footnotes are used and, most importantly, the TTs focus attention on the SL message itself, in both form (grammatical structure and stylistic pattern) and content. Some TTs have employed the exegetical translation approach through the use of additional details not explicitly mentioned by the ST (Ali, Asad, Saheeh International, Ahmad).

(ii) The major stylistic feature of the ST is the rhetorical device of metaphor represented by the expression حصيد, which is morphologically derived from the verb root حَصَدَ "to harvest" – a passive participle اسم مفعول. Semantically, however, حصيد has a negative connotative overtone. This is because in Arabic, the passive participle has the semantic role of patient; it is the entity which has suffered the action performed by the semantic role of an agent. In other words, the action of "harvest" – i.e., "to flatten, mowdown, destroy completely the inhabitants of a city" – is performed by an implicit agent known from the context of the ST as God.

(iii) Stylistically, حصيد designates the rhetorical device of implicit simile, i.e., كأنهم زرعٌ محصود literally meaning "as if they were harvested plants", and "they were mowed down". The implicit simile derives from the rhetorical device of imagery where we can have a cognitive image صورة في أذهاننا of a city whose people are bulldozed, i.e., annihilated –ß a flattened-out city. This is an implicit comparison between an empty farm after it has been harvested and a city flattened out. The TTs by Ali, Asad Saheeh International, and Abdel Haleem have managed to capture the ST's rhetorical devices of metaphor, implicit simile, and imagery.

(iv) Stylistically, the ST involves the linguistic device of ellipsis الحذف where the prepositional phrase منها is elliptted. All TTs have brought back to the TT the ST ellipted item and have provided "some, some of them" for the prepositional phrase منها.

ذلكَ من أنباء القُرى نَقُصُّهُ عليكَ منها قائمٌ و(منها) حصيدٌ

(v) A literal and slightly inaccurate translation is provided by Pickthall, Ali, Arberry, Saheeh International, Abdel Haleem, and Ahmad where they wrongly translate منها قائمٌ as "are still standing" and "are still standing 'on their feet'". The accurate translation should be "are still remaining, are still there".

2 Provide a translation for the following texts and a commentary on the stylistic differences between the STs and the TTs.

إذا قضى أمراً فإنّما يقولُ لهُ كُن فيكون (آل عمران 47)

فوكزه موسى فقضى عليه (القصص 15)

سورة آل عمران (47) Q3:47):

If He decreeth a thing, He saith unto it only: Be! and it is (Pickthall 1930:no page).
When He hath decreed a plan, He but saith to it, "Be", and it is! (Ali 1934:no page).

302 *Appendix 2*

When He decrees a thing He does but say to it "Be", and it is (Arberry 1955:26).

When He wills a thing to be, He but says unto it, "Be" – and it is (Asad 1980:120).

When He decrees a matter, He only says to it, "Be", and it is (Saheeh International 1997:70).

When He has ordained something, He only says, "Be", and it is. + a footnote (Abdel Haleem 2005:38).

When He intends to bring about a thing, He says to it: "Be" – and it is done at once (Ahmad 2010:79).

سورة القصص 15: Q28:15

So Moses struck him with his fist and killed him (Pickthall 1930:no page).

And Moses struck him with his fist and made an end of him (Ali 1934:no page).

So Moses struck him, and dispatched him (Arberry 1955:173).

Whereupon Moses struck him down with his fist, and [thus] brought about his end (Asad 1980:803).

Moses struck him and (unintentionally) killed him (Saheeh International 1997:534).

Moses struck him with his fist and killed him (Abdel Haleem 2005:246).

So Moses hit him with his fist which killed him (accidentally) (Ahmad 2010:514).

(i)   The striking stylistic idiosyncrasy of both Q3:47 and Q28:15 is the employment of the temporal conjunction ف, which is semantically oriented in Arabic and has the illocutionary force of [+ Immediate Action]; the action denoted by the verb takes place immediately. Thus, there is a stylistic and semantic distinction between the temporal conjunction ف and its counterparts – the additive conjunction و "and" and the temporal conjunction ثمّ "then" – where the latter two conjunction designate the illocutionary force of [– Immediate Action]; the action denoted by the verb does not take place immediately, but after a while. The unique example that explains the stylistic occurrence and its semantic consequence in terms of time is Q22:5, where ثمّ is employed to designate different stages of creation, for longer periods of time. The other unique example that leads to the stylistic and semantic distinction in the employment of temporal and additive conjunctions in Arabic is Q23:13–14, where we encounter the occurrence of the conjunctions ثمّ and ف.

For more details on the stylistic and semantic distinction between such conjunctions and their translation problems, see Abdul-Raof (2018:12–25, 38, 342; 2019:17; 2020:62, 85, 215, 247–252, 260).

(ii) The conjunction ف is a linguistic void and is an example of linguistic incongruity between Arabic and English at the discourse level of cohesion. In Q3:47, the ف is translated as a comma (,). However, the initial ف in Q28:15 is translated as "so, and, whereupon", while the second occurrence of ف is translated as "and". In either case, none of the TT conjunctions possess the stylistic or the semantic signification, neither do they reflect the same ST illocutionary force and the ST producer's performative intent.

(iii) Exegetical and paraphrase translation approaches are adopted by Saheeh International and Ahmad where extra details between brackets are employed.

Appendix 2 303

3   Provide a translation for the following journalistic text and a commentary on the stylistic differences between the ST and the TT.

China is moving to impose new national security laws that would give the Communist Party more control over Hong Kong, threatening to erode the freedoms that distinguish the global, commercial city from the rest of the country. The proposal, announced on Thursday, reignited the fear, anger and protests over the creeping influence of China's authoritarian government in the semiautonomous region. It also inflamed worries that Beijing is trying to dismantle the distinct political and cultural identity that has defined the former British colony since it was reclaimed by China in 1997. "National security is the bedrock underpinning the stability of the country", Mr. Zhang said. "Safeguarding national security serves the fundamental interest of all Chinese, Hong Kong compatriots included". The protests in Hong Kong started in June last year after the local government tried to enact an extradition law that would have allowed residents to be transferred to the mainland to face an opaque and often harsh judicial system. China has denounced the protests as acts of terrorism and accused western nations of fomenting the unrest. On Thursday, *The People's Daily*, the official mouthpiece of the Chinese Communist Party, and Xinhua, the state-run news agency, ran commentaries calling for the "tumor" of pro-independence sentiment in Hong Kong to be excised.

(*The New York Times*, 21 May 2020)

(i)   We propose the following translation on which our translation commentary and the textual and discourse analysis will be based:

تسعى الصين لفرض قوانين جديدة للأمن القومي من شأنها أن تمنح الحزب الشيوعي المزيد من الهيمنة على هونغ كونغ، وبهذا فإنها تقوِّضُ الحُريات التي تميز المدينة التجارية العالمية عن بقية البلاد. وقد أثار هذا الاقتراح الذي تم الأعلان عنه يوم الخميس الخوف والغضب والاحتجاجات بشأن التأثير المتسلل للحكومة الصينية الاستبدادية في الإقليم شبه المستقل. كما أشعل هذا الإقتراح المخاوف من أن بكين تحاول تفكيك الهوية السياسية والثقافية المميزة التي تتميز بها هذه المستعمرة البريطانية السابقة منذ استعادتها من قبل الصين في عام 1997. وقال السيد تشانغ "إن الأمن القومي هو الأساس الذي يقوم عليه استقرار البلاد". وأضاف قائلاً "إن حماية الأمن القومي يخدم المصلحة الأساسية لجميع المواطنين الصينيين، بمن فيهم مواطني هونغ كونغ." ويُذكر أن الإحتجاجات قد اندلعت في هونغ كونغ في يونيو من العام الماضي بعد أن حاولت الحكومة المحلية سن قانون تسليم المجرمين الذي يسمح بنقل مواطني الأقليم إلى الصين لمواجهة نظامٍ قضائي غامضٍ وغالبًا قاسٍ. ومن الجديرُ بالذكر أنَّ الصين قد نددت بالاحتجاجات ووصفتها بأنها أعمال إرهابية واتهمت الدول الغربية بإثارة الاضطرابات. ونشرت يوم الخميس صحيفة بيبولز ديلي، الناطقة باسم الحزب الشيوعي الصيني ، ووكالة أنباء شينخوا الحكومية، تعليقات تدعو إلى استئصال "ورم" المشاعر المؤيدة للاستقلال في هونغ كونغ. (عن صحيفة نيويورك تايمز الأمريكية، 21 مايو (أيار) 2020)

(ii)   Translation quality assessment based on the ST and the TT stylistic idiosyncrasies: We can observe that the TT is marked by tight texture as a stylistic idiosyncrasy through the dense clusters of many conjunctions like و ، كما، بعد, which have occurred inter-sententially and intra-sententially and at the beginning of each sentence. The grammatical

304   *Appendix 2*

unit "that would" is translated as من شأنها أن, the first comma is preserved and is translated as وبهذا فإنها, and the gerund "threatening" is translated as a verb تقوّض. The second sentence "The proposal, announced . . . " is translated with the use of a full-stop followed by the conjunction وقد followed by the verb أثار + the subject "the proposal" + the deletion of the comma and replacing it with the relative pronoun الذي + changing the past participle verb "announced" to a nominalized noun تمّ الإعلان عنه, the preposition "over" is translated as بشأن. The metaphor "reignited" is translated as a metaphor أشعلَ. The metaphor in "creeping influence" is translated as a personification التأثير المتسلّل. This is personification because the act of infiltration التسلّل is a human feature done usually by humans but it is given to a non-human abstract noun, which is "influence". The ST metaphor "inflamed" is preserved as a metaphor أشعلَ. The expression "the bedrock underpinning" involves an ellipted relative pronoun "which" + auxiliary "is" and is translated as الأساس الذي يقوم عليه, where we have used a relative pronoun تاذي + a verb يقوم. We have added the journalistic conjunction وأضاف قائلًا, the past participle "included" is translated as a prepositional phrase بمن فيهم, and the addition of the journalistic conjunction من الجديرُ بالذكر أن. The word "tumor" is translated as a metaphor ورم. The passive voice "to be excised" is translated as an active voice through the use of the nominalized noun استئصال.

4   Provide translations for the following Arabic texts and discuss the stylistic differences between the STs and the TTs.

جائحة كورونا تُخيّمُ على أجواء العيد وتسرُقُ بهجَتَهُ.

Oil rises as fears of oversupply ebb.

اسعارُ النفط ترتفعُ مع انحسار مخاوف تُخمة المعروض.

Coronavirus pandemic overshadows the Eid and snatches its festive joy.

(i)   Both the Arabic and English STs are marked by stylistic idiosyncrasies. The Arabic ST is marked by the rhetorical device of personification يُخيّم، يسرق، بهجة. However, its TT counterpart is also marked by the rhetorical device of personification. The English ST is marked by the rhetorical device of metaphor "fears ebb". However, its TT counterpart is also marked by the rhetorical device of metaphor انحسار مخاوف and personification تُخمة

(ii)   There is a subtle distinction between personification and metaphor. Personification occurs when something like an abstract, inanimate, or non-human animate thing is treated as a human being. It is thus said to be personified, as in "Justice is blind", where we have something abstract "justice" given a human quality, "the use, or loss, of sight"; therefore, the expression personifies justice. For Katie Wales (2011:314), personification is a kind of metaphor. Personification is often used in children's books. Personification makes the narration more emotional and alive (Abdul-Raof 2020:145). Metaphor, however, is a direct comparison of two different things without using the words "like" or "as". Thus, when we use a metaphor, our statement does not make sense literally. In English, polysemous words such as "heavy" in "heavy heart" can also function as metaphor. The pragmatic purpose of metaphor is to appeal to the senses, to interest, to clarify, to please, to delight, and to surprise (ibid:112).

Appendix 2 305

(iii) Based on the above personification details, the expressions يُخيِّم، يسرق، بهجة are related to a [+ Human] entity. However, the ST has given these attributes to a [– Human] entity which is جائحة كورونا. Thus, these expressions demonstrate personification. The same applies to the TT in which the expression "snatch" is usually related to a [+ Human] entity but it has been given to a [– Human] entity – the coronavirus.

(iv) Based on the above metaphor details, the expression "fears ebb" and its translation انحسار المخاوف demonstrate the rhetorical device of metaphor. Thus, the translator has preserved the ST metaphor as a metaphor in the TT.

(v) In terms of sentence structure, the Arabic ST and its TT are hypotactic (complex) sentences. Each involves two subjects and two verbs. Hypotaxis is a linguistic device in which the sentences, clauses, and phurases are subordinated and linked by either coordinating conjunctions or subordinating conjunctions. Hypotaxis is also commonly known as subordination in clauses. Hypotaxis refers to a kind of dependent element which is explicitly linked to the main clause by a conjunction – for example, "The time will come/when he will regret it".

However, the English ST and its TT are paratactic (simple) sentences. Each involves one subject and one verb. Parataxis is a literary technique in which the writer/speaker employs short simple sentences without having coordinating conjunctions or subordinating conjunctions. Thus, parataxis does not employ cohesive devices (conjunctive particles). The connection between phrases or clauses must be inferred by the reader/listener. It is worthwhile to note that although we have coordinating conjunctions like "and, but, or" used in linking paratactic sentences, we can still call such sentences paratactic. Thus, we can claim that parataxis includes simple sentences with or without coordinating conjunctions so long as they are simple structure sentences (Abdul-Raof 2020:241). On hypotactic sentences, see Abdul-Raof (2020:213).

(vi) We can also observe that both the ST and TT are marked by loose texture as a stylistic idiosyncrasy of both texts. This is because the ST is a headline, which, stylistically, usually takes less conjunctions. There is one conjunction in the ST – "as" – while the TT has no conjunction.

5   Provide a translation for the following texts and a commentary on the stylistic differences between the STs and the TTs.

هو الذي أنزلَ من السماء ماءاً (النحل 10)

(i)   The TTs are:

He it is Who sendeth down water from the sky (Pickthall 1930:no page).
It is He who sends down rain from the sky (Ali 1934:no page).
It is He who sends down water from the skies (Asad 1980:541).
It is He who sends down rain from the sky (Saheeh International 1997:354).
It is He who sends down water for you from the sky (Abdel Haleem 2005:166).
Allah sends down rain water from the sky for your benefit (Ahmad 2010:347).

(ii)   Pickthall adopts the anachronism translation approach through the employment of archaic language: "sendeth" and style "He it is Who". Asad uses the plural "skies" for the

306 *Appendix 2*

ST singular السماء. Ahmad employs the subject noun "Allah" instead of the pronoun "He" and also uses the rhetorical device of pleonasm (semantic redundancy) through the expression "rain water" where "rain" semantically designates "water"; thus, "rain water" means ماء المطر. Pickthall, Ali, Asad, Saheeh International, and Abdel Haleem have employed the style of the cleft sentence (It + is + subject + who + main verb + object). This is a style which is a marked (unusual, irregular) word order used for the perlocutionary force of affirmation (focus, saliency) through changing the unmarked (usual, regular) word order of the sentence. The TT unmarked word order is "He sends down rain from the sky". The above TTs have adopted the transposition (shift) and natural translation approaches, which allow a change (shift) in SL word order.

(iii) The ST employs the stylistic mechanism of affirmation through the marked word order where we have هو + الذي + فعل + مفعول به instead of the unmarked order where the main verb أنزلَ occurs first. The ST style of marked order is for the perlocutionary force of affirmation. The co-text (linguistic environment) of the ST is God's omnipotence (Q16:3–16), where all the sentences list for affirmation God's blessings upon His creation. The same style occurs in Q16:14 for the same pragmatic function. This stylistic pattern has also occurred in Q6:97, 98 and 99.

(iv) It is worthwhile to note that the cleft sentence stylistic structure can also occur in a no-main-verb nominal sentence such as (نحنُ لهُ عابدون البقرة 138), where we encounter the cleft sentence "It is Him we worship" (Ali 1934:no page; Mushaf Al-Madinah An-Nabawiyah 1990:55; Abdel Haleem 2005:16). However, other translators have opted for a different style: "We are worshippers of Him" (Saheeh International 1997:26), "We are His worshippers" (Pickthall 1930:no page; Ahmad 2010:38), and "We but truly worship Him" (Asad 1980:60). Another example of cleft sentence stylistic structure is Q51:58 (58 إنَّ اللهَ هوَ الرزاقُ ذو القوّةِ المتين الذاريات), whose translation is "It is Allah who is the provider, the firm possessor of strength" (Saheeh International 1997:744; Mushaf Al-Madinah An-Nabawiyah 1990:1620). Other translators have opted for an extremely bizarre and archaic style "Lo! Allah! He it is that giveth livelihood, the Lord of unbreakable might" (Pickthall 1930:no page).

6 Provide a translation for the sentences "He is as useless as a bikini in the Arctic" and (كأنَّهُم خُشُبٌ مُسَنَّدةٌ المنافقون 4) and a commentary.

(i) Stylistically, the ST "He is as useless as a bikini in the Arctic" involves the rhetorical device of simile through the simile particles "as . . . as". The pragmatically accurate intended meaning of the ST is "He is useless", which demonstrates the domestication of the ST. Also, the ST has used the expression "bikini", which we recommend deleting in the TT because it violates the TT cultural norms.

(ii) Stylistically, the ST(4 كأنَّهُم خُشُبٌ مُسَنَّدةٌ المنافقون) involves the rhetorical device of simile through the simile particle كَ. The pragmatically accurate intended meaning of the ST is "They are useless". This is because the literal translation "They are like propped-up timbers" (Q63:4) is not TL reader-oriented; it smells of foreignness and foreignization approach.

(iii) Based on the above details, we advise the translator to provide a culture-based translation based on one of the following translation approaches: communicative, dynamic equivalence, natural, acceptable, instrumental, or faithful. These translation approaches take into consideration the contextual intended meaning of the ST in order to provide

Appendix 2 307

a comprehensible TT to its audience with an acceptable natural TL style which also observes the TL cultural norms. These translation approaches aim at complete naturalness of the TT; to naturalize the TT, reduce its foreignness, and most importantly, respect the TL values. The translation should also interpretively resemble the ST without unnecessary processing effort on the part of the TL reader. Thus, we can propose the context and TL culture-based translation: إنه شخص لا فائدة منه for "He is as useful as a bikini in the Arctic". Thus, we have abandoned the ST rhetorical device of simile and we have also abandoned the ST expression "bikini". We also propose the context and TL culture-based translation "They are useless" for كَأَنَّهُم خُشُبٌ مُسَنَّدةٌ

(iv) Although we can claim that the ideal translation for كَأَنَّهُم خُشُبٌ مُسَنَّدةٌ is "They are as useful as a bikini in the Arctic" where we have converted خُشُب مُسَنَّدة to "a bikini in the Arctic", such a translation is not compatible with the religiously sensitive status of the Qur'anic ST.

7   Discuss the stylistic and semantic distinction between the interrogative particles ما and مِن in the following ST:

إِنَّكُم وما تعبُدونَ من دُون الله حَصَبُ جهنَّمَ أنتم لها واردون (الأنبياء 98)
You (disbelievers) and what you worship instead of God will be fuel for hell: that is where you will go, Q21:98.

We can argue that although there is a semantic distinction between the interrogative particles ما "what" and مِن "what", the translation of Q21:98 is accurate where ما is employed. However, Q21:98 ما designates the text producer's performative intent that the reference is made exclusively to the idols. Thus, the perlocutionary effect of ما is [– Human] – the idols. If we use مِن instead, the perlocutionary effect is [+ Human]. To eliminate ambiguity and misunderstanding of Q21:98 by the text receiver, ما is stylistically selected. Thus, the meaning of Q21:98 is "'only the disbelievers and their' idols are the fuel of hell". However, to use مِن instead, the meaning of Q21:98 is "the disbelievers, their idols, as well as other humans which you worship like some Prophets and angels are the fuel of hell".

8   In Q6:1–2, we encounter the conjunction ثُمَّ used three times. Discuss the meaning of each time this conjunction occurs and provide an accurate translation for the ST based on the different meanings of this conjunction.

الحمدُ للهِ الذي خَلَقَ السمواواتِ والأرضَ وجَعَلَ الظُّلماتِ والنُّورَ ثُمَّ الذين كَفَروا برَبِّهم يَعدِلُون. هو الذي خَلَقَكُم من طين ثُمَّ قضى أجَلاً وأجَلٌ مُسَمّىً عنده ثُمَّ أنتم تَمتَرون (الأنعام 1–2)
All praise is (due) to Allah, who created the heavens and the earth and made the darkness and the light. Then those who disbelieve equate (others) with their Lord. It is He who created you from clay and then decreed a term and a specified time (known) to Him; then (still) you are in dispute, Q6:1–2.

(i)   We have been told in Chapter 3, Section 3.5, that the conjunction ثُمَّ is a temporal conjunction and means "then, next". However, the above ST has demonstrated that ثُمَّ can also be an adversative conjunction meaning "however, but", based on the meaning of the above ST.

308 *Appendix 2*

(ii) The conjunction ثُمَّ in the ST has occurred three times. The meaning of the first ثُمَّ in the first sentence (Q6:1) is for contrast. Thus, it should be translated as an adversative conjunction meaning "however, but". This is because the meaning signifies a contrast between the first and the second notion: God created you from . . . however, the disbelievers do not believe . . .; in spite of these clear signs which demonstrate God's omnipotence in creation, they still do not believe in God. Thus, ثُمَّ designates contrast and is an inter-sentential adversative conjunction. However, the second ثُمَّ in Q6:2 signifies a temporal conjunction and means "then, and". This is because it designates passage of time from one phase to another "from the time of creation from clay to the time of death". The third time the conjunction ثُمَّ is used designates the adversative meaning and should be translated as "however, but" because it signifies contrast between the two notions: the first notion of God's omnipotence of creation and causing death to His creation, and the second notion about people's disbelief and dispute (skepticism) about creation, death, and resurrection.

(iii) We can also observe that both the ST and TT are marked by tight texture as a stylistic idiosyncrasy of both texts through the dense clusters of conjunctions "and, then" and the conjunctions و، ثُمَّ.

(iv) Based on the above textual and discourse analysis, we can propose the following accurate translation All praise is (due) to Allah, who created the heavens and the earth and made the darkness and the light. However, those who disbelieve equate (others) with their Lord. It is He who created you from clay and then decreed a term and a specified time (known) to Him. However, you are in dispute, (Q6:1–2).

9 Provide a translation for the following text and discuss the stylistic devices involved in both the ST and the TT:

Please do not lecture me on morality. If you are a priest, I'm a monk.

(i) We propose the following translation أرجو أن لا تلقي عليَّ محاضرةً في الأخلاق فإن كنتَ قسيساً فأنا راهبٌ

(ii) The ST is made up of two separate sentences: The first "Please do not lecture me on morality" is a paratactic sentence which, syntactically, has one subject "you" implicitly understood "you do not lecture me" and one main verb "lecture". The second sentence is hypotactic through the conditional particle "if" and, therefore, it has two subjects "you, I" and two verbs "are, am".

(iii) It is worthwhile to distinguish between paratactic and hypotactic sentences:

(1) A paratactic sentence has one clause (a clause simplex). Clauses that can be combined as equals, express different kinds of meaning, and are related to each other in this way are in a paratactic relationship. The paratactic relation is that of coordination, i.e., we have coordinating conjunctions "and, or, but, so".

(2) A hypotactic sentence has more than one clause (a clause complex). Clauses which are in an unequal relationship to each other, have a subordination relationship (main clause/subordinate clause), and in which the clause order can be reversed are in a hypotactic relationship. The hypotactic relation is that of subordination, i.e., we have subordinating conjunctions إذا إن، عندما، بينما، حتى، قبل، بعد، مالم، منذ، بسبب لأن، حيث، لكي، ولو أن على الرغم من "if, when, while, until, before, after, unless, since, because, where, whereas, so that, in order to, although".

Appendix 2 309

(iv) Stylistically, the second sentence involves the rhetorical device of sarcasm السُخرية whose pragmatically based and context-based meaning is "I am more knowledgeable than you in terms of morality".

(v) The ST is based on Christian theology where the monk has a higher rank than a priest. However, this fact is not known to a Muslim TL reader. Thus, the TT is literally translated and needs to be TL-oriented. To re-produce the pragmatic impact of the ST in the TT and to convey the ST intended meaning, we can translate the second ST segment as فإن كُنتَ مُؤذّناً فأنا إمامُ, whose back-translation is "If you are the person who calls for prayer, I am the Imam of the mosque".

However, we can provide a TT based on communicative, dynamic equivalence, natural, acceptable, instrumental, or faithful translation approaches. These translation approaches take into consideration the contextual intended meaning of the ST in order to provide a comprehensible TT to its audience with an acceptable natural TL style. These translation approaches aim at complete naturalness of the TT:

(فإن كُنتَ طالباً فأنا أُستاذُ).

(أرجو أن لا تلقي عليَّ محاضرةً في الأخلاق فإن كُنتَ طالباً فأنا أُستاذُ)

(vi) The full-stop after the first sentence and the comma before the main clause of the second sentence are translated as a temporal conjunction فَ.

10 Provide a translation for the following legal text and discuss the stylistic devices involved in both the ST and the TT:

The Parties to this Treaty reaffirm their faith in the purposes and principles of the Charter of the United Nations and their desire to live in peace with all peoples and all governments. They are determined to safeguard the freedom, common heritage and civilization of their peoples, founded on the principles of democracy, individual liberty and the rule of law. They seek to promote stability and well-being in the North Atlantic area. They are resolved to unite their efforts for collective defence and for the preservation of peace and security. They therefore agree to this North Atlantic Treaty.

(www.nato.int/cps/en/natolive/official_texts_17120.htm,
accessed on 16 June 2020)

(i) We propose the following translation on which our translation commentary and the textual and discourse analysis will be based:

تؤكدُ أطرافُ هذه المعاهدة من جديد إيمانها بمقاصد ومبادئ ميثاق الأمم المتحدة ورغبتهم في العيش بسلام مع جميع الشعوب وجميع الحكومات وإنهم مُصممون (عازمون) على حماية الحرية والتراث المشترك والحضارة لشعوبهم التي تستند (المستندة) على أساس مبادئ الديمقراطية والحرية الفردية وسيادة القانون وأنهم يسعون إلى تعزيز الإستقرار والرفاه في منطقة شمال الأطلسي وقد عقدوا العزم (وأنهم عازمون) على توحيد جهودهم من أجل الدفاع الجماعي والحفاظ على السلم والأمن. لذلك (ولهذا) فإنهم يوافقون على معاهدة شمال الأطلسي هذه.

(ii) Below is the translation assessment:

(a) We have the main verb (reaffirm) which has two objects: (i) their faith in the purposes and principles of the Charter of the United Nations, and (ii) their desire to live in peace with all peoples and all governments.

310 *Appendix 2*

(b) We translate the verb "reaffirm" as يُؤكد من جديد. The prefix "re-" is translated as من جديد.

(c) We put at the beginning of the TT the verb يؤكدُ followed by the subject "the Parties to this Treaty" followed by من جديد + first object + second object.

(d) We translate the modifier "all" جميع twice as it occurs in the ST جميع الشعوب و جميع الحكومات.

(e) We translate the verb "live" to a nominalized noun العيش.

(f) We translate the full-stop to the additive conjunction و.

(g) We translated the past participle "are determined" to an active participle مُصمِّمون/عازمون, which collocates with the preposition على.

(h) We translate the verb "safeguard" to a nominalized noun حماية.

(i) We translated the past participle "founded" to a relative pronoun and a verb التي تستند على/المستندة, which collocates with the preposition على.

(j) We translate the full-stop to the additive conjunction و.

(k) We translate the noun phrase "rule of law" as a noun phrase سيادة القانون.

(l) We translate the verb "promote" to a nominalized noun تعزيز.

(m) We translated the past participle "are resolved" to an active participle عازمون or a verb + a nominalized noun وقد عقدوا العزم, which both collocate with the preposition على.

(n) We translate the verb "unite" to a nominalized noun توحيد.

(o) The causal conjunction "therefore" لذلك/ولهذا is placed at the beginning of the Arabic sentence.

(iii) In terms of a statistical stylistic analysis, we provide the following analysis: The ST involves the rhetorical device of epizeuxis through the repetition of expressions like "treaty, peace, security, North Atlantic, peoples". Epizeuxis in the TT is represented by مُعاهدة، سلام، مبادئء، شعوب، شمال الأطلسي. In the ST, there are four verbs "reaffirm, seek, promote, agree", three past participle verbs "determined, founded, resolved", four infinitives "to live, to safeguard, to promote, to unite", 29 nouns "parties, treaty, faith, purposes, principles, charter, nations, desire, peace, peoples, governments, freedom, heritage, civilization, peoples, principles, democracy, liberty, rule, law, stability, well-being, area, efforts, defence, preservation, peace, security, treaty", nine noun phrases "this treaty, their faith, their desire, the freedom, common heritage and civilization, individual liberty, the rule of law, stability and well-being, their efforts", 13 prepositional phrases "in the purposes and principles, of the Charter, of the United Nations, in peace, with all peoples and all governments of their peoples, on the principles, of democracy, in the North Atlantic area, for collective defence, for the preservation, of peace and security, to this North Atlantic Treaty", and three adjectives "common, individual, collective".

In the TT, there are five verbs 12, يوافقون، عقدوا، يسعون، تستند، تؤكد nouns – هذه – أطراف المعاهدة اسم مفعول – إيمانها – مقاصد اسم مفعول – مبادئ – ميثاق – الأمم – رغبتهم – العيش – بسلام – جميع – الشعوب – جميع – الحكومات – مصممون اسم فاعل – عازمون اسم فاعل – حماية – الحرية – سيادة – القانون – تعزيز – الاستقرار – الرفاه – منطقة – شمال – الأطلسي – العزم – عازمون اسم فاعل – توحيد – جهودهم – أجل – الدفاع – الحفاظ – السلم – الأمن – ذلك – هذا – مُعاهدة اسم مفعول – جديد – المتحدة – الفردية – الجماعي and four adjectives شمال – الأطلسي.

Appendix 2 311

(iv) The ST is asyndetic inter-sententially (no conjunctions among the sentences). However, the TT is polysyndetic inter-sententially through the additive conjunction و. In the first sentence, the ST is polysyndetic intra-sententially (within the same hypotactic sentence) through the conjunctions like "and 'and their desire to live . . . '". The causal conjunction "therefore" in the final ST sentence does not create polysyndeton because the sentence in paratactic. However, the co-text "the linguistic environment" of polysyndeton is hypotaxis when we have two subjects and two main verbs. The same applies to the last sentence of the TT, which has the causal conjunction لذلك، لهذا. The whole TT is polysyndetic through the employment of the additive conjunction و.

11 Provide a translation for the following legal text and discuss the stylistic design involved in both the ST and the TT:

Article 1

The Parties undertake, as set forth in the Charter of the United Nations, to settle any international dispute in which they may be involved by peaceful means in such a manner that international peace and security and justice are not endangered, and to refrain in their international relations from the threat or use of force in any manner inconsistent with the purposes of the United Nations.

(www.nato.int/cps/en/natolive/official_texts_17120.htm accessed on 16/6/2020)

(i) We propose the following translation on which our translation commentary and the textual and discourse analysis will be based:

المادة الأولى

تتعهدُ الأطرافُ على النحو المنصوص عليه في ميثاق الأمم المتحدة، بتسوية أي نزاع دولي قد تكون طرفا فيه، بالوسائل السلمية بحيث (بطريقة) لا يتعرض فيها السلام الدولي والأمن والعدالة للخطر وأن تمتنع في علاقاتها الدولية عن التهديد أو استخدام القوة بأية طريقة (بأي شكل) تتعارض مع مقاصد الأمم المتحدة.

(ii) Below is the translation assessment:

(a) The ST numerical (1) is changed to adjective numerical in the TT الأولى. The ST is a one-hypotactic-sentence paragraph of 66 words where we have the verb "undertake", which is followed by a parenthetical clause ", as set forth . . . United Nations," الجملة الإعتراضية. The TT also employs the parenthetical clause with a comma at the beginning and a comma at the end بتسوية أي نزاع دولي قد تكون ، طرفا فيه،. The verb "undertake" has taken two infinitive verb sentences: "to settle any . . ." and "to refrain . . .". The whole text is polysyndetic through the coordinating conjunction "and", which links the two infinitive verb sentences.

(b) The first infinitive verb "to settle" is translated as a nominalized noun تسوية and the second infinitive verb "to refrain" is also translated as an infinitive, but whose structure is أن + فعل أن تمتنع. The verb "refrain" collocates with the preposition "from", while the verb يمتنع collocates with the preposition عن. The past participle "involved" is translated as a noun طرفاً فيه.

(c) The noun phrase "international dispute" is translated as a noun phrase نزاع دولي, the indefinite noun phrase "peaceful means" is translated as a definite noun phrase

312   *Appendix 2*

الوسائل السلمية, and the noun phrase "international relations" is translated as a noun phrase العلاقات الدولية. The noun phrase "the purposes of the United Nations" is translated as a noun phrase مقاصد الأمم المتحدة. However, the ST noun phrase involves an embedded (inserted) prepositional phrase "of the United Nations"; this is not compatible with Arabic style which favours dropping the preposition of and produces a style with a construct noun phrase مضاف ومضاف اليه. Thus, we get مقاصد الأمم المتحدة.

(d) The expression "in such a manner" is translated as يحيث/بطريقة.

(e) The passive voice "are not endangered" is translated as an active voice لا تتعرض للخطر. However, I have used the negation particle لا + the verb يتعرض + the sub-ject السلام الدولي والأمن والعدالة + للخطر.

(f) The adjective "inconsistent" is translated as a verb تتعارض. The adjective "inconsistent" collocates with the preposition "with" while the verb تتعارض collocates with the preposition مع.

12   Provide a translation for the following journalistic text and discuss the stylistic design involved in both the ST and the TT:

The Department of Homeland Security deployed helicopters, airplanes and drones over 15 cities where demonstrators gathered to protest the death of George Floyd, logging at least 270 hours of surveillance, far more than previously revealed, according to Customs and Border Protection data. The footage was then fed into a digital network managed by the Homeland Security Department, called "Big Pipe", which can be accessed by other federal agencies and local police departments for use in future investigations, according to senior officials with Air and Marine Operations.

(*The New York Times*, 19 June 2020)

(i) We propose the following translation on which our translation commentary and the textual and discourse analysis will be based:

وفقاً لبيانات وكالة الجمارك وحماية الحدود فإنَّ وزارة الأمن الداخلي نشرت مروحيات وطائرات مُسيَّرة (مُسيَّرات) في سماء أكثر من 15 مدينة حيث تجمَّع المتظاهرون للإحتجاج على وفاة جورج فلويد الأمريكي من أصولٍ أفريقية حيث تم تسجيل ما لا يقل عن 270 ساعة من المراقبة وهو عدد أكبر بكثير مما تم الكشف عنه سابقاً. ووفقاً لكبار المسؤولين في العمليات الجوية والبحرية يتم بعد ذلك إدخال اللقطات في شبكة رقمية تديرها وزارة الأمن الداخلي، تُسمَّى "الأنبوب الكبير"، التي يُمكن الوصول إليها من قبل الوكالات الفيدرالية الأخرى وإدارات الشرطة المحلية وذلك لاستخدامها (من أجل استخدامها) في التحقيقات المستقبلية. (عن صحيفة ذي نيويورك تايمز الأمريكية الصادرة في 19 يونيو (حزيران) 2020)

(ii) Modification (shift) in word order: The ST and the TT have distinct stylistic designs. The first and second sentences of the ST end with "according to Customs and Border Protection data" and "according to senior officials with Air and Marine Operations", respectively. However, the TT starts with these two expressions, which refer to the source of the report. Thus, stylistically, Arabic favours starting the sentence with the source of the report. This is based on natural and transposition (shift) translation approaches which allow the translator to make adjustments like shifting word order.

Appendix 2 313

(iii) The TT involves الأمريكي من أصولٍ أفريقية as additional details not explicitly mentioned in the ST; it is an explication and expansion of the ST expression "George Floyd". This is based on the exegetical translation approach.

(iv) Through mimicking the operational method of the SL jargon "helicopter", the translator has analyzed the SL jargon mechanism of taking-off. The TT jargon مروحيات/مروحية is employed since the translator is informed by its componential semantic features that the "helicopter" "uses rotating or spinning wings called blades to fly". Through this approach, we have the above TL jargon based on how this equipment works in terms of taking-off and landing. For more details on jargon translation, see Chapter 7.

(v) The use of nominalization "logging" is translated as حيث تم تسجيل; the TL nominalization pattern تم + تسجيل, while the comma followed by "far more" is translated as وهو عدد أكبر بكثير, getting rid of the comma in the TT and replacing it with the additive conjunction و. It is worthwhile to note that in the ST, we have an ellipted (relative pronoun + auxiliary) "which is" after the comma. The same applies to "managed" where the underlying meaning involves "which is managed" and "called" which is originally "which is".

(vi) The passive voice "is fed" is translated as a nominalization expression تم + ادخال. The passive voice "can be accessed" is translated as يُمكن الوصول إليها. However, the passive "called" has remained as passive in Arabic تُسمَّى.

(vii) The prepositions "over", "for", and "with" are translated as في سماء, وذلك and في respectively.

13 Provide a translation and a commentary for the following text explaining the stylistic idiosyncrasies involved in both the ST and the TT:

When it is hot cold water is the solution.

(i) It is worthwhile to note that stylistic idiosyncrasies are language-specific. For instance, what is an oxymoron in English may not be so when translated to Arabic. The ST involves the rhetorical device of oxymoron (two antonyms placed next to each other): the antonyms (hot + cold). However, this stylistic feature is lost in Arabic and has shifted to the rhetorical device of antithesis (two antonyms placed far away from each other):

عندما يكون الجوُ حاراً فالحلُ هو الماءُ الباردُ

where we have the rhetorical device of antithesis represented by the antonyms حار/بارد.

(ii) The ST ends with the noun "solution" which has been moved to the middle of the TT and is given the temporal conjunction ف affixed to it فالحلُ. Also, the TT has added the detached pronoun هو as a stylistic requirement by Arabic. However, we can propose a different style:

عندما يكون الجوُ حاراً فالماءُ الباردُ هو الحلُ

where the ST oxymoron is still lost in the TT and we still have the rhetorical device of antithesis through the antonyms حار/بارد.

14 Provide a translation for the following legal text and a translation commentary on the translation process and the stylistic idiosyncrasies of the ST and the TT.

314　*Appendix 2*

The Parties will contribute toward the further development of peaceful and friendly international relations by strengthening their free institutions, by bringing about a better understanding of the principles upon which these institutions are founded, and by promoting conditions of stability and well-being. They will seek to eliminate conflict in their international economic policies and will encourage economic collaboration between any or all of them.

(www.nato.int/cps/en/natolive/official_texts_17120.htm, accessed on 16 June 2020)

(i)　We propose the following translation on which our translation commentary and the textual and discourse analysis will be based:

ستُساهمُ الأطرافُ في زيادة تطوير العلاقات الدولية السلمية والودية من خلال تعزيز مؤسساتهما الحرة وتحقيق فهم أفضل للمبادئ التي تأسست عليها هذه المؤسسات وتعزيز ظروف الإستقرار والرفاهية. وسوف يسعون (كما سيسعون) إلى القضاء على الخلافات في سياساتهم الإقتصادية الدولية وسيشجعون التعاون الإقتصادي بين أي منهم أو جميعهم.

(ii)　The ST is made up of two sentences. Below is a translation commentary on the first sentence:

(a)　The preposition "toward" is translated as في. We have the noun phrase "the further development", where the adjective "further" – meaning "additional" – is translated as a nominalized noun زيادة. The preposition "by" occurs three times: The first preposition "by" is translated as من خلال, the second and third prepositions "by" are translated as an additive conjunction و.

(b)　There is a long noun phrase "peaceful and friendly international relations" which is translated as a noun phrase العلاقات الدولية السلمية والودية, where we have used the additive conjunction و between the last two adjectives "friendly international" of the long noun phrase. There are three other noun phrases: "their free institutions", "a better understanding of the principles", and "conditions of stability and well-being". These are translated as noun phrases: مُؤسساتهما الحُرة, فهم أفضل للمبادئ, ظروف الإستقرار والرفاهية and respectively.

(c)　The commas in the first sentence are taken out in the TT. We have three gerunds (nominalized nouns). These are "strengthening, bringing, promoting", which are translated as nominalized nouns تعزيز، تحقيق ، تعزيز, respectively.

(d)　The passive voice clause "upon which these institutions are founded" is translated as an active voice clause التي تأسست عليها هذه المؤسسات.

(iii)　Below is a translation commentary on the second sentence:

(a)　The full-stop after the first sentence is maintained but an additive conjunction و or كما is used. We have two main verbs "seek, encourage" and we have an infinitive verb "to eliminate", which is translated as a nominalized noun + a preposition القضاء على. The indefinite noun "conflict" is translated as a definite plural noun الخلافات. We have three noun phrases: "conditions of stability and well-being" ظروف الإستقرار والرفاهية, "international economic policies" السياسات الإقتصادية الدولية, and "economic collaboration" التعاون الإقتصادي.

(b)　The prepositional phrase "between any or all of them" is translated as بين أي منهم أو جميعهم where the ellipted (deleted) prepositional phrase "of them", which should

Appendix 2 315

have occurred after the word "any", is brought back in Arabic as منهم. The Arabic style for the word "any" should not involve ellipsis. The original style of the prepositional phrase "between any or all of them" is "between any <u>of them</u> or all of them".

15 Provide a translation and a translation commentary based on the translation process and the stylistic idiosyncrasies and the textual and discourse features of the following ST and TT:

كان رسولُ الله (صلى الله عليه وسلم) أشجعَ الناس. قال علي بن أبي طالب (رضي الله عنه): "كنا إذا احمرَ البأسُ، ولقي القومُ القومَ اتَّقينا برسول اللهِ (صلى الله عليه وسلم). وكان أصبرَ الناس وأسخى الناس، ما سُؤِلَ شيئاً قط، فقالَ لا. وكانَ أشد حياءً من العذراءِ في خدرِها، لا يُثبِتُ بصرَهُ في وجهِ أحد. وكان لا ينتقم لنفسهِ، ولا يغضبُ لها، إلاَ أن تُنتهك حُرُماتُ اللهِ، فيكون للهِ ينتقم. وإذا غضِبَ للهِ لم يقُم لغضبهِ أحدٌ. والقريبُ والبعيدُ والقويُ والضعيفُ عنده في الحقِّ واحدٌ. وما عابَ طعاماً قط، إن اشتهاهُ أَكلَهُ، وإن لم يشتَهِه تركهُ. وكانَ لا يأكلُ متكئاً ولا يأكلُ على خُوانٍ. ولا يمتنع من مُباحٍ، إن وجَدَ تمراً أَكلهُ، وإن وجَدَ خُبزاً أَكلهُ، وإن وجَدَ شَواءً أَكلهُ، وإن وجَدَ خُبزَ بُرٍّ أو شعيراً أَكلهُ، وإن وجَدَ لبناً اكتفى بهِ. أَكلَ البطيخَ بالرطَبِ. وكان يُحبُّ الحلواءَ والعسلَ.

خرجَ رسولُ الله (صلى الله عليه وسلم) من الدنيا ولم يشبع من خُبزِ الشعير جراء الفقر. وكان يأتي على آل مُحمد الشهر والشهران لا يُوقد في بيتٍ من بيوتِه نار، وكان قوتُهُم التمر والماء. يأكُل الهدية ولا يأكُل الصدقة، ويُكافيء على الهديةِ. لا يتأنَّق في مأكلٍ ولا ملبسٍ. يأكُل ما وجَدَ ويلبسُ ما وجَدَ. كان يخصِفُ النَّعلَ، ويرقَعُ الثُّوبَ، ويخدِمُ في مَهنةِ أهلهِ، ويعودُ المرضى. وكانَ أشدُّ الناس تواضُعاً، يُجيبُ من دعاهُ من غنيٍّ أو فقيرٍ أو دنيءٍ أو شريفٍ. وكان يُحبُّ المساكينَ، ويشهدُ جنائزَهُم، ويعُدُ مرضاهُم، ولا يهابُ ملِكاً لمُلكهِ. (المقدسي (مختصر سيرة الرسول) 2003:155)

The Messenger of Allah was the bravest of people. His cousin and fourth caliph Ali b. Abi Talib said: "When a battle raged and two opposing armies faced each other, we would fight behind the Messenger". He was from the most generous of people. Whenever he was asked for a matter, he never said no. He was the most forbearing and most generous of people. He was shier than a veiled virgin girl. He would never stare at anyone's face. He would never seek revenge for personal reasons. He would never become angry for personal issues except if the sanctuary of Allah was infringed then he would only seek revenge for Allah. He would never allow anyone to defend him on his behalf in his anger. Those that were close to him, far from him, the strong and the weak were not distinguished between with regards the truth. He would never insult food, if he liked it, he would eat it and if he didn't desire it then he would leave it. He would never eat whilst reclining. He would never eat upon a raised table (but on the floor out of humility). He would not forbid permissible things. If he found dates, he would eat them. If he found bread, he would eat it. If grilled meat was present, he would eat it. If bread made from barley and wheat was present, he would eat it. If he found milk, he sufficed himself with it. He would eat melon with ripe dates. He used to like sweet things and honey.

The Prophet left this world without even having filled his stomach with barley bread due to poverty. A month or two would pass by the family of Muhammad and a fire would not even be kindled from any of his dwellings (in order to have hot food). Their food would be dates and honey (for that period). He would accept gifts but not charity. He would reciprocate this with a gift (if he was able). He would not be extravagant in his food and clothing. He would eat and dress himself with whatever was available. He would mend his own shoes and sew his own garments. He would be at the service of his

316 *Appendix 2*

family. He used to visit the sick. He was from the humblest of people. He would answer those that called him whether they be rich, poor, with or without status. He used to love the poor people. He would attend their funerals, visit their sick and never belittle a poor person nor fear a person with authority due to his dominion.

(al-Maqdisi, Imam Abdul-Ghani 2003:155–163, 2017:4–12)

(i)   We propose the following edited version of the TT. Compare the two TT versions:

The Messenger of Allah was the bravest of people. His cousin and fourth caliph, Ali Ibn Abi Talib said: "Whenever a battle raged and two opposing armies faced each other, we would fight behind the Messenger of Allah".

The Messenger of Allah was amongst the most tolerant and generous of people. Whenever he was asked of anything, he never said no. He was shyer than a veiled virgin girl. He would never stare anyone in the face. He would never seek revenge for personal reasons. He would never become angry for personal issues, unless the sanctuary of Allah was infringed, in which case he would only seek revenge for Allah. Whenever he was angry for the sake of Allah, he would never allow anyone to defend him. He did not distinguish between those who were close to him, distant from him, strong or weak except in relation to the truth. He would never disrespect food: if he liked something, he would eat it, and if he did not, then he would leave it. He would never eat whilst reclining. He would never eat upon a raised table (but rather on the floor out of humility). He would not forbid permissible things. If ever he found dates, he would eat them. If ever he found bread, he would eat it. If grilled meat was present, he would eat it. If bread made from barley or wheat was present, he would eat it. If he found milk, he would be satisfied with it. He would eat melon with ripe dates. He used to like sweet things and honey.

The Prophet left this world without even having filled his stomach with barley bread due to poverty. A month or two would pass by the family of Muhammad and a fire would not even be kindled from any of his dwellings (in order to have hot food). Their food would be dates and honey (for that period). He would accept gifts but not charity. He would reciprocate this with a gift (if he was able). He would not be extravagant in his food and clothing. He would eat and dress himself with whatever was available. He would mend his own shoes and sew his own garments. He would be at the service of his family. He used to visit the sick. He was from the humblest of people. He would answer those who called him whether they were rich, poor, with status or without status. He used to love poor people. He would attend their funerals, visit their sick and neither belittle a poor person nor fear a person with authority due to the person's dominion.

(ii)   Stylistically, كنا إذا احمرَ البأسُ، ولقي القومُ القومَ اتقينا برسول الله involves the rhetorical device of imagery, the expression البأسُ is a metonymy for "the battle ground" and احمرَ means "become red with blood". The noun القومُ refers to the Muslim army, while القومَ refers to the disbelievers' army. The verb اتقى represents the rhetorical device of zeugma, which is a semantic ambiguity: (1) the surface meaning refers to the fear from God, and (2) the underlying meaning is (to be protected by someone/ something). Contextually, it is the second meaning that has occurred in the ST. The same applies to the verb لقيَ, which either means "to find" or "to face the enemy in battle" where, contextually, the latter meaning is required. The comparative adjectives

Appendix 2 317

are used: أصبر، أسخى. A comparative imagery is encountered in وكانَ أشد حياءً من العذراء في خدرها.

(iii) Stylistically, the ST is marked by the linguistic device of polysyndeton through the additive conjunction و at the beginning of each sentence. The second paragraph, however, is asyndetic (having no sentence-initial conjunction) خرج. The TT is asyndetic although we encounter sentence-initial subordinating conjunctions like "whenever, if". However, these conjunctions are intra-sentential (within the same sentence and not linking two separate sentences). These conjunctions within the same sentence link between the main clause and the subordinate clause. However, they have occurred at the beginning of the hypotactic sentence. We also encounter many hypotactic conditional sentences: "When a battle raged and two opposing armies faced each other, we would fight behind the Messenger . . . Whenever he was asked of anything, he never said no . . . He would never become angry for personal issues except if the sanctuary of Allah was infringed then he would only seek revenge for Allah . . . if he liked it, he would eat it and if he didn't desire it then he would leave it . . . If he found dates, he would eat them. If he found bread, he would eat it. If grilled meat was present, he would eat it. If bread made from barley and wheat was present, he would eat it. If he found milk, he sufficed himself with it . . . He would answer those that called him whether they be rich, poor, with or without status . . . He would mend his own shoes and sew his own garments . . . He would attend their funerals, visit their sick and never belittle a poor person nor fear a person with authority due to his dominion".

(iv) Stylistically, there are many TT paratactic sentences: "He was the most forbearing and most generous of people. He was shier than a veiled virgin girl. He would never stare at anyone's face. He would never seek revenge for personal reasons . . . He would never eat whilst reclining. He would never eat upon a raised table 'but on the floor out of humility'. He would not forbid permissible things . . . He would eat melon with ripe dates. He used to like sweet things and honey . . . He would accept gifts but not charity . . . He would not be extravagant in his food and clothing . . . He would be at the service of his family. He used to visit the sick. He was from the humblest of people . . . He used to love the poor people".

(v) Stylistically, the ST employs the conditional particles إذا and إن. However, these conditional subordinating conjunctions, which generate hypotactic sentences, are preceded by the additive conjunction و: وإذا غَضِبَ لله لم يقُم لغضبِهِ أحدٌ . . . إن اشتهاهُ أكلَهُ، وإن لم يشتهه تركَهُ . . . إن وجَدَ تمراً أكلهُ، وإن وجَدَ خُبزاً أكلهُ، وإن وجَدَ شواءً أكلهُ، وإن وجَدَ خُبزَ بُرٍّ أو شعيراً أكلهُ، وإن وجَدَ لبناً اكتفى به.

(vi) Both the ST and the TT have employed a double-barrel rhetorical device of zeugma and euphemism through the verb خرج "left". Semantically, this verb has a surface structure meaning "to leave a place and go somewhere else" and "to pass away", where the euphemistic meaning lies. The TT has correctly observed the second underlying context-based meaning.

(vii) Both the ST and the TT have employed the rhetorical device of metonymy through the expression لا يُوقَدُ في بيتٍ من بيوته نار, whose underlying meaning is (poverty).

(viii) The ST employs the rhetorical device of zeugma through the verb يأكل which has the surface structure meaning of "eat" and the underlying meaning "accept". It is the second meaning which has occurred in the ST. However, the TT has sacrificed zeugma and replaced it with the context-based meaning, "accept".

318 *Appendix 2*

(ix) We have a series of polysyndetic paratactic ST sentences: (.يأكُلُ ما وجدَ ويلبسُ ما وجَدَ)
كانَ يخصفُ النَّعلَ، ويرقَعُ الثَّوبَ، ويخدمُ في مَهنَةِ أهلِه، ويعُودُ المرضى ... وكان يُحِبُّ
(المساكينَ، ويشهدُ جنائزَهُم، ويعُدُ مرضاهُم، ولا يهابُ ملِكًا لمُلْكِهِ)

16 Provide different translations for the following text and a commentary on the stylistic differences between the ST and the TT.

إنَّهُم يكيدونَ كيداً. وأكيدُ كيداً. (الطارق 15–16)

Lo! they plot a plot (against thee, O Muhammad)
And I plot a plot (against them) (Pickthall 1930:no page).
As for them, they are but plotting a scheme, And I am planning a scheme (Ali 1934:no page).
They are devising guile, and I am devising guile (Arberry 1955:275).
Behold, they [who refuse to accept it] devise many a false argument [to disprove its truth]; but I shall bring all their scheming to nought (Asad 1980:1276).
Indeed, they are planning. But I am planning a plan (Saheeh International 1997:878).
They plot and scheme, but so do I (Abdel Haleem 2005:417).

(i) On the grammatical level, the ST has employed the absolute object المفعول المطلق. However, stylistically, this has led to the rhetorical device of polyptoton (a change in grammatical function from the verb يكيد to a nominalized noun كيد. Also, the ST enjoys assonance through the accusative nunation التنوين المنصوب in word-final words ... كيداً. Assonance is also depicted through the occurrence of the consonant sound ك for times in different words. These stylistic attributes are missing in the TT. Polyptoton is a grammar-based stylistic mechanism while assonance is phonetically based stylistic mechanism.

(ii) In terms of the translation process, different translation approaches have been adopted. The formal equivalence approach has been adopted by all the TTs where a source-oriented translation is given – except that by Abdel Haleem. The translation provided by Asad is based on the anachronism and exegetical translation approaches. However, Abdel Haleem has nicely observed the English cohesion system and provided a TT based on verbal substitution. For more details on verbal substitution, see Chapter 5, Section 5.6.1.1.

17 Homework assignment: The superlative adjective أعلمُ, i.e., the superlative صيغة أفعل, أفعل التفضيل, has occurred in Q6:53, 58, 117, 119, and 124. Is this a semantically based or a morphologically based hyperbole form? Compare different translations of this adjective and provide a translation quality assessment of the stylistic idiosyncrasies of the ST and TT.

18 In-class discussion: Discuss the major stylistic idiosyncrasies of Q4:133, Q25:54, Q33:27, and Q48:21, where كان + قدير on the hyperbole pattern فعيل occur: كانَ الله + قدير. على ذلكَ قديرا. Does كانَ signify a past tense? The hyperbole pattern فعيل pragmatically designates hyperbole + multitude. Can these stylistic and pragmatic functions be achieved in English? Compare different translations and provide a translation quality assessment.

Appendix 2 319

19 Homework assignment: The following texts involve two different words. Based on the distinct stylistic idiosyncrasies of Arabic and English, provide a translation quality assessment of different translations:

إِنِّي بَرِيءٌ مما تُشرِكُون (الأنعام 78)

إِنَّنِي بُراءٌ مما تَعبُدون (الزُّخرُف 26)

Take into consideration the use of إِنِّي and إِنَّنِي, the active participle بَرِيءٌ and the nominalized noun بُراءٌ, the semantic and pragmatic distinction between them, and the larger context in which each statement has occurred. For more details, see Abdul-Raof (2020), Chapter 6, Section 6.6 (context-based lexical behavior).

20 For in-class discussion: Discuss the major stylistic idiosyncrasies of the Arabic negation particles قَطُّ/أَبَداً and their English counterpart "never". Based on the stylistic idiosyncrasies and linguistic distinctions between Arabic and English, provide an assessment of the translations of examples like

ما رأيتُهُ قطُّ/لم أشرب الماءَ قطُّ as opposed to التخلُّفُ ماكِثٌ فيهم أبَداً/لن نفشل أبَداً/لا تتكلم معهم أبَداً

Note that, semantically, قطُّ signifies the past tense. Its grammatical construction is

(ما/لم) + فعل ماضي + قطُّ

However, semantically, أبَداً signifies the future and has the illocutionary force of (i) confirmation الإثبات, (ii) negation النفي, or (iii) forbidding النهي.

21 Homework assignment: Provide a translation quality assessment of the following euphemistic expressions through the assessment of different Qur'an translations:

إعتزلوا (البقرة 222)، يقرُب (البقرة 222)، آتُوهُنَّ (البقرة 222)، حرثٌ (البقرة 223)، الرفثُ (البقرة 187)، لباسٌ (البقرة 187)، أفضى (النساء 21)، لامَسَ (النساء 43)، دَخَلَ (النساء 23)، الغائِط (المائدة 6)، تغشَّى (الأعراف 189)، راوَدَ (يوسف 23)، يتماس (المُجادلة 4).

22 Classroom discussion: Discuss the difference between Arabic and English in terms of the inherent stylistic idiosyncrasy involved in the verb "to beach" through the example "Many whales beached at Hamelin Bay, southwest Australia". The verb "to beach" means جَنَحَت الحيتان الى We propose the following translation: يجنح الى الشاطيء ويعلقُ عليهِ ساحل شاطيء هامِلن باي في جنوب غرب أستراليا وعَلِقَت عليه على الساحل/الشاطيء

(i) The context-based meaning of the verb "beach" is "the whales beach themselves on dry land, i.e., head towards the beach, get stranded, and die". However, the Arabic translation of the verb "beach" favors the use of imagery, where we encounter the meaning جَنَحَ; to use the wings جناح for a specific direction or a course of action: جَنَحَت الحيتان الى شاطيء هامِلن باي في جنوب غرب أستراليا وعَلِقَت على الساحل. The verb (جَنَحَ) has occurred in the Qur'an in Q8:61 وإن جنحوا للسَّلم فاجنح لها "And if they incline towards peace, you must also incline towards it", meaning "to

320   *Appendix 2*

incline towards a course of action". However, the cognitive (mental) image we have demonstrates to us an airplane changing direction to the right or to the left through looking at the airplane's wings: الطائرةُ تجنحُ الى اليمين أو الى اليسار. Thus, "to beach" demonstrates a distinct stylistic idiosyncrasy between Arabic and English.

(ii) Because the Arabic meaning involves two verbs – يعلقُ على + يجنحُ الى الشاطيء – we need to use the subject الحيتان after the first verb جَنَحَ + the prepositional phrase الى شاطيء هاملن باي في جنوب غرب أستراليا + the conjunction و + the second verb عَلِقَت على الساحل.

(iii) There is no word-for-word equivalence for the verb "to beach". Thus, we have adopted the exegetical translation approach: يجنح الى الشاطيء الساحل ويعلقُ عليه.

23   Classroom discussion: Discuss the difference between Arabic and English in terms of the inherent stylistic idiosyncrasy involved in the following headline:

The Washington Post's media bias rating is Lean Left.
to which we propose the following translations:

تصنيف صحيفة الوشنطن بوست لتحيزها الإعلامي صحيفة يسارية

تصنيف صحيفة الوشنطن بوست صحيفة يسارية لتحيزها الإعلامي

24   For classroom discussion: Provide a translation for the following text and a commentary on the stylistic differences between the ST and the TT: "The boots are on the ground". The ST involves the stylistic (rhetorical) device of metonymy represented by the expression "boots", which is a source culture-based expression whose underlying meaning is "the military/ground forces". The other metonymy is "on the ground", whose underlying meaning is "the military zone". This gives us the meaning "The ground forces are deployed in the military zone". Thus, the TT should be تمَّ نشر القوات البرية في ساحة القتال/في ميدان المعركة

25   Homework assignment: Provide a translation and a translation quality assessment of the stylistic idiosyncrasies represented by the following three underlined metaphors and the two metonymies:

The news came as allies of Cummings and Cain said their enemies in government were "determined to set fire to [Johnson's] premiership" with a "tsunami of toxic briefings" that would ultimately undermine the government.

Another government figure said: "It's a bloodbath, isn't it?". This is evidence of how serious the internal warfare inside No 10 has become.

Ellie Price, the BBC journalist, was "head and shoulders" above the other candidates during an official selection process for the job.

(*The Guardian*, 14 November 2020)

We propose the following translation:

وقد وردت الأخبار في الوقت الذي قال فيه حلفاء كامينغز وكين إن أعداءهم في الحكومة "مصممون على إشعال (إضرام) النار في رئاسة الوزراء لحكومة جونسون (التي يترأسها جونسون)" من خلال "تسونامي من الإيجازات السامة" التي ستقوض الحكومة في النهاية.

Appendix 2 321

وقالت شخصية حكومية أخرى: "هذا (إنه) حمام دم، أليس كذلك؟". هذه بمثابة حرب داخلية داخل مقر الحكومة البريطانية.

ومن الجدير بالذكر أنَّ إيلي برايس، الصحفية في قناة بي بي سي كانت "أفضل بكثير" من المرشحين الآخرين أثناء عملية الاختيار الرسمية لهذه الوظيفة.

(عن صحيفة الغارديان البريطانية الصادرة في 14 نوفمبر (تشرين الثاني) 2020)"

26 For classroom discussion: Discuss the following ST and its proposed translation:

"He hasn't got the gig yet, we've got to be very careful", said Paul Allen, a public relations man heading the initiative. "It's a great opportunity to get another Irishman in the White House".

Biden opposed Brexit and has warned Downing Street that if it undermines the Good Friday agreement, it can kiss goodbye to a trade deal with the US – a grim scenario for Boris Johnson.

(*The Guardian*, 18 October 2020)

وقال بول ألين، رجل العلاقات العامة الذي يترأس هذه المبادرة: "لم يحصل بايدن على منصب الرئاسة بعد، ولهذا علينا أن نكون حذرين للغاية.".

وأضاف قائلاً: "إنها فرصة رائعة للحصول على رئيس آخر من أصلٍ إيرلندي في البيت الأبيض.".

ومن الجدير بالذكر أنَّ بايدن قد عارض خروج بريطانيا من الاتحاد الأوروبي وحذر الحكومة البريطانية من أنه إذا ما قوضت المملكة المتحدة اتفاق الجمعة العظيمة فإنَّ بريطانيا تكون قد ألغت الصفقة التجارية مع الولايات المتحدة وهو سيناريو قاتم لبوريس جونسون. (عن صحيفة الغارديان البريطانية الصادرة في 18 أكتوبر (تشرين الأول) 2020)

Classroom discussion: After you have read the ST and its proposed TT, discuss the stylistic idiosyncrasies of the TT in terms of the use of (i) "gig", which is rendered as منصب الرئاسة; (ii) the definite article in "the initiative", which is replaced by هذه; (iii) the first full-stop, which is replaced by وأضاف قائلاً; (iv) the second full-stop, which is replaced by the journalistic cohesive device ومن الجدير بالذكر; (v) the metonymy "Brexit", which is translated as خروج بريطانيا من الأتحاد الأوربي; (vi) the metonymy "Downing Street", which is translated as الحكومة البريطانية; (vii) the ST-culture-based expression "kiss goodbye", which is replaced by يلغي; and (viii) the ST dash (–), which is replaced by وهو.

Bibliography

Abdel Haleem, M. A. S. (2005). *The Qur'an: A New Translation*. Oxford: Oxford University Press.

Abdul-Raof, Hussein (2001). *Arabic Stylistics: A Coursebook*. Wiesbaden: Harrassowitz Verlag.

———— (2015). *Semantics: A Coursebook for Students of English as a Foreign Language*. Muenchen: Lincom Europa Academic Publications.

———— (2018). *New Horizons in Qur'anic Linguistics: A Syntactic, Semantic and Stylistic Analysis*. London and New York: Routledge.

———— (2019). *Text Linguistics of Qur'anic Discourse: An Analysis*. London and New York: Routledge.

———— (2020). *Stylistics: Arabic and English Rhetorical and Linguistic Analysis*. Muenchen: Lincom GmbH.

Ahmad, Imtiaz (2010). *The Easy Qur'an*. Farmington Hills, MI: Tawheed Center of Farmington Hills.

Ali, Abdullah Yusuf (1934). *The Holy Qur-ān: English Translation & Commentary (With Arabic Text)*. 1st edition. Kashmiri Bazar, Lahore: Shaik Muhammad Ashraf.

Arberry, Arthur John (1955). *The Koran Interpreted*. London: George Allen and Unwin.

Asad, Muhammad (1980). *The Message of the Qur'an*. On-line version.

Baker, Mona (1997). *The Routledge Encyclopedia of Translation Studies*. London and New York: Routledge.

Bassnett, S. (1998). 'The Translation Turn in Cultural Studies'. In: *Constructing Cultures: Essays on Literary Translation*. Clevedon: Multilingual Matters; pp. 123–140.

Beaugrande, R. (2003). 'On the Concept of Sensitive Translation'. *Offshoot: A Journal of Translation and Comparative Studies*, vol. 5, no. 1; pp. 1–14.

Beaugrande, Rober-Alain de and Dressler, Wolfgang (1981). *Introduction to Textlinguistics*. London: Longman.

Beekman, John and Callow, John (1974). *Translating the Word of God*. Grand Rapids, MI: Zondervan.

Bell, Richard (1937). *The Qur'an: Translated with a Critical Re-arrangement of the Surahs*. Edinburgh: T & T. Clark.

Benjamin, Walter (1968). 'The Task of the Translator'. In: *Illumination*s. Translated by Harry Zohn. New York: Schocken. In: *The Translation Studies Reader*. Edited by Lawrence Venuti (2000); pp. 15–25.

Brisset, Annie (1996). *A Sociocritique of Translation: Theatre and Alterity in Québec, 1968–1988*. Translated by Rosalind Gill and Roger Gannon. Toronto: University of Toronto Press. In: *The Translation Studies Reader*. Edited by Lawrence Venuti (2000); pp. 343–375.

Caminade, Monique and Pym, Anthony. (1998). 'Translator-Training Institutions'. In: *Encyclopedia of Translation Studies*. London and New York: Routledge; pp. 280–285.

Campbell, George (1789). *The Four Gospels*. 1 vol. London: Strahan and Cadell. In: *The Translation Studies Reader*. Edited by Lawrence Venuti (2000); p. 132.

Catford, John Cunnison (1965). *A Linguistic Theory of Translation*. Oxford: Oxford University Press.

Crystal, David (2003). *A Dictionary of Linguistics and Phonetics*. 1st edition. Oxford: Blackwell Publishing.

Bibliography   323

Dickins, James, Hervey, Sándor and Higgins, I. (2002). *Thinking Arabic Translation*. London and New York: Routledge.

Dryden, John (1680/1697/1992). *Metaphrase, Paraphrase and Imitation*. Extracts of *Preface to Ovids Epistles* (1680), and *Dedication of the Aeneis* (1697). Edited by Rainer Schulte and John Biguenet (1992); pp. 17–31.

Garvin, P. L. (ed. and trans.) (1955). *A Prague School Reader on Esthetics, Literary Structure and Style*. Washington, DC: Washington Linguistic Club. Reprinted (1964) Georgetown University Press.

Goodspeed, Edgar Johnson (1945). *Problems of New Testament Translation*. Chicago: University of Chicago Press.

Gutt, Ernst-August (1991). *Translation and Relevance: Cognition and Context*. Oxford: Blackwell.

Halliday, Michael (1971). 'Linguistic Function and Literary Style: An Inquiry into the Language of William Golding's the Inheritors'. In: *Literary Style: A Symposium*. Edited by S. Chatman. London and New York: Oxford University Press; pp. 330–365.

Halliday, Michael Alexander K. and Hasan, Ruqaiya (1976). *Cohesion in English*. London: Longman.

Hatim, Basil (1997). *Communication Across Cultures: Translation Theory and Contrastive Text Linguistics*. Exeter: University of Exeter Press.

Hatim, Basil and Munday, Jeremy (2004). *Translation: An Advanced Resource Book*. London and New York: Routledge.

Helminski, Camille Adams (2000). *The Light of Dawn: Daily Readings from the Holy Qurān*. Boston: Shambhala Threshold Book.

Hickey, Leo (ed.) (1998a). *The Pragmatics of Translation*. Clevendon: Multilingual Matters.

Hulusi, Ahmed (2013). *Decoding the Quran: A Unique Sufi Interpretation*. Translated by Aliya Atalay. https://www.ahmedhulusi.org/content/docs/decoding-the-quran.pdf. Accessed on Saturday 3rd October 2020.

Jakobson, Roman (1959). 'On Linguistic Aspects of Translation'. In: *On Translation*. Edited by Reuben Arthur Brower. Cambridge, MA: Harvard University Press; pp. 232–239. In: *The Translation Studies Reader*. Edited by Lawrence Venuti (2000); pp. 113–118.

Knox, R. A. (1957). 'On English Translation'. In: *The Translation Studies Reader*. Edited by Lawrence Venuti. Oxford: Oxford University Press (2000).

Larson, M. L. (1984). *Meaning-Based Translation: A Guide to Cross-Language Equivalence*. Lanham: University Press of America.

Larson, Mildred L. (1984). *Meaning-Based Translation: A Guide to Cross-Language Equivalence*. Lanham: University Press of America.

Levý, Jiří (1969). *Die literarische Übersetzung: Theorie einer Kunstgattung*. Translation by W. Schamschula. Frankfurt: Athenäum.

al-Maqdisi, Imam ᶜAbdul-Ghani (2003). *Mukhtasar Sirat al-Rasul*. Riyadh: Dar Balnasiyyah. *The Manners and Attributes of the Prophet Muhammad*. Translated by Abdulilah Lahmami (2017). Slough, UK: Markaz Mu'aadh Bin Jabal Islamic Centre.

McCabe, Anne (2011). *An Introduction to Linguistics and Language Studies*. London: Equinox.

Moir, Catherine (2009). 'Translational Resonance, Authenticity and Authority in the Bible and the Qur'an: Translation and Religious Change'. *New Voices in Translation Studies*, vol. 5; pp. 29–45.

Munday, Jeremy (2001). *Introducing Translation Studies: Theories and Applications*. London and New York: Routledge.

Mushaf Al-Madinah An Nabawiyah (1990). *The Holy Qur'an: English Translation of the Meanings and Commentary*. Al-Madinah: King Fahad Holy Qur'an Printing Complex.

Newman, Francis William (1861). *Homeric Translation in Theory and Practice*. London: Williams and Norgate.

Newmark, Peter (1981). *Approaches to Translation*. Oxford: Pergamon Press.

——— (1988). *A Textbook of Translation*. New York: Prentice Hall.

——— (1991). *About Translation*. Clevedon: Multilingual Matters.

Nida, Eugene (1945). 'Linguistics and Ethnology in Translation Problems'. *Word*, vol. l, no. 2; pp. 194–208.

324 *Bibliography*

———— (1964). *Toward a Science of Translating, with Special Reference to Principles and Procedures Involved in Bible Translating.* Leiden, Holland: Brill.

———— (1994). 'Translation: Possible and Impossible'. *Turjuman*, vol. 3, no. 2; pp. 147–163.

———— (2000). *The Translation Studies Reader.* Edited by Lawrence Venuti (2000); pp. 126–140.

Nida, Eugene and Taber, Charles (1969) *The Theory and Practice of Translation.* Leiden, Holland: Brill.

Nord, Christiane (1988/1991) *Textanalyse und übersetzen theoretische Grundlagen, methode und didaktische Anwendung einer übersetzungsrelevanten Textanalyse.* Heidelberg: J. Groos (trans.) (1991) as *Text Analysis in Translation: Theory, Methodology and Didactic Application of a Model fur Translation-Oriented Text Analysis.* Amsterdam: Rodopi.

———— (1997). 'A Functional Typology of Translation'. In: *Text Typology and Translation.* Edited by Anna Trosborg. Amsterdam and Philadelphia: John Benjamins Publishing Company; pp. 43–66.

Palmer, Edward (1880). *The Qur'an.* Oxford: The Clarendon Press.

Phillips, John Bertram (1953). 'Some Personal Reflections on New Testament Translation'. *Bible Translator*, vol. 4; pp. 53–59.

Pickthall, Marmaduke (1930). *The Meaning of the Glorious Koran.* On-line version.

al-Qurtubi, Abu ᶜAbd Allah Muhammad b. Ahmad (1997). *al-Jami ᶜli-Ahkam al-Qur'an.* 20 vols. Beirut: Dar al-Kitab al-ᶜArabi.

Reiss, Katharina (1971). *Möglichkeiten und Grenzen der Übersetzungskritik. Kategorien und Kriterien für eine sachgerechte Beurteilung von Übersetzungen.* Munich: Hueber. Translated by Susan Kitron. In: *The Translation Studies Reader.* Edited by Lawrence Venuti (2000); pp. 160–171.

Rieu, Emile Victor and Phillips, John Bertram (1954). 'Translating the Gospels'. *Bible Translator*, vol. 6; pp. 150–159.

Saheeh International (1997). *The Qur'an: Arabic Text with Corresponding English Meanings.* Riyadh: Abulqasim Publishing House.

Salkie, Raphael (1995). *Text and Discourse Analysis.* London: Routledge.

Shuttleworth, Mark and Cowie, Moira (1997). *Dictionary of Translation Studies.* Manchester: St. Jerome Publishing.

Sideeg, Abdunasir I. A. (2015). 'Traces of Ideology in Translating the Qurān into English: A Critical Discourse Analysis of Six Cases across Twenty Versions'. *International Journal of Applied Linguistics & English Literature*, vol. 4, no. 5; pp. 214–226.

Savory, Theodore H. (1957). *The Art of Translation.* London: Jonathan Cape and Boston: The Writer (1968). 2nd edition.

Sperber, Dan and Wilson, Deirdre (1986). *Relevance: Communication and Cognition.* Oxford: Blackwell.

Steiner, George (1998). *After Babel: Aspects of Language and Translation.* 3rd edition. Oxford: Oxford University Press.

Tancock, Leonard W. (1958). 'Some Problems of Style in Translation from French'. In: *Aspects of Translation: Studies in Communication 2.* Edited by Adam H. Smith. London: Seeker and Warburg; pp. 29–51.

Toury, Gideon (1995). *Descriptive Translation Studies and Beyond.* Amsterdam: Benjamins. In: *The Translation Studies Reader.* Edited by Lawrence Venuti (2000); pp. 198–211.

Venuti, Lawrence (1992). *Rethinking Translation: Discourse, Subjectivity, Ideology.* London and New York: Routledge.

———— (1995). *The Translator's Invisibility: A History of Translation.* London and New York: Routledge.

———— (1997). 'The American Tradition'. In: *The Routledge Encyclopedia of Translation Studies.* Edited by Mona Baker. London and New York: Routledge; pp. 305–315.

———— (1998). *The Scandals of Translation: Towards an Ethics of Difference.* London and New York: Routledge.

———— (ed.) (2000). *The Translation Studies Reader.* London and New York: Routledge.

———— (2000). 'Translation, Community, Utopia'. In: *The Translation Studies Reader.* Edited by Lawrence Venuti. London and New York: Routledge; pp. 468–488.

Bibliography 325

Vermeer, Hans J. (1978). 'Ein rahmen für eine allgemeine translationstheorie'. *Lebende Sprachen*, vol. 23; pp.99–102. 'Skopos and Commission in Translational Action'. Translated by Andrew Chesterman. In: *The Translation Studies Reader*. Edited by Lawrence Venuti (2000); pp. 221–232.

Vinay, Jean-Paul and Jean Darbelnet, Jean (1958). *Stylistique comparée du français et de l'anglais: Méthode de traduction*. Nouvelle édition revue et corrigée. Paris: Didier (*Comparative Stylistics of French and English: A Methodology for Translation*. Translated by Juan C. Sager and M.-J. Hamel (1995). Amsterdam and Philadelphia: John Benjamins).

Waard, Jan de and Nida, Eugene (1986). *From One Language to Another: Functional Equivalence in Bible Translating*. Nashville: Nelson.

Welch, Antony (1990). 'The Translatability of the Qur'an: Literary and Theological Implications of What the Qur'an Says About Itself'. In: *Translation of Scripture*. Edited by David M. Goldenberg. Philadelphia: Annenberg Research Institute; pp. 249–285.

Wilss, Wolfram (1982). *The Science of Translation: Problems and Methods*. Tübingen, Germany: Narr.

Yule, George (2006). *The Study of Language*. 4th edition. Cambridge: Cambridge University Press.

Yusufali, Abdullah (1934). *The Meanings of the Holy Qur'an*. al-Zamakhshari, Jar Allah Abu al-Qasim (1995). *al-Kashshaf*. 4 vols. Beirut: Dar al-Kutub al-ᶜIlmiyyah.

Index

absolute object 108–110, 139, 185, 318
active participle 37, 102, 117, 255–256, 310
adaptation operations 41
affirmation 90–92, 103, 115–116, 129, 133, 263
ambiguity: grammatical 183; lexical 130; semantic 130; structural 108, 114–115, 183
anaphora 173–174, 219
asyndeton 179–180, 317

back-translation 32, 65, 68, 122, 243

case ending 73
cataphora 173–174, 193
collocation 80
context 2, 4, 20–22, 34, 36, 51, 56, 87–90, 97, 122
contrastive stylistic analysis 74
co-text 83–84, 88

detached pronoun 140–141
dummy subject 129

ellipsis 105, 174, 187, 191–201
equivalence 2, 10, 11–12, 18, 24, 26, 28–37, 47, 50, 52, 56–57, 59, 104, 114, 121, 134, 261–262, 265, 309
euphemism 117

foregrounding 139, 171

hyperbaton 59, 80, 111, 114, 137, 143–144, 146
hyperbole 93–98, 118
hypotaxis 67, 159, 166–167, 172, 185, 200, 304, 308, 311

illocutionary force 23–25, 76, 88, 92, 109, 112, 115, 254, 319
intertextuality 55–56, 79, 108

jargon, types 54

marked word order 138, 146
metaphor 4, 69, 104, 124–125, 131–132, 185, 301, 304–305
metonymy 4, 125–128, 249–250, 259

neologism 68
nominalization 313, 315

over-translation 40, 48, 68, 117

parataxis 159, 218, 304, 308, 317–318
past participle 70
performative intent 15, 64, 138, 259
perlocutionary force 31, 77–79, 93, 95, 117, 127
personification 124
polysemy 65, 124–125, 127, 130–131, 295
polysyndeton 179–180, 183, 317–318
proverb 123
punctuation 9, 133–183

Qur'anic mode of reading 67

stylistic idiosyncrasy 3, 73–74, 98, 319
superlative adjective 94, 106
syntactic ambiguity 108, 114–115

texture 157
translation: procedures 12; requirements 12
translationese 135

unmarked word order 111, 138–139, 146

verbal substitution 139

Printed in the United States
by Baker & Taylor Publisher Services